PRINCIPLES OF FRENCH LAW

PRINCIPLES OF MECHANISM

Principles of French Law

Second Edition

JOHN BELL
SOPHIE BOYRON
SIMON WHITTAKER

with contributing authors
Andrew Bell, Mark Freedland
and
Helen Stalford

OXFORD
UNIVERSITY PRESS

Great Clarendon Street, Oxford OX2 6DP

Oxford University Press is a department of the University of Oxford.
It furthers the University's objective of excellence in research, scholarship,
and education by publishing worldwide in

Oxford New York

Auckland Cape Town Dar es Salaam Hong Kong Karachi
Kuala Lumpur Madrid Melbourne Mexico City Nairobi
New Delhi Shanghai Taipei Toronto

With offices in

Argentina Austria Brazil Chile Czech Republic France Greece
Guatemala Hungary Italy Japan Poland Portugal Singapore
South Korea Switzerland Thailand Turkey Ukraine Vietnam

Oxford is a registered trade mark of Oxford University Press
in the UK and in certain other countries

Published in the United States
by Oxford University Press Inc., New York

© Andrew Bell (Chapters 9 and 11), John Bell, Sophie Boyron,
Mark Freedland (Chapter 12), Helen Stalford (Chapter 8)
and Simon Whittaker 2008

The moral rights of the authors have been asserted

Crown copyright material is reproduced under Class Licence
Number C01P0000148 with the permission of OPSI
and the Queen's Printer for Scotland

Database right Oxford University Press (maker)

First published 2008

British Library Cataloguing in Publication Data

Data available

Library of Congress Cataloging in Publication Data
Bell, John, 1953-
Principles of French law / John Bell, Sophie Boyron, Simon Whittaker;
with contributing authors Andrew Bell, Mark Freedland, and Helen
Stalford. — 2nd ed.
        p. cm.
Includes bibliographical references and index.
ISBN 978–0–19–954138–6 (hardback: alk. paper)—ISBN
978–0–19–954139–3 (pbk.: alk. paper) 1. Law—France. 2. Justice,
Administration of—France. I. Boyron, Sophie. II. Whittaker,
Simon. III. Title.
KJV233.B45 2008
349.44—dc22   2008003898

Typeset by Newgen Imaging Systems (P) Ltd., Chennai, India
Printed in Great Britain
on acid-free paper by
Anthony Rowe, Chippenham, Wiltshire

ISBN 978–0–19–954138–6   ISBN 978–0–19–9541393 (pbk)

1 3 5 7 9 10 8 6 4 2

Preface

In the preface to the first edition, we expressed our ambition to write a book which sets out the underlying principles and structure of French law. So, at one level, we hoped that it would serve as an introduction for students as there is not too much detail on any one topic; but we also hoped that, at another level, the work would merit the attention of scholars as a series of essays on the basic values and structure of French law and legal thinking. In preparing this second edition, these basic orientations have not changed, but, as well as updating the text to give effect to legal changes (from legislation, case law, or scholarly writing), we also hope to give the reader a sense of the direction in which French legal thinking is moving, though this is more noticeable in some areas than in others.

We would first like to thank our contributing authors, Andrew Bell, Mark Freedland and Helen Stalford for contributing chapters to the book. Simon Whittaker would like to thank Adrien Tehrani for his invaluable work in research assistance. We all owe a debt of gratitude to our editors at OUP, John Louth and Alex Flach who have guided the work through publication with speed and efficiency.

The text reflects the law as at 1 January 2007, although some later materials have been included.

John Bell
Sophie Boyron
Simon Whittaker

8 October 2007

Contents

Detailed Contents

PART II: THE LAW

PART III: STUDYING FRENCH LAW

Notes on the Authors

Andrew Bell is a Senior Lecturer in the School of Law at the University of Manchester. He is the author of *The Modern Law of Personal Property in England and Ireland* (Butterworths, 1989) and has otherwise published in the areas of commercial law, personal property, and European and comparative law.

John Bell FBA QC (Hon) is Professor of Law (1973) at the University of Cambridge and a fellow of Pembroke College, Cambridge. He writes on French law and comparative public law and judicial institutions. In these fields, he has published *French Legal Cultures* (Butterworths, 2001), *French Administrative Law* (with L. N. Brown), 5th edn. (OUP, 1998), *French Constitutional Law* (OUP, 1992) and *Judiciaries within Europe* (CUP, 2006).

Sophie Boyron is Senior Lecturer in Law at the Birmingham Law School, University of Birmingham. She publishes articles in the areas of French public law, European and comparative law. At present she is writing a volume on the French Constitution for the series *Constitutional Systems of the World* (Hart Publishing).

Mark Freedland FBA is Fellow and Tutor in Law at St. John's College, Oxford and Professor of Employment Law at the University of Oxford. He is an editor of *Chitty on Contracts*, author of *The Contract of Employment* (OUP, 1976), and *The Personal Employment Contract* (OUP, 2003), joint author of *Labour Legislation and Public Policy* (OUP, 1993) and *Towards a Flexible Labour Market* (OUP, 2007), and has also edited and contributed to symposium works and has published articles in the areas of employment law and public law.

Helen Stalford is a Senior Lecturer at the Liverpool School of Law, University of Liverpool. She is the joint author (with L. Ackers) of *A Community for Children?: Children, Citizenship and Migration in the European Union* (Ashgate, 2004) and she has published articles and contributions to conference proceedings on English and EU family law.

Simon Whittaker is Fellow and Tutor in Law at St. John's College, Oxford and Professor of European Comparative Law at the University of Oxford. He is an editor of *Chitty on Contracts*, the joint editor (with R. Zimmermann) of *Good Faith in European Contract Law* (CUP, 2000), and author of *Liability for Products: English Law, French Law, and European Harmonization* (OUP, 2005) as well as articles in the areas of contract, tort and comparative law.

Abbreviations

The Codes are referred to in the body of the text in full, the most commonly cited being in English translation, thus, the *Code civil* becomes the Civil Code. Some codes possess two parts: a *partie législative* (the articles of which are prefixed with 'L') and a *partie règlementaire* (the articles of which are prefixed with 'R'). References to the Codes in the footnotes are abbreviated as follows (any English translations used being in brackets).

A. c. pén.	*Ancien code pénal* (Old Criminal Code)
C. assur.	*Code des assurances*
C. civ.	*Code civil* (Civil Code)
C. com.	*Code de commerce* (Commercial Code)
C. communes	*Code des communes*
C. consom.	*Code de la consommation*
C. constr. et hab.	*Code de la construction et de l'habitation*
C. éduc	*Code de l'éducation*
C.G.C.T.	*Code général des collectivités territoriales*
C. santé pub.	*Code de la santé publique* (Code of Public Health)
C. rur.	*Code rural*
C.J.A	*Code de justice administrative*
C. séc. soc.	*Code de la sécurité sociale* (Social Security Code)
C. pén.	*Code pénal* (sometimes termed *Nouveau Code pénal*) (Criminal Code or New Criminal Code)
C. pr.pén.	*Code de procédure pénale* (Code of Criminal Procedure)
N.c.pr.civ.	*Nouveau code de procédure civile* (New Code of Civil Procedure)

French cases

French cases are referred to by their deciding body and date, together with any reference where a report of the decision may be found. Sometimes this is supplemented by the name of a party (e.g. *affaire Jand'heur*), this being standard practice as regards decisions of administrative courts. We have abbreviated the month of the date to three letter English abbreviations. Many decisions of the Conseil constitutionnel, the Cour de cassation and Conseil d'Etat as well as all codified law and many individual *lois* (conveniently set out as amended) are available from the *service public* website, <http://www.legifrance.gouv.fr>.

The Conseil constitutionnel possesses a number of roles in relation to the upholding of the Constitution of the Fifth Republic of 1958 (on which see below, pp. 42–43). Its decisions are referred to by their date and often a brief description of their subject-matter. This is abbreviated here as 'C. cons.' with the date in English and any such brief description, e.g. C. cons. 6 Nov. 1962, *Election du président de la République*.

The highest court judging civil and criminal cases is the Cour de cassation, which is divided according to the subject-matter of the case. These are abbreviated in the notes as follows:

Ass. plén.	Assemblée plenière of the Cour de cassation
Ch. mixte	Chambre mixte of the Cour de cassation
Ch. réun.	Chambres réunies of the Cour de cassation
Civ. (1)	First civil chamber of the Cour de cassation
Civ. (2)	Second civil chamber of the Cour de cassation
Civ. (3)	Third civil chamber of the Cour de cassation
Com	Commercial chamber of the Cour de cassation
Req	Chambre des requêtes of the Cour de cassation
Soc	Chambre sociale of the Cour de cassation

The Cour de cassation's plenary sessions which are now called the Assemblée plénière, used to be called the Chambres réunies; until 1947 the Cour de cassation possessed a Chambre des requêtes which acted as a filter for the main court. The Chambre mixte sits to resolve divergences of interpretation and case law.

Abbreviations used for other courts

CAA	Cour d'appel administratif
CE	Conseil d'Etat
CE Ass. plén	Assemblée plenière of the Conseil d'Etat
CE Sect	Conseil d'Etat, Section du contentieux
TA	Tribunal administratif
TC	Tribunal des conflits
TGI	Tribunal de grande instance
Trib. corr.	Tribunal correctionnel

The decisions of courts of appeal are cited simply by the place of the court in question.

Where a report includes the *conclusions,* the *commissaire du gouvernement* or *rapport* of the judge assigned to report on the case to the court, this appears as '*concl.*' or '*rapp.*' respectively followed by the name of the judge in question.

English cases

The abbreviated citations to the official reports and to the *English Reports* follow the standard practice. Abbreviations of unofficial reports are contained in the general abbreviations, below.

Other abbreviations

Am. J. Comp.L	American Journal of Comparative Law
Ass. nat	Assemblée nationale de la République française
A.p-.r.	P. Catala (ed.) *Avant-projet de réforme du droit des obligaions et de la prescription* (La documentation française, 2005)

Bull. civ	Bulletin des arrêts des Chambres civiles de la Cour de cassation (a selection of the decisions of various civil chambres of the Cour de cassation which are reported in five different sections, designated by the appropriate Roman numeral). The Bulletin also reports decisions of the Assemblée plenière of the Cour de cassation noted here as 'Bull. civ. A.P.'. The references in the text refer to their numbers rather than the page.
Bull. crim	Bulletin des arrêts de la Chambre criminelle de la Cour de cassation
CPR	Civil Procedure Rules
CLJ	Cambridge Law Journal
CLY	Current Law Yearbook
Cont., Conc., Cons	Contrats, concurrence, consommation (a review annexed to Juris-Classeur, Contrats, concurrence, consommation (Editions techniques, Paris)
D	Recueil Dalloz
DA	Recueil Dalloz analytique
DC	Recueil Dalloz critique
Déc	Décret
Défrenois	Répertoire du notariat Défrenois
DH	Recueil Dalloz hebdomadaire
Dig	The Digest of Justinian
DP	Recueil Dalloz périodique
Dr. mar. fr	*Droit maritime français*
Dr. soc	*Droit social*
Droit pénal	*Droit pénal* (a review annexed to Juris-Classeur Pénal (Editions techniques, Paris))
ECJ	European Court of Justice
ECR	European Court Reports
ECHR	European Convention of Human Rights
EDCE	Etudes et documents du Conseil d'Etat
EDF	Eléctricité de France
EHHR	European Human Rights
ERPL	European Review of Private Law
GP	Gazette du palais
ICLQ	International and Comparative Law Quarterly
JCP	Jurisclasseur périodique (otherwise known as *La Semaine Juridique*) (edition générale)
J.O. Rep. fr	Le Journal officiel de la République française
Jur.-Cl. Civ.	Juris-Classeur Civil (Editions techniques, Paris)
Jur.-Cl. Proc. Civ	Juris-Classeur Procédure Civile (Editions techniques, Paris)
Jur.-Cl. Adm.	Juris-Classeur Administratif (Editions techniques, Paris)
Leb	Recueil Lebon or Recueil des décisions de la Conseil d'Etat
LQR	Law Quarterly Review
LS	Legal Studies
MLR	Modern Law Review

OJLS	Oxford Journal of Legal Studies
Ord	*Ordonnance*
RDP	*Revue de droit public et de science politique*
Procédures	Procédures (a review annexed to Juris-Classeur Procédures)
Rec	Recueil des décisions du Conseil constitutionnel
Resp. civ. et assur	Responsabilité civile et assurances (a review annexed to Juris-Classeur Responsabilité et assurance (Editions techniques, Paris))
Rev. marché commun	*Revue du Marché commun et de l'Union européenne,*
RDC	*Revue des contrats*
RFDA	*Revue française de Droit administratif*
RGAT	*Recueil général des assurances terrestes*
RIDC	*Revue internationale de droit comparé*
RSC	Rules of the Supreme Court
RTDCiv	*Revue trimestrielle de droit civil*
RTDCom	*Revue trimestrielle de droit commercial*
Rev. crit	*Revue critique de législation et jurisprudence*
S	Sirey
Sén	Sénat de la République française
SI	Statutory Instrument
Tul. L.R	*Tulane Law Review*

Special Abbreviations

1789 Declaration = *Déclaration des droits de l'Homme et du Citoyen du 26 août 1789*
1946 Constitution = *Constitution du 27 octobre 1946* (of the Fourth Republic)
1958 Constitution = *Constitution du 4 octobre 1958* (of the Fifth Republic)
Loi no. 2002–303 = *Loi* no. 2002-303 of 4 Mar. 2002 *relative aux droits des malades et à la qualité du système de santé*
Loi of 1998 = *Loi* no. 98-389 of 19 May 1998 *sur la responsabilité du fait des produits défectueux*
Loi of 5 July 1985 = *Loi* no. 85-677 of 5 July 1985 *tendant à l'amélioration de la situation des victimes d'accidents de la circulation et à l'accélération des procédures d'indemnisation*
Loi of 23 June 2006 = Loi no. 2006-728 of 23 June *2006 portant réforme des successions et des libéralités*

Note: All references in the footnotes are to page numbers unless otherwise indicated. All translations are the authors' own unless otherwise indicated.

References with Abbreviations

Works referred to in abbreviated form

Avant-projet de réforme = P. Catala (ed.), *Avant-projet de réforme du droit des obligations et de la prescription* (La documentation française, 2005)

Batteur = A. Batteur, *Droit des personnes de la famille et des incapacités*, 3rd edn. (Paris, 2007)

Bell, *French Constitutional Law* = J. Bell, *French Constitutional Law* (OUP, 1992)

Bell, *French Legal Cultures* = J. Bell, *French Legal Cultures* (Butterworths, London, 2001)

Bénabent, *Obligations* = A. Bénabent *Droit civil, Les obligations*, 10th edn. (Montchrestien, Paris, 2005)

Brown and Bell, *Administrative Law* = L. Neville Brown and J. Bell, *French Administrative Law*, 5th edn. (OUP, 1998)

Burrows, *English Private Law* = A. Burrows (ed.), *English Private Law*, 2nd edn. (OUP, 2007)

Carbonnier, *Introduction* = J. Carbonnier, *Droit Civil 1, Introduction, Les personnes, La famille, l'enfant, le couple* (PUF Coll. Quadrige, 2004)

Carbonnier, *Obligations* = J. Carbonnier, *Droit Civil 2, Les biens, Les obligations*, (PUF Coll. Quadrige, 2004)

Cartwright, Vogenauer and Whittaker = J. Cartwright, S. Vogenauer and S. Whittaker (eds.), *Reforming the French Law of Obligations, Comparative Observations on the* Avant-projet de réforme du droit des obligations et de la prescription (Hart Publishing, Oxford 2008 forthcoming)

Couchez = G. Couchez, *Procédure civile*, 14th edn. (Sirey Université, 2006)

David, *French Law* = R. David, *French Law* (Baton Rouge, 1972)

de Laubadère and Gaudemet, *Droit administratif,* Tome 2 = A. de Laubadère and Y. Gaudemet, *Traité de droit administratif, Tome 2, Droit administratif des biens*, 11th edn. (LGDJ, Paris, 1998).

Delmas-Marty report = M. Delmas-Marty, *La mise en état des affaires pénales* (Paris, 1991)

Despax and Rojot = M. Despax and J. Rojot Monograph on France, Supplement 77 to the *International Encyclopedia of Labour Law and Industrial Relations*, R. Blanpain (ed), (Kluwer, Deventer, The Netherlands, 1987).

Fabre-Magnan, *Obligations* = M. Fabre-Magnan, *Les obligations* (puf, Paris, 2004)

Fabre-Magnan, *Responsabilité civile et quasi-contrats* = M. Fabre-Magnan, *Droit des obligations 2—Responsabilité civile et quasi-contrats* (puf, Paris, 2007)

Fontaine and Viney = M. Fontaine and G. Viney (eds.) *Les sanctions de l'inexécution des obligations contractuelles, Etudes de droit comparé* (Bruyant, Bruxelles and LGDJ, Paris, 2001)

Flour, Aubert, and Savaux, *Acte juridique* = J. Flour, J.-L. Aubert & E. Savaux, *Droit civil, Les obligations,* 1. *L'Acte juridique,* 12th *edn.* (Sirey Université, Paris, 2006)

Flour, Aubert, and Savaux, *Fait juridique* = J. Flour, J.-L. Aubert & E. Savaux, *Droit civil, Les obligations,* 2 *Le fait juridique,* 11th edn. (Sirey Université, Paris, 2006)

Flour and Aubert, *Rapport d'obligation* = J. Flour and J.-L. Aubert, *Les obligations,* 3 *Le rapport d'obligation* by J.-L. Aubert, Y. Flour, and E. Savaux, 4th edn. (Sirey Université, Paris, 2006)

Gaudemet, *Droit administratif,* Tome 1 = Y. Gaudemet, *Traité de droit administratif,* Tome 1, *Droit administratif général,* 16th edn. (LGDJ, Paris, 2001)

Ghestin, Goubeaux and Fabre-Magnan, *Introduction générale* = J. Ghestin, G. Goubeaux, and M. Fabre-Magnan, *Introduction générale* in J. Ghestin (dir.), *Traité de droit civil,* 4th edn. (LGDJ, Paris, 1994)

Ghestin, *La formation du contrat* = J. Ghestin, *La formation du contrat* in J. Ghestin (dir.), *Traité de droit civil,* 3rd edn. (LGDJ, Paris, 1993).

Ghestin, Jamin, and Billiau, *Effets du contrat* = J. Ghestin, C. Jamin, and M. Billiau, *Les effets du contrat* in J. Ghestin (dir.), *Traité de droit civil*

G. Lyon-Caen = G. Lyon-Caen, *Le droit du travail—Une technique réversible* (Dalloz, Paris, 1995)

Javillier = J.-C. Javillier, *Droit du travail,* 7th edn. (LGDJ, Paris, relié 1999)

Larroumet, *Contrat* = C. Larroumet, *Droit civil,* Tome 3, *Les obligations, Le contrat,* 5th edn. (Economica, Paris, 2003)

Larroumet, *Biens* = C. Larroumet, *Droit civil,* Tome 2, *Les biens, Droits réels principaux,* 5th edn. (Economica, Paris, 2006)

Lefort = C. Lefort, *Procédure civile,* 2nd edn (Dalloz, Paris, 2007)

Le Tourneau, *Droit de la responsabilité* = P. Le Tourneau, *Droit de la responsabilité et des contrats* (Dalloz Action, Paris, 2006)

Malaurie and Aynès, *Biens* = P. Malaurie and L. Aynès, *Les Biens,* 2nd edn. (Defrénois, Paris, 2005)

Malaurie and Aynès, *Successions* = P. Malaurie and L. Aynès, *Les Successions,* 2nd edn. (Defrénois, Paris, 2006)

Malaurie, Aynès, and Fulchiron, *Famille* = P. Malaurie, L. Aynès and H. Fulchiron *La famille,* 2nd edn. (Défrenois, 2006)

Malaurie, Aynès, and Gautier, *Contrats spéciaux* = P. Malaurie, L. Aynès and P.-Y. Gautier, *Les contrats spéciaux,* 2nd edn. (Defrénois, Paris, 2005)

Malaurie, Aynès, and Stoffel-Munck, *Obligations* = P. Malaurie, L. Aynès and P. Stoffel-Munck, *Droit civil: les obligations,* 2nd edn. (Defrénois, Paris, 2005)

Marty and Raynaud, *Obligations,* = G. Marty and P. Raynaud, *Droit civil, Tome II: Les obligations, Tome I: les sources,* 2nd edn. (Sirey, Paris, 1988)

Mazeaud and Chabas, *Obligations* = H. L. and J. Mazeaud, *Leçons de droit civil*, Tome II Premier Volume *Les obligations théorie générale*, 9th edn. (Montchrestien, Paris, 1998 by F. Chabas)

Mélanges Catala = *Le droit privé française à la fin du XXe siècle, Etudes offertes à Pierre Catala* (Litec, Paris, 2001)

Meschariakoff, *Services publics* = A.-S. Meschariakoff, *Services Publics* (PUF, Paris, 1991)

Nicholas, *French Contract* = B. Nicholas, *The French Law of Contract*, 2nd edn. (OUP, 1992)

Pacteau, *Contentieux administratifs* = B. Pacteau, *Contentieux administratifs*, 5th edn. (PUF, Paris, 1985).

Pédamon, *Droit commercial* = M. Pédamon, *Droit commercial*, 2nd edn. (Dalloz, 2000).

Pélissier, Supiot, and Jeammaud = J. Pélissier, A. Supiot, and A. Jeammaud, *Droit du travail*, 23rd edn. (Dalloz, Paris, 2006)

Pradel, *Droit pénal* = J. Pradel, *Droit pénal général*, 16th edn. (Editions Cujas, 2006)

Pradel, *Procédure pénale* = J. Pradel, *Procédure pénale*, 13th edn. (Editions Cujas 2006)

Starck *et al.*, *Contrat* = B. Starck, H. Roland and L. Boyer, *Obligations*, 1. *Responsabilité délictuelle*, 6th edn. (Litec, Paris, 1998).

Starck *et al.*, *Responsabilité délictuelle* = B. Starck, H. Roland and L. Boyer, *Obligations*, 1. *Responsabilité délictuelle*, 5th edn. (Litec, Paris, 1996).

Terré, Simler, and Lequette, *Obligations* = F. Terré, P. Simler, and Y. Lequette, *Droit civil: Les obligations*, 9th edn. (Paris, Dalloz, 2005).

Vincent and Guinchard = J. Vincent and S. Guinchard, *Procédure civile*, 27th edn. (Dalloz, Paris, 2003).

Vincent and Prévault = J. Vincent and J. Prévault, *Voies d'exécution et procédures de distribution*, 19th edn. (Précis Dalloz, Paris, 1999)

Viney and Jourdain, *Conditions* = G. Viney and P. Jourdain, *Les conditions de la responsabilité* in J. Ghestin (dir.), *Traité de droit civil*, 3rd edn. (LGDJ, Paris, 2006)

Viney and Jourdain, *Introduction à la responsabilité* = G. Viney and P. Jourdain, *Introduction à la responsabilité* in J. Ghestin (dir.), *Traité de droit civil*, 2nd edn. (LGDJ, Paris, 1995)

Viney and Jourdain, *Effets de la responsabilité* = G. Viney and P. Jourdain, *Les effets de la responsabilité*, 2nd edn. (LGDJ, Paris, 2001)

Table of Cases

EUROPEAN COURT OF HUMAN RIGHTS

EUROPEAN COURT OF JUSTICE

UNITED KINGDOM

Table of Legislation

EUROPEAN COMMUNITY

Introduction: The Spirit of French Law

French law like French culture is distinctive. When legal systems are classified, the French and the English systems are not classified in the same family or group: English law is entered into the larger grouping of common law systems, while French law belongs to the loosely defined civil law systems.[1] However, they are both also very much part of a Western European tradition of law and so its distinctiveness should not be exaggerated. A common heritage from Roman law and canon law is now shaped by common adherence to the European Convention on Human Rights, the European Union, as well as to wider international obligations such as GATT, the Geneva Convention on refugees, and the United Nations Charter and declaration.

The distinctiveness of French law lies in the areas of values, legal procedure, the form of legal rules, and an attitude to law which is often described as a *mentalité*.

I. Legal Values

As part of the Judeo-Christian and Roman law traditions, French law shares most values with other Western European countries. In the area of human rights and individual freedoms, France's adherence to the European Convention on Human Rights (which is directly applicable in French courts) provides a common point of reference with other European countries and also with non-European countries which have similar frameworks for protecting rights. Membership of the European Union and agreements such as Schengen express a commitment to a whole range of common economic and social values which are directly applicable in France. Discussions on the reform of French domestic law now typically involve reference to the European Convention and the policies of the European Union. In addition, the practices and policies of other Western countries have been major influences. French writers can talk with some justification of a 'European' or 'universal' law even in such specifically national areas as criminal law.[2]

Should one say that French law is republican in spirit? As we shall note, over the 200 years or so since the Revolution of 1789 there have been a number of

---

[1] However, the grouping of the continental systems is not so easily defined. They are often subdivided themselves into Roman, Germanic and Nordic systems. See on this point K. Zweigert and H. Kötz, *An Introduction to Comparative Law,* 2nd edn. (Oxford, 1987), 69, 70. See also H. Patrick Glenn, *Legal Traditions of the World*, 2nd edn. (OUP, 2004).

[2] M. Delmas-Marty, in N. Jareborg, *Towards Universal Law* (Uppsala, 1995), ch. 10.

non-republican regimes, each of which have left their mark to a greater or lesser extent on the development of the law. Indeed, the Civil Code itself, while formally promulgated at the time of the First Republic, is often known as the *Code Napoléon* and Napoléon I clearly had a significant personal influence on a number of its provisions. On the other hand, French public law, both the administrative and constitutional, is dominated by the idea of France as a republic, a constitutional and lay (i.e. non religious) regime accepting the importance of individual human rights. And we can certainly see the impact of values associated closely with republicanism (or so associated in France). Indeed, traces of the values behind the republican motto, 'Liberty, Equality and Fraternity' may be seen in the law of contract, civil procedure, family law and labour law.

The existence of a broad commonality of policy and values does not preclude some very specific French values. Within this book, there are noted a number of social values which are distinct. In criminal and family law, there are certain specific offences which reflect social attitudes, e.g. in relation to duties to parents and to the vulnerable in society. In employment and company law, there is a great concern to protect jobs in the regulation of dismissal and insolvency. The whole area of public law with its conceptions of public service and public employment is replete with specifically French conceptions of how government should work. Constitutional law is very distinctive in many respects. There are thus distinctive values but these do not dominate the whole of law, but provide variants to the principal common values of democracy, legality, respect for the individual, the family, employment and so on.

II. Legal Procedure

Procedures adopted by different legal systems owe as much to history as they do to the values which influence their operation. In France, there are significant differences in terms of procedure which make French law different, not only from the common law, but also from other continental systems. In the case of commercial law, it is the role of lay business judges and the relative informality of proof which is distinctive. Commercial disputes are rapidly resolved by law administered by commercial men and women, rather than by professional judges. In criminal law, distinctive features are the status of the prosecutor (*procureur*) as a member of the judiciary and the role of the investigating judge in the pre-trial investigation leading to the decision to prosecute, and, more recently, the *juge de l'application des peines* in the administration of sentences and the use of conciliation procedures to avoid prosecutions. Here, the judiciary take on roles which would be given to administrators or distinct groups of officials in the management of the criminal process outside the trial phase. In employment law, distinctive features are the importance of administrative authorization by the *inspecteur du travail* before a dismissal is permitted and the composition of the employment court which has both employers and employees in equal numbers but (unless there is a tie) without a judge in the chair. Employment law is more focused on employee rights than in England. In public law, there are distinctive procedures for administrative and constitutional cases. In administrative law, the procedure is more informal and inquisitorial than in private law and less party-driven than in many legal systems. There is almost a sense in which the procedure of the administrative courts is an investigation of administrative shortcomings, rather than litigation between parties. The composition of administrative courts is also distinctive in that the members, especially of the higher courts, are not trained as judges, but are first and foremost administrators, who may move between judicial and administrative tasks. In constitutional law, the court is not composed solely of lawyers and does not have an adversarial procedure. It is an investigation conducted by those knowledgeable in constitutional matters with few formal rules of procedure.

In the case of private law (including for this purpose criminal law) and the private law courts, there is a further special and fundamental feature: the system of *cassation* ('quashing'). For while a system of appeals from decisions of first instance exists to the cours d'appel, the latters' judgments are subject only to *pourvoi en cassation* to the Cour de cassation, the nature of whose role is crucial to the exposition and the development of French private law. The starting point for understanding this is that the Cour de cassation is the 'guardian of the law' and in principle, therefore, is concerned with ensuring the proper application of the law to the facts as found by the lower courts. In this sense, then, recourse to the Cour de cassation by *pourvoi en cassation* may be thought of as similar to appeal on a point of law. Certainly, given the regional character of courts of first instance and appeal, its role is to ensure that the unity of French private law which was achieved by the promulgation of the Civil Code is maintained as a reality. However, the phrase 'appeal on a point of law' is rather too imbued with common law associations to stand without more. For the Cour de cassation does not re-decide cases submitted to it (having corrected the legal rules to be applied) but rather, as its name indicates, quashes the decisions of lower courts. In this perspective, it is a court of review, review, that is, of the legitimacy of the decision-making of the lower courts which are submitted to its control: it is 'a true judge of judgments' ('*un véritable juge des jugements*').[3] In this way, the relationship between the Cour de cassation and *juges du fond* (lower courts judging the merits) may possess a certain echo for the English lawyer of the English procedure by which a higher court reviews a lower court by way of case stated. But the importance of this system of *cassation* for the development of and understanding of the substance of French private law cannot be overestimated. For all legal propositions of private law have to be analysed so as to estabilish which issues or aspects of issues are treated as ones of fact (for the 'sovereign power of assessment' of the *juges du fond*) or of law for the control of the Cour de cassation. And while modern legislation occasionally makes clear that in coming to a particular decision (or exercising a particular

---

[3] J.-L. Aubert, 'La distinction du fait et du droit dans le pourvoi en cassation en matière civile' D 2005 Chron. 1115.

discretion) the lower courts have a 'sovereign power', for the most part it is the Cour de cassation itself which determines which propositions are within its control and which escape it. It intervenes on grounds, in ways and to an extent of which it is itself the master. Thus, whole tracts of the legal landscape (or what to a common lawyer would be the legal landscape) have been all but abandoned by the Cour de cassation to the lower courts, two striking examples of this being the interpretation of contracts and the measure and quantification of damages. In other contexts, the Cour de cassation is careful to restrict the lower courts' room for manoeuvre with rules of law whose non-observance will attract its intervention. In the result, it is one of the most salient but also one of the most frustrating aspects of French private law that many issues are decided by the lower courts behind this impenetrable veil of their 'sovereign power of assessment'. French jurists themselves sometimes observe that where an issue is put in the hands of the *juges du fond* this allows them to take into account 'equity' in their decisions, but the incidence and extent of this phenomenon must, by its nature, remain unverifiable. Be that as it may, it is clear that the boundary between law and fact in French private law practice is a function of these institutional and procedural arrangements, as much as it was in nineteenth century English civil law a function of the role (and to an extent judicial distrust) of juries. We shall see throughout our discussion of the private law this division influencing the way in which the law is exposed and discussed.

The features identified thus far reflect different, specifically French, procedures in the various areas, but there is no unifying theme. There is an effort to integrate some users of the law into the decision-making panel, by using commercial men and women, employees, administrators and politicians as judges. A more universal feature is the role of written evidence in the procedures and the relatively small part played by oral evidence and argument. The role of the 'file' in collating evidence and providing a basis for decision helps explain the rapidity of oral phases in hearings at first instance, and the ease of appeal procedures: if there is a file, it can be sent up for appeal to a higher court more easily than the oral evidence of a lower court hearing in the United Kingdom. The requirement to have a lawyer is a common, but not universal feature of many claims which can be made in the courts. This obligation restricts the scope for the litigant conducting their own case and makes easier the conduct of the case for the court.

III. The Form of Legal Rules

There are three features of French legal rules which are usually identified as distinctive, at least in relation to the common law. The first is the importance of *codification,* the second is the statement of rules in general terms, rather than in specific detail, and the third is the relative unimportance of judicial decisions compared with doctrinal legal writing, in stating the rules of the legal system.

As will be seen in the chapter on sources, French law is very heavily based on legislation, but this is not a feature peculiar to French law. The pace of social change and the importance of government direction in society and the economy has meant that most modern societies have a large amount of law-making from legislatures and government. The distinctive feature of France and a number of continental European countries is the perception that the written legislative rules provide a coherent and self-contained framework for the solution of contemporary social problems. The post-revolutionary Codes (Civil, Criminal and Commercial, together with Civil and Criminal Procedure) were the first successful attempt and have been replicated with varying success later. Rather than the classical common law conception of the law as a patchwork quilt of legislative provisions held together by thread woven out of general principles and sewn by the judges, the French civilian is thought to see the Code as the source of general principles into which judicial and later legislative decisions fit. With some exaggeration, no doubt, Philippe Malaurie has argued

Codification—above all our Civil Code—has permeated deep into our national culture. The Civil Code is part of our national heritage, just like French-style gardens, the Palace of Versailles, Philippe de Champaigne or General de Gaulle. At stake in codification is our culture and our identity. The Civil Code has been more than the symbol of national unity... The Civil Code is at the same time the cause, the witness and the consequence of our cultural unity.[4]

This picture does have some truth in that exegesis of the Code is the commonest form of civilian argument. The inter-relationship of provisions in the Code is an important test of legal arguments. But there are also difficulties with this picture. First, some of the Codes are quite old and have undergone significant change. Secondly, others have been subject to layer upon layer of textual amendment which make the underlying principles difficult to discern. Thirdly, there are whole branches of the law which do not have this kind of coherent principle, but which have the same kind of consolidating statute as can be found in English law. Lastly, as will be seen in the chapters on sources and administrative law, public law is as much a judge-made system as the English law. The texts of public law give only part of the story. The general principles of public law are the real bedrock of the system and these are as much common law as any parallel branch of English law. Thus codification and the spirit it engenders is not universal in the application of French law. All the same, codification does retain a symbolic function within French legal culture. In the view of a former Vice-President of the Commission supérieure de la codification, codification is an important element in the rule of law—permitting access to the rules which govern individuals.[5] As a result, the Commission created in 1989 has programmed some forty-two codes

---

[4] P. Malaurie, 'Les enjeux de la codification', AJDA 1997.642.
[5] See his speech of 4 December 1995, Commission supérieure de la codification, *Sixieme rapport annuel 1995* (Paris, 1996), 21.

to go alongside the five Napoleonic codes, and these will cover public authorities, public law procedures and other areas hitherto outside the existing structure of codes. All the same, most proposals are more in the form of consolidations of existing texts in a sensible order than a radical rethink of principles. This was achieved in relation to the reformed Criminal Code of 1993. The commission wants to avoid too many 'minicodes' in very discrete areas, but also the 'maxi-codes' which try to cover too many different areas.

The nature of French legal rules is the subject of repeated comment and comparison. The succinct statements of principle in the Civil Code are taken to be a model of how legislation is drafted and this is contrasted with the common law method of covering each eventuality. To be accurate, the French legislature is more likely to adopt a principled drafting style compared with the British Parliament. But the overall effect is often little different. The French resort much more to secondary legislation, which the Government has an inherent power to enact. This produces a parallel set of provisions (usually labelled R in modern codes) which are more detailed than the provisions in a *loi* (labelled L in the Code). The combination of these two sets of provisions often provides a very detailed result, even more detailed than English law. Nevertheless, the principled approach of legislation makes its purpose more evident and it is easier for the orientation of the legislation to be understood by non-lawyers.[6] Texts drafted in most common law countries are more straightforward in terms of knowing the practical impact of the legislation from a single document.

The authority of legislation as the expression of the general will and as the embodiment of general principle results in a lower status for judicial decisions. Judges as bureaucrats are meant to implement the law, not to create it. The authority of judicial decisions relates to the quality of their content, rather than to any precedential force which attaches to the jurisdiction which made it. Even the lowest courts can disregard the decisions of the highest courts if they are considered wrong. In terms of setting out the law correctly, the role of academics is also important. Doctrinal legal writing has had an influential role greater than traditionally in the common law.[7] The balance between the different actors in the legal system creates a distinctive approach to law.

IV. Attitude to Law

It has been strongly argued that there is a distinctive attitude to law which creates a different mentality among French lawyers. This feature is picked up by a number of authors.[8] Among the features identified which illustrate this difference

---

[6] See generally W. Dale (ed.), *British and French Statutory Drafting* (Institute of Advanced Legal Studies, London 1986).

[7] See R.C. Van Caenegem, *Judges, Legislators and Professors* (Cambridge, 1987), 155–7.

[8] See especially Zweigert and Kötz, (above n. 1) 71; B. Markesinis, *The Gradual Convergence* (Oxford, 1994), 10; G. Samuel, *The Foundations of Legal Reasoning* (Antwerp, 1995), 28;

of approach are the starting points for legal reasoning and the method of legal development.

As has just been stated, the common law comes across as a custom-based system in which the values of the law are recalled by the judges. In areas dominated by common law principles, specific statutory provisions have to be integrated to make a coherent whole, and may encourage the development of common law rules along similar lines to those contained in statute. But in areas dominated by statutory rules, the English judges are wary of incorporating into them common law principles by way of interpretation.[9] In much of French law, the structure of principles and values was set out in the Codes, notably the Civil, Criminal and Commercial codes, as well as the Codes of Civil and Criminal procedure. These provide the coherence of the system and it is not necessary to go further back into the legal tradition. Put in this way, there is a danger of exaggeration. French administrative law and, to a lesser extent, French constitutional law are case-based systems which operate in very similar ways to the common law, mainly because of the absence of codification in the sense of a restatement of general principles. By contrast, English company law, social security law, and tax law all operate within closely defined statutory frameworks. They may lack broad statements of principle, but they are not judge-made in the same sense as many aspects of the common law. This difference might be seen as reflecting different intellectual traditions: a rationalism in France and a traditionalism, incrementalism and pragmatism in Britain. That might be to draw the contrast too starkly, but the different traditions do originate in different periods and have been shaped by historical conditions at different times.[10] All the same, the intellectual climate in which the systems have to operate today are very close indeed and this ensures significant commonality of approach.

Samuel has argued that French law reasons from rights (*le droit subjectif*) while the common law starts from actions.[11] In France if there is a right, then a remedy can be found. In English law, traditionally there is a right only if an action and a remedy are provided by law. Thus, in English law, one can get a long way in regulating employment relationships without any conception of a right to strike.[12] However, since the writing of the first edition of this book in 1998, the Human Rights Act of the same year has reduced the impact of this contrast with French law, as English lawyers have increasingly had resort to arguments from (Convention) rights, whether as regards public law (seen for example in

---

P. Legrand, 'European Legal Systems are not Converging' (1996) 45 ICLQ 52; cf J. Bell, 'English Law and French Law—Not so Different?' [1995] CLP 63, 98–101.

[9] See J. Bell and G. Engle (eds.), *Cross on Statutory Interpretation*, 3rd edn. (London, 1995), 43–6.

[10] See R. Van Caenegem, *An Historical Approach to Private Law* (Cambridge, 1992), 187 ff.

[11] 'Le droit subjectif and English Law' [1987] CLJ 264.

[12] See below pp. 507–509.

the development of the grounds of judicial review)[13] or of private law (seen for example in the development of a law of privacy on distinctly unpromising common law foundations).[14]

Legal development in the two systems is linked to different foci of attention. The French legal structure is described in terms of concepts and the way fact situations fit into those concepts. A good example would be the importance of 'public service' in French law, a concept which is almost absent as a legal framework in English law, yet the same activities are regulated often in very similar ways. English law seems preoccupied with the resolution of fact-situations, albeit on a relatively unstructured basis. The development of the law is by analogy from facts, rather than through the logical articulation of legal concepts. Although this is accurate to some extent, there are limits to this characterization. Much of French law is case-based these days and the judges when they reason are more likely to follow methods similar to the common law in reasoning by analogy.[15]

The common law reasons by dialogue with the past, using analogies and decisions from the past in order to provide the building blocks for the future. Although this is explicit in much of what is said in a common law judgment, it is equally evident in the way lawyers reason in France. In any legal system, law operates as a tradition, a set of ideas and texts handed down and worked upon by a legal community.[16] Continuity and consistency are important legal values, though they are appreciated to different extents by different legal systems. The English common law is at the extreme of valuing legal certainty through precedent and other devices perhaps more than the achievement of justice in the individual case. The French legal tradition is even more formalist in terms of procedure, but allows a degree of latitude in the characterization of facts and the interpretation of rules by judges in individual cases. The differences are perhaps more ones of emphasis rather than radical distinctions in mentality.

V. A 'Social Model'?

Over the last decade or so in particular, French lawyers and others have raised questions as to the way in which French law should develop over the coming years. On the one hand, some are concerned to preserve what they see as valuable in their own, distinctive legal tradition, whether this is at the level of legal concepts (for example, *la cause* in contract law[17]) or, and especially, at the level

---

[13] D. Feldman, 'Standards of Review and Human Rights in English Law' in D. Feldman (ed.), *English Public Law* (Oxford, 2004), ch. 7; P. P. Craig, *Administrative Law*, 5th edn. (London, 2003), 421–425, 445–446, 465–473 and esp. 568–603.

[14] e.g. *McKennitt v. Ash* [2006] EWCA Civ 1714; [2007] 3 WLR 194.

[15] J. Bell, 'English Law and French Law—Not so Different?' [1995] CLP 63, 81–83.

[16] M. Krygier, 'Law as Tradition' (1986) 5 *Law and Philosophy* 237.

[17] Below, pp. 317 ff.

of legal values. So, for example, it would appear that a significant reason for proposals put forward in 2005 by a group of French jurists for reform of the law of obligations and prescription[18] was that French private lawyers felt left out and even left behind by developments at a European level towards a 'European Civil Code' or at least, a 'Common Frame of Reference' (proposals which are often seen as dominated by German and/or common law thinking).[19] As to legal values, there has developed a debate as to whether French law as a whole reflects and should continue to reflect a 'social model', a model different from the 'liberal' model seen as typical of 'Anglo-Saxon' law (meaning English law and the laws of the United States) and also of some of the regulations and directives emanating from the European Union.[20] But by no means all French lawyers accept the premises of this way of thinking. So, while for example some argue for a 'social' or *'solidariste'* approach to the law of contract, others counter that this way of thinking should not be allowed to contradict established *French* legal principle (notably, the binding force of contracts) and the important values of legal and contractual certainty.[21] Not surprisingly, this kind of debate is most prominent in the area of employment law, where the traditional and overtly 'social model'— reflected in the fact that *droit du travail* is seen as part of *le droit social*—is being challenged by reference to a more liberal approach.[22] As Mark Freedland explains in Chapter 12, the election in 2007 of President Sarkozy may mark a turning point in this respect.

VI. Conclusion

It would be wrong to conclude that there are no significant differences between English and French legal cultures. The traditions of codification, legal education and judicial decision-making, as well as procedure in and out of court, all have a significant impact on the way a lawyer operates. At the same time, it would be wrong to exaggerate the differences. Both systems are very much 'formalist' in terms described by Atiyah and Summers.[23] In this sense, it matters to both that the law is clear and certain (and is thus predictable), as much as it produces a fair outcome in all individual cases. The legal procedures and decision-making of

[18] P. Catala (ed.), *Avant-projet de réforme du droit des obligations et de la prescription* (La documentation française, 2005) (*'Avant-projet de réforme'*).

[19] On these proposals see in particular Report from the Commission, *First Annual Progress Report on European Contract Law and the Acquis Review* Com (2005) 456.

[20] This was particularly noticeably in some French reaction to the so-called 'Bolkenstein Directive', EC Directive 2006/123/EC of the European Parliament and of the Council of 12 December 2006 on services in the internal market.

[21] Below, pp. 300–301.

[22] Below, pp. 511–512.

[23] P.S. Atiyah and R.S. Summers, *Form and Substance in Anglo-American Law* (Oxford, 1987), 11–28.

both are clearly rule-based far more than American law. It would also be wrong to consider that the legal systems are monolithic. The chapters in this book will show that approaches in private law are different from administrative law, and areas such as employment and commercial law have specific characteristics, often because they are designed for specific groups of people who also form the body of judges who adjudicate on the application of those rules. The outcome is that France is a multi-jural society with a variety of legal cultures which have some similarities and differences. While some broad statements can be made, a better understanding is gained by closer attention to the detail of how specific branches of the system operate.

PART I
THE SYSTEM

1

Sources of Law

Comparative lawyers often distinguish legal systems according to the sources to which they refer in determining what is the law. The use of particular sources is said by Zweigert and Kötz to reflect the distinctive character of law and approach to legal thinking which is adopted in that system.[1] Though it may be doubted whether legal 'thinking' is so radically affected,[2] it is certainly true that the use of sources in different ways does alter the character of legal argument. This chapter seeks to bring out those aspects of the French approach to law and legal argument which are distinctive. Any such general presentation has to be qualified by the recognition that different branches of French law operate in different ways—the approach to case law and doctrinal legal writing is different in administrative and constitutional law (which are much more case-based systems) than civil and criminal law (which are more code-based).[3] Nevertheless, some general observations can usefully be made.

I. What is a Source of Law?

The comparative lawyer is concerned with the influences which shape the law, rather than the materials which the lawyer consults in order to discover the specific rules of law. In terms of materials, a lawyer in most systems will consult textbooks and encyclopedias, cases (frequently through databases rather than on paper), legislation and articles written by jurists, be they academics or practitioners. The lawyer uses these material sources as a database of information which provides the evidence from which a legal opinion or argument can be constructed. When lawyers talk of 'sources of law', we are referring much more to the status which attaches to the materials derived from those different sources, whether a particular item constitutes a formal or authoritative source of law.[4]

---

[1] K. Zweigert and H. Kötz, *An Introduction to Comparative Law*, 3rd edn. (Oxford, 1998), 69.

[2] J. Bell, 'English Law and French Law—Not so Different?' [1995] CLP 63, 86–90; P. Legrand, 'European legal systems are not converging' (1996) 45 ICLQ 52, 74–78.

[3] J. Bell, *French Legal Cultures* (Cambridge, 2001).

[4] R. Sacco describes the content of the various materials a lawyer may consult as 'formants', since they are only partial and incomplete statements of the law: R. Sacco, 'Legal Formants: A Dynamic Approach to Comparative Law' (1991) 39 AJCL 1, 21–24.

Is case law an influential or a binding source of law? How important are the writings of legal academics? In common law systems, lawyers are concerned with whether the various sources can be cited to judges in legal argument. If they can be cited in their own right, then they do amount to valid sources of law; if not, they are merely secondary descriptions of what the law is. In the various French legal procedures, this is an inappropriate question. Since the judge is expected to do his/her own legal researches (following the maxim *curia novit legem*), the interesting question is not what lawyers may cite in their arguments as much as what weight is attached to different sources in deciding what the law is. Given the succinct style of the French judicial decision, the answer has to be found not just by reading the judgment, but also the argument of the public representative (the *ministère public* or the *commissaire du gouvernement*) and other comments on the case made by jurists or even by the court itself, e.g. in the annual reports of the Cour de cassation or the Conseil d'Etat.

In relation to French law, it is important to draw a distinction between formal sources of law and influential sources. Formal sources are authorities which a lawyer is obliged to consider because they are binding statements of the law. Such sources cover the constitution, European Union law and international treaties, legislation, custom, and general principles of law (called by David 'supereminent principles').[5] In addition, a good lawyer will also look to case law (*la jurisprudence*) and legal writing (*la doctrine*) for reliable, but not binding, interpretation and statements of the law. The distinction between these two groups of sources rests on their constitutional status. Echoing article 2 of the Declaration of the Rights of Man and of the Citizen of 1789, article 2 of the 1958 Constitution makes clear that legal sovereignty resides in the people. In Rousseau's terms, legislation is an expression of the general will, such that a free people is only bound by the laws which they have made for themselves. The people approved by referendum the 1958 Constitution. Their representatives in Parliament enact *lois* and ratify treaties. The Executive enacts *règlements* under the authority conferred on it by the Constitution or by Parliament. Custom derives its legal force from the practice of the people who believe it is legally obligatory. General principles of law are the values which underlie enacted law. Thus it can be said that, in some form or other, all the obligatory sources of law have their origin in direct or indirect decisions of the people, and this confers on them their legitimate authority as sources of law. By contrast, case law of the courts and writings of jurists (academics or practitioners) have no claim to be in any way decisions made by the people or their representatives. They are merely views of (important) sections of the legal community about what the law is, and so lack the same constitutional legitimacy as the formal sources of law. But this does not deny that they have a great influential role in shaping our understanding of law.

    [5] R. David, *French Law* (Baton Rouge, 1972) 194–207.

The distinctiveness of a legal system lies not so much in the different sources to which its lawyers refer, but in the approach they adopt to what counts as law. Lawson suggests that the 'cast of mind' of French lawyers is shaped by the role of the written text and academic writing in the development and interpretation of law.[6] But that is not a permanent feature of the law. Since Lawson wrote those words over 50 years ago, the place of academic writing in England has significantly increased and it is now cited in the highest courts.[7] Equally, as will be seen, the written character of much of French law is rather contestable today. At best the features which will be identified represent different tendencies within French and English law, rather than sharp differences.

II. The Hierarchy of Norms

Until 1958, there were in theory only three levels of constitutional sources: the written Constitution, the *lois* passed by Parliament and the various administrative texts which aimed at implementing the acts. It emphasized the importance of *loi* ('statute', legislation passed by Parliament) over any other source; Rousseau[8] reflecting the ideas of the revolutionaries held that *lois* were the expression of the will of the Nation,[9] which was assimilated to the legislative will of the Parliament. Statutes could do no wrong and should not be controlled and they were extolled at the expense of individual decisions which were supposed to have been the cause of the arbitrariness of the *Ancien Régime*. Evolution forced the authors of the 1958 Constitution to move from this view and create a much more complex hierarchy in which the *loi* lost its primacy. This was achieved in more ways than one: the authority of the Constitution was strengthened by the creation of a constitutional control; international treaties and European legislation were given supremacy over ordinary statute, and finally, the domain of intervention of parliamentary legislation was reduced drastically.

A. The Block of Constitutional Norms[10]

France has had written constitutions for over 200 years.[11] The latest constitution, that of the fifth Republic, was adopted in 1958. But that document is not

---

[6] H. Lawson, *A Common Lawyer Looks at the Civil Law* (Ann Arbor, 1953), 66.

[7] Burrows, *English Private Law*, paras 1.103–1.104.

[8] This view was expressed in *Du contrat social* (1762), Book 2, ch 6.

[9] In French: '*l'expression de la volonté générale*' (1789 Declaration, art. 6).

[10] See generally, J. Bell, *French Constitutional Law* (Oxford, 1992), 57–77.

[11] See the list of the regimes and constitutions up until now:
3 September 1791: first written Constitution (constitutional monarchy);
24 June 1793: First Republic;
22 August 1795: Directoire;
13 December 1799: Consulate and First Empire;

an exhaustive statement of constitutional provisions, and it has become conventional in recent years for authors to talk of the 'block of constitutional provisions' (*le bloc de constitutionnalité*) to designate the totality of constitutional rules and principles. The Conseil constitutionnel refers in preference to 'principles having constitutional status' (*principes à valeur constitutionnelle*).

The 1958 Constitution mainly contains rules on the competence and functioning of the organs of government (the President, the Government, and the Parliament), the enactment of legislation, and guarantees for the independence of the judiciary. Constitutional rules are also to be found in the standing orders of both chambers of Parliament, which are approved by the Conseil constitutionnel, and in the finance legislation procedures laid down by the *ordonnance* of 7 November 1958. The 1958 Constitution affirms few fundamental values. In addition, the 1958 Constitution confirms France's adherence to the principles laid down by the Preamble to the Declaration of the Rights of Man and of the Citizen of 1789 and by the Preamble to the Fourth Republic's Constitution of 1946, to which has been added the Charter for the Environment of 2004. In brief, the Declaration of 1789 contains a list of classical liberal principles on freedom of the individual, property, and equality. The 1946 Preamble contains social and economic rights, such as the rights to health, education, to trade union activity, to work, and so on. The Charter for the Environment adds a number of environmental principles, but to which it is difficult to give concrete content.[12] But even this list is not exhaustive. The Preamble to the 1946 Constitution affirms respect for the 'fundamental principles recognized by the laws of the Republic' without enumerating them. These fundamental principles were meant to be a reference to the numerous freedoms and liberties which were recognized by the legislator during the Third Republic. However, the notion of a 'fundamental principle' is unclear, in particular to which laws (*lois*) from the preceding republics this refers. The basic test is that the relevant constitutional principle is recognized (but not necessarily laid down) by a *loi* of a republic. Thus, the Civil Code of 29 March 1804 could be a document in which such principles are recognized since it was a *loi* enacted before the proclamation of the First Empire on 18 May 1804. This requirement of a pedigree in a *loi* before 1946 leads to some unlikely points of reference. For example, the principle of freedom of education was 'discovered'

4 June 1814: Restoration—interrupted by the episode of the 'Cents jours' (return of Napoléon)—(first Constitutional Charter; constitutional monarchy);
14 August 1830: July Monarchy (2nd Constitutional Charter; constitutional monarchy);
4 November 1848: Second Republic;
14 January 1852: Second Empire;
21 May 1870: Third Republic;
27 October 1946: Fourth Republic;
4 November 1958: Fifth Republic.

[12] However, the Conseil constitutionnel has already reviewed the energy policy in the light of art. 6 and the principle of sustainable development of the Charter in C. cons. 7 July 2005, *Energy policy*.

in article 91 of the Finance Law of 31 March 1931.[13] The principle of 'separation of powers' could not be based on the most explicit text, the *loi* of 16–24 August 1790,[14] since it was adopted during the first constitutional monarchy, so it had to be based on the *loi* of 24 May 1872 concerning the Conseil d'Etat.[15] In addition, the Conseil constitutionnel refers sometimes to 'objectives of constitutional value', such as pluralism in the media, which cannot be found directly in any text, but are offered as more explicit statements of what is implicit in the various texts just cited.

As a result, it is not really possible to give a definitive list of constitutional rules and principles. The mere fact that there is a written text called 'the Constitution of the Fifth Republic' does not mean that lawyers avoid the difficulties that are encountered by their colleagues dealing with an unwritten constitution. In addition, the existence of a written text does not remove the need for conventions.[16] Such principles of constitutional morality and practice determine the actual interpretation of the constitution and sometimes create binding norms. It may even be that these conventions prevail over the text of the Constitution. Thus, article 27 of the Constitution states that the right to vote in Parliament is personal, yet it is common practice for members of the Assemblée nationale to leave their voting keys with colleagues (often party leaders) who can use them when they are absent; indeed few members need to be present for all the votes to be cast. The Conseil constitutionnel has ignored such breaches of the Constitution when *lois* have been referred to it.[17] Such conventions, however, have no formal legal validity.

The Constitution takes priority over all legislation. The Conseil constitutionnel is the only body with jurisdiction to strike down a *loi*. If the text is not referred for control, no other court can challenge its compatibility with the Constitution, and ordinary courts have to apply it. However, all courts can use the principles of the Constitution to interpret legislation, and to strike down administrative enactments (*règlements*) or decisions.[18] Ordinary courts thus have an important role in implementing the Constitution, a role which they perform without the opportunity to appeal to the Conseil constitutionnel for a ruling or an advisory opinion.

B. Treaties and European Union Law

It is conventional to divide legal systems into dualist systems (like most common law countries) in which international treaties become part of national law

[13] J. Bell, *French Constitutional Law* (Oxford, 1992), 70–71; see C. cons. 23 Nov. 1977, *Education Law*, Rec. 42.

[14] C. cons. 23 Jan.1987, *Competition Council*, Rec. 8.

[15] C. cons. 23 Jan. 1987, *Competition Law*, Rec. 8.

[16] See the discussion concerning the different interpretations of the Constitution, below pp 000.

[17] C. cons. 23 Jan. 1987, *Séguin amendment*, Rec. 13; J.-C. Nemery, 'Le principe du vote personnel dans la Constitution de la Ve République' RDP 1987.995.

[18] CE Sect. 12 Feb. 1960, *Soc. Eky*, Leb. 101.

only after specific enactment and monist systems (such as the Netherlands) in which an international treaty has automatic force in national law without specific enactment. France offers a rather hybrid picture. Following the constitutional amendments necessary to ratify the Maastricht Treaty in 1992, it is necessary to distinguish between the law of the European Union and rights and obligations arising under other international treaties.

1. Treaties

Generally, treaty commitments fall within the general provisions of article 55 of the Constitution which provides that 'treaties or other agreements duly ratified or approved shall, upon their publication, have an authority superior to that of statutes, subject, for each separate agreement or treaty, to reciprocal application by the other party'. This might appear to be a monist approach. But there are two important limitations; all treaties must be ratified: some are merely signed by the President of the Republic but others, listed under article 54 of the Constitution, require a *loi* to be adopted by Parliament. As a result, there is little practical difference between this approach and a dualist one. The main difference is the hierarchical position that international provisions benefit from within the sources of law. Once ratified, they prevail not only over previously enacted legislation, but also subsequent, inconsistent legislation. A second limitation is that the Conseil constitutionnel has ruled that it did not have jurisdiction to decide on the conformity of a statute to any international treaties;[19] in the event of a statute being incompatible with some treaty provisions, ordinary courts should apply the treaty.[20]

Furthermore, a treaty should not be ratified if it is incompatible with the Constitution. Indeed, the President of the Republic, the Prime Minister, the Presidents of either chambers or 60 members of any one chamber may refer a treaty to the Conseil constitutionnel for a decision on its compatibility with the Constitution before the ratification. In the case of the Maastricht Treaty in 1992, the Conseil constitutionnel's decision determined a revision of the Constitution, so as to grant a right for all citizens of the Union to participate in municipal elections, to transfer the appropriate powers in relation to both visa requirements for non-community nationals and monetary union.[21] Thus, treaties only have primacy within the body of constitutionally authorized sources of law. Treaties thus have a higher status than in the United Kingdom where they generally only have a degree of priority only through the principle of statutory interpretation whereby Parliament is presumed not to have wished to pass legislation inconsistent with the United Kingdom's treaty obligations.[22]

[19] C. cons. 15 Jan. 1975, *Abortion Law*, Rec. 19; Bell (above n. 13), 71 and 318–319.
[20] In fact, the Conseil constitutionnel made clear in its decisions that it was the duty of all ordinary courts to undertake this control: Bell (above n. 13), 48–53.
[21] C. cons. 9 April 1992, *Maastricht Treaty*, Rec. 55.
[22] Burrows (above n. 7), paras 1.52–1.54.

Amongst the treaties which France has ratified, the European Convention on Human Rights has a particular importance. In his speech at the beginning of 2000, the President of the Cour de cassation remarked similarly that:

Within the judicial order, it is under the impetus of [the higher law] and by a mechanism of law creation identical to the method of development in the Common Law, that the Cour de cassation as national judge reconstructs internal law on the basis of Community law or the law of the Convention by changing it profoundly.[23]

The Convention has operated in three ways. First, incompatibility with the Convention has led the legislator to change the law.[24] Secondly, even without legislative change, the Convention, as superior law, may lead the ordinary courts to disregard national legislation.[25] Thirdly, it is a source of inspiration for changes in the law.

2. *European Union law*

Article 88-1 of the Constitution of 1958 provides that the Republic shall participate in the European Communities and the European Union and exercise its competencies in common according to the treaties. Indeed, article 88-2 specifically accepts a limitation of sovereignty which membership of the EU entails. But, at the same time, in its 2004 decision on the Treaty establishing a Constitution for Europe, the Conseil constitutionnel made it clear that the supremacy of EU law is based on the Constitution of 1958 itself, which remains the superior law.[26] The label 'Constitution' given to the Treaty 'has no effect on the existence of the French Constitution and its place at the summit of the internal legal order'. All the same, an earlier decision of June 2004 had stated that the Conseil would only examine the constitutionality of a *loi* implementing an EU directive where it was manifestly contrary to constitutional principles.[27] So the requirements of the European Court of Justice on supremacy, embodied in the 2004 Treaty are satisfied.

---

[23] Canivet, Audience de rentrée, 6 January 2000, from Cour de cassation website <http://www.courdecassation.fr>, Annual Report for 1999. See generally R. de Gouttes, 'La Convention européenne des droits de l'homme et le juge français' (1999) 51 RIDC 7 and S. Bracconnier, *Jurisprudence de la Cour européenne des droits de l'homme et droit administratif français* (Brussels, 1997).

[24] See legislation on telephone tapping (loi 10 July 1991) following the European Court of Human Rights decision of 24 April 1990, *Kruslin and Hervig* (1990) EHRR 528: Bell (above n. 3), 130–131.

[25] For example, the Cour de cassation reversed previous decisions on the ability of transsexuals to change the classification of their sex on their état civil in the light of a decision of the European Court of Human Rights on 25 March 1992, see Ass. plén. 11 Dec. 1992, JCP 1993. II.21991.

[26] See C. cons. 19 Nov. 2004, Rec. 173. See J. Bell, 'French Constitutional Council and European Law' (2005) 54 ICLQ 735.

[27] C. cons. 10 June 2004, Rec. 101.

The position adopted by the Conseil constitutionnel means that the principal courts judging the compatibility of French law with European Union law are the ordinary civil and administrative courts. Although the Conseil d'Etat resisted for a long while, French courts have now accepted the supremacy of EU law over inconsistent French statutes enacted after the treaties.[28] The *S.A. Rothmans* and *S.A. Philip Morris*[29] decision of the Conseil d'Etat illustrates the point. Here a 1972 EC directive regulated price fixing by state monopolies. In an action brought by tobacco importers, the directive was held to prevail over an inconsistent French statute of 1976 concerning the state monopoly of tobacco, and the Conseil d'Etat consequently annulled some price fixing measures made under the statute because they contravened the directive.

C. Legislation

As mentioned above, for a long time *loi* (legislation enacted by Parliament) was regarded as the supreme source in constitutional theory. This supremacy was due to the fact that acts of Parliament were passed and therefore legitimized by the mechanisms of representative democracy. However, reality began to diverge from theory when the demands of a modern state could not be met within this framework. As a result, legislation now comes from a number of different sources.

1. Past experiences

During the Third Republic (1875–1940), the need to pass legislation quickly was such that the category of *décret-loi* was created. It designates a statutory instrument taken by the Government but which can amend acts of Parliament. The use of *décret-loi* was authorized by a statute delegating powers to the Government. These appeared during the First World War but were used regularly especially from 1930 in order to deal with the difficult financial and economic situation. The Constitution of the Fourth Republic sought to prohibit this controversial practice. Article 13 of the 1946 Constitution specified that the right to vote statutes could not be delegated.[30] Unfortunately, the difficult post-war political reality[31] contributed to a radical change in the interpretation of article 13. A *loi* of 17 August 1948 (*'la loi André Marie'*) created the technique of the *loi-cadre*: only the very general

---

[28] Ch. mixte 24 May 1975, *Société Cafés Jacques Vabre*, D 1975.497 concl. Touffait, [1975] 2 CMLR 336; C. cons. 21 Oct. 1988, *5e circonscription du Val d'Oise*, AJDA 1989.128 note Wachsmann; CE Ass. plén. 20 Oct. 1989, *Nicolo*, RFDA 1989.813. For the earlier history, see A.F.T. Tatham, 'Effects of European Community Directives in France: the Development of the Cohn-Bendit Jurisprudence' (1991) 40 ICLQ 907.

[29] CE Ass. plén. 28 Feb. 1992, AJDA 1992.210; see generally L. Brown and J. Bell, *French Administrative Law*, 5th edn. (Oxford, 1998), 267–270.

[30] 'Only the Assemblée nationale can adopt legislation. It cannot delegate this right'.

[31] Throughout the Fourth Republic there was no real majority in the Assemblée nationale. Coalitions might have been more stable if the cold war had not from 1947 relegated the Communist Party permanently in the opposition.

principles of a reform were to be included in the text passed by Parliament, all the rest was to be provided for by *décrets* drafted by the Government. The Parliament could oppose them within a time-limit after which they became definitive. In the same *loi* of 1948, a separation between the domain of the legislative and the domain of the executive was established. Only important subjects were left to Parliament to decide upon; the others would be permanently delegated to the executive. Moreover, Parliament was allowed to modify this classification of legislative subjects at any time.

2. *The 1958 Constitution*

The draftsmen of the 1958 Constitution took into account this past experience and decided that a number of procedures should exist in the provisions of the Constitution in order to facilitate the legislative process.[32] The Constitution was therefore written in order to ensure that the Government could override a Parliament, even where the Government did not have a supporting parliamentary majority. A number of procedures were created so as to literally bypass Parliament.

(a) A permanent divide between the domains of Parliament and of the executive in the legislative sphere: articles 34 to 37

The mechanism which been created by the *loi André Marie* had impressed the authors of the 1958 Constitution and it was reproduced there. Article 34 lists the subject matters which are left to Parliament to legislate upon. It might seem rather long at first but it is deceptive: while Parliament is limited to the list, the legislative power of the Government under article 37 consists of everything else. The executive appears to have a considerable advantage in this division.

In order for the division to be strictly respected, the authors of the Constitution established a number of procedures for the executive to protect its prerogatives. However, the political reality, a majority supporting the Government, disturbed all these plans and the divide between article 34 and article 37 was never a source of conflict between Parliament and Government. The practice turned out to be much more favourable to Parliament than the text was intended to be and the legislative domain of Parliament has been extended beyond article 34 to the extent that any important topic can be included in it.[33]

Consequently, *lois,* which are voted by Parliament according to article 34, and *règlements* which are adopted solely by the executive according to article 37 sit at the same level in the hierarchy of norms. Thus, *règlements* like *lois* come after the Constitution, treaties, and *lois organiques.*

---

[32] At the time, it was not clear that there would be a stable majority in the Assemblée nationale to ensure the effective passing of legislation.

[33] Colloque Aix-en-Provence, *Vingt ans d'application de la Constitution de 1958: le domaine de la loi et du règlement* (Marseille, 1988).

(b) A changing division: delegation under article 38

The draftsmen of the 1958 Constitution realized that theoretical purity tends to give way to constitutional pragmatism, since the technique of enacting *décret-loi* reappeared after their clear condemnation by the 1946 Constitution and so the practice should be systematized by the Constitution of the Fifth Republic. For this reason, article 38 creates a third category of ordinary legislation: *ordonnances*. Under article 38, a *loi* can define the area of intervention delegated to the Government, the general principles of the legislation and the period within which the delegated legislation (which are known as *ordonnances*) needs to be approved by Parliament. The executive has then the power to draft the legislation it wishes, but must communicate it to Parliament before the end of the deadline. If Parliament does not object to it by a vote then it is considered definitive. Furthermore, during the period of delegation, Parliament cannot legislate in the area covered by it. Parliament only recovers its full powers only once the deadline is passed. *Ordonnances* of article 38 exist in the hierarchy of norms at the same level as *lois ordinaires* and *règlements*.

D. The Phenomenon of Codification

France is often described as the country from which the trend of codification came; and it is true that the most famous of its codes, the Civil Code, was the source of inspiration in a number of other countries (where it was not actually imposed following Napoleonic conquest). It should not been forgotten however, that the idea of codification is much more ancient.[34] More recently, codification seems to be on the agenda again but a shift in its meaning can be observed.

1. The Napoleonic codifications

Codification had become badly needed at the time of the French Revolution. The territory of France was covered by many and too often conflicting legal systems: France was divided between North and South (Roman law was applied in the South, while the North was regulated by local customary law). This apparently simple divide was complicated by the fact that if in the South, Roman law rules created a relative uniformity, in the North, customs were regional and differed from the jurisdiction of one *Parlement* to the other. Throughout the centuries, the Etats Généraux had repeatedly asked that the law be codified.[35] Attempts at clarifying the legal system had been made before: in 1453, Charles VII proclaimed the ordinance of Montil-Lez-Tours by which all customs had to be written down. However, this enactment had no immediate effect and codification was

---

[34] See the codification of Roman law in the *Corpus Iuris Civilis* of Justinian (though it was not a codification in a recognizably modern sense): B. Nicholas, *An Introduction to Roman Law* (Oxford, 1962), 38–45.

[35] This demand was made at all the Etats Généraux since the 16th century (in 1560, 1579, 1640, and 1789).

fully achieved only by the end of the 16th century. In the 17th century, Colbert and a century later, d'Aguesseau, two famous government ministers drafted royal ordinances settling the law in a number of areas.[36]

Moreover, the philosophical movement of the 18th century denounced the irrationality of the system: the *siècle des lumières* wanted uniform legislation which would be easily accessible to anyone; therefore the idea of codification, that is to say all rules on one subject area contained in a single book and drafted in clear general principles, answered perfectly the philosophical and political demands of the time.

It is not therefore surprising that one of the first tasks attempted by the Constituent Assembly as early as 1791, was a general code.[37] However, it was only in 1800, and after four unsuccessful attempts, that the first Code was initiated.[38] It was written in the record time of four months and submitted to a long legislative procedure. A major political crisis slowed down the adoption of the text, but it was finally fully voted on 21 March 1804. Napoleon Bonaparte oversaw personally the project[39] and was a decisive influence in a number of areas.[40] The Civil Code is recognized by all to have been a brilliant piece of legislation. There were four more codes to be drafted soon after this (the Code of Civil Procedure in 1806, the Commercial Code in 1807, the Code of Criminal Procedure in 1808, and the Criminal Code in 1810).

The ideology behind the codes can be summarized in three propositions: each had to be clear so that anybody reading it could understand the rules which it contained, since democracy requires that laws be understood by the layman;[41] it had to be general in order to cover all sorts of situations but detailed enough so that the intervention of the courts was as little necessary as possible. In a word it was a rationalization which had to reflect an ideal but be pragmatic at the same time. In addition, the new codes introduced the ideas and ideals of the Revolution into

[36] Colbert's ordinances were as follows:
  1667: *ordonnance civile pour la réformation de la justice* (ancestor of the Code of Civil Procedure);
  1673: *ordonnance sur le commerce terrestre* (ancestor of the Commercial Code);
  1681: *ordonnance sur la marine;*
  The d'Aguesseau ordinances were:
  1731: *ordonnance sur les donations;*
  1735: *ordonnance sur les testaments;*
  1747: *ordonnance sur les substitutions.*

[37] Title 1 of the Constitution of 3 September 1791 contains the following provision: '(...) a code, applicable to the whole kingdom and containing all rules of private law will be drafted'.

[38] J. Halpérin, *French Civil Code* (trans T. Weir, Oxford, 2005).

[39] He wrote later in his memoirs: 'My true glory is not to have won forty battles, Waterloo will wipe out the memory of so many victories; nothing will cancel out, however, my civil Code that will live eternally': see B. Schwartz, *Code Napoleon and the Common Law World* (New York, 1954), 102.

[40] Particularly the provisions in relation to adoption, the civil status of soldiers, and the rules discriminating against foreigners.

[41] A layman who could read however; the greater part of the population was therefore excluded.

the law: they ensured that the established class system was abolished (for example, the rights of succession of the eldest son) and promoted the idea of property as an area for the expression of any individual's rights and liberties.

Unfortunately, the Civil Code has been little amended[42] and it is now greatly outdated. An important attempt to reform the Civil Code was made in the middle of the last century, when a committee was created[43] with the task of proposing a complete new Civil Code, but the committee's incomplete work (though published) was not implemented. Much more recently, in 2005, a group of jurists mostly drawn from French universities put forward (at the invitation of the President of the Republic) a set of reform proposals to rewrite the Civil Code's provisions governing the law of obligations and prescription, though it is yet unclear as to their fate.[44] The courts have had therefore to fill the gaps and update the text, something that they have done to a great extent, particularly in the area of delict.[45] Moreover, the Civil Code is no longer comprehensive, since a number of new areas have been regulated by legislation which has not been incorporated in it. The original ideals seems to have been slowly abandoned.

2. *Modern codification or codification* à la française

However, if political circumstances have not really allowed the adoption of a new Civil Code, it possible to perceive a new movement of codification taking place in France at the moment. The extraordinary number of legislative or administrative enactments passed every year has forced the Government to adopt a clear attitude as regards codification of new or ever changing areas. The Commission supérieure de codification was created in 1989:[46] it aims at collecting legislative and administrative enactments in specific areas so that they are ordered in a code. This exercise does not aim at redrafting the rules which already exist, but only at collecting them, organizing them rationally, and changing them only where contradictions are found between the provisions. The aim is to order the presentation of the law but not to reform it. This new trend of codification differs drastically from the previous 19th-century experience:[47] these codes merely consolidate existing texts and organize them in a logical manner, whereas the Napoleonic codifications adapted previous rules in order to reflect in the law the political changes which had occurred. The current codifications stem more from administrative necessity than from an ideological stance.

---

[42] A major exception may be found in the case of family law, see below, ch. 8.

[43] Decree of 7 June 1945.

[44] P. Catala (ed.) *Avant-projet de réforme du droit des obligations et du prescription* (La documentation française, 2005). The French text and an English translation by J. Cartwright and S. Whittaker is published in J. Cartwright, S. Vogenauer and S. Whittaker, *Reforming the French Law of Obligations* (Hart, 2008 forthcoming) and online at <http://www.justice.gouv.fr/>.

[45] See, e.g., the development of strict liability in delict: below pp. 381 ff.

[46] See *décret* no. 89-647 of 12 September 1989 as modified.

[47] See G. Braibant, 'Les problèmes actuels de codification' and B.-G. Mattarella, 'La codification du droit: réflexions sur l'expérience française contemporaine', RFDA 1994.663 and 668.

E. Custom

Custom is not a major source of law in modern French law. All the same, in areas such as commercial law, practice by the users of law is a significant element in determining what the law is. As in English law, the three prerequisites for custom are: (a) a practice of long duration; (b) a belief that the practice is obligatory (known as the *opinio necessitatis*); and (c) consistency with the law (i.e. legal principle). French judges have been very insistent that customary practices which are inconsistent with the law have no binding force.[48]

III. Other Sources of Law

A. Case Law (*la Jurisprudence*)

Case law of the courts (*la jurisprudence*) is not a binding, but merely an influential source of law. As David puts it, 'judicial decisions are not a source of law in France. Strictly speaking, they never create legal rules. Their role is always understood to be the application of pre-existing statutes or customs. In the absence of an applicable statute or custom, decisions can be based on principles of equity, reason, justice, or tradition. It is never enough, however, simply to refer to a prior judicial decision'.[49] It might be thought that this view arises because French law is a codified system and that a code claims to contain all the necessary rules and principles of law. This is not really the case in France. Nicholas suggests that 'French law, at least as presented in the Civil Code, is a complete and internally coherent system'[50] and this has some importance, but this appearance belies the reality of the broader picture which Nicholas also notes. In the first place, such codes as exist are not exhaustive; and, in the second place, there are some important branches of French law which are not codified and are judge-made, yet even here case law is not binding.

Lawson argued that 'it is wise not to take civil codes too seriously; those who have to live under them do not. This is true to a pre-eminent degree of French law'.[51] His view was endorsed by a French professor, André Tunc.[52] It would be foolish to pretend that a code contains all the answers. Indeed, those who drafted the Civil Code were clear that they had no such ambition. Introducing the final draft of the Code to the legislature, Portalis recognized that, once drafted, laws were fixed while human beings were constantly changing, such that one could

---

[48] David (above n. 6), 170.
[49] Ibid., 181.
[50] B. Nicholas, *French Law of Contract*, 2nd edn. (Oxford 1992), 13.
[51] F.H. Lawson, *A Common Lawyer looks at the Civil Law* (Ann Arbor, 1953), 56.
[52] A. Tunc, 'It is wise not to take codes too seriously...' in *Essays in Memory of F.H. Lawson* (Dordrecht, 1985), 71.

not regulate all that might occur.[53] Thus, 'to simplify everything is something on which we must agree; to foresee everything is a goal which is impossible to achieve'.[54] Accordingly, 'the function of legislation is to establish through a broad view the general maxims of the law; to establish principles rich in consequences and not to descend into the detail of questions which could arise on every question. It is up to the judge and the jurist, imbued with the general spirit of the laws, to direct their application'.[55] This role included deciding issues which were not regulated by legislation such as the Code. It was not practical or acceptable for the judge to refer the matter to the legislator. For Portalis, there was thus a distinction of roles between the legislator and judges which contributed to the creation of the law:

The science of the legislator consists in finding for each matter principles which are most favourable to the common good; the science of the judge is to put these principles into action, to develop their ramifications, to extend them by a wise and reasoned application to individual situations, to study the spirit of the law where the letter kills; and not to run the risk of being from time to time, its slave and its rebel, and to disobey it by a spirit of servility.[56]

In such an approach, the judges are clearly seen as having significant authority and not just as the bureaucratic implementers of rules established by the legislator. The Civil Code does not give judges the right to ignore the text, but only to cooperate in its implementation. The Cour de cassation is happy to endorse this approach. In its annual report for 1975, that court states that: 'we are pleased to emphasize that...whilst remaining within its role, our Court contributes to the gradual creation of the new state of law which will shape the society of tomorrow'.[57] Such a creative role for French courts is recognized both in the role they perform and in the way in which their decisions are described.

In terms of their role, the highest courts are principally responsible for making authoritative rulings on the law. In the majority of cases, they will hear appeals on a point of law (*pourvois en cassation*) against decisions of the lower courts and quash their decisions where they are wrong. This is typically described as the disciplinary role of the highest courts—to ensure that the lower courts keep in line. The court should here provide clear guidance to the lower courts. In a guide to the writing of Cour de cassation judgments, Perdriau remarks that 'these judgments must, above all, decide a legal problem by offering a clear and precise solution. To achieve this, they must, if need be, sacrifice elegance of language to the clarity of the reply and, in our opinion, they must not encumber themselves with

---

[53] J.-E.-M. Portalis, 'Discours préliminaire sur le projet de Code civil' in F. Ewald (ed.), *Naissance du Code civil* (Paris, 1989), 41.

[54] Ibid., 39.

[55] Ibid., 41–42.

[56] Ibid., 47.

[57] Cour de cassation, *Rapport annuel 1975* (Paris, 1976), 101.

too many subtleties'.[58] More recently, both the Cour de cassation and the Conseil d'Etat have acquired the role of giving advisory rulings on points of law to the lower courts. In both these roles, the courts are explicitly guardians of the law, but also have scope to develop the law by laying down principles to govern cases where legal enactments are unclear or leave gaps. At a colloquium in 1993, members of the Cour de cassation and other lawyers considered explicitly that these roles required the court to develop its own legal doctrine.[59] The role is explicitly to develop their own idea of the law. But this does not create binding precedents in the common law sense. That same colloquium contains a discussion about the 'legitimate resistance' of lower courts to the rulings of the higher courts. It is acknowledged that a refusal of lower courts to follow a ruling of the Cour de cassation can lead the latter to reconsider its views and to come up with a different solution.[60] As was said by judges of both the Cour de cassation and the cour d'appel of Lyon, the role of the lower court judge is to rebel, but not too often.[61] In addition, the highest French courts are quite willing to overturn their previous case law. For example, the Conseil d'Etat decided in 1978 that it would not give priority to EC law over inconsistent national law, yet in 1989 it reversed this position.[62] Similar cases will be noted throughout the book.[63] As the Cour de cassation has put it:

Numerous decisions bear witness to the desire not to be closed off from the world and not to be content with the cult of 'precedent'. Even though it is careful to avoid hasty reversals of case law, which would not be compatible with the need for legal certainty, the Cour de cassation does not hesitate to correct its most settled doctrines when these no longer seem to it to correspond to social or economic reality or no longer accord with the development of ideas and morals.[64]

Secondly, the description offered both by judges and lawyers more generally for decisions of the highest courts reflects their role in making authoritative rulings on the law. Conventionally, decisions are described as either *arrêts d'espèce* or *arrêts de principe*. *Arrêts d'espèce* are decisions which simply apply established principles to the large body of relatively unproblematic, routine appeals which French appeal courts receive in abundance. By contrast, *arrêts de principe* are decisions which lay down a new principle for application in subsequent cases. Judges are

---

[58] *La pratique des arrêts civils de la Cour de cassation: principes et méthodes de rédaction* (Paris, 1993), § 1317.

[59] *L'image doctrinale de la Cour de cassation* (Paris, 1994).

[60] For example, among cases discussed in this book: on the civil liability of children (Ass. plén, 5 May 1984, below p. 384), liability for things (Ch. réun. 13 Feb. 1930, *Jand'heur*, below pp. 382–383), on the dismissal of teachers in religious schools (Ass. plén. 19 May 1978).

[61] *L'image doctrinale* (above n. 59), 188–190, 191.

[62] CE 29 Oct. 1989, *Nicolo*, Leb. 190.

[63] See Ch. réun. 2 Dec. 1941, *Connot c. Franck*, DC 1942, 25 note Ripert and the fate of Civ. (2) 21 July 1982, *affaire Desmares*, D 1982, 449, below pp 383–385, 391–393.

[64] *Rapport de la Cour de cassation: Années judiciaires 1976 et 1977* (Paris, 1978), 119. See also *L'image doctrinale* (above n. 59), 123–168.

fully aware that they are laying down generally applicable rulings, and the legal community receives and comments on them with appropriate seriousness. It is therefore clear that French judges make deliberate rulings on law in a similar way to common law courts. Moreover, a consistent line of authority (*la jurisprudence constante*) is both necessary for the decision of *arrêts d'espèce* and to the creation of legal doctrine by the courts. It is through that *jurisprudence constante* that the full force of judicial law-making is seen.

Case law is obviously also important in those areas which are really judge-made. Following from what has already been said, in a code nearly 200 years old such as the Civil Code, there will be many matters on which there is little regulation. Classically, one can point to the large volume on the principles of tort liability in French private law by Geneviève Viney and Patrice Jourdain covering over 1,300 pages which relates almost entirely to a mere five articles of the Civil Code (articles 1382–1386).[65] Such an area is one where the principal point of reference for any lawyer is case law. The result is that, as Lawson argued, for many areas 'French law has become almost as much a system of judge-made law as English law. Indeed, the judges are prepared . . . to make law contra legem [against the text of the law] in a way that no English judge would do at the present day'.[66] It is even more clear that judges make law in areas where there is no code. The most obvious example is French administrative law. There are many legal enactments, some of which even call themselves 'codes', e.g. the electoral code, the code for administrative courts, and the tax code, but these are at best compilations and sometimes consolidations of disparate legislative provisions. Any general and coherent principles have been established exclusively by case law over more than 100 years by the administrative courts, principally the Conseil d'Etat. As a result, case law is the principal practical and authoritative source for a knowledge of much of administrative law.[67] More recently, the Conseil constitutionnel has developed a complex case law interpreting the Constitution and determining what belongs in the block of constitutional principles. Thus, to understand the Constitution, it is now essential to read the Conseil constitutionnel's decisions, which become a major reference point for legal discussion. Leading public lawyers fully recognize this leading role for case law in their field.[68] But as David points out, this still

---

[65] *Les conditions de la responsabilité* 3rd edn. (Paris, 2006), there is also a book of 791 pages on the consequences of liability: see *Les effets de la responsabilité* 2nd edn. (Paris, 2001).

[66] *A Common Lawyer looks at the Civil Law* (above n. 51), 82; G. Ripert, also suggested over 40 years ago, *Le régime démocratique et le droit civil moderne*, vol. 2 (Paris, 1948), 15 that: 'quite large areas of French private law have become common law, almost without our noticing it. The famous and striking opposition between sources of law recognised by Anglo-Saxon and French law respectively have been very materially reduced'.

[67] Bell (above n. 3), 175–185.

[68] See especially G. Vedel, 'Le précédent judiciaire en droit public', in *Die Bedeutung von Präjudizien in deutschen und französischen Recht (Arbeiten zur Rechtsvergleichung no. 123* (Frankfurt/Main, 1985).

does not make case law a formal source of law in this field, even if it is strongly influential.[69]

If judges are responsible (quite properly) for developing many rules of law, why do their decisions lack formal authority? Traditionally, French lawyers have referred to article 5 of the Civil Code which prohibits judges from making regulatory decisions, decisions with general legislative effect. This provision has its origins in the *loi* of 16–24 August 1790. Article 10 of that *loi* forbade the judiciary from interfering directly or indirectly in the legislative power and from refusing to enforce laws, a power which the pre-Revolutionary Parlements had enjoyed.[70] Article 12 of the same *loi* forbade the courts to make regulatory decisions, and article 121 of the Law of 27 November–1 December 1790 required judges to refer difficult questions of interpretation (those which had been quashed on two successive occasions by the Tribunal de cassation) to the legislature whose declaratory decree would bind the court. This *référé législatif* continued to operate in some form until 1837. Such provisions marked a distrust of judges, especially those who had been members of the Parlements before the Revolution in the previous year. They had blocked the reforms of the King, so it was not unreasonable for the Assembly of 1790 to fear that they might block its reforms. As Portalis made clear in his speech introducing the Civil Code to the Conseil d'Etat, this fear had receded by 1803, and realism about the role of the judges had developed. As a result, the emphasis in his speech was on the idea behind article 4 of the Civil Code under which the judge cannot refuse to decide a case simply because the legislation is obscure or has a gap, he must come to a decision, albeit in Portalis's view, this should be based on general principles of justice and the spirit of the law. As modern commentators point out,[71] there is no real objection to judicial lawmaking as long as it can be based on the Civil Code. Rather there is a distinction drawn between two types of lawmaking. In his preliminary discourse, Portalis argued:

There are two kinds of interpretation: one by way of doctrine and the other by way of authority. Interpretation by way of doctrine consists of grasping the true meaning of the laws, applying them with discernment and supplementing them in cases which they have not regulated. Without this form of interpretation, how could it be possible to carry out the office of judge? Interpretation by way of authority consists of resolving questions and doubts by means of regulations or general provisions. This is the only form of interpretation which is forbidden to a judge.[72]

---

[69] David (above n. 5), 155–156.

[70] The Parlements of pre-Revolutionary France have some similarities to the House of Lords in England and Wales, being both courts and legislative assemblies. But the Parlements were regional and were bodies which received and registered locally the laws made by the King; they thus lacked the full powers of a modern Parliament.

[71] See especially S. Belaid, *Le pouvoir créateur et normatif du juge* (Paris, 1974) and E. Severin, *De la jurisprudence en droit privé* (Lyon, 1985), 268–288.

[72] Portalis (above n. 53), 45–46.

The line may appear sharp, but in practice it is less clear. Courts may not formally aim to lay down general rules, but they know that their decisions (especially in the highest courts) will be strongly influential and will generally be respected by lawyers and lower courts. In such a case, it will be hard to see the difference between claiming authority to make general rules and acting in the knowledge that in practice one's decision will be treated as if it is a general rule. The issue turns in reality much more on the weight to be accorded to the decision of a court, rather than whether it should be treated as a source of law. The significance of the argument that judicial decisions do not constitute sources of law is that they do not constitute *binding* precedents for the lower courts. Even decisions of the highest courts, the Cour de cassation and the Conseil d'Etat do not bind the lower courts which are free to reject them if they think they are wrong, even though they typically do not do so.[73] Indeed a court is liable to have its decision quashed if its only justification for its decision is a precedent (of its own or of another court)[74]—there must be some primary support from an authoritative, formal source of law. At all events, case law is a subordinate source of law. A judge is never at liberty to give effect to his own whims, however laudable his sentiment of justice. This is vividly brought out by the Magnaud affair. Magnaud was president of the tribunal correctionnel of Chateau Thierry at the turn of the century. He was famous for his decisions in favour of the poor and weak flying in the face of the words of the law. On one occasion, he acquitted a woman of theft because her defence was that she had stolen the bread because she had not eaten for 36 hours. The cour d'appel of Amiens upheld the decision but rejected his reasoning that people could steal food if they were in need.[75]

A major limitation on the authority of case law is that discussion of precedents does not appear in the judgments of the highest courts. The following is a brief, but clear example of the style of French judgments. It is the full text of a decision concerning an action by Greenpeace France to challenge the validity of the French President's decision to hold a series of nuclear tests in 1995:

Considering that, on 13 June 1995, the President of the Republic announced his decision to proceed with a new series of nuclear tests prior to the negotiation of an international treaty; that these tests had been suspended in April 1992 to support a French diplomatic initiative concerning nuclear disarmament, and that this moratorium had been extended in July 1993 after the principal nuclear powers had themselves announced the suspension

---

[73] Exceptionally, decisions of the Assemblée plénière of the Cour de cassation do bind the lower court in the case in question, but this does not affect the status of its decisions for subsequent courts.

[74] E.g. Crim. 3 Nov. 1955, D 1956.557 note Savatier, where a Cour d'appel's decision was quashed because it had refused to exceed its normal maximum level of damages.

[75] Amiens, 22 April 1898, DP 1899.2.329 note Josserand; F. Gény, *Méthodes d'interprétation et sources en droit privé positif*, vol. 2, 2nd edn. (Paris, 1919), 287–307. The '*bon juge*' Magneaud eventually gave up his post on the bench and became a member of the Senate.

of their own tests; that thus the challenged decision is not separable from the conduct of France's international relations and, in consequence, escapes any control by the courts; that the administrative courts thus lack jurisdiction to receive the request of the association Greenpeace France seeking to annul this decision for exceeding his powers...

The style is clear in stating a reason for the decision, but offers no real argument in justification which would even hint at how the court viewed the arguments put by the parties (or indeed what it took to be the facts). Lower court judges and commentators are left to infer that argumentation from their knowledge of the law and (where published) from the arguments of the public representative (the *ministère public* or the *commissaire du gouvernement*) or the report of the reporting judge (*le juge rapporteur*),[76] which contain full discussions of the reasons for the solutions which were put to the judges.

It would be wrong to conclude that previous cases do not have a very important place in the operation of French law. Studies which have been conducted on the practice of French courts, notably the *Cour de cassation* and the *Conseil d'Etat* demonstrate that in both previous cases are included as major features both in arguments of the *ministère public* and the *commissaire du gouvernement* and in the draft opinion and arguments of the reporting judge.[77] Based on his reading of court files and the opinions of reporting judges and the *ministère public,* Lasser remarks that he did not find 'a single *conclusion* or *rapport* that does not provide citations of previous cases—i.e., of *jurisprudence*'.[78] Similar points can be made in relation to the Conseil d'Etat.[79] The written files on which the judges make their decision are usually full of photocopies of previous cases. What is more, those observations of the judicial process (which are rarely allowed to French academics) also reveal that the courts are well aware of the practical authority of their case law and will deliberately set out to define a particular line for developing the law. As David happily admitted, there is no rule of law which prohibits the citation of precedents, indeed it is very frequent as a way of ensuring that the law is applied consistently.[80] The practice of judges in the French system is not as distinct from that of their English counterparts as might be presumed from the status of case law. Given that English judges make use of distinguishing and other interpretative devices to limit the impact of binding precedents, the degree of difference is perhaps not as great as might be imagined.

There have been suggestions that the current French position is at least disingenuous if not downright dishonest and that judges should be more explicit in their reasoning when they create new rules. At present the judgment is so laconic

[76] See below, pp. 60–61.

[77] J. Bell, 'Reflections on the procedure of the Conseil d'Etat' in G. Hand and J. McBride, *Droit sans frontières* (Birmingham, 1991) and M Lasser, 'Judicial (Self-)Portraits: Judicial Discourse in the French Legal System' (1995) 104 Yale LJ 1325.

[78] Lasser, ibid., at 1376.

[79] Bell (above n. 3), 188–189.

[80] David (above n. 5), 182–183.

that few but the most expert can interpret the nuances of what has been said.[81] It has long been argued that judgments ought to be more explicit in their reasoning.[82] Little has been done to implement these ideas. In a sense, a French judgment is not written as an account of the full justification of the decision. Perdriau captures the purpose well: we do not give reasons for the reasons.[83] It suffices that the lower courts are given clear statements of what the right interpretation of the law is. The higher courts are not writing for the general public, to convince it of the correctness of its solution. The text is only comprehensible to lawyers. It is perhaps this different function of the judgment which makes French law distinctive. Lasser helpfully identifies a 'bifurcation' in judicial debates—the judgment is formalist, whilst the substantive, policy-focused justification occurs in another place.[84] Lasser's and Bell's research on court files and decisions reveals very clearly that the doctrinal, precedential and 'policy' arguments familiar to common lawyers are present in the deliberations of French judges, but they do not form part of the justification. The justification offered presents, as Lasser suggests, an 'official portrait' of the judge simply interpreting legal rules and arriving at deductive results. The reality is that the 'unofficial portrait' reveals the judge much as his German or British counterparts, concerned to adapt the law to new circumstances, a point made clearly even in official publications of the courts. It is just that the role of the judgment is not to provide that broader justification contained in common-law judgments (and even in the French *conclusions* and the *rapport*). Scholars should not be misled by the form and style of judgment to presume that the substance of the reasoning is radically different.

B. General Principles of Law

The category of the general principles of law is a creation of the courts. The expression of general principle is recognized by all French courts, but the Conseil d'Etat has resorted to them more often than any other courts.[85] This is rather logical

---

[81] For a guide to the nuances in the judgments of the Cour de cassation see A. Perdriau, *La pratique des arrêts civils de la Cour de cassation: principes et méthodes de rédaction* (Paris, 1993). For a recognition of the problems in the (similar) style of administrative court decisions: see B. Ducamin, 'Le style des décisions du Conseil d'Etat' EDCE 1984–1985.129.

[82] A. Toufait and A. Tunc, 'Pour une motivation plus explicite des décisions de justice', RTDCiv 1974.487.

[83] Perdriau (above n. 81), 1274: 'We consider ... that it is important to refrain from "giving reasons for the reasons", meaning by this that, whereas in a judicial decision the inclusion of reasons corresponds to an absolute necessity, the explanation of these reasons moves away from the sphere of law by bringing out considerations of a more or less subjective or contingent kind, and this should therefore not be done.'

[84] M. Lasser, *Judicial Deliberations. A Comparative Analysis of Judicial Transparency and Legitimacy* (Oxford, 2004), 16, 44–61.

[85] E.g. M. Letourneur, 'Les principes généraux dans la jurisprudence du Conseil d'Etat', EDCE 1951.195; R. Chapus, 'De la valeur des principes généraux du droit et autres règles jurisprudentielles en droit administratif', D 1966 Chron. 99; B. Jeanneau, 'La théorie des principes généraux du droit à l'épreuve du temps', EDCE 1981–1982.33.

since administrative law was neither codified or even legislated upon: principles were necessary in order to create a backbone for the development of rules governing the action of the administration; hence, for instance the creation of the principle of *le droit de la défense*[86] which is the equivalent to the English principle of a right to a hearing. Some of these principles were clearly taken from the constitutional texts protecting rights and freedoms: the principle of equality[87] which finds many applications in French administrative law is clearly so inspired.

Private law also recognizes general principles of law, the most famous example being the principle of unjust enrichment which led to the recognition of a separate remedy called the *action de in rem verso* even though this was not contained in the Code.[88] It seems that there is a movement towards an increased use of general principles of law in private law, although this was not really supported by the attitude of the Cour de Cassation in the past.[89]

C. Legal Writing (*la Doctrine*)

The writing of academics (which is often referred to as *la doctrine*, though this term can also be used to describe university jurists as a group) does not as such count as law, but it has an important and direct influence, and may be more so than in England, although changes can be observed.

Legislative enactments are often written in a general and open-textured manner and interpretation is often necessary so as to fit the facts to them. In order to establish the importance of legal writings as an influential source, two directions could be explored: it will be shown that academic writers have an impact on both the theories of legal interpretation and on specific judicial solutions.

1. *Theories of legal interpretation*

One of the most important contribution of academic writing has been to establish the theoretical basis for the right of interpretation of judges. As was mentioned above, after the Revolution, judges were not really trusted and their powers of interpretation were seriously curtailed as a result. The legislator also contributed to this movement, as codification which started with the drafting of the Civil Code was meant to cover all situations. Little was left to judges to decide. From this observation a school of thought came into being known as *l'école de l'exégèse* and according to which the text of enactments was most of the time simple and clear but if by accident an interpretation was necessary, the *travaux préparatoires* would provide the answer.

---

[86] CE 5 May 1944, *Trompier-Gravier*, Leb. 133.
[87] CE 30 Nov. 1930, *Couitéas*, Leb. 789.
[88] Req. 15 June 1892, DP 1892.1.596 and see below, pp. 433–435.
[89] P. Morvan, *Le principe en droit privé* (Paris, 1999).

This school of thought was superseded when it became obvious that the wording of enactments could not be relied on its own. Judges had to start adapting the text to more modern situations, situations which were not really foreseen by the authors of the codes. Another school was therefore born under the influence, among others, of Saleilles and Gény,[90] known as *l'école de la libre recherche scientifique*, according to which when a judge is faced with a real gap in legislation, he has to fill it, taking into account considerations such as the social and economic context of the time, historical precedents, future developments in this area, the state of the law in other countries, etc. This approach frees judges from the more literal interpretation supported by the *école de l'exégèse*.

This change in approach was important since to some extent academic research as to the nature of legal interpretation redefined the attitude of judges to interpretation.

2. Communities of thought

Judges do often use academic writings and especially when dealing with new situations. For instance, it is widely known that the solution put forward by the decision of the Conseil d'Etat in *Laruelle & Delville*[91] was first presented in an article by Marcel Waline.[92] The Conseil d'Etat simply applied the advice contained in the article quoted above.

Academic writings also give the possibility to judges to assess the impact of their case law. Each important decision is copiously commented on in specialized journals by the *arrêtistes*. The comments give feedback to the judges who can then refine the solution they have adopted. Judges feel also the need at times to cross the Rubicon and submit their ideas to the academic world by writing articles themselves.

Moreover, a number of famous academics have helped the organization of an entire subject. In the areas where a total reorganization was necessary, some major seminal work have literally reordered the field: for instance in delictual liability, Saleilles and Josserand clarified the application of article 1384 al. 1 on liability. for the 'actions of things'.[93]

But the integration of the legal community is much more developed than this short outline suggests. In private law, academics are sometimes said to constitute a community, rather than simply a collection of writers.[94] In administrative law, members of the Conseil d'Etat play a leading part in doctrinal

---

[90] F. Gény, *Méthodes d'interprétation et sources en droit privé positif*, 2nd edn. (Paris, 1919).

[91] CE 28 July 1951, RDP 1951.1087 note Waline.

[92] See RDP 1948.5.

[93] Below, pp. 381–393.

[94] P. Jestaz and C. Jamin, 'The entity of French doctrine: Some thoughts on the community of French legal writers' (1995) 18 LS 415.

writing. For instance, Laferièrre proposes a totally new classification of the grounds on which an administrative decision can be attacked.[95] It is a famous doctrinal text, but Laferrière was a member of the Conseil d'Etat. A number of judges have strong connections with academia: they can teach at their local university, participate in conferences, and are also involved in writing texts for students. For example, Guy Braibant and Bernard Stirn both leading past and present members of the Conseil d'Etat write a current textbook on administrative law.[96] Many leading academics have been members of the Conseil constitutionnel.[97] Indeed, it is possible to move from an academic career to the bench which has surely contributed to the creation of a more integrated community.

In some cases, scholars and judges have entered into a dialogue over the years (sometimes over decades) in order to achieve the state of the law as it is known now. For example, the establishment of the public-private divide has necessitated clear criterions to be found to delineate the jurisdictions of the private and public law courts. This was achieved through a succession of Conseil d'Etat decisions, major works and seminal articles for the last century or so.[98] It is interesting to note that the judges did not adopt some of the most extreme academic positions but that they were definitely impressed and influenced by some of the ideas and concepts which were reflected in the literature.

To conclude, there seems to be a much integrated community between judges and the academic world. But it is also true that University professors have generally a much more respected status than seems to be case in England. This might be partly explained by another circumstance: a number of academics have clear connexions with the political world. Indeed, some professors have had distinguished ministerial careers.[99]

IV. Conclusion

Although the structure of French sources might appear radically different to a reader familiar with common law practices, it would seem that the use of sources

---

[95] E. Laferrière, *Traité de la juridiction administrative et des recours contentieux*, 2nd edn. (Paris, 1896).

[96] G. Braibant and B. Stirn, *Le droit administratif français*, 7th edn. (Paris, 2005).

[97] See J. Bell, *Judiciaries within Europe* (Cambridge, 2006), 87–88

[98] Below, ch. 6.

[99] For example, R. Badinter was a well-known professor of criminal law before becoming Minister of Justice and then becoming President of the Conseil constitutionnel. R. Debré, the President of the Conseil constitutionnel appointed in 2007, was a judge before becoming a minister and then President of the Senate. The other two members appointed at the same time had been both senior judges and senior civil servants in ministries.

tend to show more similarity than might be thought at first. In fact, it might reflect a more general trend: it has often been said that differences between civil and common law systems are not as extreme as often presented, and more recently it has even been argued that continental and common law systems are in fact converging.[100] Although, the idea of convergence itself is not easily defined, the study of the sources undertaken above reveals some similarities with a common law system.

---

[100] B. Markesinis, 'Unity or Division. The Search for Similarities in Contemporary European Law' [2001] CLP 591. For a dissenting opinion, see Legrand (above n. 2).

2

Court Institutions[1]

French terminology in relation to courts can be difficult. A number of words are used to describe a 'court': *juridiction*, *tribunal*, and *cour* are the most frequent. *Tribunal* is the closest to the idea of a court as both an institution and a location. A *cour* is a name given to certain courts for historical reasons, and is the French term for a number of new courts created outside France, such as the European Court of Justice, the European Court of Human Rights, and the International Court of Justice. *Juridiction* is a technical term to describe the judicial function of an institution, identifying it as a judicial, rather than an administrative body. Some courts have other names: the Conseil d'Etat and the Conseil constitutionnel are, in practice, courts but are formally 'Councils', rather like the Privy Council and the Judicial Committee of the House of Lords are not called 'courts'.

There is a variety of court institutions which operate in different ways. This chapter seeks to identify some of the basic structural and operational principles governing the principal courts. While some of the structural principles can be said to have inspired the present arrangement of courts, other explanations are more accidental and opportunistic. The fact that some courts exist in a certain way may sometimes reflect aspects of French legal culture, but sometimes mere fashion or historical happenstance. The operational principles are perhaps most revealing about French conceptions of doing justice, both in the ideal form, and as a matter of practical implementation.

French court institutions are structured according to four basic principles, the first two of which are structural, while the last two are more operational in character. In terms of subject-matter, courts are *specialist* to varying degrees. There is a clear distinction between public law and private law courts, with further, less radical distinctions between general civil and criminal courts, and between them and specialist courts in such areas as employment, commercial and agricultural leases. In terms of territorial jurisdiction, French courts are *local or regional*, unlike their English and Scottish equivalents, the High Court in London and the Court of Session in Edinburgh. Only at the highest point in the hierarchy is there a national court in any branch of law (with the obvious exception of constitutional law). In terms of levels of court, the French adhere to the principle of

[1] J. Vincent, S. Guinchard, G. Montaigner, and A. Varinard, *Institutions judiciaires*, 8th edn. (Paris, 2005); J. Bell, *Judiciaries within Europe* (Cambridge, 2006), ch. 2.

the *right to an appeal* (*double degré de juridiction*), which entitles the litigant to a hearing at first instance and then on appeal.[2] This right of appeal on law and fact means that there is no leave required for an appeal. There are restrictions on access to the Conseil d'Etat and the Cour de cassation, the national courts at the pinnacle of the public and private law systems, but their functions are primarily to review the legal basis of decisions reached by lower courts, rather than to act as a third level of appeal on the merits.[3] Finally, in terms of *composition*, French courts are typically collegial and professional, viz. they are composed of a bench of professional judges. As will be seen, there are in fact numerous instances where there is a single judge and where non-professional judges are used.

I. Specialization

A glance at Figure 1 shows that the French have a variety of specialist courts, which match the diverse branches of law. Certain specialisms are fundamental to the structure of the French court system (and to its substantive law), others are matters more of convenience than legal principle. Three distinctions can be said to be of fundamental importance: between public law and private law, between civil law and criminal law, and between civil law and commercial law. It is within these specialist areas that the courts of general jurisdiction (*juridictions de droit commun*) are to be found. There is no court which has even residual jurisdiction over all branches of law. Within the different branches of law, the jurisdiction of courts is described as either general or as specialist. Specialist courts may be described as exceptional courts (*juridictions d'exception*) or as courts of limited jurisdiction (*juridictions d'attribution*).

A. Public Law and Private Law

Public law is the branch of law which is concerned with the powers and organization of governmental bodies, notably the state. Its central characteristic is the presence of the administration as one of the parties to the dispute. The notion of the 'administration' here covers not only national government, but also local authorities, public agencies, and public services, ranging from universities to railways or port authorities. As will be seen in Chapter 6, public law has special rules governing not only the use of powers, but also the rules of contract, the liability of public authorities and employment. By contrast, a private law dispute is one between two individuals or companies. The precise allocation of disputes to each category does pose some difficulties and there is a special court, the Tribunal des

---

[2] Below, pp. 50–51.
[3] Below, p. 91.

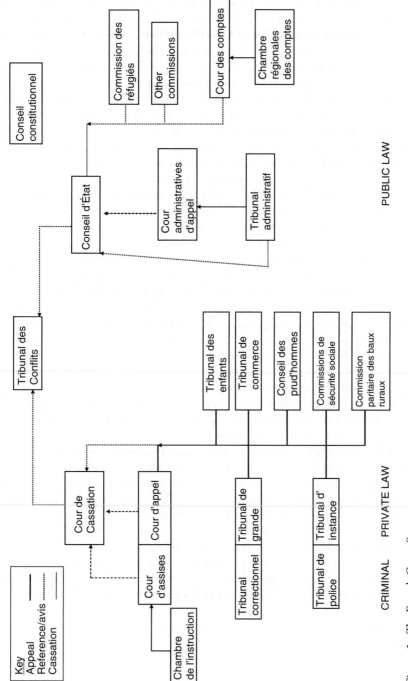

Figure 1: The French Court System

conflits, which exists to resolve them. It is made up of equal numbers of judges from the highest public and private law courts, and the Minister of Justice (*Garde des Sceaux*) has the casting vote.[4] One illustration captures the overlap. The French railways are run by a public corporation, the SNCF. In its dealings with the Government, e.g. over subsidies, it will make public law contracts. In dealings with its passengers, it makes private law contracts.

The consequence of the distinction between public and private law is two-fold: first, the rules applicable to a contract or a tort or to the use of powers are not the same for public bodies as for private bodies; secondly, any litigation is tried by different courts according to different procedures by different groups of judges whose background is distinct from that of private law judges.[5] As will be seen in Chapter 7, the origins of the principle and practice of separation date back to the monarchical period, particularly in the 17th and 18th centuries. In brief, the immunity of the sovereign or the state from action in the ordinary courts was mitigated by establishing effective remedies in the King's or the state's own courts, the Council of State (Conseil d'Etat or Conseil du Roi). This radical separation between public and private law courts, in its present form, is a feature of the French republican tradition. It was set out in a *loi* of 16–24 August 1790 and by Napoleon's creation of the Conseil d'Etat and restated by decisions of the Tribunal des conflits at the beginning of the Third Republic. More recently, it has been declared a fundamental principle recognized by the laws of the Republic by the Conseil constitutionnel. In its decision of 23 January 1987, the Conseil constitutionnel declared that this principle stipulated that the quashing of administrative decisions should be a matter for the administrative courts, though this is much narrower than the separation which currently exists.[6]

Nowadays, the distinction is of importance in terms of both substance and procedure. In terms of substance, the identification of an issue as a public law issue requires the application of different rules of law. These rules are not found in the civil or commercial codes, but are found in either a body of administrative law principles developed by the Conseil d'Etat (rather like the English common law in structure and authority) or in various legislative provisions which have been enacted from time to time. (Some of these are called 'codes' but are really no more than consolidations of disparate legal provisions developed in different periods).[7] Although there may be many similarities between private law and public law rules, e.g. on contract and tort, the rules are not the same. This distinction of substance has arisen out of and now justifies a specialist judiciary and court system which can deal with public law matters. The peculiarity of the French approach is that the specialism required has developed into a radical cleavage between public

---

[4] His casting vote is rarely required, but was used in TC 12 May 1997, *Préfet de Police de Paris*, D 1997.567.

[5] See below, Chs 3, 4.

[6] C. cons. 23 Jan. 1987, *Competition Council*, Rec. 8.

[7] Above, p. 24.

and private law courts, whilst maintaining a close connection between the judiciary of the administrative courts and the 'active administration'.

In this section, the basic structure of the public law courts will be described and this can be compared with that of the civil and criminal courts described in the next section and with the account of commercial and other specialist private law courts described in the following sections.

1. *Generalist administrative courts*

The oldest of the public law courts is the Conseil d'Etat, set up by Napoleon in 1799, but originating in the King's Privy Council. It was originally a court of first and last instance, but since the creation of the tribunaux administratifs in 1953 and the cours administratives d'appel in 1987, it has increasingly become a supervisory court, with a role as an appeal court in a small number of areas. Its jurisdiction is typically to review the decisions of the lower administrative courts and to quash them where the law has been wrongly applied. It also gives advisory opinions on the law during litigation when requested to do so on a reference from those courts. It retains some matters as a court of first and last instance, but these have become increasingly rare as the administrative appeal courts have developed. Its judges are drawn from a distinct corps of the administration[8] around 200 active members who have distinguished administrative and judicial careers. In 2005, the Conseil d'Etat decided 11,222 cases.

At the bottom of the pyramid of courts are the tribunaux administratifs. They originate in Napoleon's conseils de préfecture which advised the Prefect. There are now 36 spread across France (including in the overseas territories). They are staffed by a corps of judges drawn from the administration and, to an increasing extent, from private practice. Together with the members of the Conseil d'Etat, there were 1,125 administrative judges in 2005. Each court is made up of a minimum of a president and three or four judges, though some, such as Paris are very large. They have jurisdiction on most matters arising in their area: contracts, liability, illegal municipal elections or decisions. They now have jurisdiction to enforce their own decisions by way of *ordonnance* to the administration. In 2005, the tribunaux administratifs decided 155,562 cases.

Above these are the eight regional cours administratives d'appel. They deal with appeals on points of law and fact from the tribunaux administratifs. They are staffed by the same corps of judges, but are presided over by members of the Conseil d'Etat. In 2005, they decided 23,553 cases.

2. *Specialist administrative courts*

In addition, there are some *commissions* which function rather like tribunals in the United Kingdom. They take decisions on disputes about the application of

---

[8] The term 'administration' is preferred to 'civil service' since the latter is much narrower in meaning than the French term 'fonctionnaire'.

the law by the administration, and appeal lies to the administrative courts. In the case of the largest of these, the *Commission des réfugiés* appeal lies to the Conseil d'Etat. It deals with claims for asylum. It dealt with 38,563 cases in 2005.

Other *commissions* cover the national provision of social welfare payments (1,725 cases in 2005). The disciplinary organs of professional bodies (*avocats*, doctors, dentists, etc.) are all administrative bodies and their decisions are subject to *cassation* before the Conseil d'Etat. In 2005, there were 864 cases decided by the various professional disciplinary bodies from which appeal lies to the Conseil d'Etat.

The Cour des comptes has the function of verifying the regularity of accounts of public bodies. A small group of judges (two reporters) examine the accounts and give a judgment as to whether they are in order or in debt. If they are deficits which have not been approved the departmental accounting officer is personally responsible. The process is a judgment on the propriety of the accounts, rather than the efficiency of the accounting officer.

The Chambres régionales des comptes perform a similar function in relation to the accounts of local government accounting officers. The Cour de discipline budgétaire et financière deals with the rare case of personal fault by officials in the management of public accounts.

3. *Le Conseil constitutionnel*

The Conseil constitutionnel is not formally a 'court',[9] but a 'council'. All the same, its functions and practical status, fully set out in Chapter 5, make it a court to all intents and purposes. Unlike other courts, there is only one national court. It does not hear applications from individual citizens concerning the constitutionality of *lois* passed by Parliament in relation to concrete fact situations. Rather it reviews their constitutionality in abstract on a reference from either the President of the Republic, the Prime Minister, the President of the National Assembly, or the President of the Senate, or, more commonly, from 60 deputies or senators (usually from opposition parties). In this way it does not deal with 'cases', but rather reaches 'decisions' about the constitutionality of the *loi* taken as a whole. Since it is not formally a court, there is no procedure for reference or appeal to it from the ordinary administrative or civil courts, though there have been several proposals to this effect. The members of the court do not need to have legal qualifications and are not drawn necessarily from the ranks of the various judiciaries (as is the case in Germany or the United States). Former Presidents of the Republic are *ex officio* members, provided that they are no longer active politicians. Although not integrated into the hierarchy of courts, the Conseil does carry authority in its interpretations of the Constitution. Its rulings on the constitutionality of a *loi* must be followed by the ordinary private law and public law

---

[9] See J. Bell, *French Constitutional Law* (Oxford, 1992), 48–56.

courts, and its interpretations of provisions of the *loi* are respected by them and are typically followed as authoritative statements.

In the matter of national elections (for the President of the Republic, for the National Assembly, or for a referendum), the Conseil constitutionnel does sit as a more conventional court. It deals with petitions concerning irregularities in the electoral process and comes to individual decisions (often several hundred in relation to parliamentary elections). But this is not the principal focus of its work.

B. Civil and Criminal Law

Although criminal law involves a prosecution in the name of the state against a private individual, the courts which deal with criminal matters are connected and typically co-located with the private law courts. The private law judges thus sit in criminal and civil courts, which carry distinct names depending on whether its functions are civil or criminal. The judges involved are drawn from the corps of private law judges educated at the *Ecole Nationale de la Magistrature*.

1. First instance criminal courts

As will be seen in Chapter 7, the French distinguish between three categories of offences according to their seriousness: in ascending order of seriousness they are *contraventions, délits,* and *crimes.* This categorization is matched by the jurisdiction of criminal courts.

At the lowest level, the tribunal de police deals with the minor offences, the *contraventions.* Such offences normally carry a fine of up to €1,500. They are located in the chief town of an *arrondissment* or *département.* Cases will be tried by a single judge. The tribunal de police tried some 106,421cases in 2005. (Many minor offences are handled by way of fixed penalty fines, of which 9,985,515 were imposed in 2005.) Other minor cases are decided by the *juges de proximité.* These are non-professional judges with jurisdiction over petty crimes, especially traffic offences, involving fines, but not imprisonment, and they made decisions 319,651 in 2005.

More serious cases, involving heavy fines or imprisonment, are tried by the tribunal correctionnel. This court is located in the main town of a *département* and the judges are the same as those for the tribunal de grande instance. As will be seen in Chapter 4, this will sometimes involve the *juge d'instruction* who will prepare the case for trial. In the tribunal correctionnel, trial will be before a panel of three professional judges in most cases, though some specific offences (e.g. in the financial fraud field) are subject to special procedures. Where a trial is likely to last a long time, it may be necessary for the presiding judge to nominate some alternates who will attend the case, but only sit in judgment where one of the judges on the bench is no longer able to sit. In 2005, the tribunaux correctionnel decided some 498,278 criminal cases.

A small number of very serious cases, e.g. involving murder, are tried by the cour d'assises. This is located with the Cour d'appel and at least the presiding judge is drawn from that court. The first stage is the committal hearing before the Chambre de l'instruction which is before three judges. The trial is heard by three judges sitting with nine jurors. Jurors must be over 35 and a panel is selected at random from the electoral register for each year. One juror is selected for each 1,300 inhabitants with a minimum of 200 members for the year. (There are 1,800 jurors for Paris.) For each session of the court 35 names are chosen together with 10 substitutes. From these the jurors for a particular case are chosen by lot drawn by the president of the court. The prosecution and the defence may challenge up to four or five jurors respectively. Substitute jurors attend court and hear the case, but are only called to participate in a decision when one of the jurors is no longer able to participate. Unlike in England and Wales, the judges and jurors retire together to determine conviction and sentence according to a list of questions which the presiding judge establishes before they retire.[10] The cours d'assises dealt with 2,588 first instance trials in 2005. In addition, appeals from the cour d'assises lies to a different cour d'assises having a jury of 15 people. In 2005, there were 396 such appeals.

Young persons are tried in distinct courts which specialize in these offenders. Juvenile offenders between 16 and 18 charged with a *crime* are tried by a special formation of the cour d'assises, which has two *juges des enfants* in place of the normal assessor judges, but is otherwise similar to the cour d'assises. In 2005, some 479 cases were tried by this court. There are 155 tribunaux pour enfants. Most young offenders, however, are tried by the tribunal pour enfants or by the *juge des enfants*. Their competence is the same: serious *contraventions, délits,* and *crimes* for minors over 16.[11] Most cases can be left to the *juge des enfants* to decide on his or her own since they only result in educative measures being taken. Serious criminal penalties can only be imposed by the tribunal in which the *juge* is assisted by two lay assessors chosen from people appointed by the Minister of Justice for four-year periods on account of their expertise in relation to children. The criminal jurisdiction of the *juge des enfants* is an adjunct to his or her main function of intervening when the health, safety or moral situation of the child is threatened. The judge is seised of a case at the request of parents or guardians, the public prosecutor, or the child. The jurisdiction thus resembles the children's courts in England with their civil and criminal functions. But the criminal functions are more limited, since the criminal penalties can only be imposed by the tribunal des enfants or by the cour d'assises when the child is 16 or over. Unlike the English lay magistrates, the *juge des enfants* is a professional judge specializing in children's cases, though he is regionally based in the location of the tribunal de

---

[10] For studies on the French jury, see R. Munday, 'Jury Trial, Continental Style' (1993) 13 LS 204, 'What do the French think of their Jury?' (1995) 15 LS 65.

[11] On the significance of these different classes of criminal offences, see below, p. 205.

grande instance. In 2005, the youth courts dealt with 111,706 young people in danger and 73,161 delinquents.

2. First instance civil courts

Criminal and civil courts share the same locations and judges. There are, however, only two levels of first instance civil court.

The *tribunal d'instance* was known as the court of the *juge de paix* (justice of the peace) from the Revolution until 1958. It had long been a single-judge court hearing small civil cases. Since 1958, the judges have been drawn from the ordinary judiciary and have been grouped into 475 courts located in the main towns of *départements, arrondissements,* and important *cantons.* The jurisdiction of the court is limited to claims of €10,000. Appeal lies to the cour d'appel. In 2005, the tribunaux d'instance handed down 676,600 judgments. Of these 77,550 were decisions taken by the non-professional *juge de proximité,* and a further 73,154 were interlocutory orders (*référés*). The *loi* of 26 February 2003 created a new category of non-professional judge, the *juge de proximité.*[12] Appointed for a non-renewable period of seven years, these part-time judges will deal with small civil cases (up to €4,000).

More important civil cases, e.g. those above €10,000, are heard by the tribunal de grande instance. These are located in each *département,* though some larger ones have more than one. There are a total of 181 in metropolitan and overseas France. Some are very large—Paris has over 300 judges, and where this occurs the courts may, in practice, have specialist sections. The tribunal de grande instance is the ordinary court for family matters (marriage, divorce, affiliation, and nationality), as well as for property and patent matters. It also handles cases above the limits for the tribunal d'instance. It is a collegial court when trying such cases. But, in practice, much of its important civil work is carried on by single judges dealing with matters before the case is heard on its merits (by the *juge des référés* and by the *juge de la mise en état*). The *référé* is a rapid procedure before a designated judge who can make orders to protect the status quo pending hearing of the case, and can order either the payment of provisional damages or even the performance of contractual or other obligations.[13] Since bringing the case to trial will be expensive and time-consuming, the decision of the *juge des référés* is often in practice the definitive solution. The tribunaux de grande instance decided 953,447 cases, as well as making 115,800 *référé* orders in 2005.

3. Appeal courts

Appeals on both civil and criminal cases lie to the cour d'appel with the exception of decisions of the Chambre d'accusation and the cour d'assises which are

---

[12] *Loi* no. 2003-153 and see below, p. 63.
[13] See art. 809 C. pr. civ. on the powers of the president of the tribunal de grand instance and below pp. 97–98.

both already branches of that court. There are 35 *cours* located often where the pre-revolutionary Parlements sat, maintaining a significant element of continuity in the French legal tradition.[14] Apart from urgent matters, the cour d'appel is collegial with a minimum of three members. A typical cour d'appel will have a number of specialist chambers, dealing with civil, social, criminal, and juvenile matters. Appeal lies on law and fact. Because there is a file on the case containing all the elements of the evidence reduced to writing produced by the lower civil and criminal courts, it is easy to conduct such an appeal on fact as well as law. It is sufficient to review the file as presented by the lower court and to order such additional investigations as might seem necessary. In 2005, the cours d'appel heard 225,163 civil appeals and 51,557 criminal cases.

4. Cour de cassation[15]

A litigant may make a *pourvoi en cassation* against a decision of the cour d'appel to the cour de cassation which is the only national court in France on civil or criminal matters. As its name implies, it is not strictly an appeal court, but merely a body which quashes the rulings of appeal courts for error of law.[16] Article 3 of the *loi* of 27 November 1790 empowers it to quash all procedures breaching due form and all judgments which contain an express contradiction with a promulgated law. The Cour is made up of six chambers, five civil chambers ((i) covering contract, (ii) covering delict, (iii) covering family matters, (iv) covering commercial matters, (v) covering social matters: labour and social security law; and (vi) dealing with criminal law). The Cour has 85 *conseillers*, 39 more junior *conseillers réferendaires,* and 18 trainee *auditeurs.* The Cour sits normally in panels of five judges, though the president of the chamber may order a case to be heard by merely three judges in an appropriate case. More important cases may be heard by a larger panel of judges within a chamber. The problem of having six chambers is that they can conflict on the interpretation of the same legislation. Thus a delict case might come before the second chamber or before the fifth chamber (on the ground that the case involves the application also of provisions of the social security code); a contract case could come before the first chamber or before the fourth (if the matter is a commercial dispute). To resolve divergences of interpretation and case law, a *chambre mixte* composed of the Premier President of the Cour together with the president and three senior members of each chambre concerned (anything between 13 and 25 people in total). The Cour sits in plenary session (Assemblée plénière) where a case is appealed from a cour d'appel to which it has been remitted after *cassation*. In other important cases, it may also be involved. It

---

[14] For this reason, the location of the *cour d'appel* does not always match the major cities of modern France. For example, the *cour* in the Nord is sited in Douai and not Lille.

[15] For the work of this court, see the *Rapport Annuel* which it publishes containing statistical data and summaries of activity in major areas. The reports from 1997 are available online at <http://www.courdecassation.fr/>.

[16] The nature of *cassation* is discussed below at p. 91.

is composed of the First President, the president, oldest *conseiller* and two others from each of the six chambers, a total of 25 judges.

Since the *loi* of 15 May 1991,[17] the Cour de cassation has jurisdiction under article 151-1 of the *Code de l'organisation judiciaire* to give advice on a point of law on a reference from a lower court. This *saisine pour avis* applies where a case raises a novel legal issue of serious difficulty relevant to a number of cases. An opinion is issued within three months. The Cour sits in a particularly solemn formation to deliver such opinions, being presided over by the First president and attended by the president and oldest *conseiller* and two other members of each chamber concerned.

In recent times, two measures have been taken to reduce the time taken to decide cases submitted to the Cour de cassation. In the first place, summary decision procedures have been introduced to deal with appeals which lack merit. In 1981, article 131-6 of the *Code de l'organisation judiciaire* gave the First president or the president of chamber the discretion to refer a case to a *formation restreinte* composed of three judges instead of the normal five where the solution was obvious, but this only applies where neither party objects. Unlike a leave committee or summary judgment in the administrative courts, the court does not retain control over its business. The second reform was to give the Cour de cassation power to decide cases without referring them back to another court. The normal *cassation* procedure is that the court merely decides the disputed question of law and then refers it to a different cour d'appel. Since 1979, the Cour may enter a definitive judgment where the facts as found by the lower court enable it to apply the correct legal rule or where quashing the decision of the lower court does not require further inquiry into the facts of the case. This procedure of *cassation sans renvoi* in no way turns the Cour de cassation into a body which decides issues of fact. A further measure to avoid the use of a *pourvoi en cassation* as a delaying tactic is the power of the First President of the Cour de cassation under article 1009-1 of the Code of Civil Procedure to withdraw a case from the lists where, without good reason, the appellant has not executed the judgment against which he is appealing.

The Cour de cassation is very different from the British House of Lords. Being the only national court with no real constraint on the right to submit a *pourvoi* to it, the Cour de cassation is flooded with a large number of cases. In 2005, it decided 18,830 civil cases and 7,826 criminal cases. Its workload is much more comparable with the English Court of Appeal. Its primary function is to maintain the consistent application of the law across the numerous regional cours d'appel, and that requires a much greater intervention in the operation of the judicial system than the more measured pace of the House of Lords.

---

[17] *Loi* no. 91-491.

C. Civil Law and Commercial Law

The distinction between civil law and commercial law is much greater in France and Germany than in the United Kingdom. Although most European countries share common origins of commercial law in the customs of the medieval fairs, the ways in which commercial law has been integrated into the ordinary system of courts varies quite radically from country to country. In England, the Commercial Court is a late 19th-century innovation and is fully integrated into the ordinary court system. Recourse to arbitration outside the court system is very common and this mitigates the problems of leaving commercial matters to be resolved by ordinary judges. France adopted a different approach. As will be seen in Chapter 11, commercial law is a distinct branch of substantive law from civil law, although there are some overlaps in rules. The court system is also distinct. A system of commercial courts was established in 1563 and the courts survived with little change after the Revolution. Napoleon I's *Code de commerce* of 1807 entrusted the trial of commercial litigation to separate commercial courts staffed by businessmen. A commercial court deals with commercial matters. These are defined as disputes between commercial people (*commerçants*) or on commercial matters (company law, commercial leases) or about commercial things (e.g. patents).[18]

The 227 tribunaux de commerce are located in major towns across France. They are composed of 'consular' judges, that is to say, lay people not professional judges. As will be explained in Chapter 3, they are elected indirectly by the members of the local chamber of commerce. In large commercial centres, there may be a large number of judges. Judges are allocated to specialist sections. They sit without any professional judges in panels of at least three. There is usually a reporter judge who prepares the hearing which is oral. There is no equivalent of a magistrate's clerk who sits in with the panel, but there is a secretariat which can perform a similar support function. The idea of judgment by one's peers is popular. There are relatively few appeals to the cour d'appel. No appeal lies in cases for €4,000. In 2005, the tribunaux de commerce heard 280,274 cases. In addition, some tribunaux de grande instance have jurisdiction to hear commercial cases instead of a local tribunal de commerce, and in 2005, these courts heard a further 28,231 cases.

D. Other Specialist Private Law Courts

Three other specialist courts are worth specific mention.

1. Conseil des prud'hommes

The labour courts (which are known as conseils des prud'hommes) have their origins in pre-Revolutionary Lyon where there was a court of masters and servants

---

[18] Below, p. 455 ff.

in the silk industry. Napoleon generalized this, though the system was not completed until 1979. There are 270 *conseils* in France, with at least one in the area of each tribunal de grande instance. Each court has five different sections covering specific sectors of employment (infrastructure, industry, commerce, agriculture, and various other activities). The court is '*paritaire*', that is to say it has even numbers of representatives from the conflicting social groups, here employers and employees. The court is composed of at least eight members, four from each side. There is no professional judge present unless there is a tie, at which point a judge from the tribunal de grande instance (the *juge départiteur*) is called upon to break the deadlock. The election process is described in Chapter 3.[19] Although the judges do have some training provided by the state, they are essentially lay persons performing tasks similar to the commercial judges. Their understanding of the employment situation makes them well suited to analyse the situations of fact with which judges are principally confronted with. In 2005, the conseils des prud'hommes decided 246,290 cases. Appeal lies to the cour d'appel.

2. Le tribunal des affaires de sécurité sociale

Unlike in Britain, social security is classified as a private law matter. This is because the various social security funds (*caisses*) are private law organizations which make agreements with the state. There are social welfare tribunals within the hierarchy of the administrative courts. These deal with non-contributory social welfare payments. The social security courts (tribunal des affaires de sécurité sociale) are limited to contributory social insurance benefits; they are local and there are 113 in metropolitan France. The court is composed of representatives of employers and employees appointed by the president of the cour d'appel and is presided over by the president of the tribunal de grande instance. The representatives of employers and employees are nominated by administrations of the social security funds from lists drawn up by professional bodies. The president of the court also offers an opinion on nominations. The court sits in a panel of three: one employer, one employee, and a judge as president. Certain matters have their own special courts, e.g. the courts on invalidity litigation. The social security courts decided 95,395 matters in 2005. Appeal lies to the social chamber of the cour d'appel.

3. Comité paritaire des baux ruraux

Agricultural leases are a significant area of litigation in France. There are specialist courts composed equally of landlords' and tenants' representatives presided over by a *juge d'instance*. The landlords and tenants are designated as 'assessors' and are eligible if they are at least 26 years of age and have exercised their profession for over five years. The court deals with litigation concerning the special legislation

---

[19] Below, p. 63.

on agricultural leases. In 2004, these 413 courts dealt with 3,281 cases. Appeal lies to the social chamber of the cour d'appel.

II. The Local Character of Courts

Most legal systems attempt to bring justice as close to the litigants as possible within the limits of efficiency. The distinctive character of France compared with the United Kingdom or Eire is that there is no central first instance court in any branch of law, except for disputes concerning national parliamentary and presidential elections which are decided by the Conseil constitutionnel.[20] Those matters which the Conseil d'Etat used to deal with at first instance have mainly been transferred to lower courts: only three main categories remain—the validity of legislative or administrative decisions of the President or the Prime Minister, or decisions concerning certain high civil servants and officials appointed by decree, or where the decision covers the jurisdiction of more than one lower court. But these are minor parts of the jurisdiction of the administrative courts. Perhaps more striking is the regional character of both civil and administrative appeal courts. This leaves the supervisory court at the top of the respective hierarchies, the Cour de cassation and the Conseil d'Etat, with the function of ensuring a common application of the law across the whole national territory. Compared with the United States, there is, however, a common law across the whole country (the peculiarities of the law in Alsace-Lorraine and in overseas territories do not substantially undermine this sense of uniformity).

III. The Right of Appeal

The French adhere strongly to the idea that the litigant should have a right of appeal. Under the label, the double level of hearing (*la règle du double degré de juridiction*), this entitlement is firmly embedded as a matter of legal principle.[21] Chenot argued in his conclusions before the Conseil d'Etat in 1944 that 'the rule of the double level of hearing is a general rule of procedure which enshrines an essential guarantee for the interests of litigants and of the higher interests of justice'.[22] The principle involves a right of appeal for the losing party at first instance to a higher court. That higher court should be impartial, and so a decision which has been taken by an appeal court which includes a judge involved in the first instance case will be quashed.[23]

---

[20] Above, p. 42.
[21] Below, pp. 110–111.
[22] CE 4 Feb. 1944, RDP 1994.171 note Jèze.
[23] See Civ. (2), 3 July 1985, D 1986, 546 concl. Charbonnier.

The principle is not of universal application. There are some civil cases before the tribunal d'instance where the court hears the case in first and last instance.[24] On the other hand, the decision at first instance may already be taken by a higher court. Rare though such cases are these days, there are still some decisions taken at first instance by the Cour de cassation and the Conseil d'Etat. Further limitations include decisions on preliminary points of law (*décisions avant dire droit*) against which no appeal lies before the substantive judgment is entered, thereby saving time and avoiding an endless series of appeals before the main case is heard. But the glaring omission of any right of appeal against decisions of the cour d'assises was remedied in 2001.

The principle of an entitlement to an appeal must not be confused with the right to see cassation of a decision for error of law. Even if a decision is stated by legislation not to be susceptible to appeal, that does not preclude a *pourvoi en cassation* being lodged against the decision.[25]

The role of the Cour de cassation and the Conseil d'Etat thus offers important guarantees of the unity and correctness of the law across the whole territory. These two courts now function in both advisory and decision-making capacities. Despite efforts on the administrative law side to create new tiers of appeal courts and to devolve appeals on substance to them, both the highest public and private law courts are inundated with cases. Neither system accepts the idea that a litigant must obtain leave to appeal as in Britain. In particular, it would offend the French sense of justice if the refusal of leave were a purely administrative decision. There have been attempts in recent years to introduce speedier forms of decision-making in cases lacking merit. In the Cour de cassation, the *formations restreintes* have offered some way of reaching a judicial decision where the solution is obvious without taking up too much judicial time. The Conseil d'Etat operates with rapid decision-making procedures by *ordonnance* of the president of the court. It also has introduced the *procédure préalable d'admission* which effectively permits a small group of judges to decide on a case by way of summary judicial decision. The procedures are more akin to summary judgment than to a leave stage, but are very effective in reducing the numbers of cases requiring a full hearing.

IV. Collegiality

French courts, as will have been obvious from the summary above, are typically collegial. The old adage runs 'a single judge is an iniquitous judge' (*juge unique,*

---

[24] Below, p. 111, n. 252.

[25] See CE 7 Feb. 1947, RDP 1947.68 concl. Odent. For instance, art. 57 of the Statute of the Judiciary states that the disciplinary decisions of the Conseil supérieur de la Magistrature are not subject to appeal. But this did not prevent the Conseil d'Etat holding that it could quash the decisions of this body for error of law: CE 12 July 1969, *L'Etang*, RDP 1970.387 obs. Waline.

juge inique). There is a concern that justice should be the result of the correct application of the law and not the personal prejudices of the individual judge. But this idea has not achieved the status of a principle of law. When faced with a bill voted by Parliament which permitted the president of the tribunal de grande instance to decide whether cases would be heard by a single judge or by a panel of judges, the Conseil constitutionnel struck it down as contrary to equal treatment, not because there was anything inherently wrong with having single judge courts.[26] Indeed, there remain on the statute book a number of cases where the president of the tribunal de grande instance can still choose whether cases go to a single judge or to a collegial court.[27]

Although the principle of collegiality is highly valued, it succumbs to practical necessity to a significant degree. This is particularly true in the handling of minor cases at first instance. Both the tribunal d'instance and the tribunal de police are single judge courts. Although the full tribunal administratif is collegial, a president is permitted to delegate the trial of lesser matters such as some tax cases and litigation concerning public property or highway offences (*contraventions de grande voirie*). In both private law before the tribunal de grande instance and in administrative law, interlocutory matters are typically handled by the president of the court or a delegate as a single *juge des référés*.[28] A similar approach is adopted to interlocutory matters even before the appellate courts, largely because of the urgency of such decisions. In a number of specialist areas, there are single judge courts, e.g. the *juge aux affaires familiales* (in divorce or custody of children cases), the *juge de l'expropriation* (determining compensation for compulsory purchase), the *juge de la mise en état* (who supervises the pre-trial management of civil cases), and the *juge de l'application des peines* (who deals with the regime of prisoners in criminal cases and eventually their release). More recently, legislation has required decisions by a single judge. Thus the *loi* of 5 July 1985 on liability for traffic accidents requires that such cases be decided by a single judge in the tribunal de grande instance.

As in Britain, the French are reluctant to allow non-professional judges to sit as single judges. Thus all the courts involving lay judges are collegial.

V. Alternative Dispute Resolution

The large case-load of French courts had led to the passing of a *loi* on 8 February 1995[29] to increase the numbers of judges by 1999 and thereby reduce the number of cases awaiting trial. There has also been an interest in improving procedures to

---

[26] C. cons. 23 July 1975, *Single Judge*, Bell (above n. 9), decision 36.
[27] See art, L 311-10 of the Code de l'organisation judiciate.
[28] Below, p. 97.
[29] *Loi* no. 95-125.

resolve disputes without coming to court. In administrative law, there has been a traditional view that it was against the public interest for the administration to submit to the jurisdiction of anyone but the judge established by law. As a result, arbitration was not accepted. The Conseil d'Etat expressed the view in its opinion of 6 March 1986 on the proposed contract to govern EuroDisneyland that 'public law persons cannot escape from the rules which define the jurisdiction of national courts by submitting to the decision of an arbitrator the resolution of disputes to which they are parties which affect relationships arising from the domestic legal order'.[30] As a result, an international contract could be submitted to arbitration, but not an internal one. Certain specific public bodies such as the SNCF, the Post and France Télécom are authorized by statute to enter arbitration agreements. Conciliation, on the other hand, has been a mission of the administrative courts for many years and this was explicitly set out as the mission of the tribunal administratif in the *loi* of 6 January 1986. In tax cases, there has been great success in securing the resolution of disputes by referring them to the conciliation of the *commission départementale*. Settlements (*transactions*) are also frequently used in public works and similar areas of the life of the administration. Formally, the litigant must obtain an express or implied decision of the administration before he or she can challenge it in the administrative courts. This offers the administration a chance to put things right. A circular dated 9 February 1995 from the Prime Minister has reminded the administration of the importance of using alternative methods to resolve disputes.[31]

In criminal law, there have been experiments with *maisons de justice* to reconcile offenders and their victims.[32] The use of such techniques to encourage conciliation does not always obviate the need for the criminal process, but it does make some actions unnecessary. Article 41 al. 7 of the Code of Criminal Procedure envisages the possibility of the prosecutor encouraging mediation in order to resolve the dispute between the victim (as civil party) and the offender.

In private law, settlements have always been accepted. The parties are the primary initiators of the process. All the same, the courts have intervened to some extent to encourage settlements. The *juge de paix* used to have the formal role of conciliating the parties, but this was rendered optional in the new Code of Civil Procedure.[33] A decree of 1978 generalized the institution of non-judicial conciliators. These are voluntary workers who belong to the courts and who intervene when the parties request. There are no requirements as to the location of their work or their procedures. If the parties agree on a solution, the compromise

---

[30] CE 6 Mar. 1986, unpublished.

[31] See J. Bell, 'Reforming Judicial Procedure in French Administrative Courts' (1995) 1 European Public Law at 487–489; also *Régler autrement les conflits* (study of the *Conseil d'Etat*) (Paris, 1993).

[32] J. Faget and A. Wyvekens, 'Urban policy and proximity justice in France' (1996) 4 European Journal on Criminal Policy and Research 64.

[33] See below p. 89.

may then be referred to a *juge d'instance* who gives binding force to it. In certain areas, such as commercial, agricultural, or industrial companies which are unable to pay their debts, or individuals who have excessive debts, the courts may appoint conciliators to promote an arrangement of the payment of the debts. The *loi* of 8 February 1995 formalizes the practice of a judge appointing a mediator to resolve an issue if the parties agree. The judge sets the timetable for this action. Conciliation is also a requirement in matrimonial cases prior to divorce. Clearly there are limits to the effectiveness of formal requirements of conciliation or mediation, but they do offer some framework for cheaper and less antagonistic alternatives to a judicial decision.

3

Judicial Personnel

As a consequence of the court structure, the organization of French judicial personnel is complex and not easily recounted in the limited space of a book chapter. Furthermore, recent events have engendered serious criticisms and calls for reform. The judiciary is at a crossroads and while some reform has already been attempted, more changes are likely to be seen in the future. An investigation of these concerns is therefore necessary to assess and determine any proposal for change.

This chapter will show that French judges are more numerous and more diverse than in common law countries. Statistically, there is one judge for every 6,500 inhabitants. In 2005, there were a total of 7,526 judges in the tribunaux judiciaires (including 256 working in the Ministry of Justice) and 1,125 in the tribunaux administratifs and the cours administratives d'appel, as well as 300 in the Conseil d'Etat. This is extremely important since this might explain the tendency of the judges to behave as corporate bodies.

Before one investigates the judicial careers, it is important to identify who makes up the judicial body. The French use the terms '*juge*' and '*magistrat*' when referring to judges. Title VIII of the Constitution of 1958 refers to the '*autorité judiciaire*'. In one sense, the use of the word '*magistrat*' within that Title is broad, as it encompasses prosecutors as well as judges. On the other hand it is overly narrow, as it covers only the large body of private law judges. The definition of *magistrats* should not be limited to these judges working in the tribunaux judiciaires: first, it is also important to take into account the non-professional judges that are not directly afforded the various constitutional protections of Title VIII; and secondly, the Constitution does not mention the administrative courts or judges, though the Conseil constitutionnel has recognized their existence in its case law. In a word, the term *magistrat* needs to be understood in a broader sense than really expressed by the Constitution.

The term *juge* is also used with a different meaning from the English term 'judge'. It includes personnel who would not be called so in the English legal system: for instance, judges belonging to the *ministère public* functions as advocates of the public interest in court or as a prosecutor. However, they are *magistrats* and as such their independence is protected by the Constitution.

The division between ordinary and administrative judges is fundamental, but there is also a major division between professional and lay judges. However, all judges are under the responsibility of the *Garde des Sceaux* or Minister of Justice.

The status of the judiciary depends on certain constitutional principles that determine the status and frame the work of judges in France.

I. The Constitutional Foundations

Constitutionalism demands that judges be as independent as possible to allow them to decide cases without interference. The principle of judicial independence is meant to guarantee this freedom of decision. Although a consensus exists within Europe as to the general meaning of this principle, there is remarkable diversity in the way it is implemented. In this respect, the French Constitution of 1958 is distinctive.

A. The Independence of Judges

French constitutional law guarantees the independence of the judiciary by resorting to the principle of separation of powers. The courts are isolated structurally and functionally from the other two constitutional powers as much as possible.[1]

The Constitution of 1958 itself presents only part of the picture when it comes to the independence of the French judiciary, since it does not mention the administrative courts or their personnel at all, nor the many lay judges. The constitutional text appears to fail to protect a large number of judges. However, the Conseil Constitutionnel has largely remedied this situation.

1. The separation of powers

On the one hand, since 1790, the courts are not allowed to intervene in the activities of the legislative and executive powers. This prohibition has led both sets of courts to refuse to control the constitutionality of parliamentary legislation, for instance.[2] Neither are they at liberty to set aside a legislation that they find questionable.[3] Equally, as far as the control of administrative action is concerned, the principle of separation of the administrative and judicial authorities[4] requires that this control be undertaken exclusively by the administrative courts.

On the other hand, both the legislative and executive powers are not allowed to interfere with judicial activity. The constitutional framework, which is structured around principles and institutions, was adopted to ensure that this 'separation' be respected.

---

[1] However, the practical arrangements of a strict separation of power can be quite a challenge. It will be shown below how these are met in the French constitutional system.

[2] See CE 6 Nov. 1936, *Arrighi*, DP 1938, 3 1 and C. cass. 26 Feb. 1974 D 1974, 273, concl. Touffait.

[3] See C. cass. 30 May 1967 D. 1967, 566.

[4] See the *loi* of 16–24 August 1790.

2. *A partial protection of independence*

Article 64 of the 1958 Constitution guarantees the independence of judges working in the tribunaux judiciaires only.[5] At first sight, it would seem that this principle of independence does not apply to the judges staffing the administrative courts. This statement was true for a long period: paradoxically administrative judges whose duty consists in controlling administrative action did not benefit from the constitutional recognition and guarantees of their private law colleagues.

The limitations of this constitutional protection have been remedied. First, the Conseil constitutionnel did not hesitate to extend the principle of independence to the administrative courts;[6] as a consequence, all judges have their independence constitutionally guaranteed. Secondly, the *loi* of 6 January 1986 recognized a principle of separation of powers, in all but name, with regard to the first instance and appeal administrative courts.[7]

B. Implementation of the Principle

To guarantee judicial independence effectively, French constitutional law resorts to a web of substantive principle and institutional organization.

1. *The principle of 'irremovability'* (inamovibilité)

Beyond a general recognition of the independence of private law judges, article 64 of the Constitution also proclaims the principle of their irremovability, i.e. judges cannot be moved or removed by a decision of the executive,[8] except when authorized by law. This protection does not cover all judges. The Constitution limits the applicability of this rule to the *magistrats du siège*.[9] This excludes both the *ministère public* and all administrative judges. Consequently, many commentators in the past held the protection granted by the Constitution to be insufficient. As will be shown below, the judges of the *ministère public* are agents of the executive in the private law courts and to this effect, they are directly under the control of the Ministry of Justice. Arguably, only a limited independence is necessary. Furthermore, the exclusion of administrative judges has been remedied in the

---

[5] In addition, the Constitution invests the President of the Republic with the duty to guarantee the independence of the private law courts. One might rightly question this choice. As the President of the Republic is often the leader of the party or coalition in power, his political persona might well interfere with regard to the independence of the judiciary.

[6] See C. cons. 22 July 1980, Rec. 46.

[7] See art. L. 231-3 C. just. adm.

[8] This decision could be a suspension, dismissal, early retirement, relocation, and even promotion.

[9] Literally, this expression means the 'judges in the seat' or 'the sitting judges', i.e. the judges who issue the judgment. It is an image which refers to the fact that these judges are seated in court (as opposed to the *juge du parquet* who stands up to give his opinion). On the distinction between these different categories of judges see below pp. 60–61.

main, by the *loi* of 6 January 1986. The principle of irremovability is now proclaimed in anything but name in article L. 213-3 of the Code of Administrative Justice (CJA).[10] Even though the provision does not apply to members of the Conseil d'Etat, this is not a cause for concern; in practice, when it comes to the Conseil d'Etat, irremovability has never been infringed.[11]

It is worth pointing out, however, that the principle allows for fixed-term judicial appointments[12] and for the replacement of judges who are temporarily unable to fulfil their functions (e.g. illness, maternity leave, etc.). Furthermore, the principle does not prohibit judges from being disciplined, moved, suspended, or even revoked in case of professional failures, incompetence, or misconduct. In fact, the organization of judicial careers needs to be carefully planned to balance the requirements of irremovability with the regulation of the inevitably long judicial careers.[13]

2. *The Conseils supérieurs*

In the 1958 Constitution, the principle of judicial independence finds its institutional expression in the Conseil supérieur de la Magistrature.[14] Article 65 of the Constitution specifies the composition and the functions of the Conseil.[15] This body has a dual role: it is involved in appointments and discipline of the members of the private law courts. However, because of the differences of functions between the *magistrats du siège* and the *magistrats du parquet*, the role of the Conseil supérieur de la Magistrature is different depending on the category of judges concerned. While the Conseil is simply consulted by the Minister of Justice regarding appointments and promotions of the *magistrats du parquet*, it makes binding recommendations regarding many appointments and promotions of the *magistrats du siège*.[16] Furthermore, the same distinction applies to the disciplinary role of the Conseil supérieur de la Magistrature: for the *magistrats du siège*, the Conseil has full disciplinary jurisdiction, but for the *magistrats du parquet*, it simply issues a recommendation to the Minister of Justice.

[10] See L. 231-3 C of the *loi* of 6 January 1986.

[11] See further, Brown and Bell, *French Administrative Law*, 85.

[12] For instance, the president of a *Tribunal de Grande Instance* is appointed for seven years as it is necessary that this position experiences a certain turnover; see C. cons. 19 June 2001, Rec. 63.

[13] The recruitment procedures and practices will explained below, but the majority of French judges are recruited in their late 20s and early 30s; they will then spend their whole career in the judiciary.

[14] See art. 65 of the French Constitution.

[15] The composition of the *Conseil supérieur de la Magistrature* has been debated from the beginning of the Fifth Republic. It was felt that its appointment and composition did not guarantee its independence. In 1993, the Constitution was revised to end these criticisms. There are two different compositions of the *Conseil* depending on the role and the category of judges. Each has 12 members and of these six are elected by their peers. However, these members never all sit together: the composition differs depending on the role to be fulfilled.

[16] The Conseil supérieur de la Magistrature makes binding recommendations on all promotions from second to first grade and all appointments to new functions. For all the appointments *hors hiérarchie*, i.e. the most important positions, the Conseil selects and proposes the appointee.

Since the *loi* of 6 January 1986, the first instance and appeal administrative courts also benefit from the Conseil supérieur des tribunaux administratifs et des cours administratives d'appel.[17] This Conseil fulfils a dual role regarding appointment and discipline similar to the Conseil supérieur de la Magistrature. All promotions must be first proposed by the Conseil supérieur des tribunaux administratifs et des cours administratives d'appel. However, when it comes to discipline, the Conseil makes only a recommendation.

II. The Different Categories of Judge

The French judiciary is best understood by examining differences in jurisdiction, function, and degrees of professionalism.

A. The Jurisdictional Difference: *Juges Administratifs* vs *Magistrats Judiciaires*

The first important distinction as regards judges reflects the jurisdictional divide between the administrative courts and the private law courts (tribunaux judiciaires).[18] The *magistrats judiciaires* solve disputes of a private law nature (although private law is understood in a wide sense as it covers criminal law and labour law as well as commercial law, law of obligations, etc.). This category of judges is organized in a uniformed body, the *corps judiciaire* and a single status was granted by the *loi organique* of 22 December 1958.

The *juges administratifs* on the other hand solve administrative law disputes and their career defers quite markedly from their private law counterparts. First, as mentioned above, the 1958 Constitution is silent when it comes to the *juges administratifs*. The need for their independence however is proclaimed and safe-guarded since a decision of the Conseil constitutionnel of 1980.[19] Also, unlike the *juges judiciaires*, the *juges administratifs* are not organized in a single and uniformed *corps administratif*. For a long time, there was no legislation organizing the career of this category of judges.[20] There are in effect two major constituents: the members of the Conseil d'Etat[21] and the judges appointed to the lower courts: at first instance level, the tribunaux administratifs and at appeal level, the Cours administratives d'appel. At present, the rules regulating and organizing both careers are contained in the *Code de Justice administrative*, these rules diverge markedly and the consequent status of both categories of personnel

[17] This body has 13 members, five of whom are elected by their peers.
[18] The tribunaux judiciaires deal with civil, commercial labour, and criminal law.
[19] See C. cons. 80–119 DC of 22 July 1980, Rec. 46.
[20] This might be due to the fact that they were different *corps* within the civil service and there was no formal training as judges. Therefore, these judges were not separately identified as judges.
[21] The Conseil d'Etat is the supreme or top court of the administrative courts.

is quite different. The *juges administratifs* are not organized in a single career and although steps have been taken to allow a few to progress from the lower courts to the Conseil d'Etat, it is still difficult.

B. The Functional Difference: *Juges du Siège* vs *Juges du Parquet*

Judges in the private law courts can be subdivided into two categories of judges: the *juges du siège* and the *juges du parquet*.[22] The distinction between these two categories of judges reflects the type of judicial work performed and the functions fulfilled. In 2005, there were 7,402 magistrats, 77.8% were *juges de siège* and 25.3% were *juges du parquet*. To some extent this distinction is partially reproduced in the administrative courts with the *Commissaire du Gouvernement*.

1. *The* juges du siège

They are so named because they sit while they hear the case. By English standard, the *juges du siège* (or *magistrature assise*) are judges properly so-called, as they are the ones who hand down judgment at the end of a civil or criminal case. In order to fulfil this task, the independence of this category of judges is constitutionally protected throughout their career. Thus, article 64 of the Constitution proclaims the principle of *inamovibilité*, according to which *juges du siège* can only be dismissed, suspended, or even transferred to other duties if provided by a *loi*.

2. *The* juges du parquet

The *juges du siège* are to be contrasted with the *juges du parquet* (also called *magistrature debout* or *ministère public*). The role of the *juges du parquet* differs in criminal law cases from civil law ones. In criminal cases, the *juges du parquet* are central to the proceedings. First, the decision to initiate proceedings rests largely with the *ministère public* (however, the *juge d'instruction* has a discretion as to whether the proceedings should continue). Secondly, the *juges du parquet* represents the state during the proceedings and pleads to safeguard the interests of the state and the public interest. A request for a specific sentence will be delivered at the end of the *réquisitoire*. In civil proceedings, however, the *ministère public* can decide to be a *partie jointe* or a *partie principale*. When, the *ministère public* decides that a case is particularly significant or has serious legal implications, it can join the proceedings and become a *partie jointe*. Consequently, a *juge du parquet* will submit oral or written arguments to the *magistrats du siège*. Furthermore, in a limited number of cases, the *ministère public* will act as *partie principale* or main party and either initiate the proceedings or act as the defendant.

In order to ensure that these duties are fulfilled, a few principles regulate the work of the *juge du parquet*. First, the *ministère public* is independent from both

---

[22] This functional distinction is particularly relevant for the *juges judiciaires* but it is also found to a lesser degree among the *juges administratifs*.

the parties and from the *juges du siège*. The latter can neither give him/her orders nor have him/her removed from the case. Secondly, according to the principle of *subordination hiérarchique*, the *ministère public* is accountable to the Minister of Justice (also called the *Garde des Sceaux*). The Minister of Justice will direct the work of the *juges du parquet* through the *procureurs généraux* who will in turn keep the minister informed of developments with regard to important cases. There are two limitations to this chain of order and command: first, the head of each *parquet* gives orders freely to individual *juge du parquet* and in many cases, the ministry does not express any views;[23] secondly, any *juge du parquet* can plead freely and according to his/her conviction in court, even against Government's guidance. Still, any written submission must conform to the ministry's expressed wishes.

3. *The* Commissaire du Gouvernement

To some extent the *Commissaire du Gouvernement* plays a similar role to the *parquet* in the administrative law courts. There is not in fact a *ministère public* as such. The *Commissaire du Gouvernement* does not represent the Government and for this reason the name is badly misleading, and he has no function of prosecution. He studies and researches the case as a neutral party and delivers an opinion (called a *conclusion*) which is an argumentation on the fact and law leading to a conclusion on the case; it will explain the relevant legal provisions, establish the case law, and propose interpretations in the light of the facts of the case. The *conclusions* of the *Commissaire du Gouvernement* are always very instructive; they are well researched, well written and often very creative. The case law is assessed and proposals for change are likely to be made therein. The *conclusions* leading to important cases are likely to be published in legal journals or in the *Recueil des Arrêts du Conseil d'Etat* or in its annual report the *Études et Documents du Conseil d'État*. They are often considered as seminal doctrinal writings.

The *Commissaire du Gouvernement* does not sit as judge in the case and so does not vote in the private discussions of the judges (*délibéré*), but he or she may be present, unless a party objects (article R733-3 CJA). However, the solution put forward in the conclusions will influence the decision of the judges. It is recommended to read the Conseil d'Etat decisions, in the light of the arguments submitted to the court by the *Commissaire du Gouvernement*. He or she benefits from a totally independent status within the court in which he or she works. The list of the *Commissaires du Gouvernement* is drawn by the court to which they belong and it is published in a *décret*. The *Commissaire du Gouvernement* is also traditionally guaranteed against interference of the Government. The Conseil d'Etat has always protected its status from the attacks of the executive when necessary. They exercise these functions temporarily.

---

[23] It would even be possible for a head of *parquet* to ignore the wishes of the ministry and Government and give contradictory orders. However, disciplinary proceedings are likely to be initiated.

C. Lay Judges vs Professional Judges

The great majority of judges are professional judges and this chapter is mainly concerned with them. However, there is a small category of non-professional judges which are fully integrated to the court system. This phenomenon is restricted to the tribunaux judiciaires and to the first instance level only. Since a reform of 2002, there are two categories of non-professional judges, the lay judges who are elected by their peers and the non-professional judges who are appointed because of their suitability and legal qualifications.

1. The lay judges

To a large extent, this is an ideological legacy of the 1789 Revolution. Elections were regarded to be the optimum mechanism for choosing any appointee fulfilling a public function. With this in mind, a system of electing judges was adopted and, though later abandoned as a matter of general application, the practice survived in a few isolated cases: there, justice seemed better served by trial by peers. At present, this practice is mainly found in commercial and industrial relations matters.

The commercial courts are the oldest courts in France; they were introduced in the 15th century in order to settle any legal disputes arising during the large fairs of the day. These courts soon became permanent and survived the 1789 Revolution as the election of the judges fitted well with the ideas of the period. To this day, the principle of election has not been contested: it is said to create an environment of trust and facilitate mediation. Presently, the *juges consulaires* (the so-called judges of the commercial courts) are elected for a fixed term. The electoral system has been changed a few times, but at the moment the *juges consulaires* are elected indirectly. In the first instance, shop owners and commercial traders in the jurisdiction of each court meet to elect an electoral college. The electoral college meet with present and past members[24] of the tribunal de commerce to elect the new judges for an initial period of two years and thereafter for a period of four years. Judges may serve several terms, but after four consecutive terms, a year must elapse before they are eligible for re-election. Like English magistrates, they are unpaid. A person must be at least 30 years old and have practised in a commercial profession for at least five years. The *juges consulaires* cease their functions when their term of office comes to an end, when the court is abolished, when they become disqualified (e.g. when a judge's own company goes into liquidation), or when the national disciplinary committee orders their removal.

The Conseils de prud'hommes have jurisdiction for any litigation concerning contracts of employment between employers and employees. They aim at mediating a conciliatory agreement and to this effect all disputes are first referred to the *bureau de conciliation* to find a compromise solution. The emphasis on

---

[24] At their request, past members can be included on the electoral roll, but it is not automatic.

mediation explains the choice of elections, the organization and recruitment of the court aims to create an optimal environment to solve labour disputes. The *conseillers prud'hommes* are elected by workers registered by employment categories. To be on the electoral roll, a worker must be at least 16 years old and in employment; while to be eligible, a worker must be at least 25 years old, on the electoral roll for at least three years and have French nationality. The electorate is divided into two colleges: employers and employees. Elections take place in each of the electoral colleges with a system of proportional representation. The *conseillers prud'hommes* are elected for five years and can be re-elected. The court respects a principle of strict parity with two judges representing the employees and two judges representing the employers. The salaried members of the court have a protected status so as to fulfil their functions adequately: thus, employers must give time off to judges to sit in court, must agree to absences up to six weeks per annum for new judges to receive legal training, and cannot dismiss a judge without due cause and the approval of the *inspecteur du travail*. All *conseillers prud'hommes* receive a fee for the time spent fulfilling their judicial functions.

2. The juge de proximité

Created in 2003, the *juges de proximité* were designed to offer rapid and cheap justice on small matters. They are permitted to work up to 132 days a year and are remunerated at a daily rate. The initial plans were to recruit up to 3,300 over five years. There are a range of possible routes to become such a *juge*, notably for those over 35 with at least four years professional experience in law and qualified to apply to become a judge, or those who have worked for 25 years in a legal setting. Of the first 33, 11 were professional lawyers (avocats, huissiers, notaires), 10 had law degrees, seven were retired ordinary or administrative judges; four had worked for 25 years in a legal environment (e.g. a former secretary-general of the Suez bank group), and three were conciliators in civil courts. The typical appointee was a retired lawyer in his 60s. The character of the appointment is thus not like a lay magistracy, but rather lawyers appointed not to full judicial posts but deciding routine civil and criminal cases as a single judge

III. Recruitment

The method of recruitment of professional judges is one of the main differences between the British and French judicial professions. In France, the majority of professional judges are trained prior to holding judicial office. It reflects the belief that this profession like any other can be taught via courses and apprenticeships. This is a fundamental aspect of the judicial professions in France, and it has an impact on the homogeneity of the thinking and reasoning, methods of decision-making, and on choices made by judges in general. Long before they even reach the bench judges have been trained in very specific ways, and if they do not think alike (nothing short of brainwashing could achieve this), one might rightly think that they have already acquired a certain professional vision. However, more recently, corporatist attitudes of the judiciary have been highlighted and denounced; the choice of a career judiciary is questioned. There are concerns that the institutional independence of the judiciary has led to the creation of an unaccountable branch of Government. Calls have been heard for a more diverse recruitment to allow people with different experiences to sit on the bench. However, the reach of these reforms is still to be assessed.

A. Recruiting the *Juges Judiciaires*

Until 1958, candidates to the professional examination for the judiciary had to have completed two years traineeship at the bar; this was abolished partly because it was felt that such training was not relevant for a career in the judiciary. The new *Statut de la Magistrature* of the *ordonnance* of 22 December 1958 created a 'judicial college' and this became the Ecole Nationale de la Magistrature (ENM) in 1970. Although the great majority of private law judges are recruited by this route,[25] lately the pressure to appoint new judges and the criticisms of corporatism has meant that recruitment has had to be diversified.

In order to enter this *grande école*, one has to hold a *maîtrise*[26] or an equivalent degree, and to be successful in one of the competitions giving access to the *école*. There are three categories of competitions: the first aims at students (the *concours étudiants*), the second aims at civil servants (the *concours fonctionnaires*), and lastly, since a *loi* of 25 February 1992, a third competition aims at professionals with relevant experience: for example, an electoral mandate or a lay judicial office, etc. Competitions are normally organized every year and approximately 250 places are offered. It is not possible to enter the competition after three unsuccessful attempts.

In addition, every year a small number of applicants (between 5 and 20) are accepted into the ENM on the basis of their qualifications: these will have a *maîtrise en droit* and three or four years of relevant professional experience, for example as a university law lecturer.

On entering the ENM, the students are called *auditeurs de justice* and from this moment they are part of the *corps judiciaire* and receive a salary. They complete a programme of 31 months which is divided in two periods: one of general training (26 months)[27] and the second of specialized training (five months).

---

[25] 81% of the judges presently in office have been recruited through the ENM; 4% were recruited by extraordinary competitions; 12% were recruited directly; and 3% were recruited before 1958.

[26] The *maîtrise* does not have to be in law. This helps to widen the recruitment.

[27] This consists of two months work experience in a private company, a public corporation, or the civil service either in France or abroad so as to increase the *auditeurs'* knowledge of the 'real world'; thereafter, eight months at the Ecole Nationale de la Magistrature where technical

At the end of the first period of training, a second competition called *examen de classement*, takes place in order to rank the *auditeurs*; the top candidate is the first to make his choice of post on the list drawn to this effect: the higher the rank, the wider the choice.[28]

During the second period, the *auditeur* spends six months, in the court where his first position is going to be so as to train for the specific function.

There are also judges recruited directly into the judiciary. However, judges have always been rather suspicious of this mode of recruitment and have expressed concerns about the issue of independence. However, the government is not free to appoint whomever it wishes: there is a strict list of professions and length of working experience which apply, these appointments are limited in number, and the *commission des avancements* decides on the grade and position to which a person can be appointed. The number of people who enter the *corps judiciaire* in this way varies each year from around 10 to 30.[29] There has been call to increase the number of judges recruited by the route; it is felt that it would bring new blood and experiences to the judiciary.

The social composition of the *corps judiciaire* has been the subject of detailed study and various findings have been made; first, the main route for recruitment, through the ENM, means that judges acquire to some extent the ideology, approach, etc. of the bench while still being educated; secondly, the social origins of the *magistrats judiciaires* reveal it as a rather homogenous body, drawn mainly from the *bourgeoisie* and often with a family association with the civil service.[30]

It is worth mentioning at this stage, a major difference with the English judiciary: a process of feminization is being observed in the French judiciary. In November 2005, 54.1% of the *magistrats judiciaires* were female. But this global figure hides the fact that, on the one hand, 65.25% of the lowest grade of judges (2nd class) were women, but only 22.15% of the highest class (*hors hiérarchie*). Some fears have been expressed that this development of 'feminization' will inevitably lead to deep changes in the profession itself, but this has not occurred even though men and

---

knowledge is taught on judicial decision making; finally, a 12 months placement in court where the *auditeur* is acquainted with each and every judicial position that he might exercise on first appointment. The *auditeur* is entitled to participate in the activities of the court. He can help the *ministère public* and even plead in its name; he can participate in the *délibéré*, where he does not vote but is consulted. To widen his understanding of the justice system, the *auditeur* also spends two months in chambers to accustom himself with the task and duties of barristers (there he is entitled to plead in court), and he is seconded to a prison where he acts as prison warden.

[28] The examination board also makes for each *auditeur* a recommendation identifying the position he is best suited to fulfil.

[29] Although the possibility to appoint from outside the judiciary exists since 1960, it is only recently that it has been resorted to, partly to help with the recruitment, but also to tackle the complaint of corporatism. It is hoped that these new members when joining the private law courts will bring with them a fresh perspective and different experiences to bear on the work.

[30] See J.L. Bodiguel 'Qui sont les magistrats français? Esquise d'une sociologie de la justice', *Pouvoirs* 16, 31, and for an update see A. Boigeol, 'Les transformations des modalités d'entrée dans la magistrature: de la nécessité sociale aux vertus professionnelles' *Pouvoirs* 74, 27.

women seem often to have different approach to their career and favour different types of jobs when choosing their first posting or later promotions.[31]

B. Recruiting the *Juges Administratifs*

For a long time, each of the administrative courts recruited their personnel separately, the Conseil d'Etat, the Cour des Comptes, the conseils de préfecture, etc. each having their own competition. However, in 1945, the Ecole Nationale d'Administration (ENA) was created to unify the recruitment of the French civil service and this *grande école* became the port of entry for the *juges administratifs*. Depending on the candidates' achievements on leaving the ENA,[32] they will have a choice between positions in the civil service or in the administrative courts. The Conseil d'Etat is so prestigious that only the very best ENA graduates (or *énarques*) have the choice to become *auditeurs*, the initial grade in the Conseil d'Etat (all positions at this grade are appointed from the ENA).[33] The tribunaux administratifs are not so well regarded and a person does not have to be so high up in the final class list to obtain a position of *conseiller administratif* in one of the provincial tribunaux administratifs.

Also, many administrative judges are recruited through what is called the *tour extérieur*, which is a parallel appointment process by which civil servants may be nominated by the Government to an administrative court at any time during their career. It is a traditional route which ensures that administrative cases are tried by people who have had experience of working in the civil service and so are more likely to understand the implications of any future ruling. Indeed, this combination of experience was the basis for the initial acceptance and continued success of the Conseil d'Etat. Also, the numbers of judges appointed from ENA is too small to fill all the vacancies in the administrative courts. Still, the number of judges who can be appointed in this way is limited. As far as the Conseil d'Etat is concerned, only a quarter of the *maîtres des requêtes* and a third of the *conseillers d'Etat* can be appointed from outside.[34] Similarly, as regards the tribunaux administratifs or Cours administratives d'appel, the Government can appoint only one second class *conseiller* in three and only one first class *conseiller* in seven from the *tour extérieur*. Consequently, two other routes had to be created to help with a necessary recruitment drive: the authorization for a complementary competition, first introduced in 1980, is renewed regularly[35] and allows for the

---

[31] A. Boigeol, 'La magistrature française au féminin: entre spécificité et banalisation' (1993) 25 Droit et Société 489, 499–514. For instance, female judges are over-represented in the positions of *magistrat du siège* by opposition to the *ministère public*.

[32] This is called *concours de sortie* or *examen de classement*, and it is the same principle as for the ENM.

[33] No *auditeurs* can be appointed from the *tour extérieur* (for an explanation of this term see below).

[34] It is called the recruitement *au tour extérieur*.

[35] This competition aims at recruiting qualified professionals or civil servants who cannot enter the ENA competition because of the age limit.

permanent appointment of civil servants or private law judges on secondment to administrative courts.

The recruitment processes reflect the absence of a single career organization for the administrative courts: the members of the Conseil d'Etat are distinct from the personnel of both the tribunaux administratifs and the Cours administratives d'appel.[36] Not only is it possible to be recruited straight to the Conseil d'Etat from the ENA, but it there is no systematic promotion from a Cour administrative d'appel to the Conseil d'Etat.[37] So much so that, the number of graduates from the ENA represents approximately only 25% of the staff in the two lower courts: this seems to be a far cry from the general principle enounced in the Code de la Justice Administrative at article L233-2 which states that members of the lower courts are recruited among graduates of the ENA. As a result, members of these courts are quite uneasy as they believe that any collegial spirit is diluted by the diversity of these appointments. On the contrary, when it comes to the Conseil d'Etat, it is possible to witness a strong collective spirit.

IV. The Career: Promotion vs Independence

The fact that judges in France, unlike their English counterparts, dedicate the whole of their career to the judiciary means that a clear career structure is necessary. Also, the need for the principle of judicial independence to inform the promotion procedures, structures and practices is self-evident. In fact, many promotion decisions are framed by strict constitutional provisions. It would not do much for the legitimacy of the legal system if the Government were allowed to run a system of promotion based on arbitrariness.

As a result, all judges have a grade, which indicates the level reached in the hierarchy, and a function, which refers to the type of work undertaken. The concepts of grade and function are separate, but related: for instance, one has to have reached a certain grade in order to be appointed to perform a certain function.[38] This creates problems as in order to be promoted, a judge often has to move to a different court. Beyond the family considerations which do not always make this possible, a tension between the constitutional principle of irremovability and the need for mobility of judicial personnel must be resolved.[39] Since promotion

---

[36] This is in contrast with the situation in the private law courts.

[37] It is possible for members of the lower administrative courts to be appointed to the Conseil d'Etat either as *conseiller d'Etat* or *maître des requêtes*. However, the proportion of vacant positions which can be filled in the way is limited: one in six for the *conseiller d'Etat* and one in four for the *maître des requêtes*.

[38] For instance, to be *conseiller* or *avocat général à la Cour de Cassation*, one has to be *magistrat hors hiérarchie*. Also sometimes, the grade and the function are totally confused as for a president of a tribunal administratif.

[39] The *loi* of 25 February 1992 attempted to break a too rigid link between grade and function in the *ordre judiciaire*. In some circumstances, a judge could benefit from promotion while staying in the same function. However, today the trend has been reversed; it is felt that judges should not

is the main reason for a judge to move court and function, this could be used to circumvent the principle of irremovability, i.e. one could move a judge by promoting him/her.[40]

A. A Career in the Tribunaux Judiciaires

To prevent any breach of the principle of judicial independence, the promotion of the *magistrats du siège* must be organized so as to be either quasi-systematic or to be insulated from governmental influence. The independence of the *magistrats du siège* has been the subject of debates[41] since the beginning of the 1958 Constitution but the legislative reform of 1992 and the revision of the Constitution of 1993 has achieved a greater independence for these judges in the promotion procedure.[42]All the *magistrats judiciaires* are on the same salary scale throughout their career.[43] It has three levels. A judge might expect to pass from second grade to first grade and then rise to be *hors hiérarchie*.

Promotion between each level is strictly on the basis of seniority. In order to move from one grade to another, the name of the judge has to be put forward by the *commission d'avancement*: it draws a list (the *tableau d'avancement*) of the names of all candidates who could be considered for promotion. In order to ensure that independence is respected, the *commission d'avancement* is autonomous from the Ministry of Justice. It is composed mainly of judges elected by their peers (usually on lists drawn up by the judicial unions). The list is drawn up by the committee on the basis of each candidate's record and assessment of his work by *magistrats* of higher rank. It is then transmitted to the Conseil Supérieur de la Magistrature whose opinion is binding for the *magistrats du siège* only. The promotion system was reformed by an organic law of 26 June 2001. Under it, a judge cannot be promoted within a court in which he or she has served for more than five years, and judges cannot serve by way of transfer for longer than six years. Judges often choose to stay in a particular area for domestic reasons, so they may have to trade off promotion and mobility.

---

assume the same function for too long. To this effect, provisions of the *loi* of 25 June 2001 compel judges to a certain mobility.

[40] Both administrative judges and *magistrats du siège* can be refused a new post, even if it is a promotion.

[41] The bibliography on this theme is considerable but here are some selected examples of the literature:

See E. Bloch 'Faire carrière sous la V ème république', Pouvoirs 16, 97; F. Colcombet 'Faire carrière', Pouvoirs 74, 105; D. Soulez Larivière, Les juges dans la balance (Paris 1990), esp. ch. 5; J.-L. Bodiguel, Les magistrats, un corps sans âme (Paris, 1991).

[42] This is all the more important since less than 6% of the judges will do *une grande carrière* or reach the top jobs. See the opinion of E. Bloch about the reasons for having a successful career 'Faire carrière sous la Ve République', *Pouvoirs* 16, 97.

[43] It is contained in the *décret* no. 58-1282 of 22 December 1958 but has been modified and simplified a number of times.

The career of a judge can come to an end for a number of reasons: he or she may be dismissed, may resign or retire, or may be appointed in another government department. The retirement age is 70 for the judges of the Cour de Cassation and 67 for all others.

B. A Career in the Tribunaux Administratifs

The administrative courts are divided into two separate groups as far as recruitment, status and the general organization of the career is concerned: the Conseil d'Etat forming one category and the tribunaux administratifs and the cours administratives d'appel another. This means that unlike the junior *magistrats judiciaires*, the judges in the tribunaux administratifs or in the cours administratives d'appel will not necessarily have the opportunity to progress to the Conseil d'Etat. Still, some bridging provisions have been adopted so as to allow *juges administratifs* from the lower courts to be appointed as *maître des requêtes* or *conseiller d'Etat*.[44]

Promotions inside the Conseil d'Etat are formally made by *décret* of the *Garde des Sceaux*, on the recommendation of the *Vice-président* of the Conseil d'Etat after consultation with all the presidents of its various sections. However, these parties have little choice since a convention exists that recommendations for promotion is made in strict order of seniority, such an automatic system being thought best to ensure independence.

On the other hand, the organization within the cours administratives d'appel and the tribunaux administratifs differs, being clearly inspired from the system established for *magistrats judiciaires*. Thus, there are three grades and a judge is only allowed to be promoted one grade at a time. Again, the *juge administratif* to be promoted must appear on the *tableau d'avancement* which is drawn by the Conseil supérieur des tribunaux administratifs et des cours administratives d'appel.[45]

C. Incompatibilities

To ensure that judges are really independent professionally, financially, and politically, various rules and practices prohibit judges from undertaking specific activities. Furthermore, the pivotal role of the judiciary in the political system and its importance in society requires that judges behave in a dignified

[44] The proportion of positions reserved in either category is not high: one in six for the category of *conseiller d'Etat*, and one in four for the category of *maître des requêtes*.

[45] The Conseil supérieur des tribunaux administratifs et des cours administratives d'appel is staffed mainly by administrative judges. A number of comments can be made about its composition: first, contrarily to what happens in the ordre judiciaire, the majority of the members are not elected (and at least three appointments are likely to be highly political); this might simply be due to the fact that the membership of the Conseil Supérieur des tribunaux administratifs was established long before the CSM. was reformed. Secondly, the Conseil d'Etat is strongly represented and controls to some extent the promotion in the lower courts.

manner. While French public servants have to respect some rules of conduct, the status of judges imposes stricter restrictions. Some activities are expressly prohibited and others are incompatible with judicial office. These rules serve to establish the impartiality of the judiciary. The public must not have any doubt on this point.

1. Political activities

First, there is an obligation of *réserve* which specifies that judges should always express their political opinions moderately if in public. In general, it is prohibited for a judge to behave in a way that goes against his duties, honor, or dignity. The reason for these restrictions lies in the fact that judges should not appear to be politically biased.[46]

For the same reason, political demonstrations are prohibited for all the *magistrats judiciaires* and for the members of the Conseil d'Etat.[47] Although, the organization of strikes is expressly prohibited for the *magistrats judiciaires*, there is no such prohibition for the members of the administrative courts.

As far as a political career is concerned, a judge must resign from office if he or she is elected to either chamber of the French Parliament, to the European Parliament, or appointed to the French Economic and Social Council; However, they will be able to return to their judicial career once all political activity ceases; also, no judge can be appointed or stay in office in the constituency were her husband or his wife has been elected. In the case of local elections, these are compatible with a career in the judiciary as long as the constituency is not the one where the judge is in office. It is not unusual for a minister, especially the Minister of Justice, to be a judge.

It is interesting however, to point out that trade unions activities as such are not only allowed but fully resorted to by both the *magistrats judiciaires* and the *juges administratifs*. The fact that in France the function of judging is a career in itself and not an honour coming at the end of a successful career in advocacy means that French judges are more likely to wish to defend their career interests through the action of trade unions (also, the other prohibitions leave them little choice). There are three trade unions representing the *magistrats judiciaires*: *le Syndicat national de la Magistrature, l'Union Syndicale de la Magistrature* and the *Association Professionnelle des Magistrats*. At present, the *Syndicat de la juridiction administrative* is the main (if not sole) trade union to represent the *juges administratifs*. These trade unions have a number of aims and functions: first, they provide candidates for the elections to the various professional bodies mentioned above; secondly, they enter into collective bargaining for the *corps judiciaire*

---

[46] On the relation between judges and politics, see J. Libmann 'La "politisation" des juges: une vieille histoire?', *Pouvoirs* 16, 43.

[47] In fact the texts go even further for the magistrats judiciaires since they cannot participate in 'political debates' or 'show any hostility to the principle or form of the government of the republic' (see art. 10 of the *ord.* no 58-1273 of 22 December 1958). In fact, all civil servants have to abide by the obligation de reserve and these prohibitions are the expression of this principle. Justice cannot appear to be biased because of the pronouncements of some of its members.

or *administratif*; thirdly, they often present constructive criticisms of the legal system and put forward proposals for reform; fourthly, they are consulted by the Government when legislative proposals are drafted.

2. Other professional activities

By law, professional judges cannot have another occupation. Any other professional activity would take time away from their duties and could compromise their independence by putting them in a relation of subordination. If a judge was tempted by another career opportunity, for instance in the civil service, a public corporation or a private company, various legal provisions authorize him or her to take temporary leave of absence, and in all cases, to return to their judicial career.[48] This is particularly important for the members of the Conseil d'Etat who are often given the opportunity to spend some time in the civil service, or in managerial positions in public or private corporations. Thus, they acquire first-hand knowledge of the constraints of the administrative process or the harsh realities of industry. This is meant to help them to discern the implications of their decisions.

3. Family ties

A judge is not normally allowed to sit in the same court as his wife, husband, or relative, so as to prevent family ties from compromising their independence. Also, a judge is not allowed to hear a case when a relative represents one of the parties.

If there were doubts in the mind of the parties as regards the impartiality or independence of their judge, the parties can have the judge or judges removed from their case (*récusation*). However, in practice, judge(s) pre-empt this and tend to withdraw from such a case. If a court finds itself unable to process a case, because too many of its judges have withdrawn from it, then it will be sent to another court. Such *renvoi* is also possible if there are reasons to suspect the independence of the whole court in the circumstances of the case or for reasons of public order (e.g. if violent demonstrations were expected).

D. Duties

All judges must respect two important duties in relation to their functions: first, they must give a judgment even in the absence of any legislative provisions. Any refusal of a judge to do so constitutes a denial of justice (*déni de justice*), which is a criminal offence punished by law. Secondly, judges must keep secret any discussions

---

[48] There are three possibilities in fact:
- delegation: the person stays in the corps judiciaire or corps administratif but fulfils different functions;
- *détachement*: the person is not in the same corps anymore but all rights to promotion and pension run and that person will reintegrated at the end of it; and
- *mise en disponibilité*: it is a temporary break, promotion and pension rights are frozen but the person can come back to his or her corps at the end of it.

that take place with each other before a decision is reached.[49] This requirement of secrecy is important since decisions in France are collegiate[50] with one single judgment. It is thought necessary that no one should know which judge took what view, as otherwise any such judge might become the object of undesirable pressures.

E. Discipline

The regulation of disciplinary proceedings is fundamental to the protection of judicial independence. If a judge is at fault professionally, the principle of irremovability should not be used to shield him/her from disciplinary proceedings. On the other hand, disciplinary proceedings should not be an excuse for the Government to breach the principle of independence.

1. Magistrats judiciaires

The Conseil Supérieur de la Magistrature (CSM) is the body in charge of disciplinary matters for the *corps judiciaire*. The system is different for a *magistrat du siège* by opposition to a *magistrat du parquet*. The independence of the *magistrats du siège* must be strictly ensured and for this reason the CSM is headed by the *Premier président* of the Cour de Cassation, and the decision taken binds the Minister of Justice. On the other hand when the CSM deals with a *magistrat du parquet*, it headed by the *Procureur Général près la Cour de Cassation* and gives only an opinion to the Minister of Justice.

2. Juges administratifs

In 1963, provision was made for disciplinary proceedings to be taken against members of the Conseil d'Etat. The two least serious sanctions may be imposed directly as a result of a decision of the *vice-président* of the Conseil d'Etat. All others may be imposed only by the Minister of Justice after consultation of a committee, whose opinion while not binding, is unlikely to be ignored.

For the members of the Tribunaux administratifs and the Cours administratives d'appel, the Conseil supérieur des tribunaux administratifs et des cours administratives d'appel makes a recommendation.

V. Non-Judicial Officers of the Court

As the name indicates, an *auxilaire* is someone who helps and *auxiliaires de justice* help either the parties to put forward their arguments or the judge to make a decision.

---

[49] This duty is contained in art. 448 N.c.pr.civ. for the *magistrats judiciaires* and in the case law of the Conseil d'Etat for the *juges administratifs*; see CE 15 October 1965, *Mazel*, JCP 1966.II.14487.

[50] This means that one and only one judgment is handed down. The text is a compromise between all the judges.

The structure of French legal professions has been altered significantly both by national legislation in 1990 and in 2004[51] and by developments in European Community law.

A. The *Avocat*

The term of *avocat* cannot be fully translated into English by 'barrister'. For, while *avocats* do represent the interests of their clients in court and do possess a monopoly in doing so, they have a wider function than English barristers do. Thus, *avocats* may give legal advice on a day-to-day basis, help to negotiate and draw up contracts and draft articles of association for companies. Their profession therefore includes work performed in England by solicitors, still, with regard to these, *avocats* possess no monopoly as other *auxiliaires de justice* can give advice, draw up contracts, etc. The role of the *avocat* is protected by the Conseil constitutionnel as it is considered an essential element within a person's right to defend himself. For instance, the Conseil constitutionnel struck down a provision which allowed the President of a court to prohibit a barrister from appearing in court for a period up to two days.[52] In 2005, there were 45,818 *avocats*.

1. Access to the profession

An *avocat* must have a *maîtrise* in law (or an equivalent degree) and have passed the *Certificat d'aptitude à la profession d'avocat* (CAPA).[53] The CAPA establishes that the relevant training has been completed: it lasts 18 months and amounts to a series of taught courses and placements.

Once, the trainee has obtained the CAPA, he or she is a fully qualified barrister and can ask to be added to the list of the bar, a decision which is taken by the Conseil de l'ordre. Barristers must undertake continual education.

Until 1991, foreign lawyers could only practice in France on an occasional basis, but in 1991, it was recognized that lawyers might need to practice in France, when a case requires it, and subsequent legislation provided that they must join a French bar in order to do so.[54] If the applicant has worked three consecutive years in France, he or she is entitled to be added to the list of the bar. If, on the other hand, the applicant does not fulfil this condition, the *Conseil de l'ordre* has a discretion.

2. The organization of the profession

Avocats must feel able to express themselves freely at all times. Thus, the organization of the profession must enhance this freedom of expression. Still, the

---

[51] See *loi* no. 90-1259 of 31 December 1990 and *loi* no. 2004-130 of 11 February 2004.

[52] C. cons. 20 Jan. 1981, *loi Sécurité—Liberté*.

[53] In order to study for the CAPA, the student who has obtained a *maîtrise* takes an examination to be allowed to register in a Centre régional de formation professionnelle. The student takes the CAPA after a year.

[54] See *Arrêté* of 7 January 1993, cf. Directive 89/48/EEC.

profession must also be strictly regulated since *avocats* participate in a public service.

In order to exercise their profession, all *avocats* have to be a member of a local bar (*barreau*). There is a *barreau* attached to every tribunal de grande instance[55] in France. All *barreaux* are distinct legal entities and are organized independently: each has its own budget and internal regulations. All *barreaux* are made up of three bodies: the *assemblée générale* which is composed of its *avocats* and honorary members; it elects both the *bâtonnier* and the Conseil de l'ordre.

The *bâtonnier* is in effect the head of the *barreau* and has a number of powers: for instance, he can give a warning (*avertissement paternel*) if an *avocat* is at fault; he may mediate between colleagues entangled in a conflict; he checks the professional accounts of the *avocats*. Furthermore, the *bâtonnier* meets with judges, organizes the timetable for the hearing of cases, and checks that the organization of the court does not hinder the work of the *avocats*. Also, he is responsible for establishing a list of *avocats* available during holidays and for chairing the Conseil de l'ordre.

The Conseil de l'ordre decides on the admission of new members, on disciplinary matters, and adopts the *barreau*'s internal rules.

Finally, the Conseil national des barreaux was created to promote consistency between the various bars, and help them express their concerns and demands in one voice.

3. Practices and structures

In France, the cabinet d'*avocats* was typically organized around an individual, often working from home, maybe with a secretary. Until recently, lawyers, doctors, barristers, dentists, etc. were not allowed to organize themselves in commercial firms. Legislation now provides that *avocats* may practise through a company specifically created to this effect and this allows *avocats* to collaborate under its umbrella with chartered accountants (*experts-comptables*) and auditors (*commissaires aux comptes*). French lawyers are therefore allowed to organize themselves in powerful firms and compete with their American and British counterparts. Three methods may be used: a simple association, a *société civile professionnelle*, or a *société d'exercice libéral*. *Avocats* have traditionally worked in small offices. In 2003, outside Paris, 43.5% of *avocats* worked on their own.[56]

4. Rights and duties

In order for the *avocats* to represent successfully the interests of their clients, they enjoy an immunity with respect to anything expressed in their oral pleadings or written submissions. Also, their office may not be searched for documents establishing their client's guilt, nor may their correspondence be intercepted or read to this end.

[55] This means that there is a local bar in every French departement.
[56] B. Chambel in L. Marlière, *L'avocat en France* (Paris, 2004), 22.

The *avocats'* special position also requires a number of restrictions. First, they owe a duty of professional confidence *(secret professionnel)* to their clients; secondly, their practice as *avocat* is incompatible with most other professional activities such as membership of the civil service, salaried employment, etc. but there is no restriction on political activities; thirdly, an *avocat* may need to be protected from their clients and so they are free to decide on the legal arguments to use, and they may refuse to continue to represent a client.

B. The *Officiers Ministériels*

This expression covers various categories of practitioners who have obtained from the administration the right to perform certain legal acts, and who therefore hold public offices which bestow on them a monopoly. These *offices* have to be bought from a retiring *officier ministériel*.[57] However, a number of criteria must be met: the candidate must be French, possess a 'high morality', have completed the necessary training, and be admitted by a court. The price paid in acquiring an office is reviewed by the administration and may be reduced. The Government is responsible for the creation or cancellation of *offices* and controls their overall number.

Each profession is organized around a complex hierarchy of chambers along the lines of the old corporations. Generally, there are three levels of chambers: one at the level of the *département*, an intermediary and regional one, and a national one. Each have different functions but they deal with disciplinary matters, settle disputes between *officiers ministériels*, and voice the concerns of the profession to the relevant authorities.

1. *The* avoués près des cours d'appel

The *avoués* and *avocats* were once the equivalent of solicitors and barristers respectively. In 1971, the two professions were merged but only as regards the courts of first instance, leaving the two professions to act before the cours d'appel, still. There were only 425 members of the profession in 2005.

The *avoués* take all procedural steps necessary for the proper progress of the trial in the cours d'appel, but *avocats* can still plead and give advice to clients. Discussions regarding the merger of the two professions are heard regularly but a number of arguments in favour of retaining the distinction have been heard; for instance, in the country, cours d'appel cover a large geographical area and it is necessary to have someone permanently near where the court sits to perform all the procedural acts.

---

[57] The retiring officer will present his successor to the administration. The latter, by convention, endorses systematically the person thus presented. Arguably, this system of appointment guarantees the independence of the office-holder.

2. *The* Avocats au Conseil et à la Cour de Cassation

These *avocats* possess an *office ministériel* which entitles them to exercise the functions of both *avocat*—pleading and giving advice—and *avoué*—doing all the procedural acts necessary for a case to be heard in the Cour de Cassation or the Conseil d'Etat. Again, the exercise of these functions is restricted to the holders of these offices.

For this reason the status and organization of the profession is strictly regulated: the number of offices is limited to 60 and specific conditions have to be fulfilled to enter the profession. In 2005, there were only 91 members of the profession.

3. *The* huissiers de justice

The *huissiers de justice* fulfil a great number of functions and there were 3,259 members in 2005. First, they have the exclusive right to notify all procedural acts (such as *assignation*) in relation to legal proceedings and to execute those acts which have *force exécutoire*.

Secondly, a *huissier* is often asked by private individuals to recover unpaid debts, to establish an affidavit on matters of law or fact which might be useful for a dispute or a trial in progress.[58] Since in effect, they exercise public power (albeit a limited one), *huissiers* must obey strict rules, so that nothing which they do may compromise their independence or dignity. Any extra-professional activity when allowed by statute, is strictly controlled by the Minister of Justice.

4. *The* notaires

The *notaires* draw up legal acts (*actes notariés*) such as contracts, wills, etc. which thereby acquire two special attributes: authenticity and *force exécutoire*. As to the former, it is almost impossible to question the validity of an act drafted by a *notaire*; the procedure, which is called *procédure d'inscription en faux* is difficult and rarely used. The act drafted by a *notaire* has also *force exécutoire*, which means that a *huissier* can see to its performance without the need for a judicial decision. *Notaires* keep copies of all the acts which they have drawn up and can deliver a copy any time a party requires it.

Notaires are also often asked to give advice in relation to the situation for which an act is required. Indeed, the *notaire* has for centuries been a central figure in the social, economic, and legal life of the middle and upper classes. Nothing was decided without the advice of one's *notaire*. Today, the role of the *notaire* is not as prominent, but they are still consulted for many legal acts (particularly in relation to conveyancing).

In order to qualify as a *notaire*, one has to possess a *maîtrise en droit* and undergo three years of further training: 12 months' study leads up to a diploma

---

[58] They are often asked by new tenants to record and certify the state of the premises before they move in.

which gives a right to enter a firm (called *étude notariale*) with the title of *notaire-stagiaire*, followed by a two-year apprenticeship. In 2005, there were 8,325 *notaires*.

C. Professions Helping the Judge

A number of professions are more specifically designed to help judges discharge their duties rather than help the parties in a direct way.

1. *The* greffe

The *greffe* is in charge of all the administrative duties in relation to the decision-making process in a court of law: it keeps the files of each case up to date, looks after the various registers, and ensures that all documents are communicated between the parties.

A number of legal formalities have been made the responsibility of the *greffes* of the tribunaux judiciaires: the *registre d'Etat Civil*[59] and the *registre du commerce*.[60]

Often, the *greffe* will give advice to the parties as to how they should proceed with their case.

2. *The* administrateurs judiciaires

Administrateurs judiciaires receive authority from a court to administer the assets of a person or a company. This is particularly necessary in relation to a company which is on the brink of insolvency. *Administrateur judiciaire* tries to turn the company around so that it would trade in profit again.

3. *The* mandataires judiciaires au redressement et à la liquidation des enterprises

The *mandataire judiciaire à la liquidation des entreprises* intervenes when a company cannot be salvaged, and the *mandataire's* aim is therefore to liquidate the assets of the company in order to distribute them among its creditors.

4. *The* experts

While not a profession as such, the role of the expert is very important in French civil, criminal, and administrative procedure. A list of experts is established by each court from which an appropriate person is chosen by the court to conduct an investigation in particular cases. Use of judicially commissioned experts is a way in which the length, complexity, and expense of litigation may be reduced.[61]

---

[59] It is the register containing the status of each person (birth, death, marriage, etc.).

[60] All new companies have to be entered in the *registre du commerce* when they are created. Important changes also need to be notified.

[61] See generally, J.R. Spencer, 'Courts Experts and Expert Witnesses: Have We a Lesson to Learn from the French?' [1993] CLP 213.

VI. The Accountability of the French Judiciary

In many constitutional systems, the accountability of the judiciary has become a thorny issue. There seems to be a clear shift of expectations. This might be in part explained by the ever-increasing demands for justice and the consequent 'judicialization' of social life.[62] These demands clearly impact on and also redefine the role, behaviour, and activity of judges. Furthermore, the role played by the justice system has changed from being a tool of legitimization of the political and constitutional system, to being assimilated to 'a new stage for democracy'. Consequently, the existing mechanisms for control are thought to be insufficient.

A. The Changing Role of the French Judiciary

The judiciary in the course of the Fifth Republic have seen their role alter dramatically. This change was partly in response to demands made by society; and in turn, these responses engendered other demands, thereby fuelling change at a quick speed and on a large scale.

The functioning of the political system so clearly different from the previous constitutional experiences of the last century, left a gap in the accountability of the institutions: the French Parliament has neither the constitutional tools nor the political will to control in-depth the activity of the Government. The emergence and consolidation of constitutional review was to be expected and it has resulted in a constitutionalization of the political discourse; it has led members of the Conseil constitutionnel and their decisions to hover around the political arena. Furthermore, the changes in attitudes when it comes to responsibility and behaviour of civil servants, state officials and decision-makers has led the courts to criminalize and sanction an increasing number of political activities and has involved members of the judiciary deeper in political controversy.

Furthermore, the demand for justice has increased, to the point, that for many commentators, the whole of society has been 'judicialized'; in any event, the justice system now has the task of resolving an ever-increasing number of disputes in an ever-widening circle of societal activities. These disputes do not fit easily into established legal categories, such as 'public law' or 'private law', around which judicial institutions and procedures are organized; a sense of unease and foreboding is starting to undermine the justice system as judges are forced to intervene in a wider range of issues: moral, economic, political, scientific, etc. Not surprisingly, demands for more accountability of the judiciary soon started to be heard. The public is not satisfied any longer with the existing institutional controls over the judiciary; it is felt that judges should be made more strictly

---

[62] See G. Canivet 'The responsibility of judges in France' in G. Canivet, M. Andenas and D. Fairgrieve (eds.), *Independence, Accountability and the Judiciary* (London, 2006), 29.

accountable for their decisions. After all, judges are state officials; ironically, the move to control and criminalize the failures of civil servants, state officials and decision-makers has led to the same demands being made of judges. However, this surge in the demand for accountability has serious consequences when it comes to the principles of separation of powers and independence of the judiciary. Accountability does not sit easily with the constitutional requirement of judicial independence. This trend is all the more difficult to accommodate in that it conflicts with an earlier demand for more institutional independence as finally delivered by the constitutional reform of the Conseil supérieur de la magistrature and the general organization of the career of administrative judges.

B. The Inadequacies of the Control Mechanisms

The accountability of the judiciary must be organized carefully so as not to impede its independence. Furthermore, each legal system makes institutional choices which impact in turn on the mechanisms for accountability. For instance, the French judicial system tends to set up collective processes of judicial decision-making. In the main, French judicial decisions are the product of a court and not a single judge, and the single judgment is often the result of a compromise between members of the court.[63] Individuality of thought or opinions is arguably eliminated from the process of judicial decision-making. Consequently, the search for mechanisms of accountability has focused on collective and institutional processes[64] and traditionally little place was accorded to individual accountability. For instance, procedures for appeal and review by higher courts aim at corrected any erroneous legal interpretation, but do target individual judges. Also, the financial control performed by the Cour des Comptes on the cost and efficiency of the public service of justice is a process of accountability of large areas of the public service: if the Cour does not limit itself to check that public money is used legally, its control does not investigate the actions of individuals. Again, the supreme courts themselves report annually on their workload and the evolution of the case law; they also put forward proposals for legislative reforms in areas which have been highlighted by the courts as problematical.[65] However, this type of reporting concentrates mainly on the activity of the top courts, the role and activity of individual judges is obliterated. Finally, even when a failure of the public service of justice attributable to individual judges or a group of them, harms members of the public, the liability of the state is triggered. Individual civil servants (i.e. the judicial personnel) are not held personally responsible for

---

[63] This has often been the subject of criticism as it is impossible for any dissenting opinion to be heard.

[64] Also, these are easier to organize than processes of individual accountability.

[65] For some, these methods of accountability represent a degree of self-legitimacy; still, the annual reports of both the Cour de cassation and the Conseil d'Etat contain useful and objective information concerning the case load.

mistakes they might have committed. The state is liable in their stead; of course, there might be consequences when it comes to individual appraisal and career prospect, but the state shoulders the liability (if not the blame) for the activity of its civil servants. A recent reform tried to introduce in March 2007[66] a new category of disciplinary offence arising from judicial decision-making, thereby strengthening the individual responsibility of private law judges; the offence was triggered if a judge was found to have breached gravely and deliberately an essential procedural guarantee of the parties. However, the Conseil constitutionnel struck the new legislation down.

Furthermore the present organization of the judicial profession emphasizes and strengthens its collective identity, especially when it comes to private law courts. The recruitment from a *Grande Ecole* either the Ecole Nationale de la Magistrature (ENM) or the Ecole Nationale de l'Administration (ENA) helps to create a corporate identity that is often criticized. The tendency to corporatism (*esprit de corps*) of the courts is denounced repeatedly.[67] Also, the main values that frame the delivery of the public service of justice (e.g. equality, neutrality, continuity, respect of public utility, etc.) tend to be internalized by the judges themselves and again might exacerbate this communality of views, especially as they determine the personal obligations that judges respect in the performance of their duties.[68] Furthermore, judges are represented by well-organized trade unions that not only relay their demands efficiently but also play a major role in the system of elections to both Conseils and many professional bodies; this gives trade unions a direct influence over individual careers and strengthens the detractors' claims of latent corporatism.

VII. Conclusion

It has been alleged that the emphasis on collective accountability has enabled individual members of the judiciary to escape from the consequences of their actions. Collegiate decision-making might be regarded to promote more impartial and therefore 'better' decisions, but it is paired with secrecy. The collegiate compromise might not be clouded by personal opinions and prejudices, but it is not revealed so as to make it impossible to identify the authorship of judicial decisions. If it provides protection against individual attacks, it also engenders a lack of transparency and individual accountability. In fact as mentioned above, there is a deficit in the French judicial system when it comes to individual accountability, a deficit which is impossible to reconcile with the growing demand for

---

[66] Organic law no. 2007-287 of 5 March 2007 on the recruitment, education and responsibility of private law judges JO of 6 March 2007. This provision has not come into effect as the *Conseil constitutionnel* contested its constitutionality.

[67] Although when it comes to the lower administrative courts the situation is quite the reverse.

[68] This is clear when one analyses the rights and obligations of individual judges, see above.

responsibility of decision-makers. Consequently, attempts at increasing aspects of individual accountability have been witnessed recently. In 2003, a committee was set up to investigate the issue of judicial ethics. However, the committee did not recommend the adoption of an ethical code and moreover, the main recommendations put forward by the committee were never implemented. More recently, the *Outreau* affair[69] shook the foundations of the justice system and a reform attempted to increase individual accountability of private law judges. The organic law of 5 March 2007 meant to address the responsibility of individual judges by introducing a new disciplinary offence and by giving the responsibility to the *Médiateur* of overseeing a new mechanism to complain of the behaviour of individual judges. However, these provisions were found to infringe the principle of the independence of the judiciary and were declared unconstitutional by the Conseil constitutionnel.[70] The conciliation between individual responsibility and the independence of the judiciary is indeed quite difficult to achieve. It seems that the accountability deficit identified above will take some thought and effort before it is appropriately addressed.

[69] The sad facts of this case of incest and sexual abuse were anything but simple. Originally three children were taken away from their parents because they could not cope with the upbringing of their children. Soon, the new carers for the children reported serious suspicion of sexual abuse at the hand of the parents and a criminal investigation was triggered into the allegations. However, during the investigation, the existence of a paedophile ring seemed to emerge. The original children accused a wide circle of adults, the children of whom sometimes confirmed the allegations. In total, 16 men and women were imprisoned awaiting trial. The first instance court acquitted seven of these 16 men and women as two of the allegations were withdrawn at the last moment and most of the cases collapsed (one man died in prison while awaiting trial). However, six of the accused had to go on appeal to be freed. The case received unprecedented media attention and the miscarriage of justice was so wide-ranging and had ruined so many lives that the President of the Republic apologized officially to the families concerned in an unprecedented attempt to own up to the facts. Soon calls for the punishment of the 'responsible' judge(s) were heard. Two processes took place in parallel to answer these demands. First, a disciplinary procedure was opened against the investigating magistrate, Mr Francis Burgaud, which culminated in a decision of the Conseil Supérieur de la Magistrature. Secondly, in a unprecedented move, the Assemblée Nationale, set a committee of inquiry into the miscarriage. The committee was meant to provide an in-depth analysis of the dysfunctions that had prevailed in the case and engage in lesson-learning. It aimed to make proposal for reforms to avoid such miscarriage in the future. Beyond a very critical review of every stage of the judicial process, the report of the committee of inquiry also dealt with the thorny issue of individual responsibility of the judiciary: a whole chapter covered this point and a number of suggestions were made.

[70] C. cons. 1 Mar. 2007, Recruitment, training, and accountability of judges (not yet published).

PART II
THE LAW
(A) PROCEDURE

4

Legal Procedure

(1) Civil Procedure

I. Striking Features of the French System

[T]here is no 'trial' in the common law sense in French civil procedure.[1]

The differences between French and English civil procedure are extremely marked and very varied and themselves reflect differences in conception of and significance given to the distinction between law and fact; different perceptions as to the proper and relative roles of the parties, their representatives and the court in the gathering and preparation of evidence; and, on the French part, an intense and long-standing distrust of oral evidence and an absence of a law of contempt.[2] In the result, Beardsley's comment quoted above is clearly justified, but it relates to only a part of the story. In this section, we shall explain a few of the salient differences which have just been noted, outline the general proceeding of litigation in the civil court of general jurisdiction, the Tribunal de grande instance, and explain the availability of appeals (*appels*) and review of judgments (*cassation*), legal costs and the enforcement of judgments. It should be noted, then, that we shall not attempt to discuss the divergence from the procedure found in the Tribunal de grande instance of other special jurisdictions.[3]

What then are the most striking features of the French system of civil procedure, at least when viewed from the perspective of English law? There are at least four.

A. The Relative Roles of the Parties, the Court and the *Ministère Public*

First, there is a very different balance between the role of the parties and of the court, or as French discussions say, the 'judge'. French jurists often refer in this

---

[1] J. Beardsley, 'Proof of Fact in French Civil Procedure' (1986) 34 *Am. J. Comp. L.* 459, 480 (the author sees proceedings before the *expert* as a partial substitute in some cases: below p. 106 ff).

[2] This last feature colours the whole of the law relating to the enforcement of judicial orders: see below p. 116 ff.

[3] See above pp. 45–46 for discussion of the other civil courts.

respect to the distinction between an accusatorial and an inquisitorial model of procedure.[4] According to the accusatorial model, it is the parties who play the primary role in the process: they start it, direct it, gather what evidence they think appropriate, whether personally or by setting in motion any necessary judicial intervention to obtain it. By contrast, the judge plays only a 'passive role', overseeing the 'duel' which the parties play out. According to the inquisitorial model, the role of the judge both as to the course of the proceedings and the gathering of evidence is much more pronounced, the judge acting in the public interest to bring out the truth of a case.[5] We shall see how important the judge's role is in criminal procedure, particularly as regards the work of the *juge d'instruction*,[6] and this system is often seen as typically inquisitorial in its nature. But it is clear that the French *civil* process under the New Code of Civil Procedure, which was enacted in the early 1970s, reflects neither of these somewhat simplistic models. Certainly, the starting point is that civil litigation involves by its nature a *private* dispute, invoking the application of *private law* and this means that the initiative for starting it,[7] its subject-matter[8] and much of the course of the proceedings are the responsibility and within the choice of the parties.[9] But the judge nevertheless does possess a very important and often far from 'passive' role in the civil process, particularly as to the gathering of evidence or *les preuves*.

At this point, we should note that there is a particular difficulty in translating *'preuve'*, as it combines elements of the English terms 'proof' and 'evidence'. In English law, rules of evidence set out what types or sources of evidence may be admitted for assessment by the fact-finding body and, on occasion, what weight should be given to them. The 'persuasive' or 'legal' burden of proof has been defined as the 'obligation of a party to meet the requirement that a fact in issue be proved (or disproved) either by a preponderance of the evidence or beyond reasonable doubt as the case may be'[10] and in the civil context the 'standard of proof' is the balance of probabilities. In the French context, these notions are not sharply distinguished. A prominent distinction there is between the facts (*les faits*) on which a litigant relies and their *preuve* and here the sense of *preuve* seems to be similar to the English 'proof'. Thus, in a civil context it is for a claimant to *faire la preuve* (i.e. establish the facts) of his case; and the law sometimes

---

[4] e.g. Couchez, *Procédure civile*, 229–230.

[5] Ibid.

[6] Below, p. 127 ff.

[7] Art. 1 N.c.pr.civ: 'Only the parties may introduce a case, with those exceptions which are recognised by legislation. They are at liberty to put an end to it before it concludes by a judgment of the court or by virtue of legislation'.

[8] 'The subject-matter of the litigation is determined by the respective claims [*prétentions*] of the parties': art, 4 al. 1 N.c.pr.civ. Not all proceedings in the civil courts involve 'disputes'; see below p. 93 concerning proceedings *en matière gracieuse*.

[9] Arts. 2 and 5 N.c.pr.civ., the latter stating that '[t]he judge must pronounce on all claims put to him but on these alone'.

[10] C. Tapper, *Cross and Tapper on Evidence*, 11th edn. (London, 2007) 131.

establishes presumptions as to their proof or reverses the burden of proof.[11] On the other hand, when it comes to the actual process of establishing facts in civil cases, we shall see that the parties share with the court the responsibility for adducing *les preuves* to establish what were the facts of a dispute: here, then, *les preuves* is closer to the English notion of evidence. Interestingly, the distinction between these two significances can sometimes be seen clearly in the substantive law. So, for example, the Cour de cassation has held that the fact that one party to litigation bears the burden of proof (*la charge de la preuve*) does not mean that the other need not help in adducing evidence, as 'each party is bound to lend a hand to the means of adducing evidence [*mesures d'instruction*]'.[12] While French law generally allows any type of evidence to establish necessary facts (*preuve libre* or *preuve morale*), in some cases certain types of evidence are required, such as written evidence in order to establish the existence of a legal transaction (this being generally known as *preuve légale*).[13] Finally, we should note that in the general situation of *preuve libre*, French civil law, unlike English, does not possess any rule as to the standard of proof (proof on a balance of probabilities in English law): a fact is either proven or not, this being within the '*intime conviction*' of the *juges du fond*.[14]

The more active role of the judge in the French civil process can be most clearly seen in the case of the *juge de la mise en état*, a judge who may be appointed to oversee the preparation of the case before it is heard,[15] but it is by no means restricted to this context. Thus, while it is indeed primarily for the parties to put together their own case,[16] as article 3 of the New Code of Civil Procedure puts it: 'The judge oversees the proper running of a case; [[17]] he has the power to set periods of time [for performance of procedural acts] and to order any necessary procedural measures'.

As to the latter, as we shall see, it is for the court to decide, either of its own initiative (*d'office*) or on the application of a party, whether to order the production of a document, the examination of a witness or the commissioning of an expert report.[18] In a very real sense, then, the parties and the judge share the responsibility for gathering the facts to be judged.

More difficult, and still controversial, is the relative role of the parties and the court in relation to the *law*. Certainly, it is for the court to apply the law to the

---

[11] Aubert, *Introduction,* 228–229.

[12] Civ. (1) 20 Mar. 2005, *Procédures* 2005 no. 123. The Cour de cassation is echoing the wording of art. 10 al. 1 C. civ. on which see below, p. 101. On *mesures d'instruction* generally see below, p. 102 ff.

[13] cf. below pp. 325–326 as to the significance of written evidence for contracts generally.

[14] Malaurie, Aynès, and Morvan, *Introduction générale,* 163 ff.

[15] Below. p. 99.

[16] Arts. 1, 29 and 146 al. 2 N.c.pr.civ.

[17] *L'instance* has been translated here as 'case', but the word refers to any civil process in being, from its introduction to its termination due to settlement, judgment or otherwise: art. 384. N.c.pr.civ.

[18] See art. 10 N.c.pr.civ. and below, p. 101.

facts which come before it,[19] and while the parties may be invited to make submissions on the law applicable to their case,[20] a court is by no means restricted to the legal materials cited to it: the idea of a decision made *per incuriam* (as distinct from legally *wrong*) is simply meaningless in the French context.[21] This still leaves the problem of the relative roles of the parties and the court as regards the legal classification or characterization of the facts which they allege, the 'legal grounds' (*moyens de droit*) of their claims, For example, if a claimant has bought a television set which no longer works owing, it is alleged, to a manufacturing defect, a claimant will choose whether to put his claim for termination of the contract against his seller in terms of substantial mistake, latent defect or a 'failure to deliver conforming property,'[22] but the question arises whether the court is bound to apply the rules of law which apply to *these* legal classifications of the facts alleged, or whether it *may* or *must* choose between them or any other which it thinks legally correct. Here, article 12 of the New Code of Civil Procedure states that:

[The judge] *must* give or restore the exact classification to the facts and legal transactions[23] [*actes*] which are the subject of the litigation and not stay with the characterization suggested for them by the parties.[24]

Despite this apparent legislative clarity, the different chambers of the Cour de cassation have given different responses to these questions as to the reclassification of a claim by a court which to an extent are driven by the context in which they are made[25]: indeed, for some commentators, the Cour de cassation holds that article 12 imposes an obligation on lower courts to reclassify claims before them when it wishes to quash their decisions, but holds that it merely empowers them to do so when it does not![26] For Vincent and Guinchard, though, the proper position is that the courts *must* classify the parties' claims (i) if the parties have not done so;[27] (ii) where the parties have done so but wrongly; and (iii) where a court has exercised its discretion to pick up and rely in its decision on facts from the material before it which have *not* been specifically relied on by the parties in

---

[19] Art. 12 al. 1 N.c.pr.civ.

[20] Art. 13 N.c.pr.civ.

[21] Of course, the point of the idea of a decision made *per incuriam* in the English context is that it allows an exception to be made to the normal rules of *stare decisis* (which have no place in French law: above, p. 25 ff esp. at p. 30) R. Cross and J.W. Harris, *Precedent in English Law*, 4th edn. (Oxford, 1991) 148 ff.

[22] Mistake (art. 1110 C. civ.); latent defect (art. 1641 ff. C. civ.); 'conforming property' (*jurisprudence* based on arts. 1603 and 1615 C. civ.).

[23] e.g. whether a transaction is a gift or an 'onerous contract'; cf. below, pp. 318–319.

[24] Art. 12 al. 2 N.c.pr.civ. (emphasis added).

[25] For the details, see Vincent and Guinchard, 531 ff.

[26] R. Martin, 'L'article 6-1 de la Convention européenne de sauvegarde des droits de l'homme contre l'article 12 du nouveau code de procédure civile' D 1996.Chron.20.

[27] Since 1998, this situation is most unusual as since then art. 56 N.c.p.c. has required any claim by *assignation* to include 'an explanation of its grounds in fact and in law'. On *assignation*, see below, p. 95.

their submissions (so-called *faits adventices*).[28] On the other hand, where the parties have not relied on particular facts in their submissions and the court has not picked them up from the *faits adventices,* then the court *may* but need not classify the facts in question, for these are facts or legal transactions which the court may legitimately ignore.[29] The New Code of Civil Procedure also provides that a court is bound to keep to any legal classification or point of law submitted to it by the parties where the latter have expressly agreed to restrict their dispute in this way, subject to this not affecting any inalienable rights.[30] And once litigation has been started, the parties may agree (subject to the same conditions) that the court should decide the case as an 'honest broker' (*amiable compositeur*) and in doing so the court is entitled to decide according to the fairness (*équité*) of the case, rather than according to law, its grounds for decision escaping the control of the Cour de cassation.[31] With a similar aim, the judge is expressly encouraged to attempt to conciliate the parties so that they settle before judgment[32] and may even order them to go to mediation by a third party.[33]

Finally, we should mention the role of the *ministère public* in civil proceedings. As has been noted,[34] the roles of members of the *ministère public* (or *le parquet*[35]) are of two types.

Most commonly, the role is an auxiliary and advisory one, the *parquet* joining a case started by someone else in order to make observations (*conclusions*) 'on the application of the law to the case',[36] the *ministère public* being known as the 'joined party' even though not technically a party at all.[37] In general, the *parquet* has a broad discretion whether or not to intervene in this way,[38] but he must do so where the court seized of a case requests it[39] or in certain legally defined situations, such as in adoption.[40] The French Chancellery has encouraged the *ministère public* to intervene before the lower courts whenever feasible and in practice it always does in cases when they go before the Cour de cassation.[41] The advice

---

[28] See art. 7 al. 2 N.c.pr.civ.

[29] Vincent and Guinchard, 537–538, who term the situations where the court has an obligation to classify as involving '*moyens de pur droit*', the situation where it has merely a power to do so, '*moyens mélangés de fait et de droit*'.

[30] Art. 12 al. 3 N.c.pr.civ.; The power applies only to '*droits dont elles ont la libre disposition*'.

[31] Art. 12 al. 4 N.c.pr.civ.; Couchez *Procédure civile*, 236–237 and see Com. 9 Jan. 1979, D 1979. IR. 291 note Julien.

[32] Art. 21 N.c.pr.civ.

[33] Art. 21 al. 4 of *loi* no. 95-125 of 8 February 1995 (as inserted by *loi* no. 2002-1138 of 9 September 2002, art. 21).

[34] Above, pp. 60–61.

[35] Various titles are given to the various public servants who act for the *ministère public* and so one may see references in the reports of cases to the advice (*conclusions*) of a *procureur de la République, procureur général* or *avocat général*.

[36] Art. 424 N.c.pr.civ.

[37] Couchez, *Procédure civile,* 125.

[38] Art. 426 N.c.pr.civ.

[39] Art. 427 N.c.pr.civ.

[40] Art. 425 N.c.pr.civ.

[41] Vincent and Guinchard, 644–645.

may be either in writing or oral and, if the latter, comes last in the hearing.[42] This advisory role[43] is very important: first, of course, in persuading a court to decide in a particular way (though of course the court is not bound to follow the *ministère's* advice[44]) but secondly, when in an important judgment the *conclusions* are published, in explaining the thinking behind it.

Apart from joining proceedings in motion, the *ministère public* has a very broad discretion himself to bring proceedings (doing so as *partie principale*) 'for the defence of the public interest [*ordre public*] in situations where this has been *prejudiced*.'[45] Exceptionally, the *ministère public* may initiate proceedings, without fulfilling this condition, for example, in cases of nullity of marriage[46] or declarations as to nationality.[47]

B. The Distrust of Orality and the Construction of the *Dossier*

'A well-plied witness will come up to proof.'[48] This epigram of the sixteenth century legal writer, Loysel, may stand as the motto of all that French legal tradition distrusts in relation to orality in civil proceedings, but this distrust extends well beyond evidence given by witnesses. Indeed, French civil procedure is dominated by written evidence and written argument. As we shall see, while the parties have a right to be heard,[49] hearings before the full court (*audience*) are usually relatively brief, centering on a discussion by the parties or their counsel of their competing claims as drawn from the materials in the *dossier*. The *dossier* itself is put together by a court official, although all parties should also have copies of its contents in accordance with the *principe de la contradiction* according to which all parties should see or hear the others' facts, arguments and evidence in enough time for them to be able to counter them and defend themselves.[50] As this suggests, the *dossier* contains not merely the claimant's claims and the

---

[42] Art. 443 N.c.pr.civ. As this timing risks the *ministère public* raising an argument with-out any opportunity of reply by the parties, arts. 444 and 445 N.c.pr.civ. allow them to make written observations to this effect, on which the court may decide to re-open the discussion.

[43] There is considerably more doubt as to whether the *ministère public* has any role in relation to facts or their proof: Vincent and Guinchard, 647.

[44] A notable example of the Cour de cassation following the advice of the *ministère public* is the *affaire Desmares*, Civ. (2) 21 Jul. 1982. DS 1982. 449 *concl.* Charbonnier, note Larroumet, on which see below, p. 392. However, in a later set of cases in the same context, the Cour de cassation refused to accept Charbonnier's radical arguments, see Civ. (2) 15 Nov. 1984, D 1985. 20 *concl.* Charbonnier.

[45] Art. 423 N.c.pr.civ.

[46] Art. 184 C. civ.

[47] Art. 129 C. civ. and art. 1040 N.c.pr.civ.

[48] *'Qui mieux abreuve, mieux preuve'*: A. Loysel, *Institutes Coutumières*, reprinted edn. (Paris, 1846, M. Dupin and E. Laboulaye (eds.)), t. 2, 151.

[49] Below, p. 109.

[50] Arts. 14 and 15 N.c.pr.civ. E.g. Ch. mixte 3 Feb. 2006, *Droit et procédure* 2006.214 (absence of communication of documents in suitable time (*temps utile*)).

defendant's defences (and other documents which could be termed pleadings[51]), but also their written submissions which aim to justify their claims both as a matter of fact and of law, documentary evidence, written memoranda of depositions by witnesses and any technical reports which are commissioned. Although the court may hear witnesses (by ordering an *enquête*) at the full hearing, this is both unusual and, where it occurs at first instance, itself results in a memorandum of the evidence which is given being placed on the *dossier,* so as to be capable of supply to the court of appeal if necessary.[52]

C. The Nature of Appeals and *Pourvois en Cassation*

The construction of a *dossier* of this kind is clearly related to the different nature of appeals from decisions of courts of first instance from those allowed in English law, for a French appeal involves a complete reopening of the decisions challenged both as a matter of fact and of law. The existence of the *dossier* means that a French court of appeal is in as good a position as was the court below to decide issues which a common lawyer would term primary fact. Moreover, even more strikingly, a court of appeal may, if it thinks it necessary, order the taking of further evidence.[53] The courts of first instance are not 'trial courts' in the common law sense and they and the courts of appeal are together *juges du fond,* judges of the substance or merits of the case.

However, the nature of the procedure called *pourvoi en cassation* is very different. As we have seen,[54] the Cour de cassation is concerned with ensuring the proper application of the law to 'the facts as found by the *juges du fond:* it 'does not judge cases, but rather the decisions which are submitted to its censure. It makes sure that these have been rendered in accordance with the law.'[55] Thus, the Cour de cassation does not redecide cases submitted to it (having corrected the legal rules to be applied) but rather, as its name indicates, quashes the decisions of lower courts.[56] In this perspective, it appears rather as a court of review than one hearing appeals on points of law.

D. Who May Sue? The Requirement of 'an Interest'

While French substantive law is dominated by the language of rights, rather than of remedies.[57] French procedural law takes a different stance again, for

[51] The term is by no means perfect as it is so redolant of common law procedure. The term *plaidoiries* refers to the oral presentations by the parties for their counsel) at the hearing: below, p. 109.
[52] See below, pp. 105–106.
[53] Below, p. 111.
[54] Above, pp. 13–14, 46.
[55] Ghestin and Goubeaux, *Introduction générale,* 356.
[56] Exceptionally, the Cour de cassation may, having quashed a lower court's decision, proceed to dispose of the case: see below p. 113.
[57] Above pp. 17–18.

the requirement for bringing an *action* is the possession of a sufficient legitimate interest,[58] *action* here meaning not merely the initial claim starting proceedings[59] but a right to have a position on the merits of an issue heard, this thereby including also any defence.[60] Article 31 of the New Code of Civil Procedure provides that:

An *action* is open to all persons who have a legitimate interest in the success or failure of a claim,[61] those cases excepted in which legislation grants the right to bring an *action* exclusively to certain persons which it allows may raise or combat a claim, or in order to defend a particular interest.

A person's 'interest' is to be understood therefore as the pecuniary or 'moral' advantage which would result from a court's decision if that person's claim is accepted.[62] In modern practice,[63] the requirement of legitimacy plays the role of excluding frivolous claims, including those of pecuniary but minimal significance.[64] Otherwise, it is held that a person's interest must exist at the time of claiming (*'né et actuel'*) and must be 'direct and personal'. The first requirement expresses a concern that the courts should not be used for preventative sallies or forcing those who have time to make a decision in law to do so prematurely. On the other hand, the courts have not proved hostile to the development in appropriate cases of actions for declarations of the parties' rights.[65]

As to the 'personal' element of the requirement of interest,[66] the vast majority of those who litigate do so in order to protect their own *rights,* but it is clear that the notion of an 'interest' is broader than one of a 'right', at least as this is understood by French lawyers. The procedural rule of standing is supported by observing that a person's general liberties are not expressed in terms of an 'individual's rights': 'by no means all that is recognised by law fits exactly into the framework of "individual rights" [*droits subjectifs*]'.[67] An important consequence of the procedural rule has been the development by the courts, followed by the legislature, of an *action* to allow trade unions and trade associations to sue on behalf of the

---

[58] Art. 31 N.c.pr.civ.

[59] This is termed the *demande initiale.* art. 53 N.c.pr.civ.

[60] Art. 30 N.c.pr.civ.

[61] *'Prétention'*, i.e. a claim in the sense of a proposition put forward for the decision of the court.

[62] Ghestin, Goubeaux, and Fabre-Magnan, *Introduction*, 551.

[63] Some have appealed to this requirement in order to justify the exclusion of certain causes of action, such as in the case of the unmarried relict's claim for damages (see below p. 414), but this appeal confuses the legitimacy of a person's substantive interest to be protected by the law (e.g. of delict) and a person's procedural interest in coming before the court to see such a substantive interest protected: Vincent and Guinchard, 137–138.

[64] Ghesting, Goubeaux, and Magnan, *Introduction*, 551–552. A person may not for lack of *intérêt* appeal a decision where its effect was *more* favourable than the one for which he had asked: Civ. (2) 15 Dec. 2005, Bull. civ. II no. 327.

[65] Vincent and Guinchard, 138–440.

[66] Some jurists prefer to treat these issues as one of a person's *'qualité'* to be given judgment (Ghestin, Goubeaux, and Fabre-Magnan, *Introduction,* 554 ff) but it is difficult to disentangle this from *intérêt*: Couchez, *Procédure civile*, 160–161; Vincent and Guinchard, 140.

[67] Vincent and Guinchard, 134–135.

collective interests which they promote.[68] Subsequently a range of other types of association have by law been given similar powers, as is specifically recognized by the second part of article 31. Thus, for example, legislation allows recognized consumers' associations to sue in order to protect consumer interests (this allowing them, inter alia, to bring before a court contract terms to be condemned and annulled as unfair).[69] Outside these legally recognized categories, while the courts do not reject the possibility of allowing an action to such an association, they often find reasons for denying one.[70]

II. Proceedings in the Tribunal de Grande Instance

At this point, we shall look at proceedings before the court of general civil jurisdiction, the Tribunal de grande instance, by way of example (see Figure 4.1), though it should be noted that significant differences exist with the other courts, such as the small claims court (Tribunal d'instance) or Commercial Court (Tribunal de commerce).[71] Before the Tribunal de grande instance, there are two types of proceedings: litigation (where the parties are in dispute) and those *en matière gracieuse*. We shall first look briefly at the latter, but outline in some detail 'litigation' in the strict sense.

A court gives judgment *en matière gracieuse* when in the absence of a dispute it is seized of an application which is required by law in order to allow the court to exercise its control over the matter in question.[72] Examples of where such an application is required may be found in the case of divorce at the joint request of both spouses[73] and adoption.[74] The court may undertake of its own initiative any investigations it thinks fit; it may hear any persons who may throw light on the matter before it as well as any persons who may be affected by its decision, but it need not allow oral argument.[75] Both the hearing and the delivery of judgment are held in chambers.[76]

---

[68] Ch. réun. 5 Apr. 1913, DP 1914.1.65, *rapp.* Palcimaigne, now in art. L. 411-11 C. trav. Some jurists treat these cases as exceptions to the rule requiring 'direct and personal interest', exceptions created by the law: Vincent and Guinchard, 141.

[69] By the *loi* no. 73-1193 of 27 December 1973, the *'Loi Royer'*, art. 46. These provisions, much amended, now appear in art. L. 411-1 ff., esp. art. L. 421-6 C.consom. The Cour de cassation has recognized in the courts a power to award damages to a consumer association to compensate 'any direct or indirect loss caused to the collective interest of consumers': Civ. (1) 1 Feb. 2005, D 2005.487 note Rondey.

[70] Ghestin, Goubeaux, and Fabre-Magnan, *Introduction*, 477–481.

[71] On court institutions, see above, Ch. 2.

[72] Art. 25 N.c.pr.civ.

[73] Art. 230 C.civ. and see below, p. 249.

[74] Art. 1167 N.c.pr.civ. This rule applies both to *adoption simple* and *adoption plénière* on which see below, pp. 266–267.

[75] Arts. 27–28 N.c.pr.civ.

[76] Arts. 434 and 451 N.c.pr.civ.

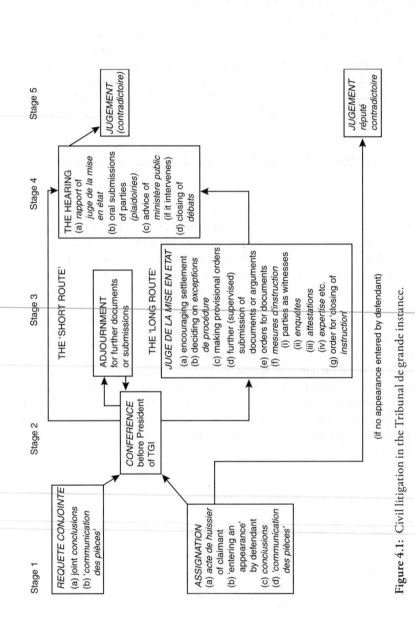

Figure 4.1: Civil litigation in the Tribunal de grande instance.

A. STAGE 1: Commencing Litigation and Written Submissions

Litigation is commenced by what is called the 'initial claim' (*demande initiale*) in one of two ways: by *assignation* or by *requête conjointe*.[77]

Assignation is by far the more common and consists of a formal document which must follow certain requirements in its content, These requirements include the name of the claimant and his *avocat*;[78] the subject-matter (*objet*) of the claim, including the factual and legal grounds (*moyens en fait et en droit*) on which it rests;[79] the court before which the claim is brought; a list of any documents on which the claim is based; and a notice informing the defendant that he must instruct and name his *avocat* and enter an appearance within 15 days on pain of judgment in his absence.[80] The *assignation* is served on the defendant by a *huissier de justice*,[81] whether in person or otherwise.[82] The defendant must then enter an appearance (*comparution*) in the proper form within the time already noted. Either party may seize the court of the case by sending to its secretary a copy of the *assignation*.[83] All other documents representing procedural steps (*actes de procédure*) and written submissions of the parties (*conclusions*), must be communicated to all parties involved in the case by the *avocat* of the party who instigates them and to the secretary of the court who places them in the case's *dossier*. The presiding judge of the court then puts down the case for a pre-trial 'conference' before him.[84] Assuming that the defendant does respond in proper form, the parties then proceed to putting in their written submissions, though the claimant does not *need* to do so as the submissions in the *assignation* may serve as *conclusions*.[85] At this stage too, the parties exchange copies of documents on which they will rely at the hearing (*communication des pièces*).[86]

The other way for litigation to commence is by *requête conjointe*. This procedure is suitable for cases where the parties cannot agree on all outstanding differences, but where their mutual attitude is less combative.[87] It is started by a *joint* submission of the parties to the court of those points on which they differ, the bases of their positions and the names of their *avocats*.[88] The court is seized of the case when this joint submission is delivered to its secretary,[89]

---

[77] Arts. 53 and 54 N.c.pr.civ. (with minor qualifications).

[78] Representation by *avocat* is required for litigation in the Tribunal de grande instance: art. 751. N.c.pr.civ.

[79] The *objet* and *moyens* are known as the *libellé* of the *acte*: Couchez, *Procédure civile*, 254, who notes that the requirement of indicating the legal grounds of a claim was specified in 1998 so as to stop the earlier practice of giving merely its factual basis.

[80] Arts, 55, 56, 752, 753 and 755 N.c.pr.civ. On the exact nature of this judgment, see below.

[81] See above p. 76.

[82] For the rules as to service, see art, 653 ff N.c.pr.civ.

[83] Art, 756 N.c.pr.civ.

[84] Arts. 758–759 N.c.pr.civ.

[85] Art. 56 al. 3. N.c.pr.civ.

[86] For the significance of these, see below p. 100 ff.

[87] Couchez, *Procédure civile*, 279–280.

[88] Arts. 57 and 793 ff N.c.pr.civ.

[89] Art. 795 N.c.pr.civ.

after which the proceedings continue in the same manner as those started by *assignation*.[90]

At this point, we should note the consequences of failure in either party in proceeding as is here envisaged. Where a defendant fails to enter an appearance in the proper form to an *assignation* then, after the possibility of correcting this omission, the case may be judged by the court immediately on the merits 'to the extent to which the court thinks it regular, admissible and well-founded'.[91] At first instance, this judgment is termed a 'judgment which is deemed to have been heard on both sides' (*jugement réputé contradictoire*) and the defendant's recourse against it lies by way of *appeal* to the court of appeal: this is not what French lawyers call a *jugement par défaut*.[92] Secondly, if *either* party fails to perform the various procedural steps which are required of him, such as failing to submit a written submission or documents in support of a case, then the court may choose either to proceed to judgment on the merits (this being considered a 'judgment heard on both sides' (*jugement contradictoire*)), or to remove the proceedings from the list (*radiation*).[93] If it is the claimant who fails in this respect, the defendant may apply to have the action declared in abeyance (*caduque*).[94]

1. *The development of the case*

A claim may be met with various responses by a defendant. Of course, he may simply dispute it on the merits (*défense au fond*) at any stage of the proceedings before the lower courts.[95] Secondly, he may rely on some significant irregularity in the proceedings as brought by the claimant, for example, challenging the jurisdiction of the court (by way of *exception de procédure*).[96] Such a defence is necessarily temporizing as it says nothing about the merits of the claim:[97] all such defences must be brought before the court at one time and before any defence on the merits has been made.[98] Thirdly, a defendant may instead (or also) challenge a claim's admissibility (by *fin de non-recevoir*), such as on the ground that the claimant's claim is time-barred or that the claimant does not have the requisite 'interest'.[99] A party may bring such a challenge at any stage in the proceedings before the *juges*

---

[90] An exception is made where the parties have requested that their case be heard by a single judge, when it is remitted to that judge: arts. 794 and 796 N.c.pr.civ.

[91] Art. 472 N.c.pr.civ.

[92] Art. 473 al. 2 N.c.pr.civ. Where the Tribunal de grande instance decides *finally* (*en premier et en dernier ressort*) without the possibility of appeal, then the decision does constitute a *jugement par défaut*, on which see below, p. 111.

[93] Arts. 381–383, 470 N.c.pr.civ.

[94] Art. 469 N.c.pr.civ.

[95] Art. 71–72 N.c.pr.civ.

[96] Contrast the use of the term *'exception'* to describe a defence granted by the substantive law: e.g. the *exception d'inexécution* in contract law (below, pp. 348–349).

[97] Couchez, *Procédure civile*, 166.

[98] Art. 74 al. 1 N.c.pr.civ. (and before any *fin de non-recevoir*).

[99] Art. 122 N.c.pr.civ. On the requirement of 'interest' see above, pp. 91–93. Another example may be found in a valid arbitration clause: Ch. Mixte 14 Feb. 2003, *Proéedures*, 2003, 22.

du fond, but may incur liability in damages if the court considers it appropriate where the challenge was dilatory.[100] Finally, a defendant may bring a claim for set-off (*demande en compensation*) or a counter-claim (*demande reconventionelle*)[101] as long as the latter is sufficiently related to the original claim.[102]

Other parties may also join the proceedings in motion and in French law, this may happen in one of two ways, though both of these are subject to a condition of a sufficient connection between the existing proceedings and the new element. First, an existing party may bring a third party into the proceedings by claiming against him, this being effected according to the same rules as for the 'initial claim' and being termed *intervention forcée*.[103] Such a procedure most frequently consists of a claim for an indemnity (*appel en garantie*[104]).[105] However, French law also allows a third party to choose to join existing proceedings (by *intervention volontaire*), as we have said, as long as there is a sufficient connection between them and his own claim.[106] While discussed here, it should be noted that the addition of new parties to a case in either of these ways may be effected at any stage in the proceedings.[107]

2. Special proceedings before litigation on the merits is commenced: the juge des référés

At this stage we should note an important type of special proceedings, those before the *juge des référés*. They take place on certain matters before the president of the court and lead to only a provisional decision, no issue on the merits being before the court, let alone taken.[108] Proceedings of this type are started by *assignation*[109] and the parties are called to a hearing, giving the defendant due time to prepare his defence.[110] They may be brought only in three situations.

First, in all urgent cases, the president of the court may order *en référé* any measure which gives rise to no serious dispute or which gives rise to a justifiable difference of opinion.[111] The condition of urgency is a matter within the 'sovereign power of assessment' of the *juge des référés*.[112] Thus, for example, where a person is concerned that the 'intimacy of his private life' is threatened then the court may

---

[100] Art. 123 N.c.pr.civ.
[101] Art. 64 N.c.pr.civ.
[102] Art. 70 N.c.pr.civ.
[103] Art. 68 al. 2 N.c.pr.civ.
[104] Art. 334 ff N.c.pr.civ.
[105] Couchez, *Procédure civile*, 370.
[106] Art. 325 N.c.pr.civ.
[107] Art. 327 N.c.pr.civ., which also provides that 'voluntary intervention' by which a person simply associates himself with an existing party's claim (*intervention accessoire*) is admissible before the Cour de cassation.
[108] Art. 484 N.c.pr.civ.
[109] Art. 485 N.c.pr.civ. and see above p. 95.
[110] Arts. 484 and 486 N.c.pr.civ.
[111] Art. 808 N.c.pr.civ.
[112] Civ. (1) 29 Apr. 1975, Bull. civ. I no. 148.

make a suitable order to protect it, such as seizing an offending publication,[113] the urgency being found in the fact that the claimant's harm being 'moral' would be imperfectly protected by an award of damages.[114]

Secondly, the president of the court may order *en référé* any measure whose aim is to preserve the status quo or to put matters in such a state as is necessary either to prevent an imminent harm or to ensure the discontinuance of a 'manifestly illegal behaviour' (*trouble manifestement illicite*), even where this order is seriously disputed.[115] As to cases of 'manifestly illegal behaviour' (an issue within the 'sovereign power of assessment' of the *juge des référés*[116]), it is to be noted that there is here no element of urgency.

Thirdly, in cases where the existence of an obligation is not seriously capable of dispute, the president of the court may order its creditor (the claimant) either a partial or full provisional award or, in the case of an obligation to do (*obligation de faire*) even order its performance[117] (again with no condition of urgency).[118] In a clear case, therefore, this type of proceeding allows the rapid obtaining of an order for the handing over of property or even the performance of services. Where a judge has made such an order *en référé*, he may not, however, later decide the case on the merits as this would threaten the principle requiring an objectively impartial tribunal.[119]

Despite their provisional nature, orders made *en référé* are very important in practice[120] and they often in fact lead to the termination of a case. In this respect, it is to be noted that the president of the court has the power to order an *astreinte* to encourage obedience of any order made, and the power to award costs.[121]

B. STAGES 2 and 3: The Preliminary Conference; the 'Short Route', the 'Long Route', and *l'Instruction*

After *conclusions* (which set out in writing the submissions of the parties both in fact and in law)[122] are submitted and documents exchanged, the case comes before the president of the court at a preliminary 'conference' at which the parties are represented, to ascertain the 'state of the case' and to decide whether it is ready to be sent immediately to be heard (*renvoi à l'audience*) or whether it requires the further collection of evidence or development of written submissions. If it is indeed ready, it

---

[113] e.g. Civ. (1) 18 May 1972, JCP 1972.II.17209 *concl.* Lindon. On the legal basis for the protection of private life, see below pp. 379–380.

[114] P. Kayser, *La protection de la vie privée par le droit*, 3rd edn. (Paris, 1995), 346.

[115] Art. 809 al, 1 N.c.pr.civ.

[116] Civ. (2) 6 Dec. 1978, Bull. civ. II, no. 204.

[117] Art. 809 al. 2 N.c.pr.civ.

[118] Civ. (2) 18 Jan. 1978, D 1979.IR. 512 (second case) note Julien.

[119] Ass. plén. 6 Nov. 1998, JCP 1998.II.10198 *rapp.* Sargos.

[120] Couchez, *Procédure civile*, 59.

[121] Art. 491 N.c.pr.civ. On the nature of *astreintes*, see below pp. 117–118.

[122] Arts. 815, 753 N.c.pr.civ. and see C. Lefort, *Procédure civile*, 2nd edn. (Paris, 2007) 215–218.

is sent to be heard without more ado; if not, the president may adjourn the conference in order to allow the parties to submit further documents or submissions if he thinks this will be enough to make the case ready and at this adjourned conference send it to be heard if it is then ready. In both circumstances, this direct route to the hearing before the full court[123] is known as the 'short route' (*circuit court*). If, on the other hand, the president of the court considers that further work is necessary before the case can be decided on its merits, he will send it to one of his colleagues on the court for directions, this judge being termed the *juge de la mise en état*.[124] This stage in the process is often called *l'instruction,* the judge responding to the parties' requests to make orders relating to the collection of evidence, but also acting on his own initiative in this respect and inviting and even requiring submissions from the parties so that the case may be made 'ready to be judged'; the evidence is gathered under judicial supervision. While, as we shall see, the powers of French judges to make such orders is not restricted to the time when the *juge de la mise en état* is seized of the case,[125] as the full court may do so after the case has been remitted to it for hearing or during the hearing itself, typically this is the stage at which such orders are made. In recent years, the powers of the *juge de la mise en état* have been extended so as to allow him to fulfil an 'active control' in the preparation of a case.[126] These include a power to hear the parties in order to try to reach a full or partial settlement, even on the judge's own initiative.[127] They also include powers to decide on *exceptions de procédure,*[128] to order provision to be made for payment in advance to a creditor of a sum of money where the debt is not seriously able to be contested,[129] and to order a number of provisional measures.[130]

The New Code of Civil Procedure distinguishes between two classes of order relating to evidence, the first relating to the gathering of documentary evidence[131] and the second to a range of other types of evidence, these alone being called *mesures d'instruction.*[132]

1. Documentary evidence: the absence of 'disclosure'

While the English law civil process (when not aborted by settlement) is dominated by the oral proceedings at trial, it also allows a very considerable use of documentary evidence. In this respect, in English law under what is now termed

---

[123] This term should not be understood to exclude the possibility of a case being heard and decided on the merits by a single judge, but in the Tribunal de grande instance, this is exceptional: see Couchez, *Procédure civile,* 281ff.

[124] Art. 763. al. 1 N.c.pr.civ.

[125] Below p. 103.

[126] Couchez, *Procédure civile,* 260 referring to *déc.* no. 98-1231 of 28 December 1998, *déc.* no. 2004-836 of 20 August 2004 and *déc.* no. 2005-1678 of 28 December 2005.

[127] Arts. 21, 767 and 768 N.c.pr.civ.

[128] On which see above, p. 96.

[129] Arts. 517–522, 771 30 N.c.pr.civ.

[130] Art. 771 N.c.pr.civ.

[131] Arts. 132–142 N.c.pr.civ.

[132] Arts. 143–322 N.c.pr.civ.

'disclosure',[133] a party must disclose '(a) the documents on which he relies; and (b) the documents which (i) adversely affect his own case; (ii) adversely affect another party's case; or support another party's case'.[134] In doing so, a party is required to make a reasonable search for documents falling within this rule, taking into account the number of documents involved, the nature and complexity of the proceedings, the ease and expense of retrieval of any particular document; and the significance of any document that is likely to be located during the search.[135] This process is a particularly demanding one and, as Lord Woolf observed in his report, *Access to Justice,* the obligation on a party to disclose documents damaging to his own interest 'comes as a surprise, sometimes as a painful surprise, to litigants from abroad'.[136] Nevertheless, as a result of disclosure a party may obtain access to documents in his opponent's possession which reveal hitherto unknown information or evidence, and this often leads to the settlement of the case. Clearly, though, this is a system for the exposure of the truth which relies for its effectiveness on a combination of the honesty of the parties and their legal advisers, and the effectiveness of forced production orders where this is in doubt.[137]

As we have said, French civil procedure is predominantly written, but, paradoxically, a party to litigation does *not* have access to a technique for the gathering of information and documentary evidence as powerful as the English law of disclosure. Instead, French law possesses two distinct procedures relating to documentary evidence.

First, the New Code of Civil Procedure seeks to ensure that a party is furnished with a copy of any document *which is to be relied on by the other party,* and that this is 'spontaneous', i.e. in principle it should occur without party request or court order (*communication des pièces*).[138] The purpose of this is to allow the other party an opportunity to consider the evidence so as to reply to it, thus giving effect in this context to the *principe du contradictoire* (right to reply or to defend oneself).[139] This purpose is reflected in the ultimate sanctions available for a party's failure to communicate a document, for the court *may* exclude from discussion at the hearing any material which has not been communicated within sufficient time for a reply (*en temps utile*)[140] and, traditionally, the courts have a

---

[133] CPR 35.5(1). The text describes 'standard disclosure' which is ordered by a court unless it directs otherwise. This mechanism replaced in 1998 'inspection and discovery' under which in principle *all* relevant document had to be produced by a party even if damaging to his own case.

[134] CPR 31.6.

[135] CPR 37.1(1) and (2).

[136] Lord Woolf, *Access to Justice* (London, 1995) 164. (this report inspiring the enactment of the new English 'code' of civil procedure, the Civil Procedure Rules of 1998).

[137] i.e. by means of the law of contempt of court: Civil Procedure Rules, Part 31 rule 12.

[138] Art. 132 N.c.pr.civ.

[139] Couchez, *Procédure civile,* 329.

[140] Art. 135 N.c.pr.civ. E.g. Civ. (2) 2 Dec. 2004, D 2005.315 (last minute disclosure of document held by party for several months which was deliberately intended to surprise the other party

duty not to rely on such documents in coming to their decisions.[141] However, this may not be entirely satisfactory from the other party's point of view, as a document not seen by him may play a part in the judge's decision and the latter would enjoy a 'presumption of regularity' and so the Code also provides that a party may request the court to order a party to communicate a document, if necessary, under the threat of *astreinte*.[142] The 'communication of documents' is clearly then, a key element in the French civil process, but it is not concerned with the gathering of evidence, but rather with the fairness of the conduct of the dispute. It allows a party to obtain useful information only incidentally and to the extent that the other party thinks it is not damaging to him to do so. Certainly, the parties' counsel do not feel under an obligation to disclose documents prejudicial to their clients' cases under the impulse of the search for truth.[143]

Secondly, a party may ask the court to order the production of a document[144] (*production forcée d'une pièce*), and at first sight this looks rather more like English law's disclosure. While its legislative underpinning appears to bear this out, the reality is very different. Traditionally, French law has been hostile to procedures which make parties to civil cases produce evidence contrary to their own interests, even where this is in the interest of truth.[145] However, legislation in the early 1970s seemed to mark a turning-point, the Civil Code being amended so as to declare that '[e]veryone is bound to lend a hand to justice in order to see the truth brought to light[146] and the New Code of Civil Procedure being enacted so as to provide for the 'forced production of documents'.[147] As to the latter, a distinction is drawn between documents in the hands of another party to the litigation and in the hands of a third party.

A party may ask the judge seized of the case[148] to order another party to produce a document (whether the original, a copy or an extract) in his hands which he considers relevant to the dispute: a court may not do so of its own initiative.[149] Once asked, the judge must decide whether such a claim is 'founded' and has a free discretion whether or not to make the order requested,[150] taking into account

excluded from consideration as this behaviour breached the party's duty of cooperation (*loyauté*) in the civil process).

[141] Couchez, *Procédure civile,* 330–331.

[142] Arts. 133–134 N.c.pr.civ. On *astreintes,* see below pp. 117–118.

[143] Beardsley, (above n. 1), 474.

[144] *Pièces* is translated here as 'documents', though in principle other types of evidence (such as a physical thing) may be included.

[145] Couchez, *Procédure civile,* 326.

[146] Art. 10 al. 1. C. civ. as substituted by *loi* no. 72-626 of 5 July 1972, art. 12.

[147] Arts. 138–142 N.c.pr.civ.

[148] In practice, this will often be the *juge de la mise en état,* about whom see above p. 99. A party may request a *juge des référés* to make such an order: *arguatur* from art. 145 N.c.pr.civ.

[149] Arts. 11 al., 138 and 142 N.c.pr.civ. Cf, the position as regards administrative courts (below p. 124) and in criminal procedure below pp. 130–132).

[150] Civ. (2) 14 Nov. 1979, D 1980, 365 note Lemée.

the usefulness of the document to the dispute[151] and the claims of 'higher principles' such as professional privilege.[152] If the judge considers it necessary, the order may be backed by the imposition of an *astreinte*.[153]

A party may also ask the judge seized of the case to order a third party to produce a document in his hands and such an order is binding on the third party immediately on its communication to him (and without prior notice).[154] However, the third party may apply to the judge to have the order set aside or modified, in particular on 'legitimate grounds' (*empêchement légitime*), which include situations of professional privilege but extend beyond it and any such further decision of the judge is itself subject to appeal.[155] Interestingly, it has been held that a public authority may be ordered to produce a document under this procedure, it being held that this does not conflict with the principle of the separation of powers, though the authority may oppose the order on the ground of respect for a person's privacy (unless disclosure is necessary for the protection of another's rights or liberties) or professional privilege.[156] To this extent, then. French civil law does not recognize anything like the English public interest immunity.

The possibility of a party benefiting from an order to produce a document against another appears to come close to disclosure, but there is a radical difference, for under the French system a party's counsel must be able to identify the particular document in question and show its relevance before its production is ordered.[157] In fact, therefore, it is rare for this possibility to be invoked.[158]

2. *Mesures d'instruction*

As we have seen, the starting-point is that it is for the parties themselves to gather the evidence which is needed to justify their allegations. However, the New Code of Civil Procedure provides several mechanisms for the collection of evidence which involve the court as much as the parties. These mechanisms are known as *mesures d'instruction,* there being four: 'personal verification' by a judge (*vérifications personnelles*); deposition by a party or parties before a judge (*comparution personnelle*); depositions by non-parties (*attestations*) and the request for technical information or advice.

Before going further, it is to be noted that the last three explain the absence of witnesses from French civil hearings. Neither the parties themselves nor third parties 'give evidence' in the common law sense (on examination and subject

[151] Couchez, *Procédure civile*, 328.
[152] Vincent and Guinchard, 795.
[153] Arts. 139, 142 N.c.pr.civ. (on *astreintes* see below pp. 117–118.
[154] Art. 140 N.c.pr.civ.
[155] Art. 141 N.c.pr.civ.
[156] Civ. (1) 21 Jul. 1987, Bull. civ. 1 no. 248 (Ministry of Telecommunications ordered to give name of holder of telephone number to a court before whom a wife had alleged that the holder was her husband's mistress).
[157] J.-J. Daigre, *La production forcée de pièces dans le procès civil* (Paris, 1979), 170–173.
[158] Beardsley, (above n. 1), 474.

to cross-examination) but *may* be allowed or required to be questioned by the *judge*.[159] *No* (potentially conflicting) expert *evidence* is given in French courts: rather the court itself commissions its own expert or experts to report on any issue which it considers necessary. Often, the results of these investigations are not heard at the time of the hearing, but are considered then in the form of a written report. And in all these matters the parties have no *right* to bring evidence before the court, but simply the possibility of requesting that a particular investigatory measure he ordered.

These four investigatory mechanisms have certain features in common. Articles 143 and 144 of the New Code of Civil Procedure state:

Art. 143: Facts on which the outcome of the litigation depends may be the object of any *mesure d'instruction* which is legally allowed, whether on the request of the parties or on the initiative of the court.

Art. 144: *Mesures d'instruction* may be ordered at any time during the case, as long as the judge does not possess sufficient material on which to decide.

Thus, while the parties may request a judge to order such a measure, he may do so 'on his own initiative', this reflecting the general statement of principle we have seen stated in article 3 of the same Code.[160] Furthermore, in principle these methods of gathering evidence may not be employed except for decisive evidence ('facts on which the outcome of the litigation depends'); they should not be used to make up for a party's failure to supply evidence himself[161] and any order or orders made must be as simple and unburdensome as possible.[162] However, in deciding whether or which measure to order a judge has a 'sovereign power of assessment' as to their appropriateness[163] and only in the case of decisions ordering an *expertise* are they the subject of a distinct appeal (distinct, that is, from any appeal from the judgment to which their results contribute).[164]

Secondly, such a measure may be ordered 'at any time in the proceedings' ('*en tout état de la cause*'). Thus, while often a *mesure d'instruction* will be ordered before the hearing (such as a *juge de la mise en état* commissioning an expert report), one may be ordered by a full court in the course of the hearing up until the time of the *mise en délibéré* and this may be either at first instance or on appeal.[165] The judge or full court which orders the measure is responsible for its putting into

---

[159] Ibid., 478–479.
[160] Above p. 87.
[161] Art. 146 N.c.pr.civ.
[162] Art. 147 N.c.pr.civ.
[163] Civ. (1) 8 May 1974, Bull. civ. 1, no. 133.
[164] Arts. 151 and 272 N.c.pr.civ. (appeal is only on a 'serious and legitimate ground').
[165] Vincent and Guinchard, 809. The *mise en délibéré* marks the ending of the hearing and the start of the 'deliberation' of the case by the court. They may also be ordered *en référé* before any litigation has been commenced: art. 145 N.c.pr.civ. On the role of the *juge des référés*, see above pp. 97–98.

effect[166] and where it requires the cooperation of one or other party, they should be called together by a court officer or, as it may be, the *expert*.[167]

Thirdly, it should be noted that whatever the nature of these investigations, they result in a written document. This may take the form of a signed memorandum (*procès-verbal*) of the questions and answers put by a judge or the full court to a party or of a report, as in the case of an *expertise*. This means that any prehearing investigations are put into a form which may go before the full court at the hearing, but it also means that investigations carried out at first instance may be properly considered on appeal. It can at this point, therefore, be clearly seen how it is possible for a French court of appeal to re-open a lower court's decisions entirely, both as to facts and the law. For the court of appeal can examine *exactly the same evidence* as went before the lower court: it is all in the *dossier*.

(a) Personal verification by judges

A judge may decide to 'verify in person' any matter which is the object of litigation, as long as the parties to the case are present or have been summoned.[168] Typically, such a verification consists of visiting land or premises which are significant in the dispute. If he considers it necessary, the judge may ask for assistance from an expert either at the time or subsequently and may hear the parties or other persons whose evidence may reveal the truth.[169]

(b) Taking evidence from people as to facts

In taking evidence from people as to non-technical facts[170] French civil procedure distinguishes between the parties to the dispute and third parties.

The parties themselves: comparution personnelle. A judge may order a party or parties to be questioned before him, either in public or in chambers,[171] subject to the general conditions for any *mesure d'instruction*.[172] It is the judge who has the initiative in asking questions of a party and while counsel for either side may make suggestions as to the questions which should be put, the judge does not have to accept them.[173] A party may be faced with an expert's views or with

---

[166] Art. 155 N.c.pr.civ.

[167] Art. 160 N.c.pr.civ.

[168] Art. 179 N.c.pr.civ.

[169] Art, 181 N.c.pr.civ.

[170] For the treatment of technical facts, see below p. 106 ff. The distinction is, of course a difficult one to maintain. In particular, as we shall see, experts often in practice report on issues of primary fact.

[171] Art. 188 N.c.pr.civ.

[172] Above pp. 102–103. *Comparution* should be distinguished from *serments* (oath-taking). In the case of *serments décisoires,* a judge may order a party, at the other party's request, to take an oath that some critical fact is or is not true. If the oath is refused, the party who has called for it prevails on the point in question; if the oath is taken, he loses. Perhaps surprisingly, it was retained by the New Code of Civil Procedure (see art. 317 ff and art. 1357 ff C. civ.), but is very rarely invoked in practice: Beardsley, (above n. 1), 472.

[173] Art. 193 N.c.pr.civ.; Civ. (2) 16 Oct. 1974, JCP 1974.IV.390.

a witness[174] and must respond to the questions put without reliance on a written outline.[175] After the investigation, the questions, answers (and failures to answer or even failure to attend) are recorded in a *procès-verbal* signed by the parties and the judge.[176] An important purpose for use of this procedure is in order to make up for the absence of written evidence of a transaction (notably, a contract) where this is necessary: for a person's declaration or silence is deemed to be equivalent to a *'commencement de preuve par écrit'*.[177]

Third parties: attestations and enquêtes. There are two means by which the evidence of non-party witnesses may be brought to the notice of the court: by *attestation* and by *enquête*. *Attestations* are written depositions signed by their authors relating to facts which they themselves witnessed or of which they have personal knowledge.[178] They are obtained expressly for the purpose of the dispute by the *parties* (not by their counsel who must abstain from contact with non-party witnesses).[179] They may be submitted to the judge (who provides the other side with a copy) by a party voluntarily or may be the subject of a court order, but if not satisfied with such a written deposition, a judge may instead summon the witness in question to be heard, by way of *enquête*.

At first sight, the procedure of *enquête* seems recognizable as the giving of oral evidence by witnesses at a common law trial, but this is a false impression. *Enquêtes* are special hearings which take place either before the *juge de la mise en état* or the full court to which both parties and their representatives are invited.[180] Although a judge may call a witness of his own initiative,[181] if a party wishes a witness to be summoned, that party must explain what evidence he hopes to obtain from this being done so that the judge may fix these relevant facts in his mind.[182] In either case, the judge decides whether or not to call a witness, this being a matter for his 'sovereign power of assessment' though it is subject to the rule that where a witness has given evidence on a particular issue, the other side are entitled to have a counter-witness (this being called *contre-enquête*).[183] Witnesses must attend the *enquête* on pain of a civil fine, excepting only those with a 'legitimate interest' in refusing to testify (including on the ground of professional privilege[184] or family or matrimonial relationship).[185] They must in general swear to the truth of

---

[174] Art. 190 N.c.pr.civ.
[175] Art. 191 N.c.pr.civ.
[176] Arts, 194, 195 N.c.pr.civ.
[177] Art. 198 N.c.pr.civ. For this requirement, see below p. 326.
[178] Art. 202 al. 1 N.c.pr.civ.
[179] Beardsley, (above n. 1), 476.
[180] Arts. 208 al. 1 and 209 N.c.pr.civ.
[181] See above p. 103 relating to *mesures d'instruction* in general.
[182] Art. 222 N.c.pr.civ.
[183] Art. 204 N.c.pr.civ.
[184] Couchez, *Procédure civile*, 350.
[185] Arts. 206 and 207 N.c.pr.civ.

their statements.[186] However, once in court (or, rather as often, in chambers), it is again the judge who asks the questions of the witness and in doing so he is not restricted to the investigation of any matters on which the summons was justified,[187] nor is he bound to put any questions suggested by the parties' themselves, doing so only if he deems it necessary.[188] The parties or their counsel are certainly not allowed to question witnesses themselves and it is therefore clearly right to say that the *enquête* does not provide anything like the possibilities of 'examination' and 'cross-examination' open to the parties or their counsel in an English civil trial:[189] they are forbidden even to address the witness directly on pain of exclusion from the hearing.[190] Once the witness has been questioned, the judge composes a memorandum of his responses,[191] but this is not a word-for-word record.[192] The witness is invited to sign it and make changes to his answers, these being noted in the margin. Finally, any written observations submitted by the parties regarding the evidence are appended to the memorandum.[193]

(c) The role of experts

A French court does not hear evidence on technical matters, such as the defectiveness of a product or the extent and nature of a claimant's personal injuries, but instead itself requests from an expert factual information (by way of *constatation*)[194] or advice (by way of *consultation*)[195] or commissions an expert or experts to report on a particular matter to it for its information (*expertise*).[196] The first two of these are relatively quick and cheap and are suitable for the settling of relatively simple matters,[197] in which they are to be preferred by a court to the more elaborate (and therefore more expensive) *expertise*.[198] Nonetheless, where commissioned the role of the *expertise* is very important, for the experts often go beyond making a limited technical report, and take a view of what a common lawyer would see as both primary and secondary fact. Indeed, despite the intrusion which this makes into the proper mission of the court itself, in the view of

---

[186] Art. 211 N.c.pr.civ (those such as minors who are 'incapable' of swearing are reminded of their duty to tell the truth).

[187] Art. 213 N.c.pr.civ. (which represented a change from the previous law).

[188] Art. 214 N.c.pr.civ.

[189] Beardsley, (above n. 1), 479.

[190] Art. 214 al. 1 N.c.pr.civ.

[191] The only exception to this rule is where the evidence is given before the full court which then decides the case, this decision not being subject to appeal: art. 219 al. 2 N.c.pr.civ.

[192] Vincent and Guinchard, 840.

[193] Art. 220 al. 4 N.c.pr.civ.

[194] Art. 249 ff N.c.pr.civ.

[195] Art. 256 ff N.c.pr.civ.

[196] Art. 263 ff N.c.pr.civ. Provisions applying to all three types of recourse to experts are found in art. 232 ff N.c.pr.civ.

[197] Couchez, *Procédure civile*, 359–360.

[198] Art. 263 N.c.pr.civ.

one common law commentator, the expert is not so much the supplier of expert evidence, as the holder of an extra-judicial trial.[199]

While a court may commission an *expertise* of its own initiative it is rare for it to do so without a party's request,[200] which may be refused in its discretion without giving any reason beyond that it would be useless or pointless.[201] Experts are not normally legally trained[202] and are selected by the court because of their special technical knowledge or experience in relation to the matter to be investigated and to this end, the court may refer to an approved list of suitable persons in different areas, though it does not have to do so.[203] Indeed, the court has a complete discretion as to whom to appoint as expert[204] and the parties are not entitled to object to the appointment of a particular person except on clearly defined grounds of relationship to the parties or involvement in the subject-matter of the litigation, grounds which are the same as any objections raised as to the judges themselves.[205]

The court also possesses a large discretion in the definition of the expert's task,[206] and, as we have said, although in principle the expert should be asked to report only on purely factual matters, they are often asked questions which require the application of legal concepts to the facts which they find.[207] Beardsley gives as an example the question whether a defendant committed 'delictual fault': as he says, before being able to do so, the expert must come to a view as to what such a fault consists of.[208] Once designated, the expert receives copies of any relevant documents from the parties and then proceeds to carry out his investigations. These may be of various types: for example, in the case of a car accident, he may examine the machines involved, the scene of the accident and, most importantly, can hold a hearing with both parties present (and their lawyers if they so desire).[209] The expert can hear the parties and others

[199] Beardsley, (above n. 1), 480 ff. According to R. Genin-Meric, 'Mesures d'instruction exécutées par un technicien, Dispositions communes, L'intervention d'un technicien dans l'instruction des litiges', Jur.-Cl. Proc. Civ., (1995) Fasc. 660, 4–5, the New Code of Civil Procedure attempted to alter this, in particular expressly forbidding the expert any role in the settlement of disputes (art. 240) and, in art. 238 al, 3 expressly stating that '[the expert] must never make any assessments of a legal nature:' ibid., but, according to Beardsley, these changes have not greatly changed practice: (above n. 1), 484.

[200] Art. 232 N.c.pr.civ. R. Genin-Meric, Mesures d'instruction exécutées par un technicien, Les trois modalités de l'intervention du technicien', Jur.-Cl. Proc. Civ., Fasc. 662 (1995) 7–8.

[201] Civ. (1) 4 Feb. 1963, JCP 1963.II. 13159 note Savatier.

[202] *Avocats* cannot be designated as *experts:* Genin-Meric, (above n. 199), 9.

[203] Ibid.

[204] Arts. 232 and 265 N.c.pr.civ.

[205] The decision to appoint an expert can be the subject of appeal under art. 272 N.c.pr.civ., but any challenge to the propriety of the person appointed must be instead by way of *récusation*: arts. 234 and 341 N.c.pr.civ.

[206] The *juges du fond* possess a *pouvoir souverain* as to this issue: Soc. 29 Nov. 1984, 1985.IV.50.

[207] Beardsley, (above n. 1), 481–3.

[208] Ibid and see below p. 364. ff on the legal significance of delictual fault.

[209] Art. 276 N.c.pr.civ.

who are in the position to know what actually has occurred[210] and the parties must be given an opportunity to ask questions of these persons,[211] but no cross-examination occurs.[212]

The court which orders the *expertise* also fixes the time-limit for the expert to submit his report,[213] which is usually in writing.[214] In principle, the court is not bound to follow its contents,[215] but it is very unusual for it to reject its findings: it is difficult for a judge to contradict an expert in his own field without recourse to the advice of another expert.[216] The court may, to this end, order a further *expertise* to examine or to re-examine issues whose treatment it considers unsatisfactory, but this is only rarely done.[217] Although a party may claim that the *expertise* be annulled either on formal or on substantial grounds,[218] again this is rare.[219] On the other hand, if the *juges du fond* fundamentally misinterpret the conclusions reached by an *expertise,* their decision will be quashed.[220]

3. *The closing of the* instruction *stage*

The *juge de la mise en état* will order the 'closure of the *instruction*' stage of a case either when he considers that the case is ready to be judged on the merits[221] or as a 'sanction' for one party's failure to execute the 'procedural acts' required of it in due time.[222] The *instruction* stage of proceedings will then cease at the time appointed by the *juge de la mise en état,* though he will continue to be seized of the case until the hearing opens.[223] Closure of *l'instruction* in principle disallows the introduction of further documentary evidence or submissions (with certain exceptions[224]), but if sufficiently serious facts appear the closure may be

---

[210] Art. 242 N.c.pr.civ.
[211] Genin-Meric, (above n. 200), 16.
[212] Beardsley, (above n. 1), 483.
[213] Art. 265 N.c.pr.civ.
[214] Art. 282 N.c.pr.civ.
[215] Art. 246 N.c.pr.civ.
[216] Genin-Meric, (above n. 199), 12.
[217] Beardsley, (above n. 1), 484.
[218] It is *not* a ground for nullity that an expert has not heard the evidence of all those whom the parties request should be heard, as it is for him to choose his sources of information, Genin-Meric, (above n. 200), 20.
[219] Genin-Meric, (above n. 200). 19–21. An *expertise* must be annulled on the application of one of the parties if it fails to uphold the *principe de la contradiction* (on which see above, p. 90): Civ. (2) 24 Feb. 2005, D 2005.737. A lower court may follow the advice of an expert even if the latter has expressed an opinion going beyond the limits of his task: Civ. (3) 5 Mar. 2003, *Procédures* 2003 no. 110.
[220] This fundamental misinterpretation is known as '*dénaturation*' and see Civ. (3) 4 Jan. 1979, JCP 1979.IV.79.
[221] Art. 779 N.c.pr.civ.
[222] Art. 780 N.c.pr.civ. If both parties' counsel fail in this respect, the *juge de la mise en état* may instead order the case removed from the list (*radiation*): art. 781 ibid.
[223] Art. 779 al. 2 and al. 3 N.c.pr.civ.
[224] Art. 783 N.c.pr.civ.

revoked by the court,[225] either of its own initiative or on the application of the parties.[226]

C. STAGE 4: The Hearing (*L'audience*)

Whether the case travels by the short route or the long route (via the *juge de la mise en état*), no case comes before the Tribunal de grande instance to be judged on its merits without a judicial order holding that it is ready (or *treated as* ready). Ideally and normally, all the evidence has been gathered and reduced to writing.

The parties have a right to an oral hearing,[227] but their *avocats* may request the court to dispense with one (where appropriate, with the additional consent of the *ministère public*), the court having a discretion whether or not to do so.[228] The hearing, which is in principle held in public,[229] may possess three elements.

First, the *juge de la mise en état* gives a summary report of the case, exposing the parties' claims, legal arguments and specifying its significant legal and factual issues. This report, which must not contain any advice on the appropriate decision on the merits, is read first.[230]

Secondly the parties' counsel speak (their interventions being called *plaidoiries*), the claimant first, the defendant next, the claimant in reply etc. without any formal restriction, though the presiding judge may stop the parties if the court is satisfied that it has heard enough argument. As we have noted, counsels' oral arguments develop their client's position, both as a matter of fact and law, and highlight particular elements from the written *dossier,* though formally they must be *invited* to make observations on the content of the law itself.[231]

Thirdly, the *ministère public* speaks, if he has *intervened* in the case.[232]

After these (or after the *plaidoiries* alone in those cases is which there is no advice of the *ministère public*) the hearing is closed.

---

[225] The 'court' refers either to the *juge de la mise en état* or the full court before which the hearing has commenced depending on which is seized of the case at the time: Couchez, *Procédure civile*, 268–269.

[226] Art. 784 N.c.pr.civ.

[227] Ass. plén. 24 Nov. 1989, D 1990.25 concl. Cabannes.

[228] Arts. 779 al. 3 and 786-1 N.c.pr.civ. (as inserted by décr. no. 2005-1678 of 28 Dec. 2005).

[229] Art. 22. N.c.pr.civ. The hearing may be held in chambers either where legislation specifically so allows or where the parties request this and the subject matter of the case would, if heard in public, either threaten 'the intimacy of their private life' or give rise to 'such disorder as to trouble the serenity of justice' art. 435 N.c.pr.civ.

[230] Art. 785 N.c.pr.civ. (as amended by décr. no. 2005-1678 of 28 Dec. 2005 which made the giving of such a report compulsory).

[231] Arts. 13 and 442 N.c.pr.civ. and above p. 88.

[232] Above, pp. 89–90.

D. STAGE 5: Deliberation and Judgment

After the closure of the hearing, the court considers the case (in secret).[233] Where more than one judge is sitting, judgment is by majority verdict,[234] though of course no record of this appears in the report. It may be unreserved or reserved to be given at a date fixed by the presiding judge.[235] Judgments must summarize the parties' claims and their legal bases and give the reasons for the court's own conclusion,[236] but they are usually very short indeed compared to an English decision of the High Court, the French case following a highly formal and logical structure which is laconic and often distinctly unrevealing.[237]

III. *Voies de Recours* (Means of Overturning a Judgment)

We have already noted that there is a significant difference between appeal of a decision of first instance and an application for review (*pourvoi en cassation*) of a decision of final resort, but French law distinguishes first in relation to the means of overturning judgments between 'ordinary' and 'extraordinary' means.[238] 'Ordinary' *voies de recours* are appeal (*appel*) and *opposition*. These have in common that in principle they arise without special legislative provision, must both be lodged within a month from the notification of the judgment to the party in question,[239] and that once lodged they suspend the enforcement of the judgment.[240]

In principle, all decisions at first instance are subject to appeal as of right on the application of any of the parties to the case who have an interest in doing so[241] and may aim either at the complete overturning of the decision of the lower court or its amendment.[242] Cross-appeals (*appels incidents*) may also be lodged by the respondent to an appeal (*intimé*) or by any other party.[243] Even, a person who was *not* a party to the case at first instance may appeal from the decision, where he has an 'interest' in doing so and, exceptionally, such a person may be *summoned* (and *lose*)

---

[233] Arts. 447–448 N.c.pr.civ.

[234] Art. 449 N.c.pr.civ.

[235] Art. 450 N.c.pr.civ.

[236] Art. 455 N.c.pr.civ.

[237] Above pp. 30–32 and below p. 527 ff

[238] Above, pp. 13–14, 91. For the sake of brevity, we shall here omit discussion of the way in which these various *voies de recours* apply to decisions made on 'incidents of procedure', keeping instead to cases where the decision on the merits (*sur le fond* or *au principal*: art. 480 N.c.pr.civ.) is challenged.

[239] Arts. 528 and 538 N.c.pr.civ. (15 days *en matière gracieuse*.)

[240] Art. 539 N.c.pr.civ.

[241] Art. 546 N.c.pr.civ. A party may renounce his right to appeal under certain conditions: art. 556 N.c.pr.civ. On the right of appeal, cf. above pp. 50–51.

[242] Art. 542 N.c.pr.civ.

[243] Arts. 548–549 N.c.pr.civ.

before the court of appeal where the 'development of the litigation requires it'.[244] The effect of an appeal is to place before the court of appeal either the entirety of the decision below or those aspects of it which are appealed and it re-decides this issue or issues (and those intimately related to them) both as a matter of fact and law.[245] This reflects the principle which is termed the *principe du double degré de juridiction* according to which a person is in principle entitled to have his case decided *twice,* on the second occasion by judges of greater experience.[246] In challenging the decision below, the parties are entitled to adduce new documentary evidence, ask the court to order appropriate *mesures d'instruction* to establish the relevant facts or put forward new legal bases for their claims.[247] A party may make explicit any claim which was implicit at first instance and may add any claim (*prétention*) which is 'accessory, consequential or complementary' to it.[248] On the other hand, in principle, an appellant may not adduce a new claim before the court of appeal,[249] though a claim is not 'new' unless it seeks a different result (*fin*) from what was sought at first instance, even if its legal basis (*fondement juridique*) is different.[250] Proceedings before the court of appeal are similar to those before the Tribunal de grande instance. Thus, a distinction is made between a 'short route' (by which the case is sent immediately for re-hearing) and a 'long route' (by which an *instruction* stage is started before a *conseiller de la mise en état* before it is so sent). The oral hearing itself is also similar. Once a court of appeal has come to its decision, its enforcement is in principle for the court from which the appeal arose.[251]

Opposition is the term given to a special procedure by which a party who has failed to enter an appearance on the other side's appeal[252] may apply to the court to set aside the judgment entered against him, provided that the appeal had *not been served in person* on him.[253] In these circumstances, such a judgment is termed a *jugement par défaut.* Once seized of a claim of *opposition,* the court who gave the default judgment looks at the case *de novo,* re-deciding questions of both fact and law.[254] On the other hand, if the appeal which gave

---

[244] Art. 555 N.c.pr.civ. Couchez, *Procédure civile,* 432 notes that the courts interpret this power narrowly as its effect is to deprive the persons so summoned of their own right of appeal. E.g. Ass. plén. 11 Mar. 2005, Bull. civ. Ass. plén. no.4, RTDCiv. 2005. 455 note Perrot where it was held that litigation does not 'develop' within the meaning of art. 555 N.c.pr.civ. without 'the revelation of a factual or legal circumstance stemming from the judgment below or after it, which modifies the juridical foundation of the litigation'.

[245] Art. 561 N.c.pr.civ.

[246] Vincent and Guinchard, 986–987.

[247] Art. 563 N.c.pr.civ. On *mesures d'instruction,* see above p. 102 ff.

[248] Art. 566 N.c.pr.civ.

[249] Art. 564 N.c.pr.civ.

[250] Art. 565 N.c.pr.civ.

[251] Art. 570 N.c.pr.civ.

[252] Or the other side's *claim* where the court before which it came decided the matter without the possibility of appeal (*en premier et en dernier ressort*), on which see Vincent and Guinchard, 989.

[253] Art. 473 al.1 and 571 N.c.pr.civ.

[254] Art. 572 N.c.pr.civ. Once the time for bringing *opposition* has expired, the person against whom judgment in default was entered may still bring a *pourvol en cassation:* art. 613 N.c.pr.civ.

rise to the judgment in the defendant's absence was served on him in person then that judgment constitutes a *jugement réputé contradictoire* and this may not be set aside by *opposition*, though it may be subject to review by the Cour de cassation in the normal way.[255]

There are three 'extraordinary' *voies de recours: tierce opposition, recours en révision* and *pourvoi en cassation,* but of these we shall discuss only the last and most important.[256] They have in common that they arise only when legislation expressly so provides[257] and that, in principle, they do not suspend the enforcement of the judgment in respect of which they are made.[258] As to *pourvois en cassation,* we have already noted the special role of the Cour de cassation in the hierarchy of the civil courts[259] and its role of 'censuring... the non-conformity of the judgment attacked [which is itself non-appealable][260] with legal rules'.[261] Here, we shall note three further aspects of the procedure of *cassation.*

First, in principle, it is only the parties to the judgment below who may bring a *pourvoi en cassation,* and these subject to the condition of possessing an interest in so doing.[262] This general rule applies also to the *ministère public,* who may therefore challenge a decision only where it is truly a party to the proceedings (*partie principale*).[263] However, there are two exceptional exceptions to this last rule. For, first, the *procureur général* attached to the Cour de cassation, himself a member of the *ministère public,* may spontaneously challenge *any* judgment by *pourvoi en cassation* (and not merely ones not subject to appeal) where the parties have failed to challenge them in the proper time[264] 'in the interest of *la loi*' to protect 'the honour of legal principles'.[265] Here censure by the Cour de cassation has

---

[255] Art. 477 N.c.pr.civ.
[256] *Tierce opposition* allows a third party prejudiced *factually* by a court's judgment to have the matter re-decided, though only as regards that third party; the original judgment remains binding as between its parties: arts. 582 ff N.c.pr.civ. *Recours en révision* is brought in order to have a judgement retracted and re-heard by the court which gave it, this being allowed only in four situations where some clear miscarriage of justice is established, such as fraud in relation to the case in the party who won: art. 593 ff N.c.pr.civ.
[257] Art. 580 N.c.pr.civ.
[258] Art. 579 N.c.pr.civ.
[259] Above pp. 46–47 ff.
[260] *Pourvois en cassation* are typically brought against decisions of a *cour d'appel* on the merits, but they may also be brought against a decision at first instance which is non-appealable (*en premier et en dernier ressort*) or against decisions taken on certain 'incidents of procedure' such as an *exception de procédure,* or *fin de non-recevoir* (on which, see above p. 96) which put an end to the proceedings in respect of the case: art. 607 N.c.pr.civ. Other decisions *en dernier ressort,* may not in general be the subject of a *pourvoi en cassation* independently of the judgments on the merits: art. 608 N.c.pr.civ.
[261] Art. 604 N.c.pr.civ. and see above pp. 3–4 and 46–47.
[262] Art. 609 N.c.pr.civ.
[263] Above p. 60.
[264] *Loi* no. 67-523 of 3 July 1967, arts. 17 and 18, itself re-enacting *loi* of 27 *ventôse* Year VIII (1800), arts. 80 and 88.
[265] Vincent and Guinchard, 1072.

no effect on the parties to the decision.[266] Secondly, the same *procureur général* may be instructed by the Ministry of Justice to challenge *any* judicial 'procedural act' by *pourvoi en cassation* on the ground of *excès de pouvoir,* i.e. that the judicial bodies have usurped the powers of either the legislature or the executive.[267] Typically this occurs when the judicial decision is by way of *arrêt de règlement.*[268] If quashed, this decision of the Cour de cassation is effective for everyone.

Secondly, a *pourvoi* is much more limited than an appeal in terms of any changes in a party's case. Thus, no new grounds or bases (*moyens*) may be put before the Cour de cassation, with the exceptions of, first, legal grounds which arise from the judgment which is challenged; secondly, new grounds which involve *ordre public* (here, the public interest or matters of public policy) as long as these result from evidential materials put to the court at first instance;[269] and, thirdly, 'grounds of pure law'.[270] Again, this accords with the proper role of the Cour de cassation, which is to judge the decision below, rather than the case: for how can the decision below be criticized by reference to grounds not put before the court?[271]

Thirdly, the Cour de cassation may take various courses once it has come to a view on the decision of the court below. It may, of course, simply uphold it and reject the *pourvoi.* If, however, it decides to quash the decision below either wholly or in part, two possibilities arise. If the facts as they were 'sovereignly found and assessed' by the lower court allow it simply to apply the correct rule of law, it may itself dispose of the case without more ado,[272] but if they do not so allow, it must send the issues to be re-heard and re-decided on the merits by a court of the same level as that of the judgment quashed (though with different judges) (*renvoi*).[273]

IV. Costs and Legal Aid

A. Costs

It was established soon after the Revolution that justice should be free (*la gratuité de la justice*)[274] and this principle is still found in modern legislation,[275]

---

[266] *Loi* no. 67-523 of 3 July 1967 art. 17 al. 2.
[267] Ibid. art. 18 and see Vincent and Guinchard, 1073.
[268] Couchez, *Procédure civile,* 466.
[269] This exception is based on case law starting with Req. 12 Dec. 1871, DP 1872.1.316.
[270] Art. 619 N.c.pr.civ.
[271] Vincent and Guinchard, 1084–1085 who distinguish from this the adducing of new *arguments.*
[272] Art. 627 N.c.pr.civ. reiterating art. L. 131-5 *Code de l'organisation judiciaire.* See further F. Luxembourg, 'La Cour de cassation, juge du fond' D 2006.2358 at n.21, who notes that from being used very rarely in the 1980s (0.6% in 1984), this power was exercised in 20% of cases of *cassation* in 2004.
[273] Art. 626 N.c.pr.civ. reiterating art. L. 131-4 *Code de l'organisation judiciaire.*
[274] *Décret* of 16–24 August 1790, Tit. II, art. 2.
[275] *Loi* no. 77-1468 of 30 December 1977, art. 1.

but all this means is that in general judges and other court officials are to be paid by the state, rather than by charging the parties to the cases with which they deal. Civil litigation in France still costs the parties money, though it appears to be much less expensive than in England. This relative cheapness results principally from the general features of the French civil process which we have already noted: i.e. its reliance on a (relatively) restricted documentation, its use of judicial expert witnesses and its very short hearings. If some of these can be criticized on the basis that they do not encourage the revelation of all the relevant facts—Beardsley went so far as to accuse the French system of 'fact-avoidance'[276]—it may be countered that civil justice is *relatively* more accessible to citizens. In terms of the fees of *avocats*, these are in principle set by agreement with their clients: there is no fixed scale set by law,[277] although an *avocat* must respect a 'principle of moderation' on pain of professional discipline.[278] However, an exception is made to this in that *avocats* may not lawfully set the whole of their fees conditionally on a decision of a court, though a conditional element may supplement a fee calculated on the basis of work done or an hourly rate.[279]

There are three central features of French law's treatment of the recovery of these costs (*frais*) in civil litigation.

First, there is a legally prescribed list of expenditures which count as *dépens*,[280] this list including any expenses incurred by witnesses, the remuneration of experts and the emoluments of *officiers publics*. Notably, however, the remuneration of a party's *avocat* counts as a *dépens* only if the remuneration is a regulated one and where recourse to an *avocat* before the court in question is compulsory.[281]

Secondly, in principle, it is the loser of a case who has to pay the *dépens* of the other side (as well as his own), but the court possesses a discretion to place either all or part of them on another party to the litigation.[282]

Thirdly, as to costs which do not count as *dépens* (such as the cost of legal advice, consultations, *avocats'* fees in general), these may be recovered by a party to a case in one of two ways. If the other (losing) party's behaviour has been unfair or vexatious, then he may be held liable in damages for the loss which this causes any other parties to the litigation.[283] Otherwise, while in principle the person who is ordered to pay the *dépens* is to be ordered to pay any other costs, a court may in its discretion, taking into account what is equitable and the economic situation of

---

[276] Beardsley (above n. 1), *passim*.
[277] *Loi* no. 71-1130 of 31 December 1971, art. 10 al. 1.
[278] S. Guinchard (ed.), *Droit et pratique de la procédure civile*, 5th edn. (Dalloz, 2006), 1279.
[279] *Loi* no. 71-1130 of 31 December 1971, art. 10 al. 3.
[280] Art. 695 N.c.pr.civ.
[281] Art. 695-7⁰ N.c.pr.civ.; Vincent and Guinchard, 1114.
[282] Art. 696 N.c.pr.civ.
[283] Vincent and Guinchard, 1115. This is expressly recognized in various particular contexts in the New Code of Civil Procedure, see arts. 32-1 (dilatory or abusive suit): 559 (dilatory or abusive appeal): 628 (abusive *pourvoi en cassation*).

the person to be subjected to such an order, make no such order or only a reduced one.[284] Thus, a person who wins his case may well still find that he bears a good deal of the costs of bringing it.

B. Legal Aid

Legal aid (*l'aide juridique*) is available in France (subject to a means test) either for legal advice (*l'aide à l'accès au droit*) or for litigation (*l'aide juridictionelle*).[285] The purpose of legal aid is to make access to justice a reality so that, in the words of Vincent and Guinchard, it is 'free (without financial impediment), equal (without discrimination on the basis of wealth) and fraternal (that is to say, equitable); it is at the heart of the application of our Republican motto in the world of justice.'[286] *L'aide juridictionelle* is available in principle for any type of litigation (including *en matière gracieuse*) and may be given in respect of any stage of proceedings. There is, moreover, no exclusion of any type of claim.[287] A person[288] must apply for *aide juridictionelle* and must show his or her lack of means[289] to specially constituted bodies, the *bureaux d'aide juridictionelle*, who are composed of *magistrats*, lawyers, public officials and 'consumers'.[290] These bodies, which are found notably at all tribunaux de grande instance and the Cour de cassation, may accept the application either completely or in part (depending on the means of the applicant): it will not be granted where a person's claim is manifestly inadmissible or without foundation, though this condition does not apply to defendants.[291] If a legally-aided person wins, then he may gain the benefit of any order as to costs to the extent to which he bears them personally, but to the extent to which they have been paid for by the state, then the latter may in principle recover them.[292] If a legally-aided person loses, and is ordered to pay costs, then he must in principle do so personally: legal aid is available only for a party's *own* costs.[293] Clearly, however, such a person's resources would be a factor in the exercise of the court's discretion *not* to order costs which we have already noted.[294]

---

[284] Art. 700 N.c.pr.civ.
[285] The main provisions are contained in *loi* no. 91-647 of 10 July 1991 (as very considerably amended, most recently by *loi* no. 2007-210 of 19 Feb. 2007).
[286] Vincent and Guinchard, 1124 (who also note the importance of access to justice under the ECHR, art. 6 and the EU Charter of Fundamental Rights, art. 47(3)).
[287] *Loi* of 10 July 1991, arts. 10 and 11; Vincent and Guinchard, 1129.
[288] It is available to non profit-making *persones morales* exceptionally: *loi* no. 91-647 of 10 July 1991, art. 2.
[289] *Loi* of 10 July 1991, arts. 4–6.
[290] Ibid., arts. 12ff.
[291] *Loi* of 10 July 1991, arts. 7 al. 1,2.
[292] *Loi* of 10 July 1991, art. 43.
[293] Ibid., art. 42; Couchez, *Procédure civile*, 419.
[294] Above, p. 114.

V. The Enforcement of Judgments

English law possesses three main mechanisms for the enforcement of judgments. In the case of orders of specific performance or injunction, wilful disobedience constitutes contempt of court and can lead to imprisonment, a fine or the sequestration of assets.[295] This reflects the idea that disobedience of a court order, even in a 'private matter' is a public wrong.[296] Not surprisingly given the potential sanctions, these orders are in the vast majority of cases obeyed. While at one time orders for the payment of *money* could lead to imprisonment for debt, this was all but abolished in 1869[297] and so for example, court orders to pay a debt or damages are now to be enforced by a series of different procedures aimed at satisfaction of the debt from the proceeds of liquidation of the debtor's property or other assets. Finally, if an English court orders a defendant to give up possession of land to the claimant, then possession will be transferred by the sheriff's officer, if need be, by force.[298]

French law possesses no law of contempt of court and has had to develop other mechanisms for the enforcement of judgments and other court orders. While the Revolution consecrated the principle of personal liberty, this being reflected in the minimizing in the Civil Code of the specific enforcement of obligations (*exécution en nature*),[299] imprisonment for debt in certain circumstances (both civil and commercial) was retained and was not abolished until 1867.[300] Here, we shall note three major features of modern French law's approach to the enforcement of judgments.

First, there are a series of different legal procedures by which a judgment debtor's property may be seized and liquidated in order to satisfy a judgment debt. The idea that a debtor's property, whether movable or immovable, is liable to seizure is expressed technically by saying that it is subject to a 'general charge' in respect of his debts,[301] but this should not be seen as giving any proprietary as opposed to personal right in the creditor nor, of course, as giving any priority in the debtor's insolvency.[302] The various procedures available for the satisfaction

---

[295] Contempt of Courts Act 1981; R.S.C. Ord. 45 and Ord. 52. (for High Court).

[296] A.H. Pekelis, 'Legal Techniques and political Ideologies' (1943) *Mich LR* 665, 668, quoted in *Source-Book,* 506–507, and see generally M. Chesterman, 'Contempt: in the common law but not the civil law' (1997) 46 ICLQ 521.

[297] Debtors Act 1869, s. 4 (with exceptions).

[298] R.S.C. Ord. 45, r. 3 (for the High Court).

[299] Art. 1142 C.civ.

[300] *Loi* of 22 July 1867. It remains available for the enforcement of criminal fines, costs in Criminal proceedings and fiscal penalties: Vincent and Prévault, 20–21. Under *loi* no. 2004-204 of 9 March 2004, new arts. 749ff C. pén. this is termed '*contrainte judiciaire*' and is subject to strict conditions.

[301] Arts. 2284-2285 C. civ. (renumbering arts. 2092–2093 C. civ. by *Ord.* no. 2006-346 of 23 March 2006). Some items of a debtor's property may not be seized, such as income necessary for food, movable property necessary for private life or work *loi* no. 91-650 of 9 July 1991, art. 14:

[302] Cf. below p. 479.

of debts against the debtor's property (*voies d'exécution* in a technical sense) were subjected in 1991–92 to major legislative reforms[303] and can be divided into three categories: those whose aim is preventative (*saisies à fin simplement conservatoire*), that is, preventative of a debtor's disposal of property in such a way as to defeat any subsequent satisfaction; those whose aim is the satisfaction of a debt (*saisies à fin d'exécution*) and those whose aim is the specific restitution of corporeal property (these being *saisies-appréhensions* and *saisies-revendications*). Of these, as can be seen, the last differ in that they aim not at the (ultimate or immediate) satisfaction of a debt, but rather the performance of an obligation. Different procedures were established by the 1991–92 legislation as to the mechanisms by which different types of property could be seized, for example, for a debtor's salary (*saisie des rémunérations du travail*), for movable corporeal property (*saisie-vente*) or immovable property (*saisie immobilière*). These all have in common the involvement of *huissiers de justice* in the process of seizure and liquidation and that the debtor's property is put under the control of the court: enforcement is not a matter of self-help for the creditor.[304] Where, as often, a *huissier de justice* encounters difficulty in seizing property, for example, if he is refused entry to premises, he cannot himself force an entry, but must request the local public (executive) authorities to 'lend a strong hand'.[305] Despite the fact that legislation in 1991 provides that 'the State must lend its concurrence in the execution of judgments', it acknowledges that it may refuse to do so.[306] Such a refusal is by no means uncommon[307] and while, as we have seen, it may give rise to liability in damages in the public (executive) authority to a person who suffers loss as a result, either with or without proof of fault, this liability is subject to restrictive rules.[308]

Secondly, in the last quarter of the nineteenth century the courts developed the technique of *astreintes* whose aim was to put indirect pressure on a person who had been ordered to perform an obligation to do or not to do and this technique was given a legislative basis (and juridical respectability) in 1972.[309] An *astreinte* is a money sum which is ordered to be paid by a court for every day, week or month during which a person fails to perform its order. While they are often ordered at the request of a party to litigation, a court may do so on its own initiative.[310] *Astreintes* are either 'provisional' or 'definitive'. An *astreinte* is 'provisional' where the sum to be paid is finally fixed by the court after the debtor

---

[303] *Loi* no. 91-650 of 9 July 1991, *Décret* no. 92-755 of 31 July 1992. These reforms have themselves been the subject of legislative amendment on a number of occasions.

[304] *Loi* of 9 July 1991, arts, 18–21.

[305] See *loi* of 9 July 1991, arts, 17 and 21.

[306] Ibid., art 16.

[307] Vincent and Prévault, 37 note that of a sample 1,229 requests for help from executive authorities, only 58 actually received it.

[308] Below pp. 194–195. This liability is expressly noted in the *loi* of 9 July 1991, art. 16.

[309] *Loi* no. 72-626 of 5 July 1972, art. 5 ff. These provisions (considerably amended) now appear in *loi* of 9 July 1991, art 33 ff.

[310] *Loi* of 9 July 1991, art. 33.

has failed to perform and its amount is then fixed taking into account the debtor's behaviour and any difficulties in performance which he may have encountered.[311] This type of order is both the default position and more common. An *astreinte* is 'definitive' when it is fixed when it is first ordered: its amount may not subsequently be changed.[312] The great advantage of obtaining an order for the payment of an *astreinte* is that it adds to a debtor's obligation 'to do or not to do' an obligation to pay a sum of money, which may be enforced by *voies d'exécution* against the debtor's property.[313] It is finally to be noted that it is the *creditor* who receives any *astreinte* which is ordered (not the state) and that it is distinct from any liability in the debtor to pay damages.[314] While the court has a 'sovereign power of assessment' both as to the appropriateness of ordering an *astreinte* and as to the amount at which it should be fixed in order to put adequate pressure on a person to perform an order, there is a dispute as to how effective their use is in practice.[315]

Thirdly, and finally, there are two situations in which a court's order seems to be more directly the subject of enforcement. First, we have noted that a person may be ordered to deliver to another specific property belonging to the first, this procedure having much in common with court orders to *do* something.[316] Secondly, a court may order a person to vacate another person's immovable property, for example, to order a former tenant from an apartment or striking employees from their place of work. Such an order is termed *expulsion*. It is an 'exceptional measure' and subject to restrictive rules.[317] Moreover, the mere fact that a court decides to order a person to vacate premises does not mean that they will have to leave: for effective expulsion is left to the local *executive* authority, which chooses whether or not to use force in the case in question.[318]

(2) Administrative Procedure

French administrative courts and their working methods traditionally have attracted a lot of attention from this side of the Channel. It is true that the special characteristics of the structure of French courts have led to the development of procedural rules which might strike the English reader as decidedly 'continental'.

---

[311] *Loi* of 9 July 1991, art. 36 al. 1.
[312] Ibid., art 36 al. 2.
[313] It is to be noted that no *voie d'éxécution* may be used to recover an *astreinte* until the latter is liquidated (though an exception is made for *voies d'éxécution* whose aim is preventative): Vincent and Prévault, 53.
[314] *Loi* of 9 July 1991, art. 34.
[315] Vincent and Prévault, 28.
[316] Vincent and Prévault, 228 (*saisie-appréhension*).
[317] *Loi* of 9 July 1991, arts. 61–66.
[318] Cf. above p. 117.

Moreover, the course of legal proceedings is quite different from that to which English administrative lawyers are accustomed to.

In reality, the function which the administrative courts attempt to fulfil has determined to a great extent the procedural rules regulating the proceedings. First, although most rules of administrative procedure were originally the product of case law and thus reflected a considerable degree of self-regulation, these are now contained in the *Code de justice administrative*.[319] This history explains the links that exist between procedural rules and substantive principles. From these principles, it is possible to detect two aims which the courts try to reconcile: on the one hand, administrative law must provide the administration with the necessary legal tools for the performance of its tasks, but on the other, administrative law must protect citizens from the possible abuse of the exercise of its powers by the administration. Not surprisingly, to a great extent the rules of administrative procedure reflect the balance which courts try to strike between these competing aims. In general, procedure in all administrative courts is quite 'user-friendly' and it is fair to say that both the organization of the court and the procedural rules have been elaborated so as to provide as fair a system as possible for the ordinary citizen. Just to give one example, judges do not rely on the parties to provide them with those arguments on which they can rely in coming to their decision ('decisive argument'): the case is constructed, the facts unearthed, and line of reasoning developed through the work of the *juge rapporteur* during the stage of the *instruction*. By contrast, other procedural rules clearly protect the administration and its activities. Since all administrative decisions are *exécutoires*,[320] a citizen will often wish to ask an administrative court to stop or delay the performance of a contested administrative action. Although, it is not easy to obtain an order from the court that an administrative decision or action should be suspended until the court has decided the case on its merits. Recent reforms have created a number of interlocutory procedures to request such a suspension. However, the conditions are still quite strict.

I. Access to the Administrative Courts

There are few limitations on access to French administrative courts. Rules of standing are interpreted generously and applicants do not have to comply with many conditions before they can bring a case to court.

---

[319] The *Code de justice administrative* was adopted on 4 May 2000. It consolidates the procedural rules concerning all the administrative courts.

[320] This means that they are directly enforceable without recourse to judicial order.

A. *Le Recours Préalable*

French administrative procedure provides potential applicants with the option of requesting the administration itself to review any particular decision before challenging it in court. This possibility, termed the *recours préalable*, should provide an opportunity for an early settlement without legal proceedings and is all the more important since, unlike the position as regards civil proceedings,[321] mediation is only resorted to occasionally before administrative courts.[322]

There are two *recours* available generally: the first consists of asking the official who took the decision complained of himself or herself to reconsider it, and the second consists of asking the superior of the official who took the decision to look into the matter and consider it afresh. In some circumstances, use of this procedure has been made compulsory and, where this is the case, it is impossible to bring an action before such a *recours* is made. In any event, use of these mechanisms of 'administrative appeals' has been encouraged by successive administrations. However, their practical success is debatable as typically public bodies do not even respond to these appeals.[323]

B. Rules of Standing

The requirement of standing in French administrative law is relatively lax:[324] the applicant needs to show only that he or she has an interest in the action and, as we have noted, this requirement has been understood generously by the courts.[325] A person's interest does not have to be strictly financial, and may, as in civil proceedings, be purely 'moral.' Moreover, the Conseil d'Etat has for a long time recognized the 'collective interest' of associations, charities, trade unions, and so on. As regards these, it is only the interest of the association which counts and this all depends on its aims: no account is taken of the standing of their individual members.

In general, a challenge to any decision relating to the public service[326] will be admissible on the application of its users. Thus, for example, in *Syndicat des Propriétaires du Quartier Croix-de-Séguey-Tivoli* of 1906,[327] an association of local residents and taxpayers was held to have standing to challenge the cancellation

---

[321] Above p. 53.
[322] The tribunaux administratifs have a role of conciliation according to the *Code de justice administrative*—see art. L.211-4 C.J.A. However, in reality, it is rarely used: see generally S. Boyron, 'The Rise of Mediation in Administrative Law Disputes: Experiences from England, France and Germany' [2006] PL 320.
[323] The silence of the administration for four months is interpreted as a refusal: see section D below.
[324] The solutions of the French case law is quite similar to those of English law.
[325] See CE 28 Dec. 1906, *Syndicat des patrons coiffeurs*, Leb. 977.
[326] Below pp. 168–169.
[327] CE 21 Dec. 1906, D. 1907.3.41 concl. Romieu.

of a tram service in Bordeaux. Although marginally wider rights to bring actions are recognized in France than in England, in all such cases an association or other body must show that the administrative decision in question has injured its interests in circumstances which are sufficiently distinct from those in which it has affected the public in general. Moreover, merely being a taxpayer is not enough to provide standing:[328] the applicant needs to be affected in a 'special, certain and direct' manner. Thus for example, a trade union does not have an interest in an employee's dismissal where the employee does not bring an action, even though the dismissal may create a precedent: any person directly affected is seen as the primary applicant.[329]

C. Legal Aid and Legal Representation

Access to justice is a rather empty notion if it is financially impossible to bring a case to court.

First, legal aid is available for proceedings in administrative courts as much as civil or criminal ones.[330] Moreover, bringing a case to an administrative court does not have to be a ruinous expense. In order to apply to the court, legal representation is not always compulsory. If one seeks the annulment of an administrative decision through the *recours pour excès de pouvoir*,[331] legal representation is not required. The lack of representation is unlikely to be damaging to a person's chances of success since, as we noted, the case is literally taken over by the court itself from the moment it is introduced. On the other hand, instruction of an *avocat* is required for all other types of *recours*, and an *avocat au conseil* is required if the case goes before the Conseil d'Etat.

D. *La Décision Préalable*

Any applicant must show that one very important condition has been fulfilled, the condition of *la décision préalable*. This condition gives expression to the rule that an applicant must seek to contest before a court an administrative act, a decision of the administration which has been taken previously. This decision may consist of the rejection of a person's request, or a refusal to take a decision as requested. In the situation where the administration has in fact taken no decision on a person's request, French law deems the request to have been refused four months after it was made. This rule was clearly necessary given the requirement

---

[328] CE 23 Nov. 1988, *Dumont*, Leb. 418.
[329] CE Ass. plén. 10 Apr. 1992, RFDA 1993.265.
[330] See above pp. 115–116.
[331] Below p. 122.

of a *décision préalable*, for otherwise the administration could protect itself simply by doing nothing in response to a request.

E. A Short Time-Limit

One of the most restrictive conditions of making applications to the administrative courts is that all *recours* must be brought within a period of two months after the decision challenged (whether real or deemed) has been taken. If this time-limit is not respected, the *recours* will not be admitted. Unlike the position in English law, the Conseil d'Etat possesses no discretion to waive the time-limit if it thinks fit.

II. Forms of Redress: *Les Recours*

Unlike the English system where there is basically one procedure which leads to a choice of remedies, French administrative lawyers classify the type of demands which applicants bring from the beginning and channel them through their own proper procedures. There are three main procedures. First, there are *recours de plein contentieux* in which there are few limitations on the powers possessed by a judge: damages may be granted, a contract may be set aside or amended so as to include new provisions.

Secondly, *recours pour excès de pouvoir* raise before an administrative court the question of the legality of an administrative decision. A court seized of such an application possesses only the possibility of quashing the decision that has been referred to their control or rejecting the application. However, it is important to note that it is not necessary for a person to start two different actions when, for example, an administrative decision which continues the application of a contract raises the question of its initial validity.

Thirdly, the courts are increasingly required to make declarations as to a person's rights. Administrative courts use declarations in specific, if a limited number, of areas: for instance, rather than annul an act the illegality of which is obvious and grave, a court instead 'declares its inexistence'. Moreover, on occasion the Conseil d'Etat may need to give an authoritative interpretation of a legal provision for another court:[332] for instance, a Tribunal judiciaire sometimes needs to ascertain the validity or proper interpretation of an administrative provision which is relevant to the case before it. Indeed, the Conseil d'Etat has even proved itself willing to provide an interpretative opinion when the relevant point of law is obscure and there is a real litigious situation. Finally, recent legislation has instituted a procedure by which both Tribunaux administratifs and Cours administratives d'appel refer interpretative questions to the Conseil d'Etat.

---

[332] For instance, a Tribunal judiciaire which needs to know the interpretation of a text before taking a decision on a relevant question.

III. Proceedings in an Administrative Court

In order to bring a *recours*, a person simply has to write a letter to the court setting out their name, address, the facts and the grounds on which the 'decision'[333] is challenged and the relief which is sought (article R. 411-1 of the *Code de justice administrative*.) It is not necessary to develop a legal argument in support of this relief as there will be plenty of opportunity for this at a later stage. However, all applications must enclose a copy of the decision under challenge which is affixed to the *recours*.

A. Interlocutory Procedures

The doctrine of the *décision exécutoire* means that any administrative decision which is subject to challenge will nevertheless be carried out unless a court orders otherwise. Interlocutory procedures (or *référés*) are therefore essential and have improved considerably over the years. A few *référés* are now available to citizens, each responding to a specific need. The *référé-liberté*, for instance, is meant to prevent the serious and clear breach of a fundamental freedom, while the *référé-suspension* is conditioned by a degree of urgency and the existence of a serious doubt as to the legality of the administrative decision. Also, the *référé-conservatoire* aims to protect the factual circumstances, if these are likely to disappear because of the performance of administrative action. Again a degree of urgency needs to be demonstrated. It is worth noting that as regards both the *référé-suspension and the référé-liberté*, a judge can issue an injunction against the administration, an exceptional remedy in French administrative law.

There are three other *référés* under the *Code de justice administrative* but this time, they are really measures to help manage the case and do not reflect much urgency: the *référé-instruction* under article R 532-1 orders that the necessary steps for the preliminary investigation of a case be taken, the *référé-constat* under articles R 532-1 and R 532-2 orders that the contested facts be established by an expert, and the *référé-provision* under articles R 541-1 to R 541-6 orders that sums of money be set aside to protect the other party.

B. *L'Instruction*

Administrative courts start the judicial process by creating a file (*le dossier*) which contains the *requête* (the claim form) and a copy of the decision which is challenged. A *rapporteur* is appointed to the case and will put together the *dossier* and prepare the case so that it can come to judgment. He will ensure that the written arguments of the applicant and the counter-arguments of the

---

[333] See above p. 121 on the necessity of a 'previous decision'.

defendant are submitted within the proper time-limits and that there is no undue delay in their exchange. The *rapporteur* will also contact the relevant administrative body, whether public corporation or local government, whose decision is challenged and obtain from it more information, their opinion and position as regards the challenge. As to this last point, all administrative courts are entitled to require the administration to hand over any document or documents which are relevant to a case.[334] Each document and *mémoire* is communicated to the other parties.

The *rapporteur* can also order a number of other measures (*mesures d'instruction*) in order to ensure that the court will ultimately reach as informed a decision as possible.[335] The most common of these is to require an expert assessment, but it is also possible for an administrative judge to decide to make a site visit (for example, to see the proposed route of a new motorway). The *rapporteur* is allowed to order *mesures d'instruction* if he considers that the file is otherwise incomplete.

Once the file is ready, the *rapporteur* has the task of producing two documents: a 'note' which outlines the facts, the arguments of both parties and then argues for the solution which the *rapporteur* favours, and secondly, a draft judgment which reflects the view of the case which he has reached.

After a first examination of the documents produced by the *rapporteur*, the case is handed over to the *Commissaire du gouvernement*.[336] The *Commissaire du gouvernement* prepares an opinion (his *conclusions*) which sets out the facts clearly and analyses in detail the points of law which are thereby raised. Because of the prestige of the office, the *conclusions* of a *Commissaire du gouvernement* carry a lot of weight.

C. The Hearing

From the above discussion, it is easy to deduce that the administrative proceedings are mainly written and that most are in fact complete by the time the case comes to be heard. The public hearing starts with the *rapporteur* reading a summary of the arguments of both parties. Then the counsel representing the applicant and the defendant are called upon by the president of the court; often, they will stand up only to say that they rely on the arguments which have been put in writing. It is rare indeed for counsel to develop oral arguments before administrative courts and this occurs only in an exceptional case where it can be justified.

---

[334] This is important. On one occasion, the administration refused to provide the relevant file and the Conseil d'Etat decided against the administration by presuming that the allegations put forward by the applicants were true since the administration was withholding the information which the Conseil had required; see CE 28 May 1954, *Barel*, Leb. 308.

[335] Cf. above pp. 102–108 in the context of civil proceedings.

[336] Contrarily to the name of the position, the *Commissaire du gouvernement* is not an agent of the executive, he is an independent judge: cf. above pp. 61.

Lastly, the *Commissaire du gouvernement*[337] reads his *conclusions*. Once the *Commissaire du gouvernement* has finished, the public hearing is concluded and the public is required to leave the courtroom. The judges then start their consideration of the case (the *délibéré*) during which the whole court discusses the case and reaches agreement not only on a solution but also on a draft judgment. The parties are entitled to respond briefly to the *conclusions*.[338] The *Commissaire du gouvernement* is not allowed to stay for the *délibéré* if one of the parties objects.[339] The discussions between the members of the court and the votes of each judge remain secret.

D. The Judgment

The judge must have regard to a number of limits when deciding a case. Thus, he cannot take a decision beyond the request of the parties but has to consider all the arguments that they put forward. If, therefore, an application is unsuccessful, all the applicant's arguments must be answered in the court's judgment.

Traditionally, French administrative judges did not possess a power to order the administration to act. As a consequence of this position, administrative courts judgments could not give a direct order to the administration. However, since a *loi* of 8 February 1995,[340] their judgment may include an injunction directed against the administration when it is necessary in order to ensure that their decisions are respected.

In order to understand administrative court judgments, it is important to outline the different parts: first, the opening *visas* refer to the legislative provisions on which the decision is based; secondly and most importantly come the *motifs* in which the reasons for the decision are stated, beginning with the word *considérant*. These *motifs* are written both very precisely and very concisely. Indeed, while it is difficult from the reading of the *motifs* to find out immediately the real reasons for a decision, their drafting is so precise that the mere change of a word of the previously accepted formulation of the legal proposition in question usually signifies a change in the case law.

---

[337] On this function, see above p. 61.

[338] It is done through a *note en délibéré*: see art. R 731-3 of the C.J.A.

[339] See art. R 732-2 of the C.J.A. The presence of the *Commissaire du gouvernement* in the hearing has been the subject of an extensive conflict between the Conseil d'Etat and the European Court of Human Rights in Strasbourg. In 2006, the Grand Chamber of the Strasbourg court in *Martinie v France*, Application no. 58675/00 insisted that the mere presence of the *Commissaire* in the private deliberations of the judges after he had already publicly taken a position on the merits of the case offended the appearance of a fair hearing. By the time of that decision, the right of a party to object to his presence during the deliberations of the judges had been included in art. R 732-2. The Conseil d'Etat has subsequently ruled that this provision is not inconsistent with the *Martinie* judgment: CE 25 May 2007, *Courty*, AJDA 2007, 1424.

[340] *Loi* no. 95-125.

E. The Aftermath

There is an obligation on the administration itself to put into effect the judgments of the administrative courts. However, this is not always done in the shortest of time. Sometimes the administration needs the guidance as to what the decision requires or as to how to proceed; other rulings of the administrative courts have major implications for the organization of the administration or for its work. Moreover, at times the administration refuses bluntly to enforce the judgments which have been made by the court. Monitoring of the administration is therefore needed.

Two *lois* have given more powers to the administrative courts in order to ensure that their judgments are enforced. Since 1980, administrative courts can fine a party who does not obey a court ruling and since 1995, they can even issue an injunction against the administration to this effect. An example of the new power to give injunctions against public bodies my be found in *Union des Associations Familiales*[341] in which the Conseil d'Etat required the Prime Minister to revalue family allowances for the year 1995.

The Conseil d'Etat has also created a special *section* which deals with this problem of enforcement of judgments. Any party who after a period of three months fails to obtain due enforcement may apply to this *section*. Once initiated, the success rate of this type of legal proceedings is high (around 80%).

IV. Conclusion

Strangely for systems of laws so different from each other, a tendency to converge seems apparent in administrative proceedings. The creation of the 'application for judicial review' in 1977 in England and Wales created somewhat by accident a procedural distinction between the public and private spheres. On the other hand, recent French procedural reforms have given more powers to administrative judges to tailor their decisions to the situation of the case. Thus, while traditionally French administrative judges felt unable to issue injunctions against the administration as a matter of respect for the principle of the separation of powers, since the 1980s there has been a move to circumvent this first by granting administrative judges the power to order *astreintes*[342] and most recently by granting them the power to issue injunctions against the administration.[343] Both powers aim at ensuring proper enforcement of judicial decisions by the administration.

---

[341] CE 28 March 1997, Leb. 124.

[342] *Astreintes* involve the imposition of payment of a sum of money to be paid by the administration after an established deadline has passed for obedience to a court order. The amount of this sum increases daily. Cf. above pp. 111–118 for *astreintes* in the context of civil proceedings.

[343] *Loi* no. 95-125 of 8 February 1995.

(3) Criminal Procedure[344]

For a common lawyer, criminal procedure is one of the most distinctive features of French law. Both common law and French law procedures have evolved over a long period and each is deeply embedded in its legal tradition. In the 1990s, the English and the French did examine each other's system officially, but considered that it would be difficult to borrow only parts of the other system.[345] Although the French national tradition originates in the 16th and 17th centuries, if not earlier, it is now subject to wider European influences. The European Convention on Human Rights sets out common standards across different legal traditions. For instance, in 1989 the Assemblée plénière of the Cour de cassation permitted the *juge d'instruction* to authorize telephone tapping without any specific basis in the Code of Criminal Procedure. The European Court of Human Rights condemned France in April 1990 on the basis that the grounds for permitting telephone tapping were inadequately clear to safeguard the rights of the suspect. Within weeks, the Cour de cassation produced a ruling setting out specific conditions which had to be satisfied before telephone tapping could be authorized.[346] The Convention has been an important point of reference in discussion of reforms and in judicial decisions ever since. Judicial Co-operation in Criminal Matters within the EU has further strengthened the need for greater similarity in the treatment of suspects and in investigation procedures. Finally, as has already been mentioned, the role of the *juge d'instruction* has come under criticism as a result of a number of high-profile cases, the most recent of which was the *Outreau* case.[347] All the same, the French are seeking to maintain the best features of their own tradition whilst striving to achieve the highest standards in compliance with internationally recognized protections of the rights of the accused and of victims.

Any legal system has to establish procedures to answer four questions: who investigates crimes; who decides whether to bring a prosecution; how is a trial conducted; and who deals with the case after trial? French criminal procedure is distinctive in the way it connects the answers to these four questions through the involvement of the judiciary. Professional judges, either as prosecutor (*procureur*) or as *juge*

---

[344] See generally J. Pradel, *Procédure pénale*, 16th edn. (Editions Cujas, 2006); M. Delmas-Marty and J. Spencer (eds.). *European Criminal Procedures* (Cambridge, 2002), ch. 4; J. Hodgson, *French Criminal Justice* (Oxford, 2005); J. Bell in C. Walker and K. Starmer (eds.), *Justice in Error*, 2nd edn. (London, 1998), ch. 17.

[345] See *La mise en état des affaires pénales* (Paris, 1991) (hereafter the 'Delmas-Marty report') and L. H. Leigh and L. Zedner, *A Report on the Administration of Criminal Justice in the Pre-Trial Phase in France and Germany* (Royal Commission on Criminal Justice, Research Study No. 1; London, HMSO, 1992).

[346] Ass. plén. 24 Nov. 1989, D 1990.34; ECHR 24 Apr. 1990, *Kruslin* and *Hervig*, 12 EHRR 528, 547; Crim. 15 May 1990, *Bacha Baroudé*, JCP 1990 II 21541 note Jeandidier. A *loi* of 10 July 1991 provided further safeguards and imposed more detailed limits on the exercise of the powers of the judge in this area.

[347] See above p. 81.

d'instruction exercise external control over police investigations, participate in the investigation process and take the decision to prosecute. Other judges preside at the trial (typically without a jury), and yet others (as the *juge de l'application des peines*) supervise the execution of a sentence and deal with matters such as parole. The central role of the judge places the French system within what might be described as the inquisitorial model of prosecution. The judge is there to ensure that the truth is arrived at and judges at all stages may order further investigation (e.g. by way of an expert's report). The judge is not the passive umpire faced with a battle between the advocates of prosecution and defence as in an accusatorial system. The French, however, would describe their system as a mix between inquisitorial and accusatorial elements.[348] The judges do interview the accused and witnesses and order investigatory measures to be undertaken, but there is an input from both prosecution and defence. As the Delmas-Marty report suggested, there can be no justice if each side is not able to put its case (the requirement of a *débat contradictoire*).[349] This feature has been strengthened over recent decades. The other distinctive feature to a common law eye is that French criminal procedure is essentially written. Materials used to establish guilt are collected in the file (*dossier*) built up in the pre-trial phase and used by trial and appellate judges alike. Indeed, as Anton put it:

The comparison between the French and Anglo-American trials is misleading for it is only a slight exaggeration to say that, while in England or in the US a *man* is on trial, in France it is a *dossier*.[350]

The existence and use of the file is both a safeguard for the accused and a permanent record of what is said. It will be about the content of this file that most debate turns in the pre-trial stage, and it is used by the trial judge.

The accumulation of evidence in the file enables its contents to be challenged before trial and the law in this area is complex. The *procureur*, the *juge d'instruction*, or the defence can apply to the *chambre de l'instruction* to strike out such items from the file during the course of investigations. Although some texts specifically impose the penalty of nullity for breach of procedural rules in the gathering of evidence, e.g. where a search has been conducted of a lawyer's office without regard to the safeguards established by law. In most cases, however, it is up to the court to decide if the breach of procedural requirements is serious enough to justify the nullity of evidence gathered for breach of public policy or of the rights of the defence. Article 171 of the Code of Criminal Procedure provides that a nullity is only pronounced where there has been a prejudice to the person concerned.[351]

---

[348] See Delmas-Marty report, 19 and 29.

[349] Ibid., 13.

[350] A. Anton, 'L'instruction criminelle' (1960) 9 Am. Jo. Comp. Law 441 at 456. For an account of the importance of the file see Hodgson, above n. 1, 191–195, 246–247.

[351] On the exclusion of evidence and the abuse of police powers, see W. Pakter, 'Exclusionary rules in France, Germany, and Italy' (1985) 9 Hastings International and Comparative Law Review 1, 8–14, 28; Pradel, *procédure pénale*, paras. 502–503.

I. Who Investigates a Crime?

There are two phases to the investigation process. In the first phase, the police make enquiries seeking to identify a suspect. This is the *enquête*. In a second phase, the prosecutor (*procureur*) or, in some serious cases, the *juge d'instruction*, seeks to establish whether there is a sufficient case to justify a prosecution. This is the phase of the *instruction*. The prosecutor or the *juge d'instruction* may become involved in the *enquête* either to authorize specific forms of investigation or in supervising the whole process in serious cases. Since both the *procureur* and the *juge d'instruction* are members of the judiciary, the investigation of crime involves judicial supervision or even direction in a way which is not found either in the common law or in a number of other civil law systems. In particular, the close connection between prosecutors and judges as members of the same profession is distinctive of France and a small number of other countries. Being a prosecutor or a *juge d'instruction* or a trial judge can be phases in the same person's judicial career, which is not true for many countries even within the civil tradition.

A. The Police

The criminal law (and associated administrative regulations) are enforced by the police. In France, there are a number of different police bodies. A number of police bodies exist whose function is to ensure the proper implementation of the law, to maintain public order and thus to pre-empt crime. These bodies are the administrative police (*police administrative*) and they are under the direction of national or local administrative authorities. Thus there are the frontier police (*police de l'air et des frontières*), traffic police, and police who guard state buildings. These have a number of powers to stop individuals or to request the production of papers, but they are not involved in the criminal process. By contrast, under article 14 of the Code of Criminal Procedure., the *police judiciaire* are involved in identifying breaches of the criminal law and in assembling evidence. There are obvious overlaps: the traffic police may note the existence of a breach of traffic regulations, or the frontier police identify false passports. But the core activities of the two bodies and their administrative structures are distinct.

The *judicial police* is made up of a number of distinct groups, some of which have these police functions as their central activity and some as a subsidiary task. The *police nationale* is under a national director and located in various *préfectures de police* across France. There are also a number of central services dealing with specialist areas such as espionage, organized crime, immigration and clandestine employment, as well as providing a strategic back-up to other forces. In addition, there is the *gendarmerie nationale* whose functions are principally to maintain order. The functions of an officer of the judicial police may be carried out by officers of the *police nationale* and the *gendarmerie nationale* of at least five years standing. Others such as mayors also have this status. The powers of the officer of the national police will be seen in the chapter on criminal procedure.

B. Judicial Supervision?

This apparent judicial control in theory is modified in practice by the delegation of authority from the *juge d'instruction* to the police by way of a *commission rogatoire*. Under article 81 al. 4, of the Code of Criminal Procedure, 'if the *juge d'instruction* is unable to carry out all the investigatory measures, he may give a *commission rogatoire* to officers of the judicial police so that they may carry out such investigatory acts as are necessary in the circumstances subject to the rules laid down for them. Certain measures cannot be delegated in this way to the police but only to another judge, especially the issuing of an arrest warrant or formally questioning the accused or witnesses.[352] Such powers of delegation have been upheld by the *Conseil constitutionnel* in relation to telephone tapping, even where the persons in question were telecommunications officials with the same status as officers of the judicial police.[353] Since there are so few *juges d'instruction* in France, it is impossible that they could cope even with the small proportion of cases which fall to them. It is necessary in most cases for the work to be undertaken by the police. In that searches, formal questioning of witnesses, requesting expert reports and so on may well be done by police officers, and yet will appear on the file which forms the basis for a judicial decision, a basic weakness in the control exercised by the *juge d'instruction* emerges, and this was noted by the Delmas-Marty report in 1991.[354] In reality, the police have more power than in England, for they are exercising the powers of a judge, but are subject to less control in that they do not require prior authorization for searches. It is in this area that the conflict is most apparent between the theory of the system as one directed by the judge and the reality of personnel and resources. As Leigh and Zedner remark, 'the reality of many of these cases probably differs little from the reality in England and Wales save that the defence may be less favoured'.[355]

C. The *Enquête*

The French system grants different powers to the police and judges depending on the nature of the offence at stake. In the ordinary procedure (*enquête préliminaire*), the police have limited powers. They can neither arrest nor search

---

[352] Art. 152 al. 2, C.pr.pén.

[353] See C. cons. 27 December 1990, *Telecommunications Law*, RFDC 1991, 118; Bell, *French Constitutional Law*, 148.

[354] Above n. 2; also Hodgson, above n, 1, 202–208.

[355] *A Report on the Administration of Criminal Justice in the Pre-Trial Phase in France and Germany*, above n. 2, 14.

without instituting a judicial inquiry (*enquête judiciaire*), i.e. involving the *juge d'instruction* who has wider powers, but the police are then constrained to act on his authority. By contrast, in the flagrant procedure (*enquête flagrante*), there are wide police powers in the early days of the inquiry, albeit under control of *procureur*, but the *juge d'instruction* must be brought in to take over the case as soon as feasible. A flagrant offence is defined by article 53 of the Code of Criminal Procedure as involving three kinds of situation: (i) either a *crime* or *délit* which is being or has just been committed;[356] or (ii) at a time very close to the commission of the offence, a person is found in possession of objects or there is other evidence that he has been involved in it; or (iii) the head of a household requires the police or *procureur* to investigate such an offence.

There are special terrorist and drugs procedures, under which the police have wider powers of search and detention, even where the offence is not flagrant. Under the *loi* of 3 September 1986, 'terrorism' is defined as individual or collective acts involving certain offences against persons or property, or with arms or explosives with the object of causing serious public disorder by intimidation or terror.

There is no power of arrest in the ordinary procedure (*enquête préliminaire*). But the judicial police have powers to stop and detain people in order to check their identity. Wide general powers under article 78-2 of the Code of Criminal Procedure enable the police to detain a person if it is necessary to verify his or her identity where he or she was about to commit a crime or where there is a threat to the safety of persons or property or to public order, or where the person is likely to be able to provide information useful for investigating an offence (*crime* or *délit*). In addition, the procureur may designate an area for a limited time within which the police can require people to prove their identity, whatever their behaviour. This last provision, introduced in 1993, responded to judicial reluctance to allow wide police powers. The Conseil constitutionnel insisted that the law could only be constitutionally valid where the decision to conduct such searches was adequately justified by the needs of public order.[357] Within 20 km of the frontier and of a number of designated ports of entry, the police have a general power to control the identity of any person. This has been rendered necessary by the abolition of frontier controls with the Schengen countries. The administrative and judicial police have more general powers in relation to foreigners. Under an *ordonnance* of 1945, foreigners are required to prove their identity at any time. The combination of these powers to control identity and to detain individuals until their identity has been established provides the judicial police with important powers .

---

[356] The central requirement is that the case is fresh, hence a rape is still flagrant if reported 28 hours after the event: Crim. 26 Feb. 1991, *Bartoli*, D. 1991. IR.115.

[357] C. cons. 5 Aug. 1993, Rec. 213.

In addition, the police do have a power in an *enquête préliminaire* under article 77 al. 1 of the Code of Criminal Procedure to detain 'any person' against whom there is evidence giving rise to a presumption that he committed the offence. In flagrant offences, in addition to a power of arrest, there is a power under articles 62 and 63 of the Code of Criminal Procedure for the police to detain anyone who they consider able to provide information, or against whom there a serious signs of guilt.

II. The Decision to Prosecute

A. The Judicial Investigation (*L'instruction*)

The stage of the police investigation is followed by a formal preparation of the case (*instruction*) before the decision to prosecute is taken and for use in the trial which is conducted in most cases by the *procureur* and in about 8% of the most serious cases by the *juge d'instruction*. In consequence, the predominant power is actually exercised by the police and the prosecutor. A flow chart of the criminal process is set out in Figure 4.2

The basic task of the *instruction* process is to decide whether there is a sufficient case to answer to warrant committal of the suspect to the courts for trial. The tasks of the *juge d'instruction* are specified in article 81 of the Code of Criminal Procedure: 'the *juge d'instruction* undertakes all investigating acts which he judges necessary to the revelation of the truth'. These acts will include gathering evidence, for example by ordering expert tests or reports, such as about ballistics, by reconstruction of the crime, or by directing further police investigation. They will also involve formal questioning of witnesses, either by taking formal statements from them one by one or even staging a confrontation of witnesses to elicit truth. Most importantly, the *juge d'instruction* will question the suspect. Apart from the first formal hearing, a lawyer will be present and the purpose is to get to the truth, and may involve challenging the suspect on statements by witnesses. The *juge* may also question witnesses directly. The *juge d'instruction* then produces a report which sets out his or her own view on what should be done and instructs the *procureur* about the next steps to be taken in the case.

The *juge d'instruction* is seized of a case by the requisition from the *procureur*.[358] This defines the ambit of the subject matter of the investigation, and the *juge* will need further instructions from the *procureur* to deal with new offences turned

---

[358] The nominee may be removed on grounds of the good administration of justice where the *procureur* or one of the parties requests, but reasons must be given for such a decision (art. 84 C.pr. pén.). The Cour de cassation has a similar power, e.g. in 1996 it removed investigation into terrorism in Corsica from the local courts to the Cour d'appel of Paris, provoking much criticism in judicial circles.

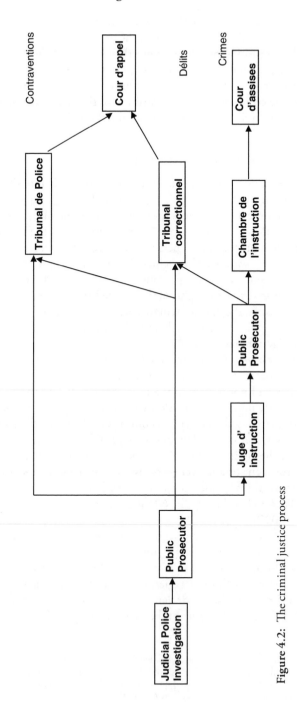

Figure 4.2: The criminal justice process

up in the course of the investigation. Unlike the English magistrates at committal, the *juge* is not limited *in personam*, as she or he may investigate both persons named in the requisition or others whom they suspect of the offence. A feature common to most civil law systems is the right of the victim of the crime to initiate the criminal process both to secure a criminal conviction and to obtain civil redress from the criminal court. A requisition to the *juge d'instruction* may thus come not only from the *procureur* but also from the civil party.

B. The Status and Rights of the Suspect

There are three stages which a person may go through before they become an accused. To begin with, the person may simply be a witness whom the police question. The moment that there is sufficient evidence of guilt, a person is 'under investigation' (*mise en examen*). Once it is established that there is sufficient evidence to sustain a prosecution, a person will be sent to court as an accused (*une personne mise en accusation*). The Delmas-Marty report noted that the rights of the suspect were not adequately protected at the time, and some improvements have been made to define the rights of the accused and to provide additional safeguards. All the same, the balance remains heavily in favour of the effectiveness of the police investigation with the rights of the accused coming to the fore once the judicial investigation has started.[359]

The *mise en examen* (formerly called *l'inculpation*[360]) is a crucial stage in the pre-trial process. From that moment, a person becomes a suspect in the eyes of the law and not merely in the eyes of the police or the civil party. The person is formally under investigation with a view to prosecution, and the *juge d'instruction* prepares the case for a committal. To be made a suspect, there must be 'serious and concordant indications' of a person's criminal liability. At that stage, the rights of the accused become stronger, notably the right to silence and the right to a lawyer. A decision to place someone formally under investigation in this way does not automatically lead to prosecution. In 2004, of the 36,125 cases handled by the 604 juges d'instruction, there was no investigation in 12,035 of them.

The stage of *mise en examen* begins with a formal interview with the *juge d'instruction*. In some cases, the person may have been questioned by the *juge d'instruction* already. Any person may be called as a witness and the necessary evidence may only arise from that questioning. Well-established case law requires that the magistrate should not declare a person a suspect 'until he has clarified whether the person did take part in the incriminating act in circumstances such

[359] For an analysis of the current law, see S. Field and A. West, 'A Tale of Two Reforms: French Defense Rights and Police Powers in Transition' (1995) 6 Criminal Law Forum 473.

[360] The term '*inculpation*' was dropped on the ground that it conveyed the impression that the judge had decided that the accused was *prima facie* guilty.

as to give rise to his criminal liability'.[361] The fact that a person has been named as a suspect when the case is referred by the *procureur* or the civil party to the *juge d'instruction* is not necessarily sufficient to justify putting him under examination. It may well be necessary for the *juge d'instruction* to check whether the allegations are substantiated.[362] In order to avoid the device of interviewing a person as a witness rather than questioning him as a suspect, with the formal constraints which that entails, article 105 of the Code of Criminal Procedure provides that neither the *juge d'instruction* nor a policeman acting under a *commission rogatoire* may hear a person as a witness where there are serious and concordant indications of guilt with the design of impeding that person's rights of defence. (Such a protection does not apply to police questioning before a person has been referred to the *juge d'instruction* or *procureur*. Here it is permitted for the police to continue questioning, even after the person has made a confession.[363])

C. Custody

A suspect may be in pre-trial custody in two ways. First, during the preliminary investigation, he or she may be in police custody (*garde à vue*). Secondly, after the stage of *mise en examen*, the suspect may be remanded in custody (*détention provisoire*), usually in prison. The rights of the suspect are significantly different at these two stages.

Detention in custody by the police may last for up to 24 hours, though it may be continued for a further 24 hours by the *procureur*. The police must inform the *procureur* of a detention as soon as possible, and must keep a record of the reasons for the detention, when it began and ended, duration of questioning and rest periods between questioning. Such records then go into the file used by the investigating and trial judges. But it is clear that there is no prohibition on the police questioning a suspect, unless he or she objects. Under legislation on serious crimes and terrorism, the 24-hour detention can be extended by two periods of 24 hours (article 706-88) by the *procureur*, but two further periods of 24 hours can only be ordered by the *juge des libertés*.

During such detention, the suspect has the rights under articles 63-2, 63-3 and 63-4 of the Code of Criminal Procedure, which must be drawn to his attention. These are the right to inform a member of his family or employer of his detention, the right to a medical examination, and the right to a lawyer. The right to a lawyer is limited. It arises only after 24 hours (and then at subsequent

---

[361] Crim. 8 Dec. 1899, D 1903.1.457, note Le Pottevin.

[362] If a person is named in the reference to the judge, but is not immediately put under examination as a suspect, he may still be interviewed by the judge. In such an interview, he is given all the same rights as would be afforded to a suspect, in particular the right to have a lawyer present and the questioning is not under oath.

[363] See Pradel, *Procédure pénale*, para. 433, and Crim. 17 Jul. 1964, JCP 1965II.14038, note P.C.

periods of 12 or 24 hours) and involves the right to have a conversation of up to 30 minutes with his lawyer or with a lawyer appointed by the head (*bâtonnier*) of the local bar. The lawyer is there to advise on the detainee's legal position, and cannot be present during the police interviews.

Once made a suspect, article 137 of the Code of Criminal Procedure provides that 'the accused shall remain free unless, for reasons of the necessities of the investigation or as a security measure, he is submitted to *contrôle judiciaire* or, exceptionally, he is remanded in provisional custody'. *Contrôle judiciaire* imposes conditions on freedom, such as might be imposed as bail conditions in the United Kingdom. Provisional custody is very significant in France. The Delmas-Marty committee received evidence that detention in custody occurred in 44% of *inculpations* in 1988.[364] In 2004, over 20,000 detentions were ordered, about 40% of those were accused of serious crime. Such detainees make up about 40% of the French prison population.

Since 1984, the *juge d'instruction* cannot take a decision to remand a person into provisional custody without hearing both sides (article 145).[365] The decision can only be justified by the need to preserve evidence, to protect public order or the accused or witnesses; reasons must be given. Furthermore, there are time-limits on the use of custody.[366] These time-limits were introduced to meet the criticism from the European Court of Human Rights that custody periods were excessive.[367] Detention in custody is reviewed by the *juge des libertés et de la détention*, not, as in the past, by the *juge d'instruction* in charge of the case.

D. Questioning

The lawyers of the parties (prosecution, defence, and civil party) have the right to attend, or at least to see the results of, any questioning. They are entitled to be present for the questioning of the suspect and the civil party, and may even suggest questions to be asked. Under article 102 of the Code of Criminal Procedure, witnesses are heard under oath by the *juge d'instruction* and his clerk alone.[368] The material produced from each question session before the *juge d'instruction* is written down and is signed by the person(s) questioned. Comments may then

---

[364] Delmas-Marty report, 48; Pradel, *Procédure pénale*, para 526.

[365] Indeed, the presence of the *procureur* with the *juge d'instruction* after the suspect has gone out may be treated as vitiating the decision to remand the suspect in custody: Crim. 19 Sep. 1990, D 1991. 91, note Mayer.

[366] In the case of *crimes* the period is a year, though this can be renewed. In the case of *délits* the period is four months, and there are special rules concerning first-time offenders.

[367] *Tomasi v France* (1992) 15 EHRR 1: here a detention of nearly five years and seven months before acquittal was held to be unjustified.

[368] The presence of the *procureur* does not invalidate such proceedings, provided that he does not intervene in the question and there is no prejudice to the rights of the accused or the civil party: Crim. 19 June 1990, D 1991.15 note Coste.

be submitted by any party on what has been said or on questions which have not been asked. These formal records and comments are kept on file and will be used at committal and trial. The defence may also ask for further expert reports to be made.

The accused's lawyer has to be informed at least four days before any proposed interview of the suspect by the *juge d'instruction*. The file is open for inspection by the *procureur* and by lawyers for the *partie civile* or the accused and they can have copies of items in it. Thus, there are no surprises, and the lawyer can prepare the case with the accused.

E. The Decision to Prosecute

The decision to prosecute is taken formally by the *procureur*, though the report of the *juge d'instruction* will be very important. Under article 36 of the of the Code of Criminal Procedure, the *procureur général de la République* can instruct the *procureur* to bring a prosecution or to undertake certain procedural steps before a court. Such instructions are included on the case file. In this way the public interest in a case is vetted. Under article 33 of the Code of Criminal Procedure the *procureur* is free to make any oral observations to the court that he or she judges appropriate, even if he or she has had to conform to instructions in presenting written arguments.

III. The Trial Process

Depending on the seriousness of the offence, criminal trials take place before differently constituted courts. In the *tribunal de police*, there will be a single judge; but in the *tribunal correctionnel* there will be a bench of judges. In the *Cour d'assises*, there will be a jury of nine people which sits with the three judges. The number of judges thus increases with the seriousness of the offence. The *procureur* sits on a raised platform, and there will be special places for the accused and the civil party.

A. The Conduct of the Trial

There are a number of distinctive features of the French criminal trial. In the first place, there is no guilty plea. The court has to be satisfied with the guilt of the accused and the procedure cannot be foreshortened by the accused's admission of guilt, unlike in the majority of English criminal trials where a guilty plea avoids the need for the evidence to be heard in depth. A procedure of plea bargaining (*plaider coupable*) was introduced in 2004, in which the defendant enters a pre-trial plea of guilty. The individual appears in court following a prior recognition of guilt (*comparution sur reconnaissance préalable de culpabilité*) under article 495-7 of the Code of Criminal Procedure made with the compulsory assistance of an *avocat*. The judge then reviews the genuineness of the facts and their legal classification before registering the declaration of the accused and the penalty proposed by the *procureur*. The order to impose the sentence is made in open court. The second feature is that the presiding judge conducts the questioning of the accused and witnesses based on the file. This means that matters stated in interviews with the investigating judge may well be raised with the witness, even if the witness has not volunteered the information at trial. All the same, the witnesses are usually heard orally at trial. The third distinctive feature is that the accused is questioned by the presiding judge before any witnesses are heard. The accused has no choice whether to face questions, though he may offer no answer. The questioning is based on previous answers provided on the file. The questions may relate to the accused's criminal record or personality, matters which might well not be admissible in a common law trial. The fourth feature is that experts are appointed by the court. Normally, they have been appointed by the *procureur* or by the investigating judge. The trial judge has power, either before or during trial, to require that further investigation be undertaken, e.g. by an expert. This status of the expert tends to reduce the place for conflicts between experts at the trial stage.[369]

That said, there are many similarities with the common law trial. The conduct of a trial is more similar to the common law in that much is oral. The judge will have the file, but witnesses will be heard and there will be oral argument by counsel for the defence and the civil party and by the prosecutor. Thus a poacher may have his own *avocat* and may face both the *procureur* and the *avocat* of the local hunting association arguing for nominal damages and a stiff penalty. The *procureur* and the parties can ask to cross-examine witnesses under the control of the judge. They can make final speeches, with the accused's lawyer having the last word.[370]

B. The Role of the Victim

Unlike common law trials, the victim in a French criminal law case can have a specific role.[371] As a civil party seeking (even nominal) damages, the victim has a full part in the pre-trial and trial stages. As an initiator of proceedings, the victim can often bring about the criminal prosecution. The victim may be an association, as well as an individual. An association has the right to bring a civil action in two cases. the first is where it is a specifically authorized litigant, e.g.

---

[369] See generally, J. Spencer, 'Court Experts and Expert Witnesses. Have we a Lesson to Learn from the French?' [1992] CLP 213.

[370] For a good account of a French trial, see the video produced by the Franco-British Lawyers' Association.

[371] For an account in English, see Whittaker, *Liability for Products*, 380–387.

associations of consumers, those concerned with national, ethnic, racial or religious, or sexual discrimination, those concerned with sexual violence or violence against children, crimes against humanity, those protecting the handicapped or fighting social exclusion, associations concerned with traffic crime or the victims of road accidents or protecting animals all have status to bring actions in some cases in relation to specific offences.[372] The criminal action can thus take the form of a major piece of social debate and not just a discrete prosecution. Represented in the pre-trial and trial phases, the victim can not only claim damages, but can add a different voice to the discussion of the wrongdoing in question and its social consequences.

The victim may not only claim damages against the author of the crime. In some cases there is a right to compensation under article 706-3 of the Code of Criminal Procedure. This applies to crimes causing personal injury (except injuries arising from traffic accidents or hunting where there is a separate insurance regime). The injury caused must cause at least incapacity of one month, and the victim must be French or a national of an EU country or a country with which there is a treaty on the matter. The behaviour of the victim is a relevant consideration. Compensation is provided by a commission, similar in function to the Criminal Injuries Compensation Board.

In recent years, there have been experiments to reconcile offenders and their victims either as an alternative or an adjunct to the criminal justice process. The use of *maisons de justice* and mediation in this area have already been discussed in Chapter 2.[373]

IV. Post-Trial

There are two features of the follow-up to a trial. The first is the rights of appeal, and the second are the ways in which as sentence is implemented.

Appeal from the decision of the *tribunal de police* or the *tribunal correctionnel* lies to the cour d'appel. The decision takes the form of a retrial based on the file and issues of conviction and sentence based on law and fact can be considered. There is no appeal against decisions of the *cour d'assises* since this is already a branch of the cour d'appel. Actions for review of decisions on a point of law may be made to the Cour de cassation.

Miscarriages of justice often lead to cases being re-opened as a result of new evidence. The procedure to re-open a case is called *révision* and was established in the wake of the *Dreyfus* and other cases in the late 1890s. The grounds for re-opening a decision are set out in article 622 of the Code of Criminal Procedure: that there is evidence that the victim of a claimed murder is still alive, that a subsequent

---

[372] See arts. 2-1–2-18, C.pr.pén.
[373] See above p. 53.

trial verdict is irreconcilable with the decision (e.g. if another person has been convicted of the same offence), that a witness has been convicted of perjury, or that there are new or previously unknown facts which place in doubt the conviction. The last ground is the most common. For example, if proof is adduced that the person convicted was in fact in hospital some distance away from the scene of the crime and his identity papers had been taken by someone else.[374] Since 1989 it has been possible for the convicted person or his family to request *révision*. Before then the procedure was restricted to a reference by the Minister of Justice. The availability of the file on the case containing the evidence makes this form of review easier than in the common law, though such a case often turns on new evidence adduced since the trial. Where new evidence is adduced, the Cour de cassation may order an *instruction* with a *commission rogatoire* given to the police to investigate the new facts and produce a report.[375]

The implementation of the sentence is supervised by the *juge de l'application des peines*. he will deal with any rectification of the sentence imposed. He will also authorize the regime of the sentence, e.g. if the condemned person is to serve part of the sentence abroad or a Frenchman is to serve a sentence imposed by a foreign court in France. In the case of release on parole (*libération conditionnelle*), this judge takes the decision on the advice of a special committee.

---

[374] Crim. 9 May 1994, Bull. crim. no. 258.
[375] J. Bell, in C. Walker and K. Starmer (eds.), *Justice in Error*, 234–236; see also J. Hodgson, *French Criminal Justice* 202–208.

PART II(B) PUBLIC LAW

PART II(D) PUBLIC LAW

5

Constitutional Law

At first sight, French constitutional law appears at the opposite end of the spectrum from British constitutional law: the written nature of the Constitution, the fully fledged constitutional review, the semi-presidential regime and the monist approach to the integration of international law in domestic law underline contrasting constitutional choices. A written constitution had become a necessity once absolute monarchy was swept away by the 1789 revolution. Only a written document could establish firmly a new political system and lay the foundations for a new model of society. From this time on, a written Constitution has been regarded in France as a means to enshrine fundamental political values and control political reality. However, the clear gap between the provisions contained in many of France's written constitutions and the reality of political practices throws an interesting light on the efficiency of written documents in constitutional law, a question upon which British lawyers might find it useful to reflect. Furthermore, the relative uncertainty arising from the ambiguity of the text of the 1958 Constitution might strengthen British lawyers in their rejection of a codified constitution. If any lesson is likely to be learnt from the French experience, it is that the adoption of a codified constitution is no easy task and no panacea. Provisions need to be carefully written if some degree of constitutional peace and harmony is to be achieved; a seemingly innocuous provision can trigger constitutional strife and instability. Further, the relative (not to say random) efficiency of the codified text must always be kept in mind: while the more careful drafting might not be able to curb the most ingrained of political practices, some other provisions might sometimes yield the more unexpected of results.

I. The Definition and Role of Constitutional Law

The teaching of constitutional law in France has been established relatively late. Even though the first chair in public law was created as early as 1773, the teaching of public law and more specifically of constitutional law encountered serious obstacles from the start. The political implications of teaching this subject matter frightened many and the chairs in public law were in turn created, abolished, and then reinstated. Public law finally took root in law faculties at the end of the 19th century. However, even then, constitutional law had quite a limited remit, being concerned solely with the interpretation and explanation of the provisions of the Constitution and the working of the institutions created by it. The constitution was the result of the process of rationalization and modernization of the 1789 Revolution, and consequently was meant to be the only rule to be applied in the constitutional space. Any practices or behaviour which diverged from the text, however slightly, were not considered a subject for legal analysis and as such were neither discussed nor evaluated. Paradoxically, constitutional law writers could not conceive of judicial review of the parliamentary expression of the will of the Nation. Consequently, constitutional rules were neither protected nor respected, and the Constitution came to be seen not as the expression of Reason but as the expression of an impossible ideal rarely to be achieved. Even though some commentators have denounced the academics of this period as obsessed with the constitutional text,[1] many important concepts and categories were created during this period (e.g. the separation of power, theory of representation, unitary and federal state, etc.). The idea of classical constitutionalism was developed then, namely that constitutional law aimed to regulate political behaviour exclusively through the use of rules and law. This approach lasted until the 1950s, when political scientists demonstrated the fallacy of such a conception, since the experiences of both the fascist and Marxist regimes forced a reassessment of such a belief. In France, this is reinforced by the unstable nature of many past constitutions and by the blatant failure of the law to constrain the behaviour of political actors.[2] The influence of American and British commentators who carry with them the message of political science is felt deeply in the discourse of French constitutional lawyers to this day.[3] Consequently, during the second part of the 20th century, the black letter analysis of the Constitution has often been neglected and even contested.

However, it has been argued that the relatively recent rise of the Conseil constitutionnel and its case law has facilitated the recognition of the importance of the law when it comes to the analysis of the Constitution.[4] The growing importance of the Conseil constitutionnel and the expansion of its case law explain this evolution. This quasi-constitutional court competes in the political arena with the other institutions and constrains the behaviour and decisions of the other institutional and political actors. By interpreting creatively the constitutional text and declaring the rights, freedoms and principles that need to be respected by all constitutional actors, the Conseil constitutionnel has paradoxically re-introduced a

---

[1]　See D. Turpin, *Droit constitutionnel* (Paris, 2003), 1–10.

[2]　This is particularly true of the Third Republic which led to the Vichy regime and the Fourth Republic which could not engender a peaceful process of independence for French colonies.

[3]　See M. Duverger, *Institutions politiques et droit constitutionnel* (Paris, 1980), vol. 1, 14: 'Constitutional law is this part of the law which regulates the political institutions of the State. To study constitutional law is to study the legal aspects of the political institutions.'

[4]　See also F. Hamon and M. Troper, *Le droit constitutionnel* (Paris, 2005), 33.

legal analysis of constitutional law.[5] However, it is worth remembering that during the first part of the 20th century, the development and teaching of public law was already driven by the case of law of the Conseil d'Etat. Even though this evolution was mostly concerned with administrative law, the decisions of the Conseil d'Etat had already developed constitutional rights and freedoms, and a certain interpretation of the principle of separation of powers.

Consequently, history plays a considerable part in constitutional law: the successive constitutions which one after the other were either perverted or had to be abandoned might have left French constitutional writers with a rich experience in constitution writing, but also with numerous myths and symbols in French constitutional law; while some institutional mechanisms are feared,[6] others are revered.[7] Still, the 1958 Constitution, in a departure from past experiences, has managed to reform itself successfully. Many constitutional amendments have been adopted since 1958 and with one exception the relevant constitutional provision framed this process of change. At last, constitutional law is able to frame constitutional change in France. The return to a legal analysis of the Constitution is doubly strengthened.

II. The Ambiguous 1958 Constitution and its Two Competing Readings

Very few constitutions have achieved the degree of ambiguity that can be found in the present French Constitution. A superficial study of the constitutional text reveals the standard mechanisms for a parliamentary system. This should be no surprise as the two preceding republics had established parliamentary regimes. The need for political consensus would have made it difficult (if not impossible) in 1958 to convince the political elite of the time to opt for a drastically different regime, such as a presidential one. Not only would politicians have been suspicious of such a system but the previous presidential system had led to the Second

---

[5] Still, this return has not been felt so clearly in constitutional textbooks and treaties: the standard works give pre-eminence still to analysis of the main institutions of the French Constitution and the functioning of the French political system. In-depth review of the case law of the Conseil constitutionnel is often severed from these and contained in works on the 'contentieux constitutionnel'. Although this dichotomy is certainly the result of the requirements of academic syllabuses, nonetheless a better integration of the case law of the Conseil constitutionnel would reflect more appropriately the evolution of the subject.

[6] It would be unconceivable to adopt a constitution with a single parliamentary chamber; the choice of a single chamber is still held responsible for the dictatorship of the Convention and the events of the Terror.

[7] The Declaration of the Rights of Man of 1789 is one of those symbolic texts which has been regularly resurrected throughout history.

Empire. The presidential system would have had to demonstrate its democratic credentials to politicians and the electorate.[8]

However, if the provisions of the 1958 Constitution are closely analysed, it is possible to read another regime between the lines. As de Gaulle was the main inspiration for the Constitution of the Fifth Republic, the seeds for a more presidential reading of the constitutional text were likely to be sown. In fact, de Gaulle had outlined his constitutional preference—a presidential regime—as early as 1946 in the *Discours de Bayeux*. Furthermore, he had refused to participate in the Fourth Republic from its inception, as he predicted that the parliamentary regime established by the 1946 Constitution would degenerate in chaos.[9] Consequently, the original text of the 1958 Constitution was drafted in a manner that allowed two competing interpretations of the constitutional provisions: it could establish either a parliamentary or a presidential regime. Even though the 1958 Constitution is the result of a political compromise, a presidential reading by the first President of the Fifth Republic, de Gaulle, was likely.

A. Bringing the Parliament Under Control

The draft constitution which was approved by referendum on 28 September 1958,[10] appears to reflect the parliamentary tradition well established by the previous constitutions. The Executive is split between the President of the Republic (Head of State) and the Prime Minister (Head of Government). This dichotomy which is often found in parliamentary regimes, signifies that while the President of the Republic has a symbolic role of State representation, the Prime Minister is responsible for Government decisions. This interpretation seems to be justified by both articles 5 and 21 of the Constitution. According to article 5,[11] the President of the Republic is a Guardian of the State and of the Constitution, while article 21[12] invests the Prime Minister with the power to decide on Government's

---

[8] The authors of the 1958 Constitution had to predict the possible reaction of the electorate as the final text would be put to a referendum. The French electorate had already rejected a earlier draft constitution on 5 May 1946.

[9] In the *Discours de Bayeux*, de Gaulle called for the creation of a strong president who would act as a referee above the parties and ensure the continuity of the Republic in the event of political upheavals and national emergencies. As none of these were adopted in the new constitution, de Gaulle withdrew from political life for most of the Fourth Republic.

[10] In the referendum 79.25% of the voters expressed their support for the draft constitution.

[11] Art. 5: 'The President shall supervise respect for the Constitution. By his arbitrament [*arbitrage*], he shall ensure the proper functioning of public authorities, as well as the continuity of the State. He is the guarantor of the Nation's independence, of the integrity of its territory, and of respect for treaties.'

[12] Art. 21: 'The Prime Minister directs the operation of Government. He is responsible for national defence. He ensures the implementation of laws. Subject to the provisions of art. 13, he exercises the power to make regulations, and decides on appointments to the civil service and the army. He may delegate some powers to ministers.

Should the occasion arise, he may deputize for the President of the Republic in presiding over the councils and committees mentioned in art. 15.

actions and policies. The President of the Republic might be said to possess some crucial constitutional powers (i.e. the power to call a referendum, to dissolve the Assemblée nationale, etc.), but these will not help with the day-to-day running of the country.

For a parliamentary regime, the Parliament of the Fifth Republic is paradoxically weak. In fact, the institution is constrained in its two main roles of legislation and control. The authors of the 1958 Constitution wanted to 'rationalize' the activities of the Parliament and ensure that it remained within the limits of its constitutional power, so as to avoid a repetition of the problems experienced during the Fourth Republic. First, the Parliament is granted a limited legislative competence: while article 34 of the Constitution lists the topics that are exclusive to the Parliament, the remaining are left to the Executive.[13] Although these provisions did not engender the constitutional revolution that was expected, they represent an extraordinary restriction on Parliament and signal the end of *la souveraineté de la loi*.[14] Secondly, the Prime Minister and the Government are given some important powers over the legislative procedure: to a large extent, the Government controls the legislative agenda; it can reject any amendment which has not been submitted at the committee stage; and finally, the Government has at its disposal a number of provisions to force through the adoption of a bill in whole or in part.[15] Thirdly, the 1958 Constitution has drawn lessons from the past by accepting that some delegation of legislative power to the Government is inevitable and provides for this in article 38.[16] Finally, the scrutiny of Government action is seriously jeopardized by the relevant constitutional provisions: committees of inquiry are created temporarily for a specific investigation and must be disbanded afterwards. This does not make for a robust and efficient system of control.

In a parliamentary regime, the Government is accountable to Parliament; this pivotal requirement is found in article 49 which lists the circumstances in which Parliament may pass a vote of no confidence on the Government. It is fair to note that the various provisions make it hard to dismiss the Government in this way. In fact, article 49 § 3 merges fiendishly the two main roles of Parliament—if the Government invokes this mechanism, a bill is considered to be adopted unless the Assemblée nationale passes a vote of no confidence by an absolute majority of its members. The impact of article 49 § 3 has been all the more controversial because, since 1962, there has been a majority supporting the Government in the

Exceptionally, he may deputize for him in presiding over the Council of Ministers by virtue of an express delegation and for a specified agenda.'

[13] See Chapter 1 at p. 21.

[14] This principle means that Acts of Parliament are an expression of sovereignty and that such provisions have consequently a high constitutional status.

[15] These provisions were included to enable the Executive to pass legislation in the absence of a supporting majority in the Assemblée nationale.

[16] Art. 38 sets up a procedure to delegate to the Government the right to legislate temporarily but exclusively on specific topics.

Assemblée nationale. Although it is infrequently used, the threat is often enough to quell the opposition or any rebellion of the parliamentary majority.

The Conseil constitutionnel is an innovation of the Fifth Republic which does not sit comfortably with the parliamentary model. However, this institution was created mainly in response to excesses perpetrated by the Parliament during the Fourth Republic. The Conseil constitutionnel was created to protect the integrity of the Constitution and to ensure that Parliament did not trespass on the province of the Government, that Acts of Parliament respected the Constitution, and that the elections were properly supervised.[17] It is interesting to note that, even though the Conseil constitutionnel created a different role for itself, it has struck down attempts by parliamentarians to bypass some of these constitutional safeguards.

In fact, many of the departures from the standard parliamentary model can be explained by the experiences of the Fourth Republic and by the wish to 'tame' the power and practices of the Parliament. In doing so, the 1958 Constitution tips markedly the institutional balance in favour of the Executive.

B. Adopting a Semi-Presidential Regime

From the beginning, the first President of the Republic, de Gaulle, favoured a presidential reading of the constitutional provisions. The personal belief of the man and the history of the previous regimes explained and justified his constitutional choices. To a large extent, the 1958 Constitution is a perfect expression of classical constitutionalism: the new Constitution was meant to redress and cure the dysfunctions which marred the end of the Third Republic and which again paralysed the Fourth Republic. A large number of provisions can indeed be explained by reference to this past.

Furthermore, the historical legitimacy of de Gaulle allowed him a certain freedom when adopting some controversial institutional practices. From the beginning of the Fifth Republic, de Gaulle favoured those interpretations which would help him transform the presidential role. Also, having been called back from retirement to end the Algerian war and address the deep constitutional crisis,[18] de Gaulle was given more political leeway and constitutional power than would be expected from the constitutional text or past practices. Consequently, he aimed first to strengthen the powers granted to the President of the Republic. By resorting to article 16 and its emergency powers longer than was warranted to contain

---

[17] This was felt necessary because of a serious incident which took place in 1956. In the parliamentary elections of that year, 11 *députés* (deputies) belonging to the (right-wing and anti-parlementarian) Pujadist political movement saw their elections annulled by the Assemblée nationale and their unsuccessful opponents elected instead. It is not surprising in the circumstances that the supervision of elections was handed over to the Conseil constitutionnel.

[18] The constitutional crisis was as serious as the Algerian war as de Gaulle narrowly averted a military coup and a possible civil war.

the attempted coup of April 1961, de Gaulle created a practice of a president with wide powers. Similarly, de Gaulle asserted his right to appoint, disagree with and dismiss the Prime Minister. Furthermore, de Gaulle sought to add to his historical legitimacy by repeatedly using referenda during his mandate.[19] Also, many referenda authorized de Gaulle to undertake a specific task (e.g. to negotiate the independence of Algeria) and thus, enhanced further the powers and role of the President.

Still, this presidential shift took place because of the difficult political circumstances. Consequently, fears were expressed that these institutional practices would not survive the departure of de Gaulle.[20] It was augured that future presidents were unlikely to possess the requisite personal legitimacy, nor gain any electoral legitimacy from the indirect suffrage of the presidential electoral system. Only a strong legitimacy would support a powerful president. Aware of this constitutional Achilles heel, de Gaulle engineered a process of normalization of the presidential reading. His most important legacy rests with the constitutional amendment reforming the electoral system for the President of the Republic. In 1962, the French people were asked whether they would accept that the President be elected by direct suffrage. Even though the choice of procedure for amending the Constitution was controversial,[21] the referendum was adopted with 62% of the votes (but only 46% of registered voters). The Conseil constitutionnel also refused to review the constitutionality of the referendum as the French people had already expressed its wish.[22] Furthermore, as the opposition voted a motion of censure and dismissed the Government to express disapproval at the use of article 11, de Gaulle retaliated by dissolving the Assemblée nationale and calling parliamentary elections. A fortunate coincidence led to the election by the Assemblée nationale, for the first time, of a strong majority supporting the President. The political phenomenon of parliamentary majority was born at last in France. This in combination with the new electoral legitimacy of the President would ensure that the presidential interpretation of the Constitution survived.

---

[19] In fact, he resigned from office in 1969 when a referendum regarding the abolition of the second chamber was negative.

[20] See M. Duverger, *La VIe République et le régime présidentiel* (Paris, 1961), 10: 'Today, everybody knows that the institutions of the Fifth Republic will not survive its founder, that there is no real institutions of the Fifth Republic, but only a personal consulate which will disappear with the Consul. "After him, what?" To this question, how many dare really answer: "A return to the parliamentary system?" '

[21] De Gaulle chose to use art. 11 of the Constitution rather than the amendment procedure contained in art. 89 of the 1958 Constitution. Art. 11 allows that changes to the organization of constitutional institutions be adopted by referendum, while art. 89 contains the procedure to follow when amending the Constitution. Art. 89 requires that both chambers agree to an amendment before a referendum is called. By resorting to art. 11, de Gaulle was in effect bypassing the Parliament which would not have assented. Arguably, this choice is unconstitutional.

[22] See C. cons. 6 Nov. 1962, *Election du Président de la République*, Rec. 27.

III. Confirming the Presidential Interpretation of the 1958 Constitution—Enter the *VI République*?

From 1962 to 1997, the presidential interpretation of the Constitution worked well. Furthermore, the election in 1981 of the socialist president, François Mitterrand confirmed this presidential reading: although considerable fears were expressed before the Socialists came to power, the left-wing parties, no longer in opposition, followed the same constitutional practices.[23] The Fifth Republic was clearly destined to remain a presidential regime as a clear political consensus seemed to have been found on the interpretation of its provisions. However, this was not to count with a constitutional accident: in 1986, for the first time since 1958, the new parliamentary elections returned a majority which differed polit-ically from the president, and contrarily to the presidential logic, Mitterrand did not resign but chose to remain in office.[24] However, as his electoral legitimacy was reduced considerably, he could only appoint a Prime Minister from the new parliamentary majority and lose many of the powers which had been acquired over the years. In one clean sweep, the presidential 'acquis' were set aside and a more parliamentary reading of the Constitution prevailed. The Prime Minister was no longer a creature of the President but the head of the parliamentary major-ity. Still, a number of important powers remained with the President: the articles 5,[25] 12,[26] 19,[27] and 64[28] contain some key provisions. In fact, some commenta-tors have argued that the resulting regime could not be labelled a parliamentary regime. Opinions can differ as to the extend of the parliamentary nature of the regime but the practice in place between 1986–88, 1993–95, and 1997–2002 left the President with marginal powers and was appropriately named 'cohabitation'. In a 'cohabitation', the Prime Minister supported by the parliamentary majority governs the country but needs to take notice of the President and on some sub-jects, they must act together. In practice, the three periods of cohabitation have been marked with tensions, struggles, and sometimes open political warfare. The experiences of the last and longest period of cohabitation (1997–2002) were such that a proposal for the revision of the Constitution was put forward. This constitutional phenomenon was the result of a discrepancy between the original

---

[23] Many commentators argued that Mitterrand adopted from the start a very Gaullist interpret-ation of his presidential office. This is all the more surprising that the presidential interpretation of the Constitution has been strongly criticized by the left-wing parties.

[24] By contrast, de Gaulle would certainly have chosen to resign.

[25] Art. 5 defines the role of the President of the Republic.

[26] Art. 12 gives the right to dissolve the Assemblée nationale to the President of the Republic.

[27] Art. 19 lists the personal powers of the President of the Republic. All other acts have to be co-signed by the Prime Minister or another responsible minister.

[28] Art. 64 specifies that the President of the Republic appoints three members of the Conseil constitutionnel, among whom is its president.

electoral mandate of the President of the Republic (seven years) and the electoral mandate of the Assemblée nationale (five years). Consequently, a parliamentary election takes place normally after five years of the presidential mandate and in both 1986 and 1993, the people returned a different majority to the Assemblée nationale. As the President of the Republic refused to resign from office, a 'cohabitation' emerged. In 1997, the situation changed as Chirac, in an attempt to pre-empt a future cohabitation, dissolved the Assemblée nationale after two years of his presidential mandate. This dissolution backfired, however, and left Chirac to manage a cohabitation for five years, the longest so far. Furthermore, as this last cohabitation was rather tense and unproductive, a consensus appeared among the main parties for a reform of the Constitution in an attempt to annihilate this practice: the mandate of the President of the Republic would be reduced to five years so as to coincide with the mandate of the first chamber. Although it would not completely avoid the recurrence of cohabitation, in practice it would make it difficult for such a situation to occur; the electorate would have to change dramatically its opinion between the presidential and parliamentary elections.[29] Also, it was argued that this reduction in the presidential mandate was necessary as seven years was too long already, especially as some presidents might be elected for two consecutive mandates—if seven years were too long, even more so were 14! The revision of the Constitution was submitted to the population by referendum and approved on 24 September 2000. Many commentators feel that this is likely to bury forever the parliamentary reading of the 1958 Constitution. It is true that with the 2000 revision of the Constitution, the presidential reading has definitely been endorsed by all as the official interpretation of the Constitution.

IV. Reaching Constitutional Maturity by Amending the Constitution

Since the 1789 Revolution, France has had a rather chequered constitutional past: coups, revolutions, and dictatorial regimes abound.[30] If constitution drafting were a sport, France would likely be world champion many times over. Consequently, many French constitutions have had a very short life and have had very little success when it came to submitting political behaviour to the Rule of Law. French history is full of instances where constitutional texts were either ignored or misapplied (so as to lead to a complete change of regime). For instance, the Constitution of the First Republic (24 June 1793) never came into force because of the period of Terror led by Robespierre and the Committee of National Security. Again, the election in 1849 of Louis-Napoleon Bonaparte (nephew of Napoleon I) as the first President of the Second Republic sealed the

---

[29] The elections of the Assemblée nationale take place immediately after the presidential ones.
[30] Since 1789, there have been 17 different regimes and five revolutions or coups in France.

fate of this regime. Finally, the 1946 Constitution was unable to reform itself and tackle the numerous dysfunctions that plagued the regime.[31] Traditionally, political change was checked and framed with difficulty by a constitution.

However, it would seem that the 1958 Constitution breaks with the past. To start with, it has lasted longer than most constitutional documents, as it is the second longest French constitution.[32] Furthermore, unlike the previous regimes, it has been able to address its main dysfunctions by amending successfully the Constitution. Also, the 1958 Constitution has proved that it could evolve with the time. Many would argue that consequently, the present constitution has achieved a certain degree of maturity. At last, the law has been allowed to frame constitutional change in France. Constitutionalism has finally prevailed.

If cohabitation was at first interpreted by many as creating a consensus across the political spectrum and a welcome sharing of constitutional power,[33] in the end, it was regarded as a systemic dysfunction, and one which needed to be stopped. The first two cohabitations lasted only two years—between 1986–88 and 1993–95—and were seen on the whole in a positive light; the numerous disagreements known to exist between François Mitterrand and Jacques Chirac during the first cohabitation and François Mitterrand and Edouard Balladur during the second did not seem to mar this assessment. However, during the 'long cohabitation' of 1997–2002, fears came to be expressed for the stability and integrity of the political system of the Fifth Republic. The return to a parliamentary logic for such a long period was felt to bring the regime too close to the perilous political practice of earlier periods. It was feared that the longer the period of cohabitation would last the more difficult it would become to return to the presidential reading of the 1958 Constitution. Furthermore, the President of the Republic was able to delay a few initiatives of the Government (e.g. the bill concerning the legal status and organization of Corsica in February 2001). He expressed many criticisms of the Government's actions[34] and legislative programme.[35] Some have argued that President and Prime Minister managed to act together as regards diplomacy and international intervention: if such coherence is evidenced by the actions in Kosovo and by the reaction to the events of 11 September 2001, the lack of political agreement was also clear during the negotiation of the Nice summit of December 2000 and is partly to blame for the poor results of the inter-governmental conference. On the whole commentators

---

[31] Article 90 of the 1946 Constitution contained a long and complex amendment procedure. A first revision amended the Constitution in 1954. However, the narrow ambit of the revision did not have much impact. Another attempt to amend the 1946 Constitution had begun in 1955 but had been abandoned as too difficult. It was chosen to change the whole regime instead.

[32] The Constitution of the Third Republic being the longest as it lasted from 1875 until 1940.

[33] See F. Luchaire, 'Réformer la Constitution pour éviter la cohabitation? C'est inutile' *Pouvoirs*, 'La cohabitation', no. 91, 1999, 119–121, but see also J. Massot 'La Vè République est-elle soluble dans la cohabitation?' in *Mélanges Ardant* (Paris, 1999).

[34] See the management of the mad cow disease in November 2000.

[35] See the introduction of the 35 hours working week in 2001.

and citizens came to believe that cohabitation was not really in the interest of the French State and that it ought to be stopped. Accordingly, the reduction of the presidential mandate aims to abandon the parliamentary reading of the French Constitution.

A. Modernizing Rights and Freedoms

Beyond these dysfunctions, the 1958 Constitution was amended so as to match contemporary changes in ideas and values.

For a long time, it was argued that the principle of equality as proclaimed by the Constitution and the Declaration of Rights of 1789 prohibited the organization of positive discrimination in favour of women or minority groups.[36] Indeed, the Conseil constitutionnel had decided in 1988 that a statute prohibiting an electoral list for local government elections with 75% or more of persons of the same sex was not compatible with the principle of equality. This interpretation was confirmed in a decision of January 1999 and led to the constitutional amendment of 8 July 1999. Article 3 of the Constitution specifies that: 'A statute is to promote the equal access of women and men to electoral mandates and electoral functions.' This drafting aimed at reversing the previous case law of the Conseil constitutionnel and this was duly accepted a year later in a decision of 30 May 2000. Provisions organizing equal access to elected offices for women and men could be compulsory and create incentives. Furthermore, although the adoption of a strict quota of female candidates was highly controversial and did not win the unconditional support of the population, the constitutional amendment only justifies equal access for both sexes in elections and authorizes Parliament to take the relevant measures. This has been achieved by requiring that any difference between the numbers of male and female candidates should be less than one in elections decided with a list system. Furthermore, this traditional understanding of equality has been closely entwined with an understanding of French citizenship; this combination is now under repeated attack because of the issue of minority representation, even if these have found no constitutional translation, as yet.

The environmental issues have also triggered another wave of modernization when it comes to rights and civil liberties: the growing concerns over the environment are clearly reflected in the Charter for the environment which is the latest declaration of rights to be adopted. The aim of the 2004 Charter[37] was to enshrine these fundamental third generation rights in the Constitution. This issue was becoming difficult to ignore. Consequently, the Charter declares that everyone has the right to live in a protected environment which respects one's

---

[36] See the decision of the C. cons. 18 Nov. 1982, Rec. 66 and for a criticism of it D. Lochak, *Droit Social* (1983), 131.

[37] It was included to the Constitution by an amendment of 1 March 2005.

health. Also, the Charter enshrines a principle of liability stating that anyone, responsible for damage to the environment must contribute to its repair. Lastly, the State can intervene in the name of the precautionary principle to prevent a possible environmental damage. Even if this new addition to rights and freedoms can be explained by the changes in attitude regarding the environment, it is fair to point out that other third generation rights, such as bio-ethical ones, ought to have been equally discussed and recognized, but were not.

B. Criminalizing the Control of Executive Action

From the beginning, the 1958 Constitution recognized that members of the Executive might need to be brought to justice for their actions as President of the Republic or as member of the Government. To this aim, a special court was provided for in the Constitution: the Haute Cour de Justice. However, it soon appeared that these provisions were extremely difficult to use: although some ministers have been charged in the past, no minister was ever brought to trial. It was therefore felt necessary to amend the Constitution so as to bring to account members of Government and the President of the Republic.

In effect, the failure of the Constitution to organize the responsibility of members of the Executive has led to the realization that an accountability gap was developing. The political phenomenon of a parliamentary majority supporting the Government has greatly diminished the mechanism of ministerial responsibility and there is no political responsibility of the President of the Republic in the Constitution. As a consequence, other processes of accountability are emerging: the criminalization of certain executive actions is meant to remedy the weak political controls. Therefore, it was important that the constitutional processes organizing this 'criminal accountability' be fully operational. The contaminated blood affair[38] made it necessary that the failings of the Haute Cour de Justice be tackled. For this reason, the Cour de Justice de la République was created and a Title X on criminal liability of the members of Government specified the rules in relation to this new form of accountability. The Cour de Justice de la République is responsible for all stages of the process: the prosecution, the investigation and the judgment.[39] This court is staffed by both judges and Members of Parliament. Still, many have criticized this membership for being too political.

This explains in part the latest amendment of the Constitution. In February 2007, both articles 67 and 68 were amended. Article 67 specifies that the President of the Republic is never liable for actions or decisions taken while acting as President of the Republic. Furthermore, he cannot take part in any judicial process during his mandate (even as a witness). Article 68 allows for the

---

[38] Three ministers were accused to have acted negligently when it came to contaminated blood: they were too slow in taking appropriate actions to avoid the use of contaminated blood. And see below pp. 405–406 on other aspects of this affair.

[39] However, the composition of the Cour de Justice de la République changes with its functions.

President of the Republic to be impeached in the event that he/she failed to fulfil his/her duties in a way manifestly incompatible with the exercise of his/her mandate. This provision softens the prohibition of Article 67. In any event, these new processes of accountability of executive action seem to reflect a deep change of attitude when it comes to the morality of political life and behaviour.

C. Towards a System of Multi-Level Governance?

In the last decade, two conflicting tendencies have united in diminishing the impact of French centralization: the demand for more power at local level and the process of European integration have meant that powers have been transferred from the central government to local entities and European Union institutions. Consequently, the French Constitution has joined the Western nations in building a vast network of powers and in recognizing a multi-level governance.

Demands of the present time have led to deep changes in central-local relations. Originally, the 1958 Constitution had not really innovated in this area; with its organization around the *communes* and the *départements*, the local government structure had hardly changed since the Third Republic. However, the creation of the regions and the strong promotion of cooperation between *communes* have dramatically altered the organisation of local power in France. Furthermore, the assertion that overseas territories can adopt a status to respect their territorial specificities and the freedom for New-Caledonia to choose specific provisions over and above national legislations in reserved areas, reflect deep constitutional changes. Consequently, the constitutional amendment of 2003 which states that '[the Republic's] organisation is decentralised'[40] should not surprise. Still, this is an important pronouncement when compared to the strong and centralizing tendency of the 1789 Revolution, still present in the original 1958 Constitution.

Lastly, a number of constitutional amendments have been necessary due to the reforms of the European Union institutions. For the first time in 1992, the Conseil constitutionnel decided that the ratification of the Maastricht Treaty required an amendment of the Constitution. Consequently, a new title XV[41] was inserted into the Constitution. The choice was made to authorize specific powers which were contrary to the Constitution rather than a blanket authorization for the European Union, its institutions and its powers. Consequently, further revisions were necessary in 1999, 2003, and 2005 (Treaty of Rome—Constitution of the European Union)[42] so as to allow specific transfer of powers to the European Union. The adoption of these amendments were also accompanied by the adoption of the constitutional provisions aiming to protect the prerogatives of French

---

[40] See art. 1 of the 1958 Constitution.

[41] Originally, the new Title was Title XIV, but the insertion in the Constitution of Title XIII in 1993 forced a renumbering of the title.

[42] The ratification of the constitutional treaty was rejected by 54.67% of the electorate in the referendum of 29 May 2005.

parliamentarians: for instance, in both 1992 and 1999, a procedure to submit and report on all legislative proposals from the European Union institutions was first created and later improved.[43]

V. An Expanding Constitutional Review

The Conseil constitutionnel has travelled a long way since its creation in 1959. Moreover, commentators agree that its present role had not been at all foreseen by the authors of the 1958 Constitution; in fact, the drafters had arguably tried to avoid such an evolution. Originally, the Conseil was meant to protect the Executive against encroachment from the Parliament and more generally, to regulate the working of the political system. It was not meant to put in place a control of constitutionality which would identify and protect constitutional rights and freedoms. The revolution which took place with the decision of 1971 was central to the redefinition by the Conseil constitutionnel of its role. The Conseil was announcing loudly and clearly that it would not content itself with a sterile role of institutional watchdog, but that it would create a control of constitutionality of the same type which is assumed by other constitutional courts. This constitutional evolution might be also regarded as another proof of constitutional maturity: the recognition that the supremacy of the Constitution must be protected judicially.

A. The Membership and the Search for Institutional Legitimacy

However, as the Conseil constitutionnel was never meant to fulfil such a role, the mode of recruitment of the Conseil never matched its present constitutional importance. Title VIII of the 1958 Constitution states that the Conseil constitutionnel is staffed by nine members appointed for one term of nine years and renewable by a third every three years. The President of the Republic, the president of the Assemblée nationale and the president of the Sénat appoint three members each. In addition, former presidents of the republic are automatically members of the Conseil unless they decide otherwise. Consequently, the strong political flavour of the appointments and the political past of many members of the Conseil constitutionnel, indicate that the issue of membership is a real one. Furthermore, there is no requirement that the appointees should have any legal qualifications. It is not surprising therefore that the legitimacy of the institution is challenged at regular intervals and that some of the most controversial

---

[43] Also, in 1999, the treaty creating the International Criminal Court required an amendment of the Constitution. Its ratification was authorized by the insertion of art. 53-2 recognizing the jurisdiction of the International Criminal Court.

appointments have been criticized.[44] Indeed, some commentators think that an in-depth reform of the institution is warranted.[45] A reform might avoid the recurrence of the legitimacy crisis as experienced in 1993 and 2000.[46]

Despite, these problems, one can safely argue that the Conseil constitutionnel benefits paradoxically from a strong output legitimacy. The institution and its existence have never been really threatened.

B. The Block of Constitutional Norms:[47] Redefining the Content of the Constitution

The block of constitutional norms contains the texts and principles which have received constitutional recognition by the Conseil constitutionnel. It was difficult for the Conseil to restrict itself to the sole text of the 1958 Constitution, as the latter did not enshrine any formal declaration or charter of rights. The Preamble of the 1958 Constitution makes a passing reference only to both the Declaration of Rights of 1789 and the Preamble of the 1946 Constitution. Still, this proved to be enough for the Conseil to engineer a quiet revolution with the decision of 16 July 1971. In 1971, Parliament tried to change the legislation regulating associations in France. Freedom of association has been recognized in France ever since the Third Republic. A *loi* of 1901 provides that the only formality resides in an official notification of the new association at the Mairie: the official systematically hands over a receipt in acknowledgment. The State then may control the aims and objectives of any association and if illegal, bans it. In 1969, the *Préfet de Paris*, acting on an order from the Interior Minister, refused to hand over the receipt when the founding member of the association '*Les amis de la cause du peuple*' came to the *Mairie de Paris* to notify it. Unfortunately for the Government of the time, the failure to act was referred to the administrative courts. The Government lost its case at first instance and decided not appeal. Instead, it sought to amend the 1901 legislation to give a power to the administration to control *a priori* the aims and objectives of any association. The Assemblée nationale had adopted the legislation in a final reading, as the Sénat had opposed it three times. The president of the Sénat forwarded the bill to the Conseil constitutionnel for control.

The Conseil was always going to have a difficult task in reviewing the constitutionality of this legislation against freedom of association. Not only did the

---

[44] The appointment of Robert Badinter as president of the Conseil constitutionnel by Mitterrand was rightly criticized. Badinter was minister for justice when he was appointed to the Conseil constitutionnel. It is widely believed that this decision was taken in view of the predicted loss of the socialist party in the impending elections.

[45] D. Rousseau, *Droit du contentieux constitutionnel*, 7th edn. (Paris, 2006), 89.

[46] In 1993, the Government and the Conseil constitutionnel clashed over the regulation of immigration. The Government sponsored a revision of the Constitution to permit the legislative changes it favoured. In 1997, the alleged involvement of the President in the Elf scandal was revealed; however, he only resigned in 2000.

[47] See J. Bell, *French Constitutional Law* (Oxford, 1992), 57–77.

1958 Constitution not recognize any declaration of rights or freedoms,[48] but also the freedom of association is not even mentioned in either the Declaration of 1789 or the Preamble of 1946. Even if the reference to these two texts in the Preamble of the 1958 Constitution might justify their integration to a block of constitutional norms, the recognition of the constitutional character of the principles contained therein would not be sufficient to constitutionalize freedom of association. Consequently, the Conseil had to go a step further and organize the importation of further principles into the block of constitutional norms. In the 1946 Preamble, the *Principes fondamentaux reconnus par les lois de la République*[49] (PFRLR) are reasserted along with the rights and freedoms contained in the 1789 Declaration. This category can be explained by the drafters' wish to insert a reference to the rights and freedoms recognized during the Third Republic, as this period witnessed a great deal of progress in relation to collective and social rights, but never had a single constitutional text.[50] The Conseil constitutionnel therefore counted freedom of association as one of these fundamental principles and struck down the new reform: by instituting prior scrutiny of the legality of any association before any legal personality be granted, the new legislation threatened the very existence of that freedom.

The category of the PFRLR allows the Conseil to determine more freely the principles which come within the block of constitutional norms. In addition, the Conseil resorts to so-called 'rules of constitutional value', 'objectives of constitutional standard' or 'objectives of constitutional necessity'. These are not mentioned in any texts but are deduced from the spirit of the Constitution. The block of constitutional norms is a remarkable and imaginative creation of the Conseil constitutionnel, but arguably does not help with its search for more legitimacy. In one single stroke, not only did the Conseil redesign its constitutional function but it also redefined the content of the 1958 Constitution. Consequently, the Conseil constitutionnel has come as close as possible to a constitutional court and the Constitution has expanded dramatically under its stewardship: it contains the 1958 Constitution, the Preamble of the 1946 Constitution, the Declaration of the rights of man of 1789, and those fundamental principles that the Conseil recognizes. For a principle to be granted this constitutional status, a statute must be adopted during a republican regime and declare a principle of constitutional importance. The decision of 16 July 1971 performed a momentous and double constitutional revolution.

Still, the decision of 1971 has been endorsed by all political actors as it was clearly underwritten by the constitutional amendment of 1974. In 1974, Valéry Giscard d'Estaing, then President of the Republic, sponsored an amendment of

---

[48] It might have been felt that it would require too much negotiation to achieve a consensus. The political circumstances were such that time was pressing.

[49] This expression may be translated by 'the principles recognised by republic legislation'.

[50] For instance, the freedom of peaceful assembly, the freedom of association, trade unions rights, etc. were recognized during this period.

the Constitution which gave the right to 60 *députés* or 60 *sénateurs* to refer a bill to the Conseil constitutionnel. Thus, the nature of the constitutional control was drastically altered, for since, the opposition has had the possibility to refer any new bill to the Conseil. The number of decisions has consequently increased steadily and with it, the Conseil constitutionnel has refined its methods of review and drawn up more precisely its 'charter' of rights and freedoms.

C. The Internal Organization of the Conseil Constitutionnel

The nine members of the Conseil constitutionnel rely on a very small administrative staff indeed. The president of the Conseil appoints a *secrétaire général*. The *secrétaire général* is generally a member of the Conseil d'Etat;[51]. not only does he direct the administrative services, but he also organizes the legal work of the Conseil constitutionnel.[52] Beyond the *secrétaire général*, the Conseil constitutionnel only benefits from a handful of legally qualified personnel: to the three lawyers who staff the legal service can be added a member of the Conseil d'Etat on secondment, a librarian, and a clerk. Many commentators have criticized this paucity of resources. Not only does the Conseil constitutionnel compare badly with its neighbour, the Conseil d'Etat, but also, by and large, with the majority of constitutional courts around the world. Although rooted in history, this organization does not reflect the present pivotal role of the Conseil.

No legal provision organizes the procedure to be followed by the Conseil constitutionnel when deciding on the constitutionality of a bill. It is, however, obliged to respect the strict time-limits imposed by the Constitution:[53] the one-month period can be shortened to eight days if the Government resorts to the emergency procedure because of the importance of the bill.[54] All other procedural choices were left at the discretion of the Conseil constitutionnel. To strengthen its legitimacy further, the Conseil decided that the procedural rules would mirror court processes as closely as possible. From the beginning, the Conseil decided to hand down fully reasoned decisions. Even though, these decisions are now argued in more detail and their text is noticeably longer, the decisions of the Conseil still follow the French tradition of judicial drafting. Furthermore, the lack of procedural codification did not deter the Conseil from developing procedural practices as adversarial as possible.[55]

Once an application is received, the president of the Conseil appoints a reporter (*rapporteur*). When choosing a reporter, the president takes into account

---

[51] However, in 1983, Daniel Mayer appointed a member of the tribunaux judiciaires. This move wished to show a certain independence from the Conseil d'Etat.

[52] He provides the *rapporteur* with all the information regarding the case which he/she needs. He is responsible for organizing meetings with the relevant government departments.

[53] Article 61 § 3 of the Constitution.

[54] These are rather short time-limits given the type of review and the issues at stake.

[55] This requires some adaptations as the Conseil does not really referee between two parties.

the specialization of each member of the Conseil. The reporter is responsible for researching the case and for suggesting a solution. To this effect, he or she will be helped by the *secrétaire général* and will receive a file containing typically: the bill, the original application, the relevant parliamentary debates, the response of the Government, the case law of the Conseil (and other French courts if relevant), a comparative review of the solutions adopted by other constitutional courts, and relevant academic writings. Often a meeting bringing together civil servants representing the relevant Government department, a representative of the secretariat of the Government, a member of the Conseil's legal service and the reporter allows some embryonic adversarial debate to take place (the reporter rehearsing the arguments contained in the application). Furthermore, beyond the informal contacts that individual reporters may establish with the parliamentarians responsible for the application, a hearing was granted, in 2004, to a parliamentary delegation wishing to put their arguments in person to the reporter. Although exceptional, this procedure enhances the adversarial character of the process. Finally, to underline this character further and introduce a degree of transparency, it was decided that the original application and the Government's response[56] would be published systematically alongside the Conseil's decision.

The reporter is further responsible for giving direction to the *secrétaire général* to produce a reasoned opinion and a draft decision. These are debated by the Conseil constitutionnel in secret. The final decision is taken by a simple majority vote.[57] No dissenting opinion is ever revealed (let alone published) and even the breakdown of the votes is a well-guarded secret. Although this principle of secrecy reflects a French procedural tradition, many find difficult to reconcile it with the requirements of transparency.

D. The Case Law of the Conseil Constitutionnel

The case law of the Conseil constitutionnel has grown in importance and has participated in the renewal of constitutional law in France.

1. A dynamic creation of rights and freedoms

For the first time in France, ordinary statutes have to respect specific constitutional rights, freedoms and principles and these are enforced judicially. Moreover, as this list or charter of rights is not pre-determined, the Conseil engages in a permanent creative dynamic. New rights and freedoms are proclaimed every year: for instance, the right to human dignity was only recognized in 1994.[58]

---

[56] While the text of the application was first published in 1983, the Government's response was only included in 1994.

[57] If there is a tie, the president carries the casting vote.

[58] See C. cons. 27 July 1994, Rec. 100.

The Conseil constitutionnel has recognized the main classical rights and freedoms: individual freedom, right to life, right to human dignity, right to the respect of private life, freedom of opinion, freedom of expression, freedom of association, freedom of communication, and the principle of free constitution of political parties. These classical rights and freedoms build a certain picture of participative citizenship. Not only are individual freedoms protected, but people benefit also from a number of rights to establish and play a part in civil society. The Conseil has also recognized alongside many economic and social rights; many of these can be found in the Preamble of the 1946 Constitution: the right to work, the right to strike, the right to trade unions, the right of workers participation, the right to family life, the right to health care, the right to asylum, the freedom of enterprise, and the right to property. Finally, the Conseil has recognized a key role to the principle of equality as early as 1973. It has used this principle extensively in order to model a certain vision of French society. There is, however, little recognition of third generation rights. If the Conseil is comfortable with the recognition of traditional rights and freedoms, it would seem that the Conseil hesitates to innovate and proclaim new rights and freedoms. Only the adoption of the Charter of the environment in 2004 has allowed the Conseil to recognize the environmental principle of sustainable development.

Furthermore, the Conseil reacts to societal changes and alter its definition and understanding of rights and freedoms to respond to new needs. For example, the issue of immigrants and their rights has become a particularly topical issue in recent years. The Conseil constitutionnel has tried to participate positively to the debate: by altering its case law, the Conseil has recognized many rights and freedoms to foreign residents. The Conseil had in the past adopted a rather wide conception of individual freedom: it regrouped freedom of movement, matrimonial freedom, the right to the respect of private life, the right to one's own body, etc. However, during the 1990s, the Conseil moved to a narrow definition of individual freedom which deals mainly with individual security and freedom from arrest. Instead, the Conseil created an overarching constitutional category on the basis of article 2 of the Constitution and included therein the rights previously attached to individual freedom (freedom of movement, right to the respect of private life, matrimonial freedom, the right to one's own body). The Conseil seems to try and create a protective constitutional status for foreign residents as this new group of fundamental rights and freedoms is recognized to all people residing on the territory of the Republic.[59] The concept of citizenship is no longer the only explanatory key to benefit from the protection of rights and freedoms. Similarly, the Conseil has used the principle of equality to promote further the rights of foreign residents in France. In the decision of 22 January 1990, the Conseil judged a legislative provision to be unconstitutional as it reserved an additional solidarity benefit to some foreign residents but not all (only those entitled

---

[59] See C. cons. 16 June 1999, Rec. 75.

to them because of Community law or reciprocal international agreements). The Conseil decided that the exclusion from this benefit of foreigners residing legally on the French territory constituted a breach of the principle of equality. The case law of the Conseil reflects the deep contemporary debate on the subject of foreign residents and their status.

2. A general theory of rights and freedoms?

As shown above the Conseil has created an impressive system of protection of rights and freedoms. Still, a list of these rights and freedoms, however complete it might be, would only reflect imperfectly the lengths to which it has gone to organize its intervention. This framework was not set up randomly: it seems to follow a logical pattern and one is tempted to claim that the Conseil constitution-nel has developed its own theory of rights and freedoms.

Early on, some commentators expressed the idea that the Conseil constitution-nel had adopted a strict hierarchy between the various rights and freedoms which it recognized. It had been argued for instance, that the rights, freedoms and prin-ciples protected in the Declaration of 1789 were superior to those protected in the Preamble of the 1946 Constitution. In reality, this does not reflect the practice of the Conseil constitutionnel and most commentators have now rejected this idea. This does not mean that all rights and freedoms have equal status and import-ance. The diverse origins of the principles making up the block of constitutional norms are responsible for contradictions and incoherence between these rights and freedoms. Often the Conseil needs to resolve these conflicts within the block of constitutional norms. It does so in different ways depending on the legisla-tive context: sometimes it is possible to reconcile some apparently contradictory rights, while in others, the Conseil will clearly state its preference for one freedom over the other. If such superiority is found in one case, it does not establish a strict and permanent hierarchy. The balance is likely to be different in another decision, in another context. In any event, most rights and freedoms encounter some limi-tations at one time or other.

Although the Conseil has not adopted a strict hierarchy of rights and freedoms, it has adopted a complex organization of the various rights around a central nexus of a few fundamental rights and freedoms. At the centre of the web, one finds a few classical rights (individual freedom, freedom of expression, right of prop-erty, etc); but many of these rights are linked to a collective or social facet of the right. For instance, the classical freedom of expression helps establish the main traits for a wider freedom of communication, a freedom which encompasses the modern media and ascertain the controls necessary over them. Similarly, the right to property has been twinned with another economic but collective free-dom: the freedom of enterprise. This allows for a control, albeit light-touch, of the occasional wave of nationalizations or privatizations. It is this web of rights and freedoms that helps the Conseil to introduce nuances and sharpen its control.

3. *The protection of the democratic space, the State and French territory*

The discussion concerning the role of the Conseil constitutionnel should not obscure the fact that the Conseil also has an important role in establishing and protecting the territory where rights and freedoms are exercised.

Many of the rights and freedoms discussed above are essential to democracy and participate to the founding of a democratic and constitutional space. For instance, the Conseil constitutionnnel watches carefully over the freedom of communication as it considers it to be: 'a fundamental freedom all the more precious that its exercise is one of the essential guarantee of the respect of other rights and of national sovereignty.'[60] To ensure that remains a plurality of opinions and ideas in the press and the media, the Conseil accepts limitations to the right of enterprise and the right of property of media owners. The Conseil will judge unconstitutional the legislation which does not have enough guarantees against media concentration.[61] In addition, the Conseil specifies that all Parliament can do to regulate the freedom of communication is to 'make its exercise more effective'; Parliament cannot curtail the freedom for any other reason. For the Conseil constitutionnel, freedom of communication must be protected to ensure that a lively and healthy democratic space exists; only a pluralist organization of the media can allow the diversity of expression and opinions which is so necessary to democracy.

The Conseil plays also an important part in defining the institutional expression of this democratic space. In its case law, the Conseil has come to regard the principle of judicial independence as a component of national sovereignty; and the care that the Conseil deploys in protecting it demonstrates the fundamental importance of this principle for the democratic space. In fact, the Conseil improved greatly the constitutional remit of the principle of judicial independence. The 1958 Constitution only proclaims the independence of private law courts; of administrative law courts nothing is mentioned. The Conseil extended the principle of judicial independence to administrative courts as well.[62]

According to the Conseil constitutionnel, the principle of judicial independence implies that the specialty and jurisdictional competence of each court system is constitutionally protected as well. It is not generally possible to transfer administrative law disputes to the private law courts and vice versa. In fact, the Conseil constitutionnel has come to regard this public-private divide as the combining effect of judicial independence and separation of power. As a consequence, the Conseil constitutionnel has had to decide on the criteria to distinguish private law cases from public law ones and in this regard it has taken a rather

---

[60] See C. cons. 10–11 Oct. 1984, Rec. 73.
[61] See C. cons. 18 Sept. 1986, Rec. 141.
[62] See C. cons. 12 Sept. 1984, Rec. 73.

controversial position. Traditionally, courts have used two criteria concurrently to determine the boundaries of the State: a criterion of public powers and one of public services. The Conseil constitutionnel has chosen to rely exclusively on the criterion of public powers. In doing so, the Conseil has adopted a narrow vision of the State, ruling out control where a public service is exercised in the absence of public powers.

Finally, the Conseil constitutionnel has also had to define another boundary as it aims to protect the integrity of the French territory. From the start, the Conseil constitutionnel was committed to soften the traditional tendency of the French State to centralization. To do so, the Conseil enshrined a constitutional principle of 'free administration of local authorities'; this principle ensured that local authorities were genuinely independent, were administered by elected bodies, and possessed independent powers. In many ways, the Conseil constitutionnel opened the way to the momentous amendment of the Constitution of March 2003. Since then, article 1 of the 1958 Constitution specifies that the organization of the French Republic is decentralized. This pronouncement has altered completely the foundations for local government law in France. Interestingly, it would seem that since the constitutional amendment, the Conseil constitutionnel has had a tendency to remind Parliament of the need to protect the unitary aspect of the French Republic, now that its decentralized nature has been clearly proclaimed. Still, it would be disingenuous to accuse the Conseil of wishing to go against the constitutional reform. The Conseil is simply expressing an understandable caution in view of the new landscape. In fact, the Conseil has always held that it would not accept that under the guise of 'free administration of local authorities', the implementation of a constitutional right or freedom could be delegated to or depend upon decisions by local authorities since these could vary widely across the French territory.[63] After all, the territorial integrity of the democratic space must be guarded effectively.

VI. The Need for Further Reforms

Although the 1958 Constitution has achieved a certain degree of maturity, there are still issues that would need addressing. A rapid investigation will reveal that the present constitution might need to be reformed further.[64]

A. Strengthening the Powers of the French Parliament

The presidential interpretation of the regime has engendered a parallel loss of power for the French Parliament. Originally, the Constitution was drafted in a

---

[63] See C. cons. 18 Jan. 1985, Rec. 36.
[64] This is reflected by the call for the adoption of the Sixth Republic.

way that would allow the Executive to govern even in the absence of a majority in the Assemblée nationale. Consequently, many constitutional provisions conspire to allow the Governments to force a bill through both chambers of Parliament or to escape full parliamentary control of the exercise of its powers. These powers have become superfluous with the phenomenon of political majority in the Assemblée nationale since 1962; in reality, the Government's powers compromise a proper functioning of parliamentary democracy. Consequently, repeated calls have been made to curb the powers of the Executive and alter the institutional balance in favour of the Parliament.

Some reforms have taken place already, particularly with the important reform of 1995: now Parliament sits continuously through the year (except for the summer recess)[65] and controls its agenda one day a month.[66] Still, many commentators recommend that further changes be made: for a start, the means of control of either chamber are limited. The authors of the 1958 Constitution were worried that future parliamentarians might abuse their powers of control and compromise the working of the Government as had happened in the past.[67] This explains why committees of inquiry can only be appointed for a maximum period of six months. This limitation has always made it hard for the Parliament to control the activities of government departments or other public bodies.[68]

Also, the Parliament's legislative role must be better protected. The powers of the Government to force the adoption of a text through Parliament are too numerous; especially, as the Government has been known to use these powers in combination to secure the swift passage of a bill.

B. From Constitutional Council to Constitutional Court?

One could not extrapolate the present role of the Conseil constitutionnel from its humble beginnings. The constitutional revolution of 1971 which was completed by the constitutional amendment of 1974 has helped shape the Conseil constitutionnel into a quasi-constitutional court. However, one cannot help feeling that the present organization and composition of the Conseil is quite inappropriate for an institution which yields such important powers. Furthermore, a lack of completeness pervades: if the parliamentary opposition can always forward a bill to the Conseil constitutionnel, individual citizens have no access to this institution, and both private and administrative courts cannot refer a *loi* to the Conseil when a case before them warrants it. Although,

---

[65] Before there were two parliamentary sessions: one in the Autumn term and one in Spring. Parliament did not sit in the Winter term and could not control government activity during this period.

[66] Consequently it can discuss private member's bills, if it wishes.

[67] During the Fourth Republic, parliamentary committees intervened in the day-to-day administration under the guise of parliamentary control and accountability.

[68] There are six permanent committees but they are concerned mainly with legislation.

François Mitterrand sponsored in 1990 a revision of the constitution which would have allowed the Conseil constitutionnel to check the constitutionality of a *loi* if referred to by either the Cour de Cassation or the Conseil d'Etat, it would not have really settled the question completely. To grant more power to the Conseil constitutionnel in its present format could only increase the legitimacy gap that has been mentioned earlier.

It is important not lose sight of the fact that the present choice of the Conseil constitutionnel reflected a strong historical reluctance in the control of constitutionality.[69] It was not really opened to the authors of the 1958 Constitution to innovate further. Consequently, the present structure of the Conseil should not be regarded as optimal. The legitimacy of the Conseil constitutionnel would be greatly enhanced if changes to its composition, its organization, research and administrative support were considered. In fact, the revision of 1990 might have been seriously detrimental: by increasing the remit and the frequency of the interventions of the Conseil constitutionnel, the amendment might have triggered a serious crisis; without the availability of further administrative support or without the legitimacy of a different appointment process, the Conseil constitutionnel might have started to unravel. The strain and demands that a procedure of reference would have imposed on the Conseil, are unlikely to leave the institution unscathed. Before any change is proposed, a thorough investigation needs to be conducted on its probable impact.

C. The New Constitutional Reform Committee

In 2007, the newly elected President of the Republic, Nicolas Sarkozy, announced his plans to reform the 1958 Constitution. To this effect, he has convened a think tank to advise him on the reforms necessary to modernize the Constitution of the Fifth Republic. The membership of this committee is political, judicial, and academic. Furthermore, there is a cross-section of political representation which should allow for a consensus to be reached if any of the proposals are to be adopted later. This committee has been asked to investigate the relationship between the President of the Republic and the Prime Minister, to propose reforms to increase the powers of the Parliament, to study the opportunity to alter the electoral system for the Assemblée nationale and to make recommendations regarding the future of the presidential powers in the event of exceptional circumstances.[70] Some of the issues go to the heart of the 1958 Constitution and any change might endanger the institutional stability which has been achieved so far. But the remit does identify an agenda of issues needing reconsideration.

The numerous constitutional amendments already made to the 1958 Constitution indicate that French constitutional lawyers, political actors, and

---

[69] This is reflected in the work of E. Lambert, *Le Gouvernement des juges* (Paris, 1921).
[70] See art. 16 of the 1958 Constitution

even the French people, have come to recognize (albeit belatedly) the influence of classical constitutionalism. Nowadays, French constitutional law is clearly able to control political behaviour and practices. Still, if the regulation of the constitutional sphere by the Conseil constitutionnel contributes to this legal revival of the constitutional analysis, it also underlines the clearly 'creative' role of the institution. This makes for an interesting constitutional paradox.

6

Administrative Law

'Whatever the new solutions and changes in the future, French administrative law must not lose its soul: the public service' (Braibant).[1]

The quotation emphasizes that administrative law is first and foremost about enabling the proper functioning of the administration in its principal activity of serving the public, rather than about the control of the administration. The French make this clear in the titles of their texts on what the English would refer to as 'administrative law'. Those concerned with the institutions and principles governing administrative conduct are designated by the label '*droit administratif*' ('administrative law') whilst those about judicial review and governmental liability have the label '*contentieux administratif*' ('administrative litigation'). This chapter is principally about the former, though the latter will feature prominently.

There are five questions which shape this brief treatment of administrative law: what is the public service or a 'public' function, in what way is it different from the private sector, and how does this affect litigation, judicial control of administrative action and governmental liability. Procedure in the administrative courts has already been discussed in Chapter 4.

I. What is the Public Service or a Public Function?

To a common law reader, it may seem strange to begin with the notion of the 'public service' since it has no specific legal connotation in our systems. As part of our political morality, the idea of 'public service' provides an ideal of conduct for civil servants and ministers, as well as their homologues in local government and non-governmental bodies. Even in the recent period of privatization, it has been recognized that private sector principles cannot provide a complete model for the public sector.[2] It is the difference in values which give rise both to different legal principles for controlling administrative action and different institutions, and,

[1] G. Braibant, 'Du simple au complexe, quarante ans de droit administratif (1953–1993)' (1994) 45 EDCE 409 at 420.

[2] The Nolan Committee talks of a 'public service culture' and 'the ethic of public service': *Standards in Public Life* (Cm 2850-I, 1995), para. 10.

once this difference is recognized, then the differences in procedure for handling claims against the administration become all the more explicable.

The idea of 'public utility' as the hallmark of the public sector goes back to Ulpian,[3] for whom there was a major distinction between what is done for the public good and what is done for private advantage. Since the Revolution of 1789, all public servants have clearly been people at the service of the State and thereby at the service of all. The public service was an activity of the State (later extended to local government and public corporations).[4] In brief, 'the public service is a legal structure by which a need of public interest is satisfied'.[5] This analysis has four crucial elements. The two principal elements are the purpose for which an activity is undertaken (the public interest) and the mechanism by which this is undertaken: the use of public power (*la puissance publique*) or contract. The two ancillary elements are the institution which decides it ought to be undertaken (the state or another public body), and those who are involved in providing the service (the civil service (*la fonction publique*) or private persons). In recent times, there has been a shift away from delivering public services through state organs and state employees, but the core features of public service and public power remain significant for European law, as well as French national law.[6]

A. Purposes of Operation

As Ulpian suggests, the public good is the principal reason for state action. That notion both justifies the more extensive powers of public bodies and constrains the actions both of those bodies and their employees. Examples of more extensive powers can be found in powers of public regulation (*pouvoirs de police*) in areas such as public health or public order, as well as in expropriation. The state has power to intervene to protect public health or public order in the public interest, and these are greater than any private individual would have. Thus, it has long been established that local mayors have powers to ensure public order, and these powers were used by analogy to justify the inherent powers of the President of the Republic which he used to require drivers to have a driving licence.[7] At the same time, the public interest constrains both decision-makers and public servants. For example, a mayor cannot use powers for private vengeance and public employees are restricted in their right to strike.

---

[3] Dig. 1.1.1.2: 'The study [of law] has two approaches, public and private. Public law is that which concerns the Roman State; private law is that which concerns individual advantage, for there are certain things useful for the public and certain things useful for private life.'

[4] See Meschariakoff, *Services publics,* 21.

[5] Conclusions Corneille in CE 7 April 1916, *Astruc,* RDP 1916.364.

[6] Case C-188/89 *Foster v British Gas plc* [1990] ECR I-3313.

[7] CE 8 Aug. 1919, *Labonne,* Leb. 373.

B. Public Service Values

The judgment about what the public interest requires rests with public officials and elected representatives. The law intervenes to establish how the decision should be made, and to rectify serious errors of judgment, but it is also concerned with the way in which the public service is delivered. The public interest gives rise to a set of values. These are set out in the *Rolland principles:* continuity, adaptability, and equality, to which neutrality is usually added.[8]

1. Continuity

Continuity in the provision of the service follows from the necessity of the activity in the public interest. If it is indeed in the public interest, the public is entitled to expect that the service will be made available. The French take this principle further than many countries. Under the *Dehaene* decision, since reinforced by the Conseil constitutionnel, the right of public sector workers to strike can be limited in order that continuity of the public service is assured.[9] This usually means that a minimum service must be maintained, even on strike days. But the principle also justifies the duty of the State to pay compensation to a contractor who meets unforeseen circumstances under a government contract which would otherwise make it impossible for him to continue (the doctrine of *imprévision* discussed below). Continuity of the service will also justify the respect of the acquired rights of users, but will not prevent adjustments to the level and price of services or the terms for obtaining them.[10]

2. Adaptability

Adaptability requires that the public authority must be able to change the specification of a service as the needs of the public interest change. In private agreements, sanctity of contract or promises is a dominant value and this means that changes to a construction contract or a service agreement must be made consensually. In public law, the public interest is paramount and its requirements can be imposed on the contractor. Thus, in *Compagnie nouvelle du Gaz de Deville-les-Rouen*,[11] the commune was authorized to change the requirements for street lighting from gas to electricity and, should the company be unable to provide it, then another company could be sought. Of course, the gas-supply contractor would be compensated, but

---

[8] See Meschariakoff, *Services publics*, 133–135.

[9] See J. Bell, *French Constitutional Law* (Oxford, 1992), 160–164; CE Ass. plén. 7 July 1950, *Dehaene*, RDP 1950.691 concl. Gazier.

[10] See Meschariakoff, *Services publics*, 176–177: e.g. students cannot complain if the rules for acquiring degrees are modified in the course of their study.

[11] CE 10 Jan. 1902, S 1903.3.17 note Hauriou; Brown and Bell, 196–197.

the existence of a contract does not prevent the local authority giving effect to the public interest.

3. *Equality of users*

Equality of users is an aspect of the general constitutional principle of equality before the public service.[12] If an activity is done for the good of the whole public, then all relevant categories of the public must have equal access to that service and be equally treated by it. If a commune runs a municipal swimming bath, then all users should be charged the same, and discrimination cannot be allowed on the ground that some people live in the commune and others do not.[13] When the *grande école*, Sciences Politiques, sought to diversify the social mix of its intake by adopting experimentally priority on admission for students from certain *lycées*, its decision was quashed because it did not define sufficiently objective criteria to respect the constitutional requirement of equality of access to education.[14]

4. *Neutrality*

Neutrality reflects the way a liberal state does not seek to impose its ideas of the good life on citizens, rather it facilitates the choice of a diversity of lifestyles. This neutrality principle has particular application in two areas. In the first place, the French state is secular (article 2 of the Constitution of 1958) and so it respects all religious beliefs. It cannot impose unreasonable restrictions on the expression of religious opinions.[15] The second area is in relation to political opinions. Clearly a public authority cannot select those who will be allowed to benefit from its services on the basis of their political opinions. Nor can they use public money or public buildings for partisan political causes, e.g. flying the flag of an independence movement on the local *mairie*.[16]

It is perfectly acceptable for a private individual to discriminate among those with whom he or she deals on grounds of religion or politics, and to offer different deals to one person or another for commercial or personal reasons (except possibly when there is an abuse of rights). But different standards apply to the conduct of a public body.

---

[12] Bell, *French Constitutional Law*, 210–211.

[13] See M. Borgetto and M. Pochard, in RFDA 1993.673 and 689. Cf. *James v Eastleigh BC* [1990] 2 All ER 607.

[14] CAA Paris, 6 Nov. 2003, *Union nationale interuniversitaire*, AJDA 2004, 343.

[15] e.g. CE 2 Nov. 1992, *Kherouaa and others*, AJDA 1992.833; CE 14 Mar. 1994, *Nesinur et Zehranur Yilmaz*, RFDA 1994.630, where a total ban on the wearing of Muslim headscarves in school was held unlawful: see further the *loi* of 15 March 2004 on the wearing of the veil in schools.

[16] CE 27 July 2005, *Commune de Sainte Anne*, AJDA 2006, 196; cf. *Wheeler v Leicester City Council* [1985] AC 1054; *R v Somerset County Council, ex p Fewings* [1995] 3 All ER 20; *R v Coventry City Council, ex p Phoenix Aviation* [1995] 3 All ER 37.

II. How is the Public Sector Different from the Private Sector

A. The State and Public Bodies

The common law does not start with a notion of the state.[17] Instead, the common law (the old French royal law) divides the world between the King or Queen and their subjects. Subjects (be they private individuals or local authorities and public corporations) require *private* Acts of Parliament to provide them with special privileges or powers, they have no fundamental differences in landholding or in contractual powers (except those more recently introduced in national and EC regulations of public works and public procurement). Many public bodies are *corporations* in a similar sense to private companies, such that the rules of *ultra vires* have been developed from common roots.[18] By contrast, it has required special rules to be applied to the Crown to make it amenable to the courts in contract and tort.

The French have a more clear-cut distinction between the state and public bodies on the one hand and private individuals on the other. A public body is an organization set up in the public interest to carry out a public service function (*mission de service public*). It may be an organ of the state or local government or be a public enterprise of an administrative or commercial kind. Public bodies are governed by distinct rules on their powers. They may have inherent powers to protect the public interest. This may entail certain privileges, for example, the privilege to act unilaterally to enforce one's decision (the *privilège du préalable*[19])—once made, an administrative decision has executory force before which the private individual must incline, unless he/she obtains an order from the courts suspending that decision.) The public body's acts will be governed by separate rules on contracts, which ensure that the public interest is served both in making the contract and in its performance, as, for example with the power to alter the terms of a concession so street lighting is by electricity and not gas. Perhaps most strangely for the common lawyer, there is the idea of public property which is distinct from private property. For example, public property is inalienable unless it has first been declassified by the Conseil d'Etat. Private rights of acquisition of land or use of public property are very much constrained. By contrast, there is almost no comparable legislation in the English common law, which uses the trust con-

---

[17] Lord Templeman, *Ross v Lord Advocate* [1986] 3 All ER 79 at 92; C. Graham and T. Prosser, *Privatizing Public Enterprises* (Oxford, 1991), 6: 'it has proved impossible to identify coherently such a legal concept [in Britain]'. Though this is not to deny that we do have highly sophisticated political theories about the state.

[18] Thus one of the leading cases cited in books on administrative law and company law is *A-G v North-Eastern Ry* (1880) 5 App Cas 473, a case about the powers of a private company.

[19] Brown and Bell, 120; G. Darcy, 'La décision exécutoire, esquisse méthodologique' AJDA 1994.663.

cept to ensure that the interests of the public are protected, much as that concept protects the interests of private beneficiaries of a settlement.

The distinctive treatment of public bodies in terms of the law applicable to their actions reflects their function to ensure the public interest is respected. But, of course, there are a variety of bodies which help to achieve such a result. To go back to the case of street lighting, the public interest was defined by the local authority, but the actual lighting was to be provided by a private company as a concessionary. By contrast, a public body may engage in activities which have little to do with the public interest—it may happen to own some land which it leases as office space at a commercial rent. In such a case, the public body is engaged in a purely private activity. The application of distinct rules to public bodies rests on the public interest activity which is undertaken, not on the mere fact that they happen to be *public* bodies.

Of course, the concept of the public sector is subject to similar evolution to other European countries. The public service not only includes the state and local authorities, but includes both public enterprises and quangos (*autorités administratives indépendantes*). Apart from public bodies, there are a number of private companies that operate in the public sphere, delivering public services. Public enterprises may not only be administrative activities running services, but also commercial activities which are not much different from private commerce. Quangos are administrative authorities which are independent of the political process. Thus the Banque de France has been deliberately given a status to control monetary policy which is distinct from the Government.[20] The regulatory functions of other bodies such as the Conseil de la concurrence (Competition Council) and the Conseil supérieur de l'audiovisuel (audiovisual authority) are very much public activities controlled by public law, but they represent a fragmentation of the public sector. The key to whether a body is to be treated distinctly from the private sector remains the extent to which it performs a *mission de service public*.

B. Public Activities

The distinctive feature of action by public bodies is that it can be *unilateral*, i.e. the state can act without consent. Expropriation (euphemistically called 'compulsory purchase' in England) is the classic illustration where the private individual is dispossessed in the public interest (albeit with compensation). The power to rule by order establishes an important relationship of subjection which is inherent in the French terminology of '*l'administration*' and '*l'administré*' (the administered).[21]

---

[20] See M. Lombard, 'Le nouveau statut de la Banque de France' AJDA 1994. 491; J.-P. Duprat, 'The Independence of the Bank of France: Constitutional and European Aspects' [1995] PL 133. More generally on French quangos, see J. Bell, 'Independent Administrative Authorities in France' [1997] 3 EPL 474.

[21] See J. Rivero, 'L'administré face au droit administratif' AJDA, special issue 20 June 1995, 147.

Of course, the administration does succeed in many cases in reaching an agreement with those it wishes to act in a certain way. Some such situations result from genuine agreements and common purposes, but others result from the use of considerable bargaining power. The result is that both the contractual and unilateral power of the state need to be subject to scrutiny.

As the state moves from areas essential to society's own survival (defence, public order, public health) and moves into areas where it makes available opportunities and services for the public, the state is less the commander as the entrepreneur ensuring the provision of basic services. Here the terminology changes, so that the French talk not of '*l'administré*' as of '*l'usager*', the user of a service. In both, a public interest function is performed, but the kind of relationship with the citizen changes. In particular, not only does the state typically not use force on citizens to carry out public services, it can often delegate the delivery of the service (as opposed to its general planning) to a private contractor. The relationship between the user and the public body becomes thus more tenuous.

The area of privatization offers a good example of the different discussion which takes place. Where a public corporation, e.g. a television station, is to be privatized, the French would be inclined to ask 'Is this still going to be a public service when it is privatized?' For the French, it makes sense to say that an activity is a public service, an activity performed in the public interest which is subject to a special legal regime, even if it is operated by private companies. English conceptions of privatization often fail to be clear on this point. For us, either a public body runs something or private individuals do. The idea of the state having a public law role in taking responsibility for defining and overseeing the public service, whilst leaving the private sector to run it has only gradually come into focus through recent policies of 'contracting out' and 'market testing'. Unlike the French, the common law has lacked an abstract idea of 'a public service' as distinct from the concrete mechanisms of its operation.

C. Public Servants

The public interest mission of the administration gives a particular status to those who carry it out. Associated with the public service, the individual official has an expertise to accomplish the missions of that service. Those who collaborate in the performance of the public service are entitled to recognition from the community which benefits from their acts. That status is protected by special regulations.[22] The 2006 Dalloz *Code de la fonction publique* collects together 1,669 pages of special rules on public servants. There is special recruitment (to ensure all have access by virtue of their abilities), special conditions of service (to ensure

---

[22] Public employment is covered more fully below in Chapter 12 and the relevance of the distinction between public and private law in that context is discussed there at length: see esp. pp. 484–488.

the public interest continues), special rules on promotion and progression (typic-ally to avoid political favouritism), special disciplinary procedures (which often provide effectively for security of tenure), and special routes for complaint (espe-cially to the administrative courts). The range of issues which can be litigated is far broader in civil service matters than in private employment. For example, the award of particular allowances, the promotions list for the year,[23] and so on can be the subject of public law litigation. Public servants cover a vast range of employments.

By contrast, the area of civil servants provides one of the best examples of how the various key features of the public service are actually recognized by non-law in the United Kingdom. There is no statute on the civil service, though there is an Order in Council governing the civil service in general. The Civil Service Code of 2006 is merely a short code of ethics covering two pages, issued by the Government and the Civil Service Commissioners, which is not a set of legal rules. As a result, there has been serious uncertainty until recent years whether being a civil servant was a status (an office under the Crown) or a contract. Ironically, the choice of the latter status is mainly due to the privatization of many aspects of civil service work.[24] Courts have argued that there may be no contract, that civil servants may be dismissed at pleasure and that they may not sue for their wages. These legal ideas bear little relationship to reality. As in France, the civil service has traditionally been a safe employment with strong protections. The difference is that this has arisen as a matter of non-law—there are a series of well-established rules and practices which operate outside the normal realms of law and the courts. Civil service discipline rarely reaches the courts (and is even more rarely successful)—it is governed by internal organs, such as the Civil Service Appeal Board. Similarly issues of pay and conditions rarely enter the courts. This idea of non-law applies equally to government contracting, where, until very recently (and only as a result of EC legislation) the procedures of public works and pro-curement have received a legislative framework. It is the idea of the public service as a non-legal, political value which really dominates many of the structures (or absence of structures) in English administrative law. By contrast the French have well-defined legal principles which operate in this area.

By having the concept of public service, the French have been able to articu-late more clearly the key features which are distinctive in public law. This can be illustrated by the notion of privatization. For the French, the English use of the term 'privatization' covers two distinct phenomena. On the one hand, the Government may wish to continue to run an activity in the public interest, but decide that the operation of that activity should be handed over to the private sec-tor, e.g. in the case of railways. On the other hand, the Government may decide

---

[23] See CE Sect. 29 July 1994, AJDA 1994.738.

[24] See M. Freedland, 'Contracting the employment of civil servants—a transparent exercise?' [1995] PL 224. '[T]he unique feature of the legal framework governing the civil service is the pau-city of statutory regulation': S. Fredman & G. Morris, *The State as Employer* (London, 1989), 23.

that an activity is no longer required in the public interest, but should be run, if at all, as a private business, e.g. in the case of the manufacture of cars. The French draw a clear distinction between the two. The former is still part of the public service and remains governed by principles of public law, especially the right of the Government to change the specification of the service to be provided. By contrast, the second is clear privatization and the principles governing the activity move from public law to private law. This distinction has a number of implications. For instance, the privatization of France Télécom involved turning a public enterprise into a private company which became the concessionary for running the public service of telecommunications. The civil servants previously responsible for the service were to work for the new private sector company. How far can the civil servants retain their status if they are under private sector management? The civil service legislation of 1958 only permitted assignment of civil servants to work under a minister or 'a subordinate authority', and, should a post be abolished, they would retain their status as civil servants. The Conseil d'Etat was of the view that for the company to be considered a 'subordinate authority' in public law terms, its chairman had to be nominated by the minister and not according to normal company law principles by the shareholders.[25] The integration of the people into the public service required an organic and not merely a functional link. By contrast, if the Government had ceased to operate telecommunications as a public service altogether (as it did with television), then the employees of the private company would have lost their civil service status altogether, since they were no longer engaged in the performance of a public service.

This attachment to the public service justifies the special treatment of civil servants compared with private law employees. In order to deal with this, they are given special procedures for appointment, promotion, and discipline. For example, the Conseil d'Etat has held that the regulations governing the paid holidays of railway workers could legitimately be different from those laid down by the *Code du travail*, for example in requiring that holidays of individuals fit in with the needs of the service.[26] The regulations in that case were typical in providing both increased benefits and detriments for public employees compared with their private sector equivalents.

III. Public Law and Private Law in Litigation

The distinctiveness of public order and public service as aspects of the public interest justify distinctive regulation in terms of rules and principles of law. The

---

[25] See further J. Bell, 'Current Developments' (1995) 1 EPL 16 at 19–20, and more generally, L. Richer, 'Le statut des agents de France Télécom' AJDA 1994.463. Shares in France Télécom were made available to the private sector by reforms in 1996.

[26] CE Ass. plén. 7 July 1995, *Damiens*, AJDA 1995.757.

French go further and adopt the view that the resolution of disputes in those areas ought to be given to distinctive courts and procedures. Public law issues are to be judged by the public law courts. There are two features involved here. There is the general idea found in other legal systems, such as Germany, that specialist rules require specialist judges, a view which is shared only to a limited extent in England by establishing the Administrative Court and reforming the tribunal system. But for the French, there is an additional feature. As has been seen in Chapter 3, the judges of the administrative courts are distinct by their recruitment and training from the civil and criminal judges, and this involves some placement in the administration. In addition, during their career, it is common that an administrative judge has spent some years in the 'active' administration, as the French term it. In this way, the administrative judge has a distinctive formation in administration and personal experience of how it works. Though this is less true today, this feature justifies the special place of administrative judges. As President Odent stated:

the interpenetration of administrative and judicial functions is fortunate: if administrative judges were isolated from the active administration, if they ceased to be in constant contact with the needs and constraints of administrative life, they would lose their specific character. Instead of building a law adapted to the necessities of the public service, they would be inspired by a fossilised law bearing no relationship to the realities of the active administration. Administrative judges must have an administrative training and they have to sustain it to retain an understanding of administrative life.[27]

The specialist character of the law and the distinctiveness of administrative judges provide modern justifications for a distinction between public law and private law courts which was originally based on an idea of sovereign immunity—the King could not be judged in his own courts and so ministers made decisions on *ex gratia* responses to requests for redress of wrongs.[28]

The distinction between the competence of administrative courts and that of civil courts has some limited constitutional status. The Conseil constitutionnel held in its *Competition Law* decision of 1987 that essential rights of due process required that issues of the legality of administrative actions should be handled by courts empowered to suspend their application. There was a fundamental principle recognized by the laws of the Republic that the quashing or reviewing of administrative decisions was a matter for the administrative courts. Since the ordinary courts could not have that power to suspend administrative decisions, they should not have exclusive jurisdiction over the decisions of the competition council.[29] But this does not cover the full scope of the jurisdiction claimed by the administrative

---

[27] R. Odent, *Contentieux administratif* (Paris, 1981), 746–747.

[28] On the ideas of sovereign immunity and the minister-judge, see Brown and Bell, 47–48 and cf. England before the Crown Proceedings Act 1947.

[29] C. cons. 23 Jan. 1987, GD 43; Bell, *French Constitutional Law*, 194. The requirement that the ordinary courts should not seek to review administrative decisions was already laid down by the edict of St. Germain-en-Laye of February 1641 which prohibited the Parlements from being

courts today, and indeed the Conseil did admit the value of grouping certain similar issues before a single court, provided adequate safeguards could be provided to the litigants. The rules of competence developed since 1873 are essentially that an issue concerning the legality of a decision of a public body go to the administrative courts, as do challenges to the substance of public service decisions where an appeal on the merits lies. Actions concerning the contractual or non-contractual liability of a public body are governed by special rules and also belong in the administrative courts. In addition, citizens may raise the illegality of an administrative decision by way of defence in a criminal action before the criminal courts.[30]

Obviously, there are difficult borderline cases. In the first place, it may be necessary to differentiate between the public and private law aspects of a public body's activity. For example, where a postman attacks the recipient of a registered parcel, is this a private law case against the individual postman concerned, or a public law case concerning the defective postal service? Where a public authority runs a summer play scheme for which parents pay, is this a public service or a private law contractual activity?

In addition, there may be problems in working out whether a body is engaged in a public law activity. An illustration is the regulation of sport. From the point of view of the sportsman or club, the body in charge of the sport has unilateral power—it makes rules which they have to obey even without their consent. On the other hand, the body may well be a private law organization. The French solution is to suggest that a body which regulates a national championship is performing a public activity and is thus governed by public law. The formal reason for this is that the minister approves the bodies which regulate national championships.[31]

The key feature is the relationship to the public service. A person may be linked to the public service either as a collaborator, a provider, or as a user. The collaborator is a person who assists as part of the public body's performance of its mission to deliver a public service. Many such individuals are employees, but some may be volunteers. For example, a local commune may put on a festival and run some events, drawing on the volunteer help of non-employees. In terms of injuries caused to such collaborators, the law makes no distinction—they are all entitled to the special protection of public law. Where the activity is delivered by a private law concessionary, then the relationship between that person and the public authority is governed by public law, since the purpose of their relationship is to deliver the public service. But the situation of the user may be different. Where

concerned with litigation 'concerning the State, administration or government which we reserve to ourselves alone and to our successor kings'.

[30] Cf. *DPP v Hutchinson* [1990] 2 AC 783.

[31] See art. L 131-8, *Code du Sport*. Compare cases on the control of sport in France, e.g. CE Sect. 25 June 2001, *Toulouse*, RFDA 2003, 47 and CE Sect. 5 May 1995, *Burruchaga*, AJDA 1995.753 with the English cases of *R v Disciplinary Committee of the Jockey Club, ex parte Aga Khan* [1993] 1 WLR 909 and *R v Football Association Ltd, ex parte Football League* [1993] 2 All ER 833.

the service is provided under concession, then the relationship with the concessionary is essentially private—the delivery of a bus journey or train ride is much the same whether a public body or a private body delivers it. But if the complaint is about the organization of the public service, then the issue properly concerns the public service functions of a public body, and is public.

The complexity of this analysis leads to numerous cases each year which are handled by a conflicts court, the Tribunal des Conflits. For example, where Gaz de France caused poisoning by fumes, the client had to sue in private law (because he had a contract with the company), but the neighbour had to sue in public law, for harm caused by a public work.[32]

IV. Control Over Administrative Action

The notion of *l'État de droit* is central to the contemporary French constitution.[33] Under this notion, the state must obtain authority for what it does from the law and is subject to the limits imposed by it.

In broad terms, the administration has two sources of authority for action: certain rather limited inherent powers and specific legislative authorization. The role of the administrative courts is to ensure that the administration stays within its competence.

A. Areas Excluded from Judicial Review

Despite this principle, there are certain decisions which the courts cannot review. Traditionally, judicial control is not exercised over certain administrative decisions which because of their importance or relative triviality are not appropriate to judicial intervention. *Actes de gouvernement* (acts of state) illustrate the politically important and sensitive decisions which are not suitable to judicial involvement. *Mesures d'ordre interne* (internal regulation) are a level of operational decision which is not appropriate to involve the courts with. Given that the right to bring complaints before an administrative judge represents an established value of French administrative law and now European law,[34] the tendency in recent years has been to diminish the number of situations which are excluded from judicial control.

1. Actes de gouvernement

Actes de gouvernement cover major politically sensitive decisions of high policy which it is not appropriate for the courts to review. Thus, the administrative

---

[32] TC 1 July 2002, *Labrousse c Gaz de France*, AJDA 2002.689.
[33] See J. Rivero, 'Etat de droit, Etat du droit' in *Mélanges Braibant* (Paris, 1996), 609.
[34] CE 17 Feb. 1950, *Lamotte*, RDP 1951.478 concl. Delvolvé; Case 188/89 *Johnstone v Chief Constable of Northern Ireland* [1990] 3 All ER 897.

courts will not review the President's decision to dissolve Parliament or to award honours or grant an amnesty.[35] Such decisions are not only discretionary and based on political reasons, but are also of high governmental responsibility. Since the decision in *Prince Napoléon* in 1875,[36] the political reason for a decision has not been in itself a sufficient ground for excluding review by the courts, it requires a high degree of sensitivity in matters in which the courts are not competent to form a judgment, e.g. national security and international relations. In international affairs, then equally the central question is not the political reasons for the decision alone, but the purpose and importance of the decision. For example, the Conseil d'Etat refused to entertain an action by Greenpeace against the decision by the President to launch a series of nuclear tests.[37] A similar decision was reached when a challenge was made to the suspension of financial aid to Iraq.[38] All the same, the courts will review some decisions connected with international affairs. They draw the distinction between aspects of the decision with an international relations effect, such as the defence policy importance of nuclear tests, and the domestic aspects. In relation to the latter, then there is scope for challenging the decisions taken by the administration which are severable (*actes détachables*) from the conduct of foreign policy. In addition, the scope of *acte de gouvernement* has been considerably reduced. Today, the granting of passports or military activities unconnected with warlike operations are subject to review.[39] Likewise, the Conseil d'Etat will examine whether a treaty has been ratified in accordance with the requirements of the Constitution.[40]

2. Mesures d'ordre interne

Mesures d'ordre interne are the internal affairs of an administrative organization which should not be the subject of judicial intervention, but rather be left to internal hierarchical procedures. This was traditionally understood in a very broad sense to cover most operational decisions within an administrative organization.[41] Gradually, the Conseil d'Etat has reduced the scope of this concept. In *Marie* and *Hardoun*,[42] the Conseil d'Etat decided that the area of internal measures not susceptible of judicial review should be reduced. Thus in *Marie*, it decided that a disciplinary penalty of confinement to a cell for eight days imposed by a prison governor was susceptible to judicial review and it was quashed on the ground that the facts did not justify the penalty imposed. In *Hardoun*, the

---

[35] CE 20 Feb. 1989, *Allain*, RFDA 1989.568; CE 10 Dec. 1986, *Loredon*, AJDA 1987.133; CE 31 Jan. 1986, *L*, AJDA 1986.396.

[36] CE 19 Feb. 1875, Leb. 155 concl. David.

[37] CE Ass. plén. 29 Sept. 1995, *Greenpeace*, AJDA 1995.749.

[38] CE 23 Sept. 1992, *GISTI-MRAP*, AJDA 1992.752.

[39] See TC 9 June 1986, *Eucat*, AJDA 1986.456.

[40] CE Ass plén. 5 March 2003, *Aggoun*, AJDA 2003.726.

[41] CE 20 Oct. 1954, *Chapou*, Leb. 541 on school uniform rules. On similar facts, *Spiers v Warrington Corporation* [1954] 1 QB 61.

[42] CE Ass. plén. 17 Feb. 1995, AJDA 1995.420 and 421.

Conseil d'Etat took a similar approach to military discipline, but did not find any illegality in the refusal by the Ministry of Defence to overturn a sailor's punishment for drunkenness. The result of these decisions is that very few disciplinary decisions of any consequence will escape control by the courts, because they will usually affect the rights of individuals. On the other hand, ordinary operational decisions in the exercise of a discretion which the administration enjoys will not be subject to review, e.g. the decision to alter the frequency of services, unless there is a breach of a legal requirement.

B. Grounds of Review

There are two elements in judicial control over administrative action: insistence that there be legal authority for taking a decision in the first place, described as 'external legality', and review of the decision taken to ensure that the decision-maker has not exceeded the powers accorded, described as control over the 'internal legality' of the decision. The external legality covers not only authority to make a decision, but also the formalities as to how a decision is taken before the decision can be validly made. But even if the decision appear to be validly made in this formal sense, it may be defective in that its content exceeds the powers of the decision-maker, e.g. because a sanction is in some sense disproportionate to the wrong committed. The French usually distinguish these two categories as external and internal legality: external in the sense that you know it is invalid without having to look at its content, internal because you have examined its content.

In terms of external legality, the basic grounds on which a decision might lack any legal basis are that the decision-maker had no authority (*incompétence*) or that he or she failed to comply with some procedural requirement in the making of the decision (*vice de forme*).

1. Incompétence

There must be a legal basis (*base légale*) for the action of any public authority. A clear example of a decision quashed for lack of competence was where a local authority financed a leaflet calling for a 'no' vote in the national referendum on whether France should ratify the Treaty of Maastricht.[43] Local authorities have no responsibility for the conduct of the external affairs of the nation.

Even if there is authority to act, it is obvious that only a properly authorized person can make a valid decision. To take a simple example, the Constitution requires that the Prime Minister signs certain decrees. If he is abroad, then he must delegate authority to sign to someone else, usually another minister. If a person who has not been duly authorized, e.g. his secretary, then the decree will be treated as never validly made. Since powers are often assigned to busy people who head large offices,

---

[43] CE 25 April 1994, *Président du conseil général du Territoire-de-Belfort*, AJDA 1994.545.

it is unrealistic to expect them to make each decision personally. Delegation of signature (as the French term it) is commonplace, but one has to be clear when this is valid and when this is not. The usual principle is that the person to whom the power was given must remain responsible for the decision reached.

More common is a mistake about the division of functions between different bodies. For instance, several administrative bodies may have planning powers—the Government for the general framework, the Region and the Department for their plans, and then the commune for it own local plan. In an individual case for planning permission, the question may arise how far it is permissible for a decision to be taken at local level. For example, for the proposal to build a barrage involving the territory of two departments, a joint commission was convened which gave a negative opinion on the public interest in its construction. Because the competence to make a final decision after the opinion of a joint commission lay with the Conseil d'Etat, the prefects of the two departments were held to have acted without authority in purporting to approve the project and the expropriation of land involved.[44] In English law terms, there was a basic lack of jurisdiction here to make the decision.

2. Vice de forme

Administrative decisions are only valid if they are made according to the right procedure. This enables the proper influences to be brought to bear on the decision-makers and the requisite information to be gathered. Most procedural requirements are set out in the authorizing legislation. Thus, in planning cases, there are set procedures which must be followed. But there are also certain general principles of procedure which apply to all administrative decisions. These principles cluster around the ideas of rights to a hearing (*droits de la défense*) and lack of bias.

The *droits de la défense* are more extensive than the common law 'right to a hearing' in that they cover both the procedures to be followed before coming to a decision and the communication of the decision itself. It thus covers (i) the duty to listen to the affected party, (ii) the duty to give reasons, and (iii) the duty to explain the citizen's rights in relation to the decision. The French courts give effect to the European Court of Human Rights' idea of 'equality of arms', though they recognize that such a principle has to apply differently to a citizen's dealings before the administration compared with before a court.[45]

(i) Duty to listen
As has been noted, the executory nature of administrative decisions is justified in the public interest. This means that, once validly made, the decision can be

---

[44]　CE Sect. 20 Mar. 1992, *Commune de Miat*, AJDA 1992.454.
[45]　See Avis of CE Sect. 31 Mar. 1995, *Ministre du Budget c. SARL Auto-Industrie Meric*, AJDA 1995.739.

implemented by the administration unless the citizen obtains a court order to suspend it. The involvement of the citizen in the decision-making process is thus the main safeguard of the citizen's rights. In emergency cases, such as major civil disorder, the administration may have to act before the affected parties can be consulted, but such situations are rare.[46] The normal principle is that the administration must give the affected person notice in advance of the case he or she has to meet and an opportunity to put his or her case. This was established in *Trompier-Gravier*[47] where the prefect revoked Mme Trompier-Gravier's concession to sell newspapers from a street kiosk in Paris as a result of complaints which he had received that she had been engaged in extortion of money from the manager of the kiosk. Although the prefect had a discretionary power to award and withdraw such concessions, his decision was invalid because he had not given her an opportunity to refute the allegations before the concession was withdrawn. This principle applies not only to disciplinary cases, but also to other administrative decisions. For example, in *Société des Etablissements Cruse*,[48] a wine producer challenged successfully a decision of the agriculture minister to downgrade the quality of his wine on the basis that no opportunity to contest the findings of the advisory committee or the experts had been granted. On the whole, this principle applies only to decisions affecting individuals. Where a decision affects a substantial group of people, then the procedures that must be followed are only those laid down in the empowering legislation.

In relation to the conduct of the hearing, the kind of opportunity afforded must be appropriate, but there are no specific general requirements as to its form. In some cases, it may be appropriate to allow representation of the person affected, e.g. in a disciplinary case.[49]

(ii) Duty to give reasons

French administrative case law, like English case law, did not require that the administration give reasons for its decisions, though specific texts, e.g. in planning law, often did. But the *loi* of 11 July 1979 provides that reasons must be given for a range of administrative decisions including individual administrative decisions restraining public liberties, imposing a penalty, imposing conditions on an authorization, withdrawing rights, or refusing benefits where someone has fulfilled the legal conditions for them.[50] This increase in transparency of administrative decisions is enhanced by a general right of access to administrative documents concerning the decisions made in relation to an

---

[46] See CE 24 July 1987, AJDA 1988.63 (New Caledonia).
[47] CE 5 May 1944, D 1945.110 concl. Chenot.
[48] CE 9 May 1980, AJDA 1980.482 concl. Genevois.
[49] CE 17 June 1988, AJDA 1989.50.
[50] This statutory duty to give reasons does not apply to all administrative bodies, only to ones for which central government is responsible: see the decision of the ECJ in Case 222/86 *UNCTEP v Heylens* [1989] 1 CMLR 401 which criticized a sporting body for failure to give reasons.

individual as well as to many general administrative documents and circulars under the *loi* of 17 July 1978.

(iii) Duties of explanation

In more recent times, French case law has been concerned to ensure the effectiveness of rights, and it has imposed on the administration a duty to explain the time-limits within which a person can appeal or lodge a request for judicial review or else it cannot use those limits as a bar to a late appeal or request.[51]

Questions concerning the internal legality of a decision relate to the justifications for a decision. Although a decision has been taken by a proper person in a proper manner, it may be unlawful because it is taken for the wrong reasons or for inadequate reasons. Such a decision may arise either because of a misinterpretation of the administrator's powers or of the facts. Where the administration has no discretion, but it merely has to be satisfied that certain specific conditions have been met, the courts will be quick to intervene, for the administration is bound to follow the requirements of the law. (The administration is described as having a *compétence liée*.) By contrast, where the administration has a discretionary power (*pouvoir discrétionnaire*), then the courts will be more reluctant to interfere with the decision-making authority of the administration. Most of the discussion here will relate to discretionary powers.

3. Détournement de pouvoir

The most flagrant case of an unlawful decision is one which is made deliberately not to benefit the public but to serve the private ends of the decision-maker. The category of *détournement de pouvoir* is reserved for such deliberately wrongful decisions either to reach the result or to use a procedure typically for the personal ends of the decision-maker. Thus in *Rault*,[52] the Conseil d'Etat struck down regulations concerning dancing made by a mayor not in the interests of public order, but merely to encourage people to use his inn. But a *détournement de pouvoir* may also occur where power is used improperly to serve the interests of the public authority itself. For example, in *Beaugé*,[53] the mayor passed regulations controlling undressing on the beach not in the interests of public decency, but to ensure bathers made use of the municipal bathing cabins. More recently, close to the date for local elections, a local authority voted to introduce a flat rate social welfare payment for low income households not for the purpose of giving individual assistance (as the statute required) but to offset a nationally determined increase in the residence tax.[54] This was an abuse of power for electoral advantage. Deliberate misuse of power of these kinds is rare and the ground of *détournement de pouvoir* is rarely invoked.

[51] CE 8 June 1994, *Moumini*, AJDA 1994.729.
[52] CE 14 Mar. 1934, Leb. 337.
[53] CE 4 July 1924, Leb. 641
[54] CE 23 Mar. 1988, *Ville de Puteaux*, RFDA 1988.729.

4. Violation de la loi

It is more common that a decision is invalid because of some misapplication of the law which is not deliberate, but arises from a mistake or from misplaced enthusiasm. In some cases, there will be a breach of rights or of some fundamental principles of law. More commonly, there will be simply a misapplication of the law. Such misapplication has three facets of this ground of review which approximate closely to facets of the ground of illegality in English law: misinterpretation of a legal power, error of fact, and erroneous classification of fact.

(a) Misinterpretation (*erreur de droit*)

In any legal system under the rule of law, an authority must construe its powers correctly and a mistake of law will lead to a decision being quashed. For instance, in *Association 'Les Amis de St. Augustin'* a prefect mistakenly thought that he had a discretionary power to refuse recognition to a charitable association, when, in law, the association has a right to be registered once it has completed the formalities for a declaration of public utility. The refusal to register the association was therefore quashed.[55]

(b) Mistake of fact (*faits matériellement inexacts*)

A decision must be sufficiently justified by the facts. At a minimum, this requires that the facts are true. Thus, in *Tissot*, a decision to dispense with the services of a senior civil servant at his own request was quashed when it turned out that he had made no such request.[56] Similarly, the application by Shaukat, a Pakistani, for naturalization was declared inadmissible on the ground that he did not reside in France. In order to be resident, it was necessary to show that his 'centre of interests' was in France. The decision alleged that this was not the case since Shaukat's family lived in Pakistan. In fact, by the time of the application, his wife and one of their children were living with him in France.[57]

(c) Classification of facts (*qualification juridique des faits*)

Rather than the facts being wrong, it is often a mistake in interpreting the facts which causes a problem. A classical example is *Gomel*,[58] in which a statute empowered a prohibition on building in order to protect an existing view of architectural value (*une perspective monumentale*). The prefect refused planning permission for a development in Place Beaveau in Paris on the ground that such a view would be interfered with. But the Conseil d'Etat quashed the decision on the ground that there was no such view of architectural value involved. The courts did review the facts and come to a different assessment of the facts on which the power to make

---

55 CE 25 Jan. 1985, Leb. 18.
56 CE 14 Dec. 1934, *Tissot*, Leb. 1185.
57 CE 26 Feb. 1988, *Shaukat* [1988] PL 638.
58 CE 4 April 1914, S 1917.3.25 note Hauriou.

a decision was based. There was no doubt about the facts, merely about the evaluation of those facts.

The administrative courts will be willing to interfere with the evaluation made by the administration in some areas more than others. The closer the evaluation is to policy, the less willing the courts are to interfere. As a result, the administrative courts have adopted a sliding scale of review over the discretion exercised by the administration.[59]

(d) Maximum control

Maximum control is exercised over decisions which affect civil liberties or other rights of the individual. In this approach, the court will ascertain both the correctness of the facts and the appropriateness of the evaluation made by the administration. For example, in *Benjamin*,[60] a notorious right-wing speaker was prohibited from addressing a public meeting organized by a literary society on a literary theme on the ground that various left-wing groups had threatened public disorder if he spoke. The Conseil d'Etat held that the grounds were insufficient to justify the decision, since it had not been shown that serious public disorder would follow and that banning the meeting was the only way to deal with the threat. This degree of review comes close to permitting the courts to challenge the merits of an administrative decision.

(e) Normal control

Normal control involves the courts ensuring that the facts are sufficient to justify the decision and that the legal powers had been interpreted. *Gomel* illustrates this degree of control quite well. There, the facts were insufficient to justify the refusal of planning permission. The administration is permitted a degree of latitude in that, as long as the facts are capable of coming within the classification, the courts will not interfere. In addition, at the very least, it must be obvious what are the reasons for the decision, and if these are so exiguous as not to permit the court to understand the basis on which a decision was taken, then the decision may be quashed.[61]

(f) Minimum control

Minimum control is exercised over decisions which contain a significant element of policy judgment or technical evaluation or form part of the internal discipline of the public service. The courts defer here to the expertise or authority of the administration and only interfere where the administration has manifestly

---

[59] See J. Bell, 'The Expansion of Judicial Review of Discretionary Powers in France' [1986] PL 99 at 104–106.

[60] CE 19 May 1933, S 1933.3.1. See also CE 17 April 1985, *Société les Éditions des Archers*, RDP 1985.1393 concl. Stirn where a similar control was exercised over the banning of a book on grounds of public policy.

[61] CE Sect. 26 Jan. 1968, *Maison Genestal*, D 1969.456 note Fromont.

exceeded its powers. Two grounds of review are usually invoked in such cases. The first is a manifest error in evaluation (*erreur manifeste d'appréciation*) whereby the court will only interfere where the assessment of the facts as falling within a legal category is manifestly erroneous. For example, in the *Pamplonne* decision,[62] planning legislation required the prefect to consider the extent to which a new building would affect public health or safety, neighbouring buildings, the countryside, or vistas of a monumental character. On the facts, the decision by a prefect to grant planning permission for the building of hotels was declared to be a manifest error in evaluation on the ground that they were very close to a beach and out of keeping with surrounding buildings. The prefect had clearly not assessed the facts in the light of the criteria set out in the planning legislation.

The other ground invoked in this area is proportionality. The courts will interfere where the decision reached is disproportionate to the facts as found. This ground is invoked particularly in the areas of disciplinary decisions and the expropriation of property. The administration is left a wide discretion, and the courts will only interfere where there is a serious disproportion in the penalty imposed or a serious divergence between the benefits to the public and the harm to individuals. A good illustration is *Vinolay*[63] in which the director of a local agricultural committee was dismissed for delay in replying to an inquiry from the Ministry of Finance. While accepting this amounted to a professional fault, the Conseil d'Etat considered that dismissal from office was a manifestly disproportionate penalty. The principle of proportionality (*le bilan 'coûts-avantages'*) was established by the Conseil d'Etat in its *Ville Nouvelle Est*[64] decision, which concerned the expropriation of a substantial area of land (including some newly constructed houses) for the construction of a university campus in Lille. In that case, no excessive disproportion was found between the benefits to the public from the construction of the university campus and the detriment caused to the property owners affected. But the principle has been applied to strike down administrative decisions. For example, in *Société civile Sainte-Marie de l'Assomption*,[65] the Conseil d'Etat struck down a plan to route a motorway slip road in such a way that a psychiatric hospital would have to be demolished in part and its site be restricted in ways which made it virtually unusable. While such a balance of advantages and disadvantages may appear to be an interference with the administration's assessment of the merits of a decision, the administrative judges are careful to suggest that it is not. Braibant argued in his *conclusions* in *Ville Nouvelle Est* that:

There is no question that you are exercising discretions which belong to the administration; questions such as whether the new airport for Paris should be built to the north or

---

[62] CE Ass.plén. 19 Mar. 1968, *Soc. du Lotissement de la Plage de Pamplonne*, AJDA 1968.341.

[63] CE 26 July 1978, Leb. 315.

[64] CE 28 May 1971, AJDA 1971.420 concl. Braibant.

[65] CE 20 Oct. 1972, RDP 1973.843 concl. Morisot; see also CE Ass. plén. 19 April 1991, *Belgacem*, RFDA 1991.497.

the south...It is only above and beyond a certain threshold, in cases where a social or financial cost is abnormally high and has not been justified, that you should intervene. What matters is that you should be able to review decisions which are arbitrary, unreasonable, or ill-considered, and that you should compel local authorities to give first of all citizens, and thereafter the courts, should the need arise, serious and plausible justifications for their projects.[66]

Proportionality is an idea that France has imported from other European countries. European Union law has led to the importing also of the precautionary principle.[67] But the French have consistently rejected the European concept of legitimate expectation and have preferred the idea of legal certainty, which is narrower.[68]

V. Administrative Liability

A. Non-contractual Liability

French administrative law starts from the premise that public authorities should not necessarily be liable for their actions on the same basis as private individuals. This was laid down as a principle in the *Blanco* decision of 1873. In that case, a young girl, Agnès Blanco was injured by a cart belonging to a state-owned tobacco factory in Bordeaux. The Tribunal des Conflits established three principles: the state was responsible vicariously for the acts of its employees, but this liability should be governed by rules which were separate and distinct from those applying to private individuals under the *Code civil*, and the jurisdiction over litigation concerning such liability lay with the administrative and not the civil courts. The principles of liability are thus to be found in distinct sources, the case law established by the administrative courts and not in the *Code civil*, but that is not to suggest that there are not many similarities between the two.[69]

The basic principles of administrative liability can be traced to the Declaration of the Rights of Man and of the Citizen of 1789. Article 4 declares that individuals are free to do what they wish, as long as they do not cause harm to others. By implication, they are liable to their victim if they do cause such harm. Article 13 sets out the principle of 'equality before public burdens', that one individual should not have to shoulder a disproportionate burden in relation to an activity done for the public good. These two principles justify a public authority being

---

[66] AJDA 1971 at 467.

[67] CE 9 Oct. 2002, *Union de l'apiculture française*, AJDA 2002.1181 and M. Franc, 'Traitement juridique du risque et principe de précaution' AJDA 2003.360.

[68] See CE Ass. plén. 24 March 2006, *KPMG*, AJDA 2006.684.

[69] In certain areas, such as motor-vehicle accidents and teachers in state schools, jurisdiction has been given to the civil courts: see *lois* of 31 December 1957 and 5 April 1957.

liable not only for the consequences of its fault, but also for the excessive burdens or risks which its actions or policies impose on individuals.

The liability of Government for its actions or inactions is only part of its responsibility to the victims of injuries or disasters.[70] Justice is not the only virtue of Government—compassion, social solidarity, and humanity are of equal value. Liability for risk needs to be distinguished from a duty to compensate individuals for losses which arise from social calamities. Paragraph 12 of the Preamble to the French Constitution of 1946 (reaffirmed in the 1958 Constitution) affirms the solidarity of individuals before national calamities. It is social solidarity, rather than justice (equality before public burdens) which has provided compensation for centuries for damage caused to individuals by riot[71] or, more recently, for state intervention and even compensation for acts of terrorism.[72] As a result, no risk-based liability arises where the loss is merely caused by a natural calamity, such as heavy rain, without proof of some state activity (such as public works on the river bank) which caused the loss to occur in that way.[73]

B. Liability for Fault

The *Blanco* decision clearly accepted that a public authority could be liable for fault. But the French are concerned to establish both the *nature* and the *degree* of fault. The nature of the fault depends on whether one is concerned with the personal fault of the agent (breach of law, failure to perform a duty adequately, etc) or fault of the service. Briefly stated, a public authority is only liable for a fault of the service. Its agents may be liable in the civil courts for a personal fault *outside the scope of their employment*, but have a defence if the activity was part of the performance of their duties. A public authority may in some circumstances only be liable for serious fault (*faute lourde*) rather than ordinary fault (*faute simple*), though the number of situations in which this higher standard of fault is required is diminishing.

Liability of the administration for fault is well established in most legal systems.[74] That fault may be either that of the public authority itself or of one of its agents for whom it is vicariously liable. Difficulties arise in both areas.

---

[70] On the basis of governmental liability, see J. Bell, 'Governmental Liability in Tort' (1995) 6 National Journal of Constitutional Law 85.

[71] See J. Mestre, *Introduction historique au droit administratif français* (Paris, 1985), 91; CAA Nantes, 3 May 1995, *Ministre de l'Intérieur et l'Aménagement du territoire*, AJDA 1995.854; cf. Riot Damage Act 1886.

[72] See T.S. Renoux and A. Roux, 'Responsabilité de l'Etat et droits des victimes d'actes de terrorisme' AJDA 1993.75 at 78 who argue: 'while there is no doubt that the victims of terrorist acts bear a burden and evidently suffer a special and abnormal loss, it is difficult to link this burden to the activity of a public body and to consider that the victims had been exposed to a risk of attack in the public interest, unless one confuses "public burdens" and "social burdens" in a misleading way.'

[73] CE 25 May 1990, *Abadie*, AJDA 1990.824.

[74] Principle I of the Council of Europe's Committee of Ministers' Recommendation of 1984 states: 'Reparation should be ensured for damage caused by an act due to a failure of a public

1. *Liability for the acts of the administration*

It seems obvious that the administration is liable for its own acts, but two problems arise. The administration can only act through people, so do you have to demonstrate the fault of a particular individual in order to establish the fault of the administration? In broad terms, French administrative law does not require demonstrable fault on the part of an individual, if the fault of the organization (*faute de service*) as a whole can be proved. In addition, one has to ask what counts as fault on the part of the administration, as opposed to a mere error of judgment.

The central concept of fault liability in French administrative law is the notion of *faute de service* or failure of the system. Used to getting round problems of proving individual fault in complex organizations, it brings out the very important feature that liability is for the failure of government to fulfil its mission. Here we are dealing not so much with the failure to comply with a specific rule, but a general failure of the system to realize its objectives. Let us take an example of where the organization of the system breaks down. A child may not be provided with education in part of the national curriculum due to staff shortages in the school, or a hospital provides a poor service due to lack of staff. In France, the victim (child or patient) obtains compensation for the failure to live up to expected standards, rather than for the blameworthy conduct of particular individuals, all of whom may have been doing their best.[75] The independence of *faute du service* from individual fault was established long ago in *Feutry*[76] where a lunatic escaped from an asylum and burnt down the hayrick of a local farmer. The *département* which ran the asylum was held responsible for the damage by way of *faute de service* without the need to demonstrate the fault of a particular official.

For there to be fault, the public body must have done more than perform its mission badly or incompetently. Negligent failure to maintain premises might be an obvious example. In these situations, the fault of a public body is very much like that of a private person. The fault is that of the organization which is responsible for the upkeep of premises, rather than of particular individuals who played a merely instrumental role. As an illustration, one might cite the controversy over the liability to those contracting AIDS from contaminated blood. The French passed legislation to compensate victims on 31 December 1991 on the basis of social solidarity. But the administrative courts had been faced with the question whether the failure of the administration to introduce heat-treatment of blood

---

authority to conduct itself in a way which can reasonably be expected from it in law in relation to the injured person. Such a failure is presumed in case of transgression of an established legal rule.'

See generally, D. Fairgrieve, M. Andenas and J. Bell (eds.), *Tort Liability of Public Authorities in Comparative Perspective* (BIICL, 2002). For a comparison between France and England, see D. Fairgrieve, *State Liability in Tort* (Oxford, 2003).

[75] See CE 27 Jan. 1988, *Ministre de l'Education national c Giraud*, RFDA 1988.321 and CE 8 Oct. 1986, *Langlet et Centre hospitalier général de Château-Thierry*, AJDA 1986.723.

[76] TC 29 Feb. 1908, *Feutry*, D 1908.3.49 concl. Teissier.

based on American techniques constituted fault giving rise to administrative liability. The Conseil d'Etat decided that there was no liability for injuries caused before the date on which serious medical evidence of the risk was brought to the attention of the administration, but that it was liable to the victims for fault in failing to act on that information once received.[77] This neatly demonstrates the point at which we move from the principle of social solidarity (on which the legislation was based) to liability (on which the courts acted). As Honoré notes,[78] the moment that we could (and should) have done something about the potential risk of injury, then we have responsibility for the outcome which can ground legal liability, and we are not merely faced with an adventitious outcome which, out of compassion and humanity, we feel compelled to respond.

The other distinctive feature of French fault liability is the way in which breach or misapplication of the law will be treated as fault. Unlike under article 215 of the EC Treaty or English law, the victim does not have to show that there was a serious error or fault in coming to an illegal decision, merely that there has been an unlawful act which caused damage. This is made clear in the case law on failure to implement an EC directive. It suffices that there is a breach of law to give rise to damages as a matter of course under French law.[79]

2. Vicarious liability

Vicarious liability makes the administration responsible for the fault of individuals. This is really part of the notion of *faute de service*. The institution takes responsibility for those whom it employs and the harm they cause. If you like, it is a risk idea—if the public authority takes the risk of employing certain people, it takes the burden of that as well. Of course there are limits. A fault may be considered 'detached' from the public service, such as when a postman attacks the person to whom he is supposed to be delivering a registered parcel.[80] But the French go very far in their interpretation of this principle of vicarious liability. They admit the notion of *cumul* (co-existence) of personal fault of the individual and fault of the service. This was made clear in *Lemonnier*[81] where the mayor of a country commune had been held liable by the civil courts to the user of a river towpath who had been injured by bullets fired at targets in the river as part of the commune's

[77] See CE Ass. plén. 9 April 1993, *M.G., M.D., M. et Mme B*, RFDA 1993.583 concl. Legal; J.M. Pontier, 'Sida: de la responsabilité à la garantie sociale', RFDA 1992.537.

[78] 'Responsibility and Luck' (1988) 104 LQR 530 at 533.

[79] See CE Ass. plén. 28 Feb. 1992, SA *Rothmans*, AJDA 1992.210, CE Ass. plén. 30 Oct. 1996, *SA Cabinet Revert* and *Ministre du Budget c Dangeville*, AJDA 1996.1044 and Case C-6/90 *Francovich* [1993] 2 CMLR 66.

[80] TC 21 Dec. 1987, *Kessler c Thebenas*, AJDA 1988.364. The French extend this principle of liability too far. For example, where two soldiers made unauthorized use of a dustcart in order to go to the cinema, it was held that the state was still liable for *faute de service* (TC 22 Nov. 1965, *Collin*, D 1966.195). The state may also be liable without fault for the risk it creates, e.g. where an off-duty policeman accidentally kills a youth with his service weapon: CE 23 Dec. 1987, *Bachelier*, AJDA 1988.364.

[81] CE 26 July 1918, D 1918.3.9 concl. Blum.

summer fête. The Conseil d'Etat held that the victim could still sue the commune for its liability over the same injury. In addition, the French have been very wide in their interpretation of what falls within the service. In *Mimeur*,[82] a conscript soldier was driving a tanker on military business when he took a large detour on his way back to base in order to visit his family. While on the detour, he went too fast round a bend and crashed, demolishing the house of the plaintiff. The Conseil d'Etat held that the soldier was still performing his duty in driving the lorry at the time, so that the state was responsible for the damage he had caused. The result of this *cumul* doctrine is not that the victim receives damages from both the state and the official, but that he or she has a choice. This choice is frequently exercised in medical cases where a doctor may be prosecuted for unlawful wounding (*coups et blessures*) when an operation goes wrong through his negligence, but the victim can not only sue him as a *partie civile* to the criminal action, but may also use the criminal judgment as the basis for an action against the hospital for *faute de service* in the administrative courts.[83]

3. Degree of fault

Until recently, French administrative law recognized that some activities of the administration were more difficult than others, e.g. the conduct of policing or medical activities, and considered that there should only be liability on proof of serious fault (*faute lourde*), rather than mere negligence (*faute simple*). This approach has been overturned in many areas since the mid-1980s. Postal services used to be protected by requiring *faute lourde* but this has been reduced, first by stretching the idea of serious fault, and then by allowing actions for negligence. Liability for medical activities now lies in principle for mere negligence, this being established by the blood transfusion cases and later put on a legislative basis (for both public and private law) by legislation in 2002.[84]

If the loss is the unintended result of a difficult exercise of discretion, then liability should only arise where the discretion was not properly exercised. In the case of the police, is it really social risk-taking to arm the police? If so, then all those injured accidentally should be compensated. (And this is the view the French are taking at least with regard to weapons which the police are obliged to keep at home.) If not, then the decision to deploy weapons in a particular situation will not give rise to liability unless it is outside the proper scope of discretion and thereby amounts to fault (which is essentially the French view by requiring *faute lourde* (serious fault) in such cases).

---

[82] The liability here is much wider than would be admitted in private law: cf. Ass. plén. 17 June 1983, *Caille*, D 1984.134 note Denis.

[83] On the *partie civile* in criminal proceedings, see above pp. 138–139.

[84] See CE Ass. plén. 10 April 1992, *Epoux V*, AJDA 1992.355; A. Toublanc, 'De la prétendue disparition de la faute lourde en matière de la responsabilité médicale' AJDA 2004.1173; *loi* no 2002-303 of 4 March 2002, art. 98 (which also set up a scheme of compensation where no fault can be established) and see below, pp. 409–410.

The area of *regulatory or supervisory failure* is also one which has traditionally had special treatment. Here the principal liability ought to lie with the person who has caused the loss. If we ask why a public body acts as a regulator, it could be simply as a policeman to scrutinize carefully a certain activity and to undertake prosecutorial discretion or other interventionist measures to ensure the rules are obeyed.

But the public body could also act as guardian of the interests of particular vulnerable people (such as children). In the latter case, the idea of the protective norm suggests that it should be liable to them for failure to live up to expectations. It is certainly in this light that the French have viewed the exercise of much regulatory power. Classically, the state has been responsible for those in its care (children, the mentally ill, and prisoners) often without proof of fault, but on the basis of some form of risk-based or vicarious liability.[85] Thus, the state was liable for failing to enact regulations in order to require the heat treatment of blood used in blood transfusions when there was strong medical evidence to show this was effective to prevent the transmission of AIDS in contaminated blood.[86] In such cases, the question has often been effectively about the level of fault required: should the regulatory authority be liable only for gross fault (given that someone is already primarily liable) or should the normal principles of fault apply. But the French are moving towards applying ordinary principles of fault in such cases.

C. Liability Without Fault

The principle of equality before public burdens is a different principle of justice from liability for fault. In its origin in medieval law, it is a principle of compensation for justified expropriation. The principle is exhibited both in the common law and in systems of a Roman law origin.[87] Where the community benefits from a lawful act at the expense of an individual, then that individual should be compensated for the forced transfer to the common weal. The justice lies in restoring the individual to his or her appropriate share of social resources which has been diminished excessively by community action.

The natural home of liability without fault is in the law on expropriation of property, but it has also been used more recently by the Conseil constitutionnel to strike down the imposition of excessive tax burdens on one section of

---

[85] Brown and Bell, 194–196. For example, TA Versailles, 18 May 2004, *Salah Z.*, AJDA 2004.2172 (liability for harm inflicted by one prisoner on another).

[86] CE Ass.plén. 9 Mar. 1993, *M.G.*, RFDA 1993.583.

[87] See J. L. Mestre, *Service public*, 28–32, 137–140, cf. *Case of the King's Prerogative in Saltpetre* (1607) 12 Co. Rep. 12. Indeed it forms Principle II of Recommendation No. R (84) 15 on Public Liability, adopted by the Committee of the Council of Ministers of the Council of Europe on 18 September 1984 (Strasbourg, 1985): 'reparation should be ensured if it would be manifestly unjust to allow the injured person alone to bear the damage, having regard to the following circumstances: the act is in the general interest, only one person or a limited number of persons have suffered damage and the act was exceptional or the damage was an exceptional result of the act.'

the community.[88] A different aspect of this principle is the principle of risk. If one creates a hazard for the public good, eg a weapons dump, then the public authority should carry the burden, irrespective of fault. This was made clear in the *Regnault-Desroziers* case,[89] in which the state was liable when an arms dump on the outskirts of Paris exploded in 1915 causing death and property damage to neighbours. Responsibility in French law lies for the conscious and lawful decision to create a risk, and the cost of that risk-taking needs to be incorporated in the cost of the activity by the actor in question, the state.

A borderline situation between the requirements of social solidarity and liability for risk or imposed public burdens comes where the state operates as a policeman. In the classic *Couitéas* case,[90] a landowner was compensated where the public authorities in Algeria refused to exercise force to remove squatters from his land following a court order that they should leave.

A duty to remove the effects of crime or social disorder (rather than just to contain it or prosecute it) is a rare requirement, even on government. The *Couitéas* principle is justified on the basis of risk in the standard texts or at least on the principle of equality before public burdens. The burden imposed is the refusal to exercise public power to benefit an individual because this would jeopardize a socially beneficial activity from which other citizens gain. French administrative law provides compensation where an abnormal and severe loss is caused to an individual which exceeds that suffered by the generality of the public. In other words, a distinction is drawn between the general run of inconvenience which we all have to tolerate and special losses sustained by an individual. To take an example, in *Sealink*, French fishermen blockaded the port of Boulogne. The port authorities refused to have recourse to force to remove the fishermen, and those who suffered loss sued the Minister of Sea Transport.[91] One firm, Jokelson et Handstaem, a local forwarding, storage, and handling company was unable to process the cargo of two ships due to the blockade and its adjacent office had to be closed for several days, but it was able to operate its other offices and cargoes in other, neighbouring ports. Such losses, though annoying, were not held to be substantial in relation to the business of the firm. By contrast, Sealink provided cross-Channel passenger ferries between Boulogne and the English coast. Its trade on the August bank holiday weekend was completely disrupted and the passengers used other companies travelling out of other ports in France and Belgium. The loss was irrecoverable. The Conseil d'Etat held this loss was abnormal and special sufficient to entitle the company to compensation for the loss sustained. It is hard to see that there is much of a public burden here. The loss is caused by the protesters; the state simply refused (for good reasons) to attempt to

[88] C cons. 16 Jan. 1986, *Cumulation of Pensions and Salaries*, Rec. 9; C cons. 13 Dec. 1985, *Eiffel Tower Amendment*, AJDA 1986.171.
[89] CE 28 Mar. 1919, RDP 1919.239 concl. Corneille.
[90] CE 30 Nov. 1923, *Couitéas*, D 1923.3.59 concl. Rivet.
[91] CE 22 June 1984, *Société Sealink UK Ltd*, Leb. 246.

alleviate the situation. Of course there was a calculation of social risk in deciding on the costs of the intervention by the navy and the likely harm to be done to the process of resolving the grievance of the fishermen.

Where harm results from the action of a public body which has taken a deliberate risk, either intending or knowing that the loss might occur in achieving its desired outcome, then no-fault liability seems appropriate—the loss is part of the price of the socially valuable outcome. The case of *indirect or unplanned harm* is more complex. Take the case of the new medical technique which is tried out on a patient and produces unanticipated side-effects. This has led to no-fault liability,[92] based on equality before public burdens. Similarly, in the *Banque Populaire de Strasbourg* case, three prisoners were released on various forms of licence or parole. They committed a bank robbery and the bank successfully sued to recover its loss.[93] Liability arose because the policy of licensing prisoners created a risk which the community ought to bear. By contrast, the English approach is to see such indirect losses as the subject for arguments about social solidarity, rather than compensation for harm caused.

D. A Single Basis of Liability?

Because of the emphasis on impersonal bases of liability which do not attribute fault to anyone, current French writers argue that the entire basis of public law liability is to be found in 'equality before public burdens' rather than in fault.[94] But, though that has conceptual elegance, such a simple statement would hide the difference between liability for expropriation, for risk-creation, and for failure of the system to fulfil its mission.

E. Contracts

The French administration can enter into both administrative contracts (*contrats administratifs*) and private law contracts (*contrats de droit privé*). The two basic criteria for the former are that the contract relates to a public service and that the contract reserves exceptional powers to the administration (it contains *clauses exorbitantes du droit commun*). Either criterion may suffice to make a contract 'administrative' in character. Despite their apparent simplicity, these criteria give rise to a complex case law which need not be explained here.

An administrative contract differs from a private law contract essentially in its importance for the public service. Litigation with regard to these administrative

---

[92] CAA Lyon, 21 Dec. 1990, *Gomez*, AJDA 1991.167; CE Ass. plén. 9 April 1993, *Bianchi*, AJDA 1993, 344.

[93] CE 9 April 1987, RFDA 1987.831 concl. Vigoroux.

[94] See R. Errera, 'The Scope and Meaning of No-Fault Liability in French Administrative Law' [1986] CLP 157 and M.A. Latournerie, in J. Bell and A.W. Bradley, *Governmental Liability* (London, 1991), 225–227.

contracts falls within the competence of the administrative courts. In addition, administrative decisions to enter into such contracts may be challenged by way of a *recours pour excès de pouvoir*,[95] but only give rise to a remedy for damages under the *pleine juridiction* of the administrative courts.

Although some administrative decisions may be reached after a process of consultation and agreement, e.g. in the regulation of pharmaceutical prices, their authority remains based on the imposition of a solution by the administration so that the French describe it as an 'acte administratif unilatéral' especially the case where a collective agreement effectively has regulatory effect. Such 'administration by collaboration' does not really lead to an extension of the domain of contract.[96] The true domain of contract remains an agreement between the administration and its collaborator.[97]

The public interest justifies a number of specific characteristics of administrative contracts in relation to their formation, terms, and termination.

1. Formation

French lawyers draw a distinction between a number of different kinds of administrative contracts. Two main categories of contract exist, *la concession de service public* and *le marché public*. The concession grants the operation of a public service to an individual (often a private person). That person is responsible for running the service within the framework settled by the public authority granting the concession, and the concessionaire is paid for the service typically out of revenue received from the users of the service. Thus, local water services in France are typically run by private companies who have concessions from local communes to provide water in their area. Water users pay these companies for the service. Although both operator and consumer are private persons and have private law contracts between them, the concession itself is an administrative contract between the local commune and the water company.

The public procurement contract (*le marché public*) is concerned with the provision of a particular object or activity for the public service. This may take the form of public works, such as constructing a road or a school, supplies, such as stationery or vehicles, or services, such as cleaning or catering. In such contracts what matters most is the quality of the product or service provided, rather than the person who makes the provision. By contrast, the concession is traditionally seen as a contract *intuitu personae* where the concessionaire is chosen for his particular characteristics by the public authority, and the concessionaire himself is

---

[95] e.g. CE 23 Mar. 1992, AJDA 1992.375: a challenge to the legality of certain clauses in the Eurodisney contract.

[96] D. Harris and D. Tallon, *Contract Law Today* (Oxford, 1988), 150 and 138–144; also R. Römi, 'La requalification par le juge des actes négociés en actes unilatéraux' AJDA 1989.9.

[97] R. Roquette, 'Contribution à la classification des contrats synallagmatiques de l'administration' AJDA 1995.483.

providing the public service. Where the concessionary changes, that is sufficient reason for the concession to be revoked.[98]

The particular nature of administrative contract gives rise to a difference in the procedure of formation of contract compared with that in private law. Whereas the private individual is free to contract with whomsoever he wills and on whatever terms he wishes, the dominant position and immense contracting power of public authorities is redressed by subjecting them to certain procedural requirements. Failure to comply with these renders the decision to enter the contract (a decision separable from the contract itself) liable to be quashed for *excès de pouvoir*.[99] A further reason for these requirements is to ensure that public money is spent in a cost-effective manner. In both concession and public procurement, these requirements govern the publicity which must be given by the public authority to its intention to make a contract so as to invite tenders from interested parties. To a great extent, thanks to EC directives, the law in France and England in this area is becoming very similar.

2. Terms of the contract

The terms of many administrative law contracts are stipulated by the *Code des marchés publics* which sets out a number of standard terms and conditions ('cahiers des clauses et conditions' and 'cahiers des charges') which bind the different administrative authorities in making contracts. All the same, there is also significant room for terms to be determined by negotiation.

The public interest as expressed in the principle of the adaptability of the public service requires that the administration should be able to review the needs of the public service and to adapt the terms of existing contracts accordingly. This unilateral and unpredictable power is mitigated by the requirement that the contractual equilibrium should be maintained and that any change imposed by the administration should be compensated appropriately. For example, in *Compagnie Nouvelle du Gaz de Deville-Lès-Rouen* which has been discussed earlier,[100] a contract for street lighting was modified to permit the gas company to use electricity instead of gas, but, if it did not do so, the municipality should be allowed to engage a third party to provide electric lighting.

This can be contrasted with the doctrine of '*fait du prince*' which applies where the administration uses its general powers in such a way that the economic basis of the contract is upset. In France, unlike in England, unless the governmental act was some general legislation affecting all citizens equally, the contractor will be entitled to a monetary indemnity or to increase the charge to the consumer. This is justified by the principle of equality before public burdens.

---

[98] e.g. CE 31 July 1996, *Société des téléphériques du massif du Mont-Blanc*, AJDA 1996.788 where the concessionary was taken over by a company which ran a concession of ski-lifts in a competing commune.

[99] See CE Ass. plén. 16 April 1986, *Cie Luxembourgeoise de télévision*, Leb. 97.

[100] Above pp. 170–171.

3. Imprévision

The principle of the continuity of the public service requires that the contractor is kept in a position so as always to be able to supply the administration, even if this involves an increase in the cost of his service. Thus, if unforeseen supervening circumstances (unconnected with the administration) arise which make it uneconomical for the 'private' party to the contract to perform his part, he will not be allowed to resile from the contract, but may be compelled to perform the contract and will then be entitled to an indemnity from the administration against his extra expenses. Thus, in the leading case of *Compagnie Générale d'Éclairage de Bordeaux*,[101] a commune had entered into a contract with a gas company for a supply of gas for the lighting of the streets in the town. Because the coalfields in Northern France had been overrun by the Germans in the early part of the First World War, the price of coal increased in 15 months from 35 francs per ton at the time when the contract was made to 117 francs per ton; an increase which, unless the company were allowed to increase the contract charges for the gas supplied, would have compelled the gas company to go into liquidation. The Conseil d'Etat took the view that it was not in the public interest that this should happen, as, if the company became defunct, the streets of Bordeaux would not be lit. Therefore the court ordered the company to continue to perform the contract, but substantially increased the price of gas charged to the commune under the contract. The eventuality of *imprévision* does not render the contract null or terminable, it merely gives rights to the concessionary to obtain some compensation from the public authority.[102]

In some circumstances, even the doctrine of *imprévision* cannot adequately salvage the situation and the concession has to be terminated by reason of the external circumstances (*force majeure*).[103]

VI. Protection of Civil Liberties Outside Courts

The role of the administrative courts is very important in France in the protection of civil liberties. The ease of access to the courts makes them a primary guardian of the rights of the citizen faced with the administration. But the courts will act typically after the event and on an individual, rather than a structured basis. In addition there are both quangos established to take a more general oversight on civil liberties as well as alternative complaints systems.

---

[101] CE 30 Mar. 1916, D 1916.3.25 concl. Chardenet.
[102] CE Sect., 4 May 1990, *CIM*, AJDA 1990.735.
[103] e.g., CE 9 Dec. 1932, *Compagnie des Tramways de Cherbourg*, D 1933.3.17, where fares could not be increased without seriously affecting the number of users of the service and so the concession was terminated.

A. Quangos Protecting Civil Liberties

There are a number of *autorités administratives indépendantes,* created in the last 30 years, which undertake a regulatory role in relation to civil liberties. The first of these was the CNIL (*commission nationale de l'informatique et des libertés*) which was established in 1978 to oversee the development of information technology and the storage of personal information. It operates as a watchdog, advising the Government on new developments and the need for reforms. It also provides redress to the individual who is wrongly denied access to information stored on him or her. Another major body is the CSA (*Conseil supérieur de l'audiovisuel*) whose role is to regulate the operation of the various licensees of television and radio channels. Among its functions is to ensure plurality of information in the interests of the public and to enforce the rules on the diversity of programming (especially material of French or European origin) and against mergers. It may receive individual complaints about broadcasting.

B. Alternative Complaints Systems[104]

The principal alternative to the courts is the *Médiateur,* the French Ombudsman, created by the law of 3 January 1973. He investigates complaints that the administration has failed to live up to its mission in both central and local government. Thus his brief is wider than British Ombudsman in that he is not just concerned with maladministration but with failure to perform its mission and he covers all tiers of government in a single institution. He has been successful in attracting more complaints than his British counterparts. In 2006, there were 33,824 complaints submitted (the major areas being justice, health, social security and employment, tax and civil service matters). Where mediation was attempted, there was success in 80% of cases.[105] In addition, the *Médiateur* makes proposals for reform to the administration arising from the matters which have come to light during his investigations. Despite this obvious success, the creation of the *Médiateur* has had only a limited impact on the administrative court system. Until recently, there has been little success in establishing alternative dispute resolution in public law. The circular of 9 February 1995 restated the importance of alternative methods of resolving disputes, focusing particularly on the need for complaints to be resolved within the hierarchy of the administration before having to go to court. To that end, each branch of the administration should have proper complaints procedures in place which are know to citizens. Indeed, there are some three million such complaints a year, of which a mere 15,000 end up in court. In addition, a report in 1993 suggested that more could be made of

---

[104] See D. Fairgrieve, above n. 74, ch. 8.
[105] Médiateur de la République, *Rapport au Président de la République et au Parlement 2006* (Paris, 2007).

conciliation, a procedure which is part of the mission of the tribunaux administratifs to encourage, but which has not been very successful.[106]

VII. Conclusion

There are many similarities between the French and other European administrative law systems, both in the common law tradition and elsewhere. The values which are enforced and which inspire administrative action are shared by many Western European liberal democracies. All the same, the French system has a number of distinctive features. Most notable among these are the distinction between the rules of public and private law (even in matters such as administrative liability) and the separation between administrative and private law courts. The concept of 'public service' is more structured and distinctive than in many systems and articulates a set of values which the British might typically see as non-legal. Indeed, the emphasis on the importance of law and the courts in establishing standards and in providing solutions to complaints is perhaps the feature which most distinguishes the French and common law systems in this field.[107]

---

[106] Section du rapport et des études, Conseil d'Etat, *Régler autrement les conflits. Conciliation, transaction, arbitrage en matière administrative* (Paris, 1993).

[107] See J. Bell, 'English Law and French Law—Not So Different?' [1995] CLP 58.

7

Criminal Law

Criminal law is concerned with the responsibility of the individual to the state. The state undertakes a prosecution in the name of society against a deviant individual. In this light, criminal law is part of public law. It is not directly concerned with the rights of individuals *inter se*. On the other hand, the courts which try criminal cases in France are, as was seen in Chapter 2, effectively the same as those trying civil cases, though carrying different names. The private law judges are members of the same corps of judges who try criminal cases. Administrative judges have no role in criminal matters. In that way, it is common to treat criminal law alongside private law. While recognizing these points, we have chosen to situate criminal law alongside public law where it belongs conceptually, if not procedurally.

French criminal law is distinctive mainly in terms of it conceptual structure, rather than its result. Unlike civil law and some aspects of public law, it is not strongly influenced by Roman law. Its structure has developed from medieval roots in royal law, but is now heavily influenced by international trends in criminality and criminology. The reform of the Criminal Code in 1994 gave a chance to modernize and systematize the treatment of issues. But there remains a strong influence of history from the Revolutionary and Napoleonic periods.

I. Values

French values in criminal law reflect liberal political philosophy, but also the utilitarian tradition of the deterrence school.

A. Individual Responsibility

Criminal law is founded on the idea of individual responsibility for actions and a retributive response for the abuse of that responsibility demonstrated in criminal wrongdoing. As we will see, this produces a resistance to any form of vicarious liability in criminal law and delayed the recognition of the criminal liability of corporations until the New Criminal Code of 1994 (hereafter, the 'Criminal Code'), since how could a non-person like a company (rather than its human directors) take responsible decisions? The treatment of children and the insane is also founded on the moral idea of personal responsibility inherited from the canon law and at the core of liberal political thinking.

B. Equality Before the Law

The other value inherited from the Revolutionary period is equality before the law. The Declaration of 1789 had at its heart the abolition of privilege, placing everyone in an equal position before the law. Aristocrats and peasants enjoyed each other's company and fate in the tumbrels and on the guillotine. There remain procedural differences in the treatment of certain offences, e.g. terrorist and political offences. Reformed in 1993, the prosecution of ministers and high state officials is before the Haute Cour de la Justice, an institution which had to be changed to deal with the highly political question of the criminal liability of ministers for actions leading to recipients of blood transfusions becoming infected with the HIV virus.[1] With this exception and the prosecution of the head of state, the criminal process gives equal treatment in terms of procedure. In terms of the applicable rules, the principle of equality is recognized. There are three principles of equality before the law—treating the same situation similarly and respecting appropriate differences, equality within the law, and equality before penalties. Difference in situation may justify difference in treatment, such as the difference drawn by article 132-76 of the Criminal Code between an ordinary attack on a person and an attack with a racist purpose. Equality within the law usually requires similar penalties and procedures to be applied to different people covered by the same legal rule. Equality before penalties requires that the same penalty be applied to similar categories of offender, and that differences be justified.[2] In truth, inequality is permissible as long as it is not significantly disproportionate. The principle of equality is tempered by mercy in one specific respect. Legislators regularly alter the tariff for offences. This means that offenders sentenced for crimes committed at different dates are liable to different penalties. All the same, the Conseil constitutionnel has affirmed the long-standing principle of the criminal courts that, where a subsequent statute reduces the penalty for an offence, the lesser penalty should be applied with immediate effect,[3] even to offences committed before the law came into force. But this principle of mercy does not require that a harsher penalty should be of immediate effect.

---

[1] J. Bell, 'The Criminal Liability of Politicians in France' (2001) 3 Cambridge Yearbook of European Legal Studies 65–78.
[2] C. cons. 3 Sept. 1986, *Criminality and Delinquency*, Rec. 130; Bell, *French Constitutional Law*, 146.
[3] C. cons. 19 and 20 Jan. 1981, *Security and Liberty*: Bell, *French Constitutional Law*, Decision 18.

C. Legal Certainty

A citizen should know in advance what is required of him or her. There are two aspects to this principle of legal certainty. Criminal laws are not generally retrospective in effect. Article 112-1 of the Criminal Code provides for non-retrospectivity, following the decision of the Conseil constitutionnel of 20 January 1981. The principal exception is the effect of lesser criminal penalties. The second feature is that penal laws are to be construed strictly. This principle is explicitly laid down in article 111-4 of the Criminal Code, but the courts had consistently reiterated it from even before the Criminal Code of 1810.[4] For example, a doctor by negligence caused a foetus to be aborted. His conviction for involuntary homicide was quashed because a foetus was not clearly 'another person' within article 221-6 of the Criminal Code capable of being the victim of such a crime.[5] Equally, where it was an offence to steal, it was not an offence to make use of the minitel telephone-based electronic information system, since there was nothing which could be 'appropriated'.[6] That said, French authors note that the conflicting imperatives of mercy and the effectiveness of the criminal law lead the courts to attenuate this principle of strict construction. In terms of mercy, defences favourable to the accused are often given a broad construction at least where they are substantive in character. For example, article 380 of the Old Criminal Code created an immunity from prosecution for theft for acts taking place within the family. Judicial interpretation extended this to cover abuse of confidential information, extortion of a signature, and fraud.[7] But the imperative of punishing acts which fall within the policy of the legislation leads the courts to resist the idea that they must interpret every ambiguity in a text in favour of the accused. This tendency is clearly visible where the accused has committed a morally reprehensible act and is seeking to rely on an apparent ambiguity to escape conviction. A good example is the taking and driving away of motor cars. Article 379 of the Old Criminal Code defined theft as 'the fraudulent removal of a thing'. Although earlier case law had insisted that for a 'fraudulent' intent an offender must intend to act definitively as owner, the Cour de cassation decided in 1959 that it was sufficient that the accused should intend to act, even momentarily, as owner. Such a momentary intention is clear in the case of taking a car and driving it away, albeit for a joyride.[8] Another clear example is the interpretation of article 309 of the Old Criminal Code which punished violent conduct, but was interpreted to cover a

---

[4] See Crim. 8 Sept. 1809, S 1809–11. 1.107: 'penal texts are to be interpreted strictly and... judges cannot proceed in this area by means of extension or analogy'.

[5] Crim. 30 June 1999, Bull. crim. no. 174; upheld by the European Court of Human Rights in *Vo v France*, App. no. 53924/00.

[6] Crim. 12 Dec. 1990, D 1991.364 note Mirabail.

[7] Crim. 4 Jan. 1930, DP 1930.1.230; Crim. 8 Feb. 1840, S 1840.1.651; Toulouse 9 April 1851, S 1851.2.348 respectively.

[8] Crim. 18 Feb. 1959, D 1959.331 note Roujou de Boubée.

person who banged on the ceiling every night for months thereby inducing a nervous condition in a neighbour.[9] Such interpretation is likely *a fortiori* where the text requires updating. A good example is the case of theft under article 379 of the Old Criminal Code which was interpreted to cover abstraction of electricity, a solution later confirmed by article 311-2 of the New Criminal Code.[10]

D. Social Order

Criminal law should be a last resort to maintain social order. The Declaration of the Rights of Man and of the Citizen of 1789 provides that 'the law shall provide only for penalties which are strictly and evidently necessary'. The ground of necessity has so far not led to criminal offences being declared unconstitutional, but it does require serious justification to be presented by the legislature. Along the same lines, the penalty must be proportionate and some penalties have been declared excessive.[11] Such an approach fits well with the revolutionary concern to protect individual liberty as far as possible. But the Conseil constitutionnel also recognizes that there are other objectives of constitutional value such as the prevention of threats to public order, especially to persons or property.[12] The role of proportionality in justifying the penal actions of the state is complemented by the requirement of proportionality in actions by citizens in relation to each other. Thus self-defence only applies where a person uses force proportionate to a threat posed by an attacker as will be seen later.

E. Legality

The principle of legality requires in France that crimes should be created by *loi*.[13] Regulation has been accepted as a legitimate source of regulatory offences (*contraventions*), even if they give rise to imprisonment. But *délits* and *crimes* must be the creation of statute. In addition, the courts have set their face against the creation of criminal offences by circulars, even if they are mere regulatory offences.

F. Moral Component

French criminal law doctrine distinguishes the 'legal component' (*l'élément légal*), the 'material component' (*l'élément matériel*) and the 'moral component' (*l'élément moral/psychologique*). The first two identify aspects of the *actus reus*:

---

[9] Crim. 22 Oct. 1936, D 1937.2.38.

[10] Crim. 3 Aug. 1912, S 1913.1.337 note Roux; also Crim. 14 Jan. 1971, D 1971.101: records were 'printed matter' within art. 23 of the Law of 29 July 1881.

[11] C. cons. 30 Dec. 1987, *Finance Law for 1988*, RFDA 1988.350 and C. cons. 19 Jan. 1989, *CSA*, Bell, *French Constitutional Law*, Decision 28.

[12] C. cons. 19 Jan. 1995, *Diversity of Habitat*, AJDA 1995.455.

[13] For the distinction between *loi* and *règlement*, see above pp. 21–22.

the events which took place and the legal characteristics which those events are required to have. The last component corresponds with the mental element in crime. A number of French authors, such as Merle and Vitu[14] and Pradel would argue that one should not discuss the mental element of a *crime*. A crime is merely an objectively verifiable breach of a legal norm. Once this is established, then the question is what to do with the offender. Only in certain circumstances will society wish to impose a criminal penalty and stigma upon an offender, and most of the relevant circumstances relate to the character of the offender in question. As a result, Pradel writes:

in the theory of the offence, the main distinction is between the act and the person (the offender). The different aspects of the act are equally components of the offence, but the psychological aspects concerning the agent have to be related not to any claimed 'moral element' of the offence, but to the offender and to his responsibility. To talk of the 'moral component' of the offence in criminal law is simply a pedagogical convenience.[15]

While this present exposition follows the 'pedagogical convenience' of the classical distinction between the physical and mental aspects of the offence, the limitations of this analysis have to be borne in mind.

II. Categories of Offences

French law distinguishes three categories of offences. The categories, stemming from 1791 are set out in article 111-1, but there is no definition. In broad terms, *crimes* are a small category of very serious offences (murder, rape, etc), *délits* are less serious offences requiring a mental element and carrying some form of moral disapproval (such as theft, fraud, assault, etc), while *contraventions* include a large range of regulatory offences often of strict liability. For example, deliberate homicide is a *crime*, while involuntary homicide is a *délit* (see section VI below), and selling drink to someone under age is a *contravention*. The category into which an offence falls is fixed by the legislation creating it and does not depend on the penalty applicable to it. The difference between these categories has primarily procedural consequences in terms of the investigation process and the allocation of the offence to a trial court, but it also has importance for the prescription period applicable. Under the Criminal Code, whereas *crimes* are not prescribed until 20 years have elapsed (article 133-2), the period for *délits* is five years (article 133-3) and for *contraventions* this is merely two years (article 133-4). Time runs from the moment when the relevant facts were known on which a prosecution could have been brought. Time never runs with regard to certain offences, notably crimes against humanity. This was made clear in

---

[14] R. Merle and A. Vitu, *Traité de droit criminel*, 7th edn. (Paris, 1997) i, no. 455.
[15] Pradel, *Droit pénal*, 347.

the *Barbie* case in which the indictment was quashed on the grounds that the Chambre d'accusation (now the Chambre de l'instruction) had erred in considering that a charge of crimes against humanity could not be pressed in 1986 relating to offences committed in 1943.[16] The relevant point is now confirmed in article 213-5 of the Criminal Code.

III. *Actus Reus*

The key feature of the *actus reus* is that it must be an unlawful act, that is to say, certain facts must be classifiable under the description of acts prohibited by the criminal law. Mere civil wrongs, without a specific criminal proscription, do not constitute criminal offences. Rather than present defences as exculpation of the accused, French lawyers suggest that defences such as self-defence, necessity, and so on demonstrate that the act committed was not an unlawful act and, therefore, does not constitute the *actus reus* of an offence.

A. The Classification of Facts

Problems of fact arise in a number of ways. In some cases, the issue will simply be about what occurred, the brute event, such as whether a man drowned or was poisoned. In many cases, however, the question may be how to classify the events which have occurred. The facts of a case only constitute a crime if they can be classified as within the definition of the *actus reus* of an offence. The element of classification is thus crucial. There are three kinds of classification issue which arise: the classification of facts in terms of ordinary usage (e.g. is this lump of metal with wheels a car?), the classification of facts in terms of ordinary legal usage (e.g. was the person who took the property already its owner?), and the classification of facts in terms of specifically criminal law usage (was the act a 'handling' (*recel*) of stolen goods?). In English law, the last two issues might be treated as questions of law, since they concern the question of whether certain facts are capable in law of constituting the *actus reus* of the offence. As such, the question might be within the purview of the judge rather than the jury. In France, the distinction between law and fact is primarily relevant in terms of deciding on the offence which is charged (*crime* or *délit*), or grounds of appeal, particularly to the Cour de cassation.

It is well recognized in French doctrine that a particular set of facts may be analysed in a number of different ways. These different 'readings' of the facts may lead to different legal consequences. The presence of more than one possible way of reading the facts does not, in itself, demonstrate a level of uncertainty sufficient to lead to an acquittal. But it may require the judge to decide which analysis is

---

[16] Crim. 20 Dec. 1985, D 1986.500 note Chapar.

to be retained. Thus some classifications of facts are mutually incompatible. For example, where a person assaults another (the delict of violence contrary to article 222-7 of the Criminal Code) and then leaves him without care for his injuries (delict of omission to assist a person in danger contrary to article 223-6 of the Criminal Code), it is generally thought that the offender should only be charged with assault (*coups volontaires*). The action in question is essentially a commission, rather than an omission.[17] Even if the interpretations of facts are not incompatible, the judge may have to choose between alternative permissible classifications for the purposes of criminal law. For example, the same set of facts may have several elements which are criminal offences in their own right, yet build together into a more complex criminal offence. Thus public drunkenness is an offence in its own right (article R. 3353-1 of the Code of Public Health) as well as a component of drunk driving contrary to article L. 234-1 of the Highway Code. While some legal authors argue that an offender is liable to punishment for as many different criminal laws as he has broken, others consider this to be excessive—only if there are a number of different moral elements in the activity which offend against distinct social values should a single set of facts give rise to more than one offence. It is this latter view which is reflected in the case law. The Cour de cassation has stated that 'any offence giving rise to a prosecution should be considered from the angle of the most serious criminal aspect of which it is capable'.[18] Thus, repeated telephone calls should be prosecuted not as abusive calls (article 222-16 of the Criminal Code), but as violence under article 222-11 if they give rise to illness.[19] Where, on the other hand, distinct social values are threatened by the same act, then it is perfectly proper to lay two distinct charges in relation to the same facts. The example often given is of a person throwing a grenade into a crowded cafe injuring some people and causing damage to the building. The Cour de cassation held that it was proper to convict him both of attempted murder and of an attempt to destroy a dwelling house by explosion, because the two offences had distinct intentions (and thus it was possible to convict him of one without automatically convicting him of the other).[20] (Naturally, the issue of classification is frequently resolved at the stage of prosecutorial discretion when one level of offence is decided on and the case is sent to an appropriate trial code. This may not, in practice, reflect the most serious criminal offence possible, but may reflect what is achievable in practice.)

B. Unlawful Act

An act may be unlawful if it breaches the injunctions of the criminal law. But there are a number of defences which are seen by French lawyers as removing the

[17] See MRMP note under D 1959.161; Douai, 30 Sept. 1954, D 1955.55; contra Crim. 24 June 1980, Bull. crim. no. 202.

[18] Crim. 13 Jan. 1953, Bull. crim. no. 12.

[19] Crim. 3 Mar. 1992, Bull. crim. no. 95.

[20] Crim. 3 Mar. 1960, *Ben Haddadi*, Bull. crim. no. 138; Pradel and Varinard, no. 19.

element of unlawfulness from an action. Such defences of legitimate authority, consent, self-defence, and necessity remove from the action any senses that it was unlawful.

1. *Legitimate authority*

Legitimate authority is specifically recognized as a ground exonerating or attenuating liability by article 122-4, al. 2 of the Criminal Code, provided that the act in question is not obviously unlawful. This defence follows on from a defence of doing what was required by statute or decree, and reflects the primary responsibility of those in authority for what they have ordered. This defence did not formally exist in the 1810 Criminal Code, and the *ordonnance* of 28 August 1944 on war crimes only recognized it as an attenuating circumstance or an excuse (and indeed article 213-4 of the Criminal Code on crimes against humanity only treats superior orders as a circumstance relevant to sentence). The case-law prior to the Code was generally more severe.[21] But the case law was not consistent and so a motorist directed by a policeman to go the wrong way up a one-way street was not held criminally (or indeed civilly) for any accident resulting.[22] Where there is legitimate authority permitting an action such as holding a suspected shoplifter until the police come, then there will be no offence, even if the person detained turns out to have committed no offence.[23] But where the person committing the offence ought to have known that the order given to him was unlawful, he will have no excuse.[24]

2. *Self-defence* (légitime défense)

Self-defence is recognized as a ground of exoneration by article 122-5 of the Criminal Code, repeating what was contained in the 1810 Code and its predecessor of 1791. But the Code expands the scope of this defence. This ground is carefully circumscribed in the Code: there must be 'an unjustified attack on himself or another' to which, at the same time, an action required by the necessity of self-defence is undertaken, but only if the action is a proportionate response. Under alinéa 2 of this article, the ground may also be used by a person undertaking a proportionate action to interrupt the performance of a *crime* or *délit* against property.

The case law demonstrates a degree of flexibility towards the person claiming this defence. Thus, although the Code talks of an 'attack', case law extends this to include the likelihood of attack provided this is based on concrete actions which led the potential victim reasonably to consider himself or another to be in danger. The approach is thus essentially subjective (did the accused believe,

[21] See Crim. 22 May 1959, *Brunel*, JCP 1959.II.11162 (Pradel and Varinard, no. 20).
[22] Cass. civ. 14 Nov. 1963, JCP 1964.II.13490.
[23] Crim. 1 Oct. 1979, *Gilbert*, D 1980.IR.334.
[24] Crim 25 Feb. 1998, *Droit pénal* 1998, 84 obs. Véron.

albeit wrongly, he was facing aggression), but it is moderated by the requirement that the belief be reasonable and not imaginary. For example, where a person was pointing a pistol at his son 'for a joke', a father was held justified in shooting what he took to be an attacker.[25] The need for immediacy is also a limitation. For example, in *Minet*[26] a jeweller living with his family in a self-contained flat over his shop heard some burglars trying to break into the shop. He surprised them from his flat window and shot them in the street as they were moving away from the doorway into a getaway car. He was not able to raise self-defence. By contrast, in another case an unarmed burglar was confronted by the householder in his kitchen. He pointed a gun at the burglar and shot him when the burglar tried to attack him with his fists. Here self-defence was allowed. These cases illustrate the fact that issues of justification and proportionality are matters of fact for the trial courts.[27] Such a situation can lead to inconsistent and surprising results. The requirement that the attack to which one responds is 'unjustified' is new in the 1994 code and so the scope for the defence is limited to actions without any pretence of legitimate authority.

Although the decision about proportionality is a matter of fact and the courts seem indulgent towards those raising the defence, there are clear limits. One cannot respond to a slap on the face by firing a revolver.[28] Where the action of the accused is disproportionate, the act committed is unlawful and so constitutes the *actus reus* of an offence. All the same, the circumstances may be such as to cause the judge to impose a lower sentence for the offence.

One area of uncertainty lies in the scope for the defence in relation to unintentional acts. Since self-defence is a deliberate response to an attack, French law has traditionally argued that it cannot be raised as a defence where the injury caused to the attacker is really one of carelessness. For example, a threatening drunk importuned a person who pushed him back forcefully, the drunk lost his balance, fell and was injured. The Cour de cassation affirmed the opinion of the lower judges who had considered this to be an unintentional injury to the drunk, and rejected the argument that this fell within the scope of self-defence.[29] In the court's opinion, 'self-defence is inconsistent with the unintentional character of the offence'.

In general, it is for the defence to raise this ground of exoneration, but in article 122-6 of the Criminal Code. French law presumes that certain actions are undertaken in self-defence where an attempt is made to force out a person who has entered a dwelling at night forcibly or by trick, or where theft or ransacking is accomplished with force. Nineteenth century case law saw this as an irrebuttable

[25] Crim. 5 June 1984, Bull. crim. no. 209; Nancy, 9 Mar. 1979, D 1981.462 note Bernadini.
[26] Crim. 11 May 1995, Gaz. Pal. 1995.2.Som 443.
[27] Req. 25 Mar. 1902, *Fraville*, D.1902.1.356 (the use of booby traps as a defence of property).
[28] Crim. 4 Aug. 1949, RSC 1950, 47 obs. Magnol.
[29] Crim. 16 Feb. 1967, *Cousinet*, JCP 1967.II.15034; more recently Crim. 28 Nov. 1991, D 1993.18.

presumption, applying it to husbands who killed their wives' lovers entering their house by stealth at night.[30] Modern case law is firmly of the view that such a presumption is rebuttable, and that the older decisions might not have the same result today. Thus, in *Reminiac*,[31] a householder refused entry to a drunken former lover of one of his servants, but the man still made efforts to climb through the windows. The householder went and got a gun, loaded it, returned to the window and fired in the dark at where he thought the would-be entrant was. By this time, the man had given up his effort and was smoking a cigarette behind a bush. The man was injured, but the Cour de cassation quashed the decision of the lower court to apply the presumption of self-defence in the case of forcible entry. The shooting was not necessary and there was no longer a serious and immediate danger of a threat to person or property.

3. Necessity

The New Criminal Code contains the first formal text admitting the defence of necessity. Article 122-7 declares a person not to be criminally liable where, 'faced with an actual or imminent danger threatening himself, another or property, he undertakes an action necessary to safeguard person or property, unless there is a lack of proportion between the means used and the seriousness of the threat'. In practice, French case law and doctrine had admitted this ground for some time. Pradel notes that this came to the fore in a decision of the Tribunal correctionnel of Colmar in 1956 where a person had been accused of erecting a dwelling without planning permission. He had been living in unsanitary conditions and this had affected the health of his child. He persisted in the construction despite an order from the local council to desist. He was acquitted since his actions had been necessary to provide his family with decent conditions for existence.[32]

The recognition given to necessity is limited. In the first place, the defence has only been admitted in case of acts against property, never harm against persons.[33] There must be an immediate danger which requires the action, and most of the cases on squatters have failed because there were alternative ways of proceeding to obtain accommodation for the homeless people. (Though such a necessity has been found in a case where a failure to submit a lorry to a technical inspection

---

[30] See Crim. 11 July 1844, S 1844.1.777; Crim. 8 Dec. 1871, D 1872.1.193.

[31] Crim. 19 Feb. 1959, D 1959.161.

[32] Trib. corr. Colmar, 27 April 1956, D 1956.500; cf. the earlier case of Amiens 22 April 1898, DP 1899.2.329 note Josserand where a decision of 'le bon juge Magneaud' to acquit a penniless woman for stealing a loaf of bread to feed her sick child on grounds of necessity ('moral constraint' under what is now art. 122-2 N.c.pén.) was revised by the Cour d'appel so that she was only acquitted for lack of criminal intent. See also Crim. 28 June 1958, *Lesage*, D 1958.693 where a father held onto his children when the door of his car flew open on a country road and prevented him being able to control the car. He was held to have a defence of necessity to breaches of the highway code and injuries caused thereby.

[33] The issue of the defence of necessity in abortion in order to save the life of the mother is treated as a specific legal authorization of an action, not as an illustration of the defence of necessity.

before it was put on the road was held justified because the locality had run out of sugar!)[34] The danger must also not have arisen through the fault of the person acting out of necessity. This was made clear in an *obiter* statement by the Cour de cassation in its 1958 decision of *Lesage* approving the principle of necessity.[35] Thus, where a driver unwisely went onto a level crossing, he could not claim necessity as a defence to a prosecution for smashing through the crossing gate in order to avoid being crushed by an oncoming train.[36]

4. Consent

As in English law and other legal systems, the consent of the victim may often remove the unlawfulness of an action. This clearly applies to offences such as rape where one of the constituent elements of the offence is that the victim did not consent. But it is unclear how far consent is otherwise a distinct defence. Pradel[37] argues that in many cases consent is not the real justification, but the lawfulness relies on custom. In the case of surgery and many sports like boxing, rugby or judo, it is the authorization by customary law which makes the assault or injuries lawful. But since the law established the permissive framework, it can also set limits which will punish actions undertaken even with the victim's consent. Thus the law used to permit only therapeutic surgery and punish experimental or aesthetic surgery, even where the surgeon acted with the victim's consent.[38] Injuries or death caused in duelling are similarly punished.[39] Unless undertaken as part of medical treatment, sterilization and sex change operations are still considered unlawful because they are against the public interest.[40]

C. An Attributable Act

To constitute the *actus reus* of an offence, the action must be the free act of an individual to whom it can thus be attributed. The action must also be the cause of the harm for which the accused is to be held criminally liable. The criminal law does not punish mere intentions which are not in some way realized.

If liability is based on a responsible action, then the action must represent the free choice of the individual. The schools of retribution and deterrence would clearly rely on this as the basis for punishment, while even the theorists of social protection are wary of using the criminal law in order to take action against

[34] Trib. corr. Coutances, 22 Oct. 1968, JCP 1969.II.15879 note Guigue.
[35] See above n. 32.
[36] Rennes, 12 April 1954, S 1954.2.185.
[37] Pradel, *Droit pénal*, para. 538.
[38] Crim. 16 April 1921, S 1923.1.143, though this is no longer accepted.
[39] Ch. réun. 15 Dec. 1837, S 1838.1.5.
[40] Crim. 1 July 1937, *The sterilised of Bordeaux*, S 1938.1.193 note Tortat; Aix, 23 April 1990 GP 1990.2.575, upheld Crim. 30 May 1991, D 1991.IR.197, commented on in D. Thouvenin, D 1991 Chr. 271. See J. Penneau, *La responsabilité du médecin* (Paris, 1992), 94–95.

individuals unless they are responsible for their acts. As a result, the law admits defences such as duress and that of necessity.

Article 122-2 of the Criminal Code excludes liability where a person has acted 'under the aegis of a threat or a constraint against which he could not resist', a formulation very similar to article 64 of the 1810 Code. Doctrinal writing distinguishes between physical and moral constraints.

Physical constraints can be external or internal. An external constraint is an event which either forces the offender to commit the offence or prevents him complying with the law. For example, in the days of lantern lamps, when a storm blew so hard that the driver of a coach could not keep his lamps lit at night, there was no offence.[41] Equally where torrential rain caused a wall to crumble onto the highway, this exculpated the owner of the wall from obstructing the public highway.[42] Internal constraints arise from the health or condition of the individual. Thus, a passenger who fell asleep on the train and went past his destination was held to have a defence to the offence of travelling without a ticket valid for the journey to the actual station at which he got off.[43]

The key features of this constraint are that it must be both irresistible and unforeseeable, requirements similar to those for *cause étrangère* in civil law. Irresistibility has traditionally been judged objectively and requires that there be no possibility of the accused complying with the requirements of the law. An extreme and much criticized application of this idea is found in *Rozoff*.[44] Here the Minister of the Interior expelled the accused, but he did not leave French territory. In his defence, he offered to show that all the neighbouring countries had refused him admission. The attitude of countries bordering on France was held to be irrelevant. The defence only applied where there was actual impossibility of complying. This is extreme compared with the view adopted in contract law.[45] A more acceptable case is that of *Genty*.[46] Here the Germans arrested a farmer and told him that they would shoot or at least take captive three fellow villagers who had been arrested after having shot at the German patrol, unless he went and spied out the position of French troops in a nearby village and reported back to them. If he did as they instructed, the Germans promised to release the villagers. Genty did go and report on the position of French troops and the Germans released the hostages The Germans attacked the French soldiers in the nearby village the following day. Genty was prosecuted for providing the enemy with information likely to harm French military operations contrary to article 206 al. 2 of the Code of military justice. The Cour de cassation rejected his claim of duress on the ground that 'at the time

---

[41] Crim. 28 Feb. 1861 DP 1861.1.140.
[42] Crim. 28 July 1881, DP 1882.1.95.
[43] Crim. 19 Oct. 1922, DP 1922.1.233.
[44] Crim. 8 Feb. 1936, DP 1936.1.44 note Donnadieu de Vabres.
[45] See below p.000.
[46] Crim. 20 April 1934, S 1935.1.138.

when he committed the criminal act ... the threat which, in reality, lay over his three fellow citizens was neither so urgent nor so direct as to remove from him all freedom of action and to prevent him evaluating the greater danger to which he was exposing the French troops and the village occupied by them in accomplishing the blameworthy act which the enemy required'. He did not have to give information to the enemy and, on balance of the evils threatened, should not have done so.

The unforeseeability of the constraint calls into question the fault of the accused in getting into a situation where an offence became inevitable. A good example is *Trémintin*[47] where a merchant sailor was convicted of desertion when he failed to board his ship at Le Havre because he had been arrested for drunkenness a few hours before it set sail. Although it was clearly impossible for him to go onboard, the situation had been created through his own fault, and so he could not rely on duress as a defence. More prosaically, a person who causes harm to another because he has failed to take precautions to avoid being physically incapable will be at fault and unable to rely on duress.[48]

Moral duress applies where a pressure removes the freedom of action of an individual. For a constraint to operate in this way, it must be both illegitimate and unavoidable.

D. Causation

Criminal law punishes results not intentions. To hold an individual liable, it is necessary that the result occurs and that it is the consequence of the actions of the accused. The result is judged not by what the criminal wanted to get out of the action, e.g. revenge or personal gain, but by reference to the social harm which is created. The notion of harm is conceived broadly, covering not only injury to people or to their property or income, but also to social order, but there must always be some such harm. For example in fraud, it is not necessary that the person deceived paid over the market price for what he received, it is sufficient that he was deprived of a free and informed choice about whether to enter the transaction or not.[49] It is the attack on freedom, rather than on the pocket which is central to the offence. The so-called cases of 'victimless' offences are typically ones where the victim has consented. It has already been seen that French law often views these as offences not against the individual harmed, but against social order. To that extent, there is a victim (society) even if the person immediately affected experiences no harm.

As in most legal systems, French criminal law has problems with a multiplicity of causes of harm. Three theories are offered by doctrinal writers. The theory of the

[47] Crim. 29 Jan. 1921, S 1922.1.185 note Roux; Crim. 6 May 1970, Bull. crim. no. 154.
[48] Crim. 8 May 1974, Bull. crim. no. 165.
[49] Crim. 20 June 1983, Bull. crim. no 189.

'proximate cause' focuses on the factor which is closest in time to the result. A person is liable if he is the close and immediate cause of the result. The case law does not accept this theory. The theory of the 'equivalence of conditions' (the 'but for' test) considers that any fact without which the event would not have materialized can be considered a cause. This is, of course, very wide in its potential scope. The case law accepts this in part. It is not necessary that the fault of the accused is the sole cause of the injury to the victim. This is seen in two ways. First, the intervening act of the victim between the action of the accused and the harm does not always exonerate the accused. For example, if the accused wounds a person who then commits suicide as a result of a pre-existing morbid condition which the attack has triggered, then the accused can be convicted of manslaughter (*homicide involontaire*).[50] This is an example of the idea that one takes one's victim as one finds him. The second illustration is where there is an intervening fault of the victim or of a third party. For instance, where a roaming dog bit a man who, careless of the rules of hygiene, died later of tetanus, the dog owner was held liable for homicide by carelessness.[51] The action of a doctor may not be the original cause of an injury, but his failure to treat the injury properly may well amount to a cause of the victim's injury sufficient to give rise to criminal liability. Thus where a man had been wounded by a bullet and was in a serious condition, a duty surgeon was held guilty of manslaughter when he delayed surgery until the following morning. The victim's death could have been avoided by his prompt action, and this gave rise to liability, even though there were other significant causes of the death.[52] All the same, it is a third, more restricted theory of causation which also holds sway. The theory of 'sufficient cause' (*cause adéquate*) focuses on the antecedent action which would produce the result in the normal course of events. In this sense, it is normally sufficient to produce the result. The question thus becomes whether the victim's harm was the natural or probable consequence of the accused's action. Particularly where the victim's own act intervenes, then the court will be attentive to the question of whether the action of the accused was sufficient to cause the harm. For example, a motorcyclist was knocked down by a drunken motorist but was not seriously injured. He ran after the driver, swearing at him and collapsed with a heart attack. The Cour de cassation refused to hold the driver guilty of homicide by carelessness on the ground that the wounds were not such as normally to cause death.[53]

E. Omissions

Omissions are less likely to be treated as causes of an injury unless some duty to act is established. French law has undoubtedly more duties to act than systems

[50] Crim. 14 Jan. 1971, D.1971.164 note Robert.
[51] Crim. 18 Nov. 1927, S 1928.1.192.
[52] Crim. 25 May 1982, Bull. crim. no. 134. The liability of the surgeon does not preclude the liability of the person who fired the bullet for the crime.
[53] Crim. 25 April 1967, GP 1967.1.343.

such as English law, so omissions are a significant branch of the law. A writer of the Ancien Régime, Loysel, wrote in his *Institutes* that '*qui peut et n'empêche pèche*' (he sins who could prevent but fails to do so). French law is less severe. This is well illustrated by the case of the 'closeted woman of Poitiers'.[54] A mentally retarded woman was kept in filthy and unsanitary conditions closeted away by her mother in a room without air or light. She was, however, well fed. Eventually she died from her treatment. Her brother, who did not live in the house, but visited it was charged with violence against his sister on the ground that he had done nothing to stop his mother's ill-treatment of his sister. The lower court found that the brother had never been allowed any responsibility for his sister which was kept strictly by his mother (who did not like him and had disinherited him). The Cour de cassation refused to find him guilty on the ground that he had merely shown passivity and an impassive coldness which prevented him taking any steps to help his sister, even though he merited 'the most severe moral censure'. Those in senior positions will only be held liable where they engaged in positive actions, not mere passive acquiescence. In *Coutant*, the president of a hunting club was charged with permitting an illegal lottery to take place. As president, he knew of the activities of the club, but took no active part in its organization. The result was a mere act of omission which was insufficient to create liability.[55]

The Bordeaux case illustrates the kind of situation in which a person's status as parent does create duties to act in relation to another, whereas other statuses, such as brother do not. The law's set of moral duties is more limited than those of a moralist. But there are specific legal duties which extend the range of people who have to take positive actions to help another.

Certain articles of the Code specifically punish omissions as well as carelessness, e.g. article 221-6 punishes the deliberate failure to comply with a legal requirement on safety. For example, a mountain guide who undertook to accompany a person was held in breach of the then equivalent of article 221-6 when he abandoned him and let him die of exhaustion.[56] But such offences have been few in number in relation to pure omission until this century. The *loi* of 7 February 1924 created the offence of abandoning one's family (now articles 227-3 and 227-17 of the Criminal Code), and the *ordonnance* of 25 June 1945 created the offence of failure to report a *crime* (now article 434-1 of the Criminal Code). Other offences include failure to prevent the commission of a *crime* or *délit* offence against the person (article 223-6, al. 1) and the failure to help a person in danger (article 223-6, al. 2), as well as the failure to give testimony in favour of the innocent person accused of an offence (article 434-11 of the Criminal Code). The *délit* of failing to help a person in danger has caused particular problems in the case of doctors. Doctors have even been convicted by the criminal courts for

[54] Poitiers, 20 Nov. 1901, *Monnier*, DP 1902.2.81 note Le Poitevin.
[55] Crim. 29 Jan. 1936, DH 1936.134.
[56] Pau, 2 Dec. 1943, JCP 1944.II.2724.

failure to provide adequate medical assistance while being acquitted of any disciplinary offence by professional bodies.[57] The reason for this may well lie in the fact that the criminal actions will have a civil party, the victim, who will obtain damages from the doctor (and his insurer) if he is convicted.

The most commonly cited provision punishing omissions is article 223-6, al. 2, which, like its predecessor, article 63 al. 2 of the 1810 Criminal Code provides:

Whoever voluntarily abstains from giving assistance to a person in danger is liable to [five years in prison or a fine of €75,000], if they could have done so without risk to themselves or to a third party, either by personal action or by summoning assistance.

This omission to help must be in the face of a danger of imminent death or serious injury to the person, such as to require immediate action. For example, a person who is present at a sexual assault but fails to intervene commits this offence.[58] The offender must clearly be aware of the danger and thus know that his or her intervention is necessary. In the case of a doctor who refused to attend upon a sick person, the offence was committed by his failure to satisfy himself by questions to the caller that there was no immediate danger to the patient.[59] The offence is frequently used to punish a failure to act by a medical person, such as a doctor who fails to visit a woman who has just given birth to a child and lives in poor housing or a pharmacist who fails to warn a doctor who has made a mistake in his prescription for a patient.[60] More controversially, the offence was used to punish the author of a guidebook on committing suicide on the ground that to give such instructions made it clear that he would not assist a desperate person.[61] This article of the Code does not expect a person to expose themselves to a disproportionate risk, but merely to act where humanity requires a possible action, rather than heroism.

F. Attempts

In dealing with attempts, the law is concerned with punishing actions which do not produce the social harm of the completed offence, but are nevertheless sufficient threats to public order in their own right to justify punishment. (The fact that it is perceived as a threat in its own right is seen by the fact that French law has always made it possible to punish attempts as severely as the completed crime.) French law is no more concerned than English law to punish bad intentions,

[57] See generally, J. Penneau, *La responsabilité du médecin*, title 3, ch. 1.
[58] Bourges 21 June 1990, *Droit pénal* 1991, 135.
[59] Crim. 21 Jan. 1954, D 1954.224; but contrast an acquittal where the information given on the telephone did not alert the doctor to the seriousness of the condition: Crim 26 March 1997, Bull. crim. no. 123.
[60] See Crim. 17 Feb. 1972, D 1972.325.
[61] Crim. 26 April 1988, D 1990.479 note Fénaux.

however much this might be a useful way of preventing harm in the future. The law is thus concerned to identify a sufficiently externalized expression of intention that constitutes harm to social order. Given the nature of most *délits* and *contraventions* which are offences of carelessness or strict liability, the scope for punishing attempts is limited mainly to *crimes* and to those *délits* where this is specified by legislation (article 121-4, al. 2.). French doctrine would identify three stages in the process of committing a crime (the *iter criminis*): the psychological stage of forming a desire to commit the offence, the preparatory stage where what is undertaken has no direct and immediate connection with the offence, e.g. hiring a car as a getaway vehicle, and the third stage is the commission of the offence.[62] It is only this third stage which is the basis for criminal liability. But it may be exhibited in a number of ways. Article 121-5 of the Criminal Code states that 'an attempt is committed where, manifested by the beginnings of its commission, it was only suspended or failed in its effect by reason of circumstances independent of the will of the offender'. There are thus two distinct kinds of attempt: a course of action which is interrupted before it can achieve its objective, and a course of action which is misdirected to achieve its objective.

1. *The beginnings of a commission*

A crime must be demonstrated by objective facts, not just by what the accused thought he was doing, since there must be more than a criminal intention involved. There must be an action which is a constituent element of the offence or of an aggravating circumstance related to it. A mere preparatory act contains no action which is part of the offence. Thus hiring a car is not a constituent element of robbery, even if the car is to be used in such a planned crime. Some French doctrine has argued that it is sufficient for an attempt if the offender has committed himself irrevocably to the crime.[63] Such a subjectivist approach focuses on the harm which the person poses to society, but is difficult to reconcile with the law's objection to punishing mere intention. The case law insists that the issue of whether there are the beginnings of a commission is a matter of law. The Cour de cassation tends to use two expressions to describe what is involved either that the accused has committed an act which 'leads directly to the offence where it is accomplished with the intention to commit it' or, more objectively, 'an action which ought to have as its direct and immediate consequence the commission of the offence'. There are thus two elements in the idea of the beginning of commission: an irrevocable commitment and a causal nexus with the completed commission of the offence. The intention involved in this commitment is shown by the facts (or from a confession). For example, where a man tricked a woman into believing he was a doctor and persuaded her to come to his 'surgery' and undress, this was treated as an attempted sexual assault, even though he had not yet moved

---

[62] Pradel, *Droit pénal*, 431.
[63] H. Donnadieu de Vabres, *Traité élémentaire de droit criminel*, 3rd edn. (Paris, 1947), 231.

to touch her. The key thing is that the commitment is evidence by actions close to the commission of the offence. Thus, where people were in a car awaiting the arrival of a person carrying money and were wearing hoods, glasses, and false noses to disguise themselves and carried guns, then an attempted robbery could be found. All that was necessary was that the person arrives before the actual offence would have been committed.[64] Although most illustrations are of cold deliberation, it is clear that the element of intention is met where the offender deliberately engages in a course of action which would typically lead to a criminal result, e.g. the panicking gunman who shoots in all directions, but does not injure anyone. In addition, the causal link must be sufficiently close, as when samples of wine are sent so as to obtain orders. If the samples claim to be of a quality of wine which is false, then an attempted fraud has taken place.[65] Where it is not, then there has only been a preparatory act. For example, where a man set fire to his own lorry, he could not be convicted of attempted fraud before he had made a claim to his insurance company in relation to the damage to the vehicle.[66]

2. *The interrupted attempt*

It is necessary that the action leading to the crime be stopped other than by the voluntary action of the accused and that this occurred before the offence was completed. The issue of the voluntary withdrawal of the accused requires that he or she desist of his or her own motion, and not just because it is perceived that the crime won't work.

The difference between these situations can be illustrated by two cases. In *Berchem*, a man was going round a supermarket; emptied three cardboard boxes with goods marked at 184 francs and filled them with goods worth 4,000 francs, before resealing them and wheeling them in his trolley towards the checkout. He was stopped by his cousin who was supposed to help him take the goods through the checkout who indicated that they had been spotted by supermarket employees. He then proceeded to leave behind his trolley and its contents and leave the supermarket. The Cour de cassation[67] held that he had been rightly convicted of attempted theft, since he had only desisted because he had appreciated that it was impossible to take the boxes through the checkout without detection. There was only an interruption of the criminal activity due to circumstances, rather than a real change of mind about whether to commit the offence. By contrast, in *Weinberg*, the accused was standing in the doorway of a tobacconists intending to break in when a friend of his happened by chance to pass by. The friend engaged him in conversation and they then walked off together. In defence to a charge of attempted theft, the accused alleged that there was no danger that his

[64] Crim. 29 Dec. 1970, JCP 1971.II. 16770 note Bouzat.
[65] Crim. 3 May 1974, *Ramel*, D 1975 Somm. 20.
[66] Crim. 27 May 1959, Bull. crim. no. 282; but there is an offence where a claim was made or begun to the insurance company: Crim. 14 June 1977, D 1978.127.
[67] Crim. 3 Jan. 1973, GP 1973.1.290.

friend would report his actions if he persisted in the theft, but he had persuaded him not to commit the offence and so he had voluntarily renounced his intended criminal enterprise. The lower court convicted him on the ground that his course of conduct had been interrupted by the intervention of a third party. The Cour de cassation,[68] however, quashed the conviction on the ground that the lower court had not adequately investigated the accused's assertion that he had voluntarily renounced his criminal enterprise. If it were true that he had been dissuaded by his friend from continuing with the theft, then this would be a voluntary renunciation and not an attempted theft. Such an approach is not that different from the English lawyer's concern to determine how far the accused has progressed in the execution of the crime. A case like *Weinberg* focuses on how to interpret the early stages of a criminal activity and demonstrates a certain indulgence towards those who are trying to extricate themselves from a criminal enterprise.

The other condition for the defence of voluntary renunciation to apply is that it must occur before the completion of the offence. Repentance after the completion of the crime is a matter for mitigation, not acquittal. A classic example is *Natal*[69] where a man obtained payment of 42,000 francs by fraud in that the money was sent by the victims in the belief that Natal was owed this sum of money by a bookseller in St. Petersburg and a result of a (non-existent) consignment of books supposedly sent by Natal to him. Natal repaid the money to his victims before criminal proceedings were commenced. All the same, the Cour de cassation held that he had been rightly convicted of fraud, since the offence had been successfully completed before Natal had a change of heart. Repentance after the event is still encouraged, and indeed there are specific provisions in the New Criminal Code reducing the penalty applicable to *repentis* ('repentant criminals'), e.g. a reduction by half for *repentis* involved in drug trafficking (article 222-43), and reductions in relation to terrorism (articles 422-1 and 422-2).[70]

3. The misdirected attempt

An action which is complete may not achieve its intended objective. This arises either because the action has failed or because it was directed at achieving something which was impossible. Article 121-5 of the Criminal Code simply assimilates the failed attempt to the category of an interrupted attempt. In the case of attempting the impossible, French case law originally did not criminalize it at all.[71] The argument was that, in the case of an action which could not possibly achieve a criminal result; there could never be the beginnings of the commission of a criminal enterprise. But gradually it moved towards treating attempting the impossible in the same way as a failed attempt. The turning point came in the

[68] Crim. 20 Mar. 1974, Bull. crim. no. 124.
[69] Crim. 11 Oct. 1872, DP 1873.1.391.
[70] See generally, Bouloc, 'Le problème des repentis. La tradition française relativement au statut des repentis', RSC 1986, 771.
[71] See, e.g, Crim. 6 Jan. 1859, S 1859.1.362.

case of *Fleury*[72] in 1928. Here a couple injected their servant girl with eau de Cologne either neat or mixed with vinegar in an attempt to induce an abortion. Such an action could not possibly achieve that result. The couple were nevertheless convicted of attempting to induce an abortion contrary to article 317 al.1 of the 1810 Criminal Code. The Cour de cassation considered that the actions of the couple undertaken with the intention and for the purpose of inducing an abortion amounted to the beginnings of the execution of the *délit*. The fact that the steps taken were insufficient to have the desired effect intended 'was merely a circumstance independent of their will as the result of which their action failed to have effect'. Since then the case law has been applied in numerous cases. *Joao*[73] provides a good illustration of the view expressed by commentators that French law now takes no account of impossibility in the area of attempts. Joao was convicted of attempted theft. He was arrested having broken into parked cars with a view to stealing their contents. Unfortunately for him, there were no objects in those cars which could be stolen, but the Cour de cassation did not consider this relevant to the conviction. It merely repeated the formula in *Fleury* that the impossibility of a successful crime arose from a circumstance independent of the will of the accused.

The impossibility in the above cases was factual. The result could not be achieved at all. But there are other situations where the result was factually achievable, but there has been an inadequate implementation, e.g. an insufficient dose of a noxious substance was given. French law treats the two as equivalent situations of impossibility and both are punished criminally.

In earlier case law, the Cour de cassation appeared to approve the theory proposed in doctrinal writing which distinguished between absolute and relative impossibility. Absolute impossibility arose where it was legally, as opposed to factually, impossible for the offence to be committed. The classical illustration was the 'murder' of a dead man. But recent case law seems to have removed even this obstacle to convicting the person who attempts the impossible. For example, the Cour de cassation has upheld the conviction of a person for attempted murder where he 'killed' someone who was already dead on the ground that the fact that the victim was already dead was merely a circumstance independent of the will of the accused.[74] There are cases where people have been acquitted of failing to assist a person in danger or even involuntary manslaughter where the victim was already dead.[75] But for those *délits*, the law has not created an attempt offence, and so the reasons for the acquittal have nothing to do with the law on attempting

---

[72] Crim. 9 Nov. 1928, D 1929.1.97 note Henry.

[73] Crim. 23 July 1969, S 1970. 361 note Roujou de Boubé, JCP 1970.II.16507bis, note Littmann.

[74] Crim. 16 Jan. 1986, D 1986.265 notes D Mayer and C. Gazounaud, J. Pradel; also Crim. 5 Oct. 1972, GP 1973.1.25.

[75] See, e.g. Crim. 1 Feb. 1955, JCP 1955.II. 8582; Crim. 12 Dec. 1972, GP 1973.1.285.

the impossible. It is merely that the substantive offence could not be committed in those circumstances.

Attempting the impossible has to be distinguished from situations in which a person does an act believing it to be unlawful, when it is in fact lawful. Here there is no offence to be committed. For example, as in English law, there is no offence where a man who has consensual intercourse with a woman of 25 believing the age of consent to be 30. The same is true of those who 'attempt' to commit offences by magic. In those cases, the only wrong lies in the intention of the person, and there is no criminal offence to be attempted.

IV. The Mental Element

Liability (*responsabilité*) in criminal law depends on both breach of duty (*culpabilité*) and *imputabilité* (causation and the freedom of the individual to act as he did, notably his intention). The degree of intentionality required depends a great deal on the character of the offence. Article 121-3 makes it clear that all *crimes* require an intention to commit the offence. As amended in 2000, this article also provides that, a person may commit a *délit* through mere careless acts (*imprudence*) or omissions (*négligence*) or by a 'breach of a particular obligation of care or safety provided by *loi* or *règlement*' which directly caused the injury and that the person did not show due diligence, given the means at his disposal. Where a physical person causes injury indirectly, he or she is only liable for committing a 'manifestly deliberate breach of a particular obligation of care or safety provided by *loi* or *règlement*' or an 'aggravated fault' (*faute caracterisée*), which 'exposed another person to a risk of which they could not have been unaware'.[76] For a contravention, there is no general requirement as to the mental element although *force majeure* is a defence in all cases. It is thus sensible to distinguish between intention and carelessness or omission as grounds of liability.

As in most legal systems, a distinction is drawn between *intention* and *motives*. If one steals property, the fact that the thief intended to give the proceeds to charity does not make the action any less of a theft. Likewise in *Lahore*, the daughter and son-in-law of the deceased were convicted of the theft of flowers which they removed from his grave and put on the rubbish heap, even though their motive was not to act as owners of the flowers, but merely to express their hatred for the deceased's cohabitee who had placed the flowers on the grave.[77] In a few cases, motives do matter, for example, terrorism is defined by the *loi* of 9 September 1986 (now article 421-1 of the Criminal Code) as a crime involving 'an individual or collective undertaking having as its purpose to disturb public order seriously

---

[76] These requirements on manifestly deliberate breach and aggravated fault apply only to human beings, as opposed to companies or public bodies.

[77] Crim. 8 Feb. 1977, RSC 1977, 590 obs. Levasseur.

by means of intimidation or terror'. There is no distinct activity of terrorism, merely a crime with a particular purpose which can only be discerned from the motives of the accused. But, even in this case, the consequences affect the procedure of trial (a non-jury trial) and the sentence which can be passed; it does not alter the constituent elements of the crime itself.

A. Intention

The deliberate intention to commit a wrong is labelled *dol* in French and involves both knowledge that something is prohibited and yet the deliberate willingness to bring about the prohibited actions. Now knowledge that something is unlawful can occur at various levels. Since there is a presumption that all citizens know the law, this element plays little practical part in the finding of criminal liability, except where (as will be seen) mistake as to law is an acceptable defence. Willingness to act (*volonté*) in practice adds little to the requirement that the action is imputable to the accused. If the action is freely undertaken by the accused, this will suffice to demonstrate willingness.[78] So the key feature in *dol* is the extent to which an action reflects an intention to act wrongfully.

French lawyers distinguish between a general intention to act unlawfully (*dol général*) and the specific intent required for certain offences (*dol spécial*). It is thus not sufficient that one has an unlawful intention; there must also be an intention to do what the specific offence prohibits. As a result, for example, it will be easier to show that someone has wrongfully come into possession of information concerning national defence contrary to article 413-11 of the Criminal Code, rather than the specific intention of handing the information over to a foreign power contrary to article 413-7.

Intention can take a variety of forms. One can distinguish premeditated acts, acts with a specific intention at the time of the offence, and ones where there is a rather indeterminate intention. *Préméditation* is defined as 'a design formed before the action to commit a specific *crime* or *délit*' (article 132-72). It serves to support the existence of the requisite intention and may be an aggravating factor relevant to sentencing, e.g. in the case of premeditated murder the penalty may be life imprisonment (article 221-3) rather than just imprisonment for 30 years (article 221-1).

Specific intention arises where, without prior planning, the offender desires both to commit the acts and to achieve the results which are constituent elements of the offence.

An imprecise intention exists where the offender wishes to commit the actions in question but either is uncertain of the result which will be achieved by them or finds that it is more serious than anticipated. In both cases, French law treats the result as intended because the acts which led to them were intended. Provided

[78] See A.C. Dana, *Essai sur la notion d'infraction pénale* (Paris, 1982), paras. 421ff.

that the offender could have or should have foreseen the consequence, he is taken to have assumed the risk of it occurring (*dolus indeterminatus determinatur eventu*). This solution is typically adopted when the results exceed what was actually intended (e.g. hitting the victim in order to hurt her, but actually causing her death). (French theorists describe this as the 'praeterintentional wrong'.) Such an outcome is sometimes rather harsh for the accused and there are situations when French law adopts an intermediate position between punishing the offender according to what was actually intended and punishing him according to the result which occurred. Thus, in relation to causing the death of the victim, instead of 'intentional homicide' (*homicide volontaire*), punished by 30 years' imprisonment under article 221-1 of the Criminal Code, a person might be convicted of intentional assault causing death (*coups volontaires*), punished by 15 years' imprisonment under article 222-7.

French law does assimilate gross indifference to intention in some cases, but this is limited to where the accused has deliberately turned a blind eye to the consequences of his actions. For example, in the case of fraud, judges have treated the mere permission to put goods on the market without checking on their quality as equivalent to an intention to deceive on the ground that there is a conscious approval of the sale.[79] This case law was relied on in the prosecution of the director of the blood transfusion service who permitted potentially HIV-contaminated blood to be given to transfusion patients, despite warnings that a method existed for detecting the risk, which he did not choose to use.[80]

It is clear that intention is really proved from the facts of the case in many cases. While formally the public prosecutor has to demonstrate the intention, this is readily assumed from the facts, e.g. if you deliberately hit your opponent, this is readily assumed to be intentional without separate enquiry. Equally, the wife of a modest household whose husband starts accumulating expensive works of art at home is readily considered to have known that they were stolen and thus be guilty of handling stolen goods.[81]

B. Recklessness

English law distinguishes between intention and recklessness on the basis that recklessness is a matter of taking a risk, demonstrating a gross indifference to the outcome, rather than a desire to achieve it. Recklessness (*dol éventuel*) usually involves the commission of one wrong which has, as a consequence, a more serious outcome of a distinct kind from that deliberately contemplated. For example, a driver shows flagrant disregard for the highway code and thereby causes the death of another motorist. For the most part, recklessness is treated as gross negligence

---

[79] See, for instance, Crim. 12 April 1976, D 1977.239 note Fourgoux.
[80] Paris, 13 July 1993, *Droit pénal* Jan 1994, 12.
[81] Crim. 6 Jan. 1992, GP 16 July 1993.

and punished as unintentional fault. This position was adopted in 1832 with regard to murder, thereby reducing the number of capital crimes. In order to deal specifically with this kind of offence, the drafters of the 1994 Code created the offence of deliberately endangering life, a *délit* punishable by one year in prison or a fine of up to €15,000. Article 223-1 makes it an offence to 'expose [another] directly to an immediate risk of death or of injuries involving permanent disfigurement or infirmity by an obviously deliberate breach of a specific obligation of safety or care imposed by law or decree'. This was intended to catch reckless drivers, but covers a number of other reckless actions where the commission of one crime has consequences which might be considered as serving as the basis for a prosecution for a more serious offence.

C. Negligence

'Ordinary fault' (*faute ordinaire*) is the typical basis of liability for *délits*. Article 121-3 was amended in 2000 to emphasize that, where a *loi* creates a *délit* committed by negligence, omission or by the failure to comply with a statutory duty of care or security, a person will only be liable if he has not shown reasonable diligence, taking account of his duties and the means at his disposal. Where the person has not caused such an injury deliberately, but has merely contributed to the situation, he will only be liable criminally if he has manifestly acted deliberately in breach of a statutory duty of care or security or has been grossly negligent in placing another in danger.

A deliberate breach of a legal duty of safety or care with regard to another may amount to gross negligence or recklessness. Thus a shipowner who fills up the ship with passengers, even though he knows it is unseaworthy, is committing this kind of wrongdoing. Deliberate breach of such a legal duty of care or safety is treated as an aggravating circumstance and the penalty is increased under the new Criminal Code (article 221-6).

French doctrinal writing has discussed how far conscious carelessness can be distinguished from recklessness. In principle, there is a difference, for in the case of conscious carelessness (*faute consciente*), the offender is aware of the risk, but calculates that it will not occur, whereas the reckless person does not discount its occurrence, but is indifferent to that eventuality. In practice, the line is subtle and a body of doctrinal writers would refuse to see a serious distinction between the two states of mind.[82]

By contrast, 'unconscious fault' (*faute inconsciente*) arises from a failure to take account of a risk when one ought to have done so. For example, the landlord who rents a flat to a tenant without inspecting the pipes, is liable where the tenant dies from gas leaking out of the pipes.[83] Such a fault may arise from breach of a general

---

[82] J. Cédras, 'Le dol éventuel: aux limites de l'intention' D 1995 Chr. 18.
[83] Crim. 9 May 1973, GP 1973.2 Somm. 232.

standard of care or from a failure to comply with an obligation of safety or care laid down by law or decree. In such a case, the failure to comply with the standard in the decree (which may only create a *contravention*) serves as the basis for the commission of a *délit*. This would be particularly relevant where death ensues from the breach of some regulation concerned with office or factory safety.

D. Strict Liability

Prior to the 1994 Code, there were some *délits* which were of strict liability, but most were *contraventions*. This led to the idea that there were certain *infractions matérielles*, offences for which strict liability existed, since the prosecution had merely to prove the occurrence of the material events which constituted the *actus reus*. Article 123-1 of the New Criminal Code implicitly rejects this idea as appropriate to *délits* and leaves strict liability as a matter for *contraventions* which carry less of a social stigma. Strict liability in the case of contraventions developed under the Code of 1810 and from 1843, the Cour de cassation often applied this standard for liability where no requirement of negligence or intention was mentioned in the legislation creating an offence.[84] Such an approach covered a wide range of offences including *délits* in areas such as hunting, lakes and forests, commercial offences (e.g. predatory pricing), planning. Such strict liability had to be considered as a presumption of liability, but it was rebutted only by proof of some external cause or *force majeure*. For example, in the case of article 434-1 of the Rural Code (pollution of a waterway), it was held in *Procureur général c. Ferrier*[85] that the offence was committed where crude oil leaked into the ground from underground pipes which had been installed consistently with best practice at the time of construction some six years earlier, despite the fact that the pipe owner did not know of the leak and was not at fault. The leak was discovered and cured at the end of 1971, but the oil which had already leaked continued to cause pollution in 1972 and 1973 by the effect of rain washing it from the soil and into the river. Although the Cour d'appel acquitted the pipe owner for lack of proof of fault, the Cour de cassation held that specific proof of fault by the prosecutor was unnecessary. The mere fact of having let toxic materials flow into the river raised a presumption of fault which could only be rebutted by proof by the defendant of *force majeure*.

The idea of strict liability applied to *délits* has been problematic. Even if the European Court of Human Rights accepts presumptions of fault, provided they do not exceed 'reasonable limits taking account of the gravity of what is at stake and maintaining the rights of the defence'.[86] The approach of the New Criminal Code of 1994 is to limit strict liability to contraventions.

[84] Crim. 12 May 1843 S 1844.1.158.
[85] Crim. 28 April 1977, D 1978. 149 note Rassat; JCP 1978.II.18931 note Delmas-Marty.
[86] ECHR 7 Oct. 1988, *Salabiaku*, Ser. A, vol. 141.

While these reforms have reduced the scope for strict liability, there remains a significant area of contraventions where this is the typical basis of liability.

E. Factors Affecting Mental Capacity

Article 122-1 of the Criminal Code declares a person to be free from criminal liability if he was 'affected, at the time of the events, by a psychiatric or neuropsychiatric disorder which removed his judgment or his control over his acts'. Psychiatric illness could be congenital or be something acquired (e.g. dementia). Such illnesses include not only permanent states of incapacity, but also temporary states, such as those arising from epilepsy. The normal procedure is that the existence of the illness is determined by an expert appointed by the court. (This need not take place at trial, but could have taken place in the investigatory phase.) Although the existence of such an illness may lead to a criminal acquittal, the court is required to inform the prefect and the committee of hospitalizations in the département that the acquittal will take place on these grounds, if the person in question could be a danger to public order or to the safety of persons. The prefect can then take such steps as are necessary, including ordering the person to be detained in a psychiatric hospital under the provisions of the Code of Public Health.

To give rise to an acquittal, the mental disorder must have been present at the time of the events constitutive of the crime, and must have caused the lack of judgment or control required for the offence. Where the illness merely contributes to the offence, then an attenuation of liability is possible. Alinéa 2 of article 122-1 provides that: 'The person who is affected, at the time of the events, by a psychiatric or neuropsychiatric disorder which reduced his judgment or impeded his control over his actions remains liable; all the same, the court shall take account of this circumstance when determining the sanction and fixing its character.'

While article 122-1 covers illnesses and permanent conditions, it is less clear how it relates to temporary disorders. Obsessions and irresistible impulses, such as kleptomania or pyromania, are not treated as illnesses nor as constraints on the will, but justify a reduced sentence.[87] Other actions affecting the will are treated similarly. If they totally remove the freedom of the individual, e.g. as under a hypnotic trance, then they justify an acquittal, but otherwise they merely count towards mitigation.[88] In the case of drunkenness, a serious disorder such as *delirium tremens* would be treated as equivalent to a mental disorder and lead to an acquittal. But someone acting on one event under the influence of drink is unlikely to be seen as so affected. Indeed, as in many countries, drunkenness and undertaking tasks such as driving while drunk are seen as offences in their own right. As a result, it is often argued that the person who is voluntarily drunk has committed a fault in getting himself into that state and cannot use that as an excuse, e.g. the drunken sailor who misses

---

[87] See Crim. 11 April 1908, DP 1908.1.271.
[88] See Trib. corr. Versailles, 13 May 1970, GP 1971.1.34 note Doucet.

his boat is still guilty of desertion, as we have seen. All the same, the courts do exercise a degree of discretion in evaluating the facts to determine the extent of the individual's guilt and this may lead it to consider that the individual did not form the necessary intention for a serious offence, even though the person was negligent in committing the act. (Indeed, article L 232-1 of the Highway Code sees driving while drunk as an aggravating circumstance for negligent conduct.)

F. Mistake

Mistake may help to explain the actions of an individual and often, as an excuse, serve to reduce culpability, but rarely will it justify the action altogether. While mistakes of fact may partially excuse or at least mitigate liability, mistakes of law will only do so where they are insuperable (*invincible*), i.e. they are matters about which the offender could not be reasonably expected to know. Where it operates, mistake serves to reduce or extinguish culpability because it affects judgments about the mental state of the accused.

1. *Mistake of fact* (erreur de fait)

In the case of intentional wrongs, the general rule is that a mistake concerning an essential element of the offence excludes liability. For example, in *Procureur général c X*,[89] a man was charged with removing a minor of under 18 years of age. The physical appearance and behaviour of the girl were such as to lead him reasonably to think that she was 19 years of age, as she claimed to be. Her parents gave her a freedom of action commensurate with the older age. The Cour d'appel held that he had made a reasonable mistake and the Cour de cassation upheld the acquittal. The courts do not require the mistake to be an insuperable error, it suffices that it is within the range of reasonable responses. Thus a farmer was acquitted of intentionally killing carrier pigeons which were feeding on his crops when he thought, without careful examination, that they were tame pigeons.[90] As long as the mistake is not gross or unreasonable, the element of intention is negated. But, of course, the mistake must be such as to negate the commission of any crime. A mere mistake as to the identity of the victim of a murder or assault in no way reduces the seriousness of the offence, since, even if the situation had been as the offender believed, he would still have been committing an offence.[91]

In the case of unintentional offences, the element of negligence still exists, even if there was a mistake. Thus, to quote Pradel, if a hunter kills one of his companions in the darkness of the forest thinking that he is a wild boar, he has still committed manslaughter (*homicide par imprudence*). The mistake is indeed evidence of the

---

[89] D 1965.323 note Vouin.

[90] Crim. 19 Nov. 1926, GP 1926.1.239.

[91] e.g. Crim. 4 Jan. 1978, Bull. crim. no.5 where a booby-trapped package blew up killing four people who were different from the intended victim: the offence of murder was still committed.

negligence required. To serve as an excuse the mistake must be insuperable, one about which the accused could not be blamed in any way. Thus, in *Genty*, hunters took part in a lawful cull of vermin and harmful animals. All the hunters fired on a wolf, but Genty killed a deer which he could not have known was there. This finding of fact that he could not have been able to find out that his shot would hit a deer before he fired was sufficient to lead to his acquittal.[92] But obviously, such insuperable mistake is not easy for the defendant to prove.

2. *Mistake of law* (erreur de droit)

Mistake of law is not easily accepted since everyone is deemed to know the law, a principle affirmed at least as early as 1820. The 1978 draft of the new Criminal Code specifically provided a defence where a person demonstrates that he thought he could lawfully commit the act and that he had no way of knowing otherwise, but this was not taken up by the final draft of 1986. But there are situations where the courts recognize that the complexity of the law is such as to permit of genuine mistakes. Thus, in *Laurent*, the directors of a company were prosecuted intentionally hampering the workings of the board of directors in having refused a union representative admission to the meeting of the central committee of the company. The *ordonnance* of 22 February 1945 provided for the representation of management, unions and shareholders on the board of directors. The directors had specifically asked the Minister of Labour for advice and he had replied that the legislation did not specifically require the presence of unions in the central committee. The Cour de cassation[93] upheld the decision of the lower court that, where the legal text was controversial in its application, and where an interpretation had been offered and followed from a responsible administrative authority, the directors could legitimately believe they were entitled to refuse the union representative entry and thus did not have the criminal intent necessary for the offence. But such an excuse could rarely arise because, in principle, the mistake of law must be insuperable. The fact that the accused believed he had a good legal argument will not suffice. Thus, in *Josserand*, a father believed he had the right in law to the custody of his child, despite a court order to the contrary (which he was in the process of appealing against). He was held guilty of intentionally refusing to comply with the court order to return his child to the mother when he claimed to retain custody until the outcome of the appeal.[94]

V. Actors

Criminal liability lies for the acts of individuals as both principals and accomplices, provided they have criminal capacity. The liability of companies and

---

[92] Crim. 16 Nov. 1866, DP 1867.1.87.
[93] Crim. 9 Oct. 1958, D 1959. 68.
[94] Crim. 8 Feb. 1966, RSC 1966, 887 obs. Légal.

public bodies has only recently been established by the 1994 Criminal Code, and, as an alternative, the liability for others remains rather limited. There are some uses of criminal liability which a non-French lawyer might find strange. For example, many medical negligence claims become criminal cases.[95] This has little to do with who may be criminally liable in France, but is affected by the advantages of the *partie civile* procedure in recovering civil damages, as well as the form of public denunciation which the relatives of victims can obtain from a criminal trial.

A. Capacity

The Code of 1810 fixed the age of full criminal responsibility at 16 (raised to 18 in 1906) and required courts to examine whether children below that age had adequate discernment. The issue of discernment was abolished in 1912 for all children under 13. The relevant legal provisions for delinquents under this age of discernment were social welfare measures authorised. Since 1898, the judge was authorised to place children in the care of a parent, individual or a charitable or public institution. The law was fundamentally reformed by an *ordonnance* of 2 February 1945. The New Criminal Code provides in article 122-8 for the two basic principles now long established: that minors found guilty of criminal acts are subject to measures of protection, assistance, supervision and education, not punishment, and that a special *loi* may provide for the circumstances under which criminal sanctions can be imposed on children over 13. The 'special *loi*' in question remains the *ordonnance* of 1945. The relevant date for determining the age of the child is the date of the offence.

The basic position is that above 18, a person is fully responsible for criminal acts. Since 1970, the law has recognized the concept of the 'young adult offender' in terms of penal practice, and also in terms of the rehabilitation of offenders, since after three years, all offences committed between the ages of 18 and 21 are removed from the criminal file. Between 13 and 18, the delinquent is presumed not to be criminally responsible, but this presumption may be rebutted by evidence of adequate discernment. The sanction imposed by a court in such a case will be essentially educative where possible, though a criminal sanction such as a fine or imprisonment may be imposed where a purely educative measure is unlikely to have effect, e.g. where the child has not responded to previous similar measures. In 2005, 19,552 young people under 18 were given custodial sentences and criminal sanctions against this age group constituted 8.6% of all convictions. Even where a sentence of imprisonment is imposed, article 20-2 of the Criminal Code limits the period to half that which would apply to an adult, and article 20-3 applies a similar rule to fines. Below the age of 13, there is an irrebuttable

[95] See J. Penneau, op. cit., 98–99. Report of Mme Ferrari in Cour de cassation, *Rapport Annuel 1999*, sect. VI.

presumption that a child cannot be criminally liable,[96] though the *ordonnance* of 1945 provides that various measures of protection and education may be ordered by the juge des enfants. The Cour de cassation has considered that, if a child has not acted with understanding and will, then protective measures are not appropriate, only educative measures. Thus if a child of six commits the *actus reus* of an offence, the court will have to examine his or her understanding and intentions in order to decide which non-criminal measures should be taken. In principle, the age of reason is taken to be between eight and ten years of age, depending on the individual and the kind of wrongdoing involved.

B. Accomplices

The participant in a criminal activity is punished even if that person cannot be charged as a principal. The activity of participation is, in itself, a social harm. Participation may be by way of conspiracy, or aid and assistance.

Conspiracy is punished by article 450-1 of the Criminal Code (*association de malfaiteurs*) which criminalizes 'any group formed or agreement established with a view to the preparation, through one or more acts, of one or more distinct *crimes* punishable by at least ten years' imprisonment or one or more *délits* punished by at least five years' imprisonment.

Accomplices are defined by article 121-7 of the Criminal Code (on *complicité*) as falling into two categories. The first is a person who 'consciously, by aid or assistance, facilitates the preparation or commission of a *crime* or *délit*. The second category is the person who 'by gift, promise, threat, order, abuse of authority or power, incites an offence or gives instructions for its commission'. The two basic elements of complicity are that there is a principal offence and that there is an act of complicity.

The requirement of a principal offence follows from the essentially derivative character of complicity as an offence. French authors suggest that the accomplice's actions derive their criminality from the existence of the principal offence and so have an *emprunt de criminalité*. There are a few offences of complicity where there is no principal offence, but these are specifically designated as independent offences by legislation. An example is incitement to suicide (which is not an offence) (article 223-13 of the Criminal Code). Before the 1994 Code, the offence involved had to be a *crime* or a *délit*, there was no general offence of complicity in a *contravention*. The text of article 121-7 now makes it clear that this remains true for aid and assistance, but instigating an offence by incitement or order is deemed more dangerous to society and this applies to all categories of offence. In addition to these general provisions, there are specific offences of

---

[96] The case law of the Cour de cassation does provide that a child of even three years can be liable for a civil wrong since discernment does not play any part in liability: Ass. plén. 9 May 1984, D 1984.525 concl. Cabannes, note Chabas: see below p. 367.

complicity which may relate to particular *contraventions*, e.g. article R 625-1 al. 3 on aiding and abetting assault.

The existence of the principal offence is a fundamental requirement. If there is no crime, there can be no accomplice to a crime. For example, in *Schieb and Benamar*,[97] Schieb tried to procure an impecunious person, Benamar, to murder his wife by an offer of money. He paid several sums of money in advance and handed over a revolver and told Benamar where his wife would be on the following day. Benamar told a friend who informed the police and Schieb and Benamar were prosecuted for attempted murder. Benamar claimed that he had never intended to kill Mme Schieb and that he had taken no steps to meet up with her. He merely intended to draw the money which Schieb was paying him and to sell the gun for money. The lower court accepted these claims and acquitted both Benamar and Schieb. The Cour de cassation upheld the acquittals. Once Benamar could not be found to have begun on the commission of the offence, there was no attempt, and Schieb could not be said to be an accomplice to an attempt. The key element is that there must be a principal offence. If the principal has not or cannot be punished, for example because it has been decided not to prosecute him or because he was a minor or insane, this does not prevent the conviction of the accomplice.[98] By contrast, where there is a legal reason why the principal did not commit an offence, then there can be no complicity. Thus, where a prosecution was brought against the editor and the members of the association for defamation contained in the articles of association of a group which had to be published by law in the *Journal Officiel*, no complicity offence was possible.[99] The editor was bound by law to publish the information and could not be liable for defamation; thus the members of the association could not be liable as accomplices. This approach of the French courts is criticized by a section of doctrinal writing which argues that the actions of the accomplice have a distinctly wrongful character and, though the seriousness character of her or his wrong is linked to the character of the offence she or he tried to bring about, there is no need to require that the principal offence has actually been committed.[100]

The act of complicity must be positive and intentional, and occur at the time of the offence. This poses particular problems in the area of aiding and abetting. The requirement of a positive act means that the accomplice is actively engaged in facilitating the offence. Where there is only passive acquiescence, then there is no

---

[97] Crim. 25 Oct. 1962, D 1963.221 note Bouzat.

[98] e.g. Crim. 12 May 1970, Bull. crim. no. 158: an accomplice was punished even though the principal offender remained unidentified; Crim. 10 April 1975, *Herment and Doucet,* Bull. crim. no. 89, where the principal's conviction by default had not become definitive, but the accomplice could still be convicted.

[99] Crim. 17 Feb. 1981, *R,* Bull. crim. no. 63.

[100] See J. Carbonnier, 'Du sens de la répression applicable aux complices selon l'article 59 du code pénal' JCP 1952.I.1034; M. Ancel, *La défense sociale nouvelle* (Paris, 1980), 207; J. Pradel, *Droit pénal,* 464–465.

liability, as in *Coutant*,[101] where the president of the club must have known about the illegal lottery organized among it members. Such acquiescence only amounts to a positive act where there is not only knowledge, but the power to do something about it which is deliberately not exercised. Thus in *Pernot*,[102] a principal shareholder and board member knew of the fraudulent claims made by the company chairman with regard to his travel expenses which were in fact paid for by means of transfers to another company of which both were also major shareholders. Since the major shareholder could have used his position on the board to object to this conduct, his failure amounted to active collusion. This case demonstrates the extent to which the case law has moved from a narrow conception of what is a 'positive' action. A similar expansion of the grounds of liability occurs in relation to the requirement that the acts of complicity should predate or accompany the offence. If there is sufficient prior agreement, then acts of assistance after the event will constitute complicity. For example, in *Moullec*,[103] an armed robber attacked a businessman on his own. His brother accompanied him in a car for several hours looking for a likely victim, bringing along a sawn-off shotgun. He also was helping to push away witnesses when his brother was apprehended. These actions amounted to assistance in the getaway and, since they were based on a prior agreement, constituted aiding and abetting the armed robbery. A similar solution was adopted where the accomplice assisted in unloading stolen goods from a lorry.[104]

The intentional character of the act requires that the accomplice knows of the illegal enterprise. Thus where a man gave another two pistols in order to frighten a debtor into paying the debt, he was not held liable as an accomplice where the pistols were used to kill the concierge who answered the door when he came to deliver the threat.[105] (The Cour de cassation remarked that, while he could have been convicted as an accomplice to attempted extortion or conspiracy to murder the debtor, there was no knowledge that the pistols would be used against the concierge.) The knowledge of the intended crime must be specifically proved. It was insufficient to establish complicity in the unlawful slaughter of animals (as part of a black market activity) in *Paemelabre* that a man drove a lorry containing pigs to a location made available by his wife, where they were slaughtered and he drove away the carcases of the dead pigs afterwards.[106] The requirement that there must be an intention to assist means that there cannot be aiding and abetting of unintentional offences (though where one person orders the commission of negligent acts by another, he can be held liable as co-principal).[107]

---

[101] Above p. 215; this is consistent with case law going back to 1810 and with art. 5 of the Declaration of the Rights of Man which permits the prohibition of *actions* harmful to society.

[102] Crim. 28 May 1980, D 1981.IR.137; see also Trib. corr. Aix, 14 Jan. 1947, JCP 1947.II.3465 note Béraud, where a policeman allowed his colleague to commit theft.

[103] Crim. 8 Nov. 1972, Bull. crim. no. 329.

[104] Crim. 31 Dec. 1920, S 1922.1.45.

[105] Crim. 13 Jan. 1955, *Nicolaï*, D 1955.291 note Chavanne.

[106] Crim. 1 Dec. 1944, D 1945.162.

[107] Crim. 24 Oct. 1956, *Guillemin and Wagner*, Bull. crim. no. 675.

Incitement is distinguished from mere advice by its content, directness and consequences. In terms of content, article 121-7 of the Code specifies certain elements which must be present (described in French as *adminicules*): gift, promise, threat, order or abuse of authority or power. Thus mere advice, however strongly presented, does not amount to incitement. A direct link with the offence is important to distinguish between general advice, e.g. a home page on the internet explaining how to make bombs, and incitement to a specific individual to commit a specific offence. Only the latter is treated as a criminal incitement. Finally, the advice must be followed by an effect. The line between giving information and incitement can be fine. For example, if one provides details about the victim, this may suffice if it is sufficiently precise to permit the commission of the offence in the near future. It is the causing of the criminal action by the principal which is the reason for French law to punish the inciter. Thus, in *Schieb and Benamar*,[108] Schieb was not held liable for incitement where Benamar had not begun on the commission of the offence. There are certain offences of conspiracy which are criminal in their own right, e.g. incitement to use drugs in sport (article L 232-26 of the Code of Sports) and on incitement not conducted in public of racial discrimination (article R 625-7 of the Criminal Code), and some of these are committed even if there are no consequences: e.g. incitement to use drugs under article L 3421-4 of the Code of Public Health.

Co-principals are distinguished from accomplices in that they are liable in their own right. It is not necessary to establish the criminal liability of the other person involved. The key difference is that the co-principal has performed the actions which constitute the offence, where the accomplice has done ancillary acts with a view to assisting the offence. Under the 1810 Code, the accomplice was liable to the same penalty as the principal. Thus a son who incites another to kill his father will be liable to the penalty for murder. Under article 121-7 of the Criminal Code, the accomplice is now punished as if he were the principal. This change of wording would lead to the (more serious) penalty for parricide in the case of a son who incites another to kill his father. While the principal is only punished for ordinary murder, the son is now punishable more seriously. There may, however, be reasons why an individual should be prosecuted as an accomplice rather than as a co-principal. An old decision of the Cour de cassation[109] stated that a co-principal was necessarily guilty of aiding and abetting his partner in crime. This idea is used where a group of people are involved in the commission of an offence, but it is not possible to identify the actual principal offender. It applies, for example, where one blow causes a severe injury, but it is not possible to identify which person caused the most serious injury. In that case, all are capable of being convicted as accomplices to the most serious offence committed by a member of the group and it is not necessary to identify the principal offender.[110]

---

[108] Above p. 231.

[109] Crim. 9 July 1848, *Igneux*, S 1848.1.527. In that case, the son-in-law who helped a daughter to kill her father was convicted as her accomplice and so was liable to the death penalty for parricide, rather than imprisonment for simple murder.

[110] See, e.g., Crim. 19 May 1978, D 1980.3 note A. Galia-Beauchesne.

C. Liability for Others

In principle, vicarious liability is inconsistent with the personal character of criminal liability. In 1976 the Conseil constitutionnel declared that there could be no criminal liability except in the case of fault of the individual in question, and this was applied in the area of criminal offences in labour law by the *loi* of 6 December 1976.[111] Now the French courts had held the employer responsible for regulatory offences committed by their employees since the middle of the 19th century.[112] The justification was that:

although in principle one can only be liable to a penalty in respect of one's own acts, it is different in exceptional cases where the legal requirements create an obligation to exercise a direct action in relation to another; in the case of regulated industries, especially demolition businesses, it is necessary to impute the criminal liability back to the head of the business because the conditions and manner of exercise of the business are imposed personally on them, and they are bound to ensure the performance of these requirements.[113]

The concept of non-delegable duty seems to lie behind much of the liability in this area. At the same time, there is also a sense that the employer is in some way at fault in failing to supervise his employees or set up an appropriate system. Case law has been strict here: 'the heads of firms must personally ensure at all times that the rules on the safety of the workers they employ are strictly and constantly respected'.[114] This has the sound of an irrebuttable presumption, but since 1902 the Cour de cassation has accepted that some delegation by the head of a firm is permissible. It is noted by Pradel[115] that the effect of the 1976 *loi* was to encourage courts even more than before to identify the fault of the employer for which he was being found criminally liable. This was the rationale identified in the 19th century, the personal omission or failure to act by the employer, and which might have become less evident as liability of directors in regulatory offences was extended. The extent to which this will remain an important area now that companies can also be principals to crimes remains to be seen.

D. Corporations[116]

French law has been slow to recognize the criminal liability of corporations. Although the Criminal Ordinance of 1670 (title 21) contained provisions establishing some circumstances in which corporate bodies could be held criminally

---

[111] C. cons. 2 Dec. 1976, *Work Accidents*, Rec. 39.
[112] See Crim. 15 Jan. 1841, S 1849.1.149; Crim. 26 Aug. 1859, S.1859.1.973.
[113] Crim. 30 Dec. 1892, S 1894.1.201.
[114] Crim. 29 Feb. 1956, Bull. crim. no. 213.
[115] Pradel, *Droit pénal*, 493–494.
[116] See generally Université de Paris 1, *La responsabilité des personnes morales*, Revue des sociétés 1993, no. 2.

liable, these were not carried forward into the Criminal Code of 1810. The basic argument was that criminal penalties were personal in character and could only be imposed on the human beings responsible, not all the members of an association of group. In practice, this argument was undermined in two ways. First, under certain specific legislation enacted in the 20th century, associations and corporate bodies could be ordered to pay the fines imposed on their members or officers, e.g. article 36 of the *loi* of 9 December 1905 allowed the court to order church authorities to pay fines imposed on priests for breach of rules on the conduct of religious services, and more recently in the *loi* of 6 December 1976 employers could be required to pay fines imposed on employees (including directors) in relation to offences against the person caused by accidents at work. Case law also started to accept the imposition of criminal liability of corporate bodies for offences not involving a mental element.

Article 121-2 of the New Criminal Code provides:

Corporate bodies, with the exception of the State, are criminally liable in the different ways set out in articles 121-4 to 121-7 [as principals, for attempts, and as accomplices] and in the cases specified by statute or decree for offences committed on their behalf by their organs or representatives.

All the same, local authorities and groupings of them can only be criminally liable for offences committed in the exercise of activities which can be the subject-matter of contracts for the delegation of public services. The criminal liability of corporate bodies does not exclude that for the same facts of the human beings who were principals or accomplices.

This article makes it clear that the criminal liability of public bodies is limited.[117] But since local public services are extensive there are significant areas for criminal liability, e.g. in water services, school transport, refuse collection. The fact that a local authority keeps the activity inhouse or provided by a group of authorities, rather than by a private company, makes no difference to the criminal liability. On the other hand, there will be no criminal liability for activities of a public order kind, such as planning, policing and inspection, supervision and so on. In the case of private bodies, the Code, unlike earlier drafts, only makes bodies with legal personality liable. *De facto* groupings cannot be held liable.

Since 2006, when the *loi* of 9 March 2004 on organized crime came into force, it is no longer necessary that legislation must specifically create the liability of corporate bodies; any offence can potentially be committed by a corporate body. In the New Criminal Code, there are provisions both in the legislative and in the regulatory sections[118] which specifically create criminal liability for corporations. The legislative provisions create liability in relation to genocide, involuntary homicide or wounding (but not voluntary offences), drug-trafficking and

---

[117] G. Gartner, 'L'extension de la répression pénale aux personnes publiques' RFDA 1994.126.
[118] The division of articles in to 'L' and 'R' articles relates to how they may be amended see above p. 21.

money-laundering, endangering life, discrimination, invasions of privacy, theft, extortion, blackmail, fraud, handling stolen goods, treason, espionage and a number of other offences. The regulatory part contains even more offences, especially involuntary harms to the person, breaches of weights and measures or currency rules, and so on. Specific statutes passed since the Code was enacted have covered areas such as environmental offences and price fixing.

The offence must be committed by an organ or representative of the company. The French law here has adopted an identification theory, that the acts of the company are those of its principal organs or representatives. Under company law (Chapter 2 of the Commercial Code), the 'organs' are the general meeting (*assemblée générale*), the board of directors (*conseil d'administration*) and the governing board (*le directoire*). The 'representatives' will be the managing director of a private company or the mayor of a local authority. An illustration would be death caused by a railway accident at a pedestrian crossing. The corporate body (SNCF) was not liable where knowledge of the potential danger of this site lay only with local engineers and managers.[119]

The offence must be committed for the benefit of the company. This precludes, in principle, acts *ultra vires* the company. The result of the conviction is that the company itself acquires its own criminal record.

VI. An Illustration: Homicide

The area of homicide can be taken as a good illustration of how French criminal law operates and the similarities (as well as the differences) with criminal law policy in the common law. The protection of life is a common value between different legal systems and the circumstances giving rise to threats to life are broadly the same. The differences arise in part out of the codified nature of French law, and partly because there are certain social values which are distinctive. French society attaches importance to certain kinds of act and French citizens are likely to resort to the criminal law in situations when the British would not, e.g. in relation to medical and sporting negligence.

French law distinguishes a large variety of different forms of homicide.

(1) At the most serious end, there are the *crimes* of genocide and crimes against humanity against which prescription does not run. Article 211-1 defines genocide as carrying out a concerted plan for the total or partial destruction of a national, ethnic, racial, religious or otherwise arbitrarily defined group. Article 212-1 includes among crimes against humanity the systematic execution of a group for political, philosophical, racial or religious motives.

---

[119] Crim. 8 January 2000, JCP 2000.II.10395.

(2) Deliberate or voluntary homicide can be of various levels of seriousness. Article 221-1 defines the *crime* of *meurtre* as 'the act of voluntarily causing the death of another' and punishes it with 30 years' imprisonment. Life imprisonment is imposed for aggravated forms of voluntary homicide: where if it accompanies or follows another *crime*, or aids the escape or impunity of someone who has committed a *délit* (article 221-2), or where the action is premeditated (article 221-3). Voluntary homicide of minors under 15, of ascendants or natural or adoptive parents, of vulnerable people, such as the physically or mentally handicapped or pregnant women, and of judges, jurors, witnesses, lawyers and other public officials involved in the legal process.

(3) Involuntary homicide is a *délit* defined by article 221-6 'the act of causing the death of another by incompetence, imprudence, carelessness, neglect or failure to observe a duty of safety or care imposed by statute or regulation'. It is punished by a maximum of three years' imprisonment and a fine of €45,000. These penalties are increased to five years' imprisonment and a fine of €75,000 for deliberate breaches of regulations and are doubled in the case of drink driving (article L. 235-1, Code de la route).

A. The Different Mental Elements

As has been stated earlier, the French distinguish four different categories of mental element in homicide. The basic distinction is between intentional and unintentional homicide. Intentional homicide (*meurtre*) has two aggravated forms: where it accompanies or follows the commission of another serious crime (*crime*), and where it is premeditated (*assassinat*).

The intentional element relates essentially to the willingness to cause death by the act in question. That momentary mental element applies equally to where the murder is part of a criminal enterprise: it is not required that murder is a planned part of the criminal enterprise, merely that it is intentional when committed. The planning involved in premeditation is thus seen as an aggravating circumstance punished by a longer period of imprisonment under article 221-3 of the New Criminal Code. Article 297 of the Old Criminal Code defined premeditation as a design formed before the act took place.

The key feature of the intention is that it is an intention to take life. It is not necessary that the victim be the person the murderer wanted to kill. For example, if a person sends a parcel bomb containing a large amount of explosive, this is clear evidence of a premeditated attempt to kill and it does not matter that the actual victims who opened the parcel were different from those whom the bomb was intended to injure.[120] Similarly, the act of releasing a driverless and unlit lorry in the direction of a group of police officers with a stone jammed onto the

---

[120] See Crim. 4 Jan. 1978, D 1978.IR.330; also Crim. 31 Jan. 1835, S 1835.1.564.

accelerator is sufficient indication of an intention when it is clear that the actor knew that the lorry would necessarily kill anyone in its path.[121]

The New Criminal Code has done away with the distinction between the involuntary homicide of a person as a result of violent acts towards him (article 311 of the Old Criminal Code) and that arising from negligence or omission (article 319 of the Old Criminal Code). The key feature is the mental element which involves the unintentional, but blameworthy breach of a standard of conduct leading to death (article 221-6 of the New Criminal Code). The standard is frequently laid down by law. Thus the conduct causing the death may be a breach of a legal requirement concerning the safety of vehicles or equipment. But it is not necessary that there is a legal standard. It is sufficient that the conduct falls below the standard of a *bon père de famille* in relation to the activity in question. For example, an anaesthetist was found guilty of involuntary homicide where he removed tubes and stopped the reanimation of a patient contrary to the standards of medical practice.[122] But mere carelessness, which is sufficient to ground private law liability is not enough. The fault giving rise to criminal liability is not fundamentally different from that which would give rise to civil liability. Indeed, the interest of the civil party in pursuing a criminal prosecution is precisely to obtain civil damages following on from the criminal conviction. This important overlap in the area of unintentional homicide has important consequences for the use of criminal law in the areas of medical and sporting negligence. The strict separation in the common law, both procedural and substantive, between civil and criminal liability does not encourage the use of the criminal law in such cases, and the coroner's inquest is an alternative public forum for attaching blame to doctor and sportsmen.

It will be recalled that article 121-3, as amended in 2000, now provides that a *délit* may be committed directly through mere careless acts (*imprudence*) or omissions (*négligence*). For indirect harm, it is also necessary that there is either a 'manifestly deliberate breach of a particular obligation of care or safety provided by *loi* or *règlement*' or by 'aggravated fault' (*faute caractérisée*), which 'exposed another person to a risk of which they could not have been unaware'. These latter provisions requiring either a manifestly deliberate breach of duty or aggravated fault apply to physical persons, not public bodies or companies. The intention was to reduce the criminal liability of public officials for mere negligence in supervising situations in which people are killed, e.g. the collapse of stands in a football ground.

There are numerous instances of criminal liability for unintentional homicide arising out of medical malpractice. For example, where the surgeon and the anaesthetist left the hospital after an operation leaving the patient in the sole care of a nurse, rather than another doctor, this was sufficient to lead to the conviction

---

[121] Crim. 10 June 1970, D 1970.533.
[122] Crim. 19 Feb. 1997, D 1998.236 note Legros.

of both when the patient died.[123] Likewise, the doctor who gave a child a second anti-tetanus injection even after he had shown an adverse reaction following the first injection was held guilty when the child died.[124]

In sport, liability can arise, for example, where a death resulted from a racing driver taking a hairpin bend at excessive speed.[125] The referee who fails to stop excessive violence in a game might also be liable.[126]

B. Characteristics of the Criminal Act

Homicide is seen as more or less serious not only in relation to the intention, but also in relation to the character of the victim or the method of causing death. Article 221-4 distinguishes five particularly heinous forms of murder which give rise to life imprisonment, rather than just to 30 years' imprisonment. The special categories of victim are children under 15, ascendants or adopted parents (the old crime of *parricide*), particularly vulnerable people (the old, the sick or pregnant women), judges, jurors, lawyers or public officers (including the police) on duty, and witnesses in a civil or criminal case. Article 221-5 singles out poisoning for more severe treatment than other forms of murder. These special cases reflect certain social values specific to French society.

C. Causation

There is clearly a need to establish a link between the act of the accused and the death of the victim. The notion of causation is extended to encompass a variety of consequences of the fault in question. A good example is where the victim has to undergo medical treatment as a result of an assault and dies or is injured further as a result of that treatment. The author of the assault is liable for the consequences of the risk of medical treatment to which the victim has become exposed. For example, where the victim of a road accident had to undergo a blood transfusion and contracted AIDS as a result of infected blood, the driver causing the accident was held criminally liable for this consequence.[127] On the other hand, there must be some connection between the criminal act and the risk to which the victim is exposed. Where the victim is at fault, then no liability arises for the injury. For example, where the victim was involved in a road accident and raced after the other car and died from a heart attack, the other car driver was held not liable. The death resulted from a rash act of the victim.[128]

---

[123] Crim. 10 May 1984, D 1985.256 note Penneau.
[124] Crim. 31 Jan. 1956, D 1956.251.
[125] Chambéry, 2 July 1987, GP 1987.2 Somm 382.
[126] See Toulouse 20 Jan. 1977, JCP 1978. II.18788 note Remplon and 18810 bis.
[127] Paris 7 July 1989, GP 1989.2.752; see more generally Crim. 10 July 1952, D 1952.618.
[128] See Crim. 25 April 1967, GP 1967.1.343.

Causation has become a particularly important issue in relation to involuntary homicide. Article 121-3 requires a manifestly deliberate breach of duty or aggravated fault where the person has not directly caused the harm, 'but who [has] created or contributed to the creation of the situation which allowed the occurrence of the damage or who [has] not taken measures allowing it to be avoided'. Thus a distinction is set up between direct causation of harm, where ordinary fault has to be shown, and indirect causation where more serious fault is required. For example, a driver was driving at excessive speed so as to be unable to control his car; he saw a wild boar, swerved to avoid it and collided with another car, killing its driver. Here there was a direct causal link between the fault of the driver and the death of the victim.[129] On the other hand, such direct causation was not found where doctors administered contaminated blood to patients from which they contracted the HIV virus. They did not know the blood was infected and it was not shown that the carelessness in checking the blood products clearly led to the infection. Accordingly the lower court judges were entitled to acquit the accused.[130]

The action involved may be an omission, but the causation must involve some diminution in life chances. So it may apply to a person who is terminally ill. Thus, where a doctor committed a gross fault in failing to diagnose the real illness and offer treatment which could at least have given the victim remission from the cancer, if not a cure, he is liable for the unintentional homicide of the patient whose death has been hastened by this fault.[131]

As will be noted later,[132] there has been a partial separation between civil and criminal fault as a result of the amendments to the Criminal Code in 2000. But in many situations, such as in the car driver example, both civil and criminal fault will be found. The presence of the civil party used to encourage a closer alignment between findings of civil and criminal fault, and perhaps a lowering of the standard involved in the latter compared with English law. It remains to be seen how far a separation will now occur.

In part, the codification, undertaken most recently in the 1994 Code, ensures a tidier classification of different kinds of offence compared with the intricacies of the common law on murder and manslaughter, both of which remain common law offences. But it remains true that there is a distinct moral agenda in France which is not replicated entirely in English law. The special place of certain victims as aggravating features of an offence, and the willingness to find criminal liability for medical malpractice and for fault by public officials represents a distinct moral role for the criminal law, even if the latter is now reduced.

---

[129] Crim. 25 Sept. 2001, D 2001 IR 3328.
[130] Crim. 18 June 2003, D 2004, 1620 note Rebut.
[131] Paris 7 Nov. 1964, D 1964 Somm. 43.
[132] Below pp. 368–373.

PART II
(C) PRIVATE LAW

8

Family Law

I. Introduction

There are multiple definitions of 'family' reflecting the immense diversity of this fundamental social and legal institution. The family is characterized variously as a biological relationship (parent and child; brother and sister), as a voluntary legal undertaking (registered partnership; adoption), or as a religious and social contract (marriage). Equally, a vast array of family constellations has emerged that challenge the prevalence and, indeed, relevance of the embedded heterosexual, marital model in French family law today. Unmarried, single-parent, reconstituted, bereaved, homosexual and polygamous relationships, as well as those expanded through medical technology, all depict a diverse patchwork of family life that is based on *de facto* biological and legal ties. The *function* of the family is also difficult to define in any concrete terms since there are so many cultural, moral, religious, political and, of course, legal variables that shape our understanding of the rights and obligations of the family as a unit and, indeed, of individuals within that unit. Furthermore, the influence of and interaction between these variables change over time in response to different pressures. For instance, there is currently a distinct political preoccupation in France with promoting the role of the family; one that manifests itself in measures to promote reproduction and to facilitate reconciliation of work and family life, with a view to curbing demographic decline and securing the workforce of the future. Equally pervasive are measures aimed at inculcating in parents a sense of responsibility for the moral and social education of their children with a view to addressing anti-social behaviour, nurturing the citizens of the future, and upholding *l'ordre public*.

So how does the law accommodate, and indeed, regulate such plurality of experience, need and purpose? Indeed, how does it strike a balance between safeguarding the private realm of family relationships whilst ensuring parental authority is appropriately monitored and family relationships adequately supported? International law has played an important role in establishing a minimum 'floor' of rights beyond which state, including legal intervention, must not venture.[1] But on a day-to-day basis, upholding family rights and ensuring family

---

[1] Art. 8 of the European Convention on Human Rights and Fundamental Freedoms 1950, for instance, provides a right to respect for private and family life and has been the source of extensive case law.

obligations are fulfilled presents an ongoing challenge, particularly in the light of so many competing perspectives on what constitutes family, and how collective family rights and responsibilities are balanced with individual autonomy. The law inevitably favours some perspectives over others, with the effect that some family forms will never be as highly valued and, therefore, as well-protected, as others.

Bearing in mind these broader issues, the aim of this chapter is to consider the legal framework governing various aspects of French family law. The first section examines the legal definition and procedure relating to marriage. The second considers the circumstances in which marriage can be dissolved and analyses some of the ancillary issues arising out of divorce, namely property division and maintenance. The third section considers parental responsibility issues such as child contact (access), residence (custody), and child maintenance. The fourth section will consider the nature and scope of different forms of unmarried partnership, notably cohabitation and civil partnership (PACS), and section five provides a brief overview of the recently reformed law of succession. Finally, section six considers the specific status of children under family law, notably the legal framework governing affiliation and adoption.

II. Marriage

Despite a widespread increase in cohabitation and other forms of non-marital union in France, marriage remains a valued institution: there were 268,100 official marriages in metropolitan France in 2006. That said, this figure manifests a gradual decline in the number of marriages over the past three decades, contrasting with 297,922 marriages in the year 2000, 334,400 in 1980 and 393,700 in 1970.[2] Marriage is governed by Title V (Articles 144–228) of the Civil Code and has undergone significant statutory reform in recent years.

A. Conditions for Contracting a Marriage

In principle, the right to marry is a fundamental freedom protected by international law.[3] However, there are certain limitations imposed on *who* can marry. For instance, according to article 144 of the Civil Code the legal age of marriage is now set at 18 years old for both men and women[4] since this is deemed to be the age at which a person is considered to be sufficiently mature, both physically and emotionally, to cope with the responsibilities associated with marriage and its

---

[2] INSEE, 2007, <http://www.insee.fr/fr/ffc/chifcle_fiche.asp?ref_id=NATCCF02302&tab_id=12>.

[3] European Convention on Human Rights 1950, art. 12; Universal Declaration of Human Rights, art. 16.

[4] *Loi* n° 2006-399 of 4 April 2006 *renforçant la prévention et la répression des violences au sein du couple ou commises contre les mineurs,* art. 1. Previously, a man had to be at least 18 years old while the age limit for a female was 15.

consequences (notably parenting). Only in exceptional circumstances may the age limit be lowered, for example in the case of a minor who is pregnant, for which parental consent is required (articles 145 and 148 of the Code). Marriage is also prohibited between all legal and biological relatives, whether legitimate or illegitimate, including relatives by marriage (articles 161–163 of the Code). The only exception to this is set out in article 164 of the Civil Code which allows the President of the Republic to authorize a marriage between relatives by marriage in direct lineage where the person who created the relationship is deceased. For instance, a man could marry his deceased wife's sister. In similarly exceptional circumstances, the President can also authorize marriages between a non-biological uncle and niece or between an aunt and her nephew.

Marriage is a strictly monogamous institution. Bigamy is a criminal offence rendering the second marriage void and imposing a one-year custodial sentence and a fine of €45,000 on the bigamist, as set out in articles 147 and 188 of the Civil Code (and article 433-20 of the Criminal Law Code).[5] Polygamous marriages conducted in other countries under other religious and cultural regimes— for example Islamic—are recognized only to a limited extent in France. For instance, certain succession rights and social security rights have been made available to more than one spouse simultaneously, but rights of entry and residence can be legitimately limited to the first spouse in the interests of public order and security.[6] Most controversially, France does not recognize marriage between same-sex couples, unlike countries such as Belgium, the Netherlands and Spain. However, a transsexual can marry a partner of the opposite sex to his/her post-operative gender.[7]

Aside from these personal criteria, a number of procedural requirements have to be fulfilled before a couple can legally marry. First and foremost, in accordance with the secularization of French civil society in the early 19th century, marriage has been detached from any religious ceremonial requirement and is only recognized on completion of a civil ceremony. This must be celebrated before a state official, usually in the town hall in the locality where one party has continuously resided or been domiciled for at least one month prior to official notification of the marriage (article 74 of the Civil Code).[8] Notification of the marriage, stating the names, occupations, domiciles and residences of the future spouses, as well as the place where the marriage is to be celebrated, is posted on the town hall door

---

[5] The civil officer will also be liable for the same punishment if she or he knowingly conducted a bigamous ceremony.

[6] For further details, see Malaurie and Fulchiron, 122.

[7] French law was amended in 1992 to allow post-operative transsexuals to request a change of their birth certificate to reflect their new gender; Ass. plén, 11 Dec, 1992, D 1993.IR.1.JCP 1993. II.21991 concl. Jéol, note Mémeteau. See *B v France* App. No. 57/1990/248/319 (1992) 16 EHRR 1, confirmed by the decision in *Goodwin v UK* App. No. 28957/95 (2002) 35 EHRR 18.

[8] The term 'domicile' refers to an individual's principal place of residence and denotes a degree of permanency. Residence, on the other hand, usually denotes a more temporary place of abode, often connected with the individual's work or the exercise of a particular function.

for at least ten days prior to the ceremony (articles 63 and 64 of the Civil Code). This confirms the public status of the procedure and, in theory, allows anyone to submit their objection to the marriage. Both parties are also required to submit a medical certificate attesting to the fact that they have undergone a medical examination for the purposes of marriage within the previous two months. Since the marriage ceremony is a public event it must take place in the presence of at least two, and at most four, witnesses (articles 75 and 165 of the Civil Code). While the civil procedure legalizes the marriage, couples can choose to supplement this with a religious ceremony. This need not (and very often does not) take place on the same day as the civil service.

B. Obligations Arising out of Marriage

Under the Civil Code, marriage gives rise to a number of spousal (articles 212–226) and parental obligations (articles 203–211). Spousal obligations are summed up by article 212 of the Civil Code as comprising mutual fidelity, support and assistance. In substance, this entails a duty to cohabit (article 215),[9] as well as joint responsibility for the financial and moral direction of the family and for the educational and future welfare of the children (article 213). Financial contributions to the household must be equal and proportionate to their respective incomes,[10] and may comprise contributions-in-kind, including, for example, daily domestic chores or childcare.

According to article 215 of the Civil Code, any disposal of matrimonial property (for instance, the sale of the house) must be concluded by joint consent. Spouses may conclude contracts on an individual basis relating to matters of household maintenance or their children's education. However, the couple remain jointly responsible for any debts incurred in the process (in accordance with the French civil law notion of *solidarité*), except where the undertaking was 'manifestly excessive' or concluded in bad faith by a third party (article 220 of the Civil Code).

C. Annulment of Marriage

Failure to comply with any of the conditions set out above potentially renders the marriage null and void. The procedure for annulling a marriage (*nullité*) differs depending on the circumstances and is divided into two groups: *nullité relative* and *nullité absolue*. The former applies in cases where consent to the marriage was improperly elicited or vitiated (*vices du consentement*),[11] or where one of the parties is under the age of 18 and did not receive appropriate authorization (including

---

[9] Clearly, exceptions are made where separate living is necessary, for example, for the pursuit of professional activities, in which case, the law will interpret this as an 'intention to cohabit'.

[10] Unless stated otherwise in a pre-nuptial agreement (art. 214 C. civ.).

[11] This may occur for instance, where consent was obtained under duress; where one party consented to the marriage without realizing that her spouse was sexually impotent (TGI Avranches

parental consent) to marry. The action of *nullité relative* is only available to the aggrieved party, that is the person whose consent to the marriage was vitiated, or to the minor's parents who did not give their authorization to the marriage.

Nullité absolue, on the other hand, is open to any party affected by the marriage since it relates to more serious concerns around the fundamental nature of the marriage and is regarded as hostile not only to the interests of the parties, but to *l'ordre public.* The Civil Code refers to a number of cases in which an action for *nullité absolue* is available (articles 184 and 191). These include cases where one of the parties is below the age of sexual consent (*impuberté*), bigamy, incest, and failure to follow correct procedures, such as publicity and conducting the ceremony in an authorized setting.[12]

The effects of both *nullité relative* and *nullité absolue* are to render the marriage null and void *ab inito,* with property divided up as between strangers and no rights of succession created. Under article 371 *et seq* of the Civil Code any children conceived during the annulled marriage are treated in the same way as if the marriage had remained intact: the couple shares parental responsibility for the child (article 371 *et seq*) while the succession rights of all children have now been assimilated (article 202).[13]

That said, nullity of marriage is relatively rare in France, with an estimated one application for every 200 applications for divorce being lodged annually.

III. Divorce

Statistical data indicates the increasingly precarious nature of marriage. Over the past 30 years, there has been a steady increase in the number of annual divorces. For instance, in 2005, there were 152,020 divorces in France compared with 119,189 in 1995 and just over 81,000 in 1980.[14] Overall more than a third of all French marriages end in divorce. Of course, the rise in the divorce rate is not necessarily indicative of the disintegration of moral values or a loss of a sense of familial responsibility in preference for emotional and financial independence. A much more plausible explanation is the significant liberalization of divorce processes; a shift in the perception of divorce as an exceptional procedure, socially acceptable in only the rarest and most extreme of cases, to being a universal *right* for all married individuals.

Suffice to say, the law of divorce in France boasts a long and varied history. It was first legalized on 20 September 1792 in the aftermath of the revolution and

---

10 Jul. 1973, D.1974. 174 note Guiho); or where one party did not reveal to the other that they suffered from a severe mental illness (TGI Rennes 9 Nov. 1976, D 1977. 539 note Cosnard).

[12] Malaurie and Fulchiron, 134–152; Batteur, 274–280.
[13] See further below, p. 262.
[14] See above n. 2.

was initially available in cases of mutual consent or simply for reasons of *incompatibilité d'humeur*.[15] Following the introduction of the Civil Code in 1804, divorce was limited to fault-based grounds such as adultery, domestic violence, and desertion. Twelve years later, divorce was prohibited following the restoration of the Bourbon monarchy and in response to pressure from Catholic conservatives,[16] and was not reinstituted until 1884 under the Third Republic.[17] Fault remained the only ground for divorce at that time, a fact that was maligned for encouraging couples to manufacture instances of fault simply to enable them to end unhappy marriages. In spite of ongoing calls for reform, grounds for divorce remained unchanged for almost a century. The long-awaited 1975 Divorce Act[18] was described by many commentators at the time as instituting 'divorce *à la carte*' in that it significantly extended the grounds for divorce to include, inter alia, divorce by mutual consent.[19] In that sense, the reformed law was redolent of the liberalized approach of the late 18th century, although fault was retained as a legitimate ground. As well as making divorce more readily available, the 1975 law also brought with it structural amendments to the family justice system, notably the institution of a new *juge aux affaires matrimoniales* (JAM) within the tribunal de grande instance, with exclusive responsibility for presiding over divorce matters. This post was replaced in 1993 by the *juge aux affaires familiales* (JAF) to reflect the broader mandate of the post beyond matters of divorce, to matters of parental responsibility and child welfare.[20]

Despite the endurance of the 1975 law, it was criticized for its complexity both in substance and procedure. Thus, after lengthy and meticulous parliamentary negotiation, a new law was adopted on 26 May 2004 and came into force on the 1 January 2005,[21] the main objectives of which were to streamline and expedite divorce procedures and to minimize conflict between the parties.[22]

A. Grounds for Divorce

The 2004 law has been incorporated into Title VI (articles 229–310) of the Civil Code and recognizes four grounds for divorce: divorce by mutual consent (articles 230–232); divorce by acceptance of the principle of marital breakdown (articles 233–236); divorce by virtue of irretrievable breakdown of communal life (articles 237–241); and divorce on grounds of fault (articles 242–246). Divorce

---

[15] *Loi* of 20 September 1792.
[16] *La Loi Bonalde* of 1816.
[17] *La Loi Naquet* of 1884.
[18] *Loi* no 75-617 of 11 July 1975 *portant réforme du divorce*.
[19] M-A Glendon, 'The French Divorce Reform Law of 1975' (1976) 24 *Am J Com Law* 199–228.
[20] *Loi* of 8 January 1993. The functions of the JAF are defined in art. 373-2-6–373-2-13 C.civ.
[21] *Loi* no 2004-439 of 26 May 2004 *relative au divorce*.
[22] C. Butruille-Cardew, 'The 2004 French Divorce Law and International Prospects' (2006) 3 *Int Fam LJ* 143–149.

by mutual consent, as the least contentious and quickest of the four grounds, is regulated separately.

1. *Divorce by mutual consent* (divorce par consentement mutuel)

Divorce by mutual consent is a legacy of the 1975 Act and is the simplest and speediest procedure since both parties are in complete agreement as to the fact and conditions of the divorce. Because it is the least adversarial, this particular ground operates under different procedural rules to the other grounds. Under article 230 of the Civil Code, a request for divorce, signed by the parties and their respective lawyers or, as the case may be, their joint lawyer, is submitted to the court. This includes the terms of the parties' agreement (*convention*) in respect of the consequences of the divorce, including issues relating to the division of matrimonial property, occupation of the marital home, custody of the children, and a specification of the date at which they wish the divorce to take effect.[23]

The procedure requires a single hearing at which the JAF officially approves the terms agreed by the parties and grants a decree of divorce if he or she is satisfied that both have provided free and informed consent and that it is in the best interests of all parties concerned, including any children involved (article 232).[24]

The divorce is effective as of the date agreed by the parties in the *convention*.

2. *The three 'contentious' grounds for divorce*

The other three grounds of divorce share a common procedure for the most part but remain distinct in some respects. The first of these grounds is divorce by acceptance of the principle of marital breakdown (*divorce accepté*). Like divorce by mutual consent, this ground is a simplified version of the 1975 law and is pursued in cases where the parties agree in principle to the divorce but are unable to reach an agreement on ancillary issues (such as division of property) or parental responsibility.

The second contentious ground is divorce by virtue of irretrievable breakdown of communal life (*divorce pour altération définitive du lien conjugal*). This is granted in cases where the spouses have been separated for at least two years prior to the application.[25]

The final contentious ground, divorce on grounds of fault (*divorce pour faute*), was retained by the *loi* of 2004 after considerable debate.[26] This procedure is favoured

---

[23] This agreement is binding on the parties as soon as the divorce is finalized (art. 1091 N.c.pr.civ.).

[24] If the JAF is not satisfied that all parties are consenting or that it is not in their best interests, he or she has the option of scheduling a further hearing to take place within a maximum period of six months (art. 250-3 C.civ; art. 1101 N.c.pr.civ.). Since a decree of 29 October 2004 the JAF is also authorized to modify aspects of the agreement which he considers to be contrary to the interests of any of the parties (art. 1099 al. 2 N.c.pr.civ.).

[25] Under the previous 1975 law, a couple was required to have endured a six-year period of separation before they could request a divorce on this particular ground.

[26] Fault-based divorced has been heavily criticized for generating unnecessary conflict between parties.

in cases of a particularly serious or repeated breach by a spouse of the obligations arising out of marriage so as to render communal living intolerable (article 242).

For divorce on these three grounds, either party submits a request for divorce to the court through their lawyer. At this stage, under article 251 of the Code they do not provide any details as to the chosen grounds for the divorce. Before official proceedings can begin, however, parties are obliged to attend a conciliation hearing.

3. The conciliation hearing

Conciliation is an extra-judicial mechanism aimed at enabling parties to negotiate matters in a non-adversarial, mutually agreeable way before the divorce is finalized. Under article 252 of the Civil Code, this *must* take place in advance of any formal judicial proceedings and may even be repeated during the proceedings if the parties have failed to reach a satisfactory agreement. Conciliation is relatively informal; it does not involve any written submissions although legal assistance is compulsory since the 2004 Act (article 252-1 Civil Code), and it takes place in the presence of the JAF who meets separately with each party before convening a general meeting.[27] During the hearing, the parties will be encouraged to agree on the terms of the divorce and on which ground they wish to divorce. A suitably qualified third party may be appointed to compile an inventory of their shared assets and to draw up a provisional agreement as to how these will be divided. At this stage, interim measures (*les mesures provisoires*) will also be determined, which involves the *temporary* allocation of financial, property and parental rights and responsibilities pending finalization of the divorce (articles 254–257 of the Code). While any agreements made during the conciliation hearing are not legally binding on either party, in the vast majority of cases they will be enforced by the JAF when the decree of divorce is issued. This is to empower the parties to make decisions on their own behalf and is regarded as a more effective means of achieving fairness and future compliance. If conciliation is successful—in the sense that the parties arrive at a mutually satisfactory agreement—one or both of the parties can lodge a petition for divorce to the JAF specifying on which of the three grounds they wish to proceed. If both parties are in agreement on the fact of the marital breakdown and the ground for the divorce, the JAF will issue a decree dissolving the marriage.[28]

If, on the other hand, the parties are unable to reach an agreement during the conciliation hearing, the JAF may request that they reconvene at a later date

[27] Conciliation should not be confused with reconciliation: the aim is not to reunite the couple or to discourage divorce, but rather to minimize the degree of acrimony involved and encourage cooperation and open negotiation. Nor should conciliation be confused with mediation (although it often is!). Mediation is a *voluntary* undertaking by the couple to discuss matters on neutral territory and in the presence of an impartial mediator (not the judge). If the couple are struggling to reach an agreement during the conciliation process, the judge may suggest that they meet with an independent mediator.

[28] For further detail on this stage of the procedure, see Malaurie and Fulchiron, 272.

following a period of reflection (article 252-2 Civil Code).[29] If the parties are still unable to reach an agreement, effectively arriving at a deadlock, they will proceed with the divorce but ancillary issues will be determined by the JAF.

The flexibility provided by the regime of multiple grounds of divorce promoted by the 2004 Act has been generally welcomed not least because it allows couples to choose the grounds that most reflects the reality of their situation. The Act of 2004 also introduced a *'passarelle'* clause, effectively creating a pathway between the different procedures and enabling parties to shift from one ground to another. Thus, parties who commence divorce proceedings on grounds of irretrievable breakdown of communal life, for example, may subsequently reach an agreement on all issues at which point they can request that the JAF issue a decree based on mutual consent. Similarly, parties can request that their divorce be pronounced on grounds of acceptance of the principle of marital breakdown despite having commenced proceedings on an alternative ground such as fault (articles 247, 247-1, and 247-2 Civil Code). Essentially, the system is designed to give the parties as much control over divorce proceedings as possible enabling them ultimately to dissolve their marriage on the least contentious ground with a view to encouraging negotiation, mutual trust and expeditious decision-making.

B. The Legal Effects of Divorce

For all procedures, once the divorce has been decreed, the decision is final.

The divorce terminates any legal relationship between the parties. Both revert to their own surname. However, a party can retain the marital name with the other's consent or with the authorization of the court if this is considered to be in their own or their children's best interests.[30] The parties are free to marry again as soon as the divorce is pronounced.[31] However, under article 263 of the Civil Code if the parties wish to re-marry each another, a new ceremony has to be performed as if marrying for the first time.

1. Children

In principle divorce should not affect the nature and scope of the parents' obligations towards the child in that both remain joint holders of parental responsibility with unconditional obligations towards the child.[32] However, pragmatic

---

[29] The recommended period of reflection may be anything from a maximum of eight days (in which case the judge suspends the hearing informally), or up to six months (requiring a more formal adjournment accompanied by interim measures).

[30] Art. 264 C. civ. amended by art. 16 of the *loi* of 2004.

[31] Prior to the *loi* of 2004., a woman had to wait for a period of at least 30 days before re-marrying, the purpose of which was presumably to avoid any uncertainty as to paternity should she become pregnant.

[32] Art. 373-2 C. civ. This section of the Civil Code, which was introduced by the 2002 Parental Authority Act, deals generally with the responsibilities of separated parents and makes no distinction between situations of divorce or otherwise (*loi* no 2002-305 of 4 March 2002 *relative*

questions as to how these responsibilities are to be *allocated* between the parties are generally addressed during the conciliation hearing. Issues to be determined include: custody (*la garde*); contact arrangements with the non-custodial parent (*le droit de visite et d'hébergement*); and the amount of financial support required to fund the child's everyday needs and education (*la pension alimentaire*). All of these decisions must be taken with a view to protecting the best interests of the child.[33] In accordance with the *loi* of 2002 on parental authority, which reinforces the equal status of both parents in respect of their parental rights and duties,[34] they must maintain a personal relationship with the child and enable the child to maintain a relationship with the other parent following the divorce (article 373-2 Civil Code).[35] Generally, the *loi* of 2002 favours a model of *garde alternée* by which the child's residence alternates between that of the mother and the father (article 373-2-9 of the Civil Code.). This is regarded as the most effective means of sustaining the child's equal relationship with both parents. Where custody is awarded to only one parent, the other parent retains all other rights and duties associated with parental responsibility, including the right to be informed and consulted about major decisions affecting the child's life. Even in the rare instance in which only one parent holds parental responsibility, contact with the other parent cannot be denied, save in very exceptional circumstances (for example, in cases of violence or abuse involving the child).[36]

The process of determining custody and access issues in particular will often require independent expert assessments from psychologists or social workers who have had an opportunity to discuss matters with the child. However, under article 388-1 al. 3 of the Civil Code a child cannot be party to divorce and parental responsibility proceedings and, in practice, more often than not the child's views are not considered at all. This is in spite of explicit reference in article 388-1 of the Civil Code[37] to the right of the competent child to be heard in judicial proceedings, a provision which is also supported by article 12(2) of the UN

à *l'autorité parentale* ('*Loi* on parental authority') incorporated into the amended arts. 371–387 C.civ.). Note that this section of the Civil Code now sets out the rules relating to *all* aspects of parental responsibility. Previously, parental duties following divorce were dealt with separately under arts. 286–295 C.civ.

[33] The obligation to act in the child's best interests is espoused by art. 3 of the UN Convention on the Rights of the Child 1989 which France signed and ratified in January 1990.

[34] The principle of joint parental responsibility in the context of divorce, separation or unmarried parents had previously been endorsed by *loi* no 93-22 of 8 January 1993 *modifiant le Code civil relative à l'état civil, à la famille et aux droits de l'enfant et instituant le juge aux affaires familiales*.

[35] See further F. Boulanger, '*Modernisation ou utopie?: la réforme de l'autorité parentale par la loi du 4 mars 2002*', D. 2002, Chr. 1571–1577.

[36] See, for instance, Civ. (1), 24 Oct. 2000, Bull. civ. I, no.262 in which the court suspended the contact rights of a father because he insisted that his daughter wear an Islamic veil against her will. Contact will not be denied purely on the basis that the child expresses a desire not to see the parent (Civ. (2) 7 Oct. 1987, Bull. civ. II, no. 190; and 22 Oct. 1997, Bull. civ. II, no. 225). In this instance, the custodial parent must make every effort to encourage the child to maintain contact with the other parent if they themselves are to escape criminal liability under art. 227-5 C. pén.

[37] Formalized by *loi* no 93-22 of 8 January 1993.

Convention on the Rights of the Child 1989. Legally, the judge can only deny a child the opportunity to be heard if they are deemed to lack sufficient maturity or capacity, or if it would jeopardize the child's health or welfare.[38] That said, any decisions taken by the JAF in relation to the child must be justified fully.[39]

2. Financial provision

A distinction is made between two types of financial provision in the event of divorce: 'compensation' for marital breakdown (*des prestations compensatoires*); and division of assets (*liquidation et partage*).

Regarding compensation, an important principle underlying French divorce law is the equitable distribution of matrimonial resources to ensure that either party is not unjustly impoverished as a result of the divorce. As such, even though marriage terminates any obligation of support between the spouses, a party can claim 'compensation' from the other to reflect the financial disparity created by the divorce. This generally takes the form of a one-off lump sum payment (determined by the JAF). A number of factors will be taken into account when determining the amount of compensation payable or, indeed, whether compensation is payable at all. For divorce on grounds of fault, the JAF may refuse to authorize any compensation payment to the wrongful party. This is a controversial feature of French divorce law, since it allows the JAF to engage in a moral evaluation of the parties' behaviour and to effectively punish the 'guilty' party and award damages to the injured, 'innocent' party (see article 270 al. 3 Civil Code). More generally, under article 271 of the Civil Code, the allocation of compensation is determined by reference to the current and projected needs and resources of each party, the length of the marriage, the age and state of health of the parties, their professional status and prospects, the extent to which one or other spouse (typically the woman) sacrificed her career to care for the couple's children, the estimated value of their joint assets, and any pension or other rights that will materialize in the future.

The compensation can be paid in one of four ways: as a one-off lump sum payment; as an interest in property (usually use of the matrimonial property) (article 274 Civil Code); as index-linked periodical payments (similar to maintenance) over a maximum period of eight years (article 275 Civil Code);[40] or, in exceptional cases, as a life annuity (*rente viagère*) operating much like a pension payment) (article 276 *et seq* Civil Code).[41] In most cases, the 'clean-break', one-off payment is the favoured option and in all other cases, the arrangement

---

[38] Civ. (1), 20 Feb. 1985, Gaz. Pal, 1985.2.756 ; Civ. (1) 2 Nov. 1994, *Defrénois*, 1995.1027.

[39] Civ. (2) 24 Feb. 1993, Bull. civ. II, no. 76.

[40] This particular method of payment is used where the *debiteur* cannot or prefers not to pay an initial lump sum amount to the other party. This can be claimed in full by the other party following liquidation of all the matrimonial assets.

[41] This form of payment is ordered where the recipient is unable to meet his or her living costs alone owing to their age and/or fragile state of health.

is reviewable to take into account subsequent changes in the circumstances of either party.

As far as division of assets is concerned, for divorce by mutual consent all matters relating to the division of assets and financial provision (*l'état liquidatif*) are agreed upon by the parties from the outset and annexed to the petition for divorce. The judge simply rubber-stamps this agreement before pronouncing the divorce, provided that it is considered to be fair. For divorce on the other three grounds, if the parties cannot agree on how to divide their assets before the divorce is finalized, the JAF will allow them to determine these issues afterwards, on condition that an agreement is reached within a year (article 267-1 Civil Code).[42] This part of the procedure is concluded by a notary rather than the JAF.[43]

In principle, all matrimonial assets (joint savings, house) will be divided equally between the spouses unless there is an agreement to the contrary between them. Gifts (for example, jewellery) made to one another during the marriage, however, will remain the property of the beneficiary. Conversely, the spouses lose any rights of succession following the dissolution of the marriage.

IV. Cohabitation

Accompanying the growing secularization of French public and private life, the past 30 years in France has seen a gradual departure from an exclusively marriage-based conception of family and relationships towards more flexible, liberalized arrangements. This process, now commonly referred to as '*démariage*',[44] has made France one of the leading exponents of cohabitation in Europe with over 50% of first children now born out of wedlock. Indeed, cohabitation (alternatively referred to as *l'union libre* or *concubinage*) is not only a common precursor to marriage (*mariage à l'essai*), but is becoming increasingly widespread across the generations as an alternative to marriage.

A. Rights and Obligations Arising out of Cohabitation

Although cohabitation has been a common practice in France since the 1960s, it was not until 1999 that it was legally defined as a union characterized by stability and continuity of two persons of either the same or opposite sexes who

---

[42] This can be extended by a further six months maximum at the verbal request of a notary (on which, see above, pp. 76–77).

[43] It is important to note that the notary has no judicial discretion in this regard and can only formalize agreements reached voluntarily by the parties. If they are unable to agree on the division of assets, the matter will be returned to the court for a judicial ruling.

[44] I. Théry, 'Droit, Justice et "Demande des Familles": Réflexions sur un objet introuvable', ch. 1 in Meulders-Klein (ed.), *Familles et Justice* (Brussels, 1997).

live together as a couple.[45] While, in general, no formality is required to establish a cohabiting relationship, couples can apply for a *certificat de concubinage* from their local town hall on production of proof of their identity and domicile.[46] This certificate does not hold any specific legal weight but rather, is obtained for purely pragmatic reasons, to enable the couple to prove their cohabitation should they wish to claim the limited social benefits detailed below.

Cohabitation is referred to as a union of 'fact' (*de fait*) rather than a legal union (*de droit*) to reflect the flexible, extra-legal nature of the arrangement. Thus, unlike married couples, cohabitants cannot use or assume the name of their partner in any official capacity, nor are they under any legal obligation to support one another or to contribute to the upkeep of their household (issues which are agreed privately at the discretion of the couple). There is no legal sanction for infidelity, and each party is regarded as *une personne célibataire* for tax purposes. Under article L 351-13 of the *Code de la sécurité sociale* pension entitlement only increases to take into account a dependent spouse, not a dependent cohabitant, while any property rights held by the couple are strictly in accordance with the terms of a rental or purchase agreement rather than the more favourable terms of the matrimonial property regime. Thus, cohabitants can only claim equal tenancy rights if both parties are named on a rental agreement.

The cleft between marriage-based rights and those associated with cohabitation is derived from the traditional Napoleonic mentality, 'if they ignore the law, the law will ignore them'. In other words, couples who want to benefit from the flexibility of unmarried cohabitation have to be prepared to accept the less secure legal status that accompanies it.[47] However, reforms have gradually been introduced since the late 1970s to align the legal status of cohabitants with that of married couples, at least in some areas. For instance, in the field of social security, reforms were introduced from the late 1970s enabling cohabiting couples to claim sickness and maternity benefits on the basis of contributions made by their cohabiting partner.[48] Later reforms further assimilated the legal position of cohabitants with married couples, but mainly in a negative way, to deny them allowances that were otherwise targeted at lone persons, particularly lone parents. As such, cohabitants now relinquish their right to lone parents' allowance (*Allocations de Parent Isolé—API*), family support allowance (*Allocation de Soutien Familial—ASF*), and the allowance for widowhood (*Pension de Reversion*) should they subsequently move in with someone else. Cohabitation will also lead to a reduction in minimum income benefit (*Revenu Minimum d'Insertion—RMI*) and housing allowances (*Allocation de logement*).

---

[45] *Loi* no. 99-944 of 25 November 1999, now enshrined in art. 515-8 Civil Code.

[46] Code des communes art. L.122–26. Some town councils require a statement from two adult witnesses attesting to the durability of the cohabiting relationship.

[47] C. Martinand and I. Théry, 'The PACS and Marriage and Cohabitation in France' (2001) 15 International Journal of Law, Policy and the Family 135.

[48] *Loi* no. 78-2 of 2 January 1978, art. 13.

Cohabitants' legal status has been enhanced perhaps most acutely in the area of parental responsibility, primarily with a view to promoting and protecting the rights of the child rather than those of the parents. Thus, the legal status of children born outside and within wedlock was assimilated in 1972 for the purposes of inheritance;[49] the right to obtain IVF treatment (*la procréation médicalement assistée—PMA*) was extended to unmarried couples in 1994;[50] and the rights and responsibilities associated with being a parent are determined independently of any marital link between the parents.[51]

In the field of employment, under articles L 226-1 and L 122–25-4 of the *Code du travail* paternity leave (*congé de paternité*) was extended to fathers in 2002 irrespective of their relationship with the mother. However, the court (in this instance, the social security tribunal) confirmed in 2006 that a similar right is not available to homosexual cohabitants who wish to take leave to care for their partner's child.[52]

Cohabitants continue to face a number of inequalities in the event of the death of their partner. Unlike legal spouses, they do not benefit from any specific matrimonial property regime, nor do they automatically benefit from any inheritance should their partner die intestate. Thus, unless the surviving partner has been explicitly named as a beneficiary on the deceased's will, taken out life insurance,[53] or benefited from a gift during the deceased's lifetime, she will have no claim to the property unless she also has made a tangible contribution to the cost of the property. The situation is slightly more secure for surviving tenants; in this case, the tenancy can be transferred to the surviving partner even if she was not a party to the original rental agreement, provided that she was living with her partner in the property for at least a year before his death.[54] Finally, a surviving unmarried partner receives no payments from a deceased partner's pension, unlike a surviving spouse.[55]

To compensate for the lack of legal protection available to cohabitants, many enter into private contracts to regulate their financial affairs.[56] These are notoriously complex, however, and are often difficult to enforce. Deference to the common law thus remains the default procedure, particularly in the event of cohabitation dissolution.

---

[49] *Loi* no. 72-3 of 3 January 1972. See further sections VI and VII below on succession and affiliation.

[50] *Loi* of 29 July 1994.

[51] Art. 373-2 C. civ. See also *loi* no. 93-22 of 8 January 1993, art. 38 following which joint parental responsibility became automatic. See above n. 32 and 34.

[52] Tribunal des affaires de la securité sociale 20 Mar. 2006 *affaire Elodie et Karine*. This involved an unsuccessful claim for paternity leave by a lesbian cohabitant in respect of the newborn child of her partner.

[53] Life insurance is exempt from the inheritance regime.

[54] *Loi* of 6 July 1989. If the surviving party was living with the deceased for less than a year, it is up to the discretion of the landlord as to whether the title will be transferred to her.

[55] Note the position of cohabitants has been enhanced for those who have concluded a PACS under the recent reform to the law of succession by *loi* of 23 June 2006. See further below, p. 258.

[56] These are in principle binding under art. 1134 C civ.

B. Rupture of a Cohabiting Relationship

Perhaps the most significant differences between marriage and cohabitation exist in the context of dissolution. Dissolution of cohabitation operates on the principles of *rupture libre et non dommageable* meaning that both parties are free to dissolve the relationship at their discretion, without a need for any special procedure or justification, and without incurring any financial or legal penalty. Thus, unlike in the case of divorce, there is no mechanism for awarding *prestations compensatoires*[57] to a party whose financial situation is damaged as a result of the relationship breakdown, save in very exceptional circumstances.[58]

The financial situation of a cohabitant may be particularly precarious if they have been living in the property owned by their partner since, unlike married couples, they have no legal rights over the property simply by virtue of having lived there with the owner. They cannot, in principle, oppose the sale or rent of the property to a third party at any time nor can they request to remain in the property or to receive a share of the value of the property.

The lack of a sufficiently effective and exhaustive remedy for protecting parties' financial situation following the cohabitation breakdown has forced couples in France to defer to the more general principles of property and contract law which are less sensitive to the relationship between the parties in conferring rights. Thus, the principles associated with *la société*[59] and *enrichissement sans cause*[60] are commonly called into play by the parties. The result is, then, that the more formalized the cohabiting couple makes their relationship, the more secure their legal position is should the relationship break up. The law provides little redress for parties who are unable to quantify in tangible economic terms the extent of their *de facto* contribution to the relationship and who simply trust that their partners will provide for them in the long term.

[57] Above p.253.

[58] See e.g. Civ. (1) 3 Nov. 1976, Bull. civ. 1, no. 322. A party may also seek compensation (*dommages-intérêts*) on the basis of art. 1382 C.civ. provided he or she can establish the existence of a fault, a direct, present and certain damage, and a causal link between the two. See further p. 364 ff. For an example of this see Cass. Civ. (1) 7 Apr. 1998, RTDciv, 1998.884 note J. Hauser.

[59] Art. 1832 C. civ. This enables a couple to conclude a contract between them to a establish a company (*société*), by virtue of which they commit their property to a common venture with a view to sharing the benefit or profiting from the saving which may result from it. The parties are also bound to contribute jointly to any losses. See further A. Barlow and R. Probert, 'Addressing the Legal Status of Cohabitation in Britain and France: Plus ça change…? (1999) 3 Web Journal of Current Legal Issues, available at <http://webjcli.ncl.ac.uk/1999/issue3/barlow3.html>.

[60] This has been developed by the case law enabling parties to claim that their partner has been unjustly enriched (and, by implication, that they themselves have been unjustly impoverished) through the relationship, for example, as a result of unpaid work carried out by the female during their relationship in support of her partner's business, or direct financial contributions made to the mortgage payments or upkeep of the house. Mere contributions in kind (such as domestic work or childcare) will rarely suffice as the basis for such a claim. For an example see Civ. (1) 15 Oct. 1996, *dame Allard*, Bull. civ. no. 357. For *enrichissement sans cause* generally, see below, p. 433 ff.

Despite the popularity of cohabitation, concerns abound as to the notorious legal and financial insecurity of such relationships. These concerns have dovetailed with growing disquiet among same-sex couples objecting to the fact that this relatively insecure arrangement was, until relatively recently, the only cohabiting option available to them. Unlike heterosexual couples, they do not have the option of getting married in order to legally validate their relationship, but rather, are confined to the casual legal uncertainty of *concubinage* in which their status is even more precarious than that of heterosexual cohabitants. The introduction of the *Pacte civil de solidarité* has therefore been welcomed as providing a long-overdue solution to this entrenched inequality.

V. *Pacte Civil de Solidarité*

Following almost a decade of vociferous campaigning and heated parliamentary debate, the *pacte civil de solidarité* (PACS) was introduced in 1999.[61] PACS is regarded by many as an important step beyond *mariage à l'essai* (typically associated with informal cohabitation), towards a completely alternative way of regulating relationships. One of the most attractive features of the PACS is that, as a binding contract, it offers a degree of legal security to unmarried couples who wish to reach a clear agreement from the outset on how they will manage any personal or financial matters between them. It also offers the only opportunity for homosexual couples to legally endorse their relationship in France. In that sense, PACS represents a kind of compromise between marriage and cohabitation, drawing on the legal security and clarity associated with the former, and the freedom and flexibility associated with the latter. It should be viewed as a dynamic process, susceptible to constant review and re-negotiation as the relationship progresses and as the financial and personal situation of the parties change.

The conditions for entering into a PACS and for dissolving it should the parties no longer wish to remain together are set out in Title XII (articles 515-1–515-7) of the Civil Code.

A. Entering into a PACS

A PACS is defined in article 515-1 of the Civil Code as a 'contract' that can be concluded between two adults (*personnes majeures*) of either the same or opposite sex. The procedure for concluding a PACS is set out in article 515-3 and requires, first of all, that the couple make a joint declaration (presented in person) to the clerk of the tribunal d'instance in the locality of their main residence. Attached to this should be two original copies of the contract (*convention*) concluded between

---

[61] *Loi* no. 99-944 of 15 November 1999 *relative au pacte civil de solidarité* ('PACS *loi* of 1999').

them,[62] the documents of civil status which attest to the fact that they qualify to enter into a PACS,[63] as well as a certificate issued by the office of the tribunal d'instance of their places of birth confirming that neither party is already bound by a PACS. Once all of this documentation has been filed, the clerk enters a declaration on a register, and then signs and dates the two copies of the original agreement before returning one to each of the parties. A declaration is also made on the register held at the tribunal d'instance of each party's place of birth.[64] The PACS becomes effective as soon as this registration process is complete which involves, in the final instance, a note being made in the margins of each party's birth certificate. The parties can amend the content of the PACS agreement at any time, in which case they must inform the clerk of the tribunal d'instance that registered the original agreement so that the change can be duly noted on the parties' birth certificates (articles 515-3, al. 4 and 515-3-1 Civil Code).

PACS have proven extremely popular since their introduction. In total, since 1999, over 270,000 PACS have been concluded in France. In 2005, 60,500 PACS were concluded, representing a 50% increase on 2004, and the figure continues to rise in contrast with a gradual decrease in the annual number of marriages. Interestingly, in 2006 approximately 21 PACS were concluded for every 100 marriages. On the other side of the coin, over 35,000 PACS have been dissolved since 1999, equivalent to approximately 13% of all PACS contracted, although this remains proportionately lower than the annual divorce rate.[65]

B. Rights and Obligations Arising out of the PACS

The status of those who have concluded a PACS (*pacsés*) has changed considerably since 1999, primarily as a result of the 2006 Successions Act[66] which has assimilated PACS more closely with marriage, transforming it from a mere contractual arrangement into more of an institution.

First and foremost, it is important to note that the PACS has no impact on the status of the *pacsés qua* parents: it does not in itself bestow on the couple a right to adopt a child together or to undergo treatment for assisted conception. Not does it automatically confer parental authority on one *pacsé* in relation to the child or children of the other. In that sense, PACS by no means provides a panacea for homosexual couples who wish to gain access to parental rights, leading some to

---

[62] The contract is drafted by the couple themselves and should make reference to the PACS *loi* of 1999 and set out clearly the terms of their financial arrangement as well as any other conditions they wish to include relating to, for instance, distribution of property upon dissolution.

[63] Art. 515-2 C. civ. prohibits PACS between parties who are direct relatives in the ascending or descending line (parents, children, grandparents), those who are *alliés* (brothers, sisters, uncles, nieces) or *collatéraux* (sisters-in-law and brothers-in-law), or with a partner who is already married or has already entered into a PACS with someone else.

[64] If either party was born outside France, the declaration is made on the register of the court office of the tribunal de grande instance of Paris.

[65] INSEE at <http://www.insee.fr/fr/ffc/ipweb/ip1118/ip1118.html>.

[66] *Loi* of 23 June 2006.

question whether it really does enhance the status of this group in any meaningful way at all.[67]

However, PACS confers on the parties a number of financial, property and succession rights and obligations *intra se* which are not otherwise extended to unmarried cohabitants. Thus, by signing the PACS, the couple undertakes to support one another materially. Prior to 2006, the extent of this obligation was determined strictly by reference to the terms of the agreement.[68] The 2006 Act amended this, however, to oblige partners to provide material support insofar as is reasonable in the light of their financial means.[69]

A PACS also has implications for the division and management of property following the 2006 Successions Act. Now, unless otherwise stated on the PACS agreement, each party retains sole responsibility for the administration and disposal of their own property and assets. This regime is referred to as '*la séparation de biens*' and replaces the previous presumption of *l'indivision* (essentially a 50/50 split) that applied to PACS agreements. Similarly, the default position on any goods or assets that are subsequently acquired by either party will always be one of *séparation de biens* unless the parties explicitly opt for *l'indivision*. That said, anything that does not belong exclusively to one or other *pacsé* is regarded as the equal property of both, in which case *l'indivision* applies. In this case, the management and administration of property that is jointly owned in this way can be negotiated within the terms of the PACS agreement.

Finally, aside from an obligation to provide mutual support to one another, the couple is also jointly liable (*solidairement*) for any debts incurred by either or both of them since signing the PACS.[70]

Despite the considerable advantages attached to the PACS, parties are affected by many of the same disadvantages that face other unmarried cohabitants, particularly in the allocation of social welfare benefits. Notably, individuals (justifiably perhaps) lose any entitlement to benefits aimed at single persons, particularly those targeting lone parents and widows, as soon as they enter into a new PACS agreement. Similarly, any social welfare benefits to which they may be entitled (such as family allowance, housing benefits, disability allowance, and unemployment benefits) are calculated, and inevitably reduced, on the basis of the couple's joint income. This is justified on the grounds that by signing the PACS, the parties undertake to provide material support to one another and, by implication, assume a reciprocal dependency. While this presumption is flawed, in the sense that there is no judicial sanction currently available should one party default on their obligation to support the other (and, in that sense, they are in a much more vulnerable legal position than a married partner), the principle is fairly clear: if

---

[67] Barlow and Probert, above n. 59.

[68] Formerly art. 515-4 C. civ.

[69] This provision is redolent of art. 214 C. civ relating to the matrimonial obligation of mutual support.

[70] Art. 515-4, modelled on art. 220 C. civ.

you want the law to recognize you as a couple, you have to relinquish any state support aimed specifically at mitigating the financial difficulties associated with being alone.

Moreover, the rights of the surviving parties following the death of their partner remain limited compared to widows; there is no automatic right of inheritance between *pacsés* couples who die intestate,[71] nor is there any entitlement equivalent to the widow's pension.

C. Dissolving a PACS

A PACS is dissolved in one of four ways: by marriage (of either party to someone else or to each other); following the death of one of the parties; by mutual consent; or at the unilateral instigation of one of the parties. The procedure for dissolving a PACS is set out in article 515-7 of the Civil Code and takes the form of one a number of simple procedures depending on the circumstances. The most straight-forward scenario—dissolution by mutual consent—involves both parties submitting a joint declaration to the tribunal d'instance where at least one of them is resident. This is then entered on the official register by the clerk and a note is made in the margin of the original instrument containing the PACS agreement. At this point, the PACS is deemed to be dissolved. If just one party wishes to put an end to the PACS, he or she must notify the other party of the decision in writing and send a copy of this to the tribunal d'instance that originally registered the agreement. The PACS will be dissolved three months from the date at which the other party was notified of the decision, provided the clerk also received a copy. The marriage of either party to another person will immediately dissolve a PACS. In this case, the newly-wed need only notify his or her *co-pacsé* of the marriage and send a copy of this notification, along with a copy of his birth certificate (on which the marriage is recorded) to the tribunal d'instance where the PACS was originally registered. Similarly, the death of one of the parties will automatically bring the PACS to an end. In this case, the surviving party must submit a copy of the death certificate to the tribunal d'instance where the PACS was originally registered.

In all of these cases, on receiving notification, the clerk will register the dissolution of the PACS in the margins of the original agreement. Dissolution immediately concludes any legal relationship between the couple and the onus is on them to liquidate their assets appropriately and equitably. There is no automatic right of compensation (*prestations compensatoires*) equivalent to that available to divorcing couples unless some form of indemnity has already been agreed between the parties as part of the PACS contract,[72] nor does either party have to provide any

---

[71] But see below p. 262 on succession.

[72] Although such clauses are likely to be construed strictly to ensure they do not compromise the parties' freedom to dissolve the PACS.

motivation or justification for dissolving the PACS. Of course, a party who has suffered significant damage can always pursue a claim for compensation by the route provided by the general law of civil liability against the other party under article 1382 of the Civil Code, provided that the fault is manifested in behaviour other than the mere fact that they dissolved the relationship.[73]

VI. Succession

Until very recently, the law of succession—that governing the disposal of an individual's estate in the event of their death—was one dimension of family law to have undergone relatively little reform for over 200 years. In fact, it had been heavily criticized for its excessive complexity, and for being out of touch with modern society and with changing patterns of family life.

The *loi* of 23 June 2006 reforming the law of succession and gifts[74] which came into effect on 1 January 2007, provided a long-overdue and significant modernization of the law in this area. Its aims are essentially three-fold: to simplify succession procedures; to provide better protection for beneficiaries; and to confer a greater degree of autonomy and flexibility on the testator.[75] That said, the core principles underpinning the law of succession remain in tact. For instance, the testator cannot freely dispose of his entire estate in his will because of the notion of '*la réserve héréditaire*'. This represents the proportion of the estate that must be set aside for certain privileged heirs, notably the children and spouse of the testator. Once this proportion is allocated, the testator can dispose of the balance (*quotité disponible*) as he or she sees fit. Article 913 of the Civil Code sets out the formula for calculating the proportion of the estate that will be used for the reserve and depends largely on the number of children the testator has: if there is only one surviving child, the reserve accounts for 50% of the estate; if there are two children, it will be two-thirds of the estate; and three-quarters is set aside for three or more surviving children. Under article 914 of the Civil Code, a surviving spouse will have an automatic right to one-quarter of the estate provided there are no other surviving descendants.[76] If there are surviving children, their claim takes precedence over that of the spouse

---

[73] See generally, below, p. 364 ff.

[74] *Loi* of 23 June 2006.

[75] There is insufficient scope in this chapter to provide a detailed exposition of the law on succession as it relates to families. However, for an exhaustive, up-to-date analysis of this area see J. Maury, *Successions et Liberalités*, (Paris, 2007); and M-C Forgeard, *Le nouveau droit des successions et des liberalités : la loi du 23 juin 2006, commentaires et formules* (Paris, 2007). For a more concise English language overview of the main reforms brought about the 2006 Act, see J. Godard, 'Reform of the Law of Succession in France' (2007) *International Family Law Journal* 50.

[76] The *loi* of 23 June 2006 removes the automatic right of reserve that previously existed in favour of ascendants (ex parents of the deceased) so they no longer have a right to any of the estate unless it is specifically bequeathed to them by the testator out of the *quotité disponible*.

who could effectively be disinherited if the deceased dies intestate.[77] However, the law at least protects the accommodation rights of the surviving spouse in this case, granting her a right to remain in the couple's joint residence (either rented or otherwise) free of charge for at least one year following the death of the testator. All costs are offset against the deceased's estate (article 763 Civil Code). Moreover, the surviving spouse has a right to receive a pension from the proceeds of the estate (article 767 Civil Code).

One of the most significant innovations of the 2006 Successions Act was the extent to which it aligned the status of *pacsés* with that of married couples. For instance, it is now possible for an individual to bequeath his entire residence to his surviving *co-pacsé* (article 515-5 al. 2 of the Code). And in the event of her partner dying intestate, the surviving *pacsé* will enjoy one year of free accommodation in any shared owned or rented residence in the same way as a surviving spouse (articles 515-6, al. 3 and 763 Civil Code). However, parties to a PACS agreement, like other unmarried cohabitants, can never be regarded as protected *héritiers* under the reserve regime. Their succession rights depend very much, therefore, on the extent of the legacy bequeathed to them by their partner from the balance left over after the reserve is accounted for.

The strict exclusivity of French succession law is justified first of all by the need to secure adequate provision for the deceased's children's future. Further, the old Napoleonic adage that the law provides optimum protection for those who assume most legal responsibility—married couples as opposed to unmarried cohabitants and *pacsés*—rings true here. In short, the law is resolutely opposed to allowing individuals to simultaneously opt for minimal legal regulation of their personal relationships while demanding optimum legal protection in the event of one or other party's death.[78]

VII. Affiliation and Adoption

A. Legitimacy and Affiliation

The law of affiliation (*filiation*), which determines the legal relationship between children and their parents, traditionally drew a distinction between children born to a married couple (*la filiation légitime*) and those born outside wedlock (*la filiation naturelle*). This latter category included children born to cohabiting couples, adopted children, and children born as a result of an adulterous relationship (*enfants adultérins*). The previous sections on divorce, parental authority and succession have highlighted how such distinctions have been gradually eroded achieving an equivalence of status for all children, regardless of the circumstances

---

[77] Batteur, 274–280.
[78] What Malaurie and Fulchiron, 219, capture in the slogan '*Vivons Pacsés, Meurons Mariés*'.

of their birth.[79] The law of affiliation has followed suit, abandoning all legal distinction between legitimate and 'illegitimate' children.[80] However, differences remain in the treatment of parents, depending on whether they are married or unmarried. Thus, the procedure for establishing parentage differs for unmarried mothers and fathers. Under article 311-25 of the Civil Code, the unmarried mother's parentage is established automatically by mere virtue of her being named on the child's birth certificate and, in that sense, does not differ at all from the status of married mothers. The unmarried father, on the other hand, has to officially register his paternity. The procedure for this is set out in article 316 al. 2 of the Civil Code and involves entering personal details (such as the father's name, date and place of birth and place of residence) on an official register alongside details about the child.[81] This process can be completed either before or at any time following the child's birth. Registering paternity beforehand merely involves attending the town hall with some identification and making a declaration of paternity which is then drafted into an official act by an official registrar. If the father decides to register paternity after the child's birth, he can be named on the birth certificate if he presents himself to the town hall in the locality in which the child has been born within three days of the birth. Beyond three days after the child's birth, the registration is completed on a separate document by the registrar, provided no other man has registered his paternity of the child.[82] The consent of the mother is not required in any of these cases and is an entirely voluntary act on the part of the father.

Conversely, a 'presumption of paternity' is preserved by articles 312, 314 and 315 of the Civil Code in relation to married fathers: the child of a married woman is presumed to be the child of her husband, provided that the child was born at least 180 days after the civil marriage ceremony and no more than 300 days following the dissolution of the marriage (as a result of death or divorce).

Either parent can contest paternity. Under article 316 of the Civil Code, if the father wishes to challenge the paternity and he is married to the mother, he must commence proceedings within six months of the child's birth if he was present at the time; within six months of his return if he was absent at the time of the child's birth; or within six months of discovering the child's birth if it was concealed from him. Should the father die before the outcome of the action is known,

---

[79] Similar developments have also occurred in relation to the attribution of family name. For further detail on this, see Batteur, 22–38. Children born as a result of artificial insemination are subject to slightly different rules contained in arts 311-19 and 311-20 C. civ. Again, there is insufficient scope in this chapter to address this issue but for a brief overview of the legal framework, see Batteur, 170–174.

[80] The most recent reforms followed the implementation on 1 July 2006 of *ordonnance* of 4 July 2005 *portant réforme de la filiation*. The principle of equality now appears at the beginning of the Civil Code provisions governing affiliation (art. 310 C. civ).

[81] See also arts. 62 and 62-1 C civ.

[82] In that case, the paternity of the father already registered would have to be contested legally in accordance with the procedure set out below.

article 316-2 of the Civil Code provides that the beneficiaries of his estate can pursue the action on his behalf within the six-month deadline.

Under article 318 of the Civil Code, the mother can also contest the paternity of her husband but only following a second marriage to the 'real' father. This action must be pursued within six months of the second marriage and before the child's seventh birthday and will normally require some expert DNA evidence to support the claim. A child has the right to establish the identity of his or her father although this is generally exercised by the mother on the child's behalf while the child is still a minor (article 340-2 Civil Code).[83] If the process is not commenced before the child's 18th birthday, under article 321 and 322 of the Civil Code, the child has a further ten years within which to act. Three specific limitations have been imposed on the child's right to establish his or her affiliation: in cases of incest;[84] if the child's mother has given birth anonymously and expressly refused to be named on the child's birth certificate;[85] or if the child has been 'fully' adopted (*adoption plénière*) (article 352 Civil Code.).[86]

Should paternity be successfully established under article 340-5 of the Civil Code the tribunal de grande instance can request that the father reimburse the mother retroactively for part of the costs associated with the child's upbringing and education. If, on the other hand, paternity (or in the rare case, maternity) is successfully contested, the judgment is noted on the child's birth certificate, a minor child will no longer be known by the man's name,[87] any rights or obligations arising out of parental authority will be withdrawn,[88] and the 'parent' can claim compensation, either from the mother or from the 'real' father if he is identified, for the injury suffered as a result of the mistaken paternity.[89]

For the child who is unable to establish the identity of one or other parent, a further action is available to them: an action for support (*l'action à fin de subsides*). This involves the child making a claim against the person who was

---

[83] A child also has the right to establish the identify of his or her mother, but this will occur only in exceptional circumstances because of the presumption of maternity; for example where the child has been abandoned at birth and brought up (but not adopted fully) by a close friend or relative.

[84] In this case, the child can only establish affiliation in respect of one parent but can claim maintenance money from the man who was engaged in an intimate (albeit incestuous) relationship with his or her mother at the time of the conception under the *action à fin de subsides* procedure (see below).

[85] *Loi* of 8 January 1993.

[86] Discussed further in part B of this section.

[87] For adult children, art. 61-3 C. civ. specifies that a change in affiliation status of this nature will only result in the loss of the family name with the child's consent. Civ. (1) 27 Nov. 2001, Bull. civ. I no. 293.

[88] Although certain contact rights may be sustained with a view to protecting the best interests of the child and enabling them to sustain a relationship with the person who brought them up (art. 337 C. civ.).

[89] Compensation for the actual amount the man invested in the child's upbringing and education is unlikely to be supported by the court, first, because of the difficulties in quantifying such an amount, and secondly, because payment of such a sum could deprive the biological parents of essential resources required for the future maintenance of the child.

involved in an intimate relationship with his or her mother at the time of his or her conception, even if the relationship was adulterous (article 342 of the Code). This is a separate action from any paternity suit and does not create any filiation link between the child and the man. It can be pursued by the child's mother on behalf of the child who is under 18 years old or, alternatively, by the child before his or her 20th birthday. The request must be lodged before the tribunal de grande instance of either the claimant's or the defendant's place of residence. If successful, the court will order payment of a grant representing the maintenance and education costs of the child, which is determined in the light of the defendant's resources (article 342-2) usually until the child reaches the age of majority or, exceptionally, until the child completes his or her studies (article 342-3). If the defendant dies before payment has been made, a claim can be made against his estate (article 342-5).

B. Adoption

Adoption is another form of affiliation but is distinguished from the type described above by virtue of its voluntary, non-biological nature. While provision on adoption was included in the original Napoleonic Code it was only in 1966 that the law in this area was properly reviewed and clarified.[90] This law instituted two forms of adoption: full adoption (*adoption plénière*) and partial adoption (*adoption simple*). The former implies the full-integration of the child into the new family and a complete severance of all ties with the biological family. The latter, on the other hand, enables the child to maintain blood ties with the biological family although legal guardianship passes to the adoptive parents.

1. 'Full' adoption

Full adoption (*adoption plénière*) is governed by articles 343–362 of the Civil Code. A number of conditions relating to both the adoptive parents and the adopted child have to be met before this form of adoption can take place.

First, a couple has to be legally married and heterosexual to adopt a child in France. They have to have been married for two years or be more than 28 years of age (articles 346 and 343 Civil Code). A single person can also adopt a child provided he or she is at least 28 years old. Additionally, a couple that already has biological children can adopt, provided they satisfy the authorities that the adoption will not jeopardize the welfare and family life of these children. While there is no upper age limit for adopting a child, there must be at least a 15-year age gap between the child and the adoptive parents. This is reduced to ten years in

---

[90] *Loi* of 11 July 1966 *portant réforme de l'adoption*. The subsequent *loi* no. 96-604 of 5 July 1996 *relative à l'adoption* further refined these rules.

respect of someone who wishes to adopt the child of their spouse.[91] Additionally, adoption is available to a relative of the child (aunt, uncle, grandparents) but, for public policy reasons, a child born of an incestuous relationship cannot be adopted by his or her biological parent.[92]

Under article 345 of the Civil Code, a child can be adopted provided that: he or she is less than 15 years old and has been placed with the adoptive family for at least six months; the biological parents have consented to the adoption (article 348); the child is in the care of the state (*les pupilles de l'État*);[93] or the child has been declared 'abandoned' in accordance with the procedure set out in article 350 of the Civil Code. A child who is older than 13 years old must give their personal consent to the adoption (article 345 dernier al. Civil Code), while a child under the age of 13 must be given the opportunity to express his or her views on the adoption.

Provided the above conditions are met, the procedure for full adoption takes place in two phases: placement with the adoptive family (article 351) and the judicial judgment. The latter phase can only take place after the child has been placed with the family for a period of at least six months. In determining whether or not the adoption should be approved, the judge of the tribunal de grande instance considers a number of factors, including whether or not the adoption would have an adverse effect on family life, particularly if there are other children already in the adopting family. The judge must deliver his decision within six months which can entail either approval of full adoption, recommendation of simple adoption (see below) or a rejection of the adoption application. All parties can appeal against the decision.

Once full adoption is approved, by article 359 of the Civil Code, the decision is irrevocable.[94] It is officially recorded on the civil register of the birth place of the adopted child and is noted on the child's birth certificate. The child is thereafter regarded as the legitimate child of the adoptive parents and all ties with the biological family are severed.[95] The child acquires exactly the same legal rights and obligations as any biological child of the parents, including those relating to succession, family name, parental authority and incestuous relationships.[96] A child adopted from a foreign country also acquires French nationality.

---

[91] This type of adoption will not entail the severance of all links with the biological parent unlike other cases of *adoption plénière* given that the biological parent is married to the adoptive parent (art. 356 al. 2 C. civ.). *Adoption plénière* will not be possible by the spouse of the child's parent if the other parent and/or his or her relatives are still alive and wish to retain links with the child (art. 345-1 C.civ).

[92] *Ord.* of 4 July 2005 *portant réforme de la filiation*.

[93] This would include orphaned and abandoned children and children taken into care as a result of, for example, parental abuse.

[94] This means that once adopted, a child cannot be adopted again, although the 1996 adoption Act recognizes the possibility of a child being subject to partial adoption (*adoption simple*) following full adoption should the adoptive parents die or should the child be taken into care for some reason following the first adoption (art. 360 C. civ.).

[95] Art. 354 C.civ., subject to the restrictions on marriage set out in arts. 161–164 C. civ.

[96] For instance, an adopted child cannot marry an adoptive parent or sibling.

2. 'Partial' adoption

This form of adoption (*adoption simple*) is much less common than full adoption and enables the child to retain affective ties with his or her biological family following integration into the adoptive family. Moreover, partial adoption adheres to much more flexible rules. First, it is available regardless of the adopted person's age, although any child over the age of 13 has to give consent (article 360 Civil Code). Additionally, there is no initial requirement that the child be placed with the adoptive family for six months before the adoption is approved.

The legal effects of partial adoption have much in common with full adoption, but with a few modifications to account for the fact that the child essentially belongs to two families simultaneously. In relation to the child's name, according to article 363 of the Civil Code the birth name can be retained and the new adoptive family's name added.[97] Parental authority transfers from the biological parents to the adoptive parents. The only exception to this is where an individual adopts the child of a spouse, in which case, the couple shares parental authority (article 365). The adoptive parents also acquire an obligation to support the child (*obligation alimentaire*). The biological parents retain some responsibility in this respect but it is enforced only if the adoptive parents are unable to provide sufficient support (article 367). This obligation of support is reciprocal however; the adopted child assumes responsibility to support both sets of parents in the future. The potential burden imposed by this is mitigated somewhat by the fact that the child acquires succession rights in respect of the adoptive parents on the same basis as any other biological children in the family[98] while retaining all inheritance rights as far as the biological family are concerned.

Finally, one of the most fundamental differences between partial and full adoption is that partial adoption can be revoked if it is justified on serious grounds at the request of either the child or the parent/s, provided the child is at least 15 years old (article 370 of the Civil Code).[99]

---

[97] Where this would lead to a multi-barrelled name, specific rules set out in art. 363 al. 2 C. civ. apply.

[98] Note, however that she or he does not acquire automatic succession rights in relation to the ascendants of the adoptive parents This reflects the fact that partial adoption creates a legal tie between the child, the adoptive parents and any other children in the family only. The child is not fully integrated into the extended family.

[99] For younger children, revocation of the adoption can be authorized by the state prosecutor (*ministère public*) if the grounds are sufficiently serious.

9

Property Law

I. Introduction

The Declaration of the Rights of Man and of the Citizen of 1789 declares that property is 'an inviolable and sacred' right (article 17) and that 'the goal of any political association is the preservation of the natural and imprescribable rights of man'. These rights are liberty, property, security and freedom from oppression (article 2). Property ownership is an essential constituent of liberal political society. While that political value has persisted, it has undergone significant changes. The economic context has altered since 1789. We are no longer dealing with an economy dominated by rural landholding and produce. The industrial, consumer and intellectual revolutions have successively created a range of movable and intangible items of property whose value is of increasing importance. The public policy context has also changed in that restrictions imposed on the use of property in the public interest are more generally accepted. Indeed, article 9 of the Preamble to the 1946 Constitution suggests that public ownership of socially important goods is imperative. We will see that this provision has had a limited impact, but policy limitations on private ownership are an important feature of the modern law of property.[1]

A. History

Contemporary French property law is the product of a number of influences. Much of the conceptual language in which property is described stems from Roman law. The Civil Code adopts most of the basic divisions of Roman law, such as possession, dominium, usufruct and servitude. This was inevitable given the developed state of civil law scholarship and the influence of Roman law scholars in the formation of the Code. All the same, the ancient customary law was not without influence. The medieval tenure system was swept away in 1789, but the protection of the family and inheritance system were strongly influenced by the ancient customary law and the desire to promote family solidarity. The Revolution gave further policy direction to property law in terms of the place of public utility

---

[1] See especially the discussion below, p. 275 below.

and the status of property. But the significance of social utility expanded during the social welfare reforms of the 1930s onwards. Nationalization also had an impact in creating new categories of publicly owned property. Public ownership here has important similarities with private property in that there is an owner (the state) whose rights the law protects. Indeed, when it came to privatization, the Conseil constitutionnel ruled that article 17 of the Declaration of the Rights of Man and of the Citizen of 1789 protected the state's property as much as that of a private individual. Accordingly, it could not be transferred to private owners for less than its true value.[2]

B. General Concepts

The French law of property as set out in the Civil Code represents the conceptual structure of Roman law applied to the needs of a predominantly agricultural society. Much has happened since 1804. France is no longer predominantly agricultural and land ownership has a much more important role as residences than as farms.[3] Whereas physical property was important in 1804, much more of modern wealth is found in intangible property: copyright, patents, designs, know-how, computer programs and other forms of intellectual property. Whereas free use of land was a relatively straightforward paradigm, the modern world has to accept more restrictions imposed for the good of the community, such as servitudes to provide electricity, gas, telephones and water, as well as planning and environmental restrictions. Although the structure of French property law remains fundamentally similar to that established in 1804, the context in which it operates is now different and the problems which arise are not always the same. In some areas, such as collective property, this has required legislation. In other areas, the broad terms of Code provisions have had to be adapted to new situations. Thus, while much of the conceptual structure established in the Civil Code remains in place, its operational context has changed radically and concepts often serve new policy objectives.

1. Bien

French law uses a number of terms to describe property. The simplest word is *chose* which identifies a physical thing. The Code prefers to use the term *bien* to designate things which are capable of being appropriated. As Portalis put it, 'things would be of no interest to the legislator without the utility which men draw from them'. Thus, article 714 of the Civil Code provides that some things are not property because they are for the common enjoyment of all, e.g. the environment. *Bien* is used to designate both tangible and intangible property.

---

[2] C. cons. 26 June 1986, *Privatization*, Rec. 61, Bell, *French Constitutional Law*, decision 30.
[3] One survey would suggest that on average 62.5% of household wealth is tied up in land, most of it residential: Malaurie and Aynès, *Les Biens*, 38.

2. Patrimoine

Legal writing since Aubry and Rau has made use of the concept of *patrimoine* ('patrimony') to describe the totality of rights which an individual possesses.[4] Rather like the notion of 'estate' used in the common law's treatment of inheritance, it combines both the assets and liabilities of an individual which go to make up her or his wealth, but excludes purely personal rights, such as parental authority. The *patrimoine* is treated normally as an indivisible whole and contains both property rights and obligations owed (debts and rights of action). In modern times, it has become possible to divide a person's patrimony into a business and a personal patrimony. This has come about thanks to the creation of the one person company by the *loi* of 11 July 1985.[5] A further example is found in the legislation which establishes the institution of *fiducie* whereby property is transferred to one person under an obligation to hold it for the benefit of another.[6] Under the new article 2011 of the Civil Code, the fiduciary holds the property and rights transferred to him 'holding them separate from his own patrimony'. A *patrimoine* normally belongs to a physical or legal person, but there are a few situations in which French law recognizes a *patrimoine d'affectation*, a free-standing estate which is dedicated to a particular objective, such as a *fondation* (the closest the French come to the equitable notion of a 'charity').

II. Types of Property

A. Corporeal and Incorporeal Property

Property is divided by authors into corporeal and incorporeal property. Corporeal property includes tangible things, such as land and chattels. Incorporeal property, on the other hand, is more complex. It embraces a wide range of intangible things, such as debts and shares, as well as intellectual property rights, such as patents and copyright. It also includes property rights less than ownership, such as hypothecs, even over tangible property rights.

While the Civil Code lays down the basic rules for property in general, an important part of the law relating to incorporeal property is to be found elsewhere. Intellectual property has distinctive characteristics which have led, in France as in England, to its being treated as a separate category of property. The special legislation in this area has recently been brought together in a 'Code of

---

[4] See E. Bartin, *Cours de droit civil*, 5th edn. (Paris, 1917), vol. IX, paras. 573–576; Malaurie and Aynès, *Les Biens*, paras. 7ff.

[5] No. 85-695. On the *entreprise unipersonnelle à responsabilité limitée* (EURL) and the *exploitation agricole à responsabilité limitée* (EARL), see below p. 470.

[6] *Loi* no. 2007-211 of 19 Feb. 2007 whose art. 1 introduces provisions into the Civil Code. See below, pp. 340–341 and for a comparison between the proposed *fiducie* and trust see Malaurie and Aynès, *Les Biens,* para. 763.

intellectual property' (*Code de la propriété intellectuelle*) which deals with the rights of authors and artists, and 'industrial property', such as patents, designs and models.

B. Movable and Immovable Property

Article 516 of the Civil Code divides property between immovable and movable property, a distinction which broadly corresponds to the distinction between real and personal property in English law.

1. Immovable property

Immovable property is essentially real property, but for convenience in an agricultural economy various items of personal property are treated as part of immovable property. Because the category of immovables was fixed in 1804, this list and the distinctions to which it has given rise may seem rather archaic, and it certainly has lost a lot of its significance in a post-industrial society.

Article 517 of the Civil Code subdivides immovable property into three categories: (a) immovables by nature, (b) immovables by destination, and (c) immovables by their object.

(a) Immovables by nature

These are the most straightforward. The principal category set out in article 518 is land and buildings which are immovable by reason of their attachment to the ground. It is not necessary that foundations are dug, provided the construction is attached to the soil. Thus, an electricity pylon even if not embedded in a concrete base is an immovable by nature.[7] Things which are attached to buildings or land are also immovables so long as they are part of it. For example, in the case of the Catalan frescoes,[8] some peasants sold the frescoes on the walls of a chapel to an antique dealer. He removed them from the walls and sold them to two Swiss museums. The original vendors claimed the property back and brought an action in the French courts on the ground that the property sold was an immovable. The museums claimed that the property was movable and that the Swiss courts had jurisdiction. The Cour de cassation decided that the frescoes were immovables by nature, but once detached from the chapel became movables. This solution parallels articles 520 and 521 of the Code in relation to crops and trees, which are treated as immovables so long as they are not cut or harvested.[9]

---

[7] Civ. 4 May 1937, DH 1937.141. See also art. 519 C.civ. which mentions windmills.

[8] Ass. plén. 15 Apr. 1988, D 1988.325 concl. Cabannes.

[9] All the same, it is possible to sell the crops as movables in anticipation of the harvest. For this purpose, case law and doctrinal writing has created the notion of a 'movable by anticipation': Malaurie and Aynès, *Les Biens*, paras. 133–136.

(b) Immovables by destination

These are movable property placed on land for the service and exploitation of land. Article 524 illustrates this idea by a list of rural examples such as animals for cultivation, rabbits, beehives together with presses, barrels and other items necessary for the production of beer or wine and tools necessary for forges, paper-making or other factories. More modern examples would cover tools of trade in a bar, hotel or clinic. In order for something to be an immovable by destination, it is necessary that the movable attached to the land and the land itself both belong to the same person, and for it to be dedicated to the land in the sense that it is indispensable to the exploitation of the land. If it is an immovable by destination, then it cannot be seized by creditors in the same way as movables. An illustration comes from the case of *Tiersonnier*[10] where a landowner placed 80 cattle on his land and claimed that they were exempt from a *saisie-exécution*.[11] It was held that, although they had been dedicated to the land, only 60 were indispensable to the exploitation of the land. The surplus 20 animals were therefore merely movables which could be seized.

(c) Immovables by their object

These are certain rights which relate to the land (*a ius ad rem*). Article 526 of the Code lists these as a usufruct of an immovable, a servitude or an action to reclaim land.

2. *Movable property*

Movable property is defined by article 527 to include things which are movable by nature and those which are movable by law. Movables by nature are things which can be moved from one place to another, whether they are moved by a human being or, like animals, can move themselves. Movables by law are those obligations and actions which concern sums of money due or movables, shares or other interests in commercial or financial companies.[12] The importance of the classification of a thing as a movable is that it can be subject to seizure, including a *saisie conservatoire*.[13] There are more limited conditions for the seizure of buildings.

C. Things Outside Commerce

A number of things are not in commerce[14] and are not treated as either movable or immovable property. So, for example, certain family heirlooms are not capable

---

[10] Req. 19 Oct. 1938, DH 1938.613.
[11] Above, p. 117.
[12] On the classification of *fonds de commerce* (the assets of a person involved in commerce) see below pp. 473–476.
[13] Above, p. 98.
[14] Art. 1128 C.civ. and cf. below, p. 317.

of being traded.[15] Moreover, public property can be subject to special treatment. Public buildings, the seashore and other land held by public bodies is part of the *domaine public* and is not capable of being bought and sold by private individuals. Such public property is governed by the *Code du domaine de l'Etat*. Public bodies do acquire some property from private individuals for their ordinary activities, e.g. an office in a public square in which the town's tourist information office is run. Such property is not part of the essential character of the state or local government and is merely private property which a public body happens for the moment to be occupying. But the office could next become a florist shop run by a private individual. In such a situation, the property is part of the *domaine privé*. Thus a public body will have some property which is integral to its activity and is part of the *domaine public*, like the town hall, and some which is merely part of the *domaine privé*. The distinction is important in terms of how the property can be transferred. If property is part of the *domaine public*, then special procedures have to be followed to declassify it as part of the *domaine public* before it can be sold to a private person. If the property is part of the *domaine privé* then it can be transferred in much the same way as any other piece of land. It is not possible to obtain title to the *domaine public* by prescription. Given the increasingly fluid line between the public and private sector in modern government, this distinction is easier to state than to apply to the range of agencies and organizations which form part of the public sector.

D. Public Property

The discussion of *domaine public* highlights the fact that private individuals do not own all the property. The state is also a major owner. In terms of land, the distinction between the *domaine public* and the *domaine privé* points out that the state is owner in some cases because of the importance of certain property to the public interest, but in other cases it has become owner for more accidental and contingent reasons. No harm is done to the public interest if the *domaine privé* is sold off to the private sector. In more recent years, the state has become owner not only of land, but also of companies and other assets. Nationalized industries and businesses have been the mechanism for running public services such as the railways and television. But the state has also acquired an interest in other companies for more contingent reasons. The most famous of these was the acquisition of the car-maker Renault after the Second World War as a punishment for the collaboration of the firm's owners with the German occupation. As with the *domaine public*, the state is the legal owner of this property either directly or by means of *entreprises publiques* which it has created to run an activity. The state has the right to use and enjoy the property in the public interest. But the acquisition and disposal of such property by means of nationalization and privatization is controlled by *loi*. Nationalization and privatization fall within the legislative province of Parliament under article 34

---

[15] e.g. Civ. (2) 29 Mar. 1995, Bull. civ. II no. 115.

of the Constitution. Despite the wide wording of paragraph 9 of the Preamble to the 1946 Constitution, the Conseil constitutionnel has required that public necessity be demonstrated to justify a nationalization of property in the private sector.[16] When it comes to privatization, the state must receive full compensation for the assets transferred to the private sector, otherwise some citizens are unequally advantaged in the distribution of public property.[17] The state is thus subject to significant restrictions in the exercise of property rights in relation to public property. As a result, it has often preferred simply to own property in the same way as private individuals, e.g. by acquiring a shareholding in a company through the operation of the market, rather than through nationalization, or to sell such shares on the open market, rather than through privatization. In consequence, the rules on private property with which this chapter is concerned are of relevance to some activities of the state and other public bodies.

III. Ownership

A. In General

Article 544 of the Civil Code declares that:

Property is the right to enjoy and dispose of things in the most absolute way, provided that it is not used contrary to statutes and regulations.

The absolute nature of property is clearly qualified by a framework of legal regulation: property is the most absolute right in relation to a thing which the law allows to an individual. The case law of the Conseil constitutionnel makes it clear that property rights can be restricted by law and that one cannot complain of a legislative restriction which is at least as great as existed before.[18] But property rights can be regulated by the legislature, e.g. by planning law or by reference to shareholder publicity rules.[19] The special status of property within the 1789 Declaration only prevents expropriation unless it is justified by a clear public necessity. The limited protection afforded to property has now been reinforced by the European Convention on Human Rights.

B. Ownership and Possession

French law has increasingly supported the position of the possessor of property, rather than the owner. In the case of movable property this is made clear by

---

[16] C. cons. 16 Jan. 1982, *Nationalizations*, Rec. 18.

[17] C. cons. 26 June 1986, *Privatizations*.

[18] C. cons. 18 Oct. 1961, Rec. 50; C. cons. 25 July 1989, *TGV Nord*, RFDA 1989.1009; Bell, *French Constitutional Law*, 176–182.

[19] Bell, *French Constitutional Law*, 182–184.

article 2279 of the Civil Code: 'In the case of movable property, possession is equivalent to title.' This makes sense since movable property can be transferred easily from individual to individual. Public order is preserved by protecting the person in possession. Obviously the rule does not apply where the transfer of property is subject to some other formality, e.g. registration of cars, but such cases are not common. In the case of immovables, a certain pragmatism applies. It is necessary to protect the person in possession to prevent social disorder. In practice, it is difficult for a person to establish that she has ownership of property, and so she will typically rely on her established possession in any action. Under article 2282, the possessor of real property is entitled to protect their interest 'without reference to the justification of their right'. Since the *loi* of 9 July 1975,[20] even the mere occupier of land (the *détenteur précaire*) is allowed to bring actions to protect his interest based on the simple fact of possession. French law distinguishes between possessory actions and proprietary actions (*action pétitoire*). It is for the claimant to choose between these if evicted from property. If he relies simply on prior possession and seeks to re-establish this, he can be defeated only by the other side demonstrating either a better right to possess or by showing that they are the owners of the property. It is not sufficient for the dispossessor to show that the possessor does not have title to the property.

The possessory actions are *réintégration, complainte, dénonciation de nouvel oeuvre*. *Réintégration* (previously called *réintégrande*) serves to re-establish the possession of a person who has been evicted by a positive act of another (whether or not it was accompanied by violence). The claimant must be unable to exercise rights over all or part of the property, and must have had peaceful enjoyment of the property at the time of eviction.[21] The *complainte* is an action to stop an actual interference with property rights or intrusion into the property (e.g. work on another's land). A possession can bring a pre-emptive action, the *dénonciation de nouvel oeuvre*, to prevent work which, if it were continued, would give rise to an interference with property rights. Both the *complainte* and the *dénonciation* require that the claimant has enjoyed possession for at least a year,[22] but this is not required for *réintégration*. The idea is to ensure that possession has been established for sufficiently long enough to be able to identify the rights involved. But public order requires that possessors should not be totally dispossessed.

C. Acquisition of Ownership

Ownership can be acquired in a number of ways. One common method of classifying these draws a distinction between cases where the title is simply derived

[20] No. 75-596.
[21] Civ. 23 Feb. 1893, *Chaumier*, DP 1893.1.376 where one neighbour forcefully resisted the use of a water conduit by the claimants so that they never did have peaceful enjoyment.
[22] Art. 1264 N.c.pr.civ.

from another person (e.g. by transfer *inter vivos* or by inheritance) and cases where it is an original (i.e. new) title, as when a person appropriates property that has no owner or ousts its existing owner. A person becomes the original owner of property as a result of his own actions and without reference to the actions of others. This is unusual in modern law, but the French law demonstrates the importance of physical control in the notion of ownership.

1. *Original title*

(a) Becoming the first owner: occupation

A person may become the first owner of movable property by taking possession of it. This is true of things which have never had an owner, such as wild birds and fish, and things which once were owned but no longer have an owner, such as abandoned property. But ownership cannot be acquired in this way in the case of immovable property: all ownerless property of this kind belongs automatically to the state.[23]

(b) Adverse possession: *usucapion*

The principal method of acquiring original title is *usucaption*, acquisition by prescription. A person acquires title to a thing by possessing it openly and peacefully over a long period (article 712 of the Civil Code). Article 2219 of the Civil Code describes prescription as a method of acquiring or losing rights by lapse of time. In *usucapion* the new owner needs not only to let time elapse passively, he needs to take some positive steps to mark out his ownership. It is not enough that the original owner has lost interest in the thing: there must be some reason why the new owner is the person whose title the law should recognize.

The justification for *usucapion* is a matter of social order. If a person has held the property for a long period then that has become a settled part of social organization and should not be disturbed. Obviously these days registration of title to land and in relation to some chattels offers an alternative and better method of determining who is the owner of which property. Nevertheless, *usucapion* can be useful in dealing with some long-standing situations. Social order requires the law to recognize long-standing possession, however it came about. Thus a person can acquire title by prescription even if he obtained possession in bad faith, e.g. by squatting on land knowing that he had no right to be there. Such a situation is extreme and French law is reluctant to recognize it. Under article 2262 of the Civil Code, the normal prescription period of 30 years applies in this case, so the original owner has plenty of time to bring an action to repossess the property. Where the person comes into possession in good faith, then the prescription period is reduced (*la prescription abrégée*). The shorter period is normally ten years under article 2265 of the Code, but where the original owner has moved from the district of the cour d'appel in which the property is situated, then the

[23] Art. 713 C.civ. (and see also art. 539).

period is extended by twice the number of years in which he has lived outside that area. Thus the maximum prescription period for a good faith possessor is 20 years. Hence the prescription period is referred to as 'prescription of 10 and 20 years' in article 2266. For the shorter prescription period to apply, it is sufficient that the possessor at the beginning of the period was in good faith. But if the vendor of land acquired it in bad faith, then even a good faith purchaser will have to rely on the full prescription of 30 years.[24]

For *usucaption* to apply, the key elements are that the claimant possessed the property in his or her own right in a peaceful and public manner.

Own right: Not every person holding a thing or occupying land does so in his or her own right. A mere occupier, such as a friend who is allowed to live in your flat while you are on holiday, clearly has no pretence of a claim to be owner. Their right to occupy the flat clearly acknowledges that you are its true owner. Similarly the tenant of land or the hirer of a thing, e.g. a hire car, derives their right from another person and cannot claim that their possession gives them any right of ownership.

Long period: The prescription period begins when the claimant or his predecessor in title came into possession of the thing. Given the long prescription period which operates, then it will be common for a claimant to rely not only on his own possession, but also that of a predecessor. The period is long in order to give the original owner every opportunity to claim the property back. Indeed, the Civil Code provides that the prescription period is suspended in certain situations in which the original owner is unable to bring an action. These situations are more limited than under the pre-Revolutionary law, but include where the owner is a child or an adult whose affairs are administered by another (a person under *tutelle*), e.g. because he is mentally incapable of handling his affairs (article 2251). A supervening event (*force majeure*) affecting the owner may suspend the prescription period, but this only applies where the event makes it absolutely impossible for the owner to react to the adverse possession by the claimant.[25]

Publicity: The effect of possession must be noticeable if the original owner is going to have a chance to react and claim the property. Possession must thus be public. It is not possible to become owner if the property is hidden or if occupation is not identifiable. For example, if there is a shared drive, the claim of one user to possess all of it can only be shown if he makes successful efforts to exclude the other from using it.

Ownership must be claimed. Once it is claimed, it is deemed to have existed from the moment the claimant moved into possession. Although this operates as a matter of law, it will usually be difficult to sell the land without the title being clarified. The claimant will thus usually have to obtain an *instrumentum* from a

---

[24] See Civ. (3), 29 Feb. 1968, Bull. civ. III no. 83.
[25] Req. 11 June 1921, S 1922.1.217 note E. Naquet.

notary which records his title. The notary will receive the statements of witnesses and will record these to demonstrate the right to ownership which is claimed.

Peaceful: Article 2233 of the Civil Code provides that prescription can never be begun by a violent act. The prescription period only begins to run from the date on which forceable occupation ceased. Not even the need to respect social stability requires force to be rewarded.

(c) Movables[26]

The acquisition of title in movables is easier than with land. Commerce requires speed and security in the transfer of items which are easily transported and may be perishable. There is not sufficient time to investigate title in the same way as with land. The transferee wants to be able to rely on apparent title. Going further than English law, which recognizes in this context various exceptions to the principle *nemo dat quod non habet*, article 2279 al. 1 of the Civil Code lays down a general rule for the protection of those who acquire possession in good faith: 'in the case of movable property, possession is equivalent to title'.

This priority of possession only applies in the case of corporeal movables. Incorporeal movables, such as shares, do not transfer in the same way. For example, in the case of *Lefèvre*,[27] Morris, the owner of shares, handed the share certificates together with a signed blank transfer form to his agent. The agent handed the documents to a colleague who used them to transfer the shares to Mme Le Marrois to repay his personal debt to her. The shares register continued to carry the name Morris. The court decided that he remained owner of the shares and that Mme Le Marrois could not rely on article 2279 to obtain title to them. That article is restricted to situations where the thing is transferred manually, rather than by changing a registration. Article 2279 does not apply even to some corporeal objects whose transfer is subject to registration, e.g. ships, river barges and aeroplanes. But these are special statutory exceptions and the category does not extend to other registered objects such as cars.[28]

Possession is a factual situation of control, but it is not lost where someone else has control over the thing on behalf of the possessor. Thus, where the purchaser of a lorry sent it to a garage for repairs, he did not lose possession. The original owner, British Leyland (France), could not claim title to the lorry against the garage on the ground that its dealer had not paid it for the lorry.[29] Whatever defect may have existed in the title of the dealer, the person who purchased the lorry

---

[26] See C.S.P. Harding and M.S. Rowell, 'Protection of Property versus Protection of Commercial Transactions in French and English Law' (1977) 26 ICLQ 354.

[27] Civ. 4 Jan. 1876, DP 1877.1.33.

[28] Civ. (1), 11 July 1960, D 1960.702 note Voirin.

[29] Civ (1), 16 Jan. 1980, Bull. civ. I no. 30. Similarly, the good faith purchaser of a stolen lorry which he handed over to the police still is considered in possession of the vehicle when the true owner wished to reclaim it: Civ. (1), 22 Nov. 1988, Bull. civ. I no. 331.

from the dealer acquired good title to it and remained in possession while the vehicle was in the garage.

To rely on article 2279, the possessor must be in good faith. Thus, where five old masters paintings were taken away from the place of safety in which they had been placed during the Second World War, the court considered that the subsequent owner could not have been unaware of the unusual origin of the paintings and must be treated as in bad faith. He could not then resist the claim by the original owner, the museums of Stuttgart.[30]

The basic principle is that, where a thief[31] or the finder of goods are still in possession of the thing, the true owner can bring an action of *revendication* to reclaim it at any time—there is no prescription period. But where the property has been passed on, then article 2279 operates to protect the good faith transferee. However, within three years of a loss or theft, the original owner can reclaim the property from the good faith possessor provided he pays the latter the price he paid for it. In that way, the good faith possessor is not out of pocket. Where goods have been bought at a fair, a market or a public sale, or from a seller trading in similar items,[32] then the original owner cannot reclaim the goods against a good faith purchaser.[33] This protects commercial dealings.

2. Acquisition by transfer

Property is usually acquired by transfer from someone who has good title. Unlike German law, French law effects transfer of title automatically by the operation of contract. Under article 1138 al. 1 of the Civil Code, the obligation to deliver a thing is accomplished by the mere consent of the parties. All the same, this is a very precarious basis for security in dealings. In the case of movable property, as we have just seen, it is moderated by the rule under article 2279 that possession is equivalent to title. So the third party can rely on possession as a basis of security for dealings. In the case of land, while contract may effect the transfer of title, the institution of registration of transactions has been introduced to provide security. If the transferee wishes to secure his or her title, he or she has to register it, since priority of interests is granted by law to priority in registration.

(a) Land registration

Land registration (*la publicité foncière*) is governed by the *décret* of 4 January 1955 (as amended). The procedures for registration of land transactions have a long

---

[30] Civ (2), 23 Mar. 1965, Bull. civ. II no. 206; also Civ. (1), 2 Feb 1965, D 1965.371 (possessor of a stolen Louis XVI desk treated as in bad faith).

[31] Where the owner has merely been tricked out of his property by fraud rather than by theft, he has no similar right to reclaim the goods by *revendication*: e.g. Req. 16 July 1884, DP 1885.1.232.

[32] Whether or not a person trades in similar items is a question of fact: see Pau 3 July 1979, *Chouchou bar*, D 1980.IR.232 where an antiques dealer had sold a Louis XV commode but admitted that his previous dealings included selling a car in a cafe called the 'Chouchou bar'.

[33] Art. 2280 C. civ.

and checkered history. In 1424, Henry VI of England and France required the registration of mortgage transactions in Paris. The *droit coutumier* of Northern France (the 'pays du nantissement') required the transcription of acts for the transfer of land onto public registers, while Brittany operated a system of publicity through bans. The *ordonnance* of Villiers-Cotterets of 1539 tried to extend these systems to the whole country, but this and later attempts were not successful. Registration of gifts was, however, uniformly required. Attempts were made during the Revolutionary period to establish a more systematic land registration system. But the *lois* of 1795 (9 messidor Year III) and 1798 (11 brumaire Year VII) failed. As Ripert and Boulanger remarked, the traditional reason for the unpopularity of land registration was that the Fisc seized upon the registration of land transactions as an opportunity to levy a tax, and this hampered the development of a proper land registration system.[34]

The Roman law tradition strongly influenced the Civil Code. Following Grotius and Domat, article 1138 of the Code provides that the transfer of property is completed simply by the agreement of the parties. Any system which subordinated the efficacy of such an agreement to the formality of registration was seen as contrary to the freedom of the parties. In addition, Bigot de Préameneu, argued in presenting the draft Code to the Conseil d'Etat in 1804 that the peace of families creates public happiness, and this moral and political ideal would be infringed by the conflicts arising from a system of registration of land transactions. For him, 'the system of publicity [of land transactions] prevents families keeping secret their affairs... this secret has always been regarded as one of the principal aspects of individual freedom'.[35] The Code contented itself with requiring the registration of gifts of property which could be mortgaged (to protect family property). Registration of mortgages and similar rights did come in the 19th century, but the land registration procedures set up in 1855 were incomplete and kept records according to the name of the landowner, rather than according to plots of land. A property register of plots of land was only created in 1807, for tax purposes. It took until 1955 to establish a system of recording all transactions by reference to plot of land.

As a consequence of this history, France has a system of registration of transactions, but this procedure does not affect their validity, merely their effectiveness against third parties. There are three distinct elements in the French registered land transaction.

In the first place, there is the agreement of the parties which suffices to transfer the property under article 1138 of the Civil Code. This agreement need not be in writing. Even when it is in writing, it need not follow any particular form and can be an *acte sous seing privé* (a private written document as opposed to

[34] G. Ripert and J. Boulanger, *Traité de droit civil*, iii, Part 2: *Publicité foncière* (Paris, 1958), 57. On the history of land registration, see H. Regnault, 'L'insinuation des actes emportant transfert de propriété à titre onéreux dans l'ancien droit français', *Mélanges Fournier* (Paris, 1929), 665.

[35] P. A. Fenet, *Receuil complet des travaux préparatoires du Code civil* (Paris, 1836), xv, 237.

a notarized act). Because validity does not depend on registration, the relevant date for all issues concerning the validity of the contract is that on which it was made, not the date of registration. Thus, where a contract agreement was made on 20 March, but the notarized act and registration was not made until 4 April, the Cour de cassation decided that the first date was the relevant one for calculating the two-year period within which an action to rescind for *lésion* had to be brought and the later notarized act and registration had no effect on this.[36]

The second element is the notarized act (*acte authentique*) by which a notary records in an official note what the parties have agreed. The notary advises the parties on the transaction. The notary effectively ensures that the requirements for the validity of the transaction have been followed. Only notarized acts or decisions of courts can be registered at the registry of charges. Certain transactions, e.g. charges on land created by agreement,[37] must be made by way of notarized act in order to be valid. Even where an agreement does not require to be in the form of a notarized act to be valid, such as a sale of land, it will have to be recorded by a notary who will verify the signatures and the identity of the parties concerned. The notary (or, in some cases, a court) will act as the gatekeeper to ensure that documents submitted for registration are in proper form.

In the third place, the transaction will be registered in the appropriate local registry of charges (*bureau de conservation des hypothèques*). Despite its name, the register contains all land transactions. The role of the *conservateur* in charge of the office is not to verify the legality of the transactions submitted for registration, but merely to check that a long list of very precise details set out in the *décret* of 14 October 1955 is included in the documentation submitted. Should the information not be included, he will simply reject the application for registration. Only in rare cases does the *conservateur* strike out a registration and this on grounds of fraud. Should this happen, the affected party has the right to challenge the decision in the private law courts.

Any transactions or court judgment which effects or records a change or the creation of real property rights or charges in real property *inter vivos* must be registered, including those subject to a condition precedent or subsequent. This includes real rights such as ownership, usufruct, usage, servitudes, and emphyteusis, and transactions such as sale, gift, exchange or accession to common property. But, in addition, certain personal rights such as a long lease for more than 12 years, as well certain loan agreements for the purchase of property (the *crédit-bail immobilier*) and land concessions , since these seriously affect the value of property. Finally, certain contracts are registered really to ensure that they continue despite changes in ownership, e.g. the contract of land promotion or the *règlement de copropriété*. In the case of charges, it is necessary to distinguish those for which registration is required and those for which it is not. Preferred credit

---

[36] Civ. (1) 18 June 1962, D 1962.608.
[37] Art. 2127 C. civ.

rights (*privilèges*) are subject to publicity, with the exception of rights set out in article 2104 of the Civil Code which predominantly relate to rights of employees. Judicial hypothecs or charges (*hypothèques judiciaires*) resulting from court decisions and charges created by agreement (*hypothèques conventionnelles*) both require to be registered to have any effect in relation to the property. In the case of legal charges (*hypothèques légales*), most require to be registered.[38]

The effect of registration is to make the transaction or charge effective (*opposable*) against third parties. It has effect from the date of registration. In many cases, the transaction is effective between the original parties or those receiving their interest by way of gift. But a third party taking by way of contract is not bound by the unregistered interest. This protective effect is clearly desirable and so, since 1959, it has been possible for people to provisionally register their rights in advance of a formal transaction. Thus, someone with an option to purchase or with an unnotarized agreement to sell land can register their interest (the system of *prénotation*).

When dealing in relation to the land, the potential creditor or purchaser (or more likely his notary) can check against the land and against the individual owner and discover all interests and charges in relation to land.

(b) Gift

Because under French inheritance law, certain members of the family have rights to a specific share in the estate, the law on gifts is more restrictive than under English law. The principal restriction is in relation to the procedure which must be followed. Under article 931 of the Civil Code, a gift must be made by way of notarized act unless there is a manual transfer. In these ways, there is a public record of the transfer which enables an heir to challenge the validity of the gift or to require the transferee to account for the gift and set it off as part of his or her benefit from the estate.

(c) Inheritance

Property passes directly to the heirs under French law. It is not held by an executor or administrator as a distinct estate which is ultimately distributed to the beneficiaries. Rather the property vests in the universal heirs (those entitled to specific shares in the estate and who inherit unspecified amounts) jointly. The property falls into *indivision* until such time as it is divided up between those heirs, and it is administered under the rules on common property discussed below. Specific heirs are legatees who receive a specific item or amount under the will. On the death of the deceased, they acquire a right to the property in question, but only can enter into possession by making a request to the heirs to hand it over.[39] Succession has been discussed in more detail in Chapter 8.[40]

---

[38] On these charges see the discussion on hypothecs on p. 291 below.
[39] Art. 1011 C. civ.
[40] Above, pp. 262–263.

D. Ownership of Collective Property

Collective property is of great significance. Property will be in collective ownership in a number of common situations: during a marriage, under an inheritance,
or where several individuals share a building, e.g. a block of apartments. The common law uses the notion of trust to handle many of the problems arising in such
situations. French law lacks such a concept and so has to regulate the situation of
common ownership (*indivision*) of the property in question. It is interesting to
observe that many of the outcomes which the common law achieves through the
use of trusts and common property are achieved in France through the careful
regulation of common ownership. The Civil Code did not favour the situation of
indivision since it does not enable an individual to exploit the property to the full.
But it has to be recognized that there are many reasons why property will remain
in *indivision* for a significant period. The most common reasons are family convenience. Where one of the heirs to property is a minor or where the widow of
the deceased is still alive, the other heirs may be happy to keep the inheritance
together until it can be shared out on the majority of the child or the death of
the widow, when it is no longer needed as a family asset. The relationship during
marriage is similar. In agricultural settings where the unit may be very small,
there are often particularly good reasons for keeping the landholding together
and running it as a single unit, rather than dividing it up. As is noted elsewhere,
French inheritance law entitles the children of the deceased to share equally and
this could lead to fragmentation of an estate unless action is taken.

The legislation laid down in the Code was altered by the *loi* of 31 December
1976 dealing with the management of *indivision*.[41]

1. The basic regime

The property held in common is described as the *masse indivise*. It is treated as a
common asset to be managed for the good of all. The way in which French law
handles this situation can be seen most clearly from the way in which it deals with
the undivided inheritance. While the common property will be constituted essentially by the original inheritance, it is likely that the composition of the assets will
change over time. Where new items are added, they become subject to the same
rules governing the *masse*. In the case of a replacement, the process is described as
subrogation réelle in the sense that the rights over the new property are exercised
by way of subrogation for the rights which existed over the original property.[42]
For instance, if a house is gutted by fire, then the money paid under the insurance

---

[41] No. 76-286.
[42] This institution of *subrogation légale* is in no way a form of restitution in the common law
sense. It merely identifies a replacement for property which has been lawfully disposed of in the
normal course of the management of the common assets. In the common law of restitution, the
concern is more commonly to provide a remedy for wrongful transfers of property. See further
below, p. 449.

policy becomes subject to the rules on *indivision* in place of the house. Equally, if the co-owners agree to sell the house, then the proceeds of sale become part of the *indivision*.[43] But if the property is sold by only one of the co-owners, then the proceeds are his, subject of course to his duty to account to the *masse* for the value of the property sold. The value is determined at the date of repayment to the *masse*. For instance, in 1936, a father sold a motor launch belonging to the inheritance he shared with his sons for 2,600 francs. He purchased another launch which he resold in 1946 for 8,000 francs. The court held he was obliged to make restitution to the *masse* for the value of the launch in 1936 assessed in terms of prices in 1954.[44]

The last case illustrates that the rights of co-owners are rights against each other, but do not prejudice third parties. Third parties can acquire good title to items of the common property sold by a co-owner.

Since 1976, the rules on the enjoyment of the fruits of the inheritance or community of property have been simplified. In broad terms, the fruits of the exploitation of the common property belong to the *masse* subject to reasonable remuneration for any services rendered by one of the co-owners. Thus it was stated in one case that, even though one required a special qualification to run a biological analysis laboratory, this did not mean that the profits from this laboratory ceased to be part of the *indivision*, subject to appropriate remuneration for the work, costs and responsibility incurred by the co-owner running it.[45] Article 815-12 of the Civil Code makes specific provision for remuneration, determined if necessary by the judge, for the co-owner who manages the property. The co-owner whose personal efforts have led to an increase in the value of the common property, e.g. a farm or a business, is entitled to a similar recompense to someone who has laid out expenditure to improve it.[46] Thus a dentist who inherits clients but improves the profitability of the firm is entitled to some remuneration, even though the increased clientele remains common property.[47] The rules are more flexible than those on the remuneration of English trustees.

The common property consists not only of assets, but also of debts. Creditors will be paid in priority from the assets (*actif*) of the estate and they may bring actions to secure the seizure and sale of common property in order to obtain repayment. Where an individual co-owner has personal debts to a third party, that creditor cannot seize any of the common property, but under article 815-17

[43] e.g. Civ. (1), 6 Nov. 1967, D 1968.36 where a house was sold for 14,944,576 (old) francs and reinvested in a business which was then sold at a loss for only 133,026 (new) francs. The value of that part of the inheritance was taken by the Cour de cassation to be the proceeds of sale of the business, since the heirs shared the gains and losses.

[44] Bordeaux 18 Feb. 1954, D 1955.151 note Weill.

[45] Civ. (1), 10 Mar. 1984, Bull. civ. I no. 152.

[46] Civ. (1), 25 May 1985, D 1988.28.

[47] Civ. (1), 26 Jan. 1994, *Epergue*, JCP 1994. IV.697.

of the Code he can petition to bring about the division of the assets and thus be repaid from the share due to his debtor.

The normal regime for the administration of common property (*le régime légal*) applies unless there is a specific agreement. Under article 815-3 of the Code 'decisions for the administration and disposal of common property require the consent of all the co-owners'. The principle of unanimity obviously poses practical problems, especially where expenses must be incurred. The same article of the Code requires an express mandate for any decision which exceeds the normal use of the thing as well as for the making and renewal of leases. In the case of routine administration of the property, an implicit mandate will be presumed to exist. Where special steps have to be taken to conserve the property, then any co-owner is considered to have authority to take the necessary action and to reclaim the costs from others.[48] Such steps have been described as 'physical or legal measures which are intended to protect the property from an immediate danger without seriously compromising the rights of the co-owners'.[49] It will be common that the common property will be entrusted to the administration of one individual, e.g. a farm is run by one of the children of a family. That person will undertake administrative tasks. For example, in the case of the estate of the painter Picasso, the legal administrator was entitled to transfer his works of art within the estate to a company specializing in managing copyright.[50] But, of course, the overriding requirement of unanimity means that there will be unresolved disputes between co-owners. The powers of the judge to intervene are limited. Under article 815-6 of the Code, the president of the tribunal de grande instance can order such urgent measures to be taken in the common interest, but this will not cover the generality of issues which arise. Wide interpretation of this general power does, however, permit the common activity to be carried forward. For example, in *de Boutiny*[51] the common property was leased to certain co-owners who would not agree to a rent increase. Another co-owner petitioned for the appointment of a legal administrator of the property to determine the proper rent and the Cour de cassation quashed the refusal by the Cour d'appel to make such an appointment. It argued that the profitability of the common assets was in the interests of all co-owners and the conflict between their interest as co-owners and their personal interest as tenants did not undermine the need to protect that common interest.

No one is obliged to remain in a situation of co-property and she or he may request severance at any time. This is the ultimate safeguard of an individual's

---

[48] Art. 815-2 C. civ.

[49] Civ. (3), 25 Jan. 1983, D 1983.IR.256: there was no immediate danger requiring the bringing of a court action where works undertaken in relation to a party wall by a neighbour would not give him an immediate right to support by prescription nor did they threaten the fabric of the common property.

[50] See Civ. (1), 4 Apr. 1991, *Picasso*, D 1992.261.

[51] Civ. (1), 13 Nov. 1984, D 1985.104.

interest, and the court may help resolve disputes about the value of the assets, usually by appointing an administrator or expert. Under article 815-9 of the Code, during the currency of the co-property, any co-owner is allowed to make use of the property provided that she accounts to the *masse* for the benefits gained.

2. Co-property in buildings

Buildings which many people share have been a major feature of French urban life for much longer than in England. The regulation of the relationship between the parties has been more developed. In order to deal with the inevitable disputes which occur between those who share the same building, the *loi* of 10 July 1965[52] provides a compulsory regime for all premises which have parts which are partly private, i.e. individually owned, and partly common. This does not apply to property which is entirely in *indivision* nor where a single company or landlord owns the whole building. The *loi* provides a framework for the management of the common parts.

(a) Enjoyment

The common parts of the property are the outside shell of the building (including the walls and roof), the stairs, terraces and all facilities for common use such as lifts. These parts are maintained for the common good. The common parts are owned by each owner in proportion to the value of his or her *lot*. Under article 22 of the 1965 *loi*, in the absence of specific provision, the building is divided into notional one-thousandth units and an owner receives a number of units according to the value of his unit in terms of its size, location, tranquility, etc. Each owner in the building has a right to enjoy the common parts, but it is not like having a servitude across someone else's land. It is rather a right to enjoy the property in common with others and to share the burdens of that common enjoyment.

The use of the property is defined in the basic instrument, the *règlement de copropriété*, and the basic purpose for which the property is dedicated. There must be this special *acte authentique* which establishes the regime under which the property is held and it will describe the property (the *lot*) and what may be done on it. For example, it may be residential property (*habitation bourgeoise*) so that no trade may be conducted on it, but a professional activity such as running a dentist's surgery is permitted within the building. It is for the parties signing the original *règlement* to explain what they intend the building to be used for. All the same, while there is wide freedom of contract, there are some clauses which are extraneous and inappropriate to regulating the use of a building, e.g. a non-competition clause in a shopping centre.

The right to enjoy property is limited of course by the right of others, and article 9 al. 1 of the *loi* makes it clear that one cannot make use of one's rights in a shared building to harm others.

---

[52] No. 65-557.

(b) Management

The management of the building is vested in an association of owners, the *syndicat de copropriété*. It has its own legal personality and can bring actions to protect the interests of the co-owners, e.g. to deal with nuisances by a neighbour or to challenge planning decisions of the local authority. The *syndicat* collects the common charges and pays third parties, e.g. for gas to heat the building. All the owners of parts of the building form part of the general assembly. Most decisions are taken by simple majority, but more serious decisions (e.g. to sack the *syndic*) are taken by a majority of all owners, and fundamental decisions, such as to alter the statutes of the *syndicat* require a three-quarters majority of all owners. The most extreme decisions, e.g. to change the character of the building, require unanimity. There is thus a way for individual owners to protect their position, a set of checks and balances to ensure administrative efficiency and no prejudice to the rights of one individual. Day-to-day administration is entrusted to an administrator, the *syndic*, who takes decisions with the support of a management committee (*conseil syndical*). The funds which are collected to pay charges are common property in which the co-owners have no individual rights. It is thus a common fund which is administered by the *syndicat*.

(c) Charges

Charges for the common parts have to be shared between the co-owners. There are two different kinds of charges which are shared in different ways. The first kind are *common services and equipment* which are linked to the enjoyment of the property, e.g. common heating, hot water, lifts and the caretaker. Such charges are divided according to the utility of the service for each *lot*. Thus a ground floor flat pays less towards the lift than a sixth floor flat. For example, where a supermarket formed part of a building but had its own security and maintenance arrangements, it was exempt from the charges for the caretaker and cleaners which applied to the rest of the building.[53] The second kind of charge relates the maintenance, upkeep and administration of the common parts. Such charges are divided according to the value of each *lot* as explained above.[54] Under article 10 of the 1965 *loi*, these categories of charge are compulsory, as is the way of dividing them among the co-owners. The statute is rigid because of the litigation which the previous legislation failed to prevent. A rule-based and unchallengeable system was the only way of reducing the number of disputes which co-ownership generates. The *syndicat* has a charge on the individual owner's property to recover the collective charges if they remain unpaid.

---

[53] Civ. (3) 1 Apr. 1987, Bull. civ. III no. 72.
[54] Above p. 287.

IV. Property Rights Less than Ownership

A. Usufruct

A usufruct is defined in article 578 as 'the right to enjoy the things which another owns like the owner himself, but with the duty to preserve its substance'. This definition is drawn from Roman law and describes a property right less than ownership. It is of great significance among older members of the family. Created often by will or agreement, an older member of the family is permitted to enjoy property such as the family home while they live before it is sold or taken over by the younger generation. Often the usufructuary (*usufruitier*) will be the widow of the deceased. Unlike the lease, which also gives the lessee the right to enjoy the property for a period of time, it is a property right which must be respected by third parties.

During the usufruct, the usufructuary has the right of enjoyment whereas the reversioner (*nu-propriétaire*) has the ultimate interest in the property. The reversioner expects to obtain the substance of the property at the end of the interest of the usufructuary. Where the property is consumable or fungible, e.g. the merchandise of a business or money, then the reversioner will not get back the things themselves but a replacement equivalent in value. This is often described as a 'quasi-usufruct'. In order to define the rights of the parties, the Code provides in article 600 for an inventory to be drawn up to determine what has been handed over, unless the document creating the usufruct provides differently. Under article 601, the usufructuary has to provide a deposit or an equivalent guarantee, unless there is a provision to the contrary.

The usufructuary enjoys the property and the benefits coming from it. The Code distinguishes between *fruits civils* (such as rents) which are enjoyed as and when they come into the estate and *fruits naturels et industriels* (such as crops either self-sown or grown by man) which are acquired when cut. In both cases they fall to the usufructuary during the period of the usufruct. But in the latter case, if the usufructuary has sown crops which are not harvested when the usufruct ends, then he or she has no right to them or to be compensated for their value.

The interests of the usufructuary and the reversioner are resolved by giving the former only rights concerning the day-to-day administration of the property. He cannot take decisions which have a permanent effect on its value. Thus, article 595 of the Civil Code prevents the usufructuary from leasing the property for more than nine years. (Of course, given security of tenure in commercial and agricultural leases, this can still be problematic.)

There are two limited forms of usufruct used in family arrangements. Under article 625, the *usage* gives the beneficiary the right to use the property and to enjoy its fruits for one's own needs and those of one's family (unless there is specific provision to the contrary). It follows the normal rules on the creation and extinction of real property rights. The right is one which is *intuitu personae* and so cannot be transferred or leased to another person. An even more limited real property right is the *habitation* which is the right to enjoy property as a dwelling for one's own benefit or for that of one's family.

B. Servitudes

Although the right to property has been described in the Civil Code as a absolute right, it had to compromise with the needs of either the neighbours or the organization of society at large.

The Civil Code created a number of *servitudes* (easements) in order to protect the owners of the contiguous land: if for instance, there is no passage to the public highway, articles 682–685 of the Civil Code provide for a systematic right of way of the plot which is so enclosed (*le fond dominant*). The right of way can only be requested by the owner or the holder of a real right (usufruct, usage, etc.) and compensation must be paid to the owner of the land over which a right of way is claimed (*le fond dominé*). Other servitudes regulate the discharge of natural water: it is prohibited to discharge the rain collected from the roof directly onto the neighbouring land (however, once on the ground it is allowed to flow naturally to the contiguous land), moreover, an owner lower down on a slope is not entitled to build anything which would stop the natural flow of the water (if it builds a wall for instance, holes need to made).

The servitudes mentioned above were particularly relevant in an era during which agriculture and land were so important. However, the industrial and economic progress has given rise to an even larger category of *servitudes*: the *servitudes* of public utility. These *servitudes*, as their name implies, are created in order to benefit the collectivity; they protect the general interest of the population. A number of rules ensures that the integrity of the public highways are respected (a certain distance has to be respected when erecting building, for instance). Property owners cannot oppose the passage of aircraft above their land. Lastly, most lands nowadays have to bear a number of ordinary *servitudes* of public utility: in the air, the passage of electricity, phone lines or pylons, and underground the domestic gas pipes, the connecting pipe to the sewage system, and so on. By contrast with the traditional *servitudes* mentioned above, owners are not compensated when a *servitude* of public utility is imposed over their property; legislation has to provide expressly for it.

V. Other Interests Affecting Property

A. Security Interests

Rights of a creditor secured against property in principle are considered to be personal rights between the creditor and debtor, rather than property rights. They are thus covered in that part of the Civil Code dealing with special contracts. Nevertheless, some such rights are property rights, e.g. hypothecs. As has been seen, in relation to immovables and to some movables, such interests may have to be registered to be effective against third parties dealing in the property.

1. Privilèges

Certain individuals are preferred creditors and thus have legally protected *privilèges*. These entitle the individual to payment (in competition with others having similar rank) in preference to secured creditors such as the holders of hypothecs. The Treasury is the most preferred creditor. Such *privilèges* can be general or special and in relation to movable or immovable property. In relation to movables, general *privilèges* arise under article 2101 of the Civil Code for example in relation to the payment of court fees, funeral expenses, the cost of medical treatment during a terminal illness, certain rights of employees, and debts owed to a spouse in relation to the development of a business. General *privilèges* in relation to immovables arise under article 2104 in similar situations in relation to court fees and the rights of employees. Special *privilèges* arise in relation to specific kinds of movable property notably in farming, or the lien of a hotelier or of a carrier of goods. In relation to immovable property, they arise under article 2103 especially in relation to loans or work done by builders and architects in relation to the construction of the property. The *décret* of 1955 on land registration has made the *privilèges* in relation to immovable property into legal charges (*hypothèques légales*) and subjected them to registration as a condition of their effectiveness. As a result, they retain their priority status, but must be publicly known.

2. Hypothèques

Hypothecs (*hypothèques*) are property rights which secure the performance of an obligation (e.g. to pay money) against some specific real property. In many ways, the hypothec resembles a common law mortgage in that it offers security, normally against land. At the ultimate extreme, the creditor has the right to seize the property in order to ensure payment of the obligation. But the scope of hypothecs is broader than a mortgage and so the term 'charge' is perhaps most appropriate. Hypothecs, as has been noted, can have any of three sources. Hypothecs arising by agreement (*hypothèques légales*) follow the formalities of a notarized act. There are restrictions on the property which may be made subject to such a charge. The notarized act must specify the property subject to the charge and its location. Article 2130 prohibits a charge on future property, but then undermines this somewhat by permitting a debtor who recognizes that his present property is insufficient to provide security for a debt to promise to charge his future property to secure the debt, as and when it falls into his possession. The agreement thus made is sufficient to generate an automatic charge on the new property from the date when it enters the patrimony of the debtor. The amount of the debt must also be specified at the time of the contract. A judicial hypothec (*hypothèque judiciaire*) is a charge which is attached by law under article 2123 of the Code to any judgment of a court (civil or administrative) or an arbitration to secure compliance by the losing party. A legal hypothec (*hypothèque légale*) is a charge which arises by law in favour of certain persons. These are specified in article 2121 of the Code as one spouse in relation to the other, for minors in relation to the property of their tutor, of the state, local government and public bodies in relation to the property of their accounting officers, a legatee against the property of a succession, and a number of other rights set out in article 2101. Most of these secure the performance of obligations owed by persons in positions of trust. There are some limits on these. For example, if there is a need to waive the spouse's charge in order to raise security on the property of the other spouse in the interests of the family, then the court can order a waiver where the spouse holds the charge under article 2139 al. 3.

B. Leases

In French law, leases are not generally interests in land, but contracts. They are thus governed by the provisions in the Civil Code on special contracts. There are one or two long leases which are property rights. That said, leases have certain consequences which make them close to interests in land, especially in relation to agricultural and business leases. Article 1743 provides that the tenant's rights prevail against a subsequent acquirer of the leased property. This offers security and is a modification of the relative effect of contracts. Since 1975 article 2283 of the Civil Code has been amended so that the tenant has been able to exercise possessory actions directly without needing to involve the landlord in the action. As has been seen above, a lease of over 12 years is subject to the requirements of land registration. These features recognize the importance of the tenant's interest in relation to the land, but it is still only a personal right. The Cour de cassation made this clear in 1861[55] when it ruled that:

A lease does not effect any disaggregation of the right to property, which remains in the hand of the landlord, for whom it is merely a means of making it productive and receiving its fruits. Unlike the emphyteusis and the usufructuary, the tenant does not have possession personally in his own right; he possesses on behalf of the owner for whom he is the representative and agent . . .

Most leases are regulated by *loi*. The controls on residential leases are discussed in Chapter 10 as an illustration of restrictions on freedom of contract.[56] Commercial leases have been subject to special regulation since 1926. This provides some security of tenure for someone who has established a business (and its associated

---

[55] Req. 6 Mar. 1861, *Syndicat Vollot*, DP 1861.1.417; Malaurie and Aynès, *Les Biens*, 98.
[56] Below p. 475.

goodwill) in connection with a specific location in business premises. The tenant has a right to compensation if a lease is not renewed. This is further discussed in Chapter 11.[57] Agricultural leases offer perhaps the nearest example of a lease which is akin to a property right. Under the regulation which has existed since 1945, the agricultural tenant has a right to the renewal of a lease except where the landlord wishes to exploit the farm himself.[58] The tenant can modify the premises and, where the landlord does not consent to this, can obtain court authorization to do this.[59] Where the landlord sells the property, the tenant has a right of pre-emption. That is to say, the tenant can require that the landlord sell to him at the price which the buyer agreed to pay.[60] Although not formally the holder of an interest in land, the agricultural tenant has much more than a personal right against the landlord.

Two forms of long lease are property rights. The emphyteusis (*bail emphytéotique*) is a lease for between 18 and 99 years under which the tenant, in return for a modest rent payment, undertakes to perform major works on the land.[61] This is similar to the construction lease where, under a lease for the same period, the tenant agrees to erect and maintain buildings in good condition on the landlord's land.[62] The formalities for the creation of these are laid down in the relevant codes governing these institutions.

---

[57] Below pp. 474–476.
[58] Article L 411-16, *Code rural.*
[59] Ibid., art. L 411-28.
[60] Ibid., art. L 412-1.
[61] Articles L 451-1–425-13, *Code rural.*
[62] Articles L 251-1 to 251-9, *Code de la construction et de l'habitation.*

10

The Law of Obligations

(1) Introduction

To a common lawyer, the French law of obligations possesses a unity all but absent from the English law of contract, torts and restitution, a unity which reflects the Roman legal tradition.[1] This approach is expressed in three major ways.

First, at the level of legal literature, the majority of French texts discuss contract, delict and 'quasi-contracts' (restitution)[2] together, rather than in separate books simply on, say, contract law. These works are themselves sometimes part of a much larger work or series of works on *droit civil,* to which there is again often a common approach and a distinct personnel; for French professors often consider themselves *civilistes* (private lawyers) or *publicistes* (public lawyers) in a more marked way than do their English counterparts.

Secondly, even though the Civil Code contains no general part governing obligations as a whole,[3] many treatises contain discussions of common aspects of the regulation of obligations, whether they arise from a contract, a delict or an event giving rise to restitution, these often being termed the 'general regime' for obligations. Although there is by no means a set content for these discussions, questions such as assignment, discharge of obligations, novation or prescription are often included. Some writers also treat the rules as to liability in damages in delict and contract together. This way of thinking has clearly influenced the drafters of a recent set of reform proposals, the *Avant-projet de réforme du droit des obligations*

---

[1] Justinian, *Inst.,* III.13.2, which distinguishes four sources of obligations: from contract; as though from contract (*quasi ex contractu*); from wrongdoing; and as though from wrong doing (*quasi ex maleficio*). The French Civil Code distinguished simply between *engagements* which arise with or without agreement, but included provisions on obligations arising from agreement (art. 1101 ff), quasi-contracts (art. 1371 ff), delicts and quasi-delicts (art. 1382 ff); but the last distinction (which is interpreted as referring to the presence or absence of intention) is not used in the modern law.

[2] On the appropriateness of referring to 'restitution' in French law, see below p. 417 ff. Most writers add a very brief discussion of the possibility of obligations arising from a 'unilateral act of will', but its status and examples are the subject of dispute: Malaurie, Aynès and Stoffel-Munck, *Obligations,* 209–211.

[3] Thus, e.g., the various provisions of the Civil Code concerning the effects of obligations (art. 1134 ff) in fact concern only *contractual* obligations, though they are sometimes applied by analogy to others.

et de la prescription (the '*Avant-projet de réforme*')[4] which treats contractual liability (*la responsabilité contractuelle*) together with delictual liability, though following wider modern practice the latter is termed *la responsabilité civile* or, where it is necessary to distinguish it, *la responsabilité extra-contractuelle*.[5]

Thirdly, there are certain common themes or concepts which the various sources of obligations possess, particularly in the case of contract and delict. Thus, there has long been a debate as to whether fault is the proper (and exclusive) basis for liability (*responsabilité*, whose moral overtones contrast with the more morally neutral English term 'liability') or whether the law should impose liabilities on some other basis, in particular, on risk. In the delictual context, this debate centres on the proper interpretation to be given to liability for the 'actions of things' under article 1384 al. 1 of the Civil Code;[6] in the contractual, whether contractual liability is based on fault and the proper content of contractual obligations.[7] But in both, we see similar arguments rehearsed and sometimes the same sets of facts being analysed as one or the other.[8] An example of a concept common to contract and delict may be found in *force majeure*, whose interpretation in delict has influenced its interpretation in contract.[9]

However, all this should not obscure the fact that the French law of obligations remains fundamentally divided, in particular, between those obligations which arise from agreement (contract) and those which do not (delict and quasi-contract). This is most apparent in relation to the conditions for the existence of these obligations, but it also affects their consequences: the 'general regime' actually governs only a relatively small number of issues[10] and even within a topic which is common to obligations in general, the substantive law may often differ markedly according to the source of the obligation in question.[11] Moreover, French law often rejects any overlap between its various categories of recovery. As Rodière observed in commenting on French law's approach to the relationship between contract and delict:[12] 'The categories of liability appear at the end of this study as strangely rigid:... the communications are cut between the various systems

---

[4] P. Catala (ed.), (La documentation française) (2005), on which see below, pp. 301–302. The French text and a English translation by J. Cartwright and S. Whittaker is published in Cartwright, Vogenauer and Whittaker, *Reforming the French Law of Obligations* (Hart, 2008 forthcoming) and online at <http://www.justice.gouv.fr/>. In subsequent quotations from the *Avant-projet*, this translation will be used.

[5] Art. 1343 ff A.-p.r.

[6] Below p. 381 ff.

[7] Below pp. 341–343.

[8] This is notably the case as regards the ambit of *obligations de sécurité*, see below pp. 331–332.

[9] Below pp. 343 and 389.

[10] Carbonnier, *Obligations*, 1907.

[11] e.g. prescription, where the general period for contractual actions is 30 years (art. 2262 C. civ., though the period is often shorter for particular situations, e.g. 10 years for the liability of *constructeurs* under art. 1792 C. civ.), but the period for delictual actions is 10 years: arts. 2270-1 and 2270-2 C. civ.

[12] Below pp. 328–329.

of liability'.[13] A similar attitude lies behind the so-called rule of 'subsidiarity' of claims based on *enrichissement sans cause*.[14] This results in part from the threat of swamping which the omnipresent law of liability for delictual fault poses to particular rules,[15] but it also reflects a preference in French lawyers for retaining the integrity and therefore the elegance of their legal categories.[16]

(2) The Law of Contract

The Civil Code's provisions on contracts reflect the philosophical and political attitudes of post-revolutionary France as well as their source in Roman law as filtered through the rationalizing and generalizing tendencies of earlier canonist writers and of the French jurists, Domat and Pothier.[17] Their ideological starting point can be glimpsed in the first two elements of the Republic's motto, *'Liberté, Egalité, Fraternité'*. Clearly, freedom to govern oneself lies at the heart of republican thinking and this had found explicit expression in Rousseau's potent idea that the legitimacy of state power rests on a 'social contract',[18] but at an individual level the idea of liberty was reflected in a concern to allow citizens the freedom to make any contract they may wish subject only to the over-riding needs of *ordre public*. Moreover, for long in this context the demands of *ordre public* were perceived to be fairly narrow and this was sometimes related to the principle of equality: if all citizens are equal, then they do not need to be protected in the making of the agreements which they conclude. As Portalis, a leading member of the commission charged with drafting the Civil Code, put it:

A man who deals with another ought to be watchful and sensible; he ought to look out for his own interest, obtain appropriate information and not neglect what is useful. The function of the law is to protect us from other people's fraud, but not to dispense us from using our own reason.[19]

These ideas had two types of impact on the law governing contracts. The first was the sweeping away of the restrictions on trade and employment of the *ancien régime*, notably relating to the rights of the guilds and the grants of monopolies.

---

[13] R. Rodière, 'Etude sur la dualité des régimes de responsabilité, deuxième partie: la combinaison des responsabilités' JCP 1950.I.868, no. 17, referring also to the exclusive approach taken to the law relating to accidents at work and art. 1386 C. civ., on which see below pp. 363–364 and 383 respectively.

[14] Ibid, and see below pp. 437–438.

[15] Ibid.

[16] A. Weir, 'Complex liabilities' in Vol. XI, *Int. Enc. Comp. Law* (Tubingen, 1982) ch. 12, 28.

[17] J. de Domat, *Les lois civiles dans leur ordre naturel* (first published 1689–94) and R.J. Pothier, *Traité des obligations* (first published 1761). For a valuable (though now rather out of date treatment of the French law of contract), see Nicholas, *French Contract*.

[18] J.-J. Rousseau, *Du contrat social* (1762), esp. ch. VI.

[19] J.-E.-M. Portalis, 'Discours préliminaire sur le projet de Code civil', reprinted in *Discours et Rapports sur le Code Civil* (Caen, 1990), 53.

The second was in the provision of a civil law which gave effect to the parties' agreements in principle. As two key provisions in the Civil Code state:

Art. 1101: A contract is an agreement by which one or more persons undertake obligations to one or more others, to transfer property, to do or not to do something.
Art. 1134 al. 1: Contracts which are lawfully concluded take the place of legislation for those who have made them.

These provisions enshrine two pre-eminent principles in French contract law: freedom of contract and the binding force of contractual obligations.

That all contracts are based on agreement and that they should bind the parties (but no-one else) were Roman ideas,[20] but the Romans did not recognize that the parties' agreement was enough to create a contract, but saw agreement as the basis of the particular 'nominate' contracts which their law recognized, such as loan, sale, hire or the formal contract of stipulation: outside these recognized types of contract, agreement did not give rise to a contract.[21] The generalization in thinking about contracts expressed in the Civil Code reflected the concern of canon lawyers for a person's keeping to what he promises as well as the tendency of the natural lawyers to generalize from the particular examples of legal phenomena found in the ancient Roman texts.[22] As a matter of substantive law, therefore, it was the Civil Code's achievement to recognize that the parties' agreement creates a contract, regardless of its form or subject-matter. This indeed reflected a triumph of consensualist thinking about contracts, thinking which came also to dominate the way in which French lawyers conceived and interpreted the Civil Code's main grounds of vitiation of the contract, these coming to be known as 'defects in consent'.[23] By the middle of the nineteenth century, this approach became centred on the principle of the *'autonomie de la volonté'*, contract as 'self-regulation' stemming from the parties' intentions.

However, the influence of Roman law on the Civil Code's provisions on contract did not stop there. For its other rules governing contracts generally and particular contracts, such as sale, partnership, agency etc., are almost entirely Romanist in character. In this way, therefore, the rules which in Roman law defined and attached to some of the nominate contracts came to define and to regulate the incidents of many contracts in modern French law, even though there are no 'gaps' between the special contracts. The Code itself therefore combines a high consensualism with a recognition of the traditional and proper role of the regulation of particular contracts once formed.[24] And both the Code and French

[20] See Dig. 2.14.1.3 (no contract without agreement); Dig, 16.3.1.6 and 50.17.23 (contract as the law of the parties); Gaius, *Inst.* 3.103 and Dig. 45.1.83 pr. (privity of contract). See further, R. Zimmermann, *The Law of Obligations, Roman Foundations of the Civilian Tradition* (Oxford, reprint, 1996), 34 ff and 563–565.
[21] J.A.C. Thomas, *Textbook of Roman Law* (Amsterdam, 1979) 215.
[22] J. Gordley, *The Philosophical Origins of Modern Contract Doctrine* (Oxford, 1991), ch. 4.
[23] These are *dol, erreur* and *violence.* see below p. 307 ff.
[24] Art. 1135 C. civ. and see below p. 330 ff.

university courses reflect the idea that French contract law has two parts: the general, *le droit commun contractuel* (dealing with issues like defects in consent, unlawfulness of subject-matter or the effects of non-performance) and the special, *le droit des contrats speciaux,* dealing with the particular incidents and effects of particular types of contracts.

We should also note that there are also two other parts to French contract law in a different way, for the Civil Code and *droit civil* in a narrow sense never did and still does not contain all the rules about French contracts. As we have seen, contracts with a public aspect are subject to special rules as well as the administrative jurisdiction.[25] Secondly, commercial contracts are governed in part by different rules, the general law of the Civil Code being supplemented by the special rules of the *Code de commerce* itself enacted in 1807.[26]

Apart from these special treatments, by the late nineteenth century, there was considerable unease in France with the idea that contracts were concerned only with party intention and from this time various other influences on the development of contract law can be discerned.[27]

First, both jurists and courts have become more and more concerned with the morality and social impact of contracts. The morality in question is not so much the making of an immoral contract, but rather immoral behaviour in making and in performing or not performing one's contractual obligations once made and it may be seen to form part of the more general theory of the 'abuse of rights'.[28] Thus, for example, while a person may in principle freely withdraw from negotiations before a contract is concluded, he may not do so *abusively*[29] and a person's purported exercise of a right to terminate a contract may, when motivated by malice, be deemed ineffective.[30] Another way of looking at these sorts of situation has been in terms of good faith, a requirement which the Civil Code makes only in relation to the performance of contracts,[31] but which has also been invoked in relation to pre-contractual dealings.[32]

We may see a concern with the social impact of contracts most clearly in juristic suggestions that contract be used in order to allow the award of damages for personal injuries or death without proof of fault, suggestions first made in the

---

[25] Although in general special treatment of administrative contracts did not develop until the late nineteenth century, even at the time of the Civil Code the law relating to public works contracts (*travaux publics*) was set apart from the *droit civil* of contracts and this dated from 1799, *loi du* 28 pluviôse, Year VIII art. 4 and see above p. 195 ff.

[26] Art. 1107 al. 2 C. civ. and see below Chapter 11.

[27] For useful discussions see Terré, Simler, and Lequette, *Obligations*, 37–57; C. Jamin, 'Une brève histoire politique des interprétations de l'article 1134 du Code civil' D 2002 Chron. 901; D. Mazeaud, 'La politique contractuelle de la Cour de cassation' in *Libres propos sur les sources du droit—Mélanges en l'Honneur de Philippe Jestaz* (Dalloz-Sirey, Paris, 2006) 371.

[28] For the impact of this notion on the law of delict, see below pp. 373–375.

[29] Below pp. 305–306.

[30] Below p. 358.

[31] Art. 1135 al. 3 C. civ.

[32] Below p. 307.

context of accidents at work but first accepted by the courts as regards transport accidents.[33] The technique used to achieve this—the finding of an *obligation de sécurité* (obligation concerning the safety of the other contractor)—is open to criticism as a fiction, but its development shows how some French lawyers came to see contract law as the proper vehicle for the relief of social problems arising from the making of contracts in a modern industrial society.

Secondly, at a political and economic level, individualism and *laisser faire* gave way to *dirigisme,* the state taking on an increased role in the regulation of economic and social affairs, most conspicuously in the control of prices and foreign exchange but extending to the regulation of the labour market and agricultural and residential leases, And while since the later 1980s this *ordre public de direction* has been somewhat in retreat, its influence is still considerable.[34]

Thirdly, French jurists noted that in many contexts the parties to contracts were *not* equal and that this was not merely occasional but systematic owing to the development of large commercial entities which offered their goods or services only on the terms which they saw fit: the other party to such a contract had no more than a choice whether to take it on the other's terms or leave it, thereby attracting the term *'contrats d'adhésion'.* Juristic reaction to this was to argue for ways of protecting *some* parties to *some* contracts and this often found legislative expression in particular contexts, such as agricultural, residential and even commercial tenancies[35] and contracts of insurance.[36] One of the legislative techniques to give effect to this overtly protectionist policy (reflecting an *ordre public de protection*) was to use formal requirements to ensure that the weaker party knew the nature and risks of the contract he entered and the rights which the law gave him in respect of it and therefore clearly marked a return to formalism in contrast to the traditional consensualism of the Civil Code. A second legislative technique was the use of collective agreements to regulate the consequences of particular contractual relationships and while this was and is most prominent as regards employment contracts, it has also been used to regulate residential tenancies.[37] Where the law recognizes the effectiveness of these collective agreements, once negotiated by the appropriate representative bodies they bind those within the class represented irrespective of any authority.[38] A third technique has been for legislation to give the public administration a power to set by decree standard contract terms (and so creating a *contrat type*) for a particular kind of

[33] Below pp. 331–332.

[34] Terré, Simler, and Lequette, 379–383.

[35] All three types of tenancies were the subject of elaborate regulation after 1945, the general policy being one of protection of tenants: A. Bénabent, *Droit civil, Les contrats spéciaux civils et commercioux,* 5th edn. (2001) 263–264.

[36] Thus, in relation to insurance the *lot* of 13 July 1930 'broke away from the principle of freedom of contract which had revealed itself too often capable of prejudicing policy-holders'; Y. Lambert-Falvre, *Droit des assurances,* 9th edn. (Paris, 1995) 73.

[37] *Loi* no. 86-1290 of 23 December 1986, art. 41.

[38] Malaurie, Aynès, and Stoffel-Munck, *Obligations,* 423–425.

contract which applies by operation of law, as in the case of contracts of carriage of goods by road.[39]

However, at times this policy of protecting parties to contracts has been taken up by the courts, this being particularly noticeable in their hostility to exemption clauses, the development of pre-contractual obligations of information and of an extensive *contractual* law of liability for defective products despite the terms of the Code's provisions on sale.[40] As these examples suggest, this protectionist attitude was given a new impetus in the course of the 1960s with the advent of overtly consumerist ideas.

All these developments have led to a considerable lessening of the importance of the ideas associated with *autonomie de la volonté* and also of the importance of the general law of contract to the benefit of the rules applicable to special contracts and of new systems of regulation, such as employment law or insurance law, which are sometimes said to have 'escaped the orbit' of the civil law of contract.[41] The collection and enactment in 1992 of a *Code de la consommation* reflects a similar evolution.

Furthermore, in the modern context, discussion of the question whether French contract law is or should be 'social' rather than 'liberal' (especially in contrast to the supposed positions adopted by 'Anglo-Saxon' laws) has formed part of wider economic and political debates in France as to the distinctiveness and utility of the French model of society and economy, both in purely domestic terms and in relation to the future development of the European Union. Should contract law reflect the needs of the (internal) market? Or should the approaches found in French labour law (itself formally part of *le droit social*[42]) be extended so that contract law reflects a principle of 'social solidarity'? For those who argue the latter, this way of thinking would in particular give new life to the *third* element of the Republican motto, *fraternité*.[43]

In the meantime, European developments in private law (and especially in the law of contract) have had two significant effects on French law. First, in common with other member states, French law has had to decide how to implement a series of directives affecting private law and so has been faced with a number of difficult formal and substantive issues: should legislative implementation be undertaken by insertion within the Civil Code, in another code (such as the *Code*

---

[39] *Loi* no. 82-1153 of 30 December 1982; *déc.* no. 99-269 of 16 April 1999. Cf. below, pp. 322–323 in relation to the *jurisprudence Chronopost.*

[40] See below pp. 322–323, 356; 309–311; and 403–404 respectively.

[41] Terré, Simler, and Lequette, *Obligations,* 40 ff.

[42] Below, p. 487.

[43] D. Mazeaud, 'Loyauté, solidarité, fraternité: la nouvelle devise contractuelle?' in *L'avenir du droit, Mélanges Terré* (Dalloz, 1999), 603; C. Jamin, 'Plaidoyer pour le solidarisme contractuel' in *Etudes offertes à J. Ghestin—Le contrat au début du XXIe siècle* (LGDJ, 2001), 441. For a critical assessment: Terré, Simler, and Lequette, *Obligations,* 44–47. The importance of social solidarity in French legal and political thought is not new: see L. Duguit, *L'état, le droit objectif et la loi positive* (Paris, 1901), 69–78.

de la consommation or the *Code de commerce*) or in special legislation? Can the implementing of legislation extend the scheme of rules required by the directive to other situations and, if so, should it do so? The advantage of amending the Civil Code is that doing so includes within the legislative *droit commun* areas of very considerable practical importance; the disadvantage is that the special (and often more detailed) rules required by the directive itself may either be extended to areas to which they are not substantively appropriate or (if implementation is limited to what is required) create internal disharmony with existing rules and threaten nevertheless to 'contaminate' existing concepts.[44] Secondly, broader European initiatives (whether private[45] or institutional[46]) have appeared to give more credence to the idea that wider European legislation (or at least *principles*) should be drafted to govern the area of private law. Though the form, the content and the significance of any such an instrument remains unclear, the possibilities range from a full European Civil Code (though it is admitted that at present the EC Treaty does not provide the competence for its enactment) to an instrument for the rationalization and interpretation of the consumer *acquis*. There have been a number of types of French response to these developments, including scathing denunciation;[47] but one important response was the construction of a *French* project for the reform of the Civil Code's law of obligations by a group of French jurists which was earlier mentioned, this being published in 2005 as the *Avant-projet de réforme du droit des obligations et de la prescription*.[48] The aim of this project was primarily to give legislative recognition to developments in *la jurisprudence* and (to a lesser extent) *la doctrine,* but it was clearly hoped that it would 'serve the purpose which will give France a civil law adapted to its time and a voice at the table of Europe'.[49] While formally welcomed by the President of the

---

[44] In the case of the EC Directive 1985/374/EEC concerning liability for defective products, implementation was effected by insertion into the Civil Code: arts. 1386-1–1386-18 C. civ. as inserted by *loi* no. 98-389 of 19 May 1998 *sur la responsabilité du fait des produits défectueux*; here, the French legislator attempted to extend the scheme of the directive but was later told by the ECJ that it was not entitled to do so: Case C-52/00 *Commission v France* [2002] ECR I-3827, below, pp. 405–406. By contrast, after considerable discussion, implementation of EC Directive 99/44/EC on certain aspects of the sale of consumer goods and associated guarantees was implemented by minimalist amendment of the *Code de la consommation* rather than wider amendment of the Civil Code's provisions governing the law of sale: arts. L. 211-09–211-11, 211-13 C. consom. as inserted by *ord*. no. 2005-136 of 17 Feb. 2005 and see further on these Whittaker, *Liability for Products*, 450–465 and 574–583 respectively.

[45] Notably, the *Principles of European Contract Law* (or 'Lando Principles' named after Professor O. Lando) and the work of the Study Group on a European Civil Code presided over by Professor C. von Bar.

[46] EC Commission, *Review of the Consumer Acquis* Com (2006) 744 final (which lists the earlier documents); EC Commission, *Second Progress Report on the Common Frame of Reference* Com (2007) 447 final.

[47] Y. Lequette, 'Quelques remarques à propos du projet de Code civil européen de M. Von Bar' D. 2002 Chron. 2002. Cf. B. Fauvarque-Cosson and S. Patris-Godechot, *Le Code civil face à son destin* (La documentation française, 2006) 137–149.

[48] Above, n. 4.

[49] P. Catala, 'Présentation générale de l'avant-projet', *Avant-projet de réforme*, 16.

Republic, the legislative fate of the *Avant-projet de réforme* is still unclear, but it nevertheless remains a useful expression of juristic ideas which may well inspire future legislative or judicial developments.

I. The Creation of Contracts

Article 1108 of the Civil Code requires four conditions for the validity of a contract:

(1) the consent of the party undertaking an obligation;
(2) his capacity to contract;
(3) a certain *objet* which forms the subject-matter of the undertaking and
(4) a legal *cause* of the obligation.

We shall look at each in turn (except capacity) but add a brief discussion as to the role of formality. At this stage it should be noted that there is no conceptual and (arguably) no functional equivalent of English law's doctrine of consideration.[50]

A. Consent and Agreement

In French law, it is customary to distinguish two elements here: that there be a meeting of minds of the parties—an *accord de volontés*—whose aim is the creation or modification of contractual obligations[51] and, secondly, that each party's consent be free from defect.[52]

1. Agreement: offer and acceptance

While the Civil Code makes clear that contracts are based on agreement,[53] it does not at present contain any rules as to how such an agreement may arise, with the recent exception of contracts concluded by electronic means.[54] French jurists have supplied the deficiency here to a certain extent, though it will be seen that considerable flexibility (and therefore uncertainty) arises from the degree to which the Cour de cassation allows issues relating to formation to lie in the 'sovereign power of assessment' of the *juges du fond*.[55] Nevertheless, we find French texts

---

[50] Below pp. 321–322.
[51] See the terms of art. 1101, quoted above p. 297. A traditional distinction between *contrats* which create obligations and *conventions* which amend or extinguish them is nowadays mentioned only to be dismissed as of no practical importance: see Terré, Simler, and Lequette, *Obligations*, 57 ff esp. at 58.
[52] Below pp. 307 ff.
[53] Art. 1101 C. civ., above, p. 297.
[54] Arts. 1369-1–139-11 C. civ. inserted by *ord.* no. 2005-674 of 16 Jun. 2005. Cf. Arts. 105-107 A.-p.r. which seeks to remedy this perceived deficiency.
[55] Nicholas, *French Contract*, 61–63.

explaining that agreements should be analysed in terms of offer and acceptance and these elements have (to a common lawyer) recognizably familiar definitions: an offer is said to be a firm and sufficiently detailed indication of a willingness to contract (as contrasted with an invitation to treat); an acceptance to be its recipient's free, informed and unqualified acquiescence (as contrasted with a rejection or counter-offer). Despite French law's concern for the parties' actual or subjective intentions (*volontés internes*), at this stage in their analysis the jurists accept that what are required are *manifestations* of these intentions, whether oral, in writing or by conduct: only if there is discordance between a manifested and an actual intention does the latter become potentially significant.[56] However, differences do exist on a closer look.

As regards offers, French law does not possess *rules* dictating whether, for example, an object displayed in a shop-window at a price does or does not constitute an offer for its sale: it *may* constitute an offer and often will, subject to any evidence as to the intentions of the parties.[57] It is, moreover, clear that an offer is capable of acceptance during any period for which it is so expressed or, in the absence of such expression, for a reasonable period in the circumstances. The position as regards revocation of offers is less clear. Some jurists say that an offeror is obliged to maintain an offer for any expressed time or, in its absence, for a reasonable time and that therefore it may be accepted despite any attempted revocation; others that this result should occur only where the period for reply is expressed, in other cases the offeree being restricted to a claim for damages for delictual fault; and others that a prematurely revoked offer should give rise only to such a claim for damages.[58] For a common lawyer, these views are most striking in their assumptions that a promise to keep an offer open should be adhered to in the absence of any return (so as to provide consideration) and that (absent contract) liability in delict may play a supporting role. Here, the *Avant-projet de réforme* seeks to create a settled position, providing that 'an offer may be revoked freely as long as it has not come to the knowledge of the person to whom it was addressed or if it has not been validly accepted within a reasonable period';[59] but 'where an offer addressed to a particular person includes an undertaking to maintain it for a fixed period, neither its premature revocation nor the incapacity or death of the offeror can prevent the formation of the contract'.[60]

As we have said, a court may find that a person has accepted an offer where he has made clear his unqualified acceptance of it and the time when this occurs may be affected by custom in the particular context.[61] It is noticeable, however, that

[56] Below pp. 311 ff.
[57] Nicholas, *French Contract*, 63–65.
[58] For the opposing views, see Bénabent, *Obligations*, 45; Terré, Simler, and Lequette, *Obligations*, 117 ff.; Flour, Aubert, and Savaux, *Acte juridique*, 101–102.
[59] Art. 1105-2 A.-p.r.
[60] Art. 1105-4 A.-p.r.
[61] Civ. (1) 15 Jan. 1963, GP 1963.1.211; cf. art. 1105-5 A.-p.r.

although French lawyers recognize the special difficulties which arise in relation to acceptance of offers made *inter absentes* and the question whether an offeree's silence may constitute acceptance, the courts have not established any firm legal rules governing these situations. Thus, as regards acceptances made *inter absentes,* the Cour de cassation has generally accepted that the time or place of acceptance (whether at posting or receipt at the offeror's address)[62] is a matter for the *pouvoir souverain d'appréciation* of the *juges du fond.*[63] While there appears to be more support in the case law for acceptance being found at the time and place of sending, treating the issue as one of fact allows the courts to decide on a case-by-case basis according to what seems fair in the circumstances.[64] By contrast, the *Avant-projet de réforme* provides that '[i]n the absence of agreement to the contrary, a contract is completed by receipt of the acceptance'.[65]

On the other hand, it is clear that in general French law does not allow an offeree's silence to constitute acceptance,[66] but it *may* do so in some circumstances where it 'in the context as a whole indicates a view which is capable of interpretation'.[67] Apart from where legislation so provides,[68] this is clearest where the parties have agreed that it should, where they have had relevant previous dealings or where the custom of the context in which they contract allows silence to constitute consent.[69] Most controversially, however, the Cour de cassation has on the odd occasion (and they have on occasion been rather odd) allowed the lower courts to find that an offeree's silence *was* acceptance where the offer was made 'in his exclusive interest',[70] an approach which has been called infrequent, contested and artificial[71] and paradoxically cannot apply to offers of gifts which the Civil Code requires must be expressly accepted.[72]

It has been said that the acceptance must be 'informed', but this does not mean that the offeree must actually know *all* the terms of the offer before a contract is

---

[62] These are referred to as the theories of *expédition* and *réception* respectively. Modern jurists do not support the theories that an acceptance is made on its mere 'declaration' nor that it must be brought to the actual notice of the offeror (the 'information' theory).

[63] Carbonnier, *Obligations,* 1971–1972 citing Civ. (1) 21 Dec. 1960, D 1961.417 note Malaurie, *Source-Book,* 319.

[64] Terré, Simler, and Lequette, *Obligations,* 172–173.

[65] Art. 1107 A.-p.r.

[66] Terré, Simler, and Lequette, *Obligations,* 132–134: Larroumet, *Contrat,* 233–234 and see Civ. 25 May 1870, D 1870.1.257, S 1870.1.241 and Com. 3 Dec. 1985, JCP. 1986.IV.65.

[67] Req. 15 Mar. 1944, S 1944.1.40 (custom); Fabre-Magnan, *Obligations,* 238–239. Cf. Civ. (1) 24 May 2005 *RDC* 2005.1107 note Mazeaud, who viewed the case as one where silence constitutes acceptance in the circumstances where the offeree has no practical choice to refuse! Art. 1105-6 A.-p.r. provides that '[i]n the absence of legislative provision, agreement between the parties, business or professional usage or other particular circumstances, silence does not count as acceptance'.

[68] Carbonnier, *Obligations,* 1975.

[69] e.g. art. 1738 C. civ. (extension of tenancy by remaining in possession).

[70] Req. 29 Mar. 1938, S 1938.1.380, DP 1939.1.5 note Voirin (tacit acceptance by tenant of remission of rent) and Civ. (1) 1 Dec. 1969, D 1970.422 note Puech, JCP 1970.II.16445 note Aubert (unconscious victim of road accident accepted offer to help by rescuer injured in the process).

[71] Malaurie, Aynès, and Stoffel-Munck, *Obligations,* 237.

[72] Art. 932 al. 1 C. civ.

made or before these terms form part of the contract, but rather that they should be brought effectively to the offeree's attention, the courts taking a hostile view to terms on the reverse of documents or in documents appended.[73] So, French law accepts in principle that a person who signs a contractual document without reading it is bound by its terms, but makes exceptions where the terms are unusual or not clearly portrayed, notably in standard-form contracts.[74]

2. Preliminary agreements, good faith and fault in negotiations

Sometimes parties to contractual negotiations make preliminary agreements before concluding any ultimate contract. French law's attitude to these is generally more favourable than is English law's owing in particular to the absence of the requirement of consideration, but even where in French law these agreements are not enforced as contracts, they may be taken into account in determining whether a party has committed a delictual fault in the course of negotiations so as to be held liable in damages on this ground to the other party. A very important example of pre-contractual agreements which are enforced as contracts are 'unilateral promises to contract' (*promesses unilatérales de contrat*).[75] Here, a person promises to contract on particular terms with another at the latter's option, this promise being binding once accepted. Of more uncertain status are 'agreements in principle' (*accords de principe*) which usually involve an agreement by the parties on certain matters and that they will continue to negotiate towards final contract.[76] While Carbonnier holds that these give rise to obligations even if provisional ones[77], other jurists argue that a failure to conclude the final contract can give rise only to liability in damages, this failure constituting a delictual fault.[78]

Even in the absence of any preliminary agreement as to the course or conduct of negotiations, French law holds the parties to a standard of proper conduct, referred to either positively in terms of the requirements of good faith[79] or negatively in terms of the parties having 'abused their right' to break off negotiations before a contract is concluded,[80] but sanctioned by an award of damages in delict. While this is not stated in the present Civil Code, the *Avant-projet de réforme* is explicit, providing that '[t]he parties are free to begin, continue and

---

[73] Bénabent, *Obligations,* 50–51.

[74] Malaurie, Aynès, and Stoffel-Munck, *Obligations,* 234–235.

[75] Others may be found in pre-emption agreements (*pactes de préférence*) and *promesses synallagmatiques de vente,* where the parties both undertake to enter a subsequent contract, notably where the latter possesses some formal requirements as in sale of land: Malaurie, Aynès, Stoffel-Munck, *Obligations,* 217, 221–222.

[76] Ibid., 215–216. Cf. art. 1104-1 A.-p.r. which expressly recognizes that '[t]he parties may, by an agreement in principle, undertake to negotiate at a later date a contract whose elements are still to be settled, and to work in good faith towards settling them'.

[77] Carbonnier, *Obligations,* 1969.

[78] Malaurie, Aynès, and Stoffel-Munck, *Obligations,* 216.

[79] Ibid., 229–230.

[80] Com. 26 Nov. 2003. D 2004. 869 note Dupré-Dallemagne.

break off negotiations, but these must satisfy the requirements of good faith'.[81] Liability is clearest in cases where one party is shown to have acted maliciously or with an intention to harm the other, but this is not always required.[82] Thus, an 'abrupt and unilateral withdrawal from advanced negotiations made without any legitimate reason' may be enough[83] and where, for example, in the course of lengthy negotiations towards purchase, a supermarket company had requested an owner of land to do works on the property but subsequently withdrew from the negotiations, the owner was held entitled to damages to compensate this expenditure without any need to prove an intention to harm.[84] But no recovery can be made for any profits expected to be made out of the putative contract on the ground that this 'loss of a chance' is not caused by the party's fault in breaking-off negotiations.[85]

3. Agreements which are not contracts

Although contracts are agreements in French law, not all agreements are contracts, but only those which create or modify a person's *obligations*. It is for this reason that it excludes purely social agreements (termed *actes de courtoisie*) such as an accepted dinner invitation, from contract.[86] More difficult, however, are cases involving the gratuitous performance of services, such as giving a person a lift in one's car or giving a person first-aid (even if one is a doctor). Generally, the courts have refused to see these types of case as contractual,[87] with the result that any claims for harm caused by the provider of the service are a matter for delict.[88] On the other hand, the courts have sometimes found that a person who rescues another from danger or attempts to catch an escaping thief does so under a 'contract of help' (*convention d'assistance*), though it is often argued that these sorts of cases are also better dealt with either through delict or 'management of another's affairs' (*gestion d'affaires*).[89] Finally, the status of 'gentlemen's agreements' is uncertain in French law, for although the courts have accepted that agreements which are expressed to be binding in honour only will not be treated as contracts

---

[81] Art. 1104 A.-p.r.

[82] Malaurie, Aynès, and Stoffel-Munck, *Obligations*, 230. And see generally B. Fauvarque-Cosson, 'Negotiation and Renegotiation: a French Perspective' in Cartwright, Vogenauer and Whittaker, Ch. 2.

[83] Com. 20 Mar.1972, JCP 1973.1.17543 note Schmidt (referring to the rules of good faith in commercial relations).

[84] Civ. (3) 3 Oct.1972, Bull. civ. III no. 491.

[85] Com. 26 Nov. 2003, D 2004.869 note Dupré-Dallemagne; Civ. (3) 28 Jun. 2006, JCP 2006. II.10130 note Deshayes. Recovery may be reduced where the person breaking off the contractual negotiations can establish contributory fault in the other party to the negotiations: Com. 15 Oct. 2002, (2003) RJDA no. 218.

[86] Malaurie, Aynès, and Stoffel-Munck, *Obligations*, 212–213.

[87] Terré, Simler, and Lequette *Obligations*, 65.

[88] Paris 27 Jun.1967, Ch. Mixte, 20 Dec.1968, *arrêt Landru*, JCP 1968.II.15487, note Boré (*transport bénévole*); Civ. (2) 18 Mar. 1992, JCP 1992.IV.1525 (farmer helping neighbour on way home from work: no contract).

[89] Below pp. 360 ff. and 425 respectively.

when made between members of a family or between friends, in other circumstances they nevertheless enforce the agreement, seeing the 'honour clause' as an illegitimate attempt to escape the legal consequences of agreements which have been made.[90]

B. The Quality of Consent and Pre-Contractual Good Faith

At first sight the 'defects in consent' which the Civil Code enumerates appear familiar to a common lawyer:[91] *dol* appears to be like fraud, *violence* like duress and *erreur sur les qualités substantielles* like fundamental mistake. However, quite apart from the curious absence of a law of innocent misrepresentation, such ready parallels are misleading where not downright wrong, for it is here that French contract law's consensualism is most in evidence.[92] This means both that its grounds of vitiation are broader than in English law and that the logic of a genuine concern for the quality of each of the parties' consent is followed through, so that, notably, its law of mistake is concerned with unilateral mistakes (unlike English law which has focused on 'common mistakes'). On the other hand, French law is not only concerned with the quality of the parties' consent, but also with the quality of their mutual behaviour, this finding expression sometimes in terms of good faith, sometimes of delictual fault. In the result, it sometimes appears that there is too much law chasing too few facts.

There is, at least in part, an historical explanation for this complex regulation. As we have said, Roman law did not recognize a general law of contracts, but instead accepted particular types of contracts[93] and these different types of contracts used different approaches to deal with pre-contractual dishonest dealing and duress. For in those contracts which were termed 'good faith contracts' (such as sale, partnership and mandate) this type of behaviour was taken account of directly, the judge being asked to decide the case taking into account the requirements of good faith;[94] whereas in 'strict law contracts' (notably, stipulation) it was taken account of only by way of special defences based either on dishonest dealing or duress.[95] The French Civil Code restricted itself to the second of these approaches, generalizing the Roman defences of dishonest dealing and duress from stipulation to all contracts, though reclothing them in consensualist

---

[90] Terré, Simler, and Lequette, *Obligations*, 65–66 citing Civ. 29 Apr. 1873, DP 1873.1.207 (insolvent person agreeing in honour with creditors prior to composition to repay later).

[91] *Lésion* appears within the same section (art. 1118 C. civ.) but is not generally thought of as going to the quality of a party's consent: see below pp. 324–325.

[92] J. Cartwright, 'Defects of Consent and Security of Contract: French and English Law Compared' in P. Birks and A. Pretto, *Themes in Comparative Law in Honour of Bernard Rudden* (OUP, 2002) Ch. 11.

[93] Above p. 297.

[94] Gaius, *Inst.*, 4.61 and Justinian, *Inst.*, IV.6.30.

[95] Gaius, ibid., 4.115–116a, 119 and see J.A.C. Thomas, *A Textbook of Roman Law* (Amsterdam, 1976), 228.

garb, becoming the 'defects in consent' of *dol* and *violence*[96] there was clearly thought to be no need to require that contracts be *made* in good faith.[97] Despite this, French jurists have revived the notion of pre-contractual good faith, using it to justify, inter alia, the construction of obligations on some parties to some contracts to inform the other of matters relating to the contract.[98] A similar process of 'double generalization' explains the very considerable overlap in French law between *erreur* and *dol*. For the Civil Code's provision on 'mistake as to substance'[99] is clearly drawn from the Roman law of *sale*, the 'substance' in question typically being the physical substance of the property sold,[100] but in the Code it governs *all* contracts.

The Civil Code provides that the sanction of all the defects in consent in contract is 'relative nullity' (*nullité relative*), i.e. the party whose consent is defective may claim that a court should annul the contract.[101] It should be noted that this is to be contrasted with 'absolute nullity' (*nullité absolue*), but that the distinction relates principally to the question who may claim annulment (*any* person being able to do so for absolute nullity) and not to the effect of annulment once declared by a court, which is the same, 'retroactive destruction' for both.[102] The significance of delict appears as the legal basis for any recovery of damages by a person suffering from a defect in consent for any loss which he has suffered. While intentional positive action such as *dol* or *violence* is necessarily wrongful for this purpose, the question whether even a deliberate omission, such as a failure to speak, is so is more difficult. On the other hand, delictual fault is not limited to intentional wrongdoing and sometimes, therefore, what a common lawyer may see as a purely innocent failure to speak may give rise to liability in damages on this basis.[103]

1. Dol

Article 1116 al. 1 of the Civil Code states that: '*Dol* is a ground of nullity of a contract where the scheming of one of the parties is such that it is clear that without it the other party would not have contracted.'

For present purposes, *dol* itself is any dishonest scheming (*manœuvres*) by one party to a contract which causes a 'decisive mistake' in the other party, i.e. one

---

[96] Arts. 1116 and 1113–1115 C. civ. respectively.

[97] cf. art. 1134 al. 3 C. civ. (contractual obligations must be performed in good faith) and see below pp. 332–334. An earlier draft of art. 1134 al. 3 C. civ. stated that '[contracts] must be *contracted* and performed in good faith' (emphasis added, see P.A. Fenet, *Recueil Complet des Travaux Préparatoires du Code Civil* (Paris, 1828) t. XIII, 8).

[98] cf. above pp. 305–306 (good faith in breaking off negotiations).

[99] Art. 1110 C. civ.

[100] Dig. 18.1.9.2 (vinegar instead of wine).

[101] Art. 1117 C. civ.

[102] For the restitutionary effects of annulment, see below p. 440 ff.

[103] Below pp. 310–312.

without which that person would not have entered the contract.[104] It therefore includes fraudulent misstatements, but is rather wider, extending to any chicanery intended to deceive as long as it was effected by the other party to the contract. Where a party's *dol* has caused the other party harm, it attracts liability in damages in delict under article 1382 of the Civil Code irrespective of whether the contract is annulled.[105]

Furthermore, and in striking contrast to English law, since the 1950s, French courts have accepted that a knowing and dishonest failure to disclose a matter which the other party has an interest in knowing and about which the latter would have difficulty in finding out for himself constitutes *dol par réticence* (fraudulent non-disclosure) and can therefore give rise to annulment and/or damages.[106] More recently the courts have tended to look to the question whether the party owed a duty to inform the other person of a particular matter, such a duty usually being termed an *obligation d'information*[107]: indeed, in 2000 the Cour de cassation appeared to assume that *dol par réticence* can be established only where there is breach of an *obligation d'information*.[108]

So stated as a ground of vitiation *dol* seems to be no more than a special case of 'mistake of substance' with the additional need to prove dishonesty,[109] but in certain circumstances *dol* can apply where *erreur* cannot, for example, in cases of mistake as to value[110] or where the other party's mistake was careless.[111] Moreover, where a party can prove the other party's dishonest behaviour, its 'decisive effect' is more readily found by the courts than where he has to rely simply on his own mistake.[112]

(a) *Obligations d'information*
Both the French legislator and French courts have imposed duties to provide information on one party to a contract to the other, this sometimes having a very

---

[104] Carbonnier, *Obligations*, 1994; Larroumet, *Contrat*, 325–330.

[105] Civ. (1) 4 Feb. 1975, D 1975, 405.

[106] Larroumet, *Contrat*, 319–324; Flour, Aubert, and Savaux, *Acte juridique*, 165–167 Carbonnier, *Obligations*, 2005–2006. See e.g. Civ. (3) 15 Jan. 1971, D 1971 Somm. 148 and Civ.(1) 10 Jun. 1987, D 1987 Somm. 445 note Aynès (no duty where recipient could easily know better).

[107] Malaurie, Aynès, and Stoffel-Munck, *Obligations*, 251–252. A variety of terms are used, including *obligation de renseignement* (which is appropriate to the supply of information as opposed to advice); *obligation d'avertir* (which is used in the context of warnings against possible dangers); *obligation de conseil* (used for advice) as well as *obligation d'information*. However, there are no fixed distinctions between them and we shall use the most general term, *obligation d'information*.

[108] Civ. (1) 3 May 2000, *affaire des photographies de Baldus*, Bull. civ. I no. 131, JCP 2001. II.10510 note Jamin, Défrenois no. 19, 1106 note Mazeaud and note Delebecque; Civ. (3) 17 Jan. 2007, JCP 2007.II.10042 note Jamin.

[109] Cf. below, pp. 311 ff.

[110] Larroumet, *Contrat*, 327–330, Ghestin, *Formation*, 525–6.

[111] Civ. (3) 21 Feb. 2001, D 2001.2702 note Mazeaud, RTD Civ. 2001.353 note Mestre and Fages (mistake caused by *dol par réticence* is always excusable). Cf. below, p. 313 on inexcusable mistake as to substance.

[112] Larroumet, *Contrat*, 327.

specific and sometimes a much broader application.[113] Typically, these duties have been imposed on *professionnels* (a term which includes all persons acting in the course of a business or a profession) towards a person who is not in the same type of business or is a consumer, but they have been imposed on *non-profession-nels* too.[114] Most striking is the first provision of the *Code de la consommation* of 1993,[115] itself no more than a confirmation of *jurisprudence* at the time.[116]

> Every business seller of property or provider of services must before the conclusion of the contract put a consumer in a position to know the essential characteristics of that property or those services.

The case law governing the incidence and content of *obligations d'information* has been developed considerably, the courts imposing them in a wide range of situations.[117] On the other hand, there appears to have been a certain retrenchment in recent years. So while, for example, a bank must inform a would-be guarantor of a debt taken out by one of its customers of the latter's irremediably precarious financial state,[118] a business does not have to disclose its own imminent receivership to a would-be contracting partner.[119] And most controversially, the Cour de cassation has held that a buyer of property does not have to inform its seller that the price he is paying is too low even when he knows it to be 'derisory' given the property's value[120] or where he is a *professionnel* and the seller is not.[121]

Breach of an *obligation d'information* can have two effects. First, breach can constitute *dol* so as to give rise to annulment of the contract but only where 'it was committed knowingly with the intention to provoke in the mind of [other party] a decisive mistake';[122] otherwise, breach has no direct bearing on the validity of the contract, though the contract may instead be annulled on the grounds of the other party's substantial mistake.[123] Secondly, breach may give rise to liability in delict for fault, *whether or not* the duty-bearer was dishonest or

---

[113] And see generally J. Ghestin, 'The pre-contractual obligation to disclose, I. French Report' in D. Tallon and D. Harris (eds.) *Contract Law Today* (Oxford, 1989) 151 and Ghestin, *Formation*, 576 ff. For a less enthusiastic view of these developments, see notably, P. Le Tourneau, 'De l'allégement de l'obligation de renseignements ou de conseil', D 1987 Chron. 101.

[114] P. Malaurie, L. Aynès and P.-Y. Gautier, *Les contrats spéciaux*, 2nd edn. (Defrénois, 2005), 200 citing as example, Civ. (1) 21 Jul. 1993, D 1994. Somm. 237 note Tournafond, though the latter considers that it could have been decided as *dol par réticence*.

[115] Art. L. 111-1 C. consom.

[116] This is made clear by the *travaux préparatoires:* see, e.g., the report of M. A. Brune, *Journal Officiel*, Ass. Nat. No. 1992 (1990–1991), 36.

[117] See Larroumet, *Contrat*, 335–343 for a useful overview.

[118] Civ. (1) 13 May 2003, Bull. civ. I no. 114, JCP 2003.I.170 note Loiseau; RTDCiv. 2003. 700 note Mestre and Fages.

[119] Com. 24 Sep. 2003, RTDCiv. 2004.86 note Mestre and Fages.

[120] Civ. (1) 3 May 2000, *affaire des photographies de Baldus*, cit. n. 108.

[121] Civ. (3) 17 Jan. 2007, 2007.II.10042 note Jamin.

[122] Com. 28 Jun. 2005, D 2006.2774 note Chauvel.

[123] Terré, Simler, and Lequette, *Obligations*, 265 and see below, pp. 311 ff.

negligent: breach of a duty itself constitutes fault,[124] although the courts have a power of 'assessment' over exactly what a person owing such a duty should have said.[125] Moreover, where a party to a contract owes a duty to inform the other party, attempts to do so, but gets it wrong, this also constitutes a breach of his duty so as to attract liability in damages and exemplifies one of the ways in which French law sanctions what a common lawyer would see as an innocent pre-contractual misrepresentation.

2. Mistake

The Civil Code allows mistake to vitiate a party's consent only when it goes to the substance of the contract or to the identity of the contractor.[126]

Mistakes of identity are operative only where the identity of the other party is the 'principal cause' of the contract and while this is a matter for the intention of the parties (and therefore the *juges du fond*), it is typically found in certain types of contract, such as gifts or employment contracts, whereas in others, such as sale in which the identity of the other party is usually irrelevant, this is exceptional.[127] A person's attributes, such as his nationality, age, marital status or even his respectability or impartiality may be an element within his 'identity' for this purpose.[128]

The courts have long seen a party's 'mistake as to a substantial quality' of the subject-matter of the contract in any element which in the intentions of the parties determined its conclusion;[129] the mistake may be one of law[130] and may relate either to what the mistaken party received or transferred.[131] Thus, in the famous

---

[124] Sometimes the courts have preferred to treat such obligations as contractual: see the discussion in Malaurie, Aynès, and Stoffel-Munck, *Obligations*, 385 *et seq.* For further discussion of 'breach of duty' as delictual fault, see below p. 373.

[125] Larroumet, *Contrat*, 348.

[126] Art. 1110 C. civ. Jurists distinguish from this *'erreur-obstacle'* which prevents agreement from arising (e.g. where A receives property from B thinking it a gift, whereas B thinks it a loan or where a seller, A, thinks a sale relates to specific property X, whereas the buyer, B, thinks it relates to specific property Y). Despite this 'obstacle' to agreement, the courts hold that such a mistake leads to *nullité relative* rather than the more logical *nullité absolue*, though it may be invoked by either party: Flour, Aubert, and Savaux, *Acte Juridique*, 147–148.

[127] Terré, Simler, and Lequette, *Obligations*, 225–226.

[128] Ibid, 226.

[129] Carbonnier, *Obligations*, 2003 dates this development to around 1870.

[130] Flour, Aubert, and Savaux, *Acte juridique*, 154. In Civ. (2) 21 Oct. 2004, Bull. civ. II no. 465, *RDC* 2005.292 note Stoffel-Munck, the Cour de cassation considered the question whether a party to a contract (a liability insurer) could claim annulment for mistake where a change in judicial interpretation of the law invalidated a term of the insurance contract (a clause 'claims made') which the party argued had been 'essential'. The court held simply that in these circumstances the insurer had made no mistake at the time of concluding the contract, the subsequent judicial declaration of invalidity notwithstanding.

[131] This is put in French works in terms of the mistake as to either the *prestation* received or supplied: Flour, Aubert, and Savaux, *Acte juridique*, 153 . The *prestation* is the subject-matter of a contractual obligation, the 'thing to be done'.

Poussin case, the owners of a painting which they had thought to be by Poussin had been told that it was merely the work of a minor school and sold it at auction as such for a small price. Later its authenticity as a Poussin was taken up and it was exhibited as such by the Louvre, which had exercised its right of pre-emption from the painting's buyer. After some 15 years of litigation, the original owners obtained the annulment of the sale by auction on the ground not that they had mistakenly sold a Poussin as of a minor school (because experts still differed as to whether it *was* a Poussin) but on the ground that they had mistakenly thought that it was *definitely not* a Poussin (when it might have been!)[132]

However, French courts do possess some means by which this potentially vast ground of vitiation may be contained in the interests of the security of transactions and fairness to the other party to the contract.[133]

First, the issue as to whether a party's mistake was essential or decisive is in principle within the discretion of the *juges du fond*[134] and this gives them considerable room to put into effect their perception of the appropriateness of annulment,[135] in particular being swayed by the prejudicial effect of the mistake on the party suffering from it.[136] On the other hand, this does not always have a restrictive effect and so, for example, while the Cour de cassation does not allow mere mistakes as to value of property bought to be relied on expressly as a ground of annulment, it has allowed a lower court to find that some quality of the property determined the buyer's consent, a quality which happened to be reflected in a disparity of value.[137]

Secondly, although a party's mistake does not need to be shared by the other, both must be aware of the factual circumstances which give rise to the essential quality of the mistake of the party applying for annulment.[138] Thus, in one well-known case, buyers of a piece of land obtained the sale's annulment on the ground that, although aware of its physical extent, they were mistaken as to its hectarage, the latter being essential for them as they were intending to sell it off in parcels, a purpose which was known to their seller.[139] Moreover, recently the Cour de cassation has clearly sought to tighten up the circumstances in which annulment is to be allowed in this sort of case.[140] So, notably, in one case a company which had bought property in order to gain fiscal advantages which did not materialize applied for annulment of the contract on the ground of *erreur*.[141] Here, the Cour

---

[132] Civ. (1) 13 Dec. 1983, JCP 1984.11.20186, Versailles 7 Jan. 1987, GP 1987. 34, *Source-Book*, 331 ff.

[133] Flour, Aubert, and Savaux, *Acte juridique*, 159–160. See further Cartwright, *op. cit.* n. 92, esp. 159–162.

[134] Civ. (1) 10 Mar. 1998, Bull. civ. I no. 97.

[135] P. Malinvaud, 'De l'erreur sur la substance', D 1972 Chron. 215 at 216.

[136] Flour, Aubert, and Savaux, *Acte juridique*, 160.

[137] e.g. Civ. (3) 29 Nov. 1968, GP 1969. 1.63, *Source-Book*, 329. Cf. art. 1112-4 A.-p.r.: 'mistake as to value is not, *in itself*, a ground of nullity' (emphasis added).

[138] Larroumet, *Contrat*, 297–299.

[139] Civ. 23 Nov. 1931, DP 1932.1.129 note Josserand, GP 1932.1,96, *Source-Book*, 324.

[140] Flour, Aubert, and Savaux, *Acte juridique*, 157–159.

[141] Civ. (1) 13 Feb. 2001, Bull. civ. I no. 31, JCP.I.330 p. 1216 note Rochfeld (who explains the decision as one of *erreur sur la cause*. Similarly, Civ. (3) 24 Apr. 2003. Bull. civ. III no. 82.

de cassation upheld the lower court's rejection of this claim, holding that 'mistake as to one's own reason for entering a contract which does not relate to the subject-matter of the contract is not a ground of its nullity, even where this reason is decisive', but it made an exception to this rule where the contract contained an express term making a party's reason a condition of the contract, the other party's knowledge of the reason not being enough.

Thirdly, a party to a contract will not be able to rely on his own mistake in order to avoid the contract where he should have known better: his mistake must not be 'inexcusable'.[142] In one case, for example,[143] a seller sold velvet to a commercial buyer which intended to use it to make women's clothes. The buyer claimed the sale's annulment on the ground that it was a furnishing fabric and therefore unsuitable for its purpose, but this was refused as the material had been sold as furnishing fabric and the buyer, which was a commercial clothing manufacturer and aware of its normal use, had therefore employed it to make clothes at its own risk.

Lastly, while proof by a party to a contract of an invalidating mistake does not in itself give rise to a claim for damages against the other party for any loss which he may have suffered, such a claim may arise in certain circumstances.[144] Again, of course, the legal basis of such a liability is delictual fault, which may be found simply in the other party's lack of care but normally will lie in his breach of a duty of information.[145] Thus, a common lawyer's 'innocent misrepresentation' may in French law give rise to liability in damages in delict, but it vitiates the contract on the ground of 'substantial mistake'.

3. Undue pressure

The Civil Code provides quite elaborately for vitiation on the ground of *violence*, which should be thought of as 'undue pressure' rather than 'duress' given the very wide range of situations which it includes.[146] The sanctions for *violence* are the same as for *dol*, i.e. 'relative nullity' and damages for delictual fault, fault being a necessary element for its existence.[147]

Article 1112 of the Civil Code states:

There is *violence* where it is of a nature to make an impression on a reasonable person and where it inspires in him the fear of exposure of his person or fortune to a considerable and present harm.

---

[142] Flour, Aubert, and Savaux, *Acte juridique*, 159–160. Cf above, p. 309 (mistake always excusable where caused by *dol*).

[143] Com. 4 Jul. 1973, D 1974.538 note Ghestin.

[144] Flour, Aubert, and Savaux, *Acte juridique*, 170.

[145] Terré, Simler, and Lequette, *Obligations*, 233–334. See e.g. Civ. (3) 29 Nov. 1968, cit. n. 137, where the court found the defendant's fault lay in his misrepresentation.

[146] Arts. 1111–1116 C. civ. French courts take a more liberal approach to the interpretation of these elements where the contract is a gift, rather than a non-gratutitous contract: Malaurie and Aynès, *Successions*, 148; art. 901 C. civ. (as amended by *loi* no. 2006-728 of 23 June 2006).

[147] Art. 1117 C. civ. (relative nullity); Terré, Simler, and Lequette, *Obligations*, 255 (damages). For the distinction between 'relative' and 'absolute' nullity, see above p. 308.

Regard is to be had for this purpose to the age, sex and condition of the person affected.

First, therefore, the threat[148] must be of an act which causes the other party to fear a 'considerable and present harm' to his person or fortune. Threats of bodily violence are, of course, included, but so are threats to a person's mental well-being (such as a threat of defamation) and threats to his economic well-being.[149] Interestingly, unlike *dol,* the threat may come from any person, whether the other party or not,[150] and may be made in respect of the person or fortune of a party's spouse, ascendants or descendants.[151] The threat must also be illegitimate.[152] and while threats of violence are necessarily so, more difficulty arises in relation to threats to exercise a right (such as to take legal proceedings) which would harm the other party's economic position. Here French law again relies on the idea of the 'abuse of rights',[153] so while in principle a threat to exercise a legal right is not *violence,* exceptions are made where either the means or purpose of its exercise are improper,[154] for example, where a person threatens to bring a vexatious law suit[155] or where he uses his right to obtain more than his due.[156] Unsurprisingly, the issue of the legitimacy of threats is much litigated.[157]

Given all this, does French law allow the vitiation of a contract for *violence* on the mere ground of force of circumstances? The Code itself assumes that *violence* consists of an act by the other party (or of a third party) rather than merely the presence of circumstances surrounding the making of the contract[158] and this is reflected in the fairly restrictive attitude of French courts, which have accepted that economic duress ('*la contrainte économique*') can attract annulment of a contract on the ground of *violence* (independently of any valid claim for *lésion*[159]) but only where there is 'an abusive exploitation of a situation of economic dependence made to make a profit from the fear of an evil which directly threatens a person's legitimate interests'.[160] So, for example, where an employee of a publisher had assigned her intellectual property rights in a work to her employer in circumstances where she could not assign them elsewhere and

---

[148] The threat must be deliberate: Carbonnier, *Obligations,* 1995.
[149] Flour, Aubert, and Savaux, *Acte juridique,* 172.
[150] Art. 1111 C. civ. cr. art. 1116 C. civ. (*dol*) above p. 308.
[151] Art. 1113 C. civ.
[152] This is often supported somewhat unconvincingly from art. 1114 C. civ., which provides that respect for one's parents is not in itself a source of *violence,* for (moderate) parental influence is legitimate: Flour, Aubert, and Savaux, *Acte juridique,* 173–174.
[153] See above p. 305 and below pp. 373 ff.
[154] Carbonnier, *Obligations,* 2007 and see Civ. (3) 17 Jan. 1984, Bull. civ. III no. 13.
[155] Civ. (1) 30 Jun. 1954, JCP 1954.II.8325.
[156] e.g. Paris 31 May 1966, D 1967 Somm. 2, RTDCiv 1967.147 obs. Chevallier.
[157] Carbonnier, *Obligations,* 2007.
[158] Arts. 1111, 1113 C. civ.
[159] Civ. (1) 30 May 2000, D 2000.879 note Chazal. On *lésion* see below, pp. 324–325.
[160] Civ. (1) 3 Apr. 2002, D 2002.1860 note Chazal, note Gridel.

where the employer was making other employees redundant, the Cour de cassation held that the contract of assignment was not to be annulled for *violence*, as the lower court had not found that she had herself felt threatened with redundancy and that her employer had taken advantage of such a circumstance to convince her to contract.[161]

Secondly, French jurists agree that the defect in the party's consent which *violence* creates is fear, the fear of the harm threatened interfering with the party's freedom of consent. While the terms of article 1112 of the Civil Code are not clear on the issue, the courts have taken a 'subjective view' to the question whether the fear which a threat causes is sufficient to satisfy *violence*, looking to see whether the *particular* person's consent was sufficiently affected by the illegitimate threat, taking into account his or her 'force of character', social position, age or sex.[162]

C. *Objet, Cause,* and *Lésion*

The Civil Code contains two further requirements for the validity of a contract, that it have both an *objet* and a lawful *cause*.[163] It then goes on to declare that *lésion* (gross disparity of undertaking) will not in principle affect the validity of a contract, though it will in specific instances.[164]

1. Objet

The Code itself does not make clear whether the requirement of *objet* (subject-matter) deals with the subject-matter of the contract, of an obligation or of its *prestation* (a difficult word to translate, but the sense is of the actual thing to be done or not done), but modern jurists say that a contract itself possesses no subject-matter but rather has only effects (its obligations)[165] and that the subject-matter of a contract's obligations are its *prestations*.[166] They therefore either talk in terms of the *objet* of a contractual obligation or of the latter's *prestation*, the two being intimately related. The *objet* of a party's *prestation* may either be a physical thing (such as the property in a seller's obligation in sale, the *prestation* here being the delivery of the property)[167] an activity or omission (such as the doing of work by an employee in employment) or a risk (in a contract such

---

[161] Ibid.

[162] Bénabent, *Obligations*, 70; Flour, Aubert, and Savaux, *Acte juridique*, 172–173; Terré, Simler, and Lequette, *Obligations*, 254. See e.g. Req. 17 Nov. 1925, S 1926.1.121 note Breton; Com. 28 May 1991, D 1991 Somm. 385 note Aynès.

[163] Arts. 1108, 1126–1133 C. civ.

[164] Art. 1118 C. civ.

[165] Flour, Aubert, and Savaux, *Acte juridique*, 185 ff.

[166] Bénabent, *Obligations*, 102 ff; Malaurie, Aynès, and Stoffel-Munck, *Obligations*, 293. Some jurists refer to the issue of *lésion* as concerning the *objet* of the contract: see Terré, Simler, and Lequette, *Obligations*, 310 ff.

[167] J. Ghestin and B. Desché, *Traité des contrats, La vente* (Paris, 1990) 365.

as insurance). French law requires both that an *objet* exists and that it be lawful, failure in either respect leading to absolute nullity (*nullité absolue*) of the contract, which means that in principle any person and not merely one or other of the parties to the contract may ask a court to annul it.[168]

(a) The existence of *objet*

French law provides for the annulment of a contract as a result of an absence of *objet* in situations which may be thought of as concerning either a lack of certainty or initial impossibility. As to certainty, the Civil Code concedes that the subject-matter of a contractual obligation may either be determined on contract or determinable at the date of performance (for example, the assignment of all the assignor's rights against a particular debtor at some set future date)[169] and may consist of 'future things' (for example, the sale of manufactured goods not yet made).[170] While French courts used to consider certainty of price as an aspect of certainty of *objet*, in 1995 the Assemblée plénière divorced these two issues and roundly declared that parties to a long-term supply contract could validly set its future prices by reference to the *supplier's* normal contract rate, subject to this right in the supplier not being exercised abusively.[171] There are, however, unresolved tensions here, and this area has become a striking context for the debate as to whether French contract law should be more 'liberal' or more 'social'.[172] For example, in one case the Cour d'appel de Paris had declared that the tripling in price of the hire of a bank safe-deposit was an abuse by the bank of its contractual right to set the price; but the Cour de cassation quashed this decision, roundly declaring that 'the bank was free to set the rates on which it intended to deal' not least as the customer was free to terminate the contract (under another of its terms) and go to one of the bank's competitors.[173] For Mazeaud, while couched in the language of liberty, the practical liberty in the circumstances was all on one side (the bank's), the court's decision not even allowing a minimal '*solidarité*' by requiring the bank to give reasons;[174] by contrast, for Martin and Synvet, the Cour de cassation's appeal to freedom of contract 'does it credit as the custodian of our fundamental liberties for it thereby sets a limit to the intolerable socio-consumerist claims which try to control other people's behaviour'.[175]

---

[168] See above p. 308.
[169] Bénabent, *Obligations*, 103.
[170] Arts. 1129 and 1130 al. 1 C. civ.
[171] Ass. plén. 1 Dec. 1995, D 1996, 13, concl. Jeol, note Aynès.
[172] Above, p. 300.
[173] Civ. (1) 30 Jun. 2004, D 2005.1828 note D. Mazeaud.
[174] D 2005.1828.
[175] D. Martin and H. Synvet, 'Droit bancaire' D 2006.155.

As well as being sufficiently certain, the *objet* must also exist at the time of the conclusion of the contract. So, where, for example, a person sells a particular item of property to another which (unknown to them both) had previously perished, the seller's obligation would fail for lack of *objet*[176] which would lead to the 'absolute nullity' of the contract.[177] However, obligations whose performance is initially impossible in other ways may also be held to lack an *objet*, as long as this impossibility is absolute rather than personal to the party in question.[178]

(b) The lawfulness of *objet*

French law requires that the subject-matter of a contract be lawful (*licite*) in the wide sense of not being contrary to law, public policy or morality.[179] Thus, some types of physical things, for example, poisons, parts of the human body and public burial-grounds, are held to be beyond the proper sphere of contract ('things outside commerce') and some non-physical *objets* may also be unlawful for example, where a person agrees to commit a crime or agrees even gratuitously to act as 'surrogate mother' for another person.[180] As we shall see, even where the subject-matter of a contract is lawful in this wide sense, the contract may be annulled owing to the unlawful reason for which one of the parties entered it.[181]

2. Cause

The notion of *la cause* in French contract law is one of the most difficult for a common lawyer to grasp and this difficulty is exacerbated by the uncertainty, dispute and disparateness which surrounds it. The Civil Code is particularly unforthcoming, merely stating that an obligation with no *cause*, a false *cause* or an unlawful *cause* can have no effect[182] and even one of these elements disappears on inspection, for it is generally agreed that a 'false *cause*' merely describes absence of *cause* from the point of view of the debtor of the obligation. It is often said that *la cause* explains *why* a debtor owes an obligation, whereas *objet* describes *what* the debtor owes and while this neat opposition is somewhat opaque, it does draw our attention to the two main ways in which *la cause* is viewed: first, 'subjectively' or 'concretely' as the determining motive for the debtor's undertaking an obligation and, secondly, 'objectively' or 'abstractly' as the legal or formal reason for the

---

[176] Where one or other of the parties had taken the risk of the existence of the property in question, then this risk is said to form the object of the obligation of that party and in these circumstances the physical destruction of the property before contract would not invalidate it: Bénabent, *Obligations*, 104.

[177] Ghestin and Desché, (above n. 167), 373.

[178] Flour, Aubert, and Savaux, *Acte juridique*, 189.

[179] Ibid., 191.

[180] Art. 1128 C. civ.; Ass. plén. 31 May 1991, D 1991.417 rapp. Chartier, note Thouvenin (surrogacy agreement).

[181] Below pp. 323–324.

[182] Art. 1131 C. civ. Cf. arts. 1124–1126-1 A.-p.r.

obligation's imposition.[183] Much of the traditional juristic debate about *la cause* centred on which of these views was right, but until fairly recently a compromise position had been reached according to which both subjective and objective understandings are taken according to the purpose for which the notion is used: a subjective one in cases of unlawful *cause* and an objective one in cases of absence of *cause*.[184] However, one of the consequences of the developing use—one could even say renaissance— of l*a cause* in both the case law and juristic writing has been a unravelling of this compromise, with subjective elements becoming relevant to cases involving absence of *cause*.[185]

What, therefore, are the purposes for which the notion of *cause* has been used? There are at least five discernable in the modern law, though some of them are closely related:

(a) for conceptual analysis and exposition;
(b) to require a minimum reciprocity at the inception of bilateral contracts;
(c) to invalidate a term of a contract (especially an exemption clause) while leaving the contract itself valid;
(d) to invalidate a contract on the ground of its unlawful purpose; and
(e) to explain the interdependence of the performance of obligations in bilateral contracts.

These will be looked at in turn, with the exception of the last which will be discussed in the context of contractual performance.[186]

(a) Conceptual analysis

Modern juristic discussions often distinguish between the *cause* of a contractual *obligation* and the *cause* of the contract itself, this being a convenient way of describing, respectively, questions of absence of *cause* and of unlawful *cause*. When talking about the *cause* of a contractual obligation, an abstract approach is taken, the *cause* being said to be the same for each type of contract, the categories for this purpose being very broad indeed. So, in *contrats réels* (such as loan or deposit), the *cause* of the obligation of the recipient of the property to restore it lies in its delivery to him[187] and in gratuitous contracts (*contrats à titre gratuit*),

---

[183] Carbonnier, *Obligations*, 2017–2018.

[184] Flour, Aubert, and Savaux, *Acte juridique*, 202, 213. And see generally the influential treatment by J. Rochfeld, 'Cause' in *Répertoire civile Dalloz* (Jan. 2005).

[185] Below, pp. 319, 321.

[186] Below, p. 348.

[187] A *contrat réel* is a contract which is concluded only after delivery of a thing: the agreement of the parties is necessary, but it is not sufficient and no obligation to deliver the thing arises. Traditionally, contracts of loan, deposit and pledge are all *contrats réels*, but the classification is now disputed and the Cour de cassation has tended to restrict its ambit: Fabre-Magnan, *Obligations*, 197; e.g. Civ. (1) 28 Mar. 2000, Bull. civ. I no. 105, D 2000.482 note Piedelièvre; Civ. (1) 5 Jul. 2006, D 2007.50 note Ghestin (loan of money by a *professionnel* is not a *contrat réel*).

including agreements to make gifts,[188] the *cause* of the promisor's obligation lies in his 'donative intention' (*intention libérale*), though this seems distinctly concrete.[189] As regards bilateral (or synallagmatic) contracts, the *cause* of one party's obligation is generally said to lie in the other's *obligation* and vice versa.[190] Clearly, for some French jurists, these assertions possess an analytical attraction, but it is understandable why others thought them useless.[191]

(b) Requiring a minimum reciprocity at the inception of bilateral contracts

However, the courts have not allowed the requirement of a *cause* of a party's obligation to go unused. For if the obligations of each type of contract possess their own abstract *causes*, where on the facts a contract's *cause* is lacking, then the contract will be subject to annulment:[192] classically, 'a court must check whether a party's obligation has a juridical basis, though it must not assess whether it is balanced by what the other party must do in return'.[193] While 'absence of *cause*' may be and has been used to annul *contrats réels* and gratuitous contracts, in neither case does it add much to analysis in terms of *objet* or absence of consent and its practical importance there has not been significant in the modern law.[194] It is rather in the area of bilateral contracts where its importance has been felt.

Here, the starting-point for the law is the formal, analytical one which has just been noted. So, if the *cause* of one party's obligation is the subject-matter (*objet*, here the *prestation* or actual thing to be done or not done) of the other party's obligation, then a lack or failure of this subject-matter entails the absence of *cause* of the latter's obligation.[195] A traditional example of the application of this way of thinking can be found in the annulment of a contract by a genealogist to find an inheritance for an heir who would certainly have heard of it anyway: the heir's obligation lacked a *cause* as anything which the genealogist would do was

---

[188] These typically also count as *contrats unilatéraux* (which are all those contracts which impose an obligation on only one party to the contract: art. 1103 C. civ.) but do not necessarily do so (e.g. *donation avec charges*). Conversely, some *contrats unilatéraux* are *contrats à titre onéreux*, for example loan at interest: the contract is for reward, but only the borrower owes obligations (to return the property lent and to pay the interest): Malaurie, Aynès, and Stoffel-Munck, *Obligations*, 193.

[189] Larroumet, *Contrat*, 444.

[190] Some say that it lies in the other's *prestation* rather than *obligation* the reason for this change being the apparent illogic of A's obligation causing B's obligation when both obligations arise at the same time, the conclusion of the contract.

[191] The most prominent of these others was M. Planiol, *Traité élémentaire de droit civil*, 10th edn. (Paris, 1926) t. II, 372 ff.

[192] On the nature of this nullity, see below, p. 321.

[193] Malaurie, Aynès, and Stoffel-Munck, *Obligations*, 307.

[194] Carbonnier, *Obligations*, 2026; Flour, Aubert, and Savaux, *Acte juridique*, 205.

[195] Terré, Simler, and Lequette, *Obligations*, 349–350. This is sometimes supported by reference to art. 1601 C. civ. which provides that 'if at the time of sale the thing sold had completely perished, the sale is null'.

entirely redundant.[196] Perhaps more surprising to a common lawyer, however, is the long-standing assimilation of a 'derisory' counterpart to no counterpart at all. So, French courts have long annulled contracts on the ground that the price stipulated was derisory,[197] though some jurists are careful to point out that the approach to *la cause* is still 'objective' as the parties' motives remain irrelevant.[198] Even here, it can be seen that French courts play an 'equitable role' ensuring a minimum degree of reciprocity in contracts where reciprocity is part of the very nature of the contract to which the parties have agreed.[199]

However, in recent years French courts have proved much more willing to annul contracts on the ground of absence of *cause*. A striking example may be found in the 'Point Club Vidéo' case of 1996 in which the owners of a shop had contracted to create a video club with a company which hired out video cassettes.[200] In these circumstances, the Cour de cassation agreed with the lower court that the contract should be annulled for absence of *cause* since the locality in which the shopowners carried on business had only 1,314 inhabitants and so 'performance of the contract according to the economic purpose (*'l'économie'*) intended by the parties was impossible' and that therefore their obligation to pay hire charges 'lacked any real counterpart'.[201] A recent case emphasizes, though, that the courts are concerned with the overall economic reality of the arrangements made by the parties, rather than just an individual contract.[202] There, a musician and composer entered three contracts for the commercial exploitation of his work: a publishing contract, a contract of assignment of his intellectual property rights and a contract of sale of 'sound tracks' which he made. The Cour d'appel had annulled the last of these contracts on the ground that its price of one franc was 'derisory' and therefore his obligation to deliver the sound tracks lacked a *cause*, but the Cour de cassation quashed this decision on the basis that

---

[196] Civ. (1) 18 Apr. 1953, D 1953.403. Cf. Civ. (1) 17 Apr. 1956, D 1956.427.

[197] Flour, Aubert, and Savaux, *Acte juridique*, 207. E.g. Civ. (3) 18 Jul. 2001, Bull. civ. III no. 101, Défrenois 2000.1421 note Savaux (annulment of sale for 'cheapness of price'); Com. 8 Feb. 2005, D 2005.639. Cf. Civ. (1) 4 Jul. 1995, *affaire Cartier*, Bull. civ. I no. 303 in which the famous jeweller sold a ring at about a third of the price at which it should have been marked: no annulment for the benefit of the seller for failure of *cause* nor on the ground of *erreur* as its mistake was as to the ring's value.

[198] Terré, Simler, and Lequette, *Obligations*, 349.

[199] Carbonnier, *Obligations*, 2019; Flour, Aubert, and Savaux, *Acte juridique*, 207.

[200] Civ. (1) 3 Jul. 1996, D 1997.500 note Reigné.

[201] Ibid.

[202] Civ. (1) 13 Jun. 2006, D 2007.277 note Ghestin. Cf. Com. 15 Feb. 2000, Bull. civ. IV no. 29 (pharmacist bought on hire-purchase a special machine from a publicity company to display advertisements to be provided by it; when the publicity company ceased trading, the machine became useless to the pharmacist; in these circumstances, the contract of hire-purchase with a finance company was annulled for lack of *cause* as it was dependent on the contract with the publicity company and this failed as the machine had become useless); Civ. (3) 13 Oct. 2004, Bull. civ. III no. 170, *RDC* 2005.1009 note Mazeaud (argued that contract of assignment by tenant of his rights under a tenancy to landlord lacked a *cause* since the assignee/landlord did not have to pay rent to himself; held, the landlord's obligation possessed a *cause* in that the contract allowed him to recover the physical enjoyment of the premises in question).

the lower court ought to have considered whether this contract formed part of an 'indivisible wider economic group' which would provide a proper counterpart to his obligations.

These cases reflect a significant change of direction as they use *la cause de l'obligation* to assess the validity of a contract which is affected by a 'subjective rather than an objective imbalance', that is, whether the contract has no point for one of the parties.[203] To a common lawyer, this looks sometimes very much like annulment on the ground of having made a foolish or bad bargain and the case law remains controversial in France, the majority of *la doctrine* regretting the way in which a party's 'subjective reasons' for contracting have become relevant to an aspect of *la cause* long seen as 'objective' and also warning against the concomitant risk to legal certainty which this entails.[204]

One of the consequences of these developments is that the traditional position according to which an absence of *cause* gives rise to 'absolute nullity' has come to be seen as inappropriate, as this classification means that in principle any person having a sufficient interest in doing so may apply to the court for the contract's annulment, that the contract may not be affirmed and that the time for bringing claims is 30 years rather than five years, as is the case with relative nullity.[205] As a result, the courts have nuanced their position, holding that where an absence of *cause* stems from 'the impossibility of receiving any benefit' from the contract, it operates only for the protection of the contracting party claiming annulment and the nullity involved must therefore be relative rather than absolute.[206]

Where a bilateral contract is annulled for absence of *cause* the latter seems to resemble (at least functionally) the common law doctrine of consideration, for it ensures a minimum reciprocity between the parties. Such a similarity is, however, only superficial, for the doctrine of consideration rules out from English contract 'gratuitous agreements', a category which its attendant authorities define, even if in a complex, clumsy and at times incoherent manner: without a supporting 'something of value in the eyes of the law', no promise other than one contained in a deed is contractually binding. *La cause*, on the other hand, does not prevent the enforcement of gratuitous agreements: indeed, it provides a 'gift-promise' with its own *cause* in the promisor's *intention libérale*, thereby confirming that such promises (once accepted) are in principle contractually binding. Moreover, the French approach to absence of *cause* may be seen as furthering or protecting the parties' intentions, for while a purely gratuitous agreement is as binding as a bilateral one, where the parties intended to create a type of contract whose *nature*

---

[203] Mazeaud, *RDC* 2005.1009.

[204] Ibid. (though the author does not agree). For further contrasting views see J. Rochfeld, 'A future for *la cause*? Observations of a French Jurist' and R. Sefton-Green '*La cause* or the length of the French judiciary's foot' in Cartwright, Vogenauer, and Whittaker, chs. 4 and 5 respectively.

[205] Terré, Simler, and Lequette, *Obligations*, 368.

[206] Civ. (3) 29 Mar. 2006, Bull. civ. III no. 88, JCP 2006.I.153 no.2 note Ghestin. Cf. art. 1124-1 A.-p.r. which provides that '[a]bsence of *cause* is sanctioned by relative nullity of the contract. Unlawfulness of *cause* taints the contract with absolute nullity'.

is bilateral, an absence of this bilaterality should lead to the contract's invalidity: they did not intend to enter that sort of agreement. The doctrine of consideration, on the other hand, can defeat the intentions of the parties by excluding their agreement from the domain of contract. Finally, French courts annul bilateral contracts where the counterpart of one party's obligation is deemed derisory, whereas in English law while the consideration for a promise must be 'real', it need not be adequate and may indeed be nominal.[207]

(c) Invalidating a term of a contract

While older examples can be found of reliance on the notion of *la cause* to invalidate a particular term of a contract judged inconsistent with a party's essential obligation,[208] it was with the first *affaire Chronopost* in 1996 which this use of *cause* became prominent.[209] There, a commercial carrier had attempted by a contract term to limit its liability for delay in delivery of packages sent by the claimant (who was also in business) by a guaranteed next-day service. The Cour de cassation upheld the lower court's decision refusing to give effect to this contract term on the ground that the carrier thereby attempted to exclude its essential obligation under the contract, this resting (implicitly) on the requirement that the consignor's obligation to pay the price had to be balanced by the carrier's essential obligation to deliver on time as otherwise it would lack a *cause*.[210] While the practical effect of this approach has not been applied to contracts of carriage governed by a *contrat type* set by legislation,[211] outside this context it has continued to flourish.[212] While most of the cases illustrating this use of *la cause* involve the invalidation of exemption clauses, the courts have applied it to other types of contract term, for example, 'anti-competition clauses' or a 'claims made' clause in a contract of liability insurance.[213] Unsurprisingly, some jurists see this case law as reflecting the concern of French courts with 'contractual justice' rather than

---

[207] G. H. Treitel, *The Law of Contract*, 11th edn. (2003), 73–75.

[208] Req. 19 Jan. 1863, S 1863.1.185 (landlord cannot exclude by contract his liability for failure to perform his essential obligation to provide premises fit for their intended purpose).

[209] Com. 22 Oct. 1996, D 1997.121 note Sériaux.

[210] Art. 1131 C. civ. headed the *arrêt*.

[211] Where these *contrats type* apply, the carrier's liability is limited to the cost of the carriage; here the courts have held that, in the absence of *dol* or *faute lourde*, this limitation is to be applied even where a stipulated limitation clause to the same effect is invalidated on the ground that it purports to exclude the carrier's essential obligation: Com. 9 Jul. 2002, D 2002.2329. Moreover, *faute lourde* for this purpose must not be seen merely in a failure to explain the delay (Ch. mix. 22 Apr. 2005, D 2005.1864 note Chevrier) nor in the carrier's failure to perform its essential obligation, but in the seriously wrongful nature of the carrier's behaviour (Com. 21 Feb. 2006, D 2006.717 note Chevrier). On *contrats type* in general, see above, pp. 299–300.

[212] Com. 30 May 2006, D 2006.2288 note Mazeaud.

[213] Flour, Aubert, and Savaux, *Acte juridique*, 208. Civ. (1) 11 May 1999, Bull. civ. I no. 156 (anti-competition clause must be 'proportionate to the legitimate interests to be protected'); Civ. (2) 30 Jun. 2004, Bull. civ. II no. 336 ('claims made' clause incompatible with insurer's obligation to indemnify in respect of insured events occurring during the life of the policy).

the formal maintenance of the principle of the binding force of contracts.[214] It is certainly given full recognition by the *Avant-projet de réforme*, which states generally that '[a]ny term of the contract which is incompatible with the real character of its *cause* is struck out'.[215]

(d) Unlawfulness of purpose

The third function of the notion of *la cause* is to provide a mechanism for the annulment of contracts whose subject-matter may not be in itself objectionable, but which one of the parties enters for a reason or reasons which are considered so. Here, a 'subjective approach' is taken to *la cause*, according to which the courts look at the actual motivation or purpose of *one* of the parties to the contract in entering it,[216] this then being termed its '*cause impulsive et déterminante*'. As would be expected, it is for a person alleging such a motive to prove it,[217] but it has been said that in reality if a court finds that any reason of a party is unlawful, it will be held to have been 'decisive'.[218] For this purpose, the notion of 'unlawful purpose' of a party to a contract is understood in the same wide sense as is found in relation to 'unlawful subject-matter' and so it includes motives which are contrary to public policy (*l'ordre public*), public morality (*les bonnes mœurs*) as well as those which are illegal in the sense of being contrary to legislation (such as hiring a sporting gun to commit a murder).[219] Clearly, this leaves French courts a very considerable discretion and *la cause* has been seen as 'an instrument for the moralization of contract... While *la cause* in its classic [abstract] sense plays a role of protecting individuals, it plays [here] a role of protecting society.'[220] Unsurprisingly, the courts' perception of public policy and public morality has changed over the years.[221] So, for example, for many years it was held that the validity of a gift by a person to his 'concubine' depended on whether it was intended to encourage the beginning or continuation of the relationship (invalid) or merely reflected a 'duty of conscience' on its ending (valid),[222] but in 2004 the Assemblée plénière of the Cour de cassation held generally that gifts to persons with whom the donor had even an *adulterous* relationship did not suffer from nullity.[223]

There has also been a more general change in the attitude of the courts to the question whether the unlawful motive of one party must be shared by the other party in order for the contract to be annulled. In the case of non-gratuitous

---

[214] Bénabent, *Obligations*, 136.
[215] Art. 1125 al. 2 A.-p.r.
[216] Bénabent, *Obligations*, 142–143.
[217] Civ. (1) 8 Jan. 1962, D 1962. Somm.97.
[218] Flour, Aubert, and Savaux, *Acte juridique*, 216.
[219] Art. 1133 C. civ., above, p. 317.
[220] Flour, Aubert, and Savaux, *Acte juridique*, 211.
[221] Ibid., 221.
[222] Req. 6 Jun. 1926, DP 1927.1.113 note Savatier; Civ. (1) 6 Oct. 1959, D 1960.515 note Malaurie.
[223] Ass. plén. 29 Oct. 2004, D 2004.3175 note Vigneau.

contracts,[224] the courts used to hold that the contract would not be annulled unless the unlawful motivation of one of the parties was known to the other party.[225] However, since 1998 the Cour de cassation has held that any contract can be annulled on the ground of the unlawful motive of one of its parties even if this was *not* known by the other party.[226] This position reflects the more generally expansive attitude of French lawyers to *la cause* and the increasingly 'subjective' way in which it is viewed,[227] but it has the undesirable effect that a person who makes a contract in good faith (without any knowledge of the other party's unlawful motive) can see the contract annulled, even on the application of the guilty party or any third party with sufficient interest in doing so,[228] since unlawful *cause* attracts 'absolute nullity'.[229] The *Avant-projet de réforme* suggests at least a partial solution here, still allowing the contract to be annulled in these circumstances, but providing that 'a party who enters into a contract with a purpose which is unlawful without the knowledge of the other must compensate all the loss caused by the annulment of the contract'.[230] Moreover, French courts already take a special approach to the questions whether either of the parties to an unlawful contract may obtain restitution of money or property transferred, or services done under it before nullity is declared, questions which we shall address in the context of their approach to restitution under a failed contract more generally.[231]

3. Lésion

Lésion is used by French lawyers in a narrow sense to refer to the loss caused to a party by the disproportion between the sides of a contract (such as far too low a price for property sold),[232] but in a wider sense to any substantive unfairness in a contract's provisions. Article 1118 of the Civil Code provides that '*lésion* does not vitiate contracts except as regards particular contracts or particular persons': in principle, therefore, making a bad bargain is not a ground for avoiding a contract in French law any more than in English,[233] although, as we have seen, French courts sometimes come close to this in their application of the doctrine of *la cause*.[234] On the other hand, while the Civil Code gives only a few examples of

---

[224] In the case of gratuitous contracts, a promisor's unlawful motive was (and still is) enough in itself for the contract to suffer from nullity.

[225] Civ. (1) 17 Jul. 1989, JCP 1990.II.21546 note Dagorne-Labbé.

[226] Civ. (1) 7 Oct. 1998, D 1998.563 concl. Sainte-Rose, D 1999 Somm.110 note Delebecque.

[227] O. Tournafond 'L'influence du motif illicite ou immoral sur la validité du contrat' D 1999. Chron.237 and cf. above, p. 318.

[228] Flour, Aubert, and Savaux, *Acte juridique*, 212–213.

[229] Bénabent, *Obligations*, 144–145.

[230] Art. 1126-1 A.-p.r.

[231] Below, p. 440 ff.

[232] Carbonnier, *Obligations*, 1996.

[233] Malaurie, Aynès, and Stoffel-Munck, *Obligations*, 256–257.

[234] Above, p. 320.

contracts where *lésion* affects the validity of a contract,[235] modern legislation has added many more. It is therefore natural for French jurists to include with their discussions of *lésion*, wider legislative intervention in the interests either of ensuring contractual fairness or of sanctioning contractual unfairness.[236] Clearly, the range of such a discussion may vary and may include such rules as those which control interest chargeable in contracts of loan, those which regulate certain classes of lease or the validity of unfair contract terms (*clauses abusives*) and as such reflect the perception already described that the liberal principles of freedom of contract and the binding force of contractual obligations have been subject to considerable inroads.[237]

D. Formal Requirements

Although acceptance by French law of agreement as both necessary and sufficient to form a contract entailed a general rejection of the need for agreement to take any particular form, formality does play a significant part in French practice, formal requirements applying to particular types of contract and being of various kinds.[238]

Thus, some contracts, such as mortgage (*contrat d'hypothèque*)[239] or 'sale and build contracts' (*vente d'immeubles à construire*)[240] have to be made before a *notaire*, this being the traditional approach for the most important contracts. Other contracts require, instead, simply signed writing (*acte sous seing privé*) and it is here that modern legislation has given rise to something of a 'renaissance of formalism',[241] examples being found in a diverse range of situations, from collective industrial agreements[242] to contracts of sale of a business (*fonds de commerce*).[243] It has also become more and more common for the law to require that warnings, statements or details (*mentions informatives*) are included in the contract aimed at ensuring that one of the parties understands the significance of

---

[235] The classic examples are contained in arts. 887 (contracts under which a joint inheritance is apportioned) and 1674 C. civ. (sales of immovable property at less than seven-twelfths of its value). The Civil Code (as amended) also uses *lésion* in the context of the contractual incapacity of mentally incapable persons and minors: see arts. 491-2 and 1305 C. civ. respectively. For restitution under contracts rescinded for incapacity, see below pp. 446–447.

[236] See, e.g. Carbonnier, *Obligations*, 2035 ff who includes under the title 'social requirements as to the content of contracts' a heading 'contractual justice' with discussion of *lésion* in the narrow sense, rules against usury and modern consumer protection and a heading 'contractual public-spiritedness' with discussion of the impact of *ordre public* and morality on contract and the doctrine of *fraude à la loi* (according to which a contract whose aim is the avoidance of some legal rule which is *d'ordre public* may sometimes not be allowed to do so).

[237] Above, pp. 299–300.

[238] For a useful discussion, see Starck *et al.*, *Contrat*, 76 ff.

[239] Art. 2416 C. civ. Cf. above pp. 291–292.

[240] Art. 1601-2 C. civ. and art. L. 261-11 C. const. et hab.

[241] Starck *et al.*, *Contrat*, 81.

[242] Art. L. 132-2 C. trav.

[243] *Loi* of 29 June 1935, art. 12 (which requires certain information to be included in the document). On *fonds de commerce* generally, see below p. 473 ff.

the contract.[244] Thus, for example, residential tenancies of unfurnished accommodation have to record, inter alia, the name and address of the lessor, the date of commencement, the rent payable and any deposit to be paid.[245]

There is, however an important recent qualification on this trend, for since 2004, the Civil Code has provided that 'where writing is required for the validity of a juridical act [a category which includes contracts], it may be established and maintained in an electronic form', subject to certain conditions and with certain exceptions.[246] These liberalizing provisions, enacted to give effect to the EC Directive on Electronic Commerce and driven by the perceived needs of the internal market, sit uncomfortably with some of the traditional protective formal requirements of French law, notably in the area of consumer law.[247]

French lawyers distinguish between those formal requirements which go to the validity of the contract (*ad solemnitatem*) and those which go to evidence of it (*ad probationem*). In some cases, the effect of failure to fulfil whatever requirements are set is made clear by the provision in question, for example, specifying 'absolute' or 'relative nullity' of the contract or, as in the case of the general requirement of writing for all legal *actes* of a value greater than €1500 being clearly a matter of evidence alone.[248] Where a formal requirment is a matter of evidence, any failure is capable of remedy by 'beginning of proof by writing' (*commencement de preuve par écrit*) or, where it is impossible to adduce written evidence, by any other evidence.[249] In many cases, though, the effect of failure to fulfil formal requirements is not made clear by the *loi* in question and the courts have had to decide the issue. Their attitude has differed over the years and according to the context. In relation to gifts,[250] they proved so hostile to formal requirements and found so many ways around them that it has been said that '[t]he requirement as it still appears in the Code serves mostly as a trap for the unwary'.[251] However, in certain other situations, the courts have been concerned to uphold and support formal requirements, this being particularly noticeable as regards suretyship (*cautionnement*).[252] Where the courts have held that a formal requirement goes to the validity of a contract, the tendency has been to hold that the effect of failure gives rise to absolute rather than relative nullity.[253]

[244] Terré, Simler, and Lequette, *Obligations*, 268.ff.

[245] *Loi* no. 98-462 of 6 July 1989, art. 3.

[246] Arts. 1108-1 and 1108-2 C. civ. as inserted by *loi* no. 2004-575 of 21 Jun. 2004, art. 25-1 and implementing Dir. 2000/31/EC of 8 June 2000 on electronic commerce, art. 9.

[247] D. Fenouillet, 'Commerce électronique et droit de la consommation: une rencontre incertaine' *RDC* 2004.955.

[248] Art. 1341 C. civ. (as amended).

[249] Arts. 1347–8, 1353 C. civ. and see Carbonnier, *Obligations*, 2080–2082.

[250] The formal requirement is made in art. 931 C. civ.

[251] J. P. Dawson, *Gifts and Promises* (New Haven and London, 1980), 82.

[252] Terré, Simler, and Lequette, *Obligations*, 155–156.

[253] Ibid., 157–159. For discussion of restitution on annulment, see below pp. 440 ff.

II. The Effects of Contracts

We shall look at the effect of contracts in French law under four headings: (A) the significance of obligations between the parties; (B) the effect of contracts beyond the parties; (C) the non-performance of obligations and its excuses and (D) judicial remedies for non-perfomance.

A. The Significance of Obligations between the Parties

French contracts are defined as agreements which give rise to obligations and, if valid, therefore, their primary effect is the creation of obligations for their parties, What is the effect of these obligations and what do they include?

1. The binding force of contractual obligation

French lawyers take obligations seriously and for them it is the nature of obligations to bind. This means that once the various and relatively high hurdles of the grounds of invalidity are crossed, a contract is not easily set aside. Thus, the courts have in principle no power to revise contracts on the ground of their substantive unfairness, whether this unfairness existed at the time of agreement or arose only subsequently. On the other hand, the nature of contractual obligation also explains the main exception to its binding force: as the often-quoted maxim puts it, *impossibilium nulla obligatio*—one cannot be bound to do the impossible—and so *force majeure* (supervening impossibility) is a general ground of excuse for contractual non-performance.[254]

The modern law, however, contains a number of significant exceptions to this stark position.

First, we should note again here that modern legislation, especially in the consumer context, controls the validity of many types of term, notably, *clauses pénales* (penalty clauses) and *clauses abusives* (unfair contract terms),[255] the latter both implementing EC legislation in the area[256] and giving legal backing to existing but rather shaky *jurisprudence*.[257] In a sense, of course, these controls do not impinge on the binding force of *obligation*, given that their effect is to invalidate particular terms so that they do not give rise to obligations. But they certainly impinge on the binding effect of agreements.

Secondly, apart from the possibility for the parties to rescind their contract by mutual consent,[258] contracts may contain a term, known as a *clause de dédit*, the effect of which is to allow one of the parties unilaterally to withdraw from the

---

[254] Below, pp. 343 ff.
[255] See art. 1152 C. civ. (as amended first in 1975) and art. L. 132-1 C. consom respectively.
[256] Dir. 93/13/EEC of 5 April 1993.
[257] Civ. (1) 14 May 1991, JCP 1991.II.21763 note Paisant, D 1991.449 note Ghestin.
[258] Art. 1134 al. 2 C. civ.

contract if he so chooses.[259] These clauses are often coupled in practice with the giving of a deposit (*arrhes*), so that, for example, if a tenant of property changes his mind and withdraws from the contract, he loses the deposit paid, whereas if the lessor withdraws, he has to pay back double the amount of the deposit.[260] Strikingly, this idea has been taken up and generalized by consumer protection legislation, so that, subject to contrary exclusion, in all contracts for the sale of movables or the supply of services by *professionnels* to consumers, any sums payable in advance are deemed to be deposits (rather than part-payment) with the effect that either party may withdraw from the contract, with the same effects we have just described.[261]

2. Non-cumul des responsabilités (contractuelle et délictuelle)

At this point, we should note the rule of *non-cumul des responsabilités*, according to which a party to a contract may not sue the other party for damages in delict, as long as the facts from which the delictual liability would otherwise arise are governed by one of the contract's obligations.[262] While sometimes the rule is supported by reference to the binding force of contract, its real reasons lie in a juristic preference for keeping legal categories distinct,[263] the need to protect both the terms and the rules of contract from the invasive effect of the extraordinary general liability in delict based on fault, and as part of the means of controlling the overweening tendencies of delictual liability for the 'actions of things'.[264] However, the *Avant-projet de réforme* proposes both to give legislative recognition to the rule of *non-cumul* in principle, but by way of exception would allow a party to a contract who suffers personal injury caused by the other party's contractual non-performance to 'opt in favour of the rules [contractual or extra-contractual] which are more favourable to him'[265]. As Viney explains in her preamble to the *Avant-projet's* provisions on civil liability, this

---

[259] Terré, Simler, and Lequette, *Obligations*, 483–485.

[260] eg. Civ. (3) 11 May 1976, D 1978.269 note Taisne (though the clause was denied effect on the grounds of bad faith). Such a clause follows the scheme in art. 1590 C. civ. for *promesse de vente* and by extension sales themselves.

[261] Art. L. 114-I al. 4 C. consom.

[262] Malaurie, Aynès and Stoffel-Munck, *Obligations*, 542 ff. The earliest clear acceptance of this rule by the courts was Civ. 11 Jan. 1922, S 1924.1.105 note Demogue. As we have seen, the rule does not prevent pre-contractural liability in delict, e.g., above p. 308. There is a further exception to the rule where a person travelling under a contract is injured in a motor-vehicle accident; such a person may rely on the special liability rules governing motor-vehicle accidents despite the presence of an *obligation de sécurité: loi* no. 85-677 of 5 Jul. 1985, art. 1 and see below, p. 400 ff.

[263] R. Rodière, 'Etude de la dualité des régimes de la responsabilité—la combinaison des deux responsabilités', JCP 1950.I.868.

[264] A. Weir, 'Multiple Grounds of Claim', Int. Enc. Comp. Law (Tubingen, 1982) Vol. XI, Chap. 12, 28 and see below pp. 364 and 381 respectively.

[265] Art. 1341 A.-p.r.

provision reflects the drafters' general concern to show a special preference to the victims of personal injuries[266].

3. The interpretation of contracts

While from time to time French lawyers do distinguish between the express and implied agreement of the parties, this is not as pervasive a distinction as is found in English law in relation to express and implied contract terms nor does it have the latter's significance. Instead, the French starting-point in determining the effects of a contract is to look into what was the common ('subjective') intention of the parties and in this respect no distinction needs to be drawn between what they expressly and what they impliedly agreed.[267] Questions of what the parties agreed are treated as ones of interpretation, whether this relates to determining what was included within their agreement or what meaning should be attributed to words which they clearly did include.

The Civil Code gives some nine principles of interpretation of contracts, requiring, for example, that the judges should 'look for the common intentions of the parties rather than keeping to the literal sense of the words which they use' or that they should prefer an interpretation which gives some effect to a clause over one which denies it any effect.[268] These principles are very broad and have been treated merely as 'advice to judges... without any mandatory character'.[269] Indeed, the Cour de cassation has accepted since 1808 that questions of inter-pretation of contracts are in principle a matter of fact for the 'sovereign power of assessment' of the *juges du fond*, and are, therefore, immune from its own interfer-ence.[270] This clearly gives the lower courts very considerable room for coming to 'equitable' results in their decisions under the cloak of deciding issues of fact,[271] though given their very nature the extent to which they take advantage of this must generally be a matter of conjecture. One striking example may, however, be found in a case concerning a contract concluded in 1957 granting a right to exploit a gravel quarry[272]. In order to calculate the annual payments to be made to the quarry's owner, the contract referred to the price per metric cube of gravel fixed according to an index which had ceased to operate. In these circumstances, the Cour de cassation held that the *juges du fond* were entitled to fix the pay-ments in their 'sovereign assessment' of the common intention of the parties by

---

[266] G. Viney, *De la responsabilité civile (Arts. 1340 à 1386), Exposé des motifs* in *Avant-projet de réforme*, 165.

[267] Mazeaud and Chabas, *Obligations*, 331.

[268] Arts. 1156 and 1157 C. civ. respectively and see arts. 1158–64 C. civ.

[269] Req. 16 Feb. 1892, S 1893.1.409 (re art. 1156 C. civ). This is not, however, true of consumer contracts which must in cases of doubt be interpreted in the way most favourable to the consumer (art. L. 133-2 C. consom.): here, the Cour de cassation intervenes if it considers that a lower court has failed to do so: Civ. (1) 21 Jan. 2003, D 2003.2600 note Claret.

[270] Ch. réun. 2 Feb. 1808, S 1808.1.183.

[271] Mazeaud and Chabas, *Obligations*, 339.

[272] Civ. (3) 12 Jan. 2005, Bull. civ. III no. 4, *RDC* 2005.1018 note Mazeaud.

reference to an index commonly in use in the industry. As Mazeaud notes, here the lower courts were allowed to revise the contract where the parties' overall bargain ('*l'économie du contrat*') needed to be rescued.[273]

However, the discretion of the *juges du fond* has two very important limits. First, the Cour de cassation will intervene in order to ensure that 'clear and precise clauses' are given their intended effect, thereby preventing the clauses' *dénaturation*.[274] Thus, in one case, the decision of a lower court which had denied effect to a perfectly clear (and standard) clause in a contract of liability insurance was quashed: the lower courts must not 'under the pretext of equity exclude the legal consequences of agreements'.[275] Secondly, the legal classification (as sale, gift or hire etc.) of what the parties have agreed is a matter of law and, therefore, within the control of the Cour de cassation: neither the parties' expressed view nor the decision of the *juges du fond* are conclusive.[276] This is of enormous importance, for many legal consequences flow from a contract's classification.

4. *The legal incidents of contracts*

French law combines a concern with looking into the true intentions of the parties with a tradition of regulation of their contracts once made. As article 1135 of the Civil Code states:

> Contracts create obligations not merely in relation to what they expressly provide, but also to all the consequences which equity, custom or legislation give to them according to their nature.

This provision therefore explicitly recognizes equity, custom and legislation as a proper source of obligations attaching to the agreement of the parties.

As to legislation, the Civil Code and subsequent laws are full of examples of legal regulation of the incidents of contracts. Thus, to take merely two examples, in contracts of sale, the seller is held to guarantee the buyer from latent defects[277] and in contracts of agency (*mandat*),[278] the agent is held to perform his commission, may be liable for its mismanagement on the basis of fault and must account to his principal.[279] These and many other legislative provisions create the incidents of the contracts to which they attach, this being the typical approach of French law to the regulation of contracts, rather than the common law use of

---

[273] *RDC* 2005.1018.

[274] Terré, Simler, and Lequette, *Obligations*, 463–464 who add that the Cour de cassation has started to create fixed interpretations for standard terms in insurance contracts. Cf. arts. 1138, 1141 A.-p.r.

[275] Civ. 4 May 1942, DC 1942. 131 note Besson.

[276] Mazeaud and Chabas, *Obligations*, 340 ff. See e.g. Civ. (3) 30 May 1969, JCP 1970.II.16173 note Hubrecht. The power of the courts to modify the parties' classification is expressly provided for by art. 12 N.c.pr.civ, and see above pp. 88–89.

[277] Art. 1641 ff C. civ.

[278] There are significant differences between *mandat* and common law agency, notably that the agent acts in the name of the principal as well as on his behalf: art. 1984 C. civ.

[279] Arts. 1991–3 C. civ.

implied term.[280] In this respect, French writers distinguish between those provisions whose effect may be modified or excluded by contrary intention (*lois supplétives*) and those whose effect may not (*lois impératives*)[281] and while most of the provisions of the Civil Code governing contracts have been held to be *supplétives*, a great deal of modern legislation is *impérative*, its provisions sometimes being designated as being a matter of *ordre public*,[282] it sometimes being stated that 'any contract term to the contrary is deemed not written'.[283] In all this, it is important to note that whether *supplétive* or *impérative*, the interpretation of any legal incident to a contract is a matter of law and therefore within the control of the Cour de cassation.

The existence and content of custom (*usage*), on the other hand, is a matter for the *juges du fond*.[284] Its importance lies particularly in the context of commercial contracts, where trade practice can fill in the gaps of what has been agreed by the parties,[285] though the courts will do so only if both parties to the contract are members of the trade.[286]

The modern significance of 'equity' as a source of contractual obligations is more controversial, this question usually focusing on the legitimacy of the creation of the two sets of obligations attributed to it, *obligations de sécurité* (obligations as to the safety of the person or property of a contracting party[287]) and *obligations d'information* (obligations to provide information to the other party).[288] Outside these established contexts the courts rarely expressly rely on it as a ground for their decisions.[289]

Obligations de sécurité are important in modern practice and demonstrate the willingness of French jurists to manipulate the legal concepts at their disposal in the interests of social policy. Their origin in the late nineteenth century lay in a concern that the law left many victims of the machine age without compensation, since the law of delict as traditionally interpreted submitted the recovery of damages to a proof of fault. While some argued for a delictual solution to this problem,[290] others argued instead that contract should be used to this effect, so that, notably, an employer would be held liable for failing to perform a contractual obligation as to the safety of his workers, such a non-performance not

---

[280] B. Nicholas, 'Rules and terms—civil law and common law' (1974) 48 Tul LR 946, 950.

[281] Mazeaud and Chabas, *Obligations*, 337.

[282] e.g. *loi* no. 89-462 of 6 July 1989, art. 2, concerning all the subsequent provisions with regard to the relations between tenant and landlord of residential premises.

[283] e.g. art. 1152 al. 2 C. civ. (as amended).

[284] Civ. (1) 15.1.1963, GP 1963.1.211.

[285] Terré, Simler, and Lequette *Obligations*, 457.

[286] Com. 18 Jan. 1972, JCP 1972.II.17072.

[287] Art. 1150 A-p.r.

[288] These obligations are sometimes based on a principle of good faith, on which see above p. 307 and below pp. 332–334.

[289] Mazeaud and Chabas, *Obligations*, 339.

[290] Below p. 381 ff.

requiring proof of lack of care.[291] This approach was followed in 1911 as regards carriers of passengers[292] and soon spread from this context to others, notably, accidents in the course of fairground rides.[293] However, in the course of the 1930s a second wave of *obligations de sécurité* can be seen, whose purpose was exactly the opposite of the first wave. For rather than allowing a victim of personal injuries to recover damages without proof of fault, the effect of this wave was to curtail the strict delictual liability for the 'actions of things' which had recently been constructed from article 1384 al.l of the Civil Code.[294] For, by constructing *obligations de sécurité* which required merely the taking of reasonable care (*obligations de moyens*)[295] and applying the rule of *non-cumul des responsabilités*, which rules out recourse to delict where a contractual obligation governs the issue in question, a claimant is prevented from reliance on this strict delictual liability, leaving only liability for contractual negligence.[296] In the modern law, therefore, *obligations de sécurité* may either impose strict liability or liability based on negligence, the courts apparently proceeding 'empirically' in deciding which to adopt, relying on their sense of the appropriateness of one or the other rather than on any general criterion,[297] although it has been said that in recent years the courts have shown themselves more willing to impose stricter liabilities in this way in the interests of ensuring compensation for the victims of personal injuries.[298]

5. Performance in good faith

Article 1134, al. 3 of the Civil Code declares laconically that '[contracts] must be performed in good faith'.[299] The traditional approach to this provision was to say that it added little to the idea that true agreement was the basis of contracts and made them binding and that good faith required merely that one keep to one's agreements and that they be interpreted according to the parties' true intentions rather than the words which they used.[300] However, while contemporary jurists recognize

---

[291] e.g. J.-E. Labbé, note, S 1885.4.25.

[292] Civ. 21 Nov. 1911, S 1912.1.73 note Lyon-Caen, D 1913.1.249 note Sarrut.

[293] Nantes 28 Jan. 1931, Rec. gén. des ass. terr. 1931. 837.

[294] Below p. 381 ff.

[295] Below p. 342 ff.

[296] Above pp. 328–329. Thus, classically, a (private) surgeon was not held strictly liable for the 'actions' of his scalpel', but was instead held to a contractual obligation to his patient to take proper care: Civ. 20 May 1936, DP 1936.1.88, *rapp.* Josserand, concl. Matter (though the effect of reclassification to contract on the facts was favourable to the patient). In 2002, the liability of medical practitioners and hospitals (whether public or private) was placed by legislation on a general basis of fault, without making clear whether the liability was contractual or extra-contractual: *loi* no. 2002-303 of 4 Mar. 2002, art. 98 creating arts. L. 1142-1 ff C. santé publique and see below, p. 408 ff.

[297] Terré, Simler, and Lequette, *Obligations*, 584.

[298] Bénabent, *Obligations*, 285.

[299] See generally Terré, Simler, and Lequette, *Obligations*, 442ff; Fabre-Magnan, *Obligations*, 63–65, 69–77.

[300] V. Marcadé, *Explication théorique et pratique du Code Napoléon*, 6th edn. (Paris, 1869) t. IV, 396; G. Marty and P. Raynaud, *Droit civil*, t. II, vol. I, *Les obligations* (Paris, 1962), 204.

this originally limited significance, they then add that good faith has acquired a much greater significance and practical importance in the modern law.[301]

First, French law recognizes the significance of good faith or (conversely) bad faith in the performance or the non-performance of contracts in particular ways. So, for example, the Civil Code provides different rules depending on whether a party's contractual non-performance is innocent and where it is *dolosive* (here meaning deliberate or dishonest[302]) to govern what a common lawyer would see as remoteness of damage and to govern how much is to be paid (whether as interest or as damages) for delay in performance of monetary obligations.[303] Conversely, a contractual debtor who fails in good faith to perform on time may be granted more time to perform (*un délai de grâce*) by a court.[304] Moreover, the general approach of French courts to the validity of exemption clauses may be seen to be related to the idea of good faith, for while in principle they are valid, an exception is made where the party in default has committed *dol* (dishonesty or deliberate default) or *faute lourde* (gross fault).[305]

Secondly, and much more controversially, the idea of contractual good faith has been taken up and put to wider use by the courts. In this respect, it has become generally accepted that good faith in performance has acquired two particular expressions in the case law: a 'duty of loyalty' (which sanctions *bad* faith) and a 'duty of co-operation' (which is a 'duty to ensure the greatest effectiveness of a contract to the benefit of both parties').[306] An example of breach of the duty of loyalty can be seen in a decision of the Cour de cassation in 1999.[307] There C had in 1977 sold her life interest in a property to her niece S, who agreed in return to pay an annual, index-linked sum, on default of which C had the power to terminate the contract on notice. In 1990 (and just before she died), C served notice on S to pay arrears for the previous 12 years and on C's death, C's daughter sued for the full amount and purported to terminate the contract under the express term. The *juges du fond* accepted this claim, but their decision was quashed by the Cour de cassation on the basis that they had failed to consider whether in the circumstances (and in particular given C's failure to claim payment over the years) reliance on the power of termination showed a lack of good faith. An example of the 'duty of cooperation' may be found in the case of a party to a contract taking advantage of the other party's failure to claim for essential services rendered under it[308] or where a person who has granted by contract an exclusive concession to another person deprives the latter of the means of operating the

---

[301] Flour, Aubert, and Savaux, *Acte juridique*, 314; Terré, Simler, and Lequette, *Obligations*, 442–443.

[302] Arts. 1150–1151 C. civ.

[303] Art. 1153 al. 4, referring to *mauvaise foi*.

[304] Art. 1244-1 C. civ and see below, p. 351.

[305] Below, p. 356.

[306] Flour, Aubert, and Savaux, *Acte juridique*, 314–315.

[307] Civ. (1) 16 Feb. 1999, Bull. civ. I no. 52.

[308] Civ. (1) 23 Jan. 1996, Bull. civ. I no. 36.

concession at competitive rates.[309] On the other hand, the Cour de cassation has held that the principle of good faith does not apply after the contract has come to an end, for example, on the satisfaction of a 'suspensive condition'.[310]

Clearly, some jurists consider that the principle of good faith is a useful way for French contract law to be or to become more 'social', even more *solidariste*, allowing the Cour de cassation to 'promote a degree of good citizenship in the relationship of parties to a contract, this being preferable to the cynicism which an exclusively economic understanding of contractual relations could bring'.[311] However, other jurists warn against the potentially subjective and uncertain nature of the concept,[312] or deny the vision of contracts as 'a little society where each party works for a common good' on the basis that 'far from being the product of an *entente cordiale*, contracts often appear as the result of a tension between antagonistic interests, the striking of a balance between divergent interests'.[313] So, 'the duty of good faith does not oblige a person to protect the interests of another person to the detriment of his own interest, as some of the partisans of the unlikely notion of "contractual solidarity" contend'.[314] Given these fundamental contrasts of approach, both the notion of good faith and its use by the courts is likely to remain contested in French law.

6. *Discharge and the timing of performance*

French lawyers usually describe the performance of a contractual obligation as its *exécution*, but where this has the effect of discharging that party from his obligation, they call it *paiement* ('satisfaction'), a term which is not, as may be imagined, restricted to the discharge of money obligations.[315] The Civil Code contains various rules relating to *paiement* in this sense,[316] concerning, for example, the question whether a third party can discharge an obligation[317] or whether the 'creditor' of the obligation has to accept partial performance when tendered.[318]

---

[309] Com. 3 Nov. 1992, Bull. civ. IV no. 338.

[310] Civ. (3) 14 Jul. 2005, D 2006.761 note Mazeaud, JCP 2005.II.10173 note Loiseau. 'An obligation contracted under a suspensive condition is one which depends on either a future, uncertain event, or an event which has already happened but is not yet known to the parties.' (art. 1181 C.civ.) Mazeaud criticizes the decision inter alia on the basis of its inconsistency with the established use of good faith at the stage of pre-contractual negotiations, on which see above, p. 305.

[311] D. Mazeaud, 'La politique contractuelle de la Cour de cassation' in *Libre propos sur les sources du droit, Mélanges en l'honneur de Philippe Jestaz* (Paris, 2006) 371, 382.

[312] Flour, Aubert, and Savaux, *Acte juridique*, 315.

[313] Terré, Simler, and Lequette, *Obligations*, 443 quoting R. Demogue, *Traité des obligations en général*, t.VI (1931), 9.

[314] Malaurie, Aynès, and Stoffel-Munck, *Obligations*, 373.

[315] Ibid., 579.

[316] Art. 1235 ff C. civ.

[317] Art. 1236 C. civ. (yes, in certain circumstances).

[318] Art. 1244 C. civ. (no).

French law's approach to the time when performance is due is also unfamiliar to a common lawyer. Its starting-point is a sharp distinction between the existence of a contractual obligation and its actionability.[319] Thus, where a party agrees to undertake an obligation, in principle performance is due immediately on contract, although in the case of obligations to perform services, the courts allow a reasonable period for performance.[320] If, though, the parties have fixed a time for performance of a party's obligation, this creates what is called a *terme suspensif*, which may be defined as that part of an agreement which delays performance of an engagement rather than suspending it.[321] The Civil Code provides that where an obligation is due only on a certain event (typically a date), its performance cannot be claimed before the occurrence of that event[322] and what this also means is that French law has no room for a doctrine akin to the common law doctrine of 'anticipatory breach', under which a party who repudiates a contract before the time for performance may be liable in damages or to have the contract terminated immediately, rather than only when performance falls due.[323]

B. Privity of Contract and the Effect of Contracts beyond the Parties

The Civil Code states clearly French law's adherence to a principle of privity of contract, known there as the 'relative effect of contracts.' Thus, article 1165 provides that, '[c]ontracts have effects only as between the contracting parties: they do not prejudice third parties and benefit them only in the situation provided for by article 1121'. In French law this principle stands on its own authority and flows from the personal nature of agreement, there being no doctrine of consideration by which it can be buttressed or with which it can be confused.[324] This also affects French law's definition of a party to a contract, who is simply someone who is party to the agreement, 'the person who by his act of will [*sa volonté*] is found at the origin of the formation of the contract'.[325]

However, article 1165 does not give a proper picture of the positive law, for while French law allows contracts to impose obligations on third parties only

---

[319] Nicholas, *French Contract*, 158–159.

[320] Bénabent, *Obligations*, 230.

[321] Art. 1185 C. civ. It is, therefore, to be contrasted with *condition* in that the latter may suspend the party's obligation itself, this suspension being dependent on the occurrence of a future but uncertain event: art. 1168 C. civ.

[322] Art. 1186 C. civ.

[323] S. Whittaker, 'How does French law deal with anticipatory breaches of contract?' (1996) 45 *ICLQ* 662.

[324] Cf. Law Commission, *Privity of Contract: Contracts for the Benefit of Third Parties* (Law Com. No 242, London, 1996) 68 ff.

[325] J. Mestre, RTDCiv 1988, 125.

exceptionally,[326] there are many situations in which it recognizes the rights of someone not party to a contract to enforce its obligations.[327]

As to the burden of French contracts, we should note that French lawyers distinguish their general denial of any *obligational* effect on third parties from their acceptance of *factual* effects. So, for example, the transfer of title to property under a contract of sale may well have effects on third parties (notably, on the seller's creditors). Similarly, French law recognizes that a person who knowingly induces a party to a contract to break it may be liable in damages for delictual fault to the other party to the contract.[328] And where a person enjoys a contractual right of pre-emption over property, he may obtain the annulment of a sale to a third party made in breach of this right where that third party knows of the pre-emptive right and of its holder's intention to exercise it; he may also obtain an order to be substituted to the rights of the third party in the same circumstances.[329] In all these cases, the contract is said to be 'opposable' against the third parties in question.[330]

There are, by contrast, five important ways in which French law allows the benefit of a contract to be enjoyed by a third party despite the principle of 'relative effect.'

First, the parties to a contract may by their agreement create rights in third parties against one or other of them (by *stipulation pour autrui*), support being found for this in article 1121 of the Civil Code, even though it is clear that this article was intended to deal with the effectiveness of such a contract as between the parties themselves.[331] French courts have, despite the terms of article 1121, accepted that the only requirement other than the parties' agreement which is required is that the promisee has a 'moral interest' in the performance of the promise and it is rare for the third party's rights to be denied by a court for the lack of such an interest.[332] What then is the test of agreement for the designation of the third party beneficiary? Three classes of third party can be discerned in theory:

(i) those who simply stand to benefit from performance of a contract, so-called incidental beneficiaries;[333]

---

[326] An exception is to be found in French law's treatment of 'collective agreements' found in labour relations and the relations of landlords and tenants: Malaurie, Aynès, and Stoffel-Munck, *Obligations*, 424–425.

[327] See generally S. Whittaker, 'Privity of Contract and the Law of Tort: the French Experience' (1995) 15 OJLS 327; D. Mazeaud, 'Contracts and Third Parties in the *Avant-projet de réforme*' and S. Vogenauer, 'The Effects of Contracts on Third Parties: the *Avant-projet de réforme* in a Comparative Perspective' in Cartwright, Vogenauer and Whittaker, *Reforming the French Law of Obligations*, Ch. 10 and 11 respectively.

[328] Below p. 380.

[329] Civ. (3) 24 Feb. 2007, *Droit des sociétés* 2007 no. 63.

[330] Terré, Simler, and Lequette, *Obligations*, 492; art. 1165-2 A,-p.r. ff.

[331] Nicholas, *French Contract*, 182–4.

[332] Malaurie, Aynès, Terré, Simler and Stoffel-Munck, *Obligations*, 411–412. See arts. 1171–1171-4 A.-p.r. which gives effect to the case law.

[333] Nicholas, *French Contract*, 190. For example, if an owner of property, A, agrees not to burn garden refuse in his garden with his neighbour, B, his other neighbour, C, may benefit factually from A and B's contract, even if they did not intend that he should do so.

(i) those who are intended by the parties to benefit from performance; and

(ii) those third parties who are intended by the parties to the contract to have rights in regard to that performance.

While the distinction between classes (ii) and (iii) is not particularly prominent in French jurists, who often talk simply in terms of 'stipulations for third parties',[334] others make clear that an intention to create a direct right in the third party must be established.[335] However, this subtle distinction does not appear in the cases, where the intention of the parties to benefit the third party lies within the 'sovereign power of assessment' of the *juges du fond*.[336] This means in practice that the lower courts possess a considerable discretion to find the existence of contracts for the benefit of third parties, ostensibly on the basis of the implied intention of the parties, but often for thinly disguised reasons of policy which have nothing to do with intention.[337] The extent to which they have been willing to do so has varied considerably over the years and can be seen as contingent on the availability or otherwise of other mechanisms for achieving the result desired, some of these other mechanisms being contractual, some delictual. After a degree of popularity in the 1930s, implied contracts for the benefit of third parties fell out of favour in the 1960s and 1970s,[338] enjoyed a certain resurgence particularly in the commercial area in the 1980s,[339] but may be on the wane again.[340]

A second important way in which the benefit of contractual rights has been extended to third parties is by *actions directes*. The Civil Code itself contains examples of these, so that, for example, a principal may sue his sub-agent directly, whether or not the latter was authorized by him.[341] However, the courts have also recognized the existence of *actions directes*, notably in the context of liability for defective products and buildings.[342] Thus, for example, a sub-purchaser of a motorcar may sue not merely its retailer, but also its distributor or manufacturer *in contract*, the initial buyer's rights in respect of latent defects being said to be transferred with the property itself as its 'accessory'. This construction may therefore be formally reconciled with privity by holding that the sub-purchaser is

---

[334] e.g. Carbonnier, *Obligations*, 2137–2140.

[335] Larroumet, *Contrat*, 964; G. Légier, 'Stipulation pour autrui', Jur.-Cl. Civ., Art. 1121, Fasc. 1 (Paris, 1986), 8.

[336] See Civ. (1) 21 Nov. 1978, D 1980.309 note Carreau.

[337] For striking examples, see Civ. 6 Dec. 1932 and Civ. 24 May 1933, S 1934.1.81 note Esmein (passenger in train contracting for right of dependent relative under carrier's strict *obligation de sécurité*); Civ. (2) 20 Oct. 2005, Bull. civ. II no. 274. (hospital contracting for right in its patient against supplier of blood contaminated with HIV virus).

[338] G. Viney, *La responsabilité: conditions* 1st edn. (LGDJ, Paris, 1982) 222–223.

[339] J. Mestre, RTDCiv 1990.71.

[340] Civ. (1) 28 Oct. 2003, D 2004.233 (no implied *stipulation pour autrui* for benefit of relatives of persons killed while abroad under a holiday travel contract).

[341] Art. 1994 al. 2 C. civ.and see Whittaker, (above n. 327), 361 ff.

[342] Civ. 12 Nov. 1884, S 1886.1.149, DP 1885.1.357; Civ. (1) 9 Oct. 1979, D 1980.IR.222 note Larroumet, GP 1980.1.249 note Planqueel (both sale); art. 1792 C. civ., as amended (buildings) confirming earlier *jurisprudence*.

suing only as the *ayant cause* (successor in title) of the original contractor, but this is far from convincing. And while this sort of *action directe* was clearly invented so as to create a direct right in sub-purchasers where none previously existed,[343] in the modern law it can sometimes work to their disadvantage. For the courts have accepted that the rule of *non-cumul des responsabilités contractuelle et délictuelle* applies to this situation, so that a sub-purchaser who holds (or held) a contractual action cannot sue in delict instead.[344] On the other hand, although for a while the Cour de cassation appeared to go further and accept the idea proposed in *la doctrine* that the members of a 'group of contracts' should be able to sue each other in contract *but only in contract* and subject to a double limit of the terms and restrictions of the two contracts under which they participate in the group,[345] in 1991 its Assemblée plénière firmly rejected it,[346] swayed in part by the inherent vagueness of the notion of a 'group of contracts' and in part by the severely prejudicial effect on those held to be within them.[347] Interestingly, though, the idea of 'contractual groups' has not entirely disappeared, as the *Avant-projet de réforme* uses it so as to give effect to exemption clauses, arbitration clauses and choice of jurisdiction clauses in a contract 'within a group of contracts' whose 'performance is necessary for the putting into effect of a group operation'.[348]

Thirdly, the courts have extended the benefit of contracts indirectly through their reinterpretation of the notion of delictual fault.[349] The traditional view of the courts was that non-performance of a contractual obligation which causes harm to a third party may or may not constitute a delictual fault so as to give rise to delictual liability to that third party, depending on the nature of the fault apart from the contract: 'as a third party cannot take advantage of the contract, any fault in a party to the contract should not be assessed by reference to the contractual standard.'[350] However, during the 1990s the First Chamber of the Cour de cassation on occasion held that non-performance of a contractual obligation (even a strict *obligation de résultat*[351]) in itself constitutes delictual fault so as to attract liability to a person not party to or otherwise within the domain of protection of the contract.[352] For example, in one case, the daughter of a person who died of AIDS having received blood contaminated by HIV from the national blood transfusion service was held to benefit from the very strict contractual liability which it had constructed for this purpose towards the recipient

---

[343] C. Jamin, 'Une restauration de l'effet relatif du contrat' D 1991 Chron. 257, 259.

[344] Civ. (1) 9 Oct. 1979, GP 1980.1.249 note Planqueel, D 1980.IR.222 note Larroumet.

[345] Civ. (1) 21 Jun. 1988, D 1989.5 note Larroumet, JCP 1988.II.21125 note Jourdain.

[346] Ass. plén. 12 Jul. 1991, JCP 1991.II.21743 note Viney.

[347] Whittaker (above, n. 327) 354–357.

[348] Arts. 1172–1172-3 A.-p.r.

[349] On which see below, pp. 364 ff more generally.

[350] Bénabent, *Obligations*, 379 and see Civ. (3) 18 Apr. 1972, Bull. civ. III no. 233; Civ. (1) 11 Apr. 1995, Bull. civ. no. 171.

[351] Below, p. 342.

[352] Civ. (1) 15 Dec. 1998, Bull. civ. I no. 368; Civ. (1) 18 Jul. 2000, Bull. civ. I no. 221.

of the blood.[353] On the other hand, in other cases the Commercial Chamber of the Cour de cassation upheld the traditional position.[354] In 2006 the Assemblée plénière of the Cour de cassation brought this uncertainty to an end, ruling firmly that 'a third party to a contract may on the basis of delictual liability invoke a contractual failure to perform whenever this failure has caused him harm'.[355] As a result, a company running a business under a contract with a tenant was held entitled to sue the landlord directly for damages to cover the cost of repairs of the premises. According to Viney, this decision made clear that any contractual non-performance could give rise to liability towards a third party and that the legal ground of this liability was delict rather than contract.[356] However, while approving the former, she criticizes the latter on the basis that the Cour de cassation's 'choice of the delictual regime allows a third party to empty a contract of part of its content and even, on occasion, substitute a strict [delictual liability] for a [contractual] liability for fault based on a failure to perform an *obligation de moyens*.'[357] As Viney observes, while formally this result does not contradict the rule of *non-cumul*,[358] it defeats its main purpose of defending the contract from the intrusive and prejudicial effects of delictual liability rules.[359] Following this way of thinking, article 1342 of the *Avant-projet de réforme* provides that:

[w]here non-performance of a contractual obligation is the direct cause of harm suffered by a third party, the latter can claim reparation from the contractual debtor on the basis of [the contractual liability provisions of the *Avant-projet*]. The third party is then subject to all the limits and conditions which apply to the creditor in obtaining reparation for his own harm.

He may equally obtain reparation on the basis of extra-contractual liability, but on condition that he establishes one of the circumstances giving rise to liability envisaged by [the delictual liability provisions].

If enacted (or if taken up and given effect by the courts) this would apparently allow a third party seeking damages to choose between relying on a contractual non-performance but subject to the contract's restrictions and relying on delict as long as the independent grounds of delict are satisfied.

Fourthly, the Cour de cassation has sometimes extended the benefit of the terms of a contract to a third party by means of the idea of the 'opposability' of the contract.[360] A good example may be found in a case where a block of apartments had been sold to buyers who had financed their purchases by loans from

---

[353] Civ. (1) 13 Feb. 2001, Bull. civ. I no. 35 and see below, pp. 403 ff.
[354] Com. 8 Oct. 2002, JCP 2003 Chron. 152 no. 3 obs. Viney.
[355] Ass. plén. 6 Oct. 2006, D 2006.2825 note G. Viney.
[356] Viney, ibid.
[357] Viney, ibid. On *obligation de moyens*, see below, p. 342.
[358] Above, pp. 328–329.
[359] Viney, D 2006.2825.
[360] Above, p. 336.

banks.[361] The contracts of sale were later annulled for fraud (*dol*)[362] and fraud was also found in the *notaire*[363] who had authenticated them. As the contracts of loan were also annulled on the ground of being dependent on the contracts of sale, one of the banks claimed damages against the *notaire* on the basis of the latter's delictual fault. However, the *notaire* successfully contended that his liability in damages was limited to the amount set by an express term in the contract of loan by way of compensation for early termination of the contract by the borrower. In the view of the Cour de cassation, this term was 'opposable' against the bank in its claim against the *notaire*: the annulment of the contract of loan could not cause the banks any greater loss than the sum deemed by the express term to compensate them on voluntary termination by the borrower. For 'while, in principle, contracts affect only the contracting parties, they constitute juridical facts from which consequences for third parties may be deduced'.[364] It is in the context of this sort of development that article 1165-2 of the *Avant-projet de réforme* should be viewed, this providing that '[c]ontracts may be invoked by and against third parties; the latter must respect them and can take advantage of them, though they do not have a right to require their performance'. The breadth of this description of the 'opposability' of contracts catches very well the attenuated force of the principle of privity of contract in modern French law, even if in rather an allusive manner.

Fifthly, after many years of discussion, a *loi* of 2007 introduced into French law provision for the creation by *contract* of *une fiducie*, a new legal device which in some quarters is represented as an equivalent of the common law trust (though to a common lawyer it lacks many of the latter's key features).[365] Under this legislation, a corporate body (the *constituant* or transferor) can by contract transfer property to a corporate financial or investment institution (the *fiduciaire* or tranferee) 'acting for a specified purpose for the benefit' of a third person (the *bénéficiaire* or beneficiary) who may be a corporate or human person.[366] The *fiduciaire* receives title to the property transferred and is responsible to account to the *constituant* and to the beneficiary in respect of the accomplishment of the purpose entrusted to him[367] and is liable personally for any fault which he commits in the

---

[361] Civ. (1) 10 May 2005, D 2006.115 note Guérgan-Lécuyer.

[362] Above, p. 308.

[363] Above, pp. 76–77.

[364] Civ. (1) 10 May 2005, cit. n. 361.

[365] Loi no. 2007-211 of 19 Feb. 2007 *instituant la fiducie* whose art. 1 introduces new provisions into the Civil Code. See further P. Bouteiller, JCP (ed. entreprise et affaires) 2007.I.1404. Perhaps the most important feature of the English trust which is lacking is that the beneficiary has no right to trace the property subject to the *fiducie* in the hands of persons to whom it is transferred in breach of its terms unless the latter was shown to have been *actually aware* that the *fiduciaire* acted beyond its authority (art. 2023 C. civ.) whereas in English law only the bona fide purchaser for value without notice (actual or constructive) takes free of the trust.

[366] Arts. 2011–2012, 2014, 2015 C. civ.

[367] Art. 2022 C. civ.

course of his task.[368] The property is protected from any insolvency proceedings affecting the *fiduciaire*.[369] Quite apart from the restrictions made in respect of the nature of the persons entitled to enter a contract of *fiducie*, the legislation further specifies that it may not be entered with the intention of conferring a gratuitous benefit on the third party beneficiary,[370] the legislator seeking to avoid any overlap or potential clash with existing French law governing gifts and succession. This means that a contract of *fiducie* will not be valid unless the third party has entered or enters another contract under which he confers a benefit on the *constituant*, unless the *constituant* and the *bénéficiaire* are the same person[371] (which is specifically permitted).[372] Indeed, while it is not possible to predict the range of uses to which the new device will be put, its main intended uses are to provide legal bases for secured suretyship (*la fiducie sûreté*)[373] and for fiduciary property management (*la fiducie gestion*).[374] Nevertheless, the new law does allow the parties to a contract of *fiducie* to confer benefits on third parties (the beneficiary) in a different way from the traditional *stipulation pour autrui*.[375]

C. Contractual Fault, Non-Performance,[376] and its Excuses

1. What is 'contractual fault'?

Traditionally French jurists have accepted that contractual liability is founded on a contractual *faute* (fault),[377] but a common lawyer needs to treat this with considerable caution, for in this general sense, *faute* means no more than a 'breach of duty', the duty in question being the obligation imposed by the contract itself[378] and it is difficult not to agree with those who say that such a broad view is taken simply in order to uphold the idea that all liability (*responsabilité*) must

---

[368] Art. 2026 C. civ.

[369] Art. 2024 C. civ.

[370] Art. 2012 C. civ (on pain of 'absolute nullity').

[371] Boutellier, cit. n. 365 at 16.

[372] Art. 2016 C. civ.

[373] Here, a 'creditor/transferee' is also designated by the contract of *fiducie* as beneficiary and therefore finds that the property transferred is protected if the debtor (the transferor) becomes insolvent: Boutellier, cit. n. 365 at 16, 17.

[374] Here, the transferor is designated by the contract of *fiducie* as the beneficiary and therefore can recover the enhanced value of the property in the hands of the *fiduciaire*, which is again protected from the latter's insolvency: Boutellier, cit. n. 365 at 16, 17.

[375] Above, pp. 336–337.

[376] The rather clumsy 'non-performance' is used for *inexécution* in preference to 'breach (of contract)' as in English law the latter by definition is capable of giving rise to liability in damages (frustration of a contract rules out breach, rather than excusing it), whereas *inexécution* of a contractual obligation will *not* give rise to damages where non-performance is excused by *force majeure*.

[377] e.g. P. Esmein, 'Le fondement de la responsabilité contractuelle rapprochée de la responsabilité délictuelle' RTDCiv 1933. 627 at 630 ff. On the debate concerning the legitimacy of the notion of *la responsabilité contractuelle*, see below, pp. 352–353.

[378] Starck *et al.*, *Contrat*, 584. Cf. a similarly broad understanding of *la faute délictuelle*, below p. 365 ff.

be based on *faute*.[379] Moreover, such an understanding of fault leaves open the question to what standard of care French law holds parties to a contract in relation to performance of what they have agreed: is it absolute, strict or based on negligence? The general provisions of the Civil Code are no clear guide on this point: article 1137 requires that a person entrusted with the keeping of property must take all the care of a *bon père de famille*, the French equivalent of the 'reasonable man', this being said to vary in intensity according to the type of contract; but article 1147 provides that where a person has failed to perform an obligation, he is liable in damages subject only to a defence of *force majeure*. Some writers reconcile these provisions by saying that in the case of the former, fault needs to be proved, whereas in the latter there is a presumption of fault, which can be rebutted only by proof of *force majeure*,[380] but by the middle of the 20th century[381] French lawyers had in general adopted an analysis of the various contents of contractual obligations,[382] into *obligations de moyens, obligations de résultat* and *obligations de garantie*. Thus, an *obligation de moyens* (or *obligation de diligence*) requires a person to take the care necessary to achieve the result envisaged by the contract, the classical example being a doctor who (in general) is bound only to take proper care of his patients, not owing them any obligation to ensure that they get better.[383] An *obligation de résultat* (or *obligation déterminée*) on the other hand, requires a person to achieve a particular result, though it allows the excuse for non-performance of *force majeure*, the typical example being a carrier who is held to deliver both goods and passengers 'safe and sound' to their destination.[384] Finally, an *obligation de garantie* requires a person to achieve a particular result come what may, so that he is liable for any failure even in the case of *force majeure*.[385] Where, as normally, a legislative source of a particular contractual obligation does not make clear into which of these categories it falls, this classification is undertaken by the courts, who treat it as a matter of law (and therefore within the control of the Cour de cassation).[386] While various suggestions have been made as to the criteria on which they should do so, none are entirely convincing, the courts appearing swayed rather by considerations of

---

[379] e.g. Starck *et al.*, *Contrat*, ibid.

[380] Carbonnier, *Obligations*, 2190; Terré, Simler, and Lequette, *Obligations*, 565–566.

[381] The distinction between *obligations de moyens* and *obligations de résultat* was R. Demogue's, see his *Traité des obligations en général* (Paris, 1923) t. V, 536 ff.

[382] Malaurie, Aynès and Stoffel-Munck, *Obligations*, 491 ff.

[383] Civ. 20 May 1936, DP 1936.1.88, *rapp.* Josserand, *concl.* Matter. In 2002 the liability of doctors and hospitals was put by *loi* on a common basis of 'fault' without specifying whether this was contractual or extra-contractual: below, pp. 408 ff. For a general definition of *obligation de moyens* see art. 1149 al. 2 A.-p.r.

[384] Art. 1784 C. civ. (goods); Civ. 21 Nov. 1911, S 1912.1.73 note Lyon-Caen, D 1913.1.249 note Sarrut (persons). For a general definition of *obligation de résultat* see art. 1149 al. 1 A.-p.r.

[385] This possibility is recognized by art. 1302 C. civ. Examples of legally imposed *obligations de garantie* of differing contents may be found in arts. 1626 ff and 1641 ff C. civ. (sale) and arts. 1693 ff C. civ. (assignment).

[386] Nicholas, *French Contract*, 54.

policy.[387] The law is further complicated in that the courts sometimes impose an obligation on a party to a contract which falls between the trichotomy and so, for example, a garage is held to an *obligation de résultat atténuée* in respect of repair of a vehicle, being liable for any failure in its repair subject to showing that all proper care was taken.[388]

This means, of course, that fault in the sense of 'lack of care' needs to be proved to establish contractual liability for non-performance only where the obligation in question is classified as an *obligation de moyens*; there is no such need as regards either *obligations de résultat* or *de garantie*. But this does not mean that fault in a party who fails to perform is irrelevant in the case of the former of these two, for it comes into the definition of *force majeure*, which is the primary excuse for the non-performance of an *obligation de résultat*.

2. Defences to non-performance

There are two main defences for non-performance of contractual obligations, in which neither performance of the obligation nor damages for non-performance may be demanded by the injured party: *force majeure* and, in bilateral contracts, the substantial non-performance by the other party to the contract.

(a) Force majeure

The Civil Code provides that *force majeure*[389] (supervening impossibility) excuses a person from paying damages for non-performance of the obligation affected,[390] but it neither defines *force majeure* nor does it explain its effect in bilateral contracts on the other party's obligations. As has been explained, *force majeure* is relevant to contractual non-performance only as regards *obligations de résultat*, for in the case of *obligations de moyens* proof by an injured party of non-performance by definition rules out *force majeure* and in the case of *obligation de garantie* the person under the obligation bears responsibility for non-performance in circumstances of *force majeure*. It was long agreed by French lawyers that for an event to constitute *force majeure* it must possess three characteristics: 'irresistibility,' unforeseeability and 'exteriority', but from the 1990s the latter two characteristics have been the subject of considerable judicial erosion. Unfortunately, two linked decisions of the Assemblée plénière of the Cour de cassation of 14 April 2006 have not freed this area of the law from the uncertainty which this has caused.[391]

---

[387] Malaurie, Aynès, and Stoffel-Munck, *Obligations*, 494–496.

[388] Civ. (1) 22 Jun. 1983, GP 1983 Pan. jur. 304 note A.P., RTDCiv 1984. 119 obs. Rémy.

[389] We shall make no attempt to distinguish between *force majeure* (which in a narrow sense applies only to the forces of nature), *cas fortuit* and *cause étrangère*, both the Civil Code and jurists appearing to use these terms interchangeably.

[390] Art. 1147 C. civ.

[391] Ass. plén. 14 Apr. 2006, Bull. civ. Ass. plén. no. 5 D 2006.1577 note Jourdain, *RDC* 2006.1083 note Laithier (contractual liability); Ass. plén. 14 Apr. 2006, Bull. civ. Ass. plén. no. 6 (delictual liability, on which see below, pp. 390–391) JCP 2006.II.10087 note Grosser.

First and foremost (and relatively uncontroversially), the supervening event, act or circumstance must be 'irresistible'.[392] This requirement has two aspects, for it demands both that the event is not one which the party could have prevented and that, once occurring, it renders performance impossible rather than simply more onerous. Thus, where a party could have prevented the supervening event, the latter is said to be 'imputable' to him and this prevents it from excusing non-performance even where performance has become impossible.[393] As to the impossibility itself, for some jurists it must be 'absolute',[394] but this means that the courts are for the most part concerned with an 'objective' even if a 'relative' impossibility, i.e. a reasonable person in the position of the actual party to the contract must find performance impossible.[395] As Malaurie, Aynès and Stoffel-Munck put it, '[i]t is clear that the law is not absolute, it does not require the debtor to be superhuman, Tarzan, Asterix, Tintin, Superman, Rambo or the Count of Monte-Cristo; on the other hand, it does not have to accept that he be subhuman, devoid of any sense of effort'.[396] While the Cour de cassation allows the lower courts a good deal of leeway in determining the question of impossibility,[397] it has quashed decisions which go too far, declaring that *force majeure* cannot be invoked where performance is simply more difficult or burdensome as opposed to being impossible.[398]

Secondly, traditionally, the supervening event must not have been foreseeable at the time of making the contract.[399] Here, again, there is some dispute as to whether this has to be 'absolute' (so as to escape the bounds of all human foresight!) or 'relative' (normally unforeseeable), but the courts in general take the latter view, sometimes judging this from the point of view of the *bon père de famille* in the debtor's position, sometimes from the point of view of the particular debtor in question.[400] Again, the Cour de cassation leaves the lower courts considerable leeway in judging the issue of foreseeability, but intervenes where the facts as found below demonstrate that the supervening event must have been foreseeable.[401] However, recently the status of unforeseeability as a required characteristic of *force majeure* has been challenged, the Cour de cassation sometimes simply asserting that '*force majeure* is characterised solely by the "irresistibility" of an event',[402] while on other occasions holding that the 'irresistibility of an event is

---

[392] Where an act of the other party to the contract (*fait du créancier*) fulfils the conditions of *force majeure* it excludes liability in the 'debtor of the obligation' and is therefore to be distinguished from an injured party's 'contributory *fault*' (*faute de la victime*), which leads to a reduction of the award of damages: Civ. (1) 31 Jan. 1973, D 1973.149 note Schmelck.

[393] Art. 1147 C. civ. See e.g. Req. 4 Jan. 1927, S 1927.1.188, DH 1927.65, *Source-Book*, 432.

[394] Carbonnier, *Obligations*, 2200.

[395] Larroumet, *Contrat*, 832.

[396] *Obligation*, 501.

[397] Terré, Simler, and Lequette, *Obligations*, 571.

[398] e.g. Com. 18 Jan. 1950, D 1950.227, GP 1950.1.320.

[399] Carbonnier, *Obligations*, 2200.

[400] Malaurie, Aynès, and Stoffel-Munck, *Obligations*, 502.

[401] e.g. Civ. (1) 5 Feb. 1957, D 1957.178.

[402] Civ. (1) 6 Nov. 2002, Bull. civ. I no. 258 (no need for a person's illness to be unforeseeable).

enough in itself to constitute *force majeure* where foreseeing it would not allow its effects to be prevented, as long as the debtor [of the contractual obligation in question] took all requisite precautions to avoid the occurrence of the event'.[403] While in its decisions of 14 April 2006 the Assemblée plénière declared roundly that an event which was both irresistible and unforeseeable *does* constitute *force majeure* so as to excuse contractual non-performance,[404] this formulation (which suggests the retention of foreseeability as a condition) remains ambiguous as to whether the combination of these two elements is actually necessary.[405]

Thirdly, the supervening event must be 'exterior', 'outside the sphere for which the debtor was responsible'.[406] Here, two aspects have been developed. Where the subject-matter of the party's obligation is a physical thing, then whatever has caused the impossibility of its performance must be physically exterior to this thing, an aspect of *force majeure* which was first upheld in the context of delict and then applied to the contractual context.[407] On the other hand, French jurists have also used 'exteriority' to deny the activities of a party's employees or other 'agents for performance' (*préposés*) to constitute *force majeure*, so that, for example, the act of a driver of a vehicle employed by a carrier will not excuse the carrier's non-performance of its *obligation de résultat*.[408] For this purpose, the courts have taken a flexible approach to the effect of a strike by a contractual party's own workforce, for example, finding 'exteriority' satisfied where the the strike is organized from outside the party's business.[409] However, in one of its decisions of 14 April 2006 the Assemblée plénière appears to have rejected any requirement that an event must be 'exterior' for it to constitute *force majeure*, defining *force majeure* exclusively in terms of 'irresistibility' and unforeseeability and allowing the serious illness of a party to a contract to constitute *force majeure* so as to excuse his failure to provide goods to be made specially to order, a decision which is incompatible with a requirement that the event (the illness) must be exterior to the person of the debtor of a contractual obligation.[410] Nevertheless, the status of 'exteriority' is not free from doubt as the Assemblée plénière did not explicitly refer to this notion either positively or negatively[411] and the context of the decision (a contractor's personal illness) had earlier been treated rather specially.[412]

---

[403] Com. 1 Oct. 1997, Bull. civ. IV no. 240. Cf. similarly art. 1349, al. 2 A.-p.r.

[404] Ass. plén. 14 Apr. 2006, Bull. civ. Ass. plén. no. 5, cit. n. 391.

[405] Laithier, op. cit. and Grosser op. cit. say yes; Jourdain, op. cit., n. 391 says no).

[406] Carbonnier, *Obligations*, 2200.

[407] Mazeaud and Chabas, *Obligations*, 667. See e.g. Poitiers 16 Dec. 1970, JCP 1972.11.17127 note Mémeteau (botulism in a poached turbot cannot be *force majeure* so as to excuse non-performance of the *obligation de sécurité* of a restaurant who served it). For the main delictual context see below pp. 390–391 ff.

[408] Larroumet, *Contrat*, 835.

[409] See the discussion of A.-G. Besnard, *concl.* to Paris 4 Jun. 1980, JCP 1980.11.19411.

[410] Ass. plén. 14 Apr. 2006, Bull. civ. Ass. plén. no. 5.

[411] Laitier, op. cit. n. 391.

[412] Larroumet, *Contrat*, 836.

More generally, while French private law has remained firm in its rejection of the public law doctrine of *imprévision* (under which administrative courts modify the terms of contracts where unforeseen supervening circumstances threaten the continuity of provision of a public service),[413] there is evidence of increasing dissatisfaction among private lawyers with *force majeure* as the sole basis on which to deal with the problems arising from supervening changes of circumstances.[414] Exceptionally, it is true, legislation empowers a court to modify a contract so as to remedy the effects of a supervening change of circumstances, as in the case of giving a contracting party owing money further time to pay[415] or the case of judicial modification of commercial rents.[416] The Cour de cassation has also raised the possibility that the principle of good faith might sometimes require a party to modify the terms on which it deals owing to supervening circumstances (in a case where a petrol company refused to lower its bulk prices to a petrol retailer even though deregulation of retail petrol prices meant that this left the retailer in a very difficult position).[417] By contrast, the *Avant-projet de réforme* picks up a practice particularly prevalent in international contracts, viz the use of express renegotiation clauses (sometimes called hardship clauses). First, the *Avant-projet* (perhaps somewhat unnecessarily) provides for the validity of express renegotiation clauses in contracts 'whose performance takes place successively or in instalments' with the view to the modification of their terms 'where as a result of supervening circumstances the original balance of what the parties must do for each other is so disturbed that the contract loses all point for one of them'.[418] It further provides that, in the absence of such an express clause, a contracting party in these same circumstances may apply to the court to order the parties to renegotiate the contract, though in the absence of bad faith, their failure to reach a successful conclusion leads merely to 'a right in either party to terminate the contract for the future at no cost or loss'.[419]

The effects of *force majeure*

The Civil Code treats *force majeure* as a defence to liability in damages for non-performance[420] and a court will not order performance of an obligation whose performance has become impossible[421] but what of the status of the contract's

---

[413] Above, p. 198. Civ. 6 Mar. 1876, *affaire Canal de Craponne*, DP 1876.1.193 note Giboulot marks the formal rejection of the administrative law doctrine by the ordinary courts.

[414] See Terré, Simler, and Lequette, *Obligations*, 468ff; Malaurie, Aynès, and Stoffel-Munck, *Obligations*, 366–368; B. Fauvarque-Cosson, 'Le changement de circonstances' *RDC* 2004.67.

[415] Art. 1244-1–1244-3 C. civ. (which also allows a court to reduce the rate of interest payable).

[416] Déc. no. 53-960 of 30 Sep. 1953 (as amended).

[417] Com. 3 Nov. 1992, Bull. civ. IV no. 338; similarly Com. 24 Nov. 1998, Bull. civ. IV no. 277, JCP 1999.II.12210 note Picod and see Fabre-Magnan, *Obligations*, 428–430. Cf. Com. 3 Oct. 2006, D 2007.765 (party to renegotiation not bound to accept other's offer; breaking off negotiation is not wrongful unless it constitutes 'abusive behaviour').

[418] Art. 1135-1 A.-p.r. and see B. Fauvarque-Cosson, 'Negotiation and Renegotiation: a French Perspective,' in Cartwright, Vogenauer, and Whittaker, Ch. 2.

[419] Art. 1135-3 al. 2 A.-p.r.

[420] Arts. 1147–8 C. civ.

[421] Art. 1184 al. 2 C. civ.

obligations? In *contrats unilatéraux* (where only one party owes an obligation and which typically are gratuitous contracts)[422] the effect is straightforward: *force majeure* extinguishes the party's obligation.[423] However, the effect in bilateral contracts of impossibility of one party's obligation on the other's is more complex, this issue being treated under the heading of the 'theory of risks'.[424] So, it is said that, for example, if A's obligation becomes impossible, but B is nevertheless held bound to his obligation, the risk of impossibility lies on B. Apart from contracts which make express provision for the allocation of the risk of supervening impossibility, a distinction is drawn between those contracts under which property passes and all others.

In the case of contracts under which property passes, the location of risk of subsequent impossibility follows the location of risk in relation to the property itself and this in principle follows title: *res periit domino*. So, for example, in a contract of sale of ascertained property, in which title in principle passes on contract,[425] where the property is destroyed by *force majeure* before delivery, the buyer remains liable to pay the price, for the risk of destruction and impossibility lie on him. In contrast, in a sale of unascertained property, such as a thousand kilos of barley, in which in principle neither title nor risk pass until delivery, in similar circumstances the buyer does not have to pay the price.

In the case of contracts under which property does not pass, in general the risk of *force majeure* lies on the 'debtor' of the obligation, this being justified by reference to the interdependence of obligations in bilateral contracts as technically expressed by the doctrine of *la cause*. Thus, when one party's obligation becomes impossible through *force majeure*, this removes the *cause* of the other party's obligations and the contract logically disappears retroactively for lack of cause.[426] However, while most jurists support this logical result,[427] since the end of the nineteenth century the courts have preferred instead to rely on article 1184 of the Civil Code, which provides for judicial termination of the contract on non-performance (*résolution judicaire*), a provision which the jurists say was intended to deal with 'imputable non-performance' rather than 'excused non-performance', though the courts aften couple this with reference to *la cause*.[428] The advantage of reliance on article 1184 is that it allows the courts to verify that the conditions of *force majeure* are fulfilled before the contract is retroactively terminated.[429]

---

[422] Above, n. 188.
[423] Larroumet, *Contrat*, 853–854 generalizing from art. 1302 C. civ.
[424] Much of the following discussion comes from Larroumet, *Contrat*, 853 ff.
[425] Art. 1138 C. civ.
[426] Larroumet, *Contrat*, 856.
[427] Terré, Simler, and Lequette, *Obligations*, 656 ff.
[428] The leading case is Civ. 14 Apr. 1891, D 1891.1.329 note Planiol, S 1894.1.391, *Source-Book*, 496.
[429] Terré, Simler, and Lequette, *Obligations*, 637–638. Bénabent, *Obligations*, 258 notes that this retroactivity does not apply to divisible contracts. For the restitutionary consequences of termination see below p. 440 ff.

Finally, it should be noted that, especially in contracts whose performance occurs over a period of time, one of the parties' obligations may become *temporarily* impossible.[430] Here, the Cour de cassation has stated that the party is not released from his obligation (nor therefore is the contract to be terminated), but rather performance is suspended until the impossibility ceases.[431] However, the application of this principle outside cases recognized by legislation has been distinctly sporadic.[432]

(b) The *exception d'inexécution*

The *exception d'inexécution* (defence of non-performance) allows a party to a bilateral contract to oppose the other party's non-performance as an excuse to his own failure to perform. The Civil Code makes no general provision for this defence, though some rules applicable to particular contracts have been seen as exemplifying it,[433] but this has made no difference to its general acceptance by both writers and the courts.[434] Its juridical basis lies in the idea of the interdependence of obligations of the parties in this type of contract, this again being expressed by the jurists in terms of the doctrine of *la cause*,[435] though some have seen it as the result of the principle of good faith in the performance of contracts.[436] There are three conditions for its application.

First, the obligations of the contract have to be 'temporally concurrent'.[437] So, for example, in a cash sale, non-payment by the buyer justifies the seller in failing to deliver the property, but in a credit sale it does not as the buyer's obligation (here expressly) does not have to be performed until some later date.[438] In general, obligations in bilateral contracts are considered concurrent.[439] Secondly, a party's non-performance must be sufficiently serious to justify the other's refusal or other failure to perform, an issue which lies within the 'sovereign power of assessment' of the *juges du fond*.[440] Thirdly, only a party in good faith may rely

---

[430] Bénabent, *Obligations*, 256–257.

[431] Civ. (1) 24 Feb. 1981, D 1982.479 note Martin (adult child agreed to house parents during their lifetime; parents divorced; child's obligation to house mother revived on death of father, it being suspended on the divorce).

[432] Malaurie, Aynès, and Stoffel-Munck, *Obligations*, 505.

[433] Arts. 1612, 1653 and 1948 C. civ.

[434] Civ. 5 May 1920, DP 1920.1.37 is the leading case.

[435] Malaurie, Aynès, and Stoffel-Munck, *Obligations*, 438. Contra Starck *et al.*, *Contrat*, 687 ff.

[436] M. Planiol, note to Req. 1 Dec. 1897, DP 1898.1.289.

[437] Terré, Simler, and Lequette, *Obligations*, 628.

[438] Art. 1612 C. civ.

[439] Starck *et al.*, *Contrat*, 691. The Cour de cassation has held that the defence may also apply where a party's contractual non-performance concerns an obligation contained in a distinct contract as long as the performance of the two contracts is linked: Com. 12 Jul. 2005, unreported no. 03-12507 noted by Libchaber, Défrenois 2006.610.

[440] Civ. (1) 29 Oct. 1990, *M.D. Fauvin*, JCP 1990.IV.424.

on the defence, which is not the case where he has caused the other party's non-performance.[441]

The importance of the defence is that it allows a party to a bilateral contract to refuse to perform until the other has done so, without the need to throw up the contract entirely either by going to court and asking for its judicial termination on the ground of non-performance (*résolution judiciaire*)[442] or by exercising a contractual right of termination under a *clause résolutoire* (if such a clause is present in the contract).[443] It is, therefore, a very useful means of putting pressure on the other party to perform.[444]

D. 'Remedies' for Non-Performance

Until recently, French lawyers have not used the language of 'remedy' ('*les remèdes*') to describe the nature of the possible responses of the law to contractual non-performance, but have instead treated these responses in terms of the different effects of or sanctions for non-performance and the possible actions to which it may give rise.[445] While there are signs of some change here,[446] for many French lawyers '*les remèdes*' bears a very 'Anglo-Saxon' ring, and (unlike '*sanctions*') does not provide a sufficient sense of the law's moral disapproval of contractual non-performance. Indeed, the constant preference of French lawyers is to attempt to ensure that a contract is performed and this means both that the approach to orders of specific enforcement of contractual obligations and to termination of contracts on the ground of non-performance (*résolution*) has been very different to that of English law and that for a French lawyer, awards of damages are very much a 'second best'. As Bénabent puts it '[t]he performance of the contract on the same terms in which it was agreed is for each party a *right* of which he may always demand enforcement'.[447]

1. Performance in kind

The modern approach to the availability of orders of performance in kind (*exécution en nature*) represents a double triumph for French lawyers over the terms of

---

[441] Malaurie, Aynès, and Stoffel-Munck, *Obligations*, 440.

[442] Art. 1184. C. civ. and see below pp. 357 ff.

[443] Below p. 358.

[444] Terré, Simler, and Lequette, *Obligations*, 624.

[445] D. Tallon, 'Remedies, French Report' in D. Harris and D. Tallon (eds.) *Contract Law Today* (Oxford, 1989), 263.

[446] The starting-point was D. Tallon, 'L'inexécution du contrat: pour une autre présentation' RTDCiv. 1994.223.

[447] *Obligations*, 262 (emphasis altered). For comparative discussions see F. Bellivier and R. Sefton-Green, 'Force obligatoire et exécution en nature du contrat en droits français et anglais: bonnes et mauvaises surprises du comparatisme' in *Le contrat au debut du XXIe siècle, Etudes offertes à Jacques Ghestin* (LDGJ, 2001), 91; Y.-M. Laithier, 'The Performance of Contractual Obligations: A French Perspective' in Cartwright, Vogenauer and Whittaker, ch. 6; L. Miller, 'The Enforcement of Contractual Obligations: Comparative Observations on the Notion of Performance', ibid., ch. 7.

the Civil Code. For the latter was inspired by a concern for freedom of the person from constraint by the state, rather than the binding force of freedom of contract and this meant that no provision was made for a law of contempt to buttress any order which a court chose to make[448] and, more specifically, that according to article 1142, the main consequence of non-performance of contract was damages.[449] As to the former, the courts developed the practice of imposing the payment of money sums (*astreintes*) for each month or each day during which a person refuses to perform their orders.[450] At one time these sums were justified as a form of damages (which they clearly were not) but when a proper legislative basis was given for the practice, while the independence of *astreintes* from damages was made clear, no change was made to the fact that the sums were to be paid to the other party to the litigation.[451] Clearly, the threat of an acculmulating liability constitutes at least some incentive to obey a court order, for that other party can himself obtain these sums by proceeding against a recalcitrant party's property.[452]

The second way in which the terms of the Civil Code have been overcome has been that article 1142 is seen as providing for the exception (damages), whereas the rule (performance) is found reflected in the two following provisions, which provide for the possibility of an injured party's being authorized to obtain substitute performance elsewhere (the *faculté de remplacement*) and for a judicial order of the destruction of work done in contravention of a contractual obligation not to do it.[453] The first of these, however, also demonstrates that the French concept of *exécution en nature* is not restricted to what a common lawyer would think of as specific enforcement of a contractual obligation, for while it concerns the actual doing of what the party's obligation requires, this actual doing is effected *by another person*.[454] Where a court actually orders the performance of a contractual obligation to do something by the party, usually backed up by the threat of *astreintes*, this is usually termed *exécution forcée en nature*.

---

[448] Originally, the Civil Code provided for imprisonment for debt (*contrainte par corps*), but this was abolished for all civil and commercial debts in 1867: see above p. 116 ff.

[449] *Obligations de faire* and *de ne pas faire*. The Code is not entirely clear on this point since art. 1184 al. 2 C. civ., while concerned with *résolution judiciaire*, reserves the right in an injured party to claim performance when it is still possible.

[450] e.g. (famously) Paris 7 Aug. 1876 and Paris 13 Feb. 1877, *affaire de Bauffremont* D 1878.2.125. On *astreintes* more generally, see above pp. 117–118.

[451] Originally, *loi* no. 72-626 of 5 July 1972, arts. 5–8, esp. art. 6, now *loi* no. 91-650 of 9 July 1991, arts. 33-37, esp. art. 34.

[452] A person's debts are said to create a 'general charge' on his property: arts. 2092–3 C. civ. and see above p. 116 ff.

[453] Arts. 1143–4. C.civ.

[454] Tallon, (above n. 445), 266. See also S. Whittaker, 'Performance of another's obligation: French and English law contrasted' in D. Johnston and R. Zimmermann, *Unjustified Enrichment, Key Issues in Comparative Perspective* (CUP, 2002), 433.

Exécution forcée en nature

In discussing the availability of actions for the enforcement of contractual obligations, distinctions are drawn according to the subject-matter of the obligation in question.

Obligations to pay a sum of money are the most straightforward, for here the courts are happy to order payment when it is due, the sum being recoverable against the debtor's property, together with damages for any delay in payment at a legally-fixed rate of interest.[455] On the other hand, French courts possess a general discretion to allow a debtor time to pay of up to 2 years on the ground of financial difficulty.[456]

Secondly, French lawyers find that the traditional category of obligations to convey property (*obligations de donner*) disappears on inspection. For, in principle in French law these obligations are 'self-executing' because title is able to pass on agreement, and where it does then they are replaced by an obligation to deliver the thing, which is itself an *obligation de faire* (obligation to do).[457] In those cases where the obligation to convey is not 'self-executing', for example, in the case of unascertained goods, it is treated as being an *obligation de faire*.

This brings us to *obligations de faire* and *obligations de ne pas faire* (those not to do something). Here, the courts will in principle order performance unless it is physically, 'morally' or legally impossible.[458] Of, these, the idea of 'moral impossibility' allows them to protect the personal liberty of parties to contracts, sometimes expressly holding that non-performance of personal obligations will give rise only to damages.[459] However, this restriction leaves many cases in which performance will be ordered, where an English court would not grant specific performance, for example, a seller being ordered to deliver ascertained property. As has been noted, negative obligations (*obligations de ne pas faire*) received special treatment in the Civil Code, article 1143 of which provides that a party may ask a court to order the destruction of the thing made in breach of them or have this done at the other party's expense.[460] Here, neither the adequacy of damages in lieu of such an order nor the interests of third parties in the maintenance of the status quo is to be taken into account by the *juges du fond* in deciding whether such an order should be made[461]: indeed, it is sometimes said that a court must not refuse a creditor's claim under article 1143.[462] On the other hand, the

---

[455] Art. 1153 C. civ. (as amended).
[456] Arts. 1244-1–1244-3 C. civ (as amended).
[457] Terré, Simler, and Lequette, *Obligations*, 1061–1062.
[458] Malaurie, Aynès, and Stoffel-Munck, *Obligations*, 615.
[459] Civ. 20 Jan. 1953, JCP 1953.II.7677 note Esmein, *Source-Book*, 504.
[460] Art. 1143 C. civ.
[461] Civ. (1)17 Dec. 1963, JCP 1964.II.13609 note Blaevoelt, *Source-Book*, 505.
[462] Malaurie, Aynès, and Stoffel-Munck, *Obligations*, 615.

principle of performance in good faith applies to this context as to others and here this means that a party in bad faith will not gain an order for performance.[463]

2. Damages

Despite the widespread availability of orders for specific enforcement of contractual obligations, damages remain a very important feature of French practice. In some cases, an order for specific enforcement is meaningless (for example, in the context of personal injuries), but in many others the injured party will have lost confidence in the quality of any performance which would be tendered by the other party. As in English law, damages are in principle available to compensate the injured party's loss caused by non-performance, this being termed *réparation par équivalent*.[464]

(a) *La responsabilité contractuelle*

While the notion of *la responsabilité contractuelle* (contractual liability) was long established in both the scholarly literature and the case law, towards the end of the 20th century it was argued that this was a 'false concept' and that awards of damages for contractual non-performance recognized by article 1142 of the Civil Code should properly fulfil the role of providing the creditors of contractual obligations with a substitute for performance and not with compensation for loss as being wrongfully caused:[465] damages for contractual non-performance should therefore be seen as a form of 'forced satisfaction' (*le paiement forcé*).[466] However, while jurists have generally accepted that the special feature of contractual damages is indeed to provide the creditor with a monetary equivalent of the *prestation*[467] of which he is deprived by non-performance,[468] the majority also accept that these damages can and should also include compensation for harm caused by the situation created by non-performance, so that there remains a sufficient similarity with *la responsabilité délictuelle* (delictual liability) for the expression *la responsabilité contractuelle* to remain appropriate;[469] and for some the rejection of this expression would be contrary to the very idea of imposing a

---

[463] Bénabent, *Obligations*, 263–264.

[464] *Réparation en nature* refers to the idea that an injured party receives neither performance itself nor its equivalent in specie, but its equivalent in kind. While on occasion this has been allowed in the contractual context (e.g. a garage being ordered to replace tyres stolen from the claimant's vehicle deposited there), generally the courts have denied it: Civ. 4 June 1924, S 1924, 1.97, *Source-Book*, 504.

[465] D. Tallon, 'L'inexécution du contrat: pour une autre présentation' RTDCiv. 1994.223; P. Rémy, 'La responsabilité contractuelle: l'histoire d'un faux concept' RTDCiv. 1997.323.

[466] Rémy, ibid., at no. 45.

[467] Above, p. 315.

[468] Flour, Aubert, and Savaux, *Acte juridique*, 124.

[469] Ibid., 123–125 and see E. Savaux, 'La fin de la responsabilité contractuelle?' RTDCiv. 1999.1. This is the position adopted by the *Avant-projet de réforme* as explained by G. Viney in *De la responsabilité civile (Arts. 1340 à 1386), Exposé des motifs* in *Avant-projet de réforme*, 163.

sanction for contractual non-performance.[470] Paradoxically, given this debate, French courts continue to fail to identify within their awards of damages the distinction between recovery in respect of a claimant's 'performance' or 'positive' interest and recovery in respect of his 'reliance' or 'negative' interest and only a handful of jurists consider this distinction worthy of discussion.[471]

(b) 'Notice to perform'

While the Civil Code in general requires an injured party to serve a notice to perform (*mise en demeure*) on the party in default before damages may be recovered,[472] this requirement is generally restricted by both courts and jurists to claims for damages for delay and is dispensed with where performance is impossible,[473] in the case of negative obligations,[474] and where the *juges du fond* consider that in the circumstances the parties have implicitly agreed to dispense with it.[475] Although more elaborate notice was originally required, an ordinary letter will now suffice.[476]

(c) The assessment of damages

The starting point of French law for the assessment of damages in both contract and delict is that the injured party should receive full reparation (*réparation intégrale*) for his losses[477] and this may be supported in the case of contract by article 1149 of the Civil Code, which allows recovery of both losses incurred and profits denied as a result of default. We therefore do not find in French texts elaborate discussions of the 'heads of damage' which may be recoverable in an action for breach of contract, for all, including *dommage moral* (mental distress, lost reputation etc.) are recoverable.[478] Indeed, for a common lawyer there is remarkably little law on the issue of quantification of damages and this is to be explained by the fact that this issue is in principle within the 'sovereign power of assessment'

---

[470] C. Larroumet, 'Pour la responsabilité contractuelle' in *Mélanges offerts à Pierre Catala* (Litec, 2001), 543 at 554.

[471] A notable example is P. Rémy-Corlay, 'Exécution et réparation: deux concepts' *RDC* 2004.13 at 27 (drawing on English and German law). On the courts' approach, see below.

[472] Art. 1146 C. civ.

[473] Nicholas, *French Contract*, 239–240.

[474] Art. 1145 C. civ.; Civ. (1) 26 Feb. 2002, Bull. civ. I no. 68, RTDCiv. 2002.809 note Mestre and Fages.

[475] Com. 8 Oct. 2003, Bull. civ. IV no. 138, RTDCiv. 2003.503 note Mestre and Fages.

[476] Arts. 1139 and 1146 C. civ. (as amended).

[477] Bénabent, *Obligations*, 487–488; Terré, Simler, and Lequette, *Obligations*, 591ff. In general, damages may not be awarded in the absence of loss caused to the claimant (Civ. (3) 3 Dec. 2003, *RDC* 2004.280 note Stoffel-Munck) although there is some dispute as to whether or not this applies to negative obligations: Civ. (1) 26 Feb. 2002, Bull. civ. I no. 68 (yes); Civ. (1) 10 May 2005, Bull. civ. I no. 201, RTDCiv. 2005.594 note Mestre and Fages; RTDCiv. 2005.600 note Jourdain (no).

[478] Malaurie, Aynès, and Stoffel-Munck, *Obligations*, 506.

of the *juges du fond*.[479] In particular, as has been noted, French lawyers do not in this context distinguish between recovery of an injured party's reliance or negative interest and his performance or expectation interest.[480] Three important issues remain.

First, the Civil Code recognizes two tests of remoteness of damage for contractual damages, so that in general a party in default is liable only for those losses which were foreseen or could have been foreseen at the time of making the contract, but where that party is guilty of *dol*, here meaning bad faith and in particular deliberate non-performance, then he will be liable for all losses which are the 'immediate and direct consequence' of his non-performance[481] and the Cour de cassation intervenes to make sure that these provisions are properly applied.[482] Thus, for example, in the case of an 'innocent non-performance', it has made clear that the requirement of foreseeability applies to the extent as well as to the type of loss suffered by the injured party, but not to its monetary value.[483]

Secondly, the courts may reduce an injured party's damages on the grounds of his contributory fault (*faute de la victime*), whatever the content of the obligation on the breach of which he relies, whether *de résultat* or *de moyens*.[484] The extent of the reduction lies, in the 'sovereign power of assessment' of the *juges du fond*.[485] So, for example, a driver injured in an accident caused in part by his vehicle's defective steering may have his damages reduced on the ground of his own careless driving.[486] Here, therefore, *faute de la victime* functions rather like the English defence of contributory negligence (to the limited extent to which it applies to actions for breach of contract).[487]

Thirdly, in contrast with their common law counterparts, French lawyers have shown considerable hostility to the idea that a claimant owes a duty to minimize (or 'mitigate') his own loss (*obligation de minimiser son propre préjudice*).[488] The reasons for this hostility are to be found partly in a concern for the integrity of the principle of 'full reparation' and partly in a sympathy for those who have suffered harm wrongfully ('*les victimes*'). The hostility has been most strikingly expressed

---

[479] Terré, Simler, and Lequette, *Obligations*, 592; Starck *et al.*, *Responsabilité délictuelle*, 524 ff.

[480] Nicholas, *French Contract*, 226–7. cf. above, p. 353.

[481] Arts. 1150–1151 C. civ.

[482] e.g. Civ. 23 Dec. 1913, D 1915.1.25, *Source-Book*, 494.

[483] Com. 4 Mar. 1965, JCP 1965.II.14219 note Rodière.

[484] Civ. (1) 31 Jan. 1973, JCP 1973.II.17450 note Starck (*obligation de résultat*); Civ. (1) 29 Jun. 1976, JCP 1978:II.18995 note Chemel (*obligation de moyens*).

[485] Civ. (2) 27 Apr. 1979, *Dame Remolu*, JCP 1979.IV.213.

[486] Civ. (1) 4 Feb. 1963, JCP 1963.II.13159 note Savatier.

[487] See *Forsikringsaktielskapet Vesta v. Butcher* [1989] AC 852.

[488] Viney and Jourdain, *Effets de la responsabilité*, 120–121; S. Le Pautremat, 'Mitigation of Damage: A French Perspective' (2006) 55 *ICLQ* 205; S. Whittaker, 'Contributory Fault and Mitigation, Rights and Reasonableness: Comparisons between English and French law' in L. Tichý (ed.) *Causation in Law* (Prague, 2007), 147.

in the context of a refusal of medical treatment in claims for personal injuries or death, where the Cour de cassation has formally declared that:

a person who causes an accident is bound to make reparation for all its harmful consequences; [and]...the victim is not bound to limit his own loss in the interests of the person liable.[489]

However, in the specifically contractual context, the reasons for French law's rejection of a duty to mitigate does not depend so much on concern for the rights of 'victims' as its incompatibility with the wider scheme of the relative rights of the injured party (the 'creditor') and the party in default (the 'debtor').[490] For while French lawyers are concerned to protect the creditor's right to performance, they are also concerned to protect the debtor's right to perform. This can be seen in the general rule that a creditor of a contractual obligation cannot simply go into the market and arrange for a substitute performance, but must in principle apply to the court for authority for 'performance by a third party' (thereby granting the *faculté de remplacement*).[491] The purpose of involving the court is to protect the debtor's interest in himself performing his own contractual obligations (which *remplacement judiciaire* prevents) rather than being held liable to pay the creditor the cost of his obtaining a substitute performance elsewhere, while at the same time protecting the creditor's interest in gaining an effective 'performance' for which he can be indemnified in advance.[492] However, not all French lawyers are as hostile to the idea of a failure to mitigate outside the context of personal injuries[493] and this is reflected in article 1373 of the *Avant-projet de réforme*[494] which provides that:

Where the victim had the possibility of taking reliable, reasonable and proportionate measures to reduce the extent of his loss or to avoid its getting worse, the court shall take account of his failure to do so by reducing his compensation, except where the measures to be taken were of a kind to have compromised his physical integrity.

---

[489] Civ. (2) 19 Jun. 2003, *Dibaoui c. Flamand*, JCP 2004.I.101 Chron. G. Viney; RTDCiv. 2003 . 716 obs. Jourdain. See also Civ. (2) 19 Jun. 2003, *Lallemand Xhauflaire c. Decrepti*, Bull. civ. no. 203 (1st case), JCP 2004.I.101 Chron. G. Viney; RTDCiv. 2003.716 note P. Jourdain. Earlier, French courts had sometimes used the defence of *faute de la victime* to reduce a claimant's damages after his refusal of medical treatment: Crim. 30 Oct. 1974, Bull. crim. no. 308, DS 1975.178 note Savatier; JCP 1975.II.18038 note Morgeon.

[490] Whittaker, op. cit. n. 488, 152–158, 163–166.

[491] Art. 1144 C. civ.; G. Viney 'Exécution de l'obligation, faculté de remplacement et réparation en nature en droit français' in Fontaine and Viney, 167–188; Civ. (3) 11 Jan. 2006, Bull. civ. III no. 9 (tenant having premises repaired where landlord failed to do so) and cf. above, p. 350. Exceptions to the requirement of judicial authority are made in the case of commercial sales of goods (e.g. Com. 20 Jan. 1976, Bull. com. no. 26) and where 'replacement' was 'urgent, indispensable and effected in the most economical way': Soc. 7 Dec. 1951, D 1952.144.

[492] Art. 1144 C. civ. *in fine*.

[493] Le Pautremat, op. cit. n. 488 at 214–215.

[494] On which see above, pp. 301–302.

The authors of the *Avant-projet de réforme* do not, however, explain how this provision relates to the retention of the judicial nature of the *faculté de remplacement*.[495]

(d) Exemption clauses

French courts have long been hostile to the effectiveness of exemption clauses and have found many ways of denying or reducing their effect.[496] First, while it is accepted in principle that such a clause may modify or exclude any contractual liability, it will not do so for delictual liability based on fault, which is held to concern the public interest (being *d'ordre public*).[497] Secondly, no clause may exclude or limit a party's contractual liability for either *dol* or *faute lourde*, the latter being a gross form of fault and including recklessness.[498] Thirdly, the courts have in particular contexts prevented those in business (*professionnels*) from excluding or limiting their liability: so, notably, while the Civil Code prevents a seller from excluding his liability for *known* latent defects,[499] the courts have extended this to all sellers in business, who are irrebuttably presumed to know of their property's defects.[500] Fourthly, the courts possess a general power to hold invalid unfair terms in consumer contracts and this can be used to protect a consumer from an exemption clause.[501] Finally, as has been seen, French courts have used the doctrine of *la cause* to invalidate exemption clauses where they judge them inconsistent with a party's essential obligation.

(e) Clauses pénales

In French law, a *clause pénale* is any clause whose aim is to ensure the performance of a contract and this is therefore considerably wider than the English notion of a penalty clause.[502] Given this aim, it should not be surprising that the Civil Code as originally drafted considered them valid.[503] However, since 1975 where a *clause pénale* takes the form of a term imposing the payment of a certain sum of

---

[495] Art. 1154-2 A.-p.r.

[496] Larroumet, *Contrat*, 643. See generally P. Delebeque and D. Mazeaud, 'Les clauses de responsabilité: clauses de non responsabilité, clauses limitatives de réparation, clauses pénales, Rapport français' in Fontaine and Viney, 361.

[497] Art. 6 C. civ. and see Civ. (2) 17 Feb. 1955, DS 1956. 17 note Esmein, JCP 1955.II.8951 note Rodière.

[498] Larroumet, *Contrat*, 646–648. *Faute lourde* must be found in the seriously wrongful nature of the party's behaviour: Com. 13 Jun. 2006, D 2006.1680. Clauses which restrict the period within which a right may be exercised when compared to the law of prescription are valid even where there is *faute lourde*: Com. 12 Jul. 2004, D 2004.2296 note Delebecque.

[499] Art. 1643 C. civ.

[500] e.g. Com. 17 Dec. 1973, GP 1974.1.429 note Planqueel, JCP 1975.II.1792 note Savatier. See further Whittaker, *Liability for Products*, 93–95 (which explains the exception to this position where the parties are in the same type of business).

[501] Art. L. 132-1 al. 1 C. consom. (as amended in 1995).

[502] Art. 1126 C. civ.; L. Miller, 'Penalty Clauses in England and France: A Comparative Study (2004) 53 ICLQ 79.

[503] Arts. 1152 al. 1 and 1226 ff C. civ.

money by way of damages, the courts may reduce or increase this sum if it appears 'manifestly excessive or derisory'.[504] The Cour de cassation allows the *juges du fond* to decide as a matter of their 'sovereign power of assessment' whether it is appropriate to intervene and, if they decide to, the amount of any award made as long as this does not fall below the injured party's actual loss.[505]

3. *Termination of the contract for imputable non-performance*

The Civil Code put in place a scheme for the termination of bilateral contracts on the ground of imputable non-performance[506] which is strikingly different from the common law's treatment of termination for major breach of contract.[507] Article 1184 provides that a 'resolutory condition' (meaning a condition whose satisfaction leads to the retroactive termination (*résolution*) of the contract in which it is contained[508]) is implied in all bilateral contracts to govern the situation where one of the parties has failed to perform: in this situation, the creditor can apply to the court to have the contract terminated, together with damages. *Résolution* of a contract therefore depends both on a choice of the creditor (who may choose instead to retain the contract and claim its enforcement[509]) *and* on a decision by a court. Where a court is seized of an application for *résolution* it first assesses whether or not the debtor's non-performance is sufficiently serious to justify termination (on which the *juges du fond* has a 'sovereign power of assessment'[510]) and then decides whether the contract should be terminated in full or instead the debtor should be given more time,[511] or some 'intermediate solution' be ordered, for example, partial *résolution* of the contract with a reduction in price.[512] The effect of full *résolution* of a contract is its 'retroactive destruction' with consequential restitution and counter-restitution of money or property transferred under it,[513] but this 'destruction' does not prevent the application of contract terms governing liability such as exemption clauses or penalty clauses (to the extent to which they are valid[514]) nor the imposition of liability in damages

---

[504] New art. 1152 al. 2 C. civ.

[505] Civ. (3) 17 Jul. 1978 and Civ. (1) 24 Jul. 1978, D 1979.IR.151 note Landraud.

[506] Non-performance is not 'imputable' where it is excused on the ground of *force majeure*, on which see above, pp. 343 ff.

[507] See generally Malaurie, Aynès, and Stoffel-Munck, *Obligations*, 443ff; Terré, Simler, and Lequette, *Obligations*, 631 ff; C. Jamin, 'Les conditions de la résolution du contrat: vers un modèle unique' in Fontaine and Viney, 451; S. Whittaker, '"Termination" for Contractual Non-performance and its Consequences: French Law Viewed in the Light of the *Avant-projet de réforme*' in Cartwright, Vogenauer and Whittaker, Ch 9.

[508] Art. 1183 C. civ.

[509] Art. 1184 al. 2 C. civ.

[510] Com. 3 Dec. 1980, JCP 1980.IV.242; Civ. (1) 15 Jul. 1999, Bull. civ. no. I no. 245.

[511] Art. 1184 al. 3 C.civ. (a *délai de grâce*).

[512] Malaurie, Aynès, and Stoffel-Munck, *Obligations*, 448. This is known in commercial sales as *réfaction*.

[513] Ibid. and see below, p. 440 ff.

[514] Above, pp. 356–357.

being seen as contractual.[515] The central feature of this traditional scheme, though, is that it gives French courts a very important role in the management of the consequences of imputable non-performance, in particular in the interests of protecting the *force obligatoire* of contracts for the benefit of contractual debtors.

However, there are three important ways in which French lawyers have side-stepped this scheme.

First, French courts have nuanced the effect of judicial termination according to the circumstances and, in particular, according to the type of contract in question. So, while termination of a contract for non-performance takes effect retroactively as regards contracts whose performance is instantaneous (*contrats à exécution instantanée*, the central example being a cash sale), in the case of contracts requiring performance over a period of time (*contrats à exécution successive ou échelonnée*, such as contracts of tenancy and contracts of insurance) the courts decide whether to order retroactive termination or instead prospective termination, known as *résiliation*, depending on when the non-performance took place.[516] Where a court orders *résiliation* rather than *résolution*, the effect is to terminate the contract from the date of the order, thereby avoiding the unravelling that has already gone on under the contract by way of restitution and counter-restitution.

Secondly, since 1860 the courts have accepted the validity in principle of express contract terms providing for termination for imputable non-performance, known as *clauses résolutoires*.[517] The advantage of such a clause is that it can set the circumstances in which termination is allowed and can (if suitably drafted) allow the creditor to terminate the contract without notice to perform or the need to go to court and so to bypass the court's decision as to whether the contract should be terminated and, if so, with what effects. *Clauses résolutoires* have become very widespread in practice and in principle take effect according to their terms (though they are restrictively interpreted[518]), the only general restriction being that a creditor's decision whether to terminate must be made in good faith.[519]

Thirdly, French courts have gradually recognized that the creditor may himself sometimes choose to terminate the contract on the ground of the debtor's

[515] Art. 1184 al. 2 C. civ.; Larroumet, *Contrat*, 819–820.

[516] Civ. (3) 30 Apr. 2003, JCP 2004.II.10031 note Jamin (*contrat à exécution successive* terminated from the beginning where the non-performance had occurred from its inception). Cf. art. 1160-1 A.-p.r. and see below, pp. 448–449.

[517] Civ. 2 Jul. 1860, DP 1860.1.284.

[518] Malaurie, Aynès, and Stoffel-Munck, *Obligations*, 456. A *clause résolutoire* may be invalid in particular contexts (e.g. in the case of farm tenancies: art. L. 411-31 C. rur.) or subject to a control of fairness (as in the case of consumer contracts: art. L. 132-1 C. consom.).

[519] Civ. (1) 31 Jan. 1995, D 1995.389 note Jamin.

non-performance despite the general requirement that *résolution* be judicial.[520] This was first recognized where *résolution* was considered urgent, where the parties' relationship was one of confidence (which had been lost), or where the creditor would otherwise suffer an irreparable loss.[521] However, in 1998 the Cour de cassation went very much further, declaring that 'the seriousness of the behaviour ['*le comportement grave*'] of a party to a contract can justify the other party in putting an end to it unilaterally at his own risk [*à ses risques et périls*]'.[522] This 'unilateral breaking-off' (*rupture unilatérale*) from a contract by a creditor can affect contracts whose performance is instantaneous or over a period which is fixed or left undetermined.[523] The significance of a creditor acting *à ses risques et périls* is that if he purports to terminate a contract for non-performance, it remains open to the debtor to go to court and ask it to refuse to recognize the creditor's act of termination: if the court holds that the creditor acted within his rights, then it will uphold his earlier *rupture unilatérale*, but if not, his earlier action will itself constitute an imputable non-performance of his own contractual obligations. However, what is not yet clear is the exact significance of the central requirement that the debtor's non-performance is 'sufficiently serious'. Some authors argue that this requirement does not differ from the condition required by courts for their own termination of contracts for non-performance,[524] but others disagree seeing the language used by the Cour de cassation as requiring some further wrongful element to the debtor's behaviour.[525] As to the effects of *rupture unilatérale* on the contract, the language used by the Cour de cassation is very neutral, as it avoids using either the term *résolution* or *résiliation*, and referring to the creditor's 'putting an end' to the contract.[526] *A priori*, the effect should depend on similar considerations as are taken into account by the courts in deciding the effects of their own termination of contracts.[527] Overall, many French jurists admit that under cover of merely qualifying article 1184 of the Civil Code, this new case law allows creditors unilaterally to terminate the contract for serious non-performance in the face of the Code's provisions subject only to the possibility of later control by a court.[528]

---

[520] Terré, Simler, and Lequette, *Obligations*, 648–651. There are also legislative exceptions to the judicial nature of *résolution*, e.g. art. 1657 C.civ. (refusal by buyer to accept goods).

[521] F. Terré, P. Simler, and Y. Lequette, *Droit civil, Les obligations*, 8th edn. (2002), 639.

[522] Civ. (1) 13 Oct. 1998, Bull. civ. I no. 300, D 1999.197 note Jamin; Civ. (1) 20 Feb. 2001, D 2001.568 note Jamin; similarly, Civ. (1) 28 Oct. 2003, Bull. civ. I no. 211, *RDC* 2004.273 note Aynès, 277 note Mazeaud; Terré, Simler, and Lequette, *Obligations*, 648–651.

[523] Civ. (1) 20 Feb. 2001, cit.; Terré, Simler, and Lequette, *Obligations*, 649.

[524] Terré, Simler, and Lequette, *Obligations*, 650; similarly, Jamin, note D 2001.568.

[525] Aynès, note *RDC* 2004.273.

[526] Civ. (1) 20 Feb. 2001, cit.

[527] Above, p. 358.

[528] Terré, Simler, and Lequette, *Obligations*, 650 and see arts. 1158–1160-1 A.-p.r. on which see Whittaker, op. cit., n. 507.

(3) The Law of Delict

The English law of torts consists of a very varied collection of particular, disparate and distinct legal wrongs, having very little in common except that they do not fall into any other legal category, such as breach of contract or breach of trust: they do indeed represent a combination of the 'unanalysed remainder' of the common law[529] and various instances in which Parliament has seen fit to impose liability. There are, therefore, torts of nuisance, negligence, trespass (to the person or property), defamation, interference with contractual relations etc., each having its own rules, its own authorities and often its own focus, whether the latter is the nature of the claimant's interest (interference with contractual relations, trespass), the way in which the harm is caused (tort of negligence) or the means by which the harm is caused (defamation or deceit). The list of torts is a long one,[530] but what is clear is that where a defendant's conduct does not come within one of them[531] (or cannot by analogous extension be said by the courts to do so),[532] that conduct however much 'at fault' does *not* give rise to liability: English law recognizes *no general principle* of liability for harm caused by fault nor any general strict liability for (dangerous) things. The closest which it has come to the recognition of general principle—the so-called 'neighbour principle' of the tort of negligence—was, of course, always restricted to cases of harm caused by *negligence* and, as has been made clear by the complex case law in relation to, notably, liability for pure economic loss or omissions, the tort itself is severely restricted both as to the type of harm and the type of behaviour which it covers. The lack of a general ground of liability for personal fault is confirmed by the fact that in English law there is no necessary connection between crime and tort. So, while all common law offences have tortious counterparts, the issue whether statutory offences may also give rise to civil liability (under the tort of breach of statutory duty) is said to turn on parliamentary intention, this being notoriously elusive in the absence of express provision. All this is not, of course, to deny that 'tortious liability' does not exist as a legal category in English law; it clearly does both at common law and

---

[529] The phrase is Sir F. Pollock's, see *The Law of Torts*, 1st edn. (London, 1887) 5 who argues (ultimately unconvincingly) against the idea.

[530] To a limited extent its membership is open to argument: e.g. breach of copyright: see A. Dugdale, M. Jones, and M.A. Simpson, *Clerk and Lindsell on Torts*, 19th edn. (2006).

[531] This statement assumes, of course, that the defendant's conduct does not constitute some other legal but non-tortious wrong such as breach of trust.

[532] An example of the considerable extension of an existing tort might have been found in the decision of the Court of Appeal in *Khorasandjian v. Bush* [1993] QB 727 (private nuisance), but this was subsequently overruled in part by the House of Lords in *Hunter v. Canary Wharf Ltd* [1997] 2 WLR 684.

by statute, both of which have attached certain incidental rules to liability on condition that it is tortious.[533] But it is a category without overarching principle.

Both the formal sources and the approach of the French law of delict could hardly be more different from this picture and are to a common lawyer at first sight bewilderingly general, not to say strikingly uninformative. For until 1998,[534] there were only five articles in the Civil Code providing for *all cases* of delictual liability (*la responsabilité délictuelle* or *la responsabilité civile*) and of these the first three are by far the most important. The key provisions state that:

Art. 1382: Any human action whatsoever which causes harm to another creates an obligation in the person by whose fault it was caused to make reparation for it.

Art. 1383: Everyone is liable for the harm which he has caused not only by his action, but also by his failure to act or his lack of care.

Art. 1384 al. 1: One is liable not only for the harm which one causes by one's own action, but also for that which is caused by the action of persons for whom one is responsible, or of things which one has in one's keeping.

Article 1384 (as amended) goes on to describe the liabilities imposed in respect of fire, of parents for their children; employers for their employees[535] and teachers for their pupils. Articles 1385 and 1386 impose liability on the owner or user of an animal for harm which it causes and the owner of a building for harm caused by delapidation owing to lack of repair or construction defects. It is a constant in all cases of civil liability (including, as we have noted,[536] where it arises from the non-performance of a contract) that a claimant must establish a causal link (*lien de causalité*) between his harm (*préjudice* or *dommage*) and whichever of these legal grounds of liability he wishes to have imposed on the defendant. These further elements will be discussed later, but for reasons of space, only briefly.

These provisions on delict in the Civil Code are indeed a triumph of generalization from the particular actions for delicts found in Roman law, which, like the common law, was based on distinct, nominate wrongs. Only the special provisions on liability for animals and ruinous buildings have recognizably particular Roman origins, the liability for personal fault under articles 1382 and 1383 being more an expression of natural lawyer theorizing about delictual responsibility

---

[533] e.g. limitation of actions (Limitation Act 1980, s. 14A); conflict of laws (*Boys v. Chaplin* [1971] AC 356, though see Private International Law (Miscellaneous Provisions) Act 1995, ss. 9–14).

[534] In 1998, legislation inserted a raft of new provisions into the Civil Code to implement Dir. 1985/374/EEC concerning liability for defective products, on which see below, p. 406 ff.

[535] These terms translate *commettant* and *préposé*, which include the relation of employer and employee but are wider than this suggests, see below pp. 395–397.

[536] Above p. 352 ff.

than a modern version of liability under the Roman *Lex Aquilia*.[537] However, if the generality of these provisions themselves is considerable, the generalizing interpretation of them by the courts has been extraordinary. In the result, it can be said that there are now three general principles of delictual liability in French law. These are: (i) liability for personal fault; (ii) liability without fault for the 'actions of things in one's keeping'; and (iii) liability without proof of fault for the actions of persons 'for whom one is responsible'.

Before we look in some detail at these 'actions which give rise to liability' (*faits générateurs de responsabilité*), it should first be said that in all three the generality of treatment to which they give rise, while genuine and important in its effects, is nevertheless considerably qualified by the special treatments given to particular types of cases underneath the umbrellas of their generality. Thus, the deliberate causing of harm does *not* always constitute 'personal fault': for example, a person is entitled to compete for the custom of his competitors and thus cause them financial loss, and so only if the competition is unfair is it said to constitute 'fault'.[538] Similarly, while liability for the actions of things applies apparently indiscriminately to all physical things, different approaches have been taken by the courts according to whether, for example, the case concerns a supermarket floor or a motor-vehicle,[539] and in the case of the latter the rules were in 1985 transformed by legislation.[540] And even though a general principle of liability for other people's actions has become established, different rules still apply to the liabilities of parents for their children and employers for their employees.[541] Thus, the bases of liability remain general in the sense that they leave no (or very few) gaps between recognized 'pockets of liability'; but they are particular in their treatment of certain types of case.

Secondly, the last 20 years or so have seen the enactment of three important special legislative regimes governing particular areas: liability for motor-vehicle accidents,[542] liability for defective products,[543] and medical liability.[544] Each of these special regimes possesses its own particular rules governing the standard of liability (whether for fault or something stricter),[545] the categories of claimant

---

[537] While liability under arts. 1382–3 C. civ. has been known at times as *responsabilité Aquilienne* it is clear that it covers the ambit of the Roman *actio iniuriarum* as well as that of the *Lex Aquilia* and its extensions (and more). On the views of the natural lawyers, see R. Zimmermann, *The Law of Obligations, Roman Foundations of the Civilian Tradition* (Oxford, reprint 1996), 1032–1034.

[538] Below pp. 380–381.

[539] Below pp. 386–388.

[540] Below pp. 400 ff.

[541] Below, pp. 393 ff.

[542] *Loi* no. 85-677 of 5 Jul. 1985 ('*loi* of 5 Jul. 1985') below, p. 400.

[543] *Loi* no. 98-389 of 19 May 1998 ('*loi* of 19 May 1998') creating arts. 1386-1–1386-18 C. civ., below, p. 406.

[544] *Loi* no 2002–303 of 4 Mar. 2002 ('*loi* of 4 Mar. 2002'); *Loi* no. 2002-1577 of 30 Dec. 2002 ('*Loi* of 30 Dec. 2002'), below, p. 409.

[545] Below, pp. 401, 406 and 409 respectively.

who can recover and types of harm recoverable, and the defences available.[546] Whether or not these regimes are included within the Civil Code[547] and whether or not they replace or co-exist with its general bases of liability,[548] they have led to a much greater specialization of treatment within the law of civil liability. Moreover, these developments in the law of liability have been paralleled by the multiplication of legislative schemes providing for the allocation of compensation in respect of death or personal injuries from special funding bodies (*fonds de garantie* or *fonds d'indemnisation*) set up for the purpose, notably, compensation for the victims of crime,[549] those contracting HIV by blood transfusion,[550] and, most recently, of some medical accidents.[551] The resulting compartmentalization and complexity of the law has led some to call for reform of the law on a more rational basis.[552] In this respect, the ambitions of the *Avant-projet de réforme* as regards civil liability are fairly modest, seeking for the most part merely to set out (very much in the same legislative style as the existing code, if at greater length) the judicial developments of the last century but to leave aside the special regimes of liability.[553]

Thirdly, great swathes of cases which in English law attract liability under the law of torts are not in French law dealt with by the law of delict at all. Sometimes, this is the result of the existence of another category of liability which is held to be exclusive of (the private law of) delict, as is the case as regards both *contractual* liability and *administrative* liability. As regards the former, we have already seen how French law has manipulated the line between contract and delict in order to impose what is considered to be the appropriate rule.[554] And as regards the latter, we have seen how the Conseil d'Etat has developed a parallel system of rules of administrative liability, rules which typically apply to the liability of the administration but which may apply also as between private individuals; but whenever they do apply they oust the private law.[555] But the ambit of the private

---

[546] See below, pp. 400 ff, 406 ff, 409 ff.

[547] The new legislation was by amendment to the Civil Code in the case of product liability (below, p. 406), but not motor-vehicle liability or medical liability (below, pp. 400, 409).

[548] The law governing motor-vehicle accidents governs the cases within its ambit to the exclusion of other bases of liability (below, p. 400); the special product liability rules exist in parallel to existing general laws of liability for delictual fault and special rules governing contracts of sale (below, pp. 406–407); and the new law on medical liability replaces earlier public and private law rules in the area (below, p. 409).

[549] This scheme is now set out in arts. 706-3–706-15 C.P.P. after many legislative changes from *Loi* no. 77-5 of 3 Jan. 1977.

[550] *Loi* no. 91-1406 of 31 Dec. 1991, art. 47.

[551] Art. 1142-1 al. II C. santé pub. inserted by the *loi* of 4 Mar. 2002 and extended by art. 1142-22 al. 2 C. santé pub. inserted by *loi* of 30 Dec. 2002.

[552] C. Radé, 'Plaidoyer en faveur d'une réforme de la responsabilité civile' D 2003.2247.

[553] G. Viney, *De la responsabilité civile (Arts. 1340 à 1386), Exposé des motifs*, in *Avant-projet de réforme*, 161, 163.

[554] Above pp. 331–332 (relating to *obligations de sécurité*).

[555] An important example was formerly found in the case of liability for private medical care which was until the *loi* of 4 Mar. 2002 exclusively contractual, below, p. 408.

law of delict is also restricted in another way, for in one major area—accidents at work—the law ensures compensation through social security payments rather than the rules of delict or contract and where this is the case, the employer enjoys a legal immunity.[556]

Finally, before looking at liability for personal fault, it should be noted that while it may indeed apply to claims for personal injuries and damage to property—for some the heartland of English tort law—most who suffer these types of injury will be able and will prefer to claim under article 1384 al.1's liability without fault or will have a claim (if at all) only in contract owing to the rule of *non-cumul*.[557] Liability in delict for personal fault *is* relevant to compensation for personal injuries, but it does not dominate it in the way that the tort of negligence does in English law.

I. Liability for Personal Fault

Articles 1382 and 1383 of the Civil Code impose liability on a person for an action or omission which constitutes a 'fault' and which causes harm (*dommage*) to the claimant and this fault may consist either in an intentional or negligent causing of harm. These bare statements are most noticeable for what they do not say, rather than for what they do.[558]

First, there is no exclusion of recovery in respect of any particular *type of harm*. Thus, a claimant may in principle claim for personal injuries, damage to or loss of property, *dommage moral* (a very broad category which includes psychiatric injury, grief, upset or mental distress), 'aesthetic harm', inconvenience or what a common lawyer would call pure economic loss. There are, indeed, in French law no special rules which apply to the recovery of any particular type of harm *as such*,[559] though special rules do apply to particular sets of circumstances in which a particular type of harm may be thought to be typically concerned.[560] Of these inclusions, of course, it is pure economic loss which seems to a common lawyer so strange as to be almost incomprehensible: does French law really recognize the general recovery of *negligently or deliberately* caused pure economic loss outside contract? Can English and French law be *quite* so different here? As we shall see, the answer is both yes and no.

---

[556] *Loi* of 30 October 1946 codified in art. 451-1 ff C. séc. soc. The only exceptions to this immunity are where the employer has committed an 'intentional or inexcusable fault' or an employee has committed an intentional fault.

[557] Above pp. 328–329.

[558] See G. Viney, 'Pour ou contre un "principe générale" de responsabilité civil pour faute?' in *Mélanges offerts à Pierre Catala* (Litec, 2001); S. Whittaker, 'La responsabilité pour le fait personnel dans l'avant-projet de réforme du droit de la responsabilité: donner voix aux silences du Code civil?' in *L'avant-projet de réforme du droit de la responsabilité* (Editions Les Manuscrit, Paris, 2006), 163.

[559] The very few exceptions to this are discussed below p. 414.

[560] See especially below p. 376 ff and p. 380.

Secondly, there is no exclusion nor indeed any special treatment in the Code of liability for even 'pure omissions' (i.e. those which do not arise in the course of an activity). Here, however, the courts have developed a special stance.

Thirdly, the courts and the vast majority of *la doctrine* do not resort to the concept of duty to define and control the circumstances in which liability for 'fault' may arise, in contrast to the 'duty of care' in the English tort of negligence. On the other hand, the concept of duty does figure in relation to defining what fault may *sometimes* be. Thus, while delictual fault may exist in the absence of breach of a duty, breach of a duty will constitute delictual fault.

All this lack of restrictions makes clear how much weight is thrust in French law onto the idea of 'fault'. So, while the requirement of a causal link between this fault and the claimant's harm may also sometimes act as a way of restricting the ambit of liability (though somewhat unprovably given the discretion of the *juges du fond* in this respect),[561] we shall concentrate here on this core notion of fault and see how under this word French law has in a sense reinvented the particularity of treatment associated with those legal systems which recognize only 'nominate delicts'. Having said this, however, it must constantly be recalled that these are islands of special treatment in a sea or seas of liability, rather than (as in the English law of torts) islands of liability in a sea of immunity. To this extent, there is a greater closeness between the French law of contract and delict than at first sight appears: for both recognize the existence of general principles and of special rules governing particular classes of case.

The various juristic definitions of delictual fault found in French texts are not particularly informative. While Planiol famously suggested that it should be defined as the non-performance of a pre-existing legal duty,[562] this definition has not generally found favour, being considered inaccurate (there being no need for a claimant to prove any such duty), unnecessary and unhelpful.[563] Instead, fault is said to consist of any 'abnormal behaviour' (*comportement anormal*) or simply failing to do what one should.[564] Such a definition is helpful only in that it emphasizes how open the question of fault may be. And while in principle the courts take an objective standard in deciding what a reasonable man (*bon père de famille*) ought to do in any particular circumstance, the looseness of this definition allows very considerable room for manoeuvre. Moreover, while it is true that the Cour de cassation reserves for itself the decision as to whether the facts as 'sovereignly decided' by the *juges du fond* 'possess the legal characteristics of fault provided for by the law'[565] and, therefore, ultimately decides what type of

---

[561] Below p. 410 ff.

[562] M. Planiol, 'Etudes sur la responsabilité civile' (1905); Rev. crit. 277, 287.

[563] Malaurie, Aynès, and Stoffel-Munck, *Obligations*, 30ff; Flour, Aubert, and Savaux, *Fait juridique*, 98. cf. Viney and Jourdain, *Conditions*, 326 ff who defines fault as the breach of a duty, explaining cases where no legal duty is broken or legal right violated as ones of 'extra-contractual duties created by *la jurisprudence*'.

[564] Flour, Aubert, and Savaux, *Fait juridique*, 99.

[565] Civ. 28 Feb. 1910, S 1911.1.329 note Appert; Civ. (2) 3 Nov. 1955, D 1956.78.

conduct *may* constitute fault, it often chooses not to disturb their findings on this issue. The lower courts themselves are often inspired by ideas of morality and fairness, if not indeed the ability of the defendant to compensate the claimant. As Carbonnier puts it:

> nowhere more than in relation to fault do the judges proceed by way of a judgment based on fairness [*équité*] condemning or pardoning in the name of society… The Cour de cassation's assessment is an overall one, acting as a court of *review of excesses in fairness*. Rather than ensuring that the law is respected, its role here appears to be to prevent (in the interest, most often—why shouldn't one say it?—of insurance companies and parties with deep pockets) an over-charitable fairness, which would let the evaluation of needs and resources come before the morality of the case.[566]

However, it would be a mistake to think that all decisions on the issue of fault are, to use the somewhat derogatory common law expression, merely 'policy decisions' on the facts. And we can indeed explain a little bit more what 'fault' means before looking more closely at particular instances.

First, it is clear that either an intention to cause harm or negligence (meaning a lack of reasonable care) *may* constitute fault but will *not always* do so.

Secondly, the breach of a pre-existing duty, whether contained in legislation, administrative regulation or in the rules of say, a professional association *will* be treated as fault: a *bon père de famille* plays by the rules.

Thirdly, and *a fortiori*, French law considers that the commission of any criminal offence itself constitutes a civil fault. This means, strangely for a common lawyer, that a claimant who can establish that the defendant's action constituted an offence may succeed in a claim for damages on the basis of delictual fault, even though he can prove neither intention nor negligence: the commission of offences of strict liability constitutes delictual fault too! As will be seen, this rule is of very considerable importance both at the level of substantive law and of procedure.[567]

Fourthly, French law sometimes looks at the issue of fault in terms of *rights* rather than *duties,* these rights being either the claimant's or the defendant's. A prime example where the starting point is the claimant's rights may be found in relation to the protection of a person's 'rights of personality', which include the right to one's image, to reputation and to a private life. Here, the law defines the claimant's rights, any violation of which by a defendant will necessarily constitute a fault so as to attract civil liability.[568] Conversely, where a defendant is exercising a particular right—such as the right to strike or to enforce a court's judgment—the courts will not hold that exercise to constitute a fault unless it can be said to have been *abused.*

All this makes clear that in fact while articles 1382 and 1383 of the Civil Code do not indicate the circumstances in which delictual liability will be imposed

---

[566] *Obligations,* 2306 (emphasis added).
[567] Below, pp. 368–373.
[568] Below pp. 376–380.

on the basis of fault, there is no shortage of law—whether legislative or judge-made—to give a much clearer picture of where it will. This law is not, however, to be found in the Code's provisions on delict—nor, it must be said, in many of the French works on *obligations,* which often content themselves with general discussions—but rather in the particular rules of the criminal law and the law as a whole. In a very real sense, therefore, much of the concrete law of delictual liability for fault is to be found scattered throughout the legal system. It is in the light of this which we should see French lawyers' attachment to the general principle of liability for fault and, indeed, its recognition by the Conseil constitutionnel as possessing a constitutional importance: for if, as article 4 of the Declaration of the Rights of Man of 1789 affirms, 'liberty consists in being able to do anything which does not harm another person', then this entails that 'any human action whatsoever which causes harm to another creates an obligation in the person by whose fault it was caused to make reparation for it'.[569]

The rest of this part will, therefore, look at various more particular circumstances in which the idea of fault has been applied. All but the first is a recognizably French category. It will be seen that, in Starck's words, 'fault' is indeed 'a veritable legal chameleon, changing according to its context'.[570]

A. Negligence

A defendant's lack of appropriate care[571] in the circumstances may certainly constitute fault so as to attract civil liability. Thus, for example, a pedestrian who is injured on the roads may recover damages against a driver whose negligence he can prove caused his injuries. The standard of care in relation to negligence is, as we have said, in principle an objective one: the *bon père de famille* placed in the same situation as the defendant.[572] But (quite apart from the questions of capacity which have given rise to considerable dispute in French law),[573] subjective factors are taken into account to a degree. So, positively, a defendant's possession of special skill or knowledge in relation to the activity from which the harm has arisen is a reason for increasing the standard of care; whereas, negatively, the limited skills, age or infirmity of the defendant may attract a lesser standard of care. However, we do not find in French discussions, whether juristic or judicial, any equivalent of the cost/benefit analysis so typical of common law negligence, under which the cost (financial and social) of avoiding the claimant's harm is

---

[569] Cons. const. 9 Nov. 1999, décision no. 99-419, *loi relative au pacte civil de solidarité,* JCP 1999.III.20173, para. 70. Cf. earlier Cons. const. 22 Oct. 1982, *Labbé* (1982) R.D.C.C. 61.

[570] B. Starck, 'Des contrats conclus en violation des droits contractuels d'autrui' JCP 1954.I.1180 at para. 38.

[571] This is usually termed *imprudence* or *manque de diligence* rather than *négligence* which has more often the sense of a failure to act in contrast to *fait,* a deed or action.

[572] Terré, Simler, and Lequette, *Obligations,* 701.

[573] Notably in relation to the mentally incapable and minors: on which see art. 489-2 C. civ. and Ass. plén. 9 May 1984. *Derguini,* D 1984.525 note Chabas respectively.

weighed against the benefit (in terms of the probability and magnitude of the claimant's harm) in so doing.[574] This should not be surprising because in cases involving claims based on the defendant's negligence, and especially where this involves the assessment of any technical or scientific aspect of the case, the report of the judicially appointed expert is usually of *decisive* importance, for only in the most extreme cases will the *juges du fond* reject the view taken by an *expertise* and either substitute its own or order a fresh report.[575] And while experts may well take into account the sort of considerations which an English court would in this respect, these considerations are not required by the law to be weighed as they are in English law.

B. Criminal Responsibility and Civil Liability

The relationship between the commission of a criminal offence and the imposition of civil liability for delictual fault has long been a very important one in French law and has been the subject of considerable controversy and, more recently, reform.[576] This relationship possesses two main aspects.

First, at the level of legal institutions and procedure, in general French law allows victims of crimes to set in motion the criminal process by accusing a person (or person or persons unknown) of committing an offence to their prejudice, this being known as 'constituting themselves as *parties civiles*' ('civil parties'); equally, they may join proceedings already started by the public prosecutor, the *ministère public*.[577] The initiation of proceedings by a *partie civile* requires the investigating magistrate, the *juge d'instruction*,[578] to decide whether a prosecution should be brought and on what charges.[579] If criminal proceedings are brought to court, a victim of the crime can claim damages against the defendant by way of what is known as an *action civile*, the victim thereby becoming a full party to the criminal proceedings, represented in court.[580] Traditionally, criminal courts could impose civil liability in damages on the defendant for the benefit of the *partie civile* who has personally suffered direct harm as a result only if the defendant was found guilty of the crime,[581] but their power to impose liability has been considerably extended (as will be explained below).[582] Practically, there have been

---

[574] Whittaker, *Liability for Products*, 186 ff.

[575] J. Beardsley, 'Proof of fact in French Civil Procedure' (1986) 24 Am J Comp Law 459, esp. at 480 ff and see above pp. 106–108. on the role of *experts*.

[576] For more detail see Whittaker, *Liability for Products*, Ch. 14.

[577] Crim. 8 Dec.1906, *arrêt Thirion*, D 1907.1.207, rapp. Laurent-Attalin and Crim. 28 May 1925, *arrêt Bencker*, DP 1926.1.121 note Leloir and see arts. 1 al. 2, 85 *et seq.* C.P.P. On the *ministère public,* see above, pp. 60–61.

[578] Above, pp. 130 ff.

[579] Arts. 176, 177, 178 al. 1, 179 al. 1, 181 al. 1 C.P.P.

[580] Art. 2 C.P.P.

[581] This power is still contained in art. 2 al. 1 C.P.P.

[582] Below, p. 370.

a number of reasons why a victim of a crime may prefer to follow this criminal route to the recovery of damages:[583] as *partie civile,* a claimant can take advantage of the considerable investigative powers of the *juge d'instruction* (at the state's expense);[584] the criminal process is generally reckoned to be quicker and cheaper than claiming in the civil courts;[585] and the criminal courts have long shown very considerable concern to ensure compensation for the victims of crime, especially in the case of personal injuries or death. Moreover, the *action civile* is seen as having a double aspect, partly aimed at compensation, partly at vengeance.[586]

Secondly, at the level of substantive law, from the beginning of the 20th century French courts and writers accepted what became termed the 'unity of criminal and civil faults'.[587] As has been seen,[588] criminal offences are said to possess three aspects, the mental element (*l'élément moral*), the 'physical' elements (*l'élément matériel*) and the 'legal' element (*l'élément légal*).[589] Where the mental element required for the commission of a particular criminal offence is satisfied there is said to be *une faute pénale* even though the offence is one of strict liability, requiring neither intention nor negligence.[590] The central consequence of the doctrine of the unity of criminal and civil faults was that the commission of a criminal offence of any kind itself constituted fault for the purposes of civil liability under articles 1382 or 1383 of the Civil Code.[591] However, for many years there were a number of other consequences associated with this doctrine, in particular that any *acquittal* of a defendant by a criminal court ruled out the imposition of civil liability for fault either by itself or by a subsequent civil court.[592] In the context of accidents causing personal injuries and death, this severe consequence of acquittal led French criminal courts for a long time to find defendants guilty of criminal offences as long as they could find a 'speck of fault' so as to ensure that the 'victims' recovered compensation;[593] it also led the legislature to change the law

---

[583] Whittaker, *Liability for Products*, 384–386.

[584] Art. 81ff C.P.P. and see above, pp. 132–133.

[585] Pradel, *Procédure pénale*, 230.

[586] F. Boulan, 'Le double visage de l'action civile exercée devant la juridiction repressive' JCP 1973.I.2563; Viney and Jourdain, *Introduction à la responsabilité*, 128–129.

[587] Viney and Jourdain, ibid., 260ff.

[588] Above, p. 204.

[589] Above, pp. 204, 206 ff.

[590] F. Desportes and F. Le Gunehec, *Droit pénal générale,* 10th. edn. (Economica, 2003), 405ff.

[591] Civ. 19 Dec. 1912, S 1914.1.249 note Morel; Viney and Jourdain, *Introduction à la responsabilité* 260 *et seq.*

[592] This result was termed *l'autorité de la chose jugée au criminel sur le civil:* S. Guinchard and J. Buisson, *Procédure pénale*, 2nd edn. (Litec, 2002), 773. Another aspect of the 'unity doctrine' was that any civil claim (even if brought before the *civil* courts) was restricted to the prescription period applicable to the criminal prosecution, but this rule was abolished in 1980: *Loi* no. 80-1042 of 23 Dec. 1980, new art. 10 C.P.P.

[593] G. Viney, *Les obligations, La responsabilité: conditions* in J. Ghestin (dir.) *Traité de droit civil* (LDGJ, Paris, 1982), 186. The criminal courts also took a more lenient view of the required causal connection between the defendant's action and the claimant's harm: R. Merle and A. Vitu, *Traité de droit criminel, Problèmes généraux de la science crimenelle, Droit pénal général,* 6th edn. (Eds. Cujas, Paris, 1984), 680 *et seq.* This difference was also noted by the senator who reported on the

so as to allow a criminal court to impose civil liability towards a *partie civile* after an acquittal on a legal basis *other than* fault, notably, liability for the 'actions of things' under article 1384 al. 1 of the Civil Code.[594]

As regards compensation in respect of death and personal injuries, there is, however, a further, crucial ingredient in the importance of the role of the criminal courts: the definition of the criminal offences themselves. From the first Criminal Code of 1810, French law has contained very broad criminal offences of non-intentional causing death and personal injuries, known as *homicide involontaire* ('involuntary homicide') and *blessures et coups involontaires* ('causing personal injuries').[595] Originally, the Code provided that a person committed a *délit* (an offence of intermediate seriousness[596]) where he caused the death of another person through 'clumsiness, imprudence, inattention, negligence or failure to observe rules'[597] (similar provision being made for causing personal injuries),[598] and these provisions lasted with some minor amendment into the new Criminal Code of 1994.[599] It can be seen how easily French lawyers could hold that the commission of such a criminal offence could *in itself* constitute delictual fault so as to attract civil liability, for it is drafted in very inclusive words reminiscent of article 1383 of the Civil Code.[600] Moreover, it became established that breach of any rule (whether legislative, professional or otherwise) satisfied this test even in the absence of lack of due care.[601] The combination of the procedural and institutional attractiveness of the *action civile* and the availability of these broad crimes has given a very considerable prominence to the criminal law as the indirect basis of the imposition of liability for death and personal injuries and to the criminal courts as the forum of choice for claimants.

However, over the last ten years, this traditional picture has been changed and made considerably more complicated. The main pressure for change came from *maires*, the elected (and unpaid) officers of the smallest local authorities, the *communes*. Their concern was that a person who suffered injuries (or the relatives of a person who died) in their area could far too easily initiate criminal proceedings against them, even though the only 'negligence' alleged against them was a failure properly to exercise their considerable local powers over health and safety— although in principle, of course, their liability in damages was not based on the *private* law of civil liability, but instead only on the administrative law of liability

---

legislative reforms of 2000 (on which see below, p. 371): P. Fauchon, *Rapport sur la proposition de loi de M. Pierre Fauchon, tendant à préciser la définition des délits non intentionnels,* Sénat No. 177 (20 Jan. 2000) para. I (B)4.

[594] *Loi* no. 83-608 of 8 Jul. 1983, new art. 470-1 C.P.P.

[595] Arts. 319–320 A.c.pén.

[596] Above, pp. 205–206.

[597] Art. 319 A.c.pén. (as originally drafted).

[598] Art. 320 A.c.pén.

[599] Art. 221-6 C.pén.; arts. R. 622-1, 625-2 C.pén.

[600] Above, p. 361.

[601] Merle and Vitu, op. cit. n. 593, 739. So, e.g. breach of the rules of rugby football was enough: Crim. 24 Jan. 1956, D 1956.197.

as assessed by the administrative courts.[602] The French legislature has intervened in three ways in attempting to deal with this situation.

First, in 1996 the existing requirements for the 'mental element' for *all délits* found in article 121-3 of the Criminal Code (which refers to *imprudence* or *négligence*[603]) was supplemented by a condition that the defendant failed to take 'normal care taking into account, where appropriate, the nature of his mission or his duties, of his abilities as well as of the power and means which he possessed'.[604] The purpose of this change was to remove the possibility of a person being held guilty of a *délit* (notably, involuntary homicide or causing serious personal injuries) by the commission of an offence of strict liability or breach of an administrative regulation by moving from an objective assessment of the negligence of the defendant for the purposes of these criminal responsibilities to a subjective assessment ('*une appréciation* in concreto').[605]

Secondly, in 2000 article 121-3 of the Criminal Code was again amended so as to provide that the mental element of *délits* committed by negligence (including involuntary homicide and causing serious personal injuries) can be satisfied only by either a 'manifestly deliberate breach of a particular obligation of care or safety provided by *loi* or *règlement*' or an 'aggravated fault' (*une faute caractérisée*) which 'exposed another person to an especially serious risk of which they could not be unaware', but these new requirements apply only where the defendant is a physical person (thus ruling out companies and public bodies) who has 'not directly caused the harm but who [has] created or contributed to the creation of the situation which allowed the occurrence of the damage or who [has] not taken measures allowing it to be avoided'.[606] The intended effect of this complex change was to reduce the incidence of criminal responsibility in public decision-makers, but it is drafted so as to apply much more generally. Where it applies it breaks the 'unity' of criminal and civil faults in the sense that sometimes the ordinary fault required by the Civil Code will no longer be enough to satisfy the special mental elements required by the Criminal Code.[607] But the break is only partial because in most cases criminal fault remains the same as civil fault (the exception being where an indirect harm is caused by an individual[608]) and, more importantly, because the divorce only works one-way: for while not all civil faults constitute criminal faults, all criminal faults still necessarily constitute civil faults.[609] This

---

[602] Above, pp. 188 ff.

[603] Art. 121-3 al. 1 C. pén.

[604] *Loi* no. 96-393 of 13 May 1996, art. 1.

[605] Desportes and Le Gunehec, op. cit. n. 590, 439–440.

[606] Art. 121-3 C. pén. inserted by *loi* no. 2000-647 of 10 July 2000 ('*loi* of 10 July 2000') art. 1.

[607] Y. Mayaud, 'Sommaire de jurisprudence sur les violences non intentionnelles après la loi du 10 juillet 2000' *Revue de science criminelle* (2001) 156, 163.

[608] Pradel, *Droit pénal*, 462.

[609] P. Jourdain, 'Autorité de la chose jugée au pénal et principe d'unité des fautes: la rupture est consommée entre faute civile et faute pénale, mais l'est-elle totalment' D 2001.Somm. comm. 2232, 2233.

means that where a criminal court finds a defendant guilty of a criminal offence of involuntary homicide or causing personal injuries it still has both the power and the substantive legal foundation for the imposition of civil liability in damages on the defendant (or those who are responsible for him[610]) to the victim.

Moreover, a third change made in 2000 might well have enhanced the importance of claims in respect of death and personal injuries being made in the criminal courts, for then it was provided that acquittal of a person of a criminal offence does not prevent a civil court from holding him liable in damages on the basis of civil fault in respect of the same action or omission,[611] the intention being to remove the incentive for a criminal court to find 'specks of fault' in the interests of compensating the *partie civile*. However, the Cour de cassation has held that this rule applies also to the criminal courts so that a victim of an alleged crime can see the defendant acquitted but then recover damages straightaway on the basis of mere civil fault.[612] This change therefore removes one of the risks of using the criminal route to obtain damages in respect of death or personal injuries.

This discussion of the role of the criminal law and criminal procedure in forming the background to the imposition of civil liability in respect of accidental death and personal injuries should not give the impression that they are not also important outside this context. For, *whenever* a person suffers personal harm caused directly by a criminal offence, he or she may become *partie civile* and claim damages by this route. In the context of offences of intention, this may not appear to add very much at a substantive level to the generality of understanding of fault in article 1382 of the Civil Code, but it can be helpful in that the existence and especially the creation of a crime can make clear what must count as unacceptable *intentional* conduct. For example, while sexual harassment had previously been relevant to the relations of employer and employee, the New Criminal Code created an offence of sexual harassment, committed when a person 'harasses another by using orders, threats or pressure with the aim of obtaining favours of a sexual nature by a person abusing the authority which his office confers on him'; and this definition was later broadened so that 'any act of harassment with the aim of obtaining favours of a sexual nature' became an offence.[613] The existence of the crime means that a victim of sexual harassment as defined by it may recover damages in delict in respect of the financial loss or *dommage moral* which it causes. So too, where an offence relating to an anti-competitive practice is committed its 'victim' may recover damages for the typically financial losses which he can prove were directly caused by it.[614] The

---

[610] i.e. employers or insurers: arts. 388-1–388-3 C.P.P.

[611] Art. 4-1 C.P.P. inserted by *loi* of 10 July 2000, art.2 .

[612] C. Roca, 'Nouvelle définition de l'infraction non intentionnelle: une réforme qui en cache une autre plus importante' *Petites affiches* (26 Oct. 2000) no. 214, 5.

[613] Art. 222-33 C. pén. amended by *loi* no. 2002-73 of 17 January 2002, art. 179.

[614] M. Delmas-Marty and G. Guidicelli-Delage, *Droit pénal des affaires*, 4th edn. (2000), 519 ff.

criminal law does not *define* what may constitute 'civil' unfair competition (*concurrence déloyale*), since a court may, as we shall see, hold a person civilly at fault on this basis in the absence of an offence;[615] but it does clearly mark out what *will* constitute unfair competition for civil as well as criminal purposes. However, if this equation of criminal intention and negligence with civil fault is conceptually unremarkable, it is more surprising that French law holds that the commission of an offence of *strict* liability (*une infraction matérielle*) in itself constitutes delictual *fault* so as to attract compensation for its victim.[616]

C. Breach of duty

French lawyers have taken a similarly broad view of the significance of breaches of duties not sanctioned by a criminal offence for the imposition of civil liability, holding that in principle *all* breaches of mandatory duties constitute 'fault' for this purpose, whether the source of the duty is legislative or regulatory[617] and whether it belongs to private or to public law.[618] So, for example, breach of planning constraints constitutes a fault in itself so as to allow a person who has suffered loss as a result to recover damages.[619] Moreover, breach of professional standards, such as the failure of a surgeon to obtain the informed consent to treatment of his patient[620] or the failure of a company auditor (*commissaire aux comptes*) to follow professional standards will themselves constitute a fault.[621] And, as has been seen, recently French courts have held that a failure to perform a contractual obligation can give rise to delictual liability for fault towards third parties to the contract, whatever the content of the obligation in question.[622]

D. The Abuse of Rights

The notion of the 'abuse of rights' (*abus de droit*) became current in French juristic debate at the beginning of the 20th century and has enjoyed an important impact on French law, both theoretically and practically. While we cannot enter the debate here, we can note that there have been three main ways in which it has been argued that a person who holds a legal right may abuse it: the person may be said (i) to have committed a 'fault in the exercise of the right'; (ii) to have possessed an intention to harm or been malicious towards another person; or (iii) to

---

[615] Below, pp. 380–381.

[616] Terré, Simler, and Lequette, *Obligations*, 374 (though with a degree of hesitation).

[617] See above, pp 21–22 for this distinction.

[618] Terré, Simler, and Lequette, *Obligations*, 705; Viney and Jourdain, *Conditions*, 375–376. And see the general definition of *la faute* in art. 1352 al. 2 A.-p.r.

[619] Viney and Jourdain, ibid.

[620] Rouen 26 Feb. 1969, JCP 1971.II.16849.

[621] Com. 27 Oct. 1992, JCP 1993.II.22026 note Jeantin. Breach of the rules of a sport do not, however, constitute fault unless they are serious: Malaurie, Aynès, and Stoffel-Munck, *Obligations*, 65.

[622] Above, pp. 338–339.

have used the right contrary to its social purpose.[623] The courts have not accepted any single view, but have taken different views depending on the context, sometimes overtly referring to the notion and sometimes not. This should not be surprising as the idea of the abuse of rights has been applied to rights arising from a wide variety of sources, notably (but by no means exclusively) the use of property, family relations, legal procedure and labour relations.[624] This general legal phenomenon is important for the French law of delict because liability in damages is a frequent, though not the only, sanction of any such abuse of rights.[625] Thus, an abuse of rights (however this is defined in the particular context) constitutes delictual fault and where it has caused the claimant harm, will attract liability.

A notable example may be found in relation to the right to strike,[626] a right which, however, it has frequently been held may be abused. Here, the issue of abuse of rights is a finely-poised one: for the whole point of a strike is deliberately to cause harm to an employer so as to persuade him to change his mind about some issue of concern to the employee. As a result, the courts have held that the right to strike may be abused either in relation to the methods which are used (strike by rota or repeated strikes where they aim at the concerted disruption of production being disapproved) or the aims which are pursued ('political strikes' being disapproved for this purpose).[627] Another important example may be found in relation to the abuse of procedural rights. So, for example, a civil action brought maliciously may give rise to liability for this abuse of process to the defendant for any harm this may have caused, a liability that was for long used to supplement the rather meagre provision in French law for the recovery of costs.[628] However, malice or an intention to harm is not always required. Thus a party to litigation who had obtained a 'non-definitive judgment' and proceeded precipitately to obtain execution of the debt on the other's property, was held liable to that other party when the judgment was overturned 'without the need to find any intention to harm'.[629]

Finally, it should be noted here that many of the cases which an English lawyer would deal with by private nuisance would in French law attract the doctrine

---

[623] For an excellent general introduction, see Ghestin, Goubeaux, and Fabre-Magnan, *Introduction,* 747 ff. For its impact on delictual liability, see especially, Starck *et al., Responsabilité délictuelle,* 153ff.

[624] Ghestin, Goubeaux, and Fabre-Magnan, *Introduction,* 775 ff. See examples in the context of contract, above, pp. 305, 314.

[625] Apart from damages, there are two other main remedies. First, a person may be ordered by a court to stop abusing his right at the request of an interested person. Secondly, an abusive exercise of a right which would otherwise lead to a particular legal result may not have this effect, for example, if a party to a contract possesses a unilateral right to terminate the contract but purports to exercise it 'abusively', the termination will be deemed not to have taken place: see above p. 358 (bad faith).

[626] cf. below p. 508.

[627] The *jurisprudence* here is abundant, but see for an example of the latter, Soc. 23 Mar. 1953, JCP. 1953.II.7709 note Delpech.

[628] Ghestin, Goubeaux, and Fabre-Magnan, *Introduction,* 788–790 and see above pp.113–115.

[629] Civ. (1) 12 May 1971, *époux Ducis,* JCP 1971.IV.158.

of *troubles de voisinage*. This doctrine is linked historically to the law of delictual fault, which was for long used as its legal basis[630] and theoretically to the idea of the abuse of rights,[631] here rights of a landowner or other occupier to enjoy his property, but French courts now accept that it is independent of both, requiring only that the defendant's activity 'exceeds the normal measure of inconvenience as between neighbours' even in the absence of any fault.[632]

E. Omissions

French jurists distinguish between cases of liability for omissions in action, such as a driver of a car failing to indicate that he is about to turn left, and for pure omissions, such as a failure in a bystander to rescue a drowning child (though the courts do not tend to do so).[633] As we have said, articles 1382 and 1383 of the Civil Code allow liability to be imposed in respect of omissions and some jurists say that even as regards pure omissions the courts impose liability whenever a *bon père de famille* placed in the same situation would have intervened,[634] citing cases like the one in which an organizer of a competition was held liable for failing to advise its participants to take out insurance.[635] Nevertheless, a defendant's inaction will clearly constitute fault only in two types of case.[636]

The first is where the defendant was in breach of duty. Such a duty may be imposed by the criminal law, as in the famous provision in the Criminal Code which makes it an offence deliberately to fail to help a person in peril where there is no risk to oneself or others in doing so.[637] However, the duty may arise in other ways and the leading case is the *affaire Branly*, even though it was arguably a case of an 'omission in action'.[638] In this case, the defendant had written a history of the development of telegraphy which had omitted all reference to the part played in this development by Branly.[639] The *juges du fond* had denied liability on the basis that it had not been shown that the defendant had been motivated by any malice or intention to harm Branly and therefore was not at fault, but this decision was quashed by the Cour de cassation which declared that a failure to act may constitute fault even in the absence of such an intention where the defendant had an 'obligation to act, whether this arose from legislation, *règlement*, an

---

[630] Carbonnier, *Obligations*, 1784–1787.

[631] See, e.g. Starck *et al.*, *Responsabilité délictuelle*, 168.

[632] Malaurie and Aynès, *Biens*, 317 ff. and see e.g. Civ. (3) 4 Feb. 1971 (2 cases) JCP 1971. II.16781 note Lindon.

[633] Flour, Aubert, and Savaux, *Fait juridique*, 106–107.

[634] Bénabent, *Obligations*, 377; similarly, Flour, Aubert, and Savaux, *Fait juridique*, 109, 112.

[635] Civ. (1) 13 Jul. 1982, D 1983. 225 note Agostini.

[636] Carbonnier, *Obligations*, 2296; Terré, Simler, and Lequette, *Obligations*, 705–707; Malaurie, Aynès, and Stoffel-Munck, *Obligations*, 36–37.

[637] Art. 63 al. 2 A.c.pén., now art. 223-6 al. 2 N.c.pén., above p. 216.

[638] Civ. 27 Feb. 1951, D 1951. 329 note Desbois.

[639] The action was brought by Branly's heirs in a representative capacity.

agreement or, in the professional context, and notably in relation to historians, by virtue of the need to inform objectively'.

The second exception is already apparent, for French jurists and courts accept that an omission made with the intention of harming another person will give rise to delictual liability.[640]

However, the courts have sometimes imposed liability for omissions which they consider reprehensible in other cases, this being related sometimes to the notion of abuse of rights which we have already noticed. So, for example, where a husband and wife are married under Jewish law as well as civilly, his failure on civil divorce to deliver to his wife a letter of *gueth* as is required by Jewish law may constitute an *abus de droit* and give rise to damages even in the absence of any intention to harm her.[641]

F. Rights of Personality

One of the most important uses to which the law of delictual liability has been put has been the recognition and protection of various 'rights of personality' of individuals and here the concept of fault in the defendant often (though by no means always) seems to bear the meaning simply of a denial of the claimant's right: so the Cour de cassation has declared that 'the mere finding of an infringement of a person's private life gives rise to a right to reparation'.[642] The category of rights of personality is a particularly large and fluid one and has important consequences outside the law of delict, but we shall look at three clear examples in which delict has been important, these being a person's right to reputation, to his or her own image and to a 'private life'. Historically, these rights, through at times paralleled by developments in national legislation[643] or international convention,[644] have been the creation of the courts, who have constructed them on the bare delictual framework of a defendant's fault causing the claimant's (usually 'moral') harm. The judge-made nature of this law remains the case even after the legislative recognition in 1970 of perhaps the most important of the rights of personality: for the grand declaration in article 9 al. 1 of the Civil Code that 'everyone has the right to respect of his private life'[645] gave legislative recognition of the work of the courts but clearly did not attempt to define the line between a person's

---

[640] Terré, Simler, and Lequette, *Obligations*, 707.

[641] Civ. (2) 15 Jun. 1988, JCP 1989.II.21223 note Morançais-Demeester. The courts have refused to order the former husband to deliver the *gueth* as he has '*une simple faculté relevant de sa liberté de conscience*': Civ. (2) 21 Nov. 1990, D 1991. 434 note Agostini.

[642] Civ. (1) 5 Nov. 1996, Bull. civ. I no. 378; Viney and Jourdain, *Conditions*, 377–378.

[643] Here, the *loi* of 29 July 1881 on the freedom of the press, art. 29 ff has been particularly important, not merely in its creation of the offences of *diffamation* and *injure* but in its recognition of the distinction between a person's private and public life.

[644] I.e. The European Convention on Human Rights, art. 8.1.

[645] *Loi* no. 70-643 of 17 July 1970, art. 22.

private and public life.[646] Needless to say what follows is a mere taste of the complex jurisprudence which has grown up around this distinction and the other two rights of personality.

1. Right to reputation

A person's right to reputation (*droit à l'honneur*) is both more and less extensively protected in French law than under the English law of defamation. Our starting-point here must be the creation in 1881 of two criminal offences, *diffamation* and *injure*.[647] *Diffamation* consists of the publication by the defendant of facts relating to the claimant, whether these facts are true or not; *injure*, on the other hand, consists of the use of 'outrageous expressions' which do not impute particular facts to the defendant (one leading text gives the calling of another a 'pedantic prig' as an example!).[648] Both offences require that the defendant was malicious or in bad faith in making the statement in question,[649] though such a 'culpable intention' is deemed to exist in the absence of proof of good faith,[650] a proof which the courts have proved reluctant to admit.[651] More surprisingly, truth is a defence only as regards those imputations which relate to a person's public life: a person's private life is protected from even truthful imputations.[652] In accordance with the general rule,[653] a defendant who commits either of these offences will be liable in damages to anyone who suffers harm as a result, though both the criminal prosecution and the civil action possess a prescription period of a mere three months.[654]

The question whether these offences circumscribe the protection given by the French civil law to a person's right to reputation has become more controversial. The traditional approach was to say that they did not.[655] So, for example, in the *affaire des scouts*,[656] the defendant published a magazine containing photographs of young people dressed in scouting uniforms participating in 'erotic games' with captions parodying scouting phrases. The Cour d'appel rejected the claim

[646] The more significant changes made in 1970 relate to the possible remedies or sanctions available to a person whose private life has been compromised: see art. 9 al. 2. C. civ. and Carbonnier, *Introduction*, 533 ff.

[647] *Loi* of 29 July 1881, art. 29 (as amended).

[648] Carbonnier, *Introduction*, 511.

[649] Carbonnier, ibid.

[650] Crim, 20 Feb. 1990, *Droit pénal*, 1990 no. 250; Malaurie and Aynès, *Personnes*, 138 ff.

[651] Véron, *Droit pénal spécial*, 114–115. Cf. Civ. (2) 14 Jan. 1998, D 1999.134 note Tavieaux-Moro (restrictive attitude to the defence of good faith in the context of personal political criticism).

[652] *Loi* of 29 July 1881, art. 35 (as amended in 1944), which also provides that truth is no defence where the imputation relates to facts more than 10 years previously or an amnestied etc. offence.

[653] Above pp. 372–373.

[654] *Loi* of 29 July 1881, art. 65 and Malaurie and Aynès, *Personnes*, 139.

[655] P. Jourdain, RTDCiv. 2000.842.

[656] Civ. (2) 5 May 1993, D 1994 Somm. 193 note Massis.

of the French scouting association[657] for damages for the upset which this publication caused on the ground that where the constitutionally recognized principle of freedom of expression was in issue, the ambit of article 1382 of the Civil Code should be restricted to cases where the claimant's fundamental personal rights were affected, but this decision was quashed by the Cour de cassation, relying simply on the generality of the terms of article 1382. While this traditional approach was maintained, the courts sometimes held a person liable under article 1382 on the basis that they had abused their right of freedom of expression by prejudicing another person's reputation (for example, referring to a journalist as the 'mouth-piece' of a government minister).[658] However, in 2005 the Cour de cassation took an altogether more restrictive approach, boldly declaring that any 'abuse of freedom of expression affecting individuals' cannot be based on article 1382 of the Civil Code.[659] But it is difficult actually to find a legal ground for this denial[660] and it remains to be seen how long this case law survives.

2. Right to one's own image

French law has long recognized that a person has a right to his or her own image,[661] which means that others have no right to use a picture (and particularly a photograph) of a person without their consent, whether this is express or implied.[662] A person whose consent has not been obtained may obtain damages in respect of its publication, as well as the possibility of seeking an order forbidding its use or providing for the destruction of the offending material. Here it is clear that the mere publication of another's image without their consent itself constitutes delictual fault: there is no need for any proof of malice and a defendant's legitimate motive is not necessarily a defence.[663] On the other hand, French courts have been concerned to balance an individual's right to his own image against the principle of the freedom of the press to inform the public of matters of public interest, though in doing so they are also concerned to protect the human dignity of the individuals in question.[664] A similar approach has been taken to

---

[657] In French law, where a defendant attacks the honour of a recognized group of persons, those persons' representative organization may sue in their place.

[658] Ass. plén. 25 Feb. 2000, JCP 2000.II.10352 note Derieux. Cf. Ass. plén. 12 Jul. 2000 *affaire 'Guignols de l'Info'* JCP 2000.II.10439 note Lepage (no liability in broadcaster of satirical television puppet show to Citroën corporation in respect of loss allegedly caused to it by the depiction of its president and its products).

[659] Civ. (1) 27 Sep. 2005, D 2006.485 & 768 note Lécuyer.

[660] Lécuyer, ibid.

[661] Seine 16 Jun, 1858, *affaire de la tragédienne Rachel*, D 1858.3.62 (in which a picture of the claimant's sister on her deathbed was offered by the defendants for public sale).

[662] Malaurie and Aynès, *Personnes*, 133.

[663] Carbonnier, *Introduction*, 510 and 527.

[664] Civ. (1) 12 Jul. 2001, D 2002.1380 (person formally questioned about criminal offence); Civ. (2) 4 Nov. 2004, D 2005.696 note Copart (road accident victim's photograph used in general article on road accidents).

a person's distinctive voice as to his image,[665] but an owner of property has no exclusive right to *its* image, though he can complain of its use by a third party where this causes him an 'abnormal problem'.[666]

3. *Right to a private life*

Perhaps the most important development by the courts was their recognition of a person's right to a private life, a development which we have seen was confirmed by the new article 9 of the Civil Code.[667] The *jurisprudence* which attempts to delineate the line between a person's (protected) private life and (unprotected) public life is plentiful and complex, but it can be said that in general a person's private life includes matters relating to personal and particularly sexual relations, to his or her family, health, origin, religion[668] and even address, but not to his or her job, business activities, financial affairs or social life.[669] Even this type of broad division is, of course, very difficult to apply where the person in question is in the public eye, notably in politics or show business.[670] A person whose private life has been exposed may recover damages against the person who has done so, whether the exposure relates to true elements or not and without any need to prove malice. Here again delictual fault is to be found in the mere infringement of the right,[671] a fault which is really illusory.[672] Moreover, while damages are usually formally based on a claimant's *dommage moral*, which is often presumed, some argue that in practice the judges include a punitive element.[673]

A few examples must suffice. In one case, the defendant made a television film relating to the everyday life of residents of a home for the mentally disabled. Here, the court held that the film constituted an intrusion into the private life of the residents, made without the consent of their legal guardians and it ordered the film to be seized and damages paid.[674] However, the privacy laws can protect public figures as well as ordinary citizens, as long as their private life is at stake. So, for example, the actress Isabelle Adjani was awarded damages against a newspaper for revealing in an article that she was

---

[665] Malaurie and Aynès, *Personnes*, 136.

[666] Ass. plén. 7 May 2004, D 2004.1545.

[667] For a discussion in English see J.M. Haugh, 'Protecting Private Facts in France: the Warren & Brandeis Tort is alive and well and flourishing in France' (1994) 68 Tul. L. Rev. 1219.

[668] Civ. (1) 6 Mar. 2001, D 2002. 248 note Duvert.

[669] Malaurie and Aynès, *Personnes*, 123–126.

[670] Ibid., 124ff.

[671] Carbonnier, *Introduction*, 519.

[672] Malaurie and Aynès Personnes, 126 ff. Thus, for Haugh, (above n. 667), 1250 'the violation of privacy is a strict liability tort in France'.

[673] P. Kayser, *La protection de la vie privée par le droit*, 3rd edn. (Paris, 1995), 366–7, 369–73. Art. 9 al. 2 C. civ. gives the courts power to order any measure in order to prevent or stop an intrusion into the 'intimacy' of a person's private life and these include injunctions, the sequestration of assets and the seizure or destruction of offending material. The courts, however, exercise these powers only in extreme cases, conscious of their effect on freedom of expression: Malaurie and Aynès, *Personnes*, 127ff.

[674] Civ. (1) 24 Feb. 1993, D 1993.614 note Verheyde.

expecting a baby: as the court affirmed, 'like everybody else, artists have a right to the respect of their private life'.[675] Finally, the right to a private life has been successfully invoked by employees against their employers. So, an employer is not entitled to find out about the content of personal e-mail messages sent by his employees, even where sent from a computer which he has provided and forbidden for private use;[676] nor may an employer subject one of his employees to surveillance by a private detective at home in order to determine whether she is making false claims as to work done and expenses incurred.[677] And more generally, an employer may not dismiss an employee on the ground of circumstances relating to his or her private life, unless these are reflected in behaviour which causes problems at work.[678]

G. Inducing Breach of Contract and Unfair Competition (*Concurrence Déloyale*)

French courts have decided that special views must be taken of what constitutes fault for the purposes of delictual liability in relation to cases of inducing breach of contract and *concurrence déloyale* (unfair competition). Thus, it is clearly established that a third party to a contract may be liable in delict for inciting or otherwise contributing to a contractor's non-performance if, but only if, that third party was aware of the existence of the contract or, as the case may be, its incompatible term:[679] while neither intention to cause harm to the party to the contract nor malice is required, mere negligence in failing to know of a contract or its term benefiting the claimant is not enough, for as Viney and Jourdain observe, to impose liability on a person who merely ought to know of another's contractual obligations would be too harmful to the certainty of transactions and, indeed, economic activity more generally.[680]

   While *concurrence déloyale* may be translated as unfair competition, it includes a wide variety of types of reprehensible business behaviour, there being no set list of situations to which it applies and it possesses blurred edges with, in particular, the protection of intellectual property (whose infringement is known as *contrefaçon*). French courts have used the notion of *concurrence déloyale* as a way of 'disciplining' the market, often adding an injunction to stop the defendant's reprehensible behaviour to an award of damages.[681] The legal basis for these damages is simply delictual fault,[682] but the deliberate or negligent infliction of (typically) financial

---

[675] Civ. (2) 5 Jan. 1983, Bull. civ. II no. 4.
[676] Soc. 2 Oct. 2001, D 2001.3148, D 2002.2296 note Caron.
[677] Soc. 26 Nov. 2002, D 2003.1858, D 2003.394 note Fabre.
[678] Soc. 9 Jul. 2002, *Droit Famille* 2003. Comm. no. 22.
[679] See generally Ghestin, Jamin, and Billau, *Les effets du contrat,* 796ff; Viney and Jourdain, *Introduction à la responsabilité,* 367ff; Bénabent, *Obligations,* 184ff esp. at 185.
[680] *Introduction à la responsabilité,* 381.
[681] For a brief introduction, Pédamon, *Droit commercial,* 532ff. esp. at 541.
[682] See above, p. 364.

harm in the market does not necessarily give rise to liability: market activity must be *unfair* to constitute a fault.[683] Not surprisingly, there is a very complex *jurisprudence* on this question, the only unifying idea behind which being that the defendant's behaviour was contrary to commercial custom or business decency.[684] On the other hand, where it was 'unfair', liability may be imposed in the absence of an intention to harm or of malice.[685] So, for example, where a claimant business complains that another (the defendant) has used its trading name, then (assuming that this would give rise to confusion in the claimant's customers) the defendant is liable without more: in this case (which is very close to infringement of a person's intellectual property rights) fault has been 'emptied of its psychological content'.[686] In other types of case, for example, where critical publicity is released about another's business or product, an intention to harm or negligence is required for liability to be imposed, these going to whether the criticism is 'good or bad' (goodness not here residing in truth but in the manner in which the criticism is made!).[687] In still other cases, the definition of unfair market behaviour requires an element of intention to harm, if not maliciousness, as in the cases of the taking of another's business know-how, trade secrets or lists of clients.[688] This is clearly not the place to expose this complex law, but even this taste is enough to show that, under the generality of articles 1382 and 1383 of the Civil Code there lurks a teeming mass of particular solutions attuned to their context.

II. Liability for the 'Actions of Things'

Article 1384 al. 1 of the Civil Code states that:

One is liable not only for the harm which one causes by one's own action but also for that which is caused by the action of persons for whom one is responsible, or of things which one has in one's keeping.

It is clear that this provision was originally intended as a preface to those which followed which deal with particular cases of liability for another person's actions and for things within one's keeping.[689] As regards the latter, articles 1385 and 1386 follow quite closely the position in Roman law[690] and impose liability without

---

[683] Starck *et al.*, *Responsabilité délictuelle*, 150.

[684] '*Un manquement aux usages du commerce et à l'honnêteté professionnelle*': Pédamon, *Droit commercial*, 532.

[685] Com. 3 May 2000, D 2001.1312 note Serra.

[686] Pédamon, *Droit commercial*, 531, e.g. Com. 19 Jul. 1971, D 1971.691.

[687] M. Malaurie-Bignal, 'Dénigrement' in Jur.-Cl. Conc. Cons., Fasc. 210 (1996) 2 and 8.

[688] Pédamon, *Droit commercial*, 535ff.

[689] Flour, Aubert, and Savaux, *Fait juridique*, 253ff.

[690] J.A.C. Thomas, *Textbook of Roman Law* (Amsterdam, 1979) 382–3 (*pauperies*) and 378–379 (*actio de posito et suspenso*).

proof of fault for harm caused by animals and the 'ruin of buildings' respectively. However, towards the end of the nineteenth century it was suggested that article 1384 al. 1 should be re-interpreted so as itself to impose liability, a liability for the actions of things within one's keeping (*garde*)', so that, for example, an employer should be liable strictly as *gardien* of factory machinery for the personal injuries which it caused, his only defences being *force majeure* and contributory fault on the part of the victim.[691] This idea was therefore the delictual expression of a juristic concern for the victims of the machine age, it being thought unjust that they should be left without compensation owing to an inability to identify and prove fault. It illustrates strikingly the inventiveness of French juristic thought when inspired by such a social concern, and the receptiveness of French judges to new ideas, for they soon adopted the new interpretation, first in relation to accidents at work and then more generally.[692] On the other hand, it must be said that in re-interpreting article 1384 al. 1 in this way French jurists and courts created a monster, a vast principle of strict liability whose only apparent restraining features were that harm be caused by a 'thing' and that it is imposed on its 'keeper'. Once created, therefore, the monster had to be tamed, this being done by distinctly peculiar interpretations of its constituent elements and by the way in which its two defences of contributory fault by the claimant and *force majeure* were applied. But if this taming led for a time to something of a return to basing liability on fault—in the sense of a lack of appropriate care—this result was not universally welcomed and by way of reaction in 1982 the Assemblée plénière in a road accident case cut down considerably the impact of the defence of contributory fault, a decision which attracted legislative support in its particular context but subsequent reversal outside it.[693]

A. A 'Presumption of Liability'

As we have said, the purpose of the new interpretation was to dispense victims of personal injuries from the need to prove fault and while it clearly stemmed from humanitarian concern, it was often justified theoretically by reference to the notion of risk, either *risque-profit* or *risque-créé*.[694] Put simply, *risque-profit* argues that liability without fault should be imposed on a person who profits from a 'thing', appealing to the principle that a person who takes the benefit should shoulder the burden, whereas *risque-créé* simply appeals to the idea that a person who has created a risk should shoulder its consequences if they transpire. While neither idea has gained universal acceptance nor featured in the reasoning of the courts,[695] they gave a certain juridical respectability to the courts' acceptance in the *arrêt*

---

[691] See below p. 389 ff. concerning these defences.

[692] Civ. 16 Jun. 1896, S 1897.1.17 note Esmein (accidents at work); Civ. 29 Jul. 1924, D 1925.1.5 note Ripert is an early example of its application to accidents on the roads.

[693] Below pp. 391–393.

[694] See Starck *et al.*, *Responsabilité délictuelle*, 31 ff for a modern discussion. cf. use of the notion of risk to impose liability without fault on the administration, above pp. 193–195.

[695] Flour, Aubert, and Savaux, *Fait juridique*, 69 ff.

Jand'heur of 1930 that article 1384 al. 1 does not rest on a presumption of fault, but rather a presumption of responsibility,[696] a choice of terminology which made clear that a defendant could not escape liability by proving that he was *not* at fault.

B. 'Things'

In principle, *all physical things*, whether movable or immovable, are caught by article 1384 al. 1 with the exception only of those things which are governed by special rules (such as animals under article 1385[697] and the 'ruin of buildings' under article 1386[698]).[699] Thus, gases, liquids, electricity and even X-rays as well as motor-vehicles, television sets, tennis balls or supermarket floors are included within its ambit; but incorporeal things are not, nor are human thoughts even if expressed in words and put into writing.[700] Moreover, the *arrêt Jand'heur* established that liability under article 1384 al. 1 is not restricted to dangerous or defective things, nor is it excluded when the thing in question (for example, a motor car) was 'guided by a human hand'.[701] However, this extraordinary inclusiveness in the law's understanding of 'things' is somewhat misleading for, as we shall see, different types of things are treated significantly differently for the purposes of article 1384 al. 1 as the result of interpretations given to the concepts of causation and *la garde*.

C. Defendants: the Notion of *la Garde*

At first it was generally assumed that it was the owner of the 'thing' on whom liability should be imposed as keeper (*gardien*), but soon after *Jand'heur* the courts had to decide whether a person whose vehicle had been left in a public place retained *la garde* of the vehicle after it had been stolen and crashed by a thief. Some jurists baulked at the idea of theft transferring *la garde*, arguing that it could only be transferred by a legal transaction (*acte juridique*), but the Chambres réunies in the *arrêt Franck* obviously thought it unjust for an owner who had lost control of the 'thing' to remain liable for it and held that theft deprived the owner of *la garde*. The court took the opportunity to define a *gardien* as a person who possessed 'the use, direction and control' of it, a formula which became accepted

---

[696] Ch. réun 13 Feb. 1930, rapp. Le Marc'hadour, concl. Matter, S. 1930.1.121 note Esmein, DP 1930.1.57, note Ripert.

[697] The difference here is only formal as the same rules apply: Terré, Simler, and Lequette, *Obligations*, 734.

[698] The courts have narrowed the ambit of this provision since it is less generous to claimants than their interpretation of art. 1384 al. 1, but they have held that where it applies it possesses an exclusive domain: Civ. 4 Aug. 1942, S 1943.1.89 note Houin; Civ. (2) 12 Jul. 1966, JCP 1967. II.15185 note Dejean de la Batie and see Malaurie, Aynès, and Stoffel-Munck, *Obligations*, 101.

[699] A further exception to this general application is found in art. 1384 al. 2 C. civ., which was introduced in 1922 and requires a proof of fault where a defendant's thing has caused harm through *fire*. For the special rules which since the *loi* no. 85-677 of 5 July 1985, arts. 1–6 have governed liability for harm involving motor-vehicles, see below, p. 400 ff.

[700] Carbonnier, *Obligations*, 2354.

[701] Ch. réun. 13 Feb. 1930, *cit.*

as a definition general for liability under article 1384 al. 1.[702] After this decision, therefore, while an owner of a thing is presumed to be its *gardien*, he can rebut this presumption by showing that garde has been transferred.[703]

In the *arrêt Franck, la garde* was transferred by changing *factual* circumstances and there are many examples of this approach being applied. So, a customer in a supermarket acquires *la garde* of the shopping-trolley which he uses (and which falls over and injures him),[704] but a person who buys a stepladder for a friend and then puts up her curtains using it does not acquire *la garde* from her (and so can recover damages against her as its *gardien* when it collapses).[705] However, it has also become apparent that particular types of contractual relationship typically attract particular treatments of who should be considered *gardien* other than the owner. Thus, in general a person who hires a thing, whether a movable or an immovable, becomes the *gardien* in substitution to the person who lets it[706] and a similar result is reached in the case of some contracts for the performance of services (*louage d'ouvrage*), so that, for example, a contract by a garage to repair a car transfers *la garde* from the car's owner to the garage, including for the purposes of a test-drive.[707] On the other hand, in the case of employees or other *préposés*,[708] the courts have held that even if they have possession of the 'thing' and appear to have its 'direction', they cannot have *la garde*, which remains in the *commettant* ('employer').[709] The technical justification for this is that being a *préposé* necessarily involves subordination to the *commettant*, and this is inconsistent with the existence of the *droit de la garde*, but the practical outcome is the retention of liability for things on the employer (who is more likely to be insured) and the avoidance of the question whether vicarious liability under article 1384 al. 5 and liability under article 1384 al. 1 can co-exist.[710] What all this means is that it is not infrequent for someone injured by a 'thing' to be himself its *gardien* and where this is the case, the *gardien*/victim will often have to look to contract

---

[702] *Connot c. Franck*, Ch. réun. 2 Dec. 1941, S 1941.1.217 rapp. Lagarde note Mazeaud, DC 1942.25 note Ripert, S 1943.51, DC 1945.117 note Tunc. This left the possibility of liability in the owner for proven fault under art. 1383 C. civ., but the courts have denied the directness of the causal link between any fault in the owner and the thief's victim's injuries: Civ. 6 Jan. 1943, D 1945.117 note Tunc.

[703] Malaurie, Aynès, and Stoffel-Munck, *Obligations*, 104–105.

[704] Civ. (2) 14 Jan. 1999, JCP 2000.II.10245 note Reifegerste.

[705] Civ. (2) 7 May 2002, D 2003.463 note Jourdain.

[706] Civ. (2) 18 Jun. 1975, *Dame Luchet*, D 1975.IR.211 and see also Starck *et al.*, *Responsabilité délictuelle*, 256 ff.

[707] Starck *et al.*, Ibid., 259 ff.

[708] This term is wider than mere employees: below p. 395.

[709] Civ. 30 Dec. 1936, *arrêt Garibaldi*, DP 1937.1.5 rapp. Josserand note Savatier, S 1937.1.137 note Mazeaud; Civ. (3) 20 Oct. 1971, D 1972.414 note Lapoyade Deschamps. Both minors (Ass. plén. 9 May 1984, *Gabillet*, D 1984.525 note Chabas—a child of three!) and those with reduced mental capacity (art. 489-2 C. civ.) may be *gardiens*.

[710] Below p. 395.

to recover damages for his own injury, many of these contractual claims being founded on the defectiveness of the thing in question.[711]

However, the position under article 1384 al. 1 is yet more complicated, for the courts have recognized that *la garde* may be split, one person being *gardien du comportement* (who is responsible for harm caused by the thing's handling) and the other *gardien de la structure* (who is responsible for harm caused by its defects).[712] In general this approach is restricted to cases where the thing in question possesses 'its own dynamism capable of manifesting itself in a dangerous way',[713] a restriction which in practice has often meant that the injury has been caused by the thing's explosion or by flammable or corrosive products.[714] Sometimes, though, the distinctions in the case law are difficult to explain: so, while the Cour de cassation has on occasion allowed this special approach to *la garde* to be applied to trees,[715] it has not done so as regards pharmaceutical products[716] nor as regards cigarettes, the latter on the basis that cigarettes cannot be said to possess 'their own dynamism' (they do not explode or implode) and with the result that only the smoker is their *gardien*![717] It is not clear, moreover, who is to be treated as the *gardien de la structure* for this purpose, sometimes this being held to be the thing's supplier, sometimes its owner and sometimes its manufacturer.[718] As Malaurie, Aynès, and Stoffel-Munck observe, this law is 'discouragingly complex'[719] and where it applies an injured person must in practice show either that the thing was structurally defective (for which the *gardien de la structure* is liable) or has been handled badly (for which the *gardien du comportement* is liable) and will therefore often have to sue both possible *gardiens*, thereby abandoning any advantage of certainty or simplicity which this strict liability as it was originally conceived was intended to possess. Furthermore, to the extent to which it allows liability to be imposed on a manufacturer, its significance has been eclipsed by other judicial and legislative developments relating to product liability.[720]

---

[711] e.g., liability under the *garantie légale* imposed by arts. 1642 ff (sale) or 1721 (hire) C. civ.

[712] Civ. 12 Nov.1975, JCP 1976.II.18479 note Viney. This idea is to be distinguished from situations in which two or more persons are held to be *co-gardiens* of the thing. A simple example of the latter may be found in respect of co-owners of property, but it has been applied also to a group of persons acting in concert, one of whom has the physical use of and control over the thing: e.g. a hunting party being held *co-gardiens* of one hunter's gun: Civ. (2) 15 Dec. 1980, D 1981.45 note Poisson-Drocourt. *Cf.* Civ. (2) 19 Oct. 2006, JCP 2007.II.10030 note Mekki (where three children each lit flaming torches made of hay in a barn, one of which was dropped and caused a fire, the cour d'appel was not entitled to hold all three children *co-gardiens* of the torch which actually caused the damage).

[713] Civ. (1) 12 Nov.1975, cit. (an exploding bottle of mineral water).

[714] Viney and Jourdain, *Conditions*, 752.

[715] Civ. (2) 18 Jun. 1975, Bull. civ. II no. 190, RTDCiv. 1976.146 note Durry.

[716] Civ. (1) 8 Apr. 1986, JCP 1987.II.20271 note Viala and Viandrier (liability in manufacturer exclusively on the basis of proven fault).

[717] Civ. (2) 20 Nov. 2003, JCP 2004.II.10004 note Daille-Duclos.

[718] Viney and Jourdain, *Conditions*, 754–756 The decisions in Civ. (1) 12 Nov. 1975 and Paris 5 Dec. 1975, JCP 1976.II.18479 note Viney both refer to the manufacturer.

[719] *Obligations*, 107.

[720] Malaurie, Aynès, and Stoffel-Munck, *Obligations*, 107 and see below, pp. 403 ff.

D. Things as Causes: the 'Actions of Things'

What then is meant by the 'action of a thing' (*fait d'une chose*)? This concept has caused no little difficulty, for it is very rare for a person to suffer physical harm, whether personal injuries or damage to property, without a physical thing being 'involved' in a broad sense and it was soon recognized that the new principle of liability would 'displace the center of delictual liability, transporting it from article 1382 to article 1384.1'.[721] While the courts have held that article 1384 al. 1 does not apply to cases where a person uses a thing *deliberately* to cause harm, such as where A assaults B with a stick,[722] apart from this the courts have taken a broad but nuanced approach to the causal relation between the thing and the injured person's harm, using causation to reflect a normative sense of the proper attribution of responsibility for the claimant's harm. They have thereby come close on occasion to a return to liability for fault.

The judicial starting-point in relation to the causal role of things was that 'as soon as it is established that the thing contributed to the occurrence of the harm, it is presumed that it is an effective cause [*cause génératrice*] unless the *gardien* proves the contrary',[723] but it soon became clear that different approaches were taken by the courts according to whether the thing in question was stationary at the relevant time, for if it were its *gardien* could escape liability by proving that it had played only a 'passive role'.[724] Over the last half century or so the courts have established a steady if complex pattern of practice, which links the causal potency of things to the idea of their *normality*. For this purpose, three groups of cases need to be distinguished.[725]

First, where the thing of which the defendant was *gardien* was in motion and impacted on the person injured or property damaged, then proof of these physical circumstances gives rise to a presumption of causation. The typical case, though overtaken by the provisions of the *loi* of 5 July 1985,[726] was of a motor-vehicle which knocks over a pedestrian or crashes into another vehicle or, for example, a brick wall: neither the pedestrian nor the owner of the wall have to show anything more to establish the necessary causal element.[727]

Secondly, where the thing of which the defendant was *gardien* was moving at the time of the injury, but did not itself come into contact with the person injured or property damaged, the absence of physical contact between the thing and the person or property does not prevent article 1384 al. 1 from applying, but the

---

[721] H. Capitant, 'La responsabilité du fait des choses inanimées d'après des Chambres réunies du 13 février 1930' DH Chron. 1930.29 at 32.

[722] Starck *et al.*, *Responsabilité délictuelle*, 224.

[723] Civ. 9 Jun.1939, DH 1939.449.

[724] Cf. Civ. 19 Feb.1941 and Civ. 24 Mar.1941, D 1941.85 note Flour.

[725] See J. Boré, note to Civ. (2) 29 May 1964, JCP 1965.II.14248, followed by Viney and Jourdain, *Conditions*, 717–728.

[726] No. 85-677 below p. 400. ff.

[727] For an example outside the context of road accidents see Paris 9 Feb.1968, JCP 1968.II.15653 note Prieur.

claimant has to show that the thing played an 'active role' in causing his injury and in practice the courts look for a defect in the thing itself or an 'abnormality in its position or behaviour'.[728]

Thirdly, where the thing is stationary, an injured party also has to show that it played an active rule in causing his harm and to do so jurists and courts again refer to whether it was 'abnormal' or 'behaved abnormally'. Two sorts of case are typical. *Immovables* are almost always stationary.[729] So, a person who claims damages from, the *gardien* of a floor must show that it played an 'active role' in causing his injuries and therefore, where a claimant slipped and was injured on a slight incline in the defendant's supermarket, her claim was rejected on the ground that she had not shown that the floor, rather than her own carelessness or the state of her shoes, was the real cause of her injury.[730] On the other hand, a stationary thing's 'abnormality' can be shown if it is defective or badly positioned.[731] An example of a *stationary movable* which has been held to have caused a claimant's harm for the purposes of liability under article 1384 al. 1 can be found in a case decided in 1980,[732] in which a trawler had lost its winching-mechanism overboard somewhere in a harbour (its owners did not know exactly where).[733] The claimant company suffered financial loss when the harbour was closed to larger vessels because of this sunken danger and it sued the owner of the trawler as *gardien* of the winching mechanism to recoup it. While the *juges du fond* rejected its claim on the ground that the mechanism in fact did not lie in such a position as to prevent access to the harbour and so did not cause the claimant's loss, their decision was quashed by the Cour de cassation: the mechanism had made the harbour as a whole unsafe because its *gardien* did not know where it was and it had therefore indeed caused the claimant's loss, despite the fact that it was both stationary and without contact with the person or any property belonging to the claimants.[734]

What are we to make of these somewhat strange sets of distinctions? Does the courts' appeal to the concept of abnormality to determine the causal significance

---

[728] Viney and Jourdain, *Conditions,* 723. See e.g. Civ. (2) 8 Jul. 1971, D 1971.690. *Cf.* Civ. (2) 10 Jun. 2004, *Resp. civ. et assur.* 2004 no. 254 (bather drowned by 2 metre waves generated by defendant's boat which was held to be the cause of his death).

[729] The stationary nature of immovables may seem axiomatic, but French courts have applied art. 1384 al. 1 to cases of *landslides* causing harm, e.g. Civ. (2) 15 Nov.1984, *Lantonnais Van Rhodes,* D 1985.20 concl. Charbonnier.

[730] Civ. (2) 19 Nov. 1964, JCP 1965.II.14022 note Rodière, D 1965.93 note Esmein. See also Civ. 11 May 1966, D 1966.735 note Azard.

[731] Civ. (2) 19 Jul.1972, D 1972 Somm.212, RTDCiv 1973. 352 obs. Durry; Civ. (2) 11 Dec. 2003, Bull. civ. II no. 386, D 2004.2181 note Godechot; Civ. (2) 24 Feb. 2005, Bull. civ. II nos. 51 and 52.

[732] Civ. (2) 19 Mar. 1980, JCP 1980.IV.216, D 1980.IR.414 note Larroumet.

[733] The typical examples in older *jurisprudence* concerned stationary motor-vehicles, where it was held that if A while driving a vehicle collides with B's stationary vehicle and is injured, B's vehicle will be said to have caused A's injuries only if the position of B's vehicle was 'abnormal;' e.g. Civ. (2) 19 May 1976, *Dorgère,* D 1976.IR.233. These cases are no longer current as regards their own context owing to the effect of the loi no. 85-677 of 5 July 1985, below p. 400 ff.

[734] And see below p. 389.

of the thing mean that they have surreptitiously transformed an apparently strict liability for things into a liability for *defective* things or even a liability for fault? Certainly, defectiveness is sometimes relevant to establishing the thing's causal role, but it is merely one example of abnormality. And certainly abnormality is, as Carbonnier observed, a notion 'tainted with morality' which can lead to the reintroduction of something very much like fault.[735] On the other hand, in cases where a thing's defectiveness suggests its causal significance, its *gardien* cannot escape liability by showing himself innocent of fault nor even that the defect existed through circumstances entirely beyond his control, as an internal defect cannot constitute *force majeure*.[736] Thus, although in some cases the courts look as though they are returning to liability for fault, this is not a general phenomenon.[737] Indeed, as long as the thing does behave 'abnormally', the injured party does not have to show *why* this is the case and only where the facts allow the *gardien* to establish *force majeure* or the claimant's contributory fault will the causes of this abnormality need to be investigated.

E. The Types of Harm Recoverable

It can be seen that compensation for personal injuries was both the reason for the invention of liability under article 1384 al. 1 and its main area of application, but can liability for the 'actions of things' extend to other types of harm? In principle, there are no restrictions on the type of harm to which it may apply and it does so to damage to property and *dommage moral* to the same extent as does liability for fault under articles 1382 and 1383.[738] More difficult, however, is the question of recovery of what an English lawyer would call pure economic loss that is, financial loss not consequential on the claimant's own personal injury or damage to his own property. There is certainly no formal exclusion of liability under article 1384 al. 1 for this category of harm and a clear example may be found in cases where the claimant suffers financial harm (such as dependency loss or even on rare occasion loss of profits)[739] in consequence of a 'primary victim's' personal injuries or death. However, apart from this sort of case, the recovery of pure economic loss under article 1384 al. 1 would appear to be rare, though no French discussion addresses the point directly. Certainly one category of pure economic loss is excluded as article 1384 al. 1 cannot apply to harm caused by deficiencies in the thing itself: so, for example, a sub-buyer cannot on *this* basis claim for the cost

---

[735] *Obligations*, 2369.
[736] Below, p. 390.
[737] A. Tunc, 'Force majeure et absence de faute en matière délictuelle', RTDCiv 1946. 171, 194–5; Carbonnier, *Obligations*, 2359; Terré, Simler, and Lequette, *Obligations*, 745.
[738] Below, pp. 412 ff.
[739] Viney and Jourdain, *Conditions*, 158 ff.

of repairs in a product as they were not caused by the 'action of the thing'.[740] On the other hand, French courts have on occasion accepted that a thing has caused economic loss not consequential on any physical harm. For example, in the case of the trawler's lost winching-mechanism already mentioned,[741] the claimant company suffered purely financial loss because of the late discharge of the cargo of its ship which closure of the port had caused, this closure being caused by the defendant's lost winching-mechanism. While the decision of the Cour de cassation turned on an issue of causation, it was not suggested either by the court or the *arrêtiste* that the type of loss suffered by the claimant was irrecoverable in principle once it could be said to have been caused by the defendant's property, the winching-mechanism.[742] A case decided in 2002 is even more striking.[743] There, rocks had fallen down from a cliff below which was a hotel owned by the claimants. The cliff belonged to the defendant local authority (as part of its *domaine privé* [744]), which formally ordered the hotel to close while it undertook works to secure the cliff. In these circumstances, the hotel owners recovered damages for their 'commercial and financial losses' while the hotel was closed on the ground that the *risk* of the rock falling from the cliff (the 'thing' for the purposes of article 1384 al. 1) was indeed the cause of these losses. Apart from the purely economic nature of these losses, the case illustrates nicely how generous French courts can be in recognizing a causal connection between the defendant's thing and the claimant's harm.[745]

F. Defences: *Force Majeure* and Contributory Fault[746]

While a *gardien* cannot escape liability simply by showing that he was not at fault, he can do so by showing *force majeure* and he may reduce or even exclude his liability by establishing the claimant's own contributory fault. Both these defences have proved important, to the extent that again some jurists have argued that where the courts have interpreted them broadly, liability is really based on something not far from fault.

---

[740] There was no application of art. 1384 al. 1 to such a case before 1979, in which year it was held that not only did a sub-buyer possess a contractual *action directe* in this situation but that this was an exclusive remedy: Civ. (1) 9 Oct.1979, *arrêt Lamborghini*, GP 1980.1.249 note Planqueel, D 1980.IR.222 note Larroumet. No claim in respect of damage caused to a product by its own defectiveness can be made under the new legislative product liability: art. 1386-2 al. 1 C. civ., on which generally see below, p. 406 ff.

[741] Civ.(2) 19 Mar. 1980, cit., above p. 387.

[742] Larroumet, D 1980.IR.414.

[743] Civ. (2) 26 Sep. 2002, Bull. civ. II no. 198, RTDCiv. 2003.100 note Jourdain.

[744] It was apparently for this reason that the case came before the ordinary courts as a matter of private law: cf. R. Chapus, *Droit administratif général,* Tome 2, 15th edn. (2001), 541.

[745] Jourdain, RTDCiv. 2003.100.

[746] French courts also accept on occasion that a claimant's acceptance of risks may affect recovery. In practice, this applies to participants in sporting competitions who are said to accept the risks of injury by the things which are used in them. e.g. a rugby football. This has the effect of excluding liability based on art. 1384 al. 1 C. civ. and subjecting liability under arts. 1382–3 to a proof of a serious breach of the rules of the game: Malaurie, Aynès, and Stoffel-Munck, *Obligations*, 64–66.

1. Force majeure

As we have seen, in the Civil Code *force majeure*[747] appears as a defence to liability in damages for non-performance of a contractual obligation, where it was traditionally held to consist of some event or act of either the creditor or a third party which was unforeseeable, could not be prevented and was not otherwise 'imputable' to the debtor of the contractual obligation (these elements together meaning that it was 'irresistible').[748] Nevertheless, when in 1896 the Cour de cassation first recognized article 1384 al. 1 as an independent source of liability, it accepted that *force majeure* could be a defence.[749] For this purpose, the courts assimilated the cases where the 'event' which was unforeseeable and 'ittesistable' was a human act (fait d'un tiers;) or the forces of nature (*force majeure* in a narrow sense).

It soon became clear, however, that the traditional contractual definition of *force majeure* was not apt for the delictual context in one important respect, for having established that a defect in the thing was not a condition of liability under article 1384 al. 1, it would have been odd to allow the existence of even an unforeseeable and unpresentable defect in the thing to constitute a means of escaping liability. To avoid such a result, the Cour de cassation redefined *force majeure*, adding a requirement that any occurrence or condition must be 'exterior to the thing'.[750] Thus, for example, a *gardien* of a car whose tyre blows out or whose brakes fail causing an accident, could not, even before the *loi* of 5 July 1985,[751] point to a manufacturing defect or an incompetent repair as a defence.[752] As one court expressed it, an inherent defect in the thing 'is included within the risks for which the *gardien* assumes liability towards third parties'.[753] Put into the modern terminology of product liability, the *gardien* is liable to those injured by his thing even for its 'development risks'.[754]

As regards defects in the thing itself, therefore, the question how unforeseeable and how unpreventable an event or third party act must be to constitute *force majeure* has not needed to arise, but outside this type of case, these questions have caused considerable difficulty. With the movement away from the idea of liability for risk which can be discerned in the later 1930s and 1940s, French courts were more ready to find *force majeure*, a readiness reflected in the assertion that it was enough if the event or act was normally unforeseeable.[755]

---

[747] As in the contractual context, we shall use *force majeure*, treating this as synonymous with *cas fortuit* and *cause étrangère*: cf. above, p. 343.

[748] Art. 1148 C. civ. and above, pp. 343 ff.

[749] Civ. 16 Jun, 1896, 1897.1.17 note Esmein, D 1897.1.433 note Saleilles, following in this respect its decision concerning art. 1385 C. civ. in Civ. 27 Oct.1885. S 1886.1.33.

[750] Req. 22 Jan. 1945, S 1945.1.57. and see above, p. 345.

[751] No. 85-677 and see below, pp. 402–403.

[752] Viney and Jourdain, *Conditions*, 261–264. e.g. Civ. 22 Jan.1945, S 1945.1.57 (incompetent repair).

[753] Civ. (2) 6 Mar. 1959, GP 1959.2.12.

[754] See below, pp. 405–406.

[755] e.g. Civ. (2) 25 Jan.1956, JCP 1956.II.9153.

This approach was particularly noticeable as regards the liability of a *gardien* of a motor-vehicle for accidents precipitated by external factors. Thus, where a car driver had to swerve after a dog ran into the road, the act of the dog was held to be *force majeure* so as to exclude liability in the driver for injuries to a passenger;[756] and in another case, oil spilt on the road and not visible was similarly held to constitute *force majeure*.[757] Even the bad driving of other road-users was on occasion held to be *force majeure*, even though this can hardly be considered at all unforeseeable,[758] though it was more common for this sort of situation to be treated as one of concurrent causation by the two vehicles involved (which led to liability *in solidum*).[759] In other cases, the claimant's own 'behaviour' was held to be *force majeure*, notably where, for whatever reason and quite apart from any question of contributory fault on his part, he was lying prone in the road.[760]

However, more recently the courts have tended to become more strict in their interpretation of the conditions of *force majeure* as a defence to liability under article 1384 al. 1, although the case law remains unsettled.[761] So, for example, where a passenger was injured in falling through the door of a train stopped at a station, the Cour de cassation quashed the decision below rejecting her claim on the basis that the leaving of the door open by a fellow passenger and her being pushed forward by another constituted acts of *force majeure*; in the Cour de cassation's view, these acts were neither unforseeable nor 'irresistible' to the train corporation.[762] There remains in this area, though, a very considerable degree of practical discretion in the *juges du fond* to nuance their interpretation and application of the conditions of *force majeure* to fit their view of whether to impose liability and, in this way, in effect they choose between whether to impose a true strict liability or one closely related to fault.[763]

2. Contributory fault in the injured party

Where an act or circumstance caused by a 'victim' of a thing constitutes *force majeure* then it excuses the *gardien*, whether or not this act constitutes fault; but

---

[756] Civ. (2) 10 Apr.1964, D 1965.169 note Tunc.

[757] Civ. (2) 28 Oct.1965, D 1966.137 note Tunc.

[758] Civ. (1) 30 Nov.1960, S 1961.142.

[759] Civ. (2) 2 Jul.1969, JCP 1971.II.16582 and see below p. 411 on the meaning of liability *in solidum*.

[760] Cf. Civ. 15 Nov.1949, JCP 1950.II.5296, in which the driver did not succeed in a defence of *force majeure* because he had seen the shadow of something on the road (the body of the injured person) and Civ. (1) 17 Dec.1963, D 1964.569 note Tunc, in which on very similar facts the Cour de cassation quashed the lower court's decision rejecting a defence of *force majeure*, referring to the normally unforeseeable nature of such an event or act.

[761] Malaurie, Aynès, and Stoffel-Munck, *Obligations*, 100; Terré, Simler, and Lequette, *Obligations*, 769–770 and *cf.* Viney and Jourdain, *Conditions*, 278–280 who see the earlier judicial approach as still current.

[762] Civ. (2) 15 Mar. 2001, Bull. civ. II no. 56. See also Civ. (2) 18 Mar. 2004, D 2005.125 note Corpart (no *force majeure* in a child's action in blocking a lift between floors, disabling its safety system, opening its gates, climbing out and falling!).

[763] Bénabent, *Obligations*, 421.

where the claimant's act is not 'unforeseeable and "irresistable" ', his contributory fault was long held to reduce any damages recoverable against the *gardien*[764] to an extent within the 'sovereign power of assessment' of the lower courts.[765] The effects of this defence of contributory fault on the strictness of liability under article 1384 al. 1 has been considerable and in a series of devastingly critical articles Tunc drew attention to the unfairness which this caused,[766] for a moment's inadvertence, such as not keeping as proper a look-out when crossing the road as was ideal, could have a severe effect on any damages recoverable. As Carbonnier concluded:

> By detaching the defence of contributory fault of a victim from the notion of *force majeure* and applying it to any type of fault, the Cour de cassation has encouraged the *juges du fond* in their ancient tendency to slice the cake in two as soon as they cannot otherwise see a clear result—and, as a consequence, to encourage in legal advisers their propensity to put in as a matter of form against all claims an allegation that the defendant is only partly responsible. This itself has led claimants, worn down by disputes, to settle on conditions imposed on them by the other side's insurers. The liability for the 'actions of things' was thus emptied of the quasi-automatic character which under *Jand'heur* ensured its considerable effectiveness.[767]

This sort of criticism did not fall on deaf ears and in 1981 the French Government set up a working group under the auspices of the new minister of justice, Badinter, on the reform of the law relating to road accident injuries,[768] but before it could reach any decision, in July 1982 in the *arrêt Desmares* the Cour de cassation itself announced a striking change in its approach, asserting that an injured party's behaviour could affect liability under article 1384 al. 1 *only* where it qualified as *force majeure* where it excluded liability.[769] This change was made in the context of a traffic accident injuring a pedestrian, where criticism of its earlier attitude was sharpest, but two years later the Cour de cassation felt unable to avoid the logic of its own previous interpretation of article 1384 al. 1 and applied the *Desmares* approach to cases other than motor traffic accidents.[770] The confusion and contradictions to which this *jurisprudence* gave rise

---

[764] Req. 13 Apr. 1934, D 1934.1.41 note Savatier marks the change from the previous position under which contributory fault in the injured party *excluded* liability in the *gardien*. Terré Simler, and Lequette, *Obligations* 774–5 record that *partage* was applied before 1982 even where the injured party's contribution to his own injury did *not* constitute fault.

[765] Ass. plén. 9 May 1984, 4th, case, *Derguini*, D 1984. 525 note Chabas (in the context of liability for fault).

[766] e.g. Grenoble 6 Dec. 1974, JCP 1975.II.18080 note Tunc and see id., D 1975 Chron. 83.

[767] *Obligations,* 2368. See also A. Tunc, ' "It is wise not to take the Civil Codes too seriously." Traffic accident compensation in France' in P. Wallington and R.M. Merkin, (eds.) *Essays in Memory of Professor F.H. Lawson* (London, 1986) 71 at 78, who deplores the fact that so many cases had to be litigated—at one stage 250 introduced every day!

[768] Tunc, ibid, at 79.

[769] Civ. (2) 21 Jul. 1982, *arrêt Desmares*, D 1982.449 concl. Charbonnier, note Larroumet.

[770] Civ. (2) 15 Nov. 1984, D 1985.20. concl. Charbonnier (3 cases).

in the lower courts prompted the legislature to intervene swiftly, though only in respect of motor-vehicle accidents, in the *loi* of 5 July 1985.[771] However, rather than giving support to *Desmares,* this limited intervention resulted two years later in yet another *revirement* in three *non-traffic* accident cases, the Cour de cassation renouncing its approach in *Desmares* and establishing a position according to which fault in an injured party may reduce a claimant's damages whether or not it was unforeseeable and 'irresistible',[772] although it may exclude them altogether only if these conditions are satisfied.[773] In the result, therefore, outside the context of moter-vehicle accidents, Carbonnier's criticisms remain valid.[774] Here, the *Avant-projet de réforme* seeks to establish a different balance, preserving the *gardien*'s complete defence where an injured party's own action qualifies as *force majeure* or where he 'deliberately sought the harm' (for example, in committing suicide by jumping in front of a train), but allowing the courts to reduce the *gardien*'s liability for death or personal injury only where the person commits a serious fault.[775]

II. Liability for Another Person's Actions

As we have seen, article 1384 al. 1 of the Civil Code announces that a person may be liable for another person's action and originally the article continued by giving the three situations in which this would apply:[776] parents for their minor children who live with them;[777] teachers and craftsmen for their pupils and apprentices[778] and masters and principals for their servants or agents.[779] In the modern law, the bases of these particular liabilities are not the same, some being based on a proof of fault, some on a rebuttable presumption of fault and some being truly vicarious. Despite this, however, in 1991 the Assemblée plénière accepted that they were no more than particular instances of a general principle of liability for the action of persons for whom one is responsible, a principle found yet again in article

---

[771] No. 85-677 and below, p. 400 ff.

[772] Civ. (2) 6 Apr. 1987, *Chauvet, Jonier, Belzedhoune,* JCP 1987.II.20828 note Chabas; Civ. (2) 6 Apr. 1987, *Waeterinckx,* D 1988.32 note Mouly.

[773] Civ. (2) 18 Mar. 2004, cit. n. 762.

[774] Above, p. 392.

[775] Arts. 1349–1351 A.-p.r.

[776] Art. 1384 was amended first in 1922 so as to introduce special rules in relation to damage by fire (above, n. 699), and in 1899, 1937 and 2002 to amend the law governing the liability of parents and teachers (see following text).

[777] The original version of the Code imposed liability on the child's father while alive, and on its mother only after the father's death. This was amended in 1970 (*loi* no. 70-459 of 4 June 1970) so as to impose liability on both parents jointly: new art. 1384 al. 4 C. civ.

[778] Art. 1384 al. 6 C. civ.

[779] Art. 1384 al. 5 C. civ.

1384 al. 1.[780] The status of such a general principle remains, however, somewhat uncertain.

A. The Established Examples

1. Parental liability

Under the Civil Code,[781] 'to the extent to which they exercise parental authority, the father and mother of minor children living with them are jointly and severally liable for the harm which the latter cause' unless they establish that 'they could not have prevented the action which gave rise to this liability'. For long, this was interpreted as creating a 'presumption of fault' on parents in relation to their children's harmful acts and the courts allowed them to escape liability on showing that there was no failure to supervise or control the child's activity nor any failure properly to educate or instruct the child.[782] However, in 1997 the Cour de cassation changed its position, holding that the liability of parents for their children, termed a *responsabilité de plein droit,* arises unless they show *force majeure* or contributory fault in the injured party.[783] There is, moreover, no need for the latter to show that the *child* was at fault (which would be difficult as regards a young child lacking sufficient capacity to understand what he or she was doing) nor even that he or she was *gardien* of a thing but simply that his or her act caused the harm.[784] This means that parents can be liable for the actions of their children even where the latter are not.[785] This special treatment of parental liability is considered justified as a counterpart of parental authority, but its existence led to it becoming common practice to take out insurance to cover it, this being known as *assurance responsabilité civile-chef de famille,*[786] and this in its turn has no doubt encouraged the courts in the strictness of their interpretation of the liability.

2. The liability of teachers

The Code originally imposed liability on teachers for their pupils' actions also on the basis of a presumption of fault,[787] but, first, liability based on this presumption was imposed on the state rather than on the teacher personally,[788]

---

[780] Ass. plén. 29 Mar. 1991, D 1991.324 note Larroument, JCP 1991.II.21673 concl. Dottenville. For the text of art. 1384 al. l, see above, p. 361.

[781] Art. 1384 al. 4 and al. 7 C. civ. (as amended most recently in 2002).

[782] See Carbonnier, *Obligations,* 2323.

[783] Civ. (2) 19 Feb. 1997, D 1997,265 note Jourdain; Ass. plén. 13 Dec. 2002, D 2003.231 note Jourdain.

[784] Ass. plén. 9 May 1984, 2nd case, *Fullenwarth,* D 1984.525 note Chabas; Civ. (2) 10 May 2001, D 2001.2851, D 2002.1315 note Mazeaud; Ass. plén. 13 Dec. 2002, cit. n. 783.

[785] Bénabent, *Obligations,* 394.

[786] Mazeaud, note, D 2002.1315.

[787] This still applies to the liability of craftsmen for their apprentices: art. 1384 al. 6 and al. 7 C. civ.

[788] This regime imposed by a *loi* of 20 July 1899 applied only to teachers in public education.

and then, in 1937, the basis of the state's liability was changed to one of proven fault in the teacher.[789]

3. Liability of commettants for préposés

As will be clear, neither the liability of parents nor of teachers for the actions of those in their charge has ever been truly vicarious: even a parent's liability is personal, though based on the action of the child. The third and most important example of liability for another's action is of *commettants* (employers or principals) for their *préposés* (employees or agents),[790] a liability which is truly vicarious. It arises if three conditions are satisfied.

First, there must be a 'relationship of subordination' between the person whose act causes the harm (the *préposé*) and the person to be held liable (the *commettant*).[791] Most jurists consider that such a relationship necessarily exists in cases of employment, but may exist elsewhere.[792] A striking example outside employment may be found in a case before the Chambre criminelle in 1976,[793] in which an election candidate was held liable in damages for the death and injuries caused by his supporters in a fight with those of his opponent, on the basis that a person may be liable for the actions of others as long as it has been found that he had the power to give them orders. The courts have, moreover, on occasion held that a family member or friend acted as *préposé* in respect of a particular task, notably driving a motor-vehicle.[794] On the other hand, it is rare for a person who acts under a contract for services (*contrat d'entreprise*) to be considered a *préposé*, owing to the independence which this usually brings him in doing the job.

Secondly, a *commettant* may be liable only if the normal conditions for liability in his *préposé* are satisfied and in practice this means that the *préposé*'s action must have constituted a *faute délictuelle*:[795] this truly vicarious liability is not imposed in respect of any stricter delictual liabilities, notably liability for the 'actions of things'.[796]

---

[789] *Loi* of 5 April 1937. E.g. Civ. (2) 23 Oct. 2004, D 2004.729 note Petit. The regime which this *loi* introduced applies as much to injuries to pupils as those caused by them. Since 1960, it has applied to 'associated' private teaching establishments. Teachers in other private schools are liable for harm caused by their pupils only on proven fault under arts. 1382–3 C. civ.: Malaurie, Aynès, and Stoffel-Munck, *Obligations*, 75.

[790] Art. 1384 al. 5 C. civ. See generally N. Molfessis, 'La jurisprudence relative à la responsabilité des commettants du fait de leurs préposés ou l'irrésistible enlisement de la Cour de cassation' in *Ruptures, movements et continuité du droit, Autour de Michelle Gobert* (Economica, 2004), 495.

[791] Malaurie, Aynès, and Stoffel-Munch, *Obligations*, 78 ff.

[792] Carbonnier, *Obligations,* 2333. cf. Terré, Simler, and Lequette, *Obligations,* 800 ff.

[793] Crim. 20 May 1976, RTDCiv 1976.786 obs. Durry.

[794] Terré, Simler, and Lequette *Obligations,* 801.

[795] Starck *et al., Responsabilité délictuelle*, 328–333. An exception is found in relation to harm caused by a *préposé* who is demented, as the latter is liable even though incapable of committing a fault: art. 489-2 C. civ.

[796] This is because liability is imposed on a *gardien*, who in these circumstances is the employer: Civ. 30 Dec. 1936, D 1937.1.5 rapp. Josserand note Savatier (art. 1384 al.1); Civ.(2) 15 Dec.

Thirdly, the *préposé* must have caused the harm complained of 'in the course of the functions for which he was employed',[797] a requirement very similar to the common law's notion of the 'course of employment'. While clear cases exist on both sides of this line, the courts have vacillated in relation to cases where the *préposé* has 'abused his functions'.[798] Here, Carbonnier concludes that in practice various factors weigh with the courts;[799] (i) the time and the place of the wrong in relation to the *préposé*'s job; (ii) whether or not the wrong was intended to further the interests of the *commettant*; and (iii) whether the means which the *préposé* uses in accomplishing the wrong were provided by his *commettant* to do the job. He adds that in some types of case the fact that the *commettant* could have foreseen and prevented the claimant's harm or that the claimant could reasonably have thought that the *préposé* acted on the *commettant*'s behalf may influence a court's decision. Given these complexities, it is important to note that the burden of proof here lies on the *commettant*.[800]

Once these three conditions are satisfied, the *commettant* is liable to the injured party for the harm which his *préposé* has caused: neither proof of absence of fault in the *commettant* nor *force majeure* as regards his ability to foresee or prevent the *préposé*'s action will excuse him from liability.[801] On the other hand, while for a hundred years the courts accepted that establishing vicarious liability in the *commettant* did not rule out recovery by the injured party from the *préposé*, the position is now more complicated.[802] In principle, if the *préposé* (even if at fault) acts within the limits of his mission, then he enjoys an immunity and therefore cannot be sued by a person harmed as a result.[803] However, an exception is made to this position where a *préposé* commits a 'personal fault', a notion borrowed from the administrative law of liability where it means 'serious and detachable from his or her functions',[804] a clear example being where a *préposé* consciously

---

1976, *Laclergerie*, JCP 1977.IV.34 (animals) and see above p. 384. cf. Terré, Simler, and Lequette, *Obligations*, 803 who argue that in some exceptional cases a person may be *préposé* and *gardien*.

[797] Art. 1384 al. 5 C. civ.

[798] Carbonnier, *Obligations*, 2334 and see Ass. plén. 17 Jun. 1983, *Communes de Chignin*, D 1984. 134 note Denis, JCP 1983.II.20120 concl. Sadon, note Chabas. cf. Ass. plén. 19 May 1988, D 1988.513 note Larroumet. For recent examples cf. Civ. (2) 3 Jun. 2004, Bull. civ. II no. 275 (lorry driver entered cab of another lorry driver out of curiosity and set it going held not to be acting within his functions); Civ. (2) 29 Mar. 2006, *Resp. civ. et assur.* 2006 no. 183 (driver stealing fuel from a petrol lorry while on a detour from a task and during working hours held to be acting within his functions).

[799] *Obligations*, 2334–5.

[800] Malaurie, Aynès, and Stoffel-Munck *Obligations*, 83.

[801] Viney and Jourdain, *Conditions*, 1013, who distinguish these situations from the case where the *préposé* could not have foreseen or prevented the harm, where there would be no liability in him for the *commettant* to guarantee. They also note that contributory fault in the injured person can reduce liability in the *commettant*.

[802] Terré, Simler, and Lequette, *Obligations*, 810–819.

[803] Ass. plén. 25 Feb.2000, *arrêt Costedoat*, D 2000.673 note Brun.

[804] Malaurie, Aynès, and Stoffel-Munck, *Obligations*, 84. On the administrative law, see above, pp. 191–192.

commits a criminal offence, even if on the orders of his *committant*.[805] These judicial developments are striking for three reasons: first, because the Cour de cassation feels entitled to recognize an immunity from liability for *la faute délictuelle* despite the generality of the terms of articles 1382 and 1383 of the Code; secondly, because in so doing it took its inspiration from the case law developed by the Conseil d'Etat; and, thirdly, because it marks a shift from the role of the liability of *committants* from acting as a guarantee against the insolvency of their *préposés* to acting as a guarantee against the harmful consequences of the wrongful action of their *préposés*.[806]

B. A General Principle of Liability for Harm Caused by Others

As we have said, before 1991 the courts refused to admit liability for another person's actions outside the instances enumerated in article 1384 of the Code, but this meant merely that liability would not be imposed on a basis *other than* for personal and proven fault under articles 1382 and 1383 whose application was clear.[807] This is important because it alters the significance of the Assemblée plénière's decision in that year in the *arrêt Blieck*, which held (at least implicity) that there could be examples of liability for another person's action other than those in the Code, this approach being based apparently on a general principle of liability for another's action itself drawn from the terms of article 1384 al. 1.[808] *Blieck* itself concerned a claim by the owner of a forest set alight by a mentally disabled person who had escaped from a *private* centre for occupational therapy (the defendant), the cour d'appel holding the centre liable on the basis of 'a principle of a presumption of liability for the actions of others' found in article 1384 al. 1. Having noted the existence of a permanent relationship of control between the centre and its residents and that the particular mentally disabled person in question was allowed completely free movement during the day, the Assemblée plénière held that the lower court was right in law to hold that the centre ought to be liable for harm caused by him under article 1384 al. 1 of the Civil Code.

The decision in *Blieck* itself may well have been influenced to an extent by the position reached a number of years previously by the Conseil d'Etat in almost identical circumstances (except for the public character of the institution from which the patient escaped),[809] but the question immediately arose as its significance more generally. In this respect, French jurists remain divided as to whether the decision and the ensuing case law establish a true general principle of liability

---

[805] Ass. plén. 14 Dec. 2001, *arrêt Cousin*, JCP 2002.II.10026 note Billiau.

[806] As to the last point see Terré, Simler, and Lequette, *Obligations*, 812.

[807] Flour, Aubert, and Savaux, *Fait juridique*, 823 ff.

[808] Ass. plén. 29 Mar. 1991, *Ass. des centres éducatifs du Limousin c Blieck*, D 1991.324 note Larroumet, JCP 1991.II.21673 concl. Dottenville. For the text of art. 1384 al. 1, see above, p. 361.

[809] CE 3 Feb. 1956, *Thouzellier*, D 1956.596 note Auby.

for harm caused by the action of a person,[810] and the case law itself has become complex and remains unsettled.[811] What has become clear is that liability (if imposed) is strict in the sense that the *gardien* cannot escape liability by showing that he himself was not at fault,[812] but he can do so by establishing *force majeure* and may have it reduced on the ground of the injured party's own contributory fault.[813]

Beyond this, it is also clear that, in common with liability for the 'actions of things', a key notion on which liability rests is *la garde*, here interpreted as referring to 'the organisation, direction, and control (whether permanent or not) of the manner of life' of another person.[814] Broadly speaking this has been applied in two groups of case in which the courts have taken significantly different approaches as to the necessity or otherwise for the need to show fault in the person whose manner of life is controlled.[815] Apparently the courts' concern in developing this case law is to impose liability where the defendant is in a position to take out liability insurance.[816]

The first group consists of cases where custody of the person who actually caused the harm has been conferred on the defendant, whether (as in *Blieck*) owing to his mental disability or owing to his age. So, for example, where custody of a child is formally entrusted to his step-parent as *tuteur* (guardian), the latter is liable for the harm which he causes without any need to show fault in the child.[817] On the other hand, it has been held that a member of the family or other person to whom a child has been entrusted to be looked after temporarily is not liable on the basis of article 1384, al. 1,[818] nor is the *tuteur* of a mentally disabled adult as he does not by reason of this position possess the requisite powers of control over the adult's manner of life.[819]

The second group is rather more eclectic and consists of cases which involve the organization of a 'specific collective activity'.[820] So, for example, in the *affaire des majorettes*, a local club of drum majorettes was held liable to one of its members for the injury which she suffered from the baton of another member during

---

[810] Cf. Flour, Aubert, and Savaux, *Fait juridique*, 251–252 (yes); P. Brun, *La responsabilité civile extracontractuelle* (Lexis-Nexis Litec, 2005) 292–293 (no).

[811] Flour, Aubert, and Savaux, *Fait juridique*, 252.

[812] Crim. 26 Mar. 1997, D 1997.496 note Jourdain.

[813] Malaurie, Aynès, and Stoffel-Munck, *Obligations*, 70.

[814] Flour, Aubert, and Savaux, *Fait juridique*, 251.

[815] Malaurie, Aynès, and Stoffel-Munck, *Obligations*, 70; Fabre-Magnan, *Responsabilité civile et quasi-contrats*, 318–324. Not all the decided cases fall within these groups: e.g. Civ. (2) 24 May 1995, JCP 1995.II.22550 note Mouly (*commune* which allowed squatters to live in property belonging to it without intervening held liable for the damage caused by fire which they lit).

[816] P. Jourdain, note, RTDCiv. 1998.388; Fabre-Magnan, *Responsabilité civile et quasi-contrats*, 324.

[817] Crim. 28 Mar. 2000, D 2000.466 note Mazeaud.

[818] Civ. (2) 18 Sept. 1996, D 1997.327 note Blanc (child staying with grandmother during holidays).

[819] Civ. (2) 25 Feb. 1998, D 1998.315 note Kessous.

[820] Malaurie, Aynès, and Stoffel-Munck, *Obligations*, 70.

a parade, it being held that there was no requirement that the activity which the club organized and controlled was dangerous.[821] Just a year later, the Cour de cassation held, though, in a case concerning the liability of a rugby club in respect of an injury caused during play to one of its players, that liability in this sort of situation would be imposed only where fault is established in one of the persons for whom the club was responsible.[822] On the other hand, it has been held that a trade union has 'neither within its objects nor its mission the organisation, direction and control of its members while on a demonstration' and is not, therefore, liable for the harm which they cause under article 1384 al. 1.[823]

Overall, what, are we to make of this further French judicial discovery of a new principle of liability? As Fabre-Magnan observes, the form of words used by the Code itself in article 1384 al. 1 that 'one is responsible for the harm … caused by the action of persons for whom one is responsible' is entirely tautologous and 'to say the least, leaves a considerable margin of appreciation for the courts. The ambit of this new principle remains for now quite rightly circumscribed, but its very existence has very much destabilized and led to considerable change in the special regimes of liability for another's action' which are actually provided by the Code.[824] Given the unsettled nature of the case law here, it is interesting to note that the *Avant-projet de réforme* takes a cautious if not actually retrogressive approach to the area. For, while article 1355 states that '[a] person is liable strictly for harm caused by persons whose way of life he governs or whose activity he organises, regulates or controls in his own interests', this very general statement is intended merely as an introductory provision to the different special cases of liability for the actions of others which it then sets out,[825] a 'suppression' of the general principle which has attracted strong criticism.[826] The *Avant-projet* provides for the established liability of parents and guardians, to which are added liability of 'physical or legal persons charged by judicial or administrative decision, or by agreement' with regulating the way of life of a minor[827] and of an adult whose condition or situation require some special supervision.[828] Otherwise, the *Avant-projet* provides that '[o]ther persons who take on the task of supervising another person in the course of business or by way of their profession are answerable for the action of the person directly behind the harm, unless they show that they did not commit any fault'.[829]

---

[821] Civ. (2) 12 Dec. 2002, D 2003.2541 note Lagarde.

[822] Civ. (2) 20 Nov. 2003, D 2004.300 note Bouché (fault was to be found in breach of the rules of the game in one of the players).

[823] Civ. (2) 26 Oct. 2006, D 2007.204 note.

[824] Fabre-Magnan, *Responsabilité civile et quasi-contrats*, 280.

[825] Art. 1355 A.-p.r.

[826] P. Le Tourneau, 'Les responsabilités du fait d'autrui dans l'Avant-projet de réforme' *RDC* 2007.109.

[827] Art. 1356 A.-p.r.

[828] Art. 1357 A.-p.r.

[829] Art. 1358 A.-p.r.

IV Special Liability Regimes

There are three main special legislative regimes governing (respectively) liability for motor-vehicle accidents, liability for defective products, and medical liability.[830]

A. Liability (or Compensation) for Motor-Vehicle Accidents

It is one of the ironies of the historical development of French civil liability that the main context for which the liability for the 'actions of things' was developed—traffic accidents—is no longer governed by it. For in 1985 legislation was enacted which introduced a special regime to govern compensation for the 'victims of a traffic accident in which a motor-vehicle is involved'.[831] While the legislative provisions were drafted in a way which left the point distinctly arguable, it is now generally accepted that the new law is 'independent' from the general law found in articles 1382 *et seq* of the Civil Code, including, of course, liability for the 'actions of things' under article 1384, al. 1.[832] What this independence means is that a claimant who finds his case falling within the ambit of the *loi* of 1985 cannot claim on any other legal basis and is instead subject to the special regime which the *loi* creates;[833] but this regime is not completely divorced from earlier and wider law, for some of the concepts which it uses (notably, *le gardien* who with the driver it is assumed must pay the compensation[834]) are interpreted in the same way as they are as regards liability for the 'actions of things'[835] and some issues are left entirely for the general law (notably, the assessment of the claimant's harm).[836]

At the time of its enactment, there were two main purposes of the new legislation: first, to simplify the law whose interpretation had become very complex; and, secondly, to improve the chance of recovery of compensation to the victims of traffic accidents (in particular, by avoiding technicalities of the vehicle's causal role and judicial use of the defences of *force majeure* and contributory fault in the

---

[830] There are others, e.g. liability for nuclear energy: *loi* no. 68-943 of 30 Oct. 1968.

[831] *Loi* no. 85-677 of 5 July 1985 ('*loi* of 1985') arts. 1–6, on which see generally Bénabent, *Obligations*, 435ff; Malaurie, Aynès, and Stoffel-Munck, *Obligations*, 149ff; Terré, Simler, and Lequette, *Obligations*, 901ff and, in English, R. Redmond-Cooper, 'The Relevance of Fault in Determining Liability for Road Accidents: The French Experience' (1989) 38 ICLQ 502. Apart from the provisions discussed in the text, the *loi* of 1985 arts. 7–48 made important provision as to procedural aspects of obtaining compensation from liability insurers.

[832] Fabre-Magnan, *Responsabilité civile et quasi-contrats*, 213.

[833] Civ. (2) 28 Jan. and 4 Feb. 1987, D 1987.187 note Groutel.

[834] Bénabent, *Obligations*, 443. This is nowhere stated in the *loi*, but art. 2 denies the defence of *force majeure* or act of a third party to 'the driver or the *gardien*' of a motor-vehicle. The notion of *force majeure* furnishes another example of where the courts resort to wider established law for the interpretation of the *loi*: Terré, Simler, and Lequette, *Obligations*, 910–911.

[835] Above, pp. 381 ff.

[836] Malaurie, Aynès, and Stoffel-Munck, *Obligations*, 149–150.

victim).[837] This second purpose is reflected in the fact that the legislation (and many commentators) avoid referring to the regime as one of *responsabilité* ('liability', though the term is rather more morally loaded), such as is imposed by articles 1382 *et seq.* of the Code, seeing it as a regime of compensation (*indemnisation*).[838] To a common lawyer at least, however, this shift in terminology reflects the reality of the reform only up to a point, for the new scheme differs from those such as for the compensation of victims of crime or contamination with HIV[839] in that it identifies persons whose relationship with a motor-vehicle (its driver or *gardien*) brings with it (in certain circumstances) a duty of compensation, though it is true that having done so the practical burden of it falls on their insurers or, if uninsured or unidentified, a special compensation fund.[840] This may not involve an 'action giving rise to responsibility' (*un fait générateur de responsabilité*), but it most certainly does involve the imposition of civil liability as a common lawyer would understand it. But have the purposes of the *loi* of 1985 been achieved? Most commentators think that a road accident victim's chances of compensation have improved, but there is certainly no reduction in the complexity of the law in question, as is attested by the intricate and at times even somewhat absurd case law interpreting all the various elements of the 'independent' regime: 'traffic', 'accident', motor-vehicle', 'driver', etc.[841] Nowhere does this complexity appear more clearly than in the 19 pages of fine print annotations setting out the case law interpreting the six short provisions of the *loi* of 1985 which are found in the Dalloz 2007 edition of the Civil Code.

Rather than try to expose this complex case law, here we shall look merely at two key aspects of the new law: its use of the notion of 'involvement' of a vehicle and its treatment of the defences of *force majeure* and contributory fault in the victim.

1. The 'involvement' of a motor-vehicle

One of the most striking aspects of the *loi* of 1985 is its substitution of the language of 'involvement' ('*implication*') for the traditional language of causation, it being provided that the new regime applies where a 'earth-bound motor-vehicle is involved in a traffic accident'.[842] While at first French courts interpreted this requirement in a way highly reminiscent of its treatment of the causal role of vehicles

---

[837] Bénabent, *Obligations*, 436; Flour, Aubert, and Savaux, *Fait juridique*, 349. Cf. above, pp. 389–393.

[838] Terré, Simler, and Lequette, *Obligations*, 908–909.

[839] Above, p. 363.

[840] The *Fonds de garantie des assurances obligatoires de dommages*: art. 421-1ff C. des assur. Liability insurance is compulsory for driving a motor vehicle: art. 211-1ff C. assur.

[841] Terré, Simler, and Lequette, *Obligations*, 911ff.

[842] *Loi* of 1985, art. 1 and see Flour, Aubert, and Savaux, *Fait juridique*, 349–360 for a particularly useful discussion. Jurists also identify a requirement that a claimant's harm is 'involved' in the victim's harm, where it occurs some time after the accident: Bénabent, *Obligations*, 440–441.

for the purposes of article 1384, al. 1,[843] from the middle of the 1990s they have interpreted it much more generously, in the spirit of helping to ensure that those injured on the roads receive compensation from the insurance companies of those who use motor-vehicles. Their current approach turns on the presence or absence of physical contact between the vehicle and the person or property harmed.[844] So, instead of distinguishing between vehicles which were or were not moving at the time (as they previously did for the purposes of liability under article 1384 al. 1[845]), the Cour de cassation has declared that any vehicle is necessarily involved in an accident as long as it entered into contact with the person or property harmed.[846] However, if there is no such contact, the claimant must show that the vehicle—again, whether moving or not—played a role in the accident or 'took part in whatever way in its occurrence'.[847] So, for example, where a passenger got out of a car which had stopped in an empty space and was then crushed to death by a rotten tree which fell on her and on the vehicle, the Cour de cassation held that the lower court was *not* entitled simply to hold the driver of the car not liable on the basis that she died from the tree-fall and 'independently of the presence of the vehicle close to where it fell'![848] Moreover, where there is a series of multiple collisions over a short period of time, *all* the vehicles affected are said to have been 'involved' in one, single accident.[849]

2. Force majeure *and fault of the victim*

Article 2 of the *loi* of 1985 states that neither a driver nor a *gardien* of a motor-vehicle can rely on the defence of *force majeure* against any victim and this rule applies to those who suffer damage to property as well as to those who suffer personal injuries and to drivers as well as to passengers or pedestrians. As a result, a *gardien* or driver is liable to compensate injuries caused when his car spins out of control on hidden ice or where it crashes owing to an 'unforeseeable and unpreventable' act of a third party.

Compared to this straightforward rule, however, the *loi*'s treatment of the significance of the victim's fault is really rather bizarre. First, where a victim who dies or suffers personal injuries is *not a driver* of a motor-vehicle, his fault can affect the liability of the driver or *gardien* of any implicated vehicle only if it was 'inexcusable' *and* the 'exclusive cause' of his injury and here liability is excluded.[850] This test is a generous one and the courts have been slow to find it satisfied, interpreting an 'inexcusable fault' as 'a voluntary fault of an exceptional seriousness

---

[843] Terré, Simler and Lequette, *Obligations*, 920.
[844] Ibid., 920–922; Flour, Aubert, and Savaux, *Fait juridique*, 353ff.
[845] Above, pp. 386–387.
[846] Civ. (2) 25 Jan. 1995, Bull. civ. II no. 27, RTDCiv. 1995.382 note Jourdain.
[847] Civ. (2) 18 Mar. 1998, Bull. civ. II no. 88.
[848] Civ. (2) 23 May 2002, Resp. civ. et assur. 2002 no. 258.
[849] Civ. (2) 21 Oct. 2004, Resp. civ. et assur. 2004 no. 369.
[850] *Loi* of 1985, art. 3 al. 1. E.g. Civ. (2) 4 Nov. 2004, Bull. civ. II no. 483, RTDCiv. 2004.152 note Jourdain.

which exposes without any reason the person who commits it to a danger of which he ought to have been aware'.[851] Secondly, however, the *loi* creates an even more generous test for those road accident victims who are less than 16 or more than 70 years old or who suffer from a registered disability of 80% or more: *their* fault will extinguish their claim to compensation only where they 'voluntarily sought the injury suffered', a clear example being where such a person is injured by a car as a result of an attempt to commit suicide.[852] As Chabas jibed, this special treatment does not flatter the elderly, whose physical infirmity had not been treated by the courts as fault under the old law and whose intellectual abilities are apparently put into question by this special treatment in the same way as are a child's![853] Unsurprisingly, the *Avant-projet de réforme* proposes that this special treatment should be abolished.[854]

On the other hand, thirdly, *drivers* of motor vehicles, and those who claim through them including their dependants,[855] are treated with less sympathy by the *loi*, as *any fault* on their part can reduce or extinguish any other vehicle driver's liability[856] (as long as it was causally relevant)[857] and the same test applies to claims for *any* person's damage to property caused by a vehicle accident.[858]

B. Liability for Defective Products

From the 1950s, French lawyers identified the liability of manufacturers and business sellers (*vendeurs professionnels*) of products as possessing a certain distinctiveness[859] and they adapted the existing bases of liability found in the Civil Code very considerably.[860] In terms of the law of delict, French courts sometimes imposed liability without fault on manufacturers by applying the distinction between *la garde de la structure* and *la garde du comportement* for the purposes of liability for the 'actions of things' (article 1384 al. 1 of the Civil Code[861]) and sometimes imposed liability for proven delictual fault, notably holding that a manufacturer's mere putting of a defective product into circulation itself constituted fault for this purpose.[862] However, the law of contract provided the

---

[851] Civ. (2) 20 Jul. 1987 (10 cases) Bull. civ. II no. 160; Ass. plén. 10 Nov. 1995, Bull. civ. A.P. no. 6, RTDCiv. 1996.187 note Jourdain.

[852] *Loi* of 1985, arts. 3 al. 2 and 3 al. 3.

[853] F. Chabas, *Le droit des accidents de la circulation*, 2nd edn. (Paris, 1988), 174.

[854] Art. 1385-2 A.-p.r.

[855] *Loi* of 1985, art. 6.

[856] Ibid., art. 4.

[857] Ass. plén. 6 Apr. 2007, D 2007.1199 note Gallmeister (state of inebriation in driver not necessarily causally relevant).

[858] *Loi* of 1985, art. 5.

[859] H. Mazeaud, 'La responsabilité civile du vendeur-fabricant' RTDCiv. 1955. 611.

[860] Whittaker, *Liability for Products*, 50–52 and Ch. 4; J.-S. Borghetti, 'French Report' in S. Whittaker (ed.), *The Historical Development of European Product Liability* (forthcoming).

[861] Above, p. 385.

[862] Civ. (3) 5 Dec. 1972, D 1973.401 note J. Mazeaud.

main legal basis of imposing liability on manufacturers and business sellers for death and personal injury (and, indeed, pure economic loss), sometimes by holding that they had failed to warn adequately of a product's risk as their *obligation d'information* required;[863] sometimes by imposing an *obligation de sécurité*;[864] and much more widely by developing the Civil Code's liability in damages for latent defects imposed on sellers (known as the *garantie légale*), by holding that business sellers are irrebutably presumed to know of defects in the property sold, that they can not exclude this liability by express term, and that all buyers within a chain of distribution can sue any seller in the chain (including the ultimate manufacturer) by *action directe*.[865] The seller's liability in particular was considered to be very strict, the seller not being able to escape liability by proving that it was impossible for him to discover the defect and so prevent the claimant's harm.[866]

Given this background, it is understandable that French lawyers faced with the need to implement the EC Product Liability Directive of 1985[867] were not impressed by the extent to which it required reform of the law in favour of the victims of products, for while it required the imposition of liability on 'producers' for the death and personal injury caused by their defective products, it provided them with a number of defences, imposed liability on mere suppliers only on a subsidiary basis and restricted the range of harm recoverable.[868] French lawyers therefore sought to ensure that the new legislative liability would at the very least be no less strict and no less broad than the law already applied by the courts.[869] As a result, the process of implementation of the Directive was particularly long and difficult and this was made worse by a major product safety scandal, the *l'affaire du sang contaminé* ('affair of the contaminated blood').[870] This *affaire* is worth noting as it still colours a good deal of French thinking about product liability.

The *affaire* arose from the supply in the mid 1980s by the French National Blood Transfusion Centre of blood and blood products contaminated with

[863] Whittaker, *Liability for Products*, 64–69 eg. Civ. (1) 11 Oct. 1983. Bull. civ. I no. 228, RTDCiv. 1984.731 note Huet.

[864] e.g. Civ. (1) 11 Jun. 1991, *Soc. Zeebrugge Caravans*, Bull. civ. I no. 201, RTDCiv. 1992.114 obs. Jourdain.

[865] Civ. 19 Jan. 1965, *l'affaire de Pont-Saint-Esprit*, D 1965.389; Civ. (1) 8 Jun. 1999, Bull. civ. I no. 198 (presumption of knowledge); Civ. (3) 27 Mar. 1969, D 1969.633 note Jestaz (exemption clauses); Civ. (1) 9 Oct. 1979, *affaire Lamborghini*, GP 1980.1.249 note Planqueel, D 1980.IR.222 obs. Larroumet (*action directe*).

[866] P. Malinvaud, note to Com. 10 Dec. 1973, JCP 1975.II.17950; J. Huet, 'Le paradoxe des médicaments et les risques de développement,' D 1987 Chron. 73, 76–77; Whittaker, *Liability for Products*, 84ff and esp. 89.

[867] Dir. 1985/374/EEC concerning liability for defective products.

[868] Ibid, arts. 3 (range of defendants); 6 ('defect'); 7 (defences); 9 ('damage').

[869] J. Ghestin, 'La directive communautaire et son introduction en droit français' in J.Ghestin (ed.) *Sécurité des consommateurs et responsabilité du fait des produits défectueux*, Colloque (LGDJ, Paris, 1987) 111.

[870] The details of this *affaire* are explained by Whittaker, *Liability for Products*, 149–151, 315–319, 324, 394–401.

HIV. Haemophiliacs and others supplied with these products and who contracted AIDS claimed that the responsible officers of this service, the Prime Minister and two other government ministers had known of the risks of this contamination at the relevant time and had delayed acting for financial reasons and/or so as to wait for a French *dépistage* test to be developed.[871] Proceedings were set in motion by the victims of contaminated blood as *parties civiles*[872] in the criminal courts alleging that various offences up to and including 'poisoning' had been committed by two officers of the transfusion centre (though only lesser offences were charged),[873] in the administrative courts (claiming damages from the state on the basis that its officials had committed a fault of a type to attract its liability[874] and against various public hospitals which supplied the blood[875]), and in the ordinary courts claiming damages from private clinics which had supplied the blood.[876]

While, as can be seen, this *affaire* did not concern liability in manufacturers in an ordinary context and, indeed, centred on liabilities in individuals and in the public administration based on fault, it made implementation of the Product Liability Directive a highly sensitive matter, especially as regards the national option (which the Directive allows[877]) of exclusion of the availability of the 'development risks' defence,[878] for while many considered that the defence should be excluded so that the French victims of products (including blood) should be no worse off after implementation, others argued that this would reduce the competitiveness of French industry which would as a result have to bear a greater burden (and cost) of liability than some of its European competitors.[879]

Interestingly, towards the end of the 1990s (while the French legislature continued to fail to act), the Cour de cassation instead 'implemented' the Directive in a series of decisions which interpreted the provisions of the Civil Code (article 1147 as between parties to a contract and article 1384 al. 1 beyond the parties) 'in the

---

[871] Crim. 22 Jun. 1994, JCP 1994.II.41 note Rassat quoting the decision of the Cour d'appel of 13 Jul. 1993 (relating to the Centre's officers) and see J.Y. Chevallier, 'L'affaire du sang contaminé' in J. Pradel (ed.) *Sang et droit pénal, A propos du sang contaminé…* (Eds. Cujas, Paris, 1995) 23 at 35. Cf. above, p. 154 on resulting reform of the 1958 Constitution.

[872] Above, p. 368.

[873] Crim. 22 Jun. 1994, cit.. The two officers were found guilty of *tromperie* (misleading trade practices). On the complex proceedings against the government ministers see Cour de Justice de la République 9 Mar. 1999, Haute Cour de Justice (Commission d'instruction) 5 Feb.1993, D. 1993.261 note Pradel, Cour de Justice de la République 9 Mar. 1999, *affaire du sang contaminé*, D 1999 IR 86 and Whittaker, *Liability for Products*, 398–401.

[874] CE Ass. 9 Apr. 1993, Req. no. 138652, D 1993.312, concl. Légal, obs. Maugüé and Touvet, AJDA 1993 Chron. 344.

[875] CE Ass. 26 May 1995, *Pavan, Consorts N'Guyen, Jouan*, Leb. 221, AJDA 1995.577–78, AJDA 1995.508 note Stahl and Chavaux, JCP 1995.II.22468 note Moreau.

[876] Civ. (1) 12 Apr. 1995, *Dupuy, Martial*, JCP 1995.II.22467 note Jourdain.

[877] Product Liability Directive, arts. 7(e), 15(b).

[878] C. Larroumet, 'La responsabilité du fait des produits défectueux après la loi du 19 mai 1998' D 1998 Chron. 311, 315.

[879] P. Fauchon, *Rapport au nom de la commission des Lois constitutionnelles* [etc.], Sénat no. 226 (21 Jan. 1998) 17–20.

light of' the Product Liability Directive.[880] Then in 1998, legislation at last implemented the Directive by inserting new provisions into the Civil Code, imposing
a distinct liability on manufacturers and other suppliers for harm caused by the
defective products which they put into circulation and setting out a number of the
defences which the Directive includes.[881] The new law reflected a number of political compromises: first, the development risks defence was retained, but with an
exception where the claimant's harm is caused by 'an element of the human body
or by its products';[882] secondly, the new basis of liability for manufacturers and
business suppliers of products was not expressed as being exclusive, so that claimants could still apparently rely on the earlier generous case law;[883] and, thirdly,
various aspects of the scheme provided by the Directive were 'improved' for the
benefit of claimants, notably (following the traditional case law) by imposing
liability on suppliers on the same basis as manufacturers (whereas the Directive
allowed the former to escape liability if they identified the manufacturer or their
own supplier in a reasonable time[884]) and by imposing liability for damage to
property of all types and with no threshold (whereas the Directive restricted
liability to 'consumer property' and set a threshold for claims of 500 ECU).[885]
However, the story of French implementation did not stop there, for in 2002 the
European Court of Justice ruled that the Product Liability Directive required
the creation in the laws of member states of a 'completely harmonised' regime of
liability in producers and suppliers[886] and therefore censured France for failing
to do so in relation to the 'improvements' to its scheme of liability brought to its
attention by the EC Commission.[887] This led to new French legislation to amend
the Civil Code provisions implementing the Directive.[888]

However, in its decisions of 2002 the European Court accepted that the
Directive 'does not preclude the application of other systems of contractual or

[880] Civ. (1) 17 Jan. 1995, D 1995.350 note P. Jourdain; Civ. (1) 3 Mar. 1998, Bull. civ. I, no. 95,
JCP 1998.II.10049 note P. Sargos; Civ. (1) 28 Apr. 1998, Bull. civ. I no. 158; Whittaker, *Liability
for Products*, 455–459. This approach is still used where the product was put into circulation before
the *loi* of 19 May 1998: Civ. (1) 23 Sept. 2003, Bull. civ. I no. 188.
[881] *Loi* no. 98-389 of 19 May 1998 *sur la responsabilité du fait des produits défectueux* ('*loi* of
19 May 1998') creating arts. 1386-1–1386-18 C. civ.
[882] New art. 1386-12 C. civ. (as enacted in 1998). The defence was also 'improved' by subjecting
its application where the defect became apparent within ten years of the product being put into circulation to a condition that the producer had taken 'measures appropriate to prevent any resulting
harm'.
[883] Art. 1386-18 C. civ.
[884] Product Liability Directive, art. 3(3); art. 1386-7 C. civ. (as enacted in 1998).
[885] Product Liability Directive, art. 9 (which defines what has been termed here 'consumer
property' more elaborately); Art. 1386-2 C. civ. (as enacted in 1998).
[886] Case C-52/00 of 25 Apr. 2002, *Commission v. France* [2002] I-3827; Case C-154/00 of
25 Apr. 2002, *Commission v. Greece* [2002] ECR I-3879; Case C-183/00 of 25 Apr. 2002, *Gonzàlez
Sanchez v. Medicina Asturiana SA* [2002] ECR I-3901.
[887] Case C-52/00 of 25 Apr. 2002, *Commission v. France,* ibid.
[888] *Loi* no. 2004-1343 of 9 Dec. 2004, art. 29 (amending art. 1386-2 C. civ.). After the ECJ's
further ruling in Case C-177/04 of 14 Mar. 2006 [2006] ECR I-02461, a further amendment was
made by *loi* no. 2006-406 of 5 Apr. 2006 (amending art. 1386-7 C. civ.).

non-contractual liability based on other grounds, such as fault or a warranty in respect of latent defects'.[889] In the French context this clearly allows a claimant to establish liability in a manufacturer or a supplier for proven delictual fault under article 1383 of the Civil Code, but does it allow the courts to retain their interpretation of these provisions according to which the supply by a manufacturer of a defective product itself constitutes fault for this purpose? Further, it clearly allows a claimant to establish liability in a manufacturer or business seller (including beyond privity) under the ordinary law of sale, but does it allow the courts to develop *obligations de sécurité* or *obligations d'information* in parallel to (and to a degree more generously than) the legislative product liability provisions? These questions are by no means settled either as a matter of EC law or as a matter of domestic French law,[890] but in the meanwhile the French government by decree amended the Civil Code's provisions governing a seller's liability for latent defects so as to replace the undefined 'short period' (*bref délai*) within which claims had had to be brought with a set period of two years from the time of discovery of the defect.[891] This change may give a new vigour to this traditional contractual route to the imposition of liability for products. Certainly, the new legislation governing product liability has not prevented the courts from developing the traditional ways of imposing liability on manufacturers of products supplied *before* the coming into effect of the law implementing the Directive. So, for example, in the *affaire du Distilbène*® a cour d'appel had held liable the manufacturer of a pharmaceutical used by pregnant mothers to their children who later contracted cancer as a result on the basis of delictual fault even though in relation to the relevant time it could not point to any scientific literature which identified the risk of cancer for unborn children associated with the product.[892] The Cour de cassation refused to quash these decisions, holding that the *juges du fond* were entitled to find in the circumstances that the manufacturer had failed in its '*obligation de vigilance*' in this way, a decision seen by some as evidence of the courts applying the 'precautionary principle' found elsewhere in the law.[893] As Viney observes, this particularly broad view of fault opens to victims of products the 'easiest of ways to escape the restrictive conditions' required for the special product liability regime.[894] On the other hand, the sympathy of French courts to the 'victims' of products does have its limits, the Cour de cassation recently holding that a heavy

---

[889] e.g. Case C-154/00, cit., para. 18 so interpreting art. 13 of the Directive 1985/374/EEC.

[890] For further discussion see Whittaker, *Liability for Products*, 461–465; C. Larroumet, 'Introduction' in 'La responsabilité du fait des produits défectueux (loi du 19 mai 1998)' *Petites affiches, La Loi* no. 155 (28 Dec. 1998) 3; J.-S. Borghetti, 'La responsabilité des fournisseurs du fait du défaut de sécurité de leurs produits' (2006) *RDC* 835, 839–840.

[891] Art. 1648 C. civ. as amended by *ord.* no. 2005-136 of 17 February 2005, art. 3.

[892] CA Versailles 30 Apr. 2004, *Legifrance* (2 cases); Civ. (3) 7 Mar. 2006, Juris-Classeur Responsabilité civile et assurances (May 2006) 14 note Radé.

[893] Radé, ibid.

[894] G. Viney, 'La mise en place du système française de responsabilité des producteurs pour le défaut de sécurité de leurs produits' in *Mélanges offerts à Jean-Luc Aubert* (Dalloz, 2005) 331, 353.

smoker of many years could not recover damages against the French national monopoly supplier of tobacco at the time ('SEITA'[895]) either on the ground of article 1383 of the Civil Code (on the basis that the lower court had 'sovereignly assessed the evidence' and found no fault in relation to its duty to warn) nor article 1384 al. 1 (on the basis, as earlier noted, that only the smoker himself was *gardien* of the cigarettes).[896]

C. Medical Liability

Following the division of liability declared by the Tribunal des conflits in the *arrêt Blanco* in 1873,[897] French law long treated the civil liability of doctors and hospitals differently according to whether the health care which they provided was private or public, the Cour de cassation supervising the private law and the Conseil d'Etat the administrative law.[898] As regards the private law, until 1936 liability was based on delictual fault, but in that year the Cour de cassation instead held that the liability of medical practitioners was exclusively contractual, based on an obligation to provide 'conscientious and attentive care, which accords (save exceptionally) with the accepted scientific position', an obligation seen as typical of an *obligation de sécurité de moyens*.[899] However, from the 1960s the courts recognized a number of situations where liability would be imposed on a stricter basis. So, doctors were held to bear a duty to inform their patients of the possible risks of any treatment proposed and the burden of proving that they had done so[900] and both doctors and hospitals were held to owe a strict safety obligation to their patients in respect of any hospital-acquired infection (*infection nosocomiale*).[901] Moreover, doctors and hospitals were held to a strict safety obligation (an *obligation de sécurité de résultat*) as to injury caused by the equipment which they *used* in the course of their investigations and treatment,[902] although generally they were held liable for injury caused by the products which they *supplied* only on the basis of proof of fault.[903] Overall, even just within the private law, the basis of liability (strict or fault) varied considerably according to the circumstances.

[895] Societé Nationale d'Exploitation Industrielle de Tabacs et Allumettes.

[896] Civ. (2) 20 Nov. 2003, JCP 2004.II.10004 note Daille-Duclos and cf. above, p. 385.

[897] TC 8 Feb. 1873, DP 1873.3.17, above, p. 188.

[898] See Whittaker, *Liability for Products*, 141ff.

[899] Civ. 20. May 1936, DP 1936.1.88, rapp. Josserand, concl. Matter. On *obligation de sécurité*, see above, pp. 331–332.

[900] Civ. (1) 29 May 1984, D 1985.281 note Bouvier; Civ. (1) 27 May, 1998, Bull. civ. I no. 187.

[901] Civ. (1) 29 Jun. 1999, rapp. Sargot, JCP 1999.II.10138.

[902] Seine 3 Mar. 1965, JCP 1966.II.14582 note Savatier; Civ. (1) 9 Nov. 1999, Bull. civ. I no. 1; D 2002.117 note Jourdain.

[903] Civ. (1) 23 May 1973, JCP 1975.II.17955 note Savatier, GP 1973.2.885 note Doll. This remained the case even where liability for the supply of contaminated blood was imposed on a strict *obligation de sécurité de résultat* on the blood transfusion service: Civ. (1) 12 Apr. 1995, *Dupuy, Martial*, JCP 1995.II.22467 note Jourdain. Cf. Civ. (1) 4 Feb. 1959, JCP 1959.II.11046 note

However, in 2002 legislation was enacted which appeared to simplify the position considerably, unifying the substantive law governing liability for private and public health care.[904] Generally, the legislation provided that doctors, dental surgeons and midwives and 'any establishment, service or bodies in which individual acts of prevention, diagnosis or care take place are liable for the harmful consequences of acts of prevention, diagnosis or care only in the case of fault'.[905] Two important exceptions were made for liability in respect of the supply of defective products (owing to the impact of the Product Liability Directive[906]) and in respect of hospital-acquired infections where liability was imposed on the hospital or other institution unless they show *cause étrangère* (i.e. *force majeure*).[907] These liability provisions were coupled with an obligation on all those providing medical services, whether private or public, to insure against their liability, with the exception of the state itself.[908] It also set up a special fund for the compensation of those suffering very serious harm as a result of contracting a hospital-acquired infection or a medical accident where liability was not established.[909]

However, despite the relatively conservative nature of this law, the French insurance industry law soon began to refuse to cover medical institutions and hospitals and so at the very end of 2002 further legislation was enacted[910] to transfer the cost of liability in three situations from insurers to the national compensation fund: liability for Creuztfeldt-Jakob disease transmitted to some 2,000 patients treated with human growth hormone between 1973 and 1988;[911] liability for the intervention of medical practitioners 'in exceptional circumstances' (for example, at a roadside accident);[912] and liability for hospital-acquired infections except in relatively minor cases.[913] Apart from these adjustments, it still remains unclear as to the exact basis of liability which the new law generally sets out, for while it refers to 'fault', it does not say whether fault must be proved or may be presumed.[914]

Nevertheless, the law governing liability for harm caused in the course of the provision of medical care reflects a number of the broader features of developments

Savatier, D 1959.153 note Esmein (which took a stricter approach in the context of the injection of an impure serum).

[904] *Loi* no. 2002-303 of 4 Mar. 2002, art. 98 creating new tit. IV of book 1 of the legislative part of the C. santé pub. and see Whittaker, *Liability for Products*, 151ff.

[905] Art. L. 1142-1 al. I 1° C. santé pub.

[906] Above, p. 406.

[907] Art. L. 1142-1 al. I 2° C. santé pub.

[908] Art. L. 1142-2 C. santé pub.

[909] Art. L. 1142-1 al. II C. santé pub.

[910] *Loi* no. 2002-1577 of 30 Dec. 2002.

[911] New art. L. 1142-22 al. 2 C. santé pub..

[912] New art. L. 1142-1-1 2° C. santé pub.

[913] New art. 1142-1-1 1° C. santé pub.

[914] P. Mistretta, 'La loi no. 2002-303 du 4 mars 2002 relative aux droits des malades et à la qualité du système du santé, Réflexions critiques sur un droit en pleine mutation,' JCP 2002.I.141, 1080; P. Sargos, 'Le nouveau régime juridique des infections nosocomiales, loi no. 2002-303 du 4 mars 2002' JCP 2002 Actualité, 1117.

in French civil liability over the last century: a general trend from fault to stricter liabilities; a tendency towards the harmonization if not unification of public and private liability for accidents; and the growth in legal duties to take out liability insurance.

V. Causation and Harm

As we have noted,[915] to recover damages in delict a claimant must show not merely some action giving rise to liability (*fait générateur de responsabilité*), whether this lies in the defendant's fault or 'action of his thing', but also that this caused his harm. Let us take these further elements in turn.

A. Causation

French jurists have never really had quite the same taste for theorizing about causation as have their German counterparts.[916] This means that, while they sometimes note different theories of causation, they are usually happy to conclude that French courts proceed 'empirically', not formally adopting any one approach, through in practice adopting the so-called 'adequate cause' approach.[917] Accordingly, the courts look to 'relate the claimant's harm to one of its antecedents which, normally, according to the natural course of events, was of a nature to produce it, in contrast to other antecedents of the harm, which would lead to it only as a result of exceptional circumstances'.[918] While the Cour de cassation does intervene as to certain aspects of causation, this still leaves the *juges du fond* a very considerable area for their own assessment[919] (guided often by the report of any expert commissioned).[920] In this respect, Carbonnier notes that the courts are swayed by considerations of fairness as much as causal potency, so that 'as between two faults, of unequal moral seriousness, and *a fortiori,* as between two acts, one a fault and one not, the courts always tend to believe it makes better justice to direct the causal relationship towards the fault, or towards the most serious fault'.[921]

---

[915] Above p. 361.

[916] F.H. Lawson and B.S. Markesinis, *Tortious Liability for Unintentional Harm in the Common Law and the Civil Law* (Cambridge, 1982) Vol. I, 106. For a discussion of these theories, see H.L.A. Hart and T. Honoré, *Causation in the Law,* 2nd edn. (Oxford, 1985) chs. XVI–XVII.

[917] Carbonnier, *Obligations,* 2288. Malaurie, Aynès, and Stoffel-Munck, *Obligations,* 45–48. Cf. Civ. (2) 27 Mar. 2003, Bull. civ. II no. 76, where the Cour de cassation explicitly referred to and applied 'the principle of the equivalence of *causes*' (emphasis added).

[918] Terré, Simler, and Lequette, *Obligations,* 834–835.

[919] Carbonnier, *Obligations,* 2283.

[920] On the role of *experts,* see above, pp. 106–108.

[921] Carbonnier, *Obligations,* 2289.

Here, we shall just note French judicial approaches to three situations of possible multiple causation: acts of third parties, acts of the injured party and *force majeure*.

As in English law, an act of a third party may either be held to have contributed together with the defendant to the production of the claimant's harm or instead to have intervened, as we would say, so as to break the chain of causation. So, for example, where two drivers' fault contributed to the accident in which the claimant was injured, the claimant may recover damage representing the totality of his loss against either driver, as the two 'authors of the harm' are jointly and severally liable (*obligations in solidum*).[922] On the other hand, a third party's act may break the chain of causation between any *fait générateur* of the defendant and the claimant's harm. So, for example, the owner of a car left at the curb, stolen and then crashed by a thief is not liable to a person injured in the crash, even if the owner was at fault.[923]

Secondly, as we have noted in relation to liability in contract, in principle an injured party's own action can either exclude or reduce any claim for damages which he may otherwise enjoy.[924] Thus, where his own action (whether a 'fault' or not) is the exclusive cause of his own harm, then he can recover nothing; but where his own *fault* is a partial cause of his own harm, then his damages will be reduced to an extent which is for the *juges du fond* to determine.[925] This means, therefore, that a claimant's action which merely contributes to his own injury and which does not constitute a fault has no effect on his recovery.[926]

Thirdly, an act of nature (*force majeure* here in a narrow sense) may also contribute together with the defendant's *fait générateur*, to the claimant's harm. In the famous *arrêt Lamoricière*, the claimant's husband drowned in the sinking of a vessel of that name, whose *gardien* was the defendant, but her claim for damages under article 1384 al.1 of the Civil Code was reduced by one fifth on the ground that the sinking was caused to this extent by the extreme storm in which the vessel had gone down.[927] However, although this approach has been followed,[928] it has not had a widespread application and is treated by some authors as no longer

---

[922] Civ. 4 Dec. 1939, DC 1941.124 note Holleaux; Civ (2) Mar. 1971, D 1971.494 note Chabas; Civ. (3) 5 Dec. 1984, JCP 1986.II.20543 note Dejean de la Bâtie. The right of full recovery is known as the *droit de poursuite du créancier* and applies to both *obligations solidaires* (which arise only by the agreement or by legisation: art. 1202. C. civ.) and *obligations in solidum*, which are the creature of *la jurisprudence*; Malaurie, Aynès, and Stoffel-Munck, *Obligations*, 707 ff. and see further Whittaker, *Liability for Products*, 546–549.

[923] Civ. 6 Jan. 1943, S 1943. 51, DC 1945.117 note Tunc.

[924] Above, p. 354 cf. above, pp. 391–393 in relation to art. 1384 al.1 C. civ.

[925] Req. 8 Feb. 1875, DP 1875.1.320; Civ. (2) 25 Jun. 1998, Bull. civ. II no. 238 and see above, pp. 402–403 as to the role of the injured party's fault as regards liability under the *loi* of 5 July 1985 governing motor-vehicle accidents. See also above, pp. 354–356 on the general hostility of French law to a duty to mitigate in the injured party.

[926] Civ. (2) 12 Feb. 1970, Bull. civ. II, no. 50.

[927] Com. 19 Jun. 1951, S 1952.I.89 note Nerson.

[928] Civ. (2) 13 Mar. 1957, D 1958.73 note Radouant (in the context of liability for fault); Com. 14 Feb. 1973, D 1973.562 note Viney.

current.[929] If it were not followed, then a defendant would be liable in full where an act of nature merely contributes to the claimant's harm, though he would not be liable at all if the act of nature were held to be the exclusive cause of his harm.

B. The Claimant's Harm: *Préjudice and Réparation*

Traditionally, French lawyers distinguish between *préjudice* and *réparation*. Under *préjudice,* they address the question what types of harm caused by the defendant's action[930] will be susceptible to reparation whereas under *réparation*, they discuss the means of 'repairing' that harm, which generally refers to the quantification of damages needed to compensate the claimant.

1. Préjudice

As we have said, French law does not rule out any type of harm from recovery in delict, whatever the legal ground on which damages are claimed: in particular, pure economic loss and *dommage moral* are included.[931] On the other hand, it is accepted that the particular harm suffered by the claimant must be 'direct, certain and lawful'.[932] Here we can only glance at the significance of these restrictions.

First, the claimant's harm must be 'direct', a requirement which some writers relate to the issue of causation, noting that here the concern is with how far causation should be said to go from the defendant's act.[933] While the test is one of directness, thereby differing from the test generally applicable to claims for contractual non-performance,[934] it has been said that in fact the courts tend to use the same criterion of reasonable foreseeability as is found there.[935] Indeed some go further, so that for Malaurie, Aynès, and Stoffel-Munck, 'in practice, the classification of a loss as direct is often determined more by a sense of fairness than by any strict criteria'.[936]

We should note, however, that the requirement of directness plays an important role in restricting particular claims in respect of *dommage par ricochet,* i.e. where A claims in respect of harm caused by B's injury or damage itself caused by the defendant's (C's) act. This type of claim may be based on mental

---

[929] Malaurie, Aynès, and Stoffel-Munck, *Obligations,* 100 but cf. Terré, Simler, and Lequette, *Obligations,* 771–772.

[930] The term 'action' is used here for convenience and the propositions in the text should be understood mutads mutandis, as applying also to liability for the actions of things and of other people for whom one is responsible.

[931] Above, pp. 364 and 388–389.

[932] Req. 1 Jun. 1932, DP 1932.1.102 rapp. Pilon, S 1933.49 note Mazeaud ('certain and direct').

[933] Malaurie, Aynès, and Stoffel-Munck, *Obligations,* 49 ff.

[934] Above, p. 354.

[935] Carbonnier, *Obligations,* 2284.

[936] Malaurie, Aynès, and Stoffel-Munck, *Obligations,* 49.

distress or grief suffered as a result of the injury or death of a relative or friend (and in one case, even the claimant's *racehorse*),[937] but may also include purely financial losses caused by another's personal injury or damage to property: for French lawyers, therefore, a claim by a dependant of someone killed by the defendant is one *par ricochet*.[938] Even more surprisingly for an English lawyer, French courts have gone further and have accepted that in principle a person may recover a purely business loss suffered as a consequence of another person's injury or death. One famous example may be found in the professional football club which recovered damages for loss of a possible transfer fee and the gate-money resulting from the death of their star player;[939] another, in the employees who recovered damages for the wages (and tips) lost while they were laid off when the hairdresser's shop where they worked was closed for repairs after the defendant's car had smashed into it.[940] However, claims like these are not often successful, the courts taking a fairly restrictive interpretation of the requirement of 'directness' in this context.[941] Thus, in another case the court rejected the claim of a creditor of two persons killed in a road accident against the person responsible for the accident for money which he could not recover in full from the direct victims' heirs.[942]

Secondly, the issue of 'certainty' of a claimant's harm most commonly arises in modern practice in relation to the question of recovery of 'loss of a chance'. Although at one time the courts rejected recovery of lost chances altogether, they now allow it as long as the chance is a real and serious one so as to constitute a certain loss which calls for reparation and once this is established, they award a fraction of this advantage according to the degree of its probability.[943] A typical example of this arising in delict may be found in relation to recovery by a victim of personal injuries of damages for no longer being in contention for promotion at work (based on a percentage of the larger salary thereby obtainable).[944] Another example may be found in the recovery of lost chances owing to negligent medical treatment.[945] A final example may be found in cases against professional advisers, so that, for example, a client may lose his chance of success before the Cour

[937] Civ. (1) 16 Jan. 1962, *affaire Lunus*, JCP 1962.II.12557, note Esmein, D 1962.199 note Rodière.

[938] Bénabent, *Obligations*, 466–467. Cf. the possibility for Caisses de sécurité social (social security bodies) of recovery in respect of money or benefits paid to the injured party against the defendant by legislative subrogation: art. 376-1 C. de séc. soc.

[939] Colmar 20 Apr. 1955, D 1956.723 note Savatier.

[940] Nanterre 22 Oct. 1975, GP 1976.1.392 note Planqueel.

[941] Viney and Jourdain, *Conditions* 162–163.

[942] Civ (2) 21 Feb. 1979, D 1979.IR.344 note Larroumet.

[943] Terré, Simler, and Lequette, *Obligations*, 690.

[944] e.g. Crim. 3 Nov. 1983, JCP 1985.II.20360 (2nd case) note Chartier (where recovery was refused on the ground that it was too doubtful whether the claimant would have got the job).

[945] e.g. Civ. (1) 17 Nov. 1982, JCP 1983.II.20056 note Saluden. On the bases of liability here, see above, pp. 400–403.

de cassation because his *avocat* fails to put in the necessary document in time.[946] These cases demonstrate that for French lawyers the concept of a 'loss of a chance' goes to the issue of quantification of damages, rather than causation.[947]

Thirdly, it is often said that a claimant's harm must be lawful, this sometimes being linked to the procedural rule that actions are open to 'all those who have a *legitimate* interest in the success or rejection of a claim'.[948] For many years the standard (and decidedly isolated) example of rejection of a claimant's recovery of a particular type of harm was where a person claimed damages based on a lost dependency or *dommage moral* based on a extra-marital relationship (with a '*concubine*'), but this law was firmly overturned in 1970.[949] A contemporary example may be found in the Cour de cassation's rejection of recovery for the birth of a healthy child even where the 'fault' of her doctor prevented the mother from having the abortion which she desired, holding that the existence of the child cannot, in itself, constitute for a mother a 'legally compensatable harm' (*préjudice juridiquement réparable*).[950] Moreover, a particular element of a claim has also been held to be 'unlawful', for example, where a claim for lost future earnings included money lost from a job which had not been declared to the tax authorities.[951]

2. Réparation

Once a court has decided that a claimant's harm is 'certain, lawful and direct', then in principle there must be 'full reparation' (*réparation intégrale*). As the Cour de cassation has declared:

> The proper function of civil liability is to re-establish as exactly as is possible the balance of things destroyed by the harm and to replace the victim, at the expense of the person held liable, in the situation in which he would have been if the harm had not occurred.[952]

---

[946] Civ. (1) 18 Jul. 1972, Bull. civ. I, no. 188 (though recovery was denied on the facts on the ground that his claim would have been hopeless).

[947] Civ. (1) 17 Nov. 1982, cit.; Civ. (1) 4 Nov. 2003, D 2004.601 note Penneau.

[948] Art. 31 N.c.pr.civ. (emphasis added); Terré, Simler, and Lequette, *Obligations*, 693 cf. above p. 92, where it is argued that this confuses the legitimacy of a person's substantive interest to be protected by the law and a person's procedural interest in coming before the court.

[949] Ch. mixte 27 Feb. 1970, *arrêt Dangereux*, D 1970. 201 note Combaldieu.

[950] Civ. (1) 25 Jun. 1991. D 1991.566 note Le Tourneau. Cf. Ass. plén. 17 Nov. 2000, *affaire Perruche* JCP 2000.II.10438 rapp. Sargos, concl. Sainte-Rose, note Chabas which held a doctor and clinic liable for the loss resulting from the disability of a child born to a mother who had not been told of her infection with rubella and who had therefore been deprived of her choice of an abortion. The *loi* no. 2002-303 of 4 Mar. 2002, art. 1 (I) appeared to reverse this decision as to the child's claim by providing that 'no-one can rely on a loss by reason solely of the fact of his own birth', but then made further provision for recovery by a disabled child and the parents in certain circumstances: see further (with a full bibliography) Fabre-Magnan, *Responsabilité civile et quasi-contrats*, 117–119.

[951] Civ. (2) 24 Jan. 2002, D 2002.2559 note Mazeaud.

[952] Civ. (2) 8 Apr. 1970, Bull. civ. II no. 111. See generally Viney and Jourdain, *Effets de la responsabilité*, 111ff.

'Reparation' can be of two types here: either in kind (*en nature*) or by an equivalent sum (*par équivalent*), i.e. damages. Unlike the position we have seen in relation to contract, *réparation en nature* is generally accepted as a possibility for the *juges du fond* in some cases of liability in delict. Thus, if the defendant has damaged the claimant's property and offers to replace it, a court may order the claimant to accept a replacement rather than damages, as long as it is adequate to 'repair' his harm.[953] But 'reparation' may be of other types, so that, for example, a claimant who has suffered some 'moral or commercial harm' may persuade the court to order the defendant to publicize its own decision so as to attempt to 'repair' the damage done by his wrongdoing.[954]

In the case of *réparation par équivalent,* it is clear that, far more than in English law, the process of determing the size of an award is treated as one of fact, for a person's loss is one of fact, and it lies therefore, in principle within the 'sovereign power of assessment' of the *juges du fond.*[955] Behind this veil, the lower courts are able in fact to exercise a discretion as to the amount which should be recovered, reducing the award where appropriate.[956] In practice, the issue of a claimant's harm is often put to an expert, whether for property damage or loss or personal injuries and it is very rare that the resultant report is not followed, though in principle the *juges du fond* are not bound by it.[957] On the other hand, the Cour de cassation does intervene in the assessment of a claimant's harm (and therefore of his damages) where the lower court has taken a wrong approach in law. Thus, since the aim of an award of damages is to compensate the claimant, not to punish the defendant, the seriousness of any fault in the defendant must remain formally irrelevant,[958] even though it may be thought that it is indeed taken into account off the face of the record, especially in relation to recovery of *dommage moral.*[959] Secondly, the Cour de cassation affirms that lower courts must assess the claimant's harm as at the date of judgment, rather than the date of first suffering it.[960] However, French courts do sometimes order the payment of periodic payments (*rentes viagères*) and where they do the amount of the payments may be linked to an index of incomes.[961] Thirdly, in the case of the assessment of personal injuries,

---

[953] Terré, Simler, and Lequette, *Obligations*, 877, e.g. Civ. 20 Jan. 1953, D 1953.222, JCP 1953. II. 7677 note Esmein.

[954] e.g. Req 6 Jun. 1896, DP 1897.1.72.

[955] Crim. 3 Dec. 1969, JCP 1970.II.16353; Viney and Jourdain, *Effets de la responsabilité*, 125ff.

[956] Malaurie, Aynès, and Stoffel-Munck, *Obligations*, 128–129 referring to this as 'equivalent to the moderating power (*le pouvoir modérateur*) which always existed in the law of liability since the *ancien régime*'.

[957] See above, pp. 106–108.

[958] Civ. (2) 8 May 1964, JCP 1965.II.14140 note Esmein.;

[959] Terré, Simler, and Lequette *Obligations,* 881; Carbonnier, *Obligations*, 2397–2398.

[960] Civ. 15 Jul. 1943, DA 1943.81.

[961] Ch. mixte 6 Nov. 1974, JCP 1975.II.17978 *concl.* Gégout, note Savatier; Viney and Jourdain, *Effets de la responsabilité*, 148ff.

the lower courts do in fact often rely on conventional scales of award, but they must be careful not to refer to them as rules of law on pain of *cassation*.[962]

However, the very considerable degree of discretion allowed to the *juges du fond* and the opaqueness of their decision-making as regards awards of damages has been the subject of criticism[963] and this is reflected in the proposals of the *Avant-projet de réforme*, of which we shall note two.[964]

First, while the traditional understanding of damages as based on compensation for loss is retained in principle,[965] provision is included for the courts to possess a power to award punitive damages. Article 1371 of the *Avant-projet* states that:

A person who commits a manifestly deliberate fault, and notably a fault with a view to gain, can be condemned in addition to compensatory damages to pay punitive damages, part of which the court may in its discretion allocate to the Public Treasury. A court's decision to order payment of damages of this kind must be supported with specific reasons and their amount distinguished from any other damages awarded to the victim. Punitive damages may not be the object of insurance.

Not surprisingly, this proposal has proved highly controversial.[966]

Secondly, it is provided (in the context of damages based on loss) that

The court must assess distinctly each of the heads of loss claimed of which it takes account. Where a claim concerning a particular head of loss is rejected, the court must give specific reasons for its decision.[967]

And,

In the case of personal injuries, the victim has the right to reparation for his financial, business or professional losses and in particular to those losses which relate to expenses incurred and future outlay, to loss of income and to lost profits, as well as to reparation for his non-financial and personal losses such as physical impairment, pain and suffering, disfigurement, any specific lost pursuit or pleasure, sexual impairment and any costs of investigation of the injury.[968]

The extent of physical impairment is to be determined according to a scale of disability established by decree.[969]

In making these recommendations, the authors of the *Avant-projet* seek 'to give a proper legal framework to the assessment of compensation for personal injuries which is now almost entirely abandoned to the unfettered discretion of the lower

---

[962] Carbonnier, *Obligations*, 2402 ff.
[963] Viney and Jourdain, *Effets de la responsabilité*, 135ff.
[964] Art. 1367 ff A.-p.r.
[965] Art. 1370 A.-p.r.
[966] E.g. Y. Lambert-Faivre, 'Les effets de la responsabilité (Les articles 1367 à 1383 Nouveaux du Code civil)' (2007) *RDC* 163, 164–165.
[967] Art. 1374 A.-p.r.
[968] Art. 1379 al. 1 A.-p.r.
[969] Art. 1379-1 A.-p.r.

courts. The intention [of the provisions] is to restore to this area legal certainty, an equal treatment to all litigants and the effectiveness of reparation.'[970]

(4) *Quasi-Contrats* and *Enrichissement Sans Cause:* A 'French Law of Restitution'?

1. Introduction

The English law of restitution has emerged only fairly recently as a recognizable and distinct basis of recovery. In order to do so, three major hurdles had to be overcome. First, the damaging association with fictitious contract had to be repudiated. Secondly, a unifying but manageable principle had to be found on which to base recovery, this being the unjust enrichment of the defendant at the claimant's expense. And, thirdly, the kaleidoscope of common law and equitable material—whether put in terms of actions or concepts—had to be collated and structured (and criticized) so as to provide guidance as to *when* this principle of unjust enrichment would apply and to dispel the suspicion that the notion of *unjust* enrichment was irredeemably vague. There is still a good deal of debate as to how the material should be organized and what the various triggers for the obligation to make restitution should be; but the need for an overall framework is now generally recognized and a good deal of work has been done.[971] We can say, therefore, that the 'law of restitution' in the English context refers to that body of rules which relate to recovery based on the defendant's unjust enrichment at the claimant's expense and the courts are willing on occasion to add new examples of this type of recovery where these are justified.[972] On the other hand, it remains true that English law does not recognize unjust enrichment at the claimant's expense as a general *legal basis* for recovery, so that a person who can establish that the defendant was enriched at his expense and that this can be said in a general way to be 'unjust' or 'unjustified' may recover without more: there are instead 'pockets of recovery' for restitution.

French lawyers have long been aware of the idea that obligations may be founded on a defendant's unjust enrichment. However, while Pothier, Domat and other jurists of the *ancien régime* knew the Roman jurist Pomponius' famous observation that 'this is indeed by nature fair, that nobody should be made richer

---

[970] *Avant-projet de réforme*, 183.

[971] See especially, P. Birks, *An Introduction to the Law of Restitution,* revsd edn. (Oxford, 1989), ch. 1; A. Burrows, *The Law of Restitution*, 2nd edn. (OUP, 2005) ch. 1. For a dissenting voice see S. Hedley, 'Unjust Enrichment as the Basis of Restitution—An Overworked Concept' (1985) 5 *Legal Studies* 56.

[972] e.g. *Lipkin Gorman v. Karpnale Ltd* [1991] 2 AC 548; *Woolwich Building Society v. IRC* [1993] AC 70.

through loss to another',[973] in general they were not favourably disposed towards claims on this basis.[974] As a result, the Civil Code did not include any grand declaration concerning unjust enrichment to parallel the provisions on contract or delict,[975] though some particular Roman legal rules which could be thought of as reflecting such a principle did find their way into it. As Ripert put it, 'like a subterranean river, [the principle of unjust enrichment] nourishes detailed rules and these show that it exists, but it never comes to the light of day'.[976] However, to the law has moved on very considerably since the Code's enactment and to find the modern law of restitution one needs to look at modern legislation and *la jurisprudence,* as well as the Code itself.

Nevertheless, a good place to start is the section in the Civil Code concerning the two 'quasi-contracts (*'quasi-contrats'*), *gestion d'affaires* (unrequested management of another person's affairs) and *répétition de l'indu* (recovery of undue payments). Of these two, *gestion d'affaires* is, as we shall see, only in part concerned with restitutionary issues, but recovery of undue payments is both truly restitutionary and broader than its name suggests, applying to the undue discharge of any legal or contractual obligations other than those to perform services. It also is at least related to some claims for restitution under failed contracts.[977]

Secondly, other provisions in the Civil Code may be seen as reflecting the idea of unjust enrichment, these being scattered through its provisions on property law,[978] contracts in general[979] and particular contracts, such as sale,[980] deposit[981] or agency (*mandat*).[982]

Thirdly, and most remarkably, the Cour de cassation in the famous *arrêt Boudier* in 1892 felt able to correct the 'defect' in the Code by itself declaring a general principle of *enrichissement sans cause* based simply on *équité* as an

---

[973] Dig. 12.6.14 (Birks' translation, (above n. 971), 22); Dig. 50.17.206 on which see R. Zimmermann, *The Law of Obligations, Roman Foundations of the Civilian Tradition* (Oxford, reprint 1996) 851ff.

[974] Zimmermann (above n. 973), 883.

[975] J. Dawson, *Unjust Enrichment: a Comparative Analysis* (Chicago, 1951) 95ff. cf. the B.G.B., para. 812 (1). For contract, see art. 1101; delict, arts. 1382–3. C. civ. above, pp. 297 and 361 respectively.

[976] G. Ripert, *La règle morale dans les obligations civiles*, 4th edn. (Paris, 1949) 246.

[977] Below, p. 440 ff.

[978] Art. 554 (construction of building etc. with another's materials on one's own land); art, 555 (construction of building etc. with one's own materials on another's land); art. 599 al. 2 (restitution denied to usufructuary); art. 861 (restitution to donee who has to return a gift as the result of the application of rules relating to succession rights of heirs); art. 1469 (concerning *récompenses* granted to former spouses after the division of matrimonial property where marriage was made under the regime of community property).

[979] Notably, art. 1312 C. civ. (which gives to a person who has made a contract with a minor or person under *tutelle* which has been rescinded a right to reimbursement for property transferred under it to the extent to which this 'has turned to the profit' of the minor etc.).

[980] Art. 1673 C. civ. (buyer's rights to restitution on exercise by seller of power to buy back the property (*faculté de rachat*)).

[981] Art. 1926 C. civ.

[982] Art. 1993 C. civ.

independent ground of imposing obligations,[983] recovery under the principle becoming known as the *action de in rem verso*. In that case, the claimant had supplied fertilizer to a tenant farmer who used it on his fields. On termination of the lease for non-payment of rent, the claimant was held able to recover the price of the fertilizer from the owner of the property who had leased it to the farmer (who himself was insolvent), this being treated as the 'value' of the fertilizer which was reflected in the latter's enrichment through the improvement of the soil.[984] As we shall see, recognition of this general principle has certainly allowed restitutionary recovery in a wide variety of situations. Yet, without denying its generality in this sense, it should be noted that it possesses two very considerable limitations: first, the enrichment must be *sans cause*, that is, without any legal justification, whether this be a contract, the claimant's generosity or self-interest, or the law itself[985] and, secondly, recovery under it is 'subsidiary', in the sense that it is available only if the claimant possesses no other action in respect of his 'impoverishment', on whatever conceptual basis this may be founded.[986] These restrictions have meant that the actual number of successful claims on the basis of the general principle of unjust enrichment have not been very many so that for some authors while recovery may no longer be 'subterranean', it is a trickle rather than a river.[987] On the other hand, for other authors the last few years have seen a greater willingness to allow claims on this basis, at least in cases where otherwise injustice would go unremedied.[988]

Fourthly, both the legislature and the courts have at times recognized personal obligations on defendants which are clearly related to the idea of unjust enrichment, though this relationship is not usually an explicit one. An example of legislation may be found in the rules created for the compensation of tenants in respect of improvements made to the landlord's property. In this situation the legislature has appeared often to consider recovery under the general principle too restricted, for it has elaborated more generous rules for particular contexts.[989] Another example may be found in the right of children of farmers who work without pay on the family farm to claim a 'deferred salary' against their parents' estate on the latters' death.[990] These legislative 'examples' of the principle of unjust enrichment create their own special problem. For, where the law creates a ground of recovery but sets limits on it, does this mean that recovery under the general principle of

---

[983] *Arrêt Boudier,* Req. 15 Jun.1892, S 1893.281 note Labbé, below, p. 435.

[984] See below pp. 436–437 on the question whether this enrichment could be said to be *sans cause.*

[985] Below, pp. 435–437 ff.

[986] Below, pp. 437–438.

[987] Malaurie, Aynè and Stoffel-Munck, *Obligations,* 566.

[988] Fabre-Magnan, *Responsabilité civile et quasi-contrats,* 419 referring to J. Mestre and B. Fages, note RTDCiv. 2003.297 commenting on Civ. (1) 14 Jan. 2003, Bull. civ. I no. 11.

[989] See Art. L. 411-69 C. rur. (farm leases); *Décret* no. 53-960 of 30 September 1953, art. 37 (commercial leases); *Loi* no. 67-561 of 12 July 1967, art. 5 (residential leases); Flour, Aubert, and Savaux, *Fait juridique,* 53.

[990] *Décret loi* of 29 July 1939, art. 63 ff.

enrichissement sans cause should or should not be allowed (assuming that its conditions are otherwise satisfied)? For example, if the law restricts recovery to farmers' *children,* what should the position be of a farmer's *nephew* or *neice?* Should their claims be allowed simply by applying the general principle on the basis of *équité* or rather rejected as making nonsense of the legislation's restrictions?[991]

Moreover, the courts themselves have sometimes recognized what looks very much like recovery on the basis of unjust enrichment, but which they expressly distinguish from any of the legal grounds of recovery which we have already mentioned including *enrichissement sans cause.* One example of this may be found in the Cour de cassation's treatment of recovery by a person who pays another's debt without request and without an interest in doing so, where in 1990 it simply declared that the discharging effect of payment gave rise to a right of recovery in the payer against the debtor;[992] later, however, it brought this example of recovery firmly within the fold of *enrichissement sans cause.*[993] Another very important set of situations in which restitution is ordered, but where the precise legal basis of this is disputed, is found in respect of transfers of money or other property and work done under contracts which are later annulled or terminated for non-performance.[994] As we shall see, the rules which are applied here, while to an extent inspired by those found in the Civil Code, have been adapted by the courts to suit this contractual context.[995]

In all, therefore, the French law of restitution contains a striking paradox. For while it recognizes *enrichissement sans cause* as a distinct and 'general' ground of recovery, the wider picture of the French law of restitution (if we can properly call it that) is remarkably disparate and unsystematic, in particular when compared to its law of contract and delict.[996] There has, moreover, been in general little attempt to relate, let alone to integrate, the various legal grounds of the reversal of unjust or unjustified enrichments. Nowhere is the resulting diversity more apparent than in the measure or rather various measures of recovery which are permitted in French law.[997] Thus, in the case of recovery of undue payments, the measure of recovery depends, in particular, on a distinction between the defendant's good or bad faith or other fault;[998] a minor's restitutionary obligation under a rescinded contract is restricted to any surviving value[999] and the defendant to a claim based on *enrichissement sans cause* is in principle liable for the *lesser* sum as between the cost of the procuring of the defendant's enrichment and any

---

[991] Flour, Aubert, and Savaux, *Fait juridique,* 53 ff.

[992] Civ. (1) 15 May 1990, JCP 1991.II.21628 note Petit, D 1991.538 note Virassamy.

[993] Civ. (1) 2 Jun. 1992, D 1992.Somm. 407 note Delebecque; Civ. (1) 4 Apr. 2001, D 2001.1824 note Billiau.

[994] Below, p. 440 ff.

[995] Below, p. 440 ff.

[996] Above, pp. 296 and 361.

[997] cf. Birks (above n. 971), chap. III, who distinguishes between 'receipt value' and 'survival value'.

[998] Below, pp. 431–432.

[999] Below, p. 447.

increase in value which it may have caused the defendant.[1000] This diversity and lack of overall justifying principle may well in part be due to the way in which the Code was written, but it may also be due to the special role given to the principle of *enrichissement sans cause* in French law as a specific and independent, but therefore necessarily severely restricted, cause of recovery. For the avoidance of doubt, in the following discussion the phrase *enrichissement sans cause* will be used to refer to the particular legal ground of recovery, rather than any principle underlying recovery on the basis of unjust or unjustified enrichment more generally.

Clearly, then, we cannot examine all of the variety of situations in which unjust enrichments are reversed in French law and so the present discussion will be restricted to four areas of recovery: *gestion d'affaires;* undue payments; *enrichissement sans cause* and failed contracts. Before doing so, three further preliminary points arise.

First, in English law it has been said that some restitutionary remedies are personal (actions *in personam*) but others are proprietary (actions *in rem*.)[1001] As we shall see, at times French law allows a claimant an action which is considered to be based on unjust enrichment, but where the claimant is said either to *retain* or to *regain* title to the property which forms the substance of the enrichment in question.[1002] A notable example of the latter is the case where a party to a subsequently annulled or terminated contract has transferred ascertained and still identifiable property under it: on annulment or *résolution*[1003] the transferor, A, regains title to the property possessed by the other party, B, and is said to owe an *obligation de restitution en nature,* i.e. an obligation to restore the particular property. Here, though, great care must be taken. For while the dissolution of the contract does have proprietary effects, any temptation to think of recovery under this obligation as *in rem* must be resisted: by their nature, *obligations* are the correlative of *droits de créance* or rights *in personam*. Thus, the revesting of title to the property in the transferor merely forms the background to a personal claim based on the other party's unjust enrichment. If the transferor wishes to rely on his regained rights *in rem* (or *droits réels*), notably so as to avoid the other party's insolvency or to claim the property from third party transferees, he must do so by way of a proprietary claim, commonly known as *revendication*.[1004] The idea of a claim *in rem* based on the principle of unjust enrichment would strike a French lawyer as a contradiction in terms.

Secondly, while the term *'obligation de restitution'* is sometimes used, as in the previous paragraph, in cases in which the other party has a right of recovery based

[1000] Below, p. 439.
[1001] Birks, (above n. 971), 49ff.
[1002] An example of the *retention* of title to property transfered may be found as regards the recovery of undue payments, below, pp. 442, 448, 449 ff.
[1003] Below, p. 448.
[1004] Above, pp. 451–452. The risk of confusion in French law is aggravated by the occasional use of *restitution* to refer to a proprietary as much as to a personal restoration: e.g., M. Malaurie, *Les restitutions en droit civil* (Paris, 1991), 81.

on unjust enrichment, it is by no means restricted to this context.[1005] So, for example, a party to certain contracts—such as loan, hire or deposit—owes the other party an *obligation de restitution,* but these obligations are contractual.[1006] The expression *obligations de restitution* is not, therefore, used to refer to the body of law concerning the reversal of unjust enrichments in the way in which 'restitution' is in English law.

Finally, while for most of the 20th century French jurists generally considered that the notion of *quasi-contrat* itself added little to legal vocabulary (Josserand even referring to it as a 'legendary monster' which should be banished[1007]), over the last few years it has enjoyed something of a renaissance in part of *la doctrine* and then in 2002 found new expression in a remarkable creation of *la jurisprudence.* So, for example, Malaurie, Aynès, and Stoffel-Munck have suggested that *quasi-contrat* can be used to describe certain categories of legal relations which, while failing to be contracts in the classical and 'voluntary' sense, are nevertheless rather like contracts, as in the case of the relationship between a landlord and tenant where the latter remains in possession after the expiry of the term:[1008] here, the relationship is expressly recognized by legislation, but does not easily fit into any other category. Bénabent, on the other hand, sees the judicially recognized doctrine of apparent authority (*la théorie de l'apparence*) as underpinned by the notion of *quasi-contrat,* an example of this doctrine being the ostensible authority of agents.[1009] Generally, these suggestions have met with a somewhat lukewarm reception from other jurists, but then in 2002 the Chambre mixte of the Cour de cassation appeared to invent its own new example of a *quasi-contrat.*[1010] In this case, the principal claimant[1011] was an individual who had received from the defendant mail-order company promotional material which clearly indicated to him that he had won just over 100,000 francs in a lottery and that this sum would be paid to him if he sent in his acceptance; the claimant sent in his acceptance, but despite his requests, he received no prize. On claiming damages, he was awarded only 5,000 francs against the company by the *juges du fond* under article 1382 of

---

[1005] See especially, Malaurie, ibid., 51 who observes that '[t]he relationship between *enrichissement sans cause* and *restitution* cannot be denied; but *enrichissement sans cause* is only a poor relation, a particular institution which does not reflect the general law applicable to *restitutions.* Outside certain particular cases, *restitution* is not measured according to the debtor's enrichment. It ensures a return of property to its original *patrimoine*'.

[1006] See arts. 1875 C.civ. (loan for use); art. 1902 C.civ. (loan for consumption); art. 1915 (deposit); arts. 1730-1 C.civ. (hire). However, e.g., a borrower still owes an *obligation de restitution* even after nullity of the contract of loan, with the result that a guarantor of such a loan remains liable (Civ. (1) 25 May 1992, JCP 1992.IV.21-12) but as M. Fabre-Magnan D 1992 Chron, 366, argues that this obligation is not contractual but arises as a legal consequence of annulment.

[1007] F. Josserand, *Cours de droit civil français,* T. II (1933) no. 10.

[1008] *Obligations,* 548–549.

[1009] Bénabent, *Obligations,* 341.

[1010] Ch. *mixte* 6 Sep. 2002, D 2002.2963 note Mazeaud and see E. Terrier, 'La fiction au secours des quasi-contrats ou l'achèment d'un débat juridique' D 2004.1179; M. Tchendjou, 'La responsabilité civile des organisateurs de loteries publicitaires' in *Mélanges offerts à Jean-Luc Aubert* (Dalloz, 2005), 311.

[1011] A leading consumers' association, U.F.C., also claimed damages.

the Civil Code on the ground of the uncertain nature of his harm.[1012] However, the Chambre mixte quashed this decision, citing article 1371 of the Code, which introduces the provisions on *gestion d'affaires* and *répétition de l'indu* by stating that 'quasi-contracts are purely intentional human actions which result in some kind of engagement towards a third party, and sometimes a reciprocal engagement of two parties'. They then sent the case to another cour d'appel to determine the loss of the claimant on the basis that the company had 'failed to indicate that there was any risk of getting nothing'; and a later decision of the Cour de cassation has both confirmed this case law and made clear that in these circumstances the claimant should recover the prize which he had been promised itself.[1013]

Does this line of cases therefore represent the judicial recognition of a new *quasi-contrat*? Some jurists think so; others are less certain and less enthusiastic about using article 1371 in this way, even if they are sympathetic to the aim of the courts in sanctioning the unfair commercial practice perpetrated by these false promises of prizes.[1014] In his note to the original decision of 2002, Mazeaud notes that the radical change is that the basis of quasi-contractual obligation in the case does not rest on any unjustified enrichment in the defendant (which he sees as underpinning the traditional *quasi-contrats* and *enrichissement sans cause*) but on 'the illegitimate illusion created in the claimant as a result of a deliberate and self-interested act on the part of the defendant', a 'sanction for short-lived promises'.[1015] So, even if a French law of restitution is to be found in part in the law governing *quasi-contrats*, the latter category may now stretch beyond the reversal of unjustified enrichments.

II. Unrequested Management of Another Person's Affairs (*Gestion d'Affaires*)

The quasi-contract of *gestion d'affaires* arises where a person (the *gérant*) voluntarily and intentionally does something useful for the benefit or on behalf of another (the *maître*). The 'something' may be either physical, as in mending a neighbour's roof, or 'administrative', as in making a contract on behalf of the other.

The justification for the obligations imposed on *both* parties by *gestion d'affaires* is said to lie in a policy of encouraging citizens to help each other by requiring some recompense when they attempt to do so: it fosters, therefore, a limited altruism. This lies behind the requirement of an intention to act on behalf

---

[1012] On which see above, pp. 364 ff and 413–414.

[1013] Civ. (1) 13 Jun. 2006, D 2006.1772.

[1014] Bénabent, *Obligations*, 349–351 (treating it as an example of a *quasi-contrat* created by *la jurisprudence*); Terré, Simler, and Lequette, *Obligations*, 993–995 (who see the *théorie de l'apparence* as a better legal basis); Fabre-Magnan, *Responsabilité civile et quasi-contrats*, 424–425 (considering *quasi-contrat* 'the least appropriate classification of all').

[1015] D. 2002.2963.

of or for the benefit of ('*pour le compte*') the *maître* and it also distinguishes *gestion d'affaires* from recovery under *enrichissement sans cause* where no such require-ment is made.[1016] However, while therefore it will not arise where a person acts exclusively in his own interest, it may do so where he acts also in the interests of the would-be *maître*.[1017] Moreover, in the absence of self-interest, the courts have sometimes taken a very generous view of this requirement of intention to act on behalf of the other, holding, for example, that a customer of a large shop who attempted to catch escaping armed robbers did so for the shop, rather than in the public interest as a whole.[1018] The 'voluntary' requirement as to the *gérant's* action excludes cases where he acts under a contractual or legal duty. So, for example, an employer who paid for medical treatment of one of its employees who had fallen seriously ill while working abroad was held unable to recoup these payments from the employee's estate as it had a contractual obligation to provide for a scheme of help in these circumstances.[1019]

Gestion d'affaires may arise whether or not the *maître* is aware of the *gérant's* intervention,[1020] but if he consents to it, the relationship between the parties becomes contractual, usually being the contract of agency (*mandat*). On the other hand, while a traditional example of *gestion d'affaires* may be found in the situ-ation where a person mends his neighbour's roof after a storm whilst the neigh-bour is away, this does not mean that it may arise only when the *maître* is absent or uncontactable, for it may do so where the *maître* is present but incapable of consent (e.g. a minor or unconscious).

Clearly, such a means of imposing obligations on others without their consent could easily become a busy-bodies' charter or, as a leading text more elegantly puts it, 'philanthropy . . . must not serve as a screen for illtimed, inappropri-ate or selfish interventions'.[1021] The requirement (which is ultimately Roman) which enables French courts to keep *gestion d'affaires* under control is that the *gérant's* action be 'useful' (*utile*), a requirement whose fulfilment is within the 'sovereign power of assessment' of the *juges du fond*. As one would expect, this element is judged at the time of intervention and so, where it was appropriate at the time, the *maître* will be liable to the *gérant* even if it turns out that it

---

[1016] Malaurie, Aynès, and Stoffel-Munck, *Obligations*, 552 and see below, p. 433 ff.

[1017] Civ. (1) 28 May 1991, Bull. civ. I no. 167; Com. 12 Jan. 1999, Bull. civ. IV no. 7, Défrenois 1999.754; Civ. (1) 18 Apr. 2000, Bull. civ. I no. 113, Défrenois 2000.1384 note Delebecque. A legislative example may be found in art. 815-4 al. 2 C. civ. which provides that a co-owner of immovable property may act on behalf of the other incapable co-owners 'according to the rules of *gestion d'affaires*' despite the fact that in these circumstances it would be usual for the *gérant* to wish to act in his own interest as well as that of the others.

[1018] Civ. (1) 26 Jan. 1988, JCP 1989.II.21217 note Martin.

[1019] Soc. 11 Oct. 1984, D 1985.IR.442. Cf. Bénabent, *Obligations*, 312 who doubts the valid-ity of this exclusion. An important exception is found as regards the actions of relatives of those adjudged incapable of looking after their own affairs which are treated as giving rise to *gestion d'affaires* even though the relatives have a legal duty to do so: art. 491-4 C. civ.

[1020] Art. 1372 al. 1 C. civ.

[1021] Starck *et al.*, *Contrat*, 750.

was unprofitable to him.[1022] Here, then, the *maître*'s obligation arises in the absence of enrichment.

What are the effects of *gestion d'affaires*? Strikingly, the Civil Code declares that a *gérant* must finish a task which he starts.[1023] Thus, where a handbag was handed in as lost property by some customers to a supermarket employee, the latter was held to an obligation to complete the job of ensuring that it reached its owner, and therefore should not have given it back to its finders on their assurance that they would do so.[1024] More generally, the Code assimilated the *gérant*'s liabilities to the *maître* in respect of the intervention to those of a contractual agent and he is therefore liable to account for profits and to the standard of the *bon père de famille* in doing the task.[1025] However, two concessions are made to the altruistic character of the *gérant*'s action: first, if, as is normal, it is gratuitous, this tends to lower the standard of care imposed[1026] and, secondly, the court possesses a discretion to reduce the quantum of damages payable if the circumstances so demand.[1027] Thus, in the lost handbag case already noted, the court held the supermarket liable for *its* loss, but not for the loss of its valuable contents.[1028]

The Civil Code provides that the *maître* must indemnify the *gérant* for 'useful and necessary' expenses which he has incurred in intervening. As we have mentioned, these may well exceed any surviving or indeed original enrichment of the *maître,* as long as the intervention was useful at the time. The courts have, moreover, accepted that a *gérant* may recover compensation for either damage to property or personal injuries suffered in the course of any physical intervention for the *maître.* So, for example, where A rescues B from a burning vehicle but dies as a result, A's personal representative may recover damages on this basis for his injuries as long as B *neither consented to nor refused* to be rescued. If B had refused the assistance, this would rule out *gestion d'affaires,* but if he had consented, then A's claim would normally be based on a 'contract to rescue'!.[1029] On the other hand, while a *gérant* can recover expenses or damages, he cannot recover remuneration for any work which he has done, even if acting in the course of a business or profession.[1030]

In treating the effect of contracts and other legal *actes* made by a *gérant* as regards third parties, *gestion d'affaires* again follows the law of agency. So,

[1022] Civ. 28 Oct. 1942, DC 1943.29.

[1023] Art. 1372 C.civ.

[1024] Civ. (3) 3 Jan.1985, GP 1985 Pan.jur.90.

[1025] Arts. 1372 al. 2 and 1374 al.1 C. civ. The legal classification of this liability is far from clear: see D. Acquarone, 'La nature juridique de la responsabilité civile du gérant d'affaire dans ses rapports avec le maître de l'affaire' D 1986 Chron. 21, who assumes that it must be either contractual or delictual.

[1026] Art. 1992 C. civ. (agency).

[1027] Art. 1374 al. 2 C. civ.

[1028] Civ. (3) 3 Jan. 1985, cit.

[1029] Civ. (1) 27 May 1959, JCP 1959.II.11187 note Esmein and cf. above, p. 306.

[1030] Civ. (1) 18 Apr. 2000, Bull. civ. I no. 113, Défrenois 2000.1384 note Delebecque.

where A contracts with B on behalf of C, *in C's name* but without his consent, if the contract is 'useful' to C so that *gestion d'affaires* arises, he (C) is liable on it to B, but A is not.[1031] On the other hand, if the contract is not 'useful', A but not C may be liable to B and then only on the basis of fault. And if A contracts with B on behalf of C but *in his own name,* then only A will be liable to B. This last situation can no more be *gestion d'affaires* than it can be contractual agency.[1032]

In all, it may be thought that *gestion d'affaires* sits rather uneasily astride the modern categories of contract, delict and unjust enrichment. The enrichment of the *maître* at the expense of the *gérant* may be thought in many cases to justify the former's liability, but the one is not a necessary condition of the other and its measure is not set at the amount of his enrichment, but rather at either the expenses which the *gérant* has incurred or the loss which he has suffered in effecting the intervention. While the obligations which arise from *gestion d'affaires* are not contractual (for lack of the *maître's* consent) the *gérant's* obligation to complete the job and the assimilation of its effects for many purposes to agency shows how very closely related it is to this particular contract. Finally, in some cases, a finding of *gestion d'affaires* by a court seems to be aimed solely at procuring a legal basis for a claim for damages for personal injuries, a type of claim which some jurists consider the appropriate object of delict.[1033] Here, then, it may indeed be said that, in the absence of a claim in contract or delict, quasi-contract 'finds a home for lost causes'.[1034]

III. Recovery of 'Undue Payments' *(Répétition de l'Indu)*

Roman law possessed an elaborate set of rules regarding the recovery of undue payments and recovery (*répétition*) on this basis found its way into the Civil Code as a 'quasi-contract'.[1035] Traditionally, this recovery was justified on the idea of unjust enrichment[1036] and most modern French writers say that it is at least closely related to recovery under the principle of *enrichissement sans cause,*[1037] though it may differ from this basis of recovery in some ways, notably in that the

---

[1031] Art. 1375 C. civ.

[1032] Contractual agency (*mandat*) requires A to act in C's name: art. 1984 C. civ.

[1033] Carbonnier, *Obligations*, 2412.

[1034] D. Martin, note to Civ. (1) 26 Jan. 1988, JCP 1989.II.21217 at p. 405.

[1035] Arts. 1376-81 C. civ.

[1036] e.g. R.J. Pothier, *Traité des contrats de bienfaisance,* Troisième partie, Du quasi-contrat appelé *promutuum* et de *l'actio conditio indebiti,* in *Oeuvres complètes de Pothier* (Paris, 1821) t. 8, 222.

[1037] Malaurie, Aynès, and Stoffel-Munck, *Obligations* 560; Starck, *Régime,* 123. Terré, Simler, and Lequette, *Obligations,* 1009.

payer may sometimes recover *more* than the payee's enrichment.[1038] At the outset of this discussion, we should note that the Civil Code's rules on the measure of restitution in cases of undue payments possess a strong moral dimension.

According to article 1235 of the Civil Code, 'every *paiement* supposes a debt: what has been paid without being due is subject to recovery'. Of course, in a typical case the payer (often termed *solvens* in French discussions, the payee being termed *accipiens*) pays an 'undue debt' only because he mistakenly thinks that he owed it and such a mistake is indeed mentioned in article 1377. However, as we shall see, at least in one class of case, modern French law no longer requires the payer to show a mistake to obtain restitution.

A. Paiement

What, then, is meant by *paiement*? As we have seen,[1039] in French law this word has a much broader meaning than the English 'payment' (which refers to a transfer of *money*) or, indeed, than it does in ordinary French usage. In its broadest legal sense, *paiement* refers to the process and effect of performing *any* obligation, not merely one to pay money and is therefore best translated as 'satisfaction'. Moreover, while typically it is contractual, it need not be: payment of damages to compensate a victim of personal injuries is also *paiement*. However, in the context of the right to recover undue payments its sense is somewhat more limited, referring to the performance of obligations to transfer property, whether movable or immovable, but not to the provision of services, which are said to be incapable of being returned to their provider; this means that where a person performs 'undue services' he may claim only on the basis of and subject to the conditions of *enrichissement sans cause*.[1040] In the present context, we shall for convenience use the English 'payment', but this much broader sense of the French term should be remembered.

Secondly, it should be noted that, while in the case of payments made in money and other unascertained movable property (*choses de genre*),[1041] title passes to the payee on delivery, in the case of those made in immovable or ascertained movable property (*corps certain*) some jurists hold that title does not pass to the payee.[1042]

[1038] Below, pp. 431–433 (payee in bad faith).

[1039] Above p. 334.

[1040] Starck *et al., Régime*, 123 and cf. below p. 433 ff. Bénabent criticizes this reason for denial of *répétition de l'indu* on the basis that while the services may not be returned, their value may be: *Obligations*, 318.

[1041] This category includes such things as a quantity of corn which is mixed with the payee's own stocks.

[1042] Malaurie, (above n. 1004), 73–4; Mazeaud *et al., Obligations*, 799. Retention of title is restricted in this way because title is conditional on the ability of the owner to *identify* its subject matter, which must therefore be in existence and 'individualized': Carbonnier, *Obligations*, 1700. When property such as money or other *choses de genre* are transferred to another person (even in payment of a non-debt) it ceases to be identifiable and therefore title passes. By contrast, when

If this position is taken, this means that the payer may bring a proprietary action (*revendication*) rather than the personal *action en répétition*.[1043] The present discussion, however, will be limited to the payer's *personal* claims.

1. Undue payments and mistake

Recovery rests on the payment being *not due*. For example, A pays €50 to B, a shop-keeper, thinking he owes it under a contract to deliver groceries and forgetting that he has already paid the bill: A can recover the €50 from B.[1044] However, as has been indicated, recovery is not restricted to cases of *contractual* non-debts and may equally apply, for example, to the case of an heir who mistakenly pays money under a legacy which he subsequently discovers was not legally due. Nevertheless, this broad rule of recovery which is found in article 1235 of the Civil Code and quoted above must be qualified in four ways.

First, where payment is made in performance of a 'natural obligation' (which is not itself enforceable) no recovery is allowed.[1045] So, for example, an heir may not recover back a legacy from its recipient where it was the testator's wish but was unenforceable for lack of writing.[1046]

Secondly, any payment made of a debt which is time-barred is irrecoverable.[1047]

Thirdly, where payments are due when made but *subsequently* become undue, notably, by reason of the retroactive effect on contracts of annulment or *résolution,* restitution is allowed in principle, even though the payer made no mistake at the time. Here, though, there is some dispute as to whether recovery here is a true example of *répétition de l'indu* and we shall deal with this topic separately.[1048]

Fourthly, does the maker of an undue payment have to show that he made it under a mistake? For this purpose *doctrine* distinguishes two classes of case. The first is called *l'indu absolu ou objectif.* Here, A pays a debt to B which either has never existed or at least no longer exists on payment (because it had been paid), as in the case of the doubly-paid grocery bill already mentioned: the 'non-debt' is 'absolute' in the sense that *no-one* owes it. In this type of case, in 1993 the Assemblée plénière appeared to hold in general terms that the payer is *not*

---

ascertained and individual property (*corps certain*) is transferred in payment of a non-debt, title to it remains with the transferor as long as it remains in this state.

[1043] As against the payee himself, the main reason for wishing to bring the proprietary action would be found in the case of his insolvency, for in principle if the property which has been paid remains the payer's it does not form part of the debtor's estate (*patrimoine*) for the purposes of satisfying the creditors' claims: the owner has a *droit de préférence*. If the payer retains title to the property, he also may claim it back from third parties (*droit de suite*), though this is severely qualified by art. 2279 C. civ.; Carbonnier, *Obligations,* 1701 cf. below, pp. 449 ff on the issues which arise in respect of proprietary claims on annulment or *résolution* of a contract.

[1044] For the question of interest, see below, p. 431 ff.

[1045] Art. 1235 al. 2 C. civ.

[1046] Civ. (1) 27 Dec. 1963, GP 1964.1.340.

[1047] Soc. 11 Apr. 1991, Bull. civ. V no. 192.

[1048] Below, p. 440 ff.

required to show any mistake in making the payment, though his right to restitution may be defeated by proof by the payee that the payer intended it as an act of generosity (having thereby an *intention libérale*).[1049] Apart from textual arguments from the general terms of the Code,[1050] this approach is supported on the basis that to require proof of mistake in such a case would give an arbitrary priority to *one* of the explanations of such a payment being made: apart from mistake, it may, for example, have been made, to avoid a criminal sanction.[1051]

The second class of cases is called *l'indu relatif ou subjectif,* these having in common that a debt is in fact owing, but not in the way which the payer sees it: the 'non-debt' is therefore 'relative'. The 'relativity' may arise in one of two ways:

(1) where A pays €50 to B, which in fact he *owes to C.* Here, A is 'true debtor', but he pays to a 'false creditor'; and

(2) (which is the converse case) where A pays €50 to B, who *is* owed this sum but *not by A.* Here, A is a 'false debtor' and pays to B, a 'true creditor'.

In both these situations, it is agreed that A, the payer, must show a mistake before he will be allowed to recover the payment from B.[1052]

It should be noted that where mistake has been required by the courts for the purposes of *répétition de l'indu* it has been held to include mistake of law as much as of fact and perhaps somewhat oddly also cases of duress,[1053] the latter being justified on the basis that recovery is also based on a defect in the 'will' (*volonté*) of the payer.[1054] Traditionally, the payer's mistake must be as to his own indebtedness,[1055] though it has been suggested that a mistake as to the capacity in which the payee receives the payment will suffice.[1056] However, a restriction of recovery to mistakes of indebtedness does not have the ramifications which it would have in English law.[1057] In particular, it should be recalled that in French law gifts (*donations*) rest on a contractual foundation[1058] and that where a gift is made on the basis of a mistake, the contract on which it rests may be annulled either for *erreur* (usually as to the person), *dol* or, more rarely, absence of *cause.*[1059] On annulling such a contract, a court will in principle order the return of

---

[1049] Ass. plén. 2 Apr. 1993, JCP 1993. II.22051, concl. Jéol; Civ. (1) 20 Jan 1998, Bull. civ. I no. 18 and see Malaurie, Aynès, and Stoffel-Munck, *Obligations,* 562.

[1050] Arts. 1235 and 1376 C. civ.

[1051] Flour, Aubert, and Savaux *Fait juridique,* 23, Carbonnier, *Obligations,* 2428. For doubts as to the generality of impact of this decision see A. Sériaux, 'Beaucoup de bruit pour rien' D 1993 Chron. 229.

[1052] Flour, Aubert, and Savaux, *Fait juridique,* 26 (for the second this is expressly required by art. 1377 C. civ.) But cf. below, pp. 430–431.

[1053] Ibid., 26.

[1054] Marty and Raynaud, *Obligations,* 660–661.

[1055] Starck *et al., Régime,* 128; Bénabent, *Obligations,* 321

[1056] Starck *et al., Régime, ibid.*

[1057] On the status of this rule in English law, see Burrows (above n. 971), pp. 130–134.

[1058] This is implicit in art. 931 C. civ. and see above, pp. 318–319.

[1059] Above, pp. 308–309, 311, 317.

property transferred under it, though whether this should be considered an example of *répétition de l'indu* or merely related to it is the subject of dispute.[1060] Finally, it should be noted that payments made under settlements of disputed rights (*transactions*) may not be recovered even if subsequently it becomes clear that the settlement was made at a different amount than was actually due.[1061]

B. No 'Subsidiarity'

As we shall see, an important restriction on recovery under *enrichissement sans cause* is that it is said to be 'subsidiary', which means, inter alia, that it will not be allowed where a claimant has or *has had* a claim on another legal basis.[1062] No such restriction is made on recovery of undue payments[1063] and this may be important to a claimant as in general it enjoys a prescription period of 30 years![1064]

C. Parties to the Claim

Typically, of course, it is the *payer* who claims recovery of the undue payment from the *payee*. However, in certain circumstances other persons may wish to claim a payment unduly made and persons other than the payee may appear as a suitable defendant. Let us take first the case where A in fact owes a debt to B, but mistakenly pays it to C: can B, the true creditor, claim the payment directly from C? Here, the answer is clearly in the negative and B is therefore restricted to recovery by way of *action oblique* like any other of A's creditors[1065] (which does not avoid any insolvency in A)[1066] or the possibility of a claim on the basis of *enrichissement sans cause*.[1067] What of the converse case, where A mistakenly thinks he owes a debt to B, this debt in fact being owed to B *by C*: can A recover his payment directly from C, the true debtor? In this respect, the Civil Code expressly provides that where B has destroyed his instrument of title to the debt (*titre de créance*), A can recover *only* against C, as B's action prevents any claim *by him* against C.[1068] Outside this particular case, the Cour de cassation has vacillated somewhat as to the legal nature

---

[1060] Above, p. 428 ff. and below, p. 440 ff.

[1061] Civ. (3) 2 Jul. 1970, D 1971.41.

[1062] Below, pp. 437–438.

[1063] Starck *et al.*, *Régime*, 129.

[1064] Art. 2262 C. civ., e.g. Civ. (1) 19 Oct. 1983, JCP 1983.IV.359; Ch. mixte 12 Apr. 2002, D 2002.2433 note Aubert de Vincelles, who explains that shorter periods sometimes apply, as in the case of commercial relations (where prescription is in principle ten years, art. 110-4 (I) C. com.) or social security (where prescription is sometimes as short as two years, e.g. art. L 332-1 C. séc. soc. (recovery of false health insurance benefits)).

[1065] Art. 1166 C. civ.

[1066] Flour, Aubert, and Savaux, *Fait juridique*, 27.

[1067] Civ. 17 Nov. 1914, S 1918–1918.52 and see below, p. 433 ff.

[1068] Art. 1377 al. 2 C. civ.

of any claim by A against C, the effect of which, it is accepted, discharges C.[1069] Putting aside cases where A had an interest in paying (such as a surety) where the Code subrogates A into B's rights by law,[1070] a decision of the Cour de cassation in 1990 appeared to allow A's recovery against C to rest simply on the discharging effect of his payment.[1071] However, after toying with placing recovery here on the basis on *répétition de l'indu*, in 2001 a further decision made clear that the proper basis could only be *enrichissement sans cause* with the addition of a requirement that the payment by A be made by mistake.[1072] Rather oddly given the clear terms of article 1377 al. 1 of the Code which allows a person who mistakenly believes himself debtor to recover any amount paid from the *creditor*, the Cour de cassation has also held (in the context of claims by insurers) that where A can claim against C (the true debtor) he cannot recover any payment from B, on the basis that 'in reality [C] has benefited from the payment'.[1073] Such a result remains open to considerable criticism[1074] and the *Avant-projet de réforme* suggests instead that the A (the payer) should have a choice whether to claim against B (the creditor/payee) or against C (the true debtor).[1075]

D. The Measure of Recovery and Counter-Recovery

The first, somewhat surprising, aspect of recovery in respect of undue payments is that where payment was made by way of transfer of corporeal property, whether immovable or movable (though excluding money), and this still exists in the hands of the payee the latter owes an obligation to make specific restitution (*obligation de restitution en nature*), though as has been explained, this does not mean that the payer's remedy to enforce it is proprietary.[1076] Where, however, payment was in money or when specific restitution is no longer possible, recovery is of its value (*en valeur*).

The measure of recovery against the payee either beyond or instead of specific restitution depends on his good or bad faith and in this context, good faith is found where a payee *receives* a payment thinking that it was due. Thus, where corporeal property transferred in payment has deteriorated or been destroyed, a

---

[1069] Arts. 1236–7 C. civ. on which see S. Whittaker, 'Performance of another's obligation: French and English law contrasted' in D. Johnston and R. Zimmermann (eds.), *Unjustified Enrichment, Key Issues in Comparative Perspective* (CUP, 2002), 433, 436–439.

[1070] Art. 1236 al. 1 C. civ.

[1071] Civ. (1) 15 May 1990, JCP 1991.II.21628 note Petit, D 1991.538 note Virassamy.
Civ. (1) 13 Oct. 1998, D 1999.500, D 1999.116 note Aynès. Cf. Soc. 31 Jan. 1996, D 1997.306 note Thullier which denied recovery on the basis of *répétition de l'indu*.

[1072] Civ. (1) 4 Apr. 2001, D 2001.1824 note Billiau, JCP 2002.I.134 note Barthez; Civ. (1) 23 Sep. 2003, Bull. civ. I no. 185.

[1073] Civ. (1) 9 Mar. 2004, Bull. civ. no. 81, Défrenois 2004.996 note Libchaber; Civ. (1) 23 Sep. 2003, D 2004.3165 note Harmand-Luque.

[1074] See notes by Libchaber and Harmand-Luque, cit. n. 1073.

[1075] Art. 1332 A.-p.r.

[1076] Art. 1379 C. civ. On the nature of the claim, see above, pp. 421–422.

payee in good faith is liable for its value only if this occurred through his fault;[1077] if he sells it, he is liable only for the price at which he has done so[1078] (and not to its value if this is higher) and if he gives it away he need pay nothing.[1079] Moreover, a person who receives property in good faith in principle is *not* liable to reimburse the payer for its 'fruits',[1080] to pay an indemnity for its enjoyment nor, in the case of money, to pay interest on it.[1081]

Conversely, bad faith is in the first instance found in a payee where he *knew* that it was not due on payment and where this is the case it has a radical effect on the measure of his liability, creating, according to one text, 'a veritable private penalty'.[1082] So, a payee in bad faith is liable for the full value of property transferred as at the date of judgment, whether he has sold or given it away[1083] and whether it has deteriorated or was destroyed by *cas fortuit* (a supervening unforeseeable and 'irresistable' event).[1084] He is, moreover, also liable to reimburse the payer in respect of the payment's 'fruits' (including interest on money) from the time of receipt of the payment.[1085] Secondly, however, the courts consider it bad faith for a person who has received payment in good faith, to refuse to reimburse the payer on it being reclaimed. In this situation, the payee will therefore be held liable under the rules of recovery for good faith until such a time, but after it he will be liable according to the rules for bad faith.[1086]

Given this strict treatment of a payee in bad faith, it is all the more surprising that the Civil Code provides that where property is restored to the payer, a payee *even if in bad faith* is entitled to be reimbursed for 'necessary and useful expenses incurred for the preservation of the property', this being justified on the need to avoid the payer being unduly enriched.[1087] The payee may claim for all the cost of *necessary* expenses and *useful* ones either according to their cost or to the extent that they result in an increase in value to the property, this choice resting with the payer.[1088] A payee may, furthermore, claim damages in delict for any fault committed by the payer in making the payment, fault for this purpose including but not being limited to negligence,[1089] and this means that in principle the payer's fault reduces the payee's obligation to make restitution according to the

---

[1077] Art. 1379 C. civ.

[1078] Art. 1380 C. civ.

[1079] Terré, Simler, and Lequette, *Obligations,* 1017.

[1080] This term includes such things as crops in the case of agricultural land, offspring in the case of animals or rent in the case of a house: cf. art. 547 C. civ, which stipulates that these 'fruits' belong to the owner of property by accession.

[1081] Art. 1378 C. civ. *a contrario*. An exception to this rule is found in art. L. 122-3 C. consom, where the payer is a consumer and the payee is a business seller or provider of services.

[1082] Starck *et al., Régime,* 134.

[1083] Art. 1380 C. civ. *a contrario*.

[1084] Art. 1379 C. civ. and see above, pp. 343 ff.

[1085] Art. 1378 C. civ.

[1086] Flour, Aubert, and Savaux, *Fait juridique,* 29.

[1087] Art. 1381 C. civ.; Flour, Aubert, and Savaux, ibid., 30.

[1088] Starck *et al., Régime,* 135.

[1089] Flour, Aubert, and Savaux, *Fait juridique,* 31 and see above pp. 364 ff.

latter's loss[1090] (as is also the case in general for claims based on *enrichissement sans cause*).[1091] However, use of delict here is by no means trouble-free and some decisions restrict the payer's liability to the payee's 'abnormal loss' caused by the payment, for, it is argued, to allow the payee to recover all losses caused by returning the payment risks emptying the Code's provisions on undue payments of their substance.[1092] It has also been suggested that a distinction is drawn by the courts between *l'indu objectif* (where the payer's fault reduces his recovery) and *l'indu subjectif* (where it excludes his recovery).[1093]

The payee's good faith is therefore no defence to his obligation to make restitution, but it curtails its extent. So, while French law does not possess a defence of 'change of position' by the payee, where payment is made in corporeal property its alienation in good faith limits the payee's liability to whatever was received in return. Conversely, where the payer is at fault in making the payment or in claiming it back this does not exclude liability to make restitution, but it may lead to its reduction. To the extent to which it does, liability in delict may act so as to protect the payee's reasonable reliance: as Bénabent puts it, 'the payee cannot keep what was not owing to him, but the financial difficulties which restitution would cause him lead to its reduction'.[1094]

IV. *Enrichissement Sans Cause*

Since the *arrêt Boudier* in 1892 French law has overtly recognized a general principle of recovery on the basis of the defendant's unjustified enrichment,[1095] and it remains a remarkable example of *la jurisprudence*, even though possessing historical and contemporary juristic support.[1096] However, in the modern law, this principle is general only in the sense that it is not restricted to any particular factual or legal context. For while the Cour de cassation in the *arrêt Boudier* put the principle in extraordinarily wide terms, in 1914 it took care to restrict it not merely to cases where the claimant's 'impoverishment' was reflected in the defendant's enrichment, but also where this occurred

---

[1090] Civ. (1) 5 Jul. 1989, D 1991 Somm. 322 note Aubert; Civ. (1) 27 Feb. 1996, Bull. civ. I no. 105 (both cases of *l'indu objectif*).

[1091] Below, p. 438.

[1092] J.-B. Donnier's note to Com. 19 Nov. 1991, JCP 1993.II.2012 at 99 who sees the conflicting decisions as reflecting different views in the *chambres* of the Cour de cassation.

[1093] Bénabent, *Obligations*, 322, 325; Terré, Simler, and Lequette, *Obligations*, 1014–1015, an example of the latter being found in Com. 12 Jan. 1988, Bull. civ. IV no. 22. Cf. Fabre-Magnan, *Responsabilité civile et quasi-contrats*, 411.

[1094] *Obligations*, 322.

[1095] Req. 15 Jun 1892, S 1893.281 note Labbé and see above, pp. 418–419.

[1096] The *arrêt Boudier* and the decision Civ. 12 May 1914, S 1918.1.41 note Naquet were clearly modelled on the position of C. Aubry and C. Rau, *Cours de droit civil français d'après la méthode de Zachariae*, 4th edn. (Paris, 1873) t. VI, 246 who were themselves inspired by the German writer Zachariä von Lingenthal: Zimmermann, (above n. 973), 884.

'without a legitimate justification' (*sans cause légitime*) and where the claimant enjoys 'no other action arising from a contract, a quasi-contract, a delict or a quasi-delict'.[1097] These last two restrictions prevent *enrichissement sans cause* from becoming, in Flour's well-known phrase, a 'mechanism for exploding the law'[1098] and this combination of elements, with a few additions and qualifications, still reflects the position in the modern law.

A. The Claimant's Impoverishment and the Defendant's Enrichment

The claimant must show that the defendant was enriched at his expense, in the sense that the defendant's enrichment was caused by or was the correlative of the claimant's impoverishment,[1099] but French courts have taken a very wide view both of what may constitute impoverishment and enrichment and the causal relationship between them, so that it is sometimes said that any 'movement of value' from the claimant to the defendant will satisfy these requirements.[1100] A common example is where the claimant has done work on the defendant's property which increases its value, but the performance of 'pure services' with no proprietary result may also satisfy the test. For example, in a case decided in 1982, A, an anaesthetic nurse married B, a surgeon, under a regime of separate property and for some 10 years worked in that capacity for him without pay:[1101] after their divorce, she was held entitled to recover an indemnity in respect of the value of these unpaid services on the basis of *enrichissement sans cause* as they went beyond the duty to contribute to the household and other expenses (the *charges du mariage*) as required of spouses by the Civil Code.[1102] The defendant's enrichment may also consist in the mere use or enjoyment of the claimant's property[1103] or the decrease in the defendant's debts or obligations.[1104] Finally, it is sometimes said that a merely 'moral' enrichment may suffice. The two examples usually cited are the 'moral benefit' of increasing a pupil's knowledge by teaching[1105] and a very curious case decided in 1960.[1106] In the latter, the claimants owned a shop in Normandy and fled before the advance of the invading German army in 1940. A local councillor later ordered that the shop

---

[1097] Civ. 12 May 1914, cit.

[1098] Quoted by Bénabent, *Obligations,* 332.

[1099] Civ. (1) 25 Jan.1965, GP 1965.1.198.

[1100] Flour, Aubert, and Savaux, *Fait juridique,* 38.

[1101] Civ. (1) 26 Oct. 1982, JCP 1983.II.1992 note Terré. On the measure of recovery, see below p. 440 n. 1147.

[1102] Art. 214 C. civ. and see above p. 246.

[1103] Bénabent, *Obligations,* 334; Malaurie, Aynès, and Stoffel-Munck, *Obligations,* 568; Req. 11 Dec. 1928, DH 1929.18 (use of claimant's water pipes for distribution); Civ. 6 Jul. 1927, S 1928.1.19 (use of claimant's copyright beyond period of licence).

[1104] e.g. Civ. (1) 1 Feb. 1984, D 1984.388 (natural father held liable to indemnify former husband of mother in respect of maintenance of legitimated child).

[1105] Flour, Aubert, and Savaux, *Fait juridique,* 38 (with hesitations).

[1106] Civ. (1) 18 Jan. 1960, D 1960.753 note Esmein.

should be re-opened and food and other supplies should be distributed to the local population, sometimes for a charge and sometimes for free. The claimants returned some 2 months later and successfully claimed an indemnity for their losses from the *commune* by way of *action de in rem verso,* the measure of its enrichment being the benefit in having the goods distributed rather than the limited proceeds for them which it had received.[1107]

Clearly, in many cases, a claimant's impoverishment is directly related to the defendant's enrichment, as in the case of the wife's services as nurse for her surgeon husband. Sometimes, however, it is 'indirect' in the sense that the value flowing from the claimant 'passes though another's estate (*patrimoine*)'[1108] before bene-fitting the defendant;[1109] but here too French law in principle allows recovery. For example, in the *arrêt Boudier* the claimant fertilizer merchant was held able to recover against the *landlord* of the tenant farmer, despite it being the latter who had bought, received and consumed the fertilizer whose value led to the landlord's enrichment.[1110] Similarly, in a case decided in 1940, A sold land to B who instructed a builder, C, to carry out works of improvement on it. On *résolution* of the sale, A regained possession, but was ordered to pay C for these improvements on the basis of *enrichissement sans cause,* B being insolvent.[1111] However, it should be noted that many claims for 'indirect enrichment' fail for other reasons, notably because the enrichment in question possesses a 'legitimate justification'.

B. 'Without a Legitimate Justification'

A first important restriction on *enrichissement sans cause* is suggested by the name itself as recovery is excluded where the defendant's enrichment possessed a legit-imate justification (*une cause légitime*) which explains it. Such a justification is most commonly found in a contract between the claimant and defendant and this means that neither a gift[1112] nor a bad bargain[1113] can be undone by invok-ing the principle of recovery for enrichment. The justification of a defendant's enrichment may also be found in the law itself and so, for example, a genealogist cannot recover anything for work done in uncovering a person's right of succes-sion to property, since the latter's enrichment is said to have a justification in the rules of succession.[1114] What, however, is the position where there is no justifica-tion for the defendant's enrichment, but there is a justification for the claimant's

---

[1107] The quantum was ordered to be assessed by *experts:* see below, p. 439.

[1108] On the concept of *patrimoine,* see above, p. 271.

[1109] Starck *et al., Contrat,* 770 ff.

[1110] See above, p.

[1111] Req. 11 Sept. 1940, DH 1940.150, S 1941.1.121 note Esmein.

[1112] Gifts possess a contractual basis in French law: above, pp. 318–319.

[1113] Civ. 17 May 1944, GP 1944.2.71.

[1114] Civ. (1) 28 May 1991, JCP 1991.IV.290 and cf. art. 599 al. 2 C. civ. (no indemnity for improvement for usufructuaries).

impoverishment, notably, where it has been suffered under a contract with some-one other than the claimant? Certainly, where a claimant acts in his own interest as well as the interest of the defendant he will not recover under *enrichissement sans cause*, this interest sometimes being said to constitute the justification for his impoverishment.[1115] However, the Cour de cassation in 2003 quashed a decision below for rejecting a claim under *enrichissement sans cause* on the ground that the claimant's impoverishment possessed a justification in a contract with someone other than the defendant.[1116]

An interesting group of cases lie at the borders of law and non-law, con-tract and *enrichissement sans cause*. As we have noted, French law sometimes excludes agreements between friends and family from the domain of con-tract, this being justified on the basis that the parties had no intention to be bound.[1117] Sometimes this context may also exclude a remedy based on the defendant's enrichment; a *cause* of a defendant's enrichment may be found in his friendship with the claimant,[1118] this giving rise to a presumption of an *intention libérale*. However, in other cases, particularly those which concern family relations which have broken down, recovery is rejected in contract but is allowed on the basis of *enrichissement sans cause,* an example being found in the case of the former wife suing her ex-husband in respect of work done for him as a nurse.[1119] Similarly, the courts have allowed a claim on this basis by an adult child against the estate of his parents to whom he had given constant help before their death 'beyond the demands of filial piety'.[1120] And a woman who cohabited with a man and worked in his café without pay for a number of years, was held able to recover in respect of the benefit which this work gave him on the basis of *enrichissement sans cause.*[1121]

Finally, we should note that many cases of 'indirect enrichment' do not give rise to recovery because a *cause* for the enrichment is found in a contract *other than* with the claimant. So, for example, if A sells wine to B who sells or gives it to C, if A is not paid by B, he cannot sue C in respect of the latter's enrich-ment in receiving the wine, since this has a *cause* in B's sale or gift.[1122] To this extent, therefore, the actual decision in the *arrêt Boudier* would not go the same way today, as any enrichment in the landlord possessed a justification in his

---

[1115] Starck *et al*, *Contrat*, 773 citing Civ. (3) 8 Feb. 1972, JCP 1972.IV.70. Bénabent, *Obligations*, treats an absence of personal interest in the claimant as a separate condition for recovery under *enrichissement sans cause*.

[1116] Civ. (1) 25 Feb. 2003, D 2004.1766 note Peis and see Bénabent, *Obligations*, 337.

[1117] Above, p. 306.

[1118] Civ. (3) 1 Mar.1989, JCP 1989.IV.163 (friendship between claimant and defendant's father).

[1119] Above, p. 434 and see also Civ. (1) 19 Jan. 1953, D 1953.234.

[1120] Civ. (1) 12 Jul. 1994, D 1995.623 note Techendjou; Civ. (1) 3 Nov. 2004, JCP 2005. II.10024 note Boulanger.

[1121] Civ. (1) 15 Oct. 1996, Bull. civ. I no. 357.

[1122] B. Nicholas, 'Unjustified Enrichment in the Civil Law and Louisiana Law' (1962) 36 Tul. LR 605, 629.

contract with his (insolvent) tenant.[1123] Another illustration may be found in cases where improvements of premises are done by a builder on the instruction of their tenant, these improvements becoming the landlord's by accession. In principle, the builder may recover against the owner of the premises so improved, but if the lease includes a clause which states that all work becomes the landlord's 'without compensation', then the landlord's enrichment has a *cause* in the contract of lease itself.[1124] Of course, the major effect of recognizing such a claim is to allow privity of contract (and the intervening tenant's insolvency) to be circumvented[1125] and to this extent *enrichissement sans cause* should be seen as an alternative technique to contractual *actions directes*.[1126]

C. 'Subsidiarity'

A second important restriction on the ambit of recovery under *enrichissement sans cause* is that it is said to be 'subsidiary'. There is a degree of disagreement as to quite what this means, but three points emerge from the courts' decisions.[1127]

First, a person who possesses an effective action on some other legal ground against the 'enriched defendant' (such as non-performance of a contract, delict or *répétition de l'indu*) may not rely on *enrichissement sans cause* as otherwise the legal incidents of the other action in question would be nullified. This means, inter alia, that where a defendant's enrichment consists of the receipt of an undue payment of money or other property in the sense already explained,[1128] then recovery in respect of this enrichment is subject to the conditions and possesses the effects governing this quasi-contract rather than those which apply to *enrichissement sans cause*.

Secondly, a person for whom the law has provided an action against the enriched defendant which cannot be used owing to some 'legal obstacle' may not overcome that obstacle by relying on *enrichissement sans cause*.[1129] So, for example, where A alleges that she loaned money to B to construct a building, but fails in her claim on the contract of loan for lack of written evidence, she cannot succeed on the basis that B has been enriched by application of the loan in improving his property.[1130] Similarly, a claimant cannot use the *action de in rem verso* after the

---

[1123] Malaurie, Aynès, and Stoffel-Munck, *Obligations*, 573.

[1124] Starck *et al., Contrat*, 773, Civ. (3) 28 May 1986, GP 1986.2 Pan.jur. 186.

[1125] Starck *et al., Contrat*, 778.

[1126] See especially the position of *approved* building sub-contractors claiming against the *maître d'ouvrage* under *loi* no. 75-1334 of 31 December 1975, arts. 11–13 and the discussion in P. Dubois's note to Civ. (3) 11 Jun. 1985, D 1986. 456. On *actions directes* generally, see above pp. 337–338.

[1127] See the useful discussion in Flour, Aubert, and Savaux, *Fait juridique*, 49–55.

[1128] Above, pp. 428–430.

[1129] Civ. (3) 29 Apr. 1971, GP 1971.2.554.

[1130] cf. Civ. 12 May 1914, S 1918.1.41 note Naquet (whose facts were complicated in that the borrower was a religious foundation which was dissolved by law, its property thereby being vested in its liquidator, 'third party' to the contract of loan).

expiry of the prescription period of another action in respect of the same facts. However, this aspect of subsidiarity appears to have suffered a degree of attrition. So, for example, the woman who worked in her cohabitee's café was allowed to recover on the basis of *enrichissement sans cause* even though she failed in her claim to establish a *société de fait* (informal partnership).[1131] And the Cour de cassation has held that a claimant's failure to establish delictual liability in the defendant because of an absence of fault does not prevent recovery on the ground of *enrichissement sans cause*.[1132]

On the other hand, thirdly, the Cour de cassation continues to hold that, in principle, a person cannot claim on the basis of *enrichissement sans cause* against a defendant where he has an effective claim against *another* person, for example, a surety.[1133] However, the courts distinguish from this situation the case where the claimant cannot *in fact* claim against the other party on some practical ground, notably, the latter's insolvency.[1134]

Given all this complexity, it is understandable that it has been argued that the 'hazy notion of subsidiarity' should be abandoned as a control mechanism of *enrichissement sans cause*,[1135] but the *Avant-projet de réforme* retains it, providing (somewhat laconically) that 'a person at whose expense a benefit is conferred has no action [on the ground of *enrichissement sans cause*] where another means of recourse available to him encounters a legal obstacle such as prescription'.[1136]

D. The Claimant's Conduct

Formerly it was held that any fault in a person claiming would bar recovery on the basis of *enrichissement sans cause*, but the majority view of *la doctrine* is that the courts have abandoned this position and now generally hold that mere negligence in a claimant (as opposed to *dol* (dishonesty) or serious fault) does not bar recovery but merely leads to its reduction.[1137] This change brings *enrichissement sans cause* into line with *répétition de l'indu*.[1138]

[1131] Civ. (1) 15 Oct. 1996, Bull. civ. I no. 357.

[1132] Civ. (1) 3 Jun. 1997, JCP 1998.II.10101 note Viney.

[1133] Bénabent, *Obligations*, 339; Terré, Simler, and Lequette, *Obligations*, 1029.

[1134] Com. 10 Oct. 2000, D 2000.409 note Avena-Robardet.

[1135] Viney, note, JCP 1998.II.10101.

[1136] Art. 1338 A.-p.r.

[1137] Malaurie, Aynès, and Stoffel-Munck, *Obligations*, 572; Fabre-Magnan, *Responsabilité civile et quasi-contrats*, 417–418; Bénabent, *Obligations*, 338. For the decisions see Civ. (1) 11 Mar. 1997, D 1997.407 note Billiau; Civ. (1) 19 May 1998, JCP 1998.II.10102 note Viney; Civ. (1) 13 Jul. 2004, Bull. civ. I no. 208. The Chambre commerciale appears to retain the former position holding that any fault bars recovery: Com. 18 May 1999, D 2000.609 note Djoudi.

[1138] Above, pp. 432–433.

E. What does the Claimant Receive?

If the conditions of recovery under *enrichissement sans cause* are restrictive, its rules as to the measure of recovery are both restrictive and really a little odd. French discussions distinguish two questions here. What is the measure of recovery and at what time is this asssessed?

1. *The measure of recovery*

Since the 1950s French courts have accepted that the claimant in the *action de in rem verso* can receive only the lesser sum as between his own impoverishment and the defendant's enrichment, thereby creating a double limit on recovery.[1139] In some cases, the claimant's impoverishment will have the same value as the defendant's enrichment, but this is by no means always the case. So, for example, where A does work worth €25,000 which increases the value of B's property by only €10,000, A may receive only €10,000.[1140] Conversely, where A does work worth €10,000 which increases the value of B's property by €25,000, A may receive only €10,000.[1141] No very convincing reason is given for this rule; it is simply said that to give the claimant more than his impoverishment would lead to his own (unjust) enrichment and that it would be unjust for the defendant to pay more than his enrichment.[1142] This rule is particularly restrictive when combined with those which govern the time at which these assessments are to be made.

2. *The time (or rather, times) of assessment*

After some hesitation, the courts now as a rule assess the claimant's impoverishment at the time of *impoverishment*,[1143] but the defendant's enrichment at the time of the claimant's *bringing a claim*[1144] though exceptions are made.[1145] Thus, in the case we noted earlier of the local councillor who ordered the distribution of a trader's goods during wartime, their value on claiming (in the early 1940s) was put at some 40,000 F, but on judgment (in the late 1950s) their value would have been 1,104,749 F![1146] Clearly, then, by restricting the claimants to the lesser

---

[1139] Civ. (1) 19 Jan. 1953, D 1953.234.

[1140] Ibid.

[1141] For a striking example of this, see Civ. (1) 25 May 1992, 1992 Cont., Cone., Cons, no. 174 noted below, p. 446. where the *juges du fond* tempered the impact of this rule by putting a very generous figure on the claimant's impoverishment.

[1142] Flour, Aubert, and Savaux, *Fait juridique*, 56. cf. f. Goré, 'Les lois modernes sur les baux et la réparation de l'enrichissement aux dépens d'autrui', D 1949 Chron. 72 (who argues that the defendant's enrichment should form the measure of recovery in the context of legislative liabilities of landlords in respect of tenants' improvements).

[1143] Civ. (1) 15 Feb. 1973, D 1975. 509.

[1144] Civ. (1) 18 Jan. 1960, D 1960. 753 note Esmein.

[1145] Flour, Aubert, and Savaux, *Fait juridique*, 57ff; Malaurie, Aynès, and Stoffel-Munck, *Obligations*, 571. Cf Terré, Simler, and Lequette, *Obligations*, 1030–1.

[1146] Civ. (1) 18 Jan. 1960, cit. These figures are complicated by the fact that the experts in the case wrongly included goods stolen from the shop and not merely those distributed by the local counsellor.

sum as calculated in this way, the courts exclude a revaluation of the impoverishment to take account of inflation or other movements in the value of any property in question. Moreover, taking the date of the claimant's impoverishment rather than the date of claim for the assessment of this element, means that any delay in claiming may severely reduce the value of an award, though where this aspect of the rule could cause genuine unfairness, notably where the facts on which the claim is made extend over a period of time, the courts make exceptions.[1147] On the other hand, by taking the date of claim as the time for assessing the defendant's enrichment, things which affect the enrichment before this date affect recovery, those doing so afterwards do not. For example, if A does work on B's house and thereby increases its value, but before claiming, B's house is destroyed. A can recover nothing:[1148] B may have *received* an enrichment, but nothing of it survives on claiming. However, if in the same case the fire destroyed B's house after A had claimed an indemnity but *before judgment,* then he would still recover as though B was still enriched.

These rules as to the time of assessment of the 'double limit' for recovery are widely criticized, the date of judgment being preferred[1149] and this is certainly the basis on which some modern 'legislative examples' of unjust enrichment are made.[1150] By contrast, the *Avant-projet de réforme* provides that '[t]he enrichment and the impoverishment are to be assessed as at the date of the claim. Nevertheless, where the person enriched was in bad faith, his enrichment shall be assessed at the time when he derived the benefit from it'.[1151]

V. Restitution as Between Parties to a Failed Contract

In English law one of the most important sets of situations in which restitutionary remedies are found is where a contract is ineffective or has been terminated and what has been done under the contract therefore requires partial or complete unravelling. There are many reasons for such an unravelling of a contract and various terms are used to describe the process. So a contract may be rescinded for misrepresentation, duress or mistake; void for mistake; unenforceable or void for failure to fulfil a requirement of form; tainted with illegality (no general term may be used to describe the varied effects here); subject to termination (*aliter*

[1147] e.g. Civ. (1) 26 Oct.1982, JCP 1983.II.1992 note Terré (the case of the nurse who worked professionally for her husband for 10 years without pay, in which the value of her work was assessed as at the time of the parties' divorce, it being held to be 'morally impossible' to do so on some earlier basis). Another possible exception is where the defendant is in bad faith, where it is said that the defendant's enrichment should be assessed as from its receipt whatever happens to it subsequently: Terré, Simler, and Lequette, *Obligations*, 1030.

[1148] Assuming the destruction was *force majeure*: Starck *et al.*, *Contrat*, 780.

[1149] Carbonnier, *Obligations*, 2444; Malaurie, Aynès, and Stoffel-Munck, *Obligations*, 571.

[1150] e.g. *loi* no. 60-464 of 17 May 1960, art.1 amending inter alia art. 555 C. civ.

[1151] Art. 1339 A.-p.r.

rescission or repudiation) for major breach of contract or discharged by operation of the doctrine of frustration.

As we have seen, French law also recognizes that a contract may be unravelled for various reasons and, where it does, it holds in principle that the parties must restore property received under the contract in question. In common with English law, there are a number of terms used to describe the process by which this unravelling takes place,—*nullité*[1152] *rescision*,[1153] *résolution*,[1154] *rédhibition*[1155]— but for French law an important general distinction is between nullity (whether 'relative or absolute') and *résolution*.

So, as we have seen, where a contract lacks either *cause* or *objet*, was induced by *dol*, *erreur* or *violence*, possesses an unlawful *cause* or (exceptionally) gives rise to *lésion* it may be brought before a court and annulled.[1156] The 'relative or absolute' nature of nullity in any of these cases goes principally to the question of who may bring this action and not to the effects of nullity once declared, which are (with the exceptions which will be noted later) the same for all the various legal grounds on which it may be requested. Moreover, where the conditions of a particular ground of nullity are fulfilled, a court has no discretion to refuse it nor to order 'intermediate solutions' such as the reduction of a price, but must declare it.

Résolution is the term used to describe the termination of bilateral contracts on the ground of their non-performance, whether this is 'imputable' and therefore attracts liability in damages or excused by the presence of *force majeure*.[1157] As has been explained, according to the traditional scheme set out in article 1184 of the Civil Code, in the absence of express contractual provision, *résolution* requires a judicial decision, but in recent years French courts have recognized that a creditor may terminate the contract unilaterally on the ground of non-performance by the debtor 'at his own risk'.[1158] In contrast to the position regarding annulment, where a court is asked to 'resolve' the contract by the creditor, it has a considerable discretion as to whether or not to do so and whether to order some 'intermediate solution'.[1159]

[1152] Art. 1117 C. civ.

[1153] This term is generally reserved in modern practice to claims for termination of a contract on the ground of *lésion*, whether this is in the context of incapacity (art. 1305 C. civ., minors) or otherwise (art. 1674 C. civ.).

[1154] This term is used to describe termination on the ground of non-performance: art. 1184 C. civ.

[1155] The *action rédhibitoire* is the action for termination of a contract of sale by a buyer on the ground of the property's latent defects under arts. 1644 and 1648 C. civ.

[1156] Above, pp. 308, 311, 313, 315, 321 and 323.

[1157] Above, pp. 347 and 357.

[1158] Above, pp. 357–359.

[1159] Above, p. 357.

However, it is striking to a common lawyer that in principle the *effects* of a declaration of nullity[1160] or *résolution* (putting aside for this purpose the 'intermediate solutions' of the latter) are the same: the retroactive destruction of the contract between the parties with the consequence, where the contract has been performed in whole or in part, that both the parties are to be put back into the position which they were in before the contract was made (*mise en état antérieur*).[1161] The logic of retroactivity means that in principle where property transferred under the contract remains indentifiable, title to it reverts to its transferor, but quite apart from the availability of any proprietary action,[1162] personal claims arise either for specific restitution of the property or its value if this is not possible. The legal nature of this restitution and counter-restitution remains a matter of some controversy both in *la doctrine* and *la jurisprudence*. It is sometimes said that recovery here resembles *répétition de l'indu* but possesses certain special features[1163] and the courts have at times actually referred to the terminology and provisions relating to this *quasi-contrat* in describing the restitutionary consequences of annulment of a contract.[1164] However, in 2002 the question arose as to the prescription period applicable to a claim for restitution of property after annulment of a contract: is it the one applicable to actions for annulment (five years) or the one applicable to *répétition de l'indu* (30 years)?[1165] Here, the Cour de cassation declared roundly that 'restitution following annulment does not involve *répétition de l'indu* but only the rules of nullity' and it therefore held the shorter prescription period applicable. This decision is seen by some jurists as representing a clear declaration of position, the Cour de cassation adopting a view that restitution following annulment of a contract belongs exclusively to its own body of law, the law of nullity.[1166] However, in Aubert's view, the Cour de cassation was concerned to make sure that restitution could not be claimed without prior annulment of the contract and this means that (unless annulment had already been granted) any claim for restitution has to be subjected to the prescription period applicable to actions for annulment, but that this logic does not apply to the case where a claim for restitution is brought later (and beyond the

---

[1160] Here, we are concerned with the nullity of the whole contract. In some cases which concern illegality in its broad English sense or other ineffectiveness by law, French courts hold that only part of the contract is to be declared null. This is clearest where a law itself states that a particular clause or type of clause is to be 'deemed not written' etc: the contract is preserved, but the clause is void. However, where the effect of the nullity of a clause on the contract as a whole is not specified in the legislation in question, the courts determine this issue according to whether or not the clause in question was a '*condition impulsive et déterminante*': Terré, Simler, and Lequette *Obligations*, 419–423.

[1161] Starck *et al., Contrat*, 373.

[1162] Below, pp. 449 ff.

[1163] Malaurie, Aynès and Stoffel-Munck, *Obligations*, 346; Carbonnier, *Obligations*, 2100.

[1164] Civ. (1) 4 Apr. 1991, Cont., cons. conc. 1991 no. 137; Com. 19 May 1998, D 1999.406.

[1165] Civ. (1) 24 Sep. 2002, D 2003.369 note Aubert (who notes that the court oddly assumed that the longer period was ten years).

[1166] Terré, Simler, and Lequette, *Obligations*, 425; G. Kessler, 'Restitutions en nature et indemnité de jouissance' JCP 2004.I.154.

prescription period for nullity) but *after* annulment has already been declared.[1167] So, he argues, the Cour de cassation's declaration was particular to its context and so where the law of nullity does not provide for any rule governing restitution, the law of *répétition de l'indu* should naturally and properly be called in aid.[1168] Here, the *Avant-projet de réforme* appears to represent faithfully the diversity of views within *la doctrine*, for while its section governing *répétition de l'indu* provides that 'restitution may take place where the debt which justified payment has subsequently been annulled or retroactively terminated, or loses its justification in any other way',[1169] its earlier provisions governing contract law appear to take the opposite view and (following the views of the particular contributor, Serinet) set out really quite elaborately and in a separate section a dedicated set of special rules to govern restitution following annulment and *résolution*.[1170]

What then are the basic rules of personal recovery and what exceptions are made to them because of their contractual context? Let us start with the general position as regards the effects of annulment.

A. Restitution on Annulment of a Contract

The retroactive destruction of the contract which results from judical declaration of its nullity means both that any price paid must be returned (without any increase to take account of its loss of value through inflation) and that any other property transferred under the contract must, if still in the hands of the other party, be returned (this being termed *obligation de restitution en nature*). Formerly, the courts considered a party's inability to return any property transferred a reason for refusing annulment,[1171] but since the 1970s they have accepted instead that the party's obligation to make specific restitution merely metamorphosizes into an obligation to pay the value of the property in question (whether or not this value was reflected in the contract price)[1172] at the time of its transfer.[1173] Such an obligation will arise where this inability is caused by consumption, physical destruction of the property through the fault of its

---

[1167] J.-L. Aubert, note, D 2003.369 and see Flour, Aubert, and Savaux, *Acte juridique*, 298–300.

[1168] Ibid.

[1169] Art. 1331 A.-p.r.

[1170] Arts. 1161–1164-1 A.-p.r. and see the explanatory preamble by Y.-M. Serinet to the section 'Restitution following the Destruction of a Contract' and id., 'L'effet rétroactif de la résolution pour l'inexécution en droit français' in Fontaine and Viney, 611ff (in the context of *résolution*).

[1171] Civ.(1) 23 Feb. 1970, D 1970.604 note Etesse.

[1172] Com. 29 Feb. 1972, D 1972.623; Com. 18 Nov. 1974, D 1975.625 note Malaurie.

[1173] Starck *et al.*, *Contrat*, 381; Com. 14 Jun. 2005, D 2005.1775 note Lienhard (which refers to the value as at the date of the juridical act annulled). Cf. art. 1163-1 A.-p.r. which provides that '[t]he amount of restitution is calculated taking into account the direct and indirect benefits which the parties were able to derive from performance of the contract, assessed as at the date of restitution'.

possessor or by *force majeure*,[1174] or by its resale[1175] even in the absence of bad faith. Similarly, a claimant for restitution of property which has deteriorated in the other party's hands is entitled to the cost of its repair even in the absence of any fault in the other party.[1176] For in all these cases the claimant is entitled to be put in the position as if the contract had not been made and therefore as though he was still in possession of the property in its state when transferred. As may be seen, these results differ from the effect of the rules found in the Civil Code concerning *répétition de l'indu* proper, for there the measure of recovery is limited where a recipient is in good faith, in the case of resale to its price, and in the case of destruction or deterioration to where this is caused by the payee's fault.[1177] It is also important to note that these restitutionary claims are available to *either* party to a contract which is annulled, the courts in principle not distinguishing between those who have 'caused the nullity' nor, in the case of relative nullity, between those who are entitled to claim nullity and those who are not.[1178] However, a party's good or bad faith does affect his liability for 'fruits'.

1. Liability of a party for 'fruits' of property transferred

Here, the courts apply the scheme of rules in the Civil Code which concern the liability of a possessor of property to its true owner.[1179] According to these, a mere possessor of property, whether immovable or movable, will become the owner of its fruits only when in good faith in the sense of possessing it 'as owner by virtue of a conveyance [*titre translatif de propriété*] of whose defects he is unaware', though as soon as the possessor becomes aware of these defects, his good faith is deemed to cease.[1180] In a majority of cases of nullity of a contract, therefore, a party who has received property under it will be liable for its fruits to the other party only from the time of any claim for its nullity.[1181] Moreover, even in the case of a recipient in bad faith, who must restore the property's fruits or their value as at the date of reimbursement to the other party,[1182] an exception is made where these result from the recipient's own work; for an owner (and therefore a 'former owner' under an annulled contract) is entitled only to

---

[1174] Strack *et al.*, *Contrat*, 378.

[1175] Com. 29 Feb.1972, cit. n. 1172.

[1176] Civ. (1) 2 Jun. 1987, D 1987.IR.152. This also means, however, that no deduction from the price should be made on the basis of any wear and tear in the property returned: Com. 29 Feb. 1972, cit.

[1177] Above, pp. 431–432.

[1178] But see below pp. 446 and 447–448 concerning 'immoral contracts' and liability in delict for fault in relation to annulled contracts.

[1179] Arts. 549–50 and see Starck *et al.*, *Contrat*, 381 ff. As Larroumet, *Biens*, 122 notes, in the case of claims after annulment or *résolution* the claimant does not need to show his title to the property but merely that annulment or *résolution* has occurred.

[1180] Art. 550 al. 1 C. civ. For the meaning of 'fruits' see above, p. 432, n. 1080.

[1181] An exception may be found in the case where a recipient of property is aware of the immorality of the contract under which it passes and therefore of its 'defect': below, p. 447.

[1182] Art. 549 C. civ.

those fruits which would have been produced by the property in the state which it was found when it was received.[1183] Finally, a person who enjoys property under a contract which is subsequently annulled does not have to pay any recompense for this enjoyment.[1184]

Similar rules are applied in respect of claims for restitution of money under annulled contracts, for here interest is recoverable where its recipient was in good faith only from the time of the claim for annulment (from which time bad faith is imputed), but where in bad faith from the time of receipt.[1185] This is the same rule as is found for *répétition de l'indu* proper.[1186]

2. *Restitution for services?*

So far it has been assumed that the contract which is annulled imposed only obligations to pay money or transfer property; but what is the position where work has been done under a contract or in reliance on it, a situation particularly marked in respect of contracts whose performance is due to occur over a number of years? Here, the courts have sometimes held that this is a reason for the contract to be terminated only *prospectively*, leaving payments of money, property transferred and work done to stand without any attempt at restitution and this is what the Civil Code expressly provides for the contract of partnership.[1187] However, the more general approach has been to retain the retroactive nature of nullity, but allow restitution and counter-restitution in respect of both property and services.[1188] Thus, where a contract of employment is annulled for breach of rules of labour law, the employer is entitled to recover the wages paid and the employee is entitled to an indemnity in respect of the work done. In principle, recovery in respect of work done is a matter for the 'sovereign power of assessment' of the *juges du fond* rather than determination according to any contractual rate that may be discerned: this is certainly the logical result of nullity which obliterates the contract.[1189] Often, though, the *juges* in fact choose the 'contract rate' and, where they do, the practical effect is the same as prospective termination.[1190] A

[1183] Civ. (1) 20 Jun. 1967, D 1967.32 note Bredin, who argues that a better solution would be to allow recovery of the value of the fruits coupled with a counterclaim by the possessor in respect of the work done.

[1184] Starck *et al., Contrat,* 382; Ch. mixte 9 Jul. 2004, D 2004.2175 note Tuaillon, Défrenois 2004.1402 note Libchaber, *RDC* 2005.280 note Stoffel-Munck (though the Chambre mixte accepted that in principle liability for delictual fault could apply so as to compensate a party incurring loss caused by annulment, on which see below, p. 446.) Art. 1164-2 A.-p.r. provides for restitution in respect of the enjoyment of property transferred under an annulled or 'resolved' contract. And see generally Kessler, *op. cit.* n. 1166.

[1185] Starck *et al., Contrat,* 382 and see arts. 1164-1, 1164-2 A. p.r.

[1186] Above, p. 432.

[1187] Art. 1844-15 C. civ.

[1188] Terré, Simler, and Lequette *Obligations,* 426–427.

[1189] Soc. 8 Apr. 1957, GP 1957.2.143.

[1190] Terré, Simler, and Lequette, *Obligations,* 427.

very striking example of recovery for work done in *reliance* on the existence of a contract subsequently annulled, rather than done in performance of obligations arising from it, may be found in the case concerning the painting known as 'Le Verrou'.[1191] This painting was sold by its owners to a Paris dealer for 55,000 F on the understanding that it was 'of the school of Fragonard', but after restoration and research the dealer identified it as by Fragonard himself and resold it to the Louvre Museum for just over 5 million F! The sellers of the painting succeeded in having the sale with the dealer annulled on the ground of their mistake (*erreur sur les qualités substantielles*)[1192] and recovered the value of the painting from the dealer which was set at the price which he received from the Louvre for it (though the price they had received was deducted from this in their award). The dealer, however, recovered on the basis of *enrichissement sans cause* some 1.5 million Francs from the sellers who had benefited so amply from his labours.

3. Delictual fault (again!)

We have noted that in principle a party's fault does not bar the restitutionary effects of nullity (though on occasion it may exclude nullity itself).[1193] However, it should be noted that where a party to a contract which has been annulled has committed a fault, this may attract liability in damages for losses which this may cause in delict and where both parties are at fault, this may lead either to a reduction of one party's claim or, where appropriate, a counter-claim.[1194] Most commonly, this fault consists of a party to a contract entering it knowing of the defect which may lead to its nullity[1195] and a typical example would be where one party has committed *dol* or *violence*, both of which require a deliberate wrongful element.[1196] Where this is the case, only the party who is in good faith can recover damages for delictual fault.[1197]

4. Qualifications to the rules of recovery on annulment: incapacity and illegality

There are two major qualifications to these rules.

First, special rules apply to contracts made by minors and by those whose mental condition requires their subjection to *tutelle*.[1198] Although the Civil Code makes

---

[1191] Civ. (1) 25 May 1992, Cont., Conc., 1991 no. 174 note Leveneur.

[1192] Above pp. 311 ff.

[1193] Some jurists say that the courts allow *réparation en nature* in respect of this delict, meaning that they would uphold the contract and thereby refuse both annulment and restitution: Mazeaud and Chabas, *Obligations*, 327. An example may be found as regards the 'inexcusable fault' in a claimant for *erreur:* Terré, Simler, and Lequette, *Obligations*, 437; Flour, Aubert, and Savaux, *Acte juridique*, 309. Others see the claimant's inexcusable fault simply as excluding nullity for *erreur*: Malaurie, Aynès, and Stoffel-Munck, *Obligations*, 249.

[1194] Arts. 1382–3 C. civ. and see Terré, Simler, and Lequette, *Obligations*, 436–437.

[1195] Ibid., 437.

[1196] Above, pp. 309 and 311.

[1197] Ch. mixte 9 Jul. 2004, cit. n. 1184.

[1198] On the legal protections given to the disabled more generally, see P. Malaurie, *Les personnes, les incapacités*, 2nd edn. (Défences, 2005) 205 ff.

capacity to enter a contract one of the four essential conditions of its validity,[1199] lack of capacity on the ground of minority[1200] does not lead to absolute nullity, but rather in general to the possibility of an *action en rescision pour lésion* on the ground of the contract's prejudicial effect.[1201] Where a court orders a contract rescinded on this ground,[1202] the minor may obtain restitution of money or other property transferred, but the minor's liability to make counter-restitution is limited to money or property which he has received and 'turned to his profit'.[1203] This means that minors are liable only for surviving value in their hands and so, for example, a minor who sells property for €5,000 and dissipates €3,000 of its proceeds is liable only up to the remaining €2,000 in his hands, a rule which is justified on the basis that a liability to make full restitution would make the minor's protection illusory.[1204]

Secondly, the restitutionary effects of annulment on the ground of illegality depend on a broad distinction between immoral and merely unlawful contracts.[1205] Where a contract is immoral, the courts apply the traditional maxims *nemo auditur propriam turpitudinem allegans* ('nobody may be heard relying on his own wrongdoing') and *in pari causa turpitudinis cessat repetitio* ('restitution ceases where both parties are equally in the wrong'). As a result, while a contract may still be annulled, its parties will not succeed in a claim for restitution for money or other property transferred, the other party possessing the so-called *exception d'indignité*. On the other hand, if the contract is merely unlawful, this does not deprive the parties of their restitutionary rights.[1206] As one would expect, the line between immoral and unlawful contracts is a distinctly malleable one: indeed, 'the case law is difficult to synthesize... Rejection or acceptance [by a court] of an action for restitution on the ground of immorality or unlawfulness is decided purely empirically, the courts assessing, in each case, the appropriateness of applying the maxim *nemo auditur*'.[1207] The distinction has not, moreover, always been strictly observed by the courts.[1208] Finally, sometimes delictual liability is yet again brought in to help: so, for example, in one case a prostitute recovered damages in delict against her procurer with whom she had agreed to share her receipts, the damages representing the money and other property which she

---

[1199] Art. 1108 C. civ.

[1200] The position as regards mental incapacity is more complex: see art. 488 ff C. civ.

[1201] Art. 1305 C. civ.; Starck *et al., Contrat,* 158–9, who note that an exception is made for particularly important transactions which require special authorization, the absence of which leads to relative nullity even in the absence of *lésion.*

[1202] This effect applies also to contracts made by a person over the age of majority who is under *tutelle*: art. 1312 C. civ.

[1203] Art. 1312 C. civ.

[1204] Terré, Simler, and Lequette, *Obligations,* 429.

[1205] Terré, Simler, and Lequette, *Obligations,* 429–432.

[1206] Civ. (1) 27 Nov. 1984, GP 1985.2 Pan. jur. 135 note Chabas.

[1207] Starck *et al., Contrat,* 380.

[1208] Terré, Simler, and Lequette, *Obligations,* 432.

gave to him under this agreement: here, his fault (for which he was convicted of a criminal offence) was held to have caused the annulment of their agreement on the ground of immorality.[1209]

B. Restitution on *Résolution* of a Contract[1210]

A contract may be terminated by a court on the ground of its non-performance on the application of the injured party[1211] and the effects of this are in principle the same as for nullity: retroactive termination of the contract.[1212] Thus, any money or other property transferred under the contract must be restored to its transferor (the rules of liability for 'fruits' are also the same).[1213] However, even putting aside 'intermediate solutions' between *résolution* and its refusal (notably, where the courts reduce the contract price payable by one party on the ground of other's non-performance),[1214] the courts have taken a somewhat different approach to contracts which involve doing work or the performance of a service over a period of time, which are considered to be of two types: contracts with continuous performance (*contrats à exécution successive*) or instalment contracts (*contrats à exécution échelonnée*).[1215] As regards instalment contracts, it is generally agreed that the courts decide whether to order retroactive termination of the contract (*résolution*) or instead merely prospective termination (*résiliation*) depending on whether the contract was intended to be divisible or indivisible by the parties.[1216] Moreover, in 2003 the Cour de cassation held that a court may sometimes order *résolution* rather than *résiliation* of a contract for continuous performance, there, a contract for the tenancy of premises.[1217] Where a court orders prospective termination of such a contract (*résiliation*) as from the date of judgment, there is no restitution in respect of what has been transferred or done under it before the date.[1218] On the other hand, where the court orders *résolution*, the injured party may recover damages (which are treated as contractual) in respect of any loss which this causes him;[1219] and, in

---

[1209] Crim. 7 Jun. 1945, JCP 1946.II.2955 note Hémard (the prostitute claimed as *partie civile*).

[1210] For reasons of space, this discussion will be limited to cases of *résolution* for imputable non-performance, thereby excluding ones of *force majeure*.

[1211] Art. 1184 C. civ. and see above p. 357.

[1212] Malaurie, Aynès, and Stoffel-Munck *Obligations*, 448–450.

[1213] Ibid, and see above, p. 444 ff.

[1214] Above, p. 444.

[1215] Above, p. 358.

[1216] Terré, Simler, and Lequette, *Obligations*, 645; Malaurie, Aynès, and Stoffel-Munck, *Obligations*, 450.

[1217] Civ. (3) 30 Apr. 2003, JCP 2004.II.10031 note Jamin.

[1218] Terré, Simler, and Lequette, *Obligations*, 645.

[1219] Above, pp. 357–358. The injured party could instead choose to ask for performance of the contract: above, p. 349.

contrast to the present position as regards annulment, the Cour de cassation has recognized that the *juges du fond* are entitled to award the party whose non-performance gave rise to termination an 'indemnity' in respect of the injured party's occupation of the premises during the period when the contract was thought to exist at a sum which they are to determine rather than at the contractual rate.[1220]

C. The Effect of Annulment or *Résolution* of the Contract on Third Parties

In some cases, a party to a failed contract will not be satisfied with a personal claim. The main advantages of a claim *in rem* is that it may be effective against third party transferees (the *droit de suite*) and will not suffer abatement in the defendant's insolvency (the *droit de préférence*). However, French law allows a party to a contract such a proprietary claim only in very limited circumstances. For, a party can possess a right *in rem* only where he can still identify what he has transferred under the contract as his property and this will only be the case as regards *corps certain,* which, in particular, excludes money.[1221] Moreover, French law does not allow a claimant under a former contract to identity *as his* other property in the hands of a defendant which was exchanged for the property which he transferred: French does not allow a person to 'trace' the value representing his former property in this way.[1222] So, for example, if A sells an antique desk to B who exchanges it for a painting with C, A cannot (on annulment of the sale) claim the *painting* as his because it represents his desk's substitute: any rights *in rem* which he may possess lie against the desk's present holder, C. Furthermore, even where a party to a former contract can identify his property in the hands of either the other party or a third party, French law closely circumscribes the availability or effects of any proprietary claim.[1223]

1. *The right to avoid the insolvency of the other party to the contract*

In English law, where A can identify property in B's hands as his property, he can avoid any possible insolvency in B and a complex body of law has arisen which governs when A can do so, whether at law or in equity. French law accepts

---

[1220] Civ. (3) 30 Apr. 2003, cit. n. 1217 and cf. above, p. 445.

[1221] See above, p. 427–428.

[1222] French law accepts the idea that in certain circumstances property acquired as a substitute for other property which is governed by a particular system of rights remains governed by that system of rights (or does so to a degree), this being termed *subrogation réelle,* but this is a limited technique, recognized by the law only in certain cases: Malaurie and Aynès, *Biens,* 40ff; Carbonnier, *Obligations,* 1629–1630. For an example in the context of property held in common, see above, pp. 284–285.

[1223] Below.

the same starting-point, A's title to property giving rise to an *action en revendica-tion*.[1224] Moreover, as we have said, French law accepts that both annulment and *résolution* revest title to property transferred under the contract in its transferor, though this revesting is subject to a condition of identification of that property (not its substitute or its proceeds) and is limited to *corps certain*.[1225] This means, for example, that where A delivers chairs or land under a contract of sale to B, who pays the price and the contract is subsequently annulled for mistake or retro-actively terminated for non-performance, title to the chairs or land reverts to A, but title to the money does *not* revert to B, money being the typical example of a *chose de genre*.[1226] This occasional proprietary effect of *résolution* applies not merely when a contract is terminated by the court under article 1184 of the Civil Code but also when terminated by the injured party under an express *clause résolutoire*.

For an English lawyer, this effect is particularly surprising as regards *résolu-tion*: for it means that B's non-performance of a contract may allow A to avoid B's insolvency.[1227] Here, sometimes termination of the contract may well be much more attractive for the injured party than enforcement! However, con-siderable limits do exist on this important right. So, for example, the *right to terminate* a contract of sale of an immovable on the ground of non-payment of the price is subjected to a condition of registration.[1228] Secondly, where the debtor is a *commerçant*,[1229] the law of insolvency suspends the bringing of any *action en résolution* for non-payment of money (though *not* any *action en nullité*) from the time of the judicial decision which opens the insolvency proceedings (*redressement judiciaire*).[1230] On the other hand, the question remains unset-tled as to whether a creditor may successfully invoke an express *clause résolu-toire* for non-payment of money or whether any subsequent court proceedings to establish the effectiveness of retroactive termination in these circumstances are caught by this rule of suspension.[1231] Finally, special restrictions apply to claims by unpaid commercial sellers of goods, notably restricting such a per-son's *action en revendication* to a 3-month period from the opening of insolvency proceedings.[1232]

[1224] For the commercial law concerning insolvency proceedings, see art. L. 624-9ff C. com. and M. Jeantin and P. Le Cannu, *Enterprises en difficulté*, 7th edn. (Dalloz, 2006), 451ff.

[1225] Above, p. 450.

[1226] Carbonnier, *Obligations*, 1571.

[1227] Larroumet, *Contrat*, 814–815.

[1228] Below.

[1229] See below p. 454 ff. Insolvency proceedings have been extended to certain other classes of person, but do not apply generally.

[1230] Arts. L. 622-13 and 622-21 C. com.

[1231] Jeantin and Le Cannu, op. cit. n. 1224, 272–3.

[1232] Art. L. 624-9 C. com.

2. *The right to follow the property into the hands of third parties*

English law recognizes that where a contract is rescinded *ab initio*[1233] (as opposed to being terminated as from some later date, notably for breach or frustration) title to any property other than money transferred under it reverts to its transferor,[1234] but such a divesting cannot prejudice third party transferees of the property because the existence of third party rights is a bar to rescission being allowed.[1235] In French law, by contrast, the transfer of property received under a contract to a third party is *not* a reason for refusing either annulment or *résolution*. Logically, therefore, where property which has been transferred under an annulled or 'resolved' contract remains identifiable as *corps certain,* title to it in principle reverts to its transferor, tearing it from any ultimate transferee and causing a 'cascade of nullities' of the intervening transactions.[1236] In principle, therefore, a party to the original contract may claim what has become once again his property in the hands of third parties, this claim being by way of *action en revendication.* Given the considerable harm which this logic would cause to the security of transactions and of possession, it is not surprising that French law has found many ways of avoiding it.

As to corporeal movable property, a very considerable restriction on its potential effect is found in the famous rule that 'in the case of movable property, possession is equivalent to title'.[1237] This rule means that a person who receives this type of property in good faith from a non-owner will nevertheless acquire title to it, as long as the owner originally allowed it to leave his possession voluntarily;[1238] it therefore protects many persons who receive property from another who possessed title at the time, but who subsequently lost it as a result of the annulment or *résolution* of the contract. As to immovable property, the position is more complex, publicity requirements being only a partial protection. When a contract has been annulled, the third party's position is precarious, for only some grounds of nullity (such as *lésion* but not, for example, *erreur*) will appear from the entry of the public register of the transaction.[1239] 'Public registration does not in fact have the power to purge transactions or registered rights of any defects which affect them, nor to render their annulment inopposable to third parties'[1240] and so here the third party will be sure of his title only on expiry of the periods for *usucaption.*[1241] However, the opposite is the case as regards a contract of sale of

---

[1233] This is the case notably for rescission for misrepresentation, duress or undue influence.

[1234] Burrows (above n. 971), pp. 58–59.

[1235] *Clough v. L. and N. W. Rly.* (1871) LR 7 Ex 26. This is to be contrasted with a contract 'void for mistake' under which title is deemed never to have passed: *Cundy v. Lindsay* (1878) 3 App Cas 459.

[1236] Starck *et al., Contrat,* 374.

[1237] Art. 2279 C. civ. and above, p. 276.

[1238] This is the combined effect of arts. 2279 and 2280 C. civ.: Carbonnier, *Obligations,* 1870–1871.

[1239] Starck *et al., Contrat,* 375 ff.

[1240] Terré, Simler, and Lequette, *Obligations,* 435.

[1241] Above, pp. 277 ff.

immovable property which has been terminated on the ground of non-payment of the price, for here the Civil Code provides that the *action résolutoire* cannot be exercised against a third party whose contract has been properly published unless the seller's right to payment was registered.[1242] There are, furthermore, various other ways which affect both movable and immovable property by which the third party's rights may be protected.[1243]

[1242] Arts. 1654, 2379 C. civ.
[1243] Terré, Simler, and Lequette, *Obligations*, 646.

11

Commercial Law[1]

Exactly what is meant by 'commercial law' is something over which English lawyers (or at least English academic lawyers) can and do differ. One eminent writer has defined it as 'that branch of law which is concerned with rights and duties arising from the supply of goods and services in the way of trade'.[2] On the other hand, 'commercial law' is often used in a looser, broader sense, equivalent to 'business law', embracing not only the law of commercial transactions but also other topics, such as company law. In French law, *droit commercial* is understood in this wider sense. As such, it is a vast domain, covering a multitude of diverse topics: sale, hire, banking, insurance, partnership and company law, commercial leases, competition law and more. To give a detailed account of all these matters is clearly beyond the scope of this book, so what follows is necessarily highly select-ive. To begin with we shall look at a number of fundamental issues: the place of commercial law within the general scheme of French private law, its scope and, in general terms, the practical implications of its application. We shall then consider a limited number of specific topics: the persons involved in commerce, the special characteristics of the property they employ in their business and, in conclusion, the regime applied to businesses in difficulty (including the law of insolvency).

I. Introduction: The Notion and Significance of *Droit Commercial*

A. *Droit Commercial* as a Division of the Law

It is sometimes questioned whether commercial law is really a distinct branch of English law at all. On the surface at least, it can appear to be the simple applica-tion of the general law of contract, tort, property, etc to commercial situations. In this respect, English commercial law bears the clear marks of history. The growing centralization of the administration of justice led in the 18th century

---

[1] For a good general introduction, see M. Pédamon, *Droit commercial: Commerçants et fonds de commerce. Concurrence et contrats du commerce*, 2nd edn. (Paris, 2000). Detailed works include G. Ripert and R. Roblot, *Traité de droit commercial* t. 1, vol. 1, 18th edn. by L. Vogel (Paris, 2001); t. 1, vol. 2, 18th edn. by M. Germain (Paris, 2002); t. 2, 17th edn. by P. Delebecque and M. Germain (Paris, 2004). For works on partnership and company law, see note 56.

[2] R. Goode, *Commercial Law*, 3rd edn. (London, 2004), 8.

to the absorption of the once distinctive law merchant into the common law and to the demise of the special commercial courts that applied it. This effectively put an end to any formally distinct commercial law. In France, however, the historical development was quite different.[3] The royal interest in commercial law led to considerable codification as early as the end of the 17th century,[4] and the segregation of commercial law from the general law was further encouraged by the King's establishment of commercial courts separate from the regional *parlements*. Thus, by the time of Napoleon, commercial law had established itself as a distinct branch of the law, and this was confirmed in 1807 by the adoption of a Commercial Code (*Code de commerce*) to stand alongside the new Civil Code. However, although a potent symbol of the distinctiveness of commercial law, the Code was not to prove vital. Over the years, the Code dwindled in importance as separate legislation was enacted to deal with huge swathes of what was nevertheless recognized as a commercial law, subject to the jurisdiction of the tribunaux de commerce, the distinctive courts whose function it is to administer justice in commercial matters.[5] By the end of the 20th century, the law relating to important matters such as commercial companies and insolvency[6] was to be found outside the Code. But in the 21st century, the picture has changed radically, as a result of a process of re-codification.[7] The Code has absorbed the disparate pieces of separate legislation and has emerged once more as the central embodiment of a distinct commercial law.

B. The Scope of *Droit Commercial*

One might have expected to find in the Code a definition of what is, and what is not, commercial law. In fact, no such definition is given, at least not directly. What French lawyers look to instead are the provisions of the Code relating to 'commercial acts' (*actes de commerce*). It is in this concept of commercial acts that the key to the scope of commercial law is to be found, for commercial law is essentially about these acts and the *commerçants* who engage in them. However, the Code does not give a coherent definition of what a commercial act is, but rather simply gives a list of acts deemed to be commercial, a list which has been interpreted liberally. The courts and writers have devoted much energy to identifying and classifying the different types of act. Some acts are considered commercial by virtue of their nature, i.e. taking account of what is done and by whom (*actes de*

---

[3] A good account of the history of French commercial law can be found in J. Hilaire, *Introduction historique au droit commercial* (Paris, 1986).

[4] In the form of the Ordinance of 1673 (known as the *Code Savary*) dealing with commerce generally and the Ordinance of 1681 dealing with maritime commerce.

[5] See above p. 48.

[6] Dealt with by *loi* no. 66-537 of 24 July 1966 and *loi* no. 85-98 of 25 January 1985, respectively.

[7] The *partie législative* was re-codified by *ordonnance* no. 2000-912 of 18 September 2000 and the *partie réglementaire* by *décret* no. 2007-431 of 25 March 2007.

commerce par nature). Certain acts are automatically deemed to be commercial because of the form of the act itself or of the organization involved: *actes de commerce par la forme*. In addition, acts which would normally be regarded as civil (i.e. not commercial) will be categorized as commercial if they are done as an ancillary part of a commercial activity: *actes de commerce par accessoire*.

The significance of the various categories will be examined more fully below, but it should stressed at the outset that in practice the task of classifying acts as commercial or civil is often much more straightforward than the elaborate theory of commercial acts might suggest. This is because the types of partnership and company whose acts are automatically considered to be commercial by virtue of their form are very common and indeed account for most large and medium-sized businesses.

1. Actes de commerce par nature

At least as they have come to be interpreted, the acts listed in the Commercial Code which are commercial in nature have certain features in common: they involve an element of speculation, and they constitute a participation in the circulation of wealth (goods, services, etc). In addition, it is assumed that they are only commercial if they are done on a regular basis (as English lawyers might say, 'in the course of business').[8]

(a) Activities recognized as commercial

Turning to specifics, and putting aside the specialized area of shipping and maritime law,[9] the list of commercial acts, originally in article 632, now occupies pride of place in the very first provision of the newly refurbished Code, article L 110-1.[10] This starts with what is the most basic commercial activity, the buying and selling of movable property (e.g. goods) with a view to making a profit. Dealings with immovable property, on the other hand, were originally excluded, following the general tradition of treating matters to do with land as civil. Nevertheless, this rigid stance has been relaxed in modern times, and in 1967 the buying and selling of immovable property was added to the list, though this is subject to the proviso that buying land with a view to building on it and then reselling it is still civil.[11]

Manufacturing is also commercial. This is largely covered by the provision dealing with buying and selling movable property, for this makes it clear that it covers reselling property in its original form or as processed and made into a product. In addition, article L 110-1 mentions manufacturing as a commercial act in its own right, and this is understood rather more broadly than simply

---

[8] e.g. Com. 13 May 1970, D 1970. 644 note X.L.

[9] Dealt with by art. L 110-2 C.com.

[10] The old art. 632 was tucked away in the middle of the Code immediately after the provisions relating to the jurisdiction of the *tribunaux de commerce*, which it helped to define.

[11] This proviso was added by *loi* no. 70-601 of 9 July 1970. It does not cover simply renovating existing buildings: Trib. com. Paris, 18 Apr. 1991, *Dr. Sociétés* 1992, no. 179 obs. Chaput.

buying materials and processing them. Thus, it extends to processing someone else's goods (e.g. making wine from a farmer's grapes), provided that the processor brings to bear resources of his own (workforce and/or machinery).[12]

The provision of a wide range of services is also characterized as commercial: the carriage of goods or passengers; hiring out movable property (but, following the traditional approach noted above, not letting out immovable property); banking, insurance[13] and public entertainment. In addition, the activities of certain intermediaries figure in the list: *courtiers* (those who bring parties together but do not make contracts on their behalf);[14] *commissionaires* (commission agents who conclude contracts for their principals, but do so in their own names); *agences* and *bureaux d'affaires* (general agencies, such as travel agents); auctioneers; and intermediaries involved in the purchase, underwriting or sale of immovable property, businesses, or shares in real estate companies (*sociétés immobilières*).[15]

(b) Excluded activities

A number of what one might regard as business activities are civil and not commercial. To begin with, while those who deal in goods and those who transform goods to make new products are governed by commercial law, those from whom the goods originate are not. Agriculture has traditionally been classified as a civil activity, and this is confirmed by article L 311-1 of the Rural Code. Similarly, the extraction of materials from the ground, as by quarrying or abstracting mineral water,[16] has traditionally been regarded as civil; however, an important exception was introduced in 1919 in the case of mining.[17]

Also considered to be civil are the activities of *artisans*, those who provide manual skills, such as repairers and decorators. The basic idea is that, provided that such persons derive their profit from their labour rather than from any materials used, they will not be *commerçants*. In addition, the so-called liberal professions, whose skills are intellectual and who are typically paid by an *honorarium*, are held to be civil. This category embraces a number of professional activities, such as doctors, lawyers, accountants, architects and teachers.[18]

---

[12] Req. 11 Dec. 1944, D 1945.213 note Gabolde. If these requirements are not met, the person in question will be a non-commercial *artisan* (see below).

[13] This is not mentioned in art. L 110-1, but marine insurance figures in art. L 110-2 and analogies are drawn from that for insurance generally.

[14] Marriage bureaux have been held commercial under this head: e.g. Com. 3 Apr. 1984, Bull. civ. IV no. 122.

[15] Paradoxically, the activities of *agents commerciaux* (independent agents who negotiate contracts on behalf of manufacturers and merchants) have been held to be civil, on the ground that they act in the name of their principals and on their behalf: Com. 29 Oct. 1979, D 1980.69; RDC 1980.68 obs. Derruppé.

[16] Req. 27 Mar. 1866, DP 1866.1.428.

[17] *Loi* of 9 September 1919; see now art. 23 *Code minier*.

[18] Including driving instructors: Com. 3 June 1986, D 1986.IR.417 obs. Honorat; RTD com. 1986.513 obs. Derruppé.

2. Actes de commerce par la forme[19]

In a restricted number of cases, an act will be considered to be automatically commercial simply because of the form the act takes, irrespective of whether it is part of a regular commercial activity, i.e. whether or not the party involved is a *commerçant*. The clearest example of this kind of intrinsically commercial act is the bill of exchange, which article L 110-1 expressly declares to be a commercial act 'between all persons'. But whether this category of commercial acts extends beyond bills of exchange is controversial. It is sometimes argued that dealings with a *fonds de commerce* (the global assets of a commercial business)[20] are also acts commercial in form, but this is not settled,[21] and in any event the vast majority of such dealings would be commercial under a different head.[22]

More important in practice is the category of acts which are automatically commercial by virtue of the form of the person involved. As will be seen in more detail later (in the section dealing with commercial persons), article L 210-1 declares certain common types of partnerships and companies to be commercial.[23] Whether a business is such a *société commerciale* depends simply on its form (e.g. whether it is the equivalent of a public limited company) and not on what it does. Thus, if a firm of accountants (a liberal profession and therefore normally civil) were to incorporate itself in one of the specified forms, it would become commercial.[24] This commercial character of the business in turn makes its acts commercial.[25]

3. Actes de commerce par accessoire

In the case of *commerçants*, commercial law embraces not only their principal, commercial activity, but also acts that are ancillary to it. A wide range of contracts will be caught under this heading.[26] So, for example, if a commercial business takes out an insurance policy on its property[27] or borrows money,[28] this will be a commercial act. On the other hand, if a shopkeeper buys goods for his

---

[19] See A. Piravano, 'L'ambiguïté des actes de commerce par la forme' D 1976 Chron. 249.

[20] Discussed in detail below, p. 473 ff.

[21] Compare Aix 20 July 1943, D 1946.233 note Tunc, with Paris 27 Nov. 1962, D 1963.49.

[22] The sale of a business, for example, would normally be ancillary to the commercial activity of both the seller and the buyer. The difficulties arise if the seller has ceased to operate as a *commerçant* or is a private individual who has simply inherited the business. See M. Pédamon, *Droit commercial*, 2nd edn., para. 217.

[23] See further pp. 464 ff below.

[24] Com. 18 Feb. 1975, Bull. civ. IV no. 48; RDC 1975.466 obs. Jauffret.

[25] Ibid. But, given the traditional association of immovable property and civil law, this is subject to reservations in relation to activities involving land: see W. Jeandidier, 'L'imparfaite commercialité des sociétés à objet civil et forme commerciale' D 1979 Chron. 7.

[26] But the application of this rule to dealings with land has proved problematic: for example, compare Com. 25 Apr. 1983, D 1984.1, note Jourdain, with Civ. (3), 14 June 1989, Bull. civ. III no. 141.

[27] Civ. 24 Jan. 1865, DP 1865.1.72.

[28] Civ. 30 July 1907, DP 1908.1.161.

personal use, this will be a civil act.[29] The category of *actes de commerce par acces-soire* is not limited to contracts, however. If a *commerçant* becomes subject to a liability in delict or restitution arising out of the conduct of the business, that will also constitute an ancillary act. This obviously extends the scope of commercial law considerably, encompassing, amongst other things, questions of unfair competition.

The above acts are commercial because of the status of the party involved as *commerçant*, and for that reason they are known as *subjective* ancillary acts. More exceptionally, acts of someone who is not a *commerçant* may nevertheless be considered commercial, because of their connection with the commercial activity of someone else. These acts are known as *objective* ancillary acts, and the typical case in practice is that of the guarantee (*cautionnement*) of a commercial loan. If, for example, (as is common) a director[30] or a shareholder[31] in a commercial company gives a personal guarantee in respect of a loan to the company, the guarantee will be considered commercial, provided that the guarantor has a personal interest in the loan being granted. Similarly, the rights of the beneficiary of a *stipulation pour autrui* will be governed by commercial law if the contract is commercial for the *stipulant*, even though the beneficiary is not a *commerçant*.[32] Thus, where a manufacturer entrusted goods to a carrier for delivery to a non-commercial customer, it was held that the customer's claim for non-delivery against the carrier was governed by the rules of commercial law.[33]

C. The Practical Implications of Applying *Droit Commercial*

The French insistence on commercial law being a distinct branch of the law might lead one to expect it to be a comprehensive set of rules, but in fact many aspects of many commercial acts have no special text to govern them, as is the case as regards commercial sales of goods, and here one has to have recourse to the provisions of *droit civil*. This incompleteness of commercial law is perhaps unsurprising, given the wide range of acts that come within its ambit; nevertheless, it does diminish the significance of its status as a separate branch of the law.

Much of the interest of commercial law naturally lies in the detailed rules on specific topics. But there are a number of diverse rules which apply generally to commercial acts, and these are considered below. As will become apparent, in recent times there has been a noticeable trend towards assimilating private law and commercial law, so that some traditional differences have disappeared or have at least been diluted.

---

[29] Art. L 721-6 C. com.
[30] e.g. Com. 7 July 1969, D 1970.14.
[31] e.g. Com. 10 Feb. 1971, D 1971.605, note Coutin and Hovasse.
[32] On *stipulation pour autrui* more generally, see above pp. 336–337.
[33] Com. 1 Feb. 1955, D 1956.338, note Durand; JCP 1955.II.8772, note Hémard.

1. *General rules applicable to commercial acts*

There has traditionally been a marked difference between the general rules of evidence and those applied to commercial acts. Article 1341 of the Civil Code requires acts such as contracts[34] to be proved by means of a signed or notarized document, but article L 110-3 of the Commercial Code simply allows a commercial act to be proved by any means ('*par tous moyens*'). A number of justifications are given for this difference: commercial transactions need to be carried out rapidly and with the minimum of formality, business persons are capable of looking after their own interests, and in any event *commerçants* are obliged to keep accounts. However, the difference is not as sharp as it may seem in the light of changes made in recent years: in particular, the requirement of documentary proof now only applies where the sum involved exceeds €1,500. Moreover, there are a fair number of specific acts to which special formalities apply, even though they are carried out by a *commerçant*, such as the sale of a business (*fonds de commerce*).[35]

Secondly, a relaxation of formalities has similarly figured traditionally in relation to the effecting of a *mise en demeure*. Article 1139 of the Civil Code originally required the creditor either to employ the services of a *huissier* to serve notice on the debtor or to do an equivalent act. In commercial matters, however, no formality was required, so that a simple letter would suffice.[36] Nevertheless, in modern times there is no sharp distinction between commercial and private law: the courts came to interpret the requirement of an equivalent act liberally even in non-commercial cases, and this has now been endorsed by the legislature, article 1139 being modified by the *loi* of 9 July 1991, so that a letter is acceptable generally, provided that its intent is clear.[37]

Thirdly, article 1202 of the Civil Code provides that co-contractors are not jointly and severally liable unless this is expressly agreed, whereas in the case of commercial obligations the rule is reversed.[38]

Fourthly, compound interest on debts (*l'anatocisme*) is exceptional in the general law, but it is more readily accepted in commercial dealings. Article 1154 of the Civil Code allows the charging of compound interest where there is an agreement to that effect and the debt has been due for at least a year. By contrast, compound interest can be charged freely in commercial matters where there is a current account between the parties.[39] There used to be a further difference

---

[34] The requirement does not apply to claims in quasi-contract or delict: art. 1348 C. civ. Cf. above p. 326 on the differing significance of requirements of form in relation to contracts.

[35] Art. L 141-1 C.com. For an explanation of the exact nature of a *fonds de commerce*, see below, p. 473 ff.

[36] Req. 28 Oct. 1903, D 1904.1.14.

[37] On the significance of *mise en demeure*, see above, p. 353.

[38] Req. 20 Oct. 1920, D 1920.1.161.

[39] Civ. 14 May 1850, D 1850.1.157; Com. 22 May 1991, Bull. civ. IV, no. 168; D 1991.428, note Gavalda.

between private and commercial law, as the legal rate of interest was 1% higher in relation to commercial debts, but since 1975[40] the same rate is applied to all cases.

Fifthly, the general limitation period is 30 years for contract claims and ten years for non-contractual liability.[41] However, the need in business for disputes to be raised and settled quickly has led to the introduction of a short limitation period of ten years for all commercial obligations laid down in article L 110-4 of the Commercial Code. This corresponds to the period laid down in article L 123-22 during which *commerçants* must retain records.

Finally, French private law traditionally adopted a cautious attitude to arbitration clauses. Where a contract contained a *clause compromissoire*, i.e. one that provided that any disputes must be referred to arbitration, article 2061 of the Civil Code declared the clause to be void. But those involved in commerce appreciated the benefits of arbitration, and the *loi* of 31 December 1925 was passed to allow *clauses compromissoires* in commercial contracts.[42] This distinction was significantly eroded in 2001, however, by a radical revision of article 2061,[43] which now declares arbitration clauses to be valid in a contract made '*à raison d'une activité professionelle*'.

2. General rules applicable to commerçants

Those who engage in commerce on a regular basis must be registered in the *Registre de commerce et des sociétés*.[44] The Register is organized on a local basis, being the responsibility of the clerk of every *tribunal de commerce* or *tribunal de grande instance* with commercial jurisdiction.[45] The consequences of registration, and the sanctions for non-registration, vary according to whether the *commerçant* is an individual (i.e. a natural, physical person) or a moral person, such as a company. In the case of commercial partnerships and companies and *groupements d'intérêt économique*,[46] registration is essential in order for the business to acquire legal personality. In the case of an individual, on the other hand, registration is simply a declaration of his activity and it gives rise to a presumption that the individual's acts are commercial acts.[47] Failure to register will mean that the individual will not enjoy the benefits of the status of *commerçant*, such as the special rights of a tenant under a commercial lease,[48] and it may lead to criminal

---

[40] *Loi* no. 75-619 of 11 July 1975. See now art. L 313-2 *Code monétaire et financier.*
[41] Arts 2262 and 2270-1 C.civ.
[42] See now art. L 721-3 C.com.
[43] By *loi* no. 2001-420 of 15 May 2001.
[44] See art. L 123-1 ff. C.com.
[45] The information in this locally based register is used to compile a national register in Paris, which is a valuable source for, amongst others, government departments.
[46] See below, pp. 464, 471. Civil *sociétés* also require registration in order to acquire personality.
[47] Art. L 123-7 C.com.
[48] See below, p. 475.

sanctions[49] (though this is not usual in practice). *Commerçants* are also required by article L 123-12 ff. of the Commercial Code to keep accounts and to produce an annual statement of account.

The special regime applicable to *commerçants* who cannot pay their debts has long been a distinguishing feature of commercial law. Until recently, the general law made scant provision for insolvency. There was no orderly procedure for the realization of the debtor's assets and payment of creditors on an equal footing, so that creditors had to take their chance and the Devil took the hindmost. Equally, there was little done to help the debtor ride out financial problems. In the case of *commerçants*, however, special rules evolved. Initially, the emphasis was on the protection of creditors: in the interest of commerce, it is important to ensure that business creditors are not unduly prejudiced by their debtor's insolvency, and so procedures for the winding-up of insolvent businesses were provided for by the Commercial Code. In modern times, however, the law of insolvency has seen major reforms. As we shall see in detail later,[50] the emphasis has shifted towards enabling businesses to survive their financial difficulties and, indeed, if possible to avoid insolvency altogether.

Although the existence of special procedures relating to insolvency has been a traditional hallmark of commercial law, it is to be noted that the distinction between commercial and private law is no longer as pronounced as it once was. On the one hand, the rules outlined above are no longer confined to *commerçants*: they apply equally to businesses that are not commercial (such as those of *artisans* and professionals), as well as to legal persons generally. At the same time, the legislature has introduced a number of measures to deal with the *surendettement* of private individuals. The *Code de la consommation* thus sets out a procedure for amicable composition with creditors and also allows for a judicial rescheduling of debts and for the *rétablissement personnel* of an insolvent individual.[51]

D. The Application of Commercial Law to a Party who is not a *Commerçant*

Particular difficulties can arise in determining how far commercial law should apply when a party is involved who is not a *commerçant*. There are two distinct problematic situations here. The first relates to so-called 'mixed' acts, where an act is commercial for one party involved, but civil for the other (e.g. a sale by a business to a consumer). The second situation relates to acts which are commercial for a person even though he is not a *commerçant*: acts which are commercial in form (bills of exchange) and objective ancillary acts (such as personal guarantees of commercial loans).

---

[49] Art. L 123-4 C.com.
[50] See below, pp. 476–480.
[51] See art. L 331-1 ff. C.consom.

While the application of special rules tailored to the needs of commerce is unproblematic when both parties are *commerçants*, a nuanced approach is clearly called for in respect of dealings between one party who is a *commerçant* and one who is not. It would be wrong in a consumer contract, for example, to allow the business to rely on a rule of commercial law to the prejudice of the consumer. The general approach that is adopted is to apply commercial law to the *commerçant* and the general civil law to the other party. Thus, the *commerçant* is bound by the rules of commercial proof, so that the other party can prove acts by all means; the *commerçant*, on the other hand, must observe the rules of the Civil Code.[52] Similarly, which court has jurisdiction will depend on who the defendant is: if it is the non-*commerçant* the action must be brought in a civil court, but if it is the *commerçant* the action may be brought in the commercial court.[53] In some cases, however, this 'dualist' approach is not appropriate, and a choice has to be made in favour of one rule or the other. For example, in the context of limitation periods, the ten-year commercial rule prevails.[54]

In the case of acts which are commercial for a person even though he is not a *commerçant*, in general commercial law applies so that, for example, the commercial courts have jurisdiction. However, the application of specific rules will depend on how they are framed: some apply to all commercial acts, but others apply only to *commerçants*. Thus, the rules on commercial proof only apply to *commerçants*.[55]

II. Commercial Persons[56]

As in English law, those involved in commerce come in many different guises. An individual wishing to engage in business may act on his own as a sole trader or he may combine with others in setting up some kind of business organization. A wide variety of business organizations are possible under French law, most being legal persons, i.e. having a legal personality in their own right, distinct from that of the natural persons involved. As we have seen already, some organizations are automatically considered to be *commerçants*, and their acts are deemed to be commercial acts subject to commercial law. For others, however, their character as *commerçants* derives from the nature of their activities. Before embarking

[52] Art. L 110-3 C.com.

[53] Civ. 8 May 1907, DP 1911.1.222. The non-commercial plaintiff is not compelled to sue in the commercial courts, however, and may elect to sue in the civil courts.

[54] Art. L 110-4 C.com.

[55] G. Parléani, 'Un texte anachronique: le nouvel art. 109 C.com.' D 1983 Chron. 65 (discussing the predecessor of art. L 110-3 C.com.).

[56] See M. Pédamon, *Droit commercial*, 2nd edn., pt. 1, t. 1, ch. 1. For a more detailed account, see the general works on commercial law suggested in note 1 and also (in English) J.-P. Le Gall and P. Morel, *French Company Law*, 2nd edn. (London, 1992) and (in French) P. Merle, *Droit commercial: Sociétés commerciales*, 10th edn. (Paris, 2005).

on an examination of which organizations fall into these two categories, it will be useful to outline the broad categories of legal person that may be involved in commercial activity.

A. Legal Persons Engaged in Commerce

1. Sociétés

The general term used in French law for a profit-making organization is *société*. It is generally established by a contract between two or more persons (the *associés*), although it is possible, in certain exceptional cases laid down by legislation, for it to be established by a single person,[57] and the *société* becomes a legal person through being registered. It is tempting to translate *société* as 'company', but this would in fact be misleading, for it encompasses what English lawyers would recognize as partnerships as well as companies. This is not to say that French law does not distinguish between these different types of organization: it is only natural to draw a distinction according to the nature of the participation involved, and partnerships find their equivalent in the category of *sociétés de personnes*. Nevertheless, this is simply a sub-species of the single genus, *société*, and the fact that French lawyers do not draw a sharp distinction here in the way that English lawyers do is significant, for it reflects the differing approaches the two systems have adopted historically to the question of legal personality. Although the picture has now been changed by the introduction of the limited liability partnership in 2001, in English law, the distinction between partnerships and companies has been vital because the former have traditionally not had personality, whereas the latter have. In French law, on the other hand, *sociétés de personnes* are capable of having legal personality (although this is not mandatory).

Not every *société* is involved in commerce. French law draws a distinction between civil and commercial *sociétés*, the former governed by *droit civil* and the latter by *droit commercial*. Whether a *société* is commercial, a *commerçant*, depends in part on the nature of the *société* and in part on what it does. As we have already seen, certain types of *sociétés* are commercial in form, i.e. they are automatically considered to be commercial; the rest, like natural persons, are only considered to be commercial if they engage in *actes de commerce*.

The purpose of making profits (or at least making savings through the formation of the organization)[58] is not the only requirement for a *société*. Article 1832 of the Civil Code provides that the participants must contribute assets or labour to the common enterprise; they must share in its profits and losses; and they must have an *affectio societatis*, an intention to act in common. These requirements can sometimes prove unduly restrictive in practice. Businesses may seek to pool resources

---

[57] Art. 1832 C.civ. See below, pp. 468 (SASU), 470–471 (EURL) and 469 (a *société européenne* created as a wholly-owned subsidiary).

[58] Art. 1832 C.civ., as amended by *loi* no. 78-9 of 4 January 1978.

in a project, such as joint research, which has no immediate profit-making goal, or joint activities may be embarked on which do not call for contributions of capital. In these cases, recourse must be had to a different form of collaborative structure, such as the *association* or the *groupement d'intérêt économique*.

2. Associations

The general form of non-profit making organization is the *association*. *Associations* are created for many different purposes, ranging from the charitable, the social or recreational to the political. Many *associations* will engage in commercial activities to a greater or lesser extent, either in an ancillary way (e.g. selling items as a fund-raising activity) or as a more central part of what they do. As we shall see, some difficulty has been experienced in reconciling such commercial activity with the supposed non-profit-making character of an *association*, but it has been increasingly recognized that *associations* can be subject to *droit commercial*. One disadvantage of an *association*, however, is that, while being capable of having legal personality, it does not enjoy the full rights that other moral persons do.

3. Groupements d'intérêt économique

An intermediate type of organization is the *groupement d'intérêt économique*, designed as an appropriate vehicle for collaborative projects between businesses. Its purpose is to promote the economic activities of its participants, as in the case of joint marketing or joint research projects. Its advantages are that it is free from the restrictive requirements of a *société*, such as the need for a profit-making purpose or a contribution of capital, but at the same time it has the full rights of a legal person, unlike the *association*. Not every *groupement d'intérêt économique* is involved in commerce: its character as a *commerçant* will depend on the nature of its activities.

B. Organizations that are Commercial because of their Form

Sociétés commerciales are governed by Book Two of the Commercial Code. Article L 210-1 provides that the following are commercial by virtue of their form: *sociétés en nom collectif, sociétés en commandite simple, sociétés à responsabilité limitée* and *sociétés par actions*. These can conveniently be divided into three groups: *sociétés de personnes*, which involve the coming together of individuals in a common project, where the identity of the members is important; *sociétés par actions*, where the *associés* are purely investors, contributing capital to the common undertaking and having shares which are, in principle, freely transferable; and *sociétés à responsabilité limitée*, which are a hybrid of the two.

1. Sociétés de personnes

As noted above, *sociétés de personnes* (also known as *sociétés par intérêts*) are the equivalent of English partnerships. French law recognizes three types: *sociétés en participation, sociétés en nom collectif* and *sociétés en commandite simple*. The first of these is the closest to the traditional English partnership in that it involves a collaboration between participants without the adoption of a separate legal personality for the organization. This we shall look at later, however, because, unlike the other two, it is not a *société* that is commercial in form. *Sociétés en nom collectif* (SNC) and *sociétés en commandite simple* (SCS) are both forms of partnership where the partners have sought legal personality for their enterprise. The distinction between the two lies in the degree of participation of the *associés*. In the case of a SNC, there is full participation by all: prima facie all are involved in the management of the *société* and, under article L 221-1, all are liable without limit for its debts and are personally liable to creditors. The degree of participation is so great that the partners are all *commerçants* as well as the *société* itself. Article L 222-1 provides that, in the case of the much rarer SCS, which is similar to the English limited partnership, some of the *associés* limit their participation, in the sense that their liability is limited to the amount of their investment in the undertaking. These limited members are very much 'sleeping' partners, not being involved in the management of the *société* (indeed, they are forbidden by article L 222-6 to deal with third parties on behalf of the *société*) and not being considered *commerçants*. However, there must be at least one *associé* with full participation, and such a general member will be subject to the same rules as a member of an SNC.

In both types of *société* the personality of all the *associés* is important; nevertheless, as one would expect, the personality of the limited members of a *société en commandite simple* is not seen as being as vital as that of the full members. Thus, the general rule is that no participant can assign his share in the business without the unanimous consent of the others; however, under article L 222-8, the statutes of an SCS can allow this rule to be relaxed in the case of a limited member. Similarly, subject to contrary provision in the statutes of the *société*, article L 221-15 states that the death of a member of an SNC or a full member of an SCS will terminate its existence, but under article L 222-10 the death of a limited member does not have this effect.

As already indicated, the rules governing the management of the two *sociétés* are somewhat different. Both have one or more managers (*gérants*), who have wide powers and who are subject to the control of the partners. In the case of an SNC, article L 221-3 provides that all the partners are managers, but this is subject to contrary provision in the statutes of the partnership, and in practice the management is put in the hands of a limited number of partners or possibly someone who is not even a member. In the case of an SCS, the position is similar, save that, as already noted, the limited members are not permitted to be managers.

2. Sociétés par actions

There are several different types of *société par actions* (also known as *sociétés de capitaux*). The principal form is the *société anonyme* (SA), which corresponds to the

English public limited company: all members have assignable shares and their liability is limited. Recently, however, the complexities associated with this type of *société* have led to the introduction of a simplified version, the *société par actions simplifiée* (SAS). There is also an older alternative to the *société anonyme* which was popular in the early 19th century when the formation of a *société anonyme* required government approval, but which is little used today: the *société en commandite par actions* (SCA). This is analogous to the *société en commandite simple*: there are again two distinct groups of members, one having unlimited liability and the other with limited liability. In addition, French law recognizes the new European Public Limited Company, the *societas europaea* or *société européenne* (SE).

(a) The *société anonyme* (SA)

The designation '*société anonyme*' is a reflection of the impersonal character of the members' involvement: whereas the SNC traditionally had to include the names of its members in its name, the name of an SA indicated its purpose, not its members (who would be a potentially fluctuating body).[59] The SA is the form favoured by large companies, and one of its main attractions is the fact that, in common with the SCA, an SA can 'go public', raising money by inviting the public to invest in shares or debentures. However, to be able to do this, an SA must satisfy certain criteria, and not every SA does so; and, in any event, the members may prefer to remain private. This distinction between private and public SAs is increasingly important in practice, because the latter are subject to special rules; and, it may be added, the existence of such a distinction clearly means that the standard equation of the SA with the English public limited company is not entirely accurate.

For the creation of an SA, there must be at least seven shareholders, who may be natural or moral persons.[60] During the lifetime of the *société*, the number of members may drop temporarily below this figure, but if the deficiency is not rectified within a year, any interested party can apply for the *société* to be wound up.[61] There are also restrictions with respect to the share capital of the *société*: if it is to raise money from the public, the share capital must be at least €225,000, otherwise it must be €37,000.[62]

The traditional management structure of an SA is based on the *conseil d'administration*, the equivalent of the English board of directors. Article L 225-25 of the Code provides that its members (*administrateurs*) must all be

---

[59] In modern times the distinction is not so clear-cut: the name of an SNC does not have to include the names of its *associés* (art. L 221-2 C.com.), and that of an SA may include members' names (art. L 224-1). Under the *ancien droit*, the term *société anonyme* was used to refer to *sociétés en participation*, where the anonymity was not that of the members, but of the *société* itself, for the members acted in their own names: see Hilaire, *Introduction historique au droit commercial*, 191–192 and 209–210.

[60] Art. L 225-1 C.com.

[61] Art. L 225-247 C.com.

[62] Art. L 224-2 C.com.

shareholders and article L 225-18 provides that they are elected by the share-holders' meeting. There must be at least three such *administrateurs*, and the stat-utes of the *société* may provide for as many as 18 (article L 225-17). The statutes may also provide for the appointment of worker directors, and in certain cases they are obligatory.[63] Article L 225-35 accords the *conseil* wide powers to act in the interests of the *société*. Nevertheless, the effective day-to-day management of the *société* is in the hands of the chairman (*président*) of the *conseil* or a *directeur général* appointed by the *conseil*,[64] assisted by up to five executive officers (*direct-eurs généraux délégués*).[65] The *directeur général* and the *directeurs généraux délégués* need not be members of the *conseil*.

While preserving the traditional management structure, the *loi* of 24 July 1966 introduced as an alternative a new structure which follows the model of German law.[66] Now governed by the Commercial Code, this involves a two-tier arrange-ment which draws a sharp line between those controlling and those carrying out the management of the *société*. In place of the single *conseil d'administration* there is a supervisory board (*conseil de surveillance*), similar in size to the *conseil d'administration*,[67] and a smaller executive board (*directoire*).[68] Like the members of the *conseil d'administration*, the members of the supervisory *conseil de surveil-lance* must be shareholders (article L 225-72), but since they are not involved directly in the management of the *société*, article L 225-257 provides that they can only be held personally liable for negligence in supervision. The members of the executive *directoire*, for their part, do not have to be shareholders: they are, in effect, specialist managers. The memberships of the two bodies are mutually exclusive (article L 225-74).

The majority of SAs continue to use the traditional structure. Those that adopt the new form must indicate the fact in their corporate name.[69]

The members of an SA hold transferable shares. These may take a number of forms, including preference shares (*actions de préférence*)[70] and, for loyal members who have remained with the *société* for at least two years, shares with double vot-ing rights (*actions avec droit de vote double*).[71] Given that the identity of the indi-vidual members is not critical to the success of the *société*, shares are, in principle,

---

[63] See arts. L 225-27 (optional) and 225-23 (obligatory) C.com.

[64] Art. L 225-51-1 C.com.

[65] Art. L 225-53 C.com.

[66] The German *Aktiengesellschaft* has a *Vorstand* (managing board of directors) and an *Aufsichtsrat* (supervisory board). See N. Horn, H. Kötz and H.-G. Leser, *German Private and Commercial Law: An Introduction* (Oxford, 1982), 258 *et seq.*

[67] Art. L 225-69 C.com.

[68] The rules for the size of the *directoire* vary according to the share capital of the *société* and according to whether the shares are traded on a regulated market: art. L 225-58 C.com.

[69] An SA using the new structure must be designated as a '*société anonyme à directoire et conseil de surveillance*': art. R. 123-238 C.com.

[70] Art. L 228-11 C.com., which also provides for non-voting preference shares (*actions de préférence sans droit de vote*).

[71] Art. L 225-123 C.com.

freely transferable. Nevertheless, in practice the element of personality may be reintroduced by the statutes of the SA, which may contain a *clause d'agrément* subjecting transfers to third parties to the approval of the *société*.[72] This acts as a filter for new shareholders; however, it cannot be used to lock in a member who wishes to leave: if a transfer is disapproved, the *société* must buy the shares itself or provide a third party who is willing to do so.[73] In the case of SAs traded on a regulated market, *clauses d'agrément* cannot be relied on.

(b) The *société par actions simplifiée* (SAS)

The rules governing an SA impose many restrictions, particularly for the protection of minority shareholders. The SAS was introduced in 1994[74] to provide a flexible framework for joint operations between large undertakings, which are in a position to protect themselves. In this form of organization, the statutes of the *société* can therefore determine freely how it is governed and how decisions are taken.[75] The SAS has subsequently been made more widely available and the shareholders can now be small or medium-sized businesses or individuals.[76] Since the joint ventures for which an SAS may be used involve a significant personal element, the statutes may impose certain restrictions on the transfer of shares: they can be made non-transferable for a period up to ten years, and transfers can be made subject to the agreement of the *société* (articles L 227-13 and 227-14).

Sociétés have traditionally required more than one member, but this has been relaxed in recent years and it is now possible to have an SAS with a single shareholder.[77] This is commonly referred to as a *société par actions simplifiée unipersonnelle* (SASU) and is useful, for example, for a wholly-owned subsidiary.

(c) The *société en commandite par actions* (SCA)

As with the *société en commandite simple* discussed earlier, there are two groups of members in an SCA: the *commandités*, who are fully liable for the debts of the *société*, and the *commanditeurs*, whose liability is limited. However, whereas in the case of the SCS the personality of the limited members is of some importance, justifying restrictions on the transfer of their interests in the business, the personality of the *commanditeurs* in an SCA is not of the essence, and they have freely transferable shares. The ability of the SCA to raise money from the public naturally has its advantages and enables the development of a much larger business than an SCS. As already indicated, the SCA is no longer as popular as it was in the early 19th century, having been largely superseded by the SA. Nevertheless, there are some well-known businesses that continue in this form,

---

[72] Art. L 228-23 C.com.
[73] Art. L 228-24 C.com.
[74] By *loi* no. 94-1 of 3 January 1994.
[75] See arts. L 227-5 and L 227-9 C.com.
[76] This change was made by the *loi* no. 99-587 of 12 July 1999. See now art. L 227-1 C.com.
[77] This possibility was also introduced by the *loi* of 12 July 1999. See now art. L 227-1 C.com.

including Michelin and Eurodisney, and it has seen something of a revival in recent years.

There must be at least one *commandité*. Like the full members of an SCS, the *commandités* are *commerçants* and they are jointly liable, indefinitely, for the debts of the *société*. There must be at least three *commanditaires*, who are shareholders and who have only limited liability. In addition, the SCA is subject to the same requirements as an SA as to its minimum share capital.

An SCA is managed by a *gérant*, who has a general power to act in the name of the *société*. This important figure is appointed by the general assembly of the members, but reflecting their prominent role, the appointment must have the agreement of all the *commandités*. However, the *gérant* is subject to the control of a *conseil de surveillance*, made up of at least three *commanditaires* (article L 226-4).

(d) The *societas europaea or société européenne* (SE)

As elsewhere in the European Union, the law in France makes provision for the *societas europaea* (SE), introduced by the EU Regulation on the Statute for a European Company.[78] Referred to by the Code as a *société européenne*,[79] this organization is for business activities involving more than one member state. It may be formed by the merger of SAs or equivalent foreign public limited companies; it may be a holding company created by SAs or SARLs or equivalent foreign public or private limited companies; or it may be formed as a joint subsidiary of a wide range of entities. In these cases, at least two of the founding businesses must be governed by the laws of different member states or else (except in the case of a merger) have subsidiaries or branches in different member states. Alternatively, an SE may be the result of the conversion of an SA which has a subsidiary governed by the law of another member state. An SE can also be created as a subsidiary of an existing SE.

In France, the SE is in general governed by the rules applicable to SAs.[80]

3. Sociétés à responsabilité limitée

The *société à responsabilité limitée* (SARL) is the most popular form of *société*, and it is something of a hybrid, having some of the qualities of a *société de personnes* and a *société par actions*. On the one hand, the members' shares are not freely transferable, but on the other hand they enjoy limited liability and they do not have the status of *commerçants*. Traditionally, a SARL (like any other *société*) had to have at least two members. Since the *loi* of 11 July 1985 (the '1985 *loi*'), however, sole traders have been able to incorporate themselves as a SARL and benefit from limited liability, in which case the *société* is known as an *entreprise unipersonnelle à responsabilité limitée* (EURL).

---

[78] Council Regulation 2157/2001/EC of 8 October 2001.
[79] See art. L 229-1 ff. C.com.
[80] Arts L 229-1 al. 2 and 229-7 C.com.

(a) The traditional *société à responsabilité limitée*

The *société à responsabilité limitée* is a form available to businesses both small and large.[81] However, it may have no more than 50 members (if it grows too large it must be converted into another type of *société*, typically an SA, or else be dissolved).[82] There are certain limits to the permissible activities of a SARL: for example, insurance companies and savings institutions cannot take this form.[83]

The management of a SARL is in the hands of one or more managers (*gérants*), who have extensive powers as set out in article L 223-18 of the Commercial Code. The managers, who need not be members, are appointed by the membership. Unlike the case of the SA, there is no special body monitoring the managers: they are simply under the control of the members.

Unlike the members of an SA, the members of a SARL do not have freely negotiable *actions*. A member may assign his share in the *société*, but only subject to limitations. Transfers to someone who is not already a member generally require the consent of a majority of the membership who must hold between them at least half of the capital of the *société* (article L 223-14). But, as where a *clause d'agrément* figures in the statutes of an SA, this requirement of consent cannot be used to lock an unwilling member in. If consent is refused, the other members must find a buyer or buy his share themselves, or else reduce the capital of the *société*. By contrast, subject to restrictions imposed by the statutes of the *société*, transfers can be made freely by one member to another (article L 223-16) or by one member to his or her spouse, ascendants or descendants (article L 223-13).

(b) The *entreprise unipersonnelle à responsabilité limitée* (EURL)[84]

French law has traditionally seen a *société* as founded on a contract, and therefore as requiring more than one member. Unlike in English law, therefore, the sole trader could not incorporate his business and benefit from limited liability. This was all changed by the 1985 *loi*, which altered the basic definition of a *société* in article 1832 of the Civil Code and made provision for a SARL with only one member. In general, this *entreprise unipersonnelle à responsabilité limitée* is governed by the same rules as apply to the traditional form of SARL. Nevertheless there are some necessary modifications: thus, the provisions relating to shareholders' meetings do not apply.[85]

In practice, the EURL has found only limited popularity. In part, this is because the limited liability achieved by incorporation is compromised by the fact that institutions making loans to an EURL will usually require the single

---

[81] There used to be a minimum share capital requirement, but this restriction was removed by *loi* no. 2003-721 of 1 August 2003: see art. L 223-2 C.com.

[82] Art. L 223-3 C.com.

[83] Art. L 223-1 C.com.

[84] See P. Serlooten, 'L'entreprise unipersonnelle à responsabilité limitée' D 1985 Chron. 187; J.-J. Daigre, 'La société unipersonnelle en droit français' (1990) RIDC 665.

[85] Art. L 223-31 C.com.

member to provide a personal guarantee. In addition, the single member will usually be the *gérant* and will therefore be personally liable as such notwithstanding the limited liability of the *société*.

C. Organizations that are Commercial because of their Activities

1. Sociétés *without a commercial form*

Sociétés which are not commercial in form may nevertheless be commercial by virtue of their activities.[86]

The category of *sociétés* which may or may not be commercial includes the *société en participation* (SP), which, as noted earlier, is the equivalent of the traditional English partnership. The SP, which is governed by article 1871 of the Civil Code, lacks legal personality, but it remains a flexible business structure. No special form is laid down for an SP. The partners must each make a contribution to the common venture, but as an SP has no personality, it cannot own property and in general the partners therefore retain ownership of what they contribute.[87] Partners deal with third parties in their own name, and the others will not be bound unless they act openly as a partnership.[88]

2. Groupements d'intérêt économique *(GIE)*

The *groupement d'intérêt économique* (GIE) was first introduced into French law in 1967.[89] As noted earlier, this provides a more flexible framework for attaining the benefits of legal personality without having to satisfy the strict requirements for a *société*, such as the contribution by each *associé* of assets or labour to the common enterprise.

As its name suggests, the purpose of a GIE must be economic. The purpose is not, however, to make profits for itself: rather, it is 'to facilitate or develop the economic activity of its members', and to do this as an auxiliary to the members' activity rather than as the primary manifestation of it.[90] It thus provides a means for individuals or organizations to set up joint research or marketing activities, and it has proved a successful device, having been used for high profile ventures such as the Airbus and the *carte bleue* (a credit card organization). Not every economic activity is commercial, however: a GIE can be used for civil purposes, such as the promotion of agricultural activity. Whether a GIE is a *commerçant* will depend on whether it engages in *actes de commerce*, and there is no presumption that it is commercial.[91]

---

[86] Art. L 210-1 C.com.
[87] Art. 1872 C.civ. In the case of money held in common, the managers will owe the partner the amount of the contribution.
[88] Art. 1872-1 C.civ. In that case, they will be jointly and severally liable if the SP is commercial.
[89] By *ordonnance* no. 67-821 of 23 September 1967. See now art. L 251-1 ff. C.com.
[90] Art. L 251-1 C.com.
[91] Art. L 251-4 C.com. and above p. 454 ff.

The position of the members of a GIE is similar to that of members of an SNC: they are personally liable for the debts of the *groupement* without limit[92] and their participation is considered to be personal in character. Thus, their shares in the *groupement* are not freely assignable and cannot be represented by negotiable certificates. The extent to which existing members can leave the organization and new members join it is determined by its statutes.

3. Groupements européens d'intérêt économique *(GEIE)*

In 1985, with a view to encouraging cooperation between businesses in different member states, the Council of the European Communities enacted Regulation 2137/85 of 25 July 1985 providing for a new entity, the *groupement européen d'intérêt économique* (GEIE). Very similar to the existing French GIE, the GEIE has the distinctive feature that, by virtue of its registration in any one member state, it can have full legal personality in all. This Regulation came into effect in 1989, and the measures necessary for its full implementation in France were contained in the *loi* of 13 June 1989, now incorporated into the Commercial Code.[93]

Although the purpose of a GEIE is defined in the same way as that of a GIE, there are a number of differences between the two organizations. To begin with, the European character of the GEIE is reflected in several requirements. Thus, its members must be natural persons carrying out a professional activity in the European Union or moral persons having their registered or statutory office and their central administration in the Union; and, since the GEIE was invented to enhance cross-border cooperation, the members must be drawn from at least two member states. Moreover the registered office of the GEIE must be situated in a member state.

There are also additional restrictions on the size and funding of the GEIE. It must have no more than 500 employees, and it may not invite investment by the public. On the other hand, unlike the GIE, the GEIE can be set up for an indefinite period.

4. Associations[94]

The principal forms of *association* are those governed by the *loi* of 1 July 1901. As noted earlier, although these *associations* are intended to be non-profit-making, in practice many do in fact supply goods or services for profit. In some cases, this profit-making is only incidental to the main purpose of the *association*, as where a voluntary organization raises funds by selling publications or other articles. This limited kind of profit-making poses no real difficulty, being discounted as being

---

[92] Art. L 251-6 C.com.
[93] Art. L 252-1ff C.com.
[94] See O. Simon, 'La commercialité de l'association du 1er juill. 1901' D 1977 Chron. 153; M. Pédamon, *Droit commercial*, paras. 112 *et seq.*

merely ancillary to the main (civil) purpose of the *association*.[95] The real difficulties arise, however, when the profit-making activity becomes regular. According to the general criteria for applying *droit commercial*, one would think that such activity would then be classified as commercial, but there is the added complication of reconciling such a classification with the supposed non-profit-making character of an *association*. It has indeed been argued that a profit-making organization should be regarded as a *société*, requiring registration as such to achieve legal personality. The dominant view, however, puts weight on the fact that the *loi* of 1 July 1901 only forbids the *distribution* of profits to the members of the *association*, and it is accepted that, provided this prohibition is respected, an *association* can properly engage in commerce. In line with this view, the courts have come to accept the application of *droit commercial*. Thus, for example, the commercial rules of proof were applied to the Moslem Institute of the Paris Mosque, an *association*, in a dispute relating to a shop that it had set up to sell meat slaughtered in accordance with Islamic precepts.[96] However, it is held that an *association* cannot be registered as a *commerçant*, not because they cannot be *commerçants*, but because only organizations that are required to register can do so, and there is no such requirement for *associations*.[97]

III. Commercial Property

A. The *Fonds de Commerce*

A distinctive feature of French commercial law is the *fonds de commerce*. This embraces the various movable assets of a business. However, the *fonds de commerce* is not simply a convenient collective term to describe the property of a business, in the way that 'assets', for example, is in English. The *fonds* is conceived of as a form of property in its own right, over and above the individual assets that make it up, and since the *loi Cordelet* of 17 March 1909 it has had its own distinctive legal regime dealing with its sale or use as a security.[98]

The *fonds de commerce* is a dynamic concept, in the sense that it refers not simply to a collection of assets, but to assets in use, directed to the common goal of serving the customers of the business. The clientele are thus fundamental to the *fonds*. Accordingly, a *fonds de commerce* will not come into being until the business has commenced trading, and a business that has ceased to trade and no longer has customers will cease to have a *fonds* distinct from its individual assets.[99] More specifically, the clientele must be real and certain, rather than merely potential,[100]

---

[95] Com. 13 May 1970, D 1970.644 note X.L.
[96] Com. 17 March 1981, D 1983.23.
[97] See, for example, Com. 1 Mar. 1994, D 1994.528, note Coutant.
[98] Referred to as *nantissement du fonds du commerce*.
[99] Civ. (3) 18 May 1978, Bull. civ. III, no. 205; RDC 1978, 559 obs. Derruppé.
[100] e.g., Com. 27 Feb. 1973, D 1974.283 note Derruppé.

and the customers must be personal to the business.[101] In addition, the clientele must be licit, excluding, for example, the case of an unauthorized gaming house.

Being made up of movable assets, the *fonds de commerce* is itself regarded as a species of movable property. However, although many of its components may be tangible assets, it is itself treated as intangible property. The disposition of a *fonds* will generally[102] be an *acte commercial* and will be subject to the jurisdiction of the commercial courts.

B. The Components of the *Fonds de Commerce*

The *fonds* can be made up of a variety of different types of property. The Commercial Code[103] identifies certain obvious tangible assets, plant and equipment (*matériel*) and stock (*marchandises*), together with a number of intangible assets, the name and logo of the business, its rights to its leased commercial premises (*droit au bail*), industrial property rights, such as patents (*brevets*), trade marks (*marques de fabrique, de commerce ou de service*), models and designs, and literary or artistic property rights. It is generally agreed, however, that this list is not exhaustive; and the detailed composition of any specific *fonds* will naturally vary according to the nature of the business. Be that as it may, there is one clear limit: the *fonds* will not include any form of immovable property which the business may own. It may be added that there is some controversy as to the precise status of the clientele in this context: although its existence is clearly of fundamental importance to the existence of the *fonds* itself, there is some debate as to whether it is actually an element of the *fonds*, in the way that goodwill is part of the assets of a business in English law.

Where, as is commonly the case, a business leases its premises, the lease will be a significant element within the *fonds de commerce*. It will be an asset of not inconsiderable economic value, but it will also have considerable practical importance, for the ability to operate from a settled location is generally vital to the maintenance of a clientele. This practical concern has led to the creation of a special legal regime for commercial leases (*les baux commerciaux*), which distinguishes them from other leases and gives them a particular interest in the study of French commercial law.[104]

Originally, commercial leases were subject to the general law, which meant that, when a lease expired, the owner was free to evict the tenant without

---

[101] e.g. Ass. plén. 24 Apr. 1970, D 1970.381 note R.L.; JCP 1970.II.16489 note Boccara.

[102] For discussion of the view that such a disposition is automatically a commercial act, even if, for example, it is being sold by a private individual who has simply inherited the business, see M. Pédamon, *Droit commercial*, 2nd edn., para. 217.

[103] See arts. L. 141-5 and 142-2 C.com.

[104] It should be noted, however, the special protection afforded to commercial leases has in fact been extended in a rather piecemeal fashion to leases held by certain persons other than *commerçants*, such as *artisans*: see arts. L 145-1 and 145-2 C.com.

compensation and without offering a renewal of the lease. Special rules for the protection of commercial tenants were gradually introduced from 1926 onwards, and the law was reformed and codified by a *décret* of 30 September 1953, which has since been incorporated into the Commercial Code.[105] The position now is that, provided that certain conditions are satisfied, a tenant has the right to have the lease renewed or to be paid an indemnity (*indemnité d'éviction*), and there are controls over the length of leases, as well as provisions for the review of rents.

A business cannot claim the protection of the special rules on commercial leases unless the lease forms part of its *fonds de commerce*. Thus, the lease of a business which does not have a *fonds* because it does not satisfy the requirements as to clientele is not protected.[106] Furthermore, the protection only extends to leases of premises to which customers have access and not to accessory premises, such as storage facilities, unless their location is essential to the business. Thus, a driving school's lease of a garage to keep its cars in has been held not to be protected.[107]

A tenant's first lease of premises is not necessarily protected. Provided that this initial lease is restricted to no more than two years, the parties are free to derogate in whole or in part from the special regime.[108] Nevertheless, if the lease is renewed or if the tenant is simply left in possession at its expiry without protest on the part of the landlord, a protected tenancy will come into being.

Article L 145-4 of the Code aims to promote the stability of businesses by providing that the minimum duration of a protected commercial lease is nine years. This rule is *d'ordre public* and cannot be excluded by contract. However, there is a certain amount of flexibility, particularly in favour of a commercial tenant. Unless the parties agree otherwise, such a tenant has the opportunity every three years to give notice, and he can give notice at any time in the event of retirement or invalidity. The landlord, on the other hand, although able to give notice to quit every three years, can do so only for limited reasons, such as for the purposes of building works.

The parties are free to fix the initial rent payable. At the end of every three-year period, either party can then request a revision of the rent. If they cannot agree on a new rent, it will be determined by the courts.[109]

At the expiry of the lease, the tenant has the right to have the lease renewed or to be paid an indemnity.[110] This right is generally described, no doubt rather loosely, as the tenant's *propriété commerciale*. If the lease is renewed, it will be for a period of at least nine years and the parties must agree on a new rent, in default of which one will be set by the courts. If, on the other hand, the landlord refuses to renew, the tenant is generally entitled to an indemnity for any harm suffered, such as the costs

---

[105] Art. L 145-1 ff. C.com.
[106] e.g. Ass. plén. 24 Apr. 1970, D 1970.381 note R.L.
[107] Com. 4 Dec. 1967, D 1968 Somm. 33.
[108] Art. L 145-5 C.com.
[109] Art. L 145-37 and art. R. 145-20 C.com.
[110] Arts. L 145-8 ff. C.com.

of relocating to other premises or the diminution in the value of the business. But the landlord will not be obliged to pay an indemnity if he has good cause for not renewing the lease, as where the tenant has been in breach of his obligations.

IV. Businesses in Difficulty[111]

Special procedures dealing with insolvency have been a traditional hallmark of French commercial law. The modern law, however, is concerned not only with managing insolvency, but also with facilitating and even imposing solutions to financial problems before a business becomes insolvent. The relevant provisions in the modern Commercial Code focus therefore on 'businesses in difficulty' (*entreprises en difficultés*). They begin with procedures designed to prevent difficulties and then pass on to deal with a series of procedures, commonly referred to as *procédures collectives*, involving judicial imposed solutions to financial difficulties, both before and after the onset of insolvency.

As noted earlier, the modern procedures are not confined to *commerçants*. The detail of how they apply will vary according to the nature of the procedure, but in general they apply equally to *artisans* and they apply broadly to moral persons of all kinds.

A. Procedures Designed to Prevent Difficulties

The strategy of the law relating to the prevention of difficulties is effectively two-fold: to ensure that those in charge of a business are alerted to problems and to allow the business to negotiate its way out of its problems by reaching an amicable settlement with its creditors.

The purpose of a warning procedure (*procédure d'alerte*) is to inform those in charge of the business that there are problems and to compel them to address them. The procedure can be initiated by a number of persons or bodies. It can take the form of an intervention from outside the business. Thus, under article L 611-2 of the Code, in the case of a commercial *société*, a *groupement d'intérêt économique* or a business run by a *commerçant* or an *artisan*, the president of the commercial court can sound an alert (perhaps because of actions brought against the business). In this case, the management will be summoned to discuss the difficulties being faced by the business. In most cases, however, the procedure will be essentially an internal affair, set in motion by the auditor of the business (*commissaire aux comptes*)[112] or by

---

[111] For a useful introduction to this topic, see M. Jeantin and P. Le Cannu, *Droit commercial: Entreprises en difficulté*, 7th edn. (Paris, 2007).

[112] This is dealt with by diverse provisions in the Code: arts. L 234-1 (*sociétés anonymes*), L 234-2 (other commercial *sociétés*), L 251-15 (*groupements d'intérêt économiques*) and L 612-3 (other moral persons having an economic activity and *associations* or public bodies of a commercial or industrial character in receipt of public funds).

its workers' committee (*comité d'entreprise*).[113] The detail of how these internal procedures operate will vary according to the structure of the business and the person sounding the alert. Suffice it to say that, if satisfactory responses are not forthcoming from the management of the business, the concerns raised may be transmitted to the shareholders or other members.

The Code also establishes a framework for a business facing difficulties to reach an amicable settlement (*conciliation*)[114] with at least its principal creditors. If they see fit, those in charge of the management of the business can apply to the president of the court[115] to allow an amicable settlement to be attempted, identifying the problems they face and outlining how these might be countered. If the president accedes to this request (which he generally will do unless the business is already insolvent),[116] he will appoint a conciliator (*conciliateur*) who will oversee and promote negotiations between the business and its creditors. If a settlement is agreed, this may simply be reported to the court or the court may be asked to approve it.[117] Although in principle a settlement is a contractual matter, an approved settlement (*accord homologué*) can have effects on third parties. Thus, those who provide the business with credit under the settlement or agree to new contracts to supply it with goods or services are given priority if there is a turn for the worse and *procédures collectives* are commenced.[118]

B. *Procédures Collectives*

1. *Protection proceedings* (sauvegarde)

The *sauvegarde* procedure, the first of the *procédures collectives* dealt with by the Code, is in fact the most recent, the centrepiece of reforms in 2005.[119] Inspired by Chapter 11 proceedings in the United States and similar procedures adopted elsewhere in Europe, *sauvegarde* is available to a business which is not yet insolvent and provides it with protection from its creditors while a plan is drawn up to

---

[113] Art. L 432-5 C.trav. (in the revised Code, taking effect by 1 March 2008 at the latest, see art. L 2323-78 ff). If there is no committee, the alert can be given by the delegates of the workforce (*délégués du personnel*): art. L 422-4 C.trav. (in the revised Code, see art. L 2313-14). For the role of these generally see below pp. 504, 506–507.

[114] Prior to the reforms made by *loi* no. 2005-845 of 26 July 2005, this procedure was referred to as *règlement amiable*.

[115] If the business is commercial or engages in the activities of an *artisan*, the relevant court is the commercial court (art. L 611-4 C.com), otherwise it is the *tribunal de grande instance* (art. L 611-5).

[116] If the business is discovered to be insolvent, the president can *ex officio* start insolvency proceedings: arts. L 631-5 and 640-5 C.com.

[117] Art. L 611-8 C.com.

[118] Art. L 611-11 C.com. The suppliers or lenders are described as having a *privilège de conciliation*.

[119] As to which, see P. Omar, 'French insolvency law and the 2005 reforms' (2005) 16 ICCLR 490.

keep the business going. On application by the business,[120] the court[121] will normally make an order commencing proceedings (*jugement d'ouverture*), the effect of which will be to prevent most creditors from bringing or enforcing claims against the business.[122] The court will appoint a judge to act as *juge-commissaire*, overseeing what is done, as well as a *mandataire judiciaire* to represent the interests of the creditors. There will then follow an observation period[123] during which the state of the business will be examined and a restructuring plan will be drawn up, if possible, under which the business can continue.[124] The procedure followed will vary according to the size of the business. In the case of larger businesses, the court must appoint a judicial administrator (*administrateur judiciaire*) who will produce a report on the state of the business and in the light of that draw up proposals for a restructuring plan.[125] Small businesses,[126] on the other hand, are subject to a simpler procedure:[127] the court is given a choice as to whether an administrator is to be appointed; if no such appointment is made, proposals for what is to be done are drawn up by the management and the *juge-commissaire* reports to the court, giving a reasoned opinion on them. The final decision as to the fate of the business is taken by the court after hearing representations from interested parties. If a plan is approved, the court will appoint an official to ensure that it is carried out (*commissaire à l'exécution du plan*).[128]

2. Redressement judiciaire

Redressement judiciaire is the counterpart of *sauvegarde* for insolvent businesses and is similar to it in many respects,[129] including in protection against creditors.[130] There are, however, important differences. Unlike with *sauvegarde*, proceedings can be instituted not only by the business,[131] but also by any creditor, by the *Procureur de la République* or by the court itself acting *ex officio*.[132] The same provisions relating to the length of the observation

---

[120] Art. L 620-1 C.com.

[121] The commercial court has jurisdiction in relation to a *commerçant* or an *artisan*, but otherwise the relevant court is the *tribunal de grande instance*: art. L 621-2 C.com.

[122] Art. L 622-21 C.com.

[123] The maximum duration of the observation period is normally six months (art. L 621-3 C.com.), but the court has the power to extend it.

[124] Cf. art. L 620-1 C.com.

[125] Arts L 621-4 and 623-1-623-3 C.com. On the plan, see art. L 626-1 ff.

[126] Defined by arts. L 621-4 and R. 621-11 C.com. as those having less than 20 employees and having a turnover below €3m.

[127] See arts. L 627-1–627-4 C.com.

[128] Art. L 626-25 C.com.

[129] See, for example, art. L 631-9 C.com., applying inter alia the rules in art. L 621-4 relating to the *jugement d'ouverture* and the appointment of the *juge-commissaire*, the *mandataire judiciaire* and the *administrateur judiciaire*.

[130] Art. L 631-14 C.com.

[131] The business is indeed obliged to petition within 45 days of becoming insolvent: art. L 631-4 C.com.

[132] Art. L 631-5 C.com.

apply,[133] but they are qualified by the requirement for the court to give a ruling within two months as to whether the business has sufficient resources to allow the observation period to continue.[134] The plan that is produced may involve a simple restructuring of the business, but it would appear that it may equally involve its sale.[135]

3. *Winding up* (liquidation)

The final *procédure collective*, and ideally the last resort, is *liquidation*. It will commonly be instituted where an attempted *sauvegarde* or *redressement judiciaire* has failed, but exceptionally it may be initiated without any preliminary stage if the business is in an obviously hopeless state.

The court will appoint a liquidator (*liquidateur*) whose task it is to realize the assets of the business and to pay its creditors. This can be a lengthy process, but since 2005 a fast-track procedure has been available for small businesses.[136] There may be many claims on the business and, as in English law, some will have priority over others.[137] The ranking of claims is too complex a matter to go into in detail here. In outline, however, there are four groups of creditors. At the bottom of the pile are the ordinary unsecured creditors of the business (*créanciers chirographaires*); ahead of them come secured creditors (*créanciers hypothécaires*); and ahead of them are the so-called privileged creditors (*créanciers privilégiés*). The first to be paid, however, are the workforce who, at least in respect of certain claims (principally for pay for the preceding 60 days),[138] are said to have a *superprivilège*.

The effect of winding-up on the insolvent person will depend on the nature of the latter. In the case of natural persons (such as an individual trader), the final court order that brings the winding-up to an end extinguishes all claims against the business,[139] so that the businessman can then carry on his life without fear of being pursued by unsatisfied creditors. However, as we shall see below, his future activities may be restricted if he has been guilty of misconduct. In the case of a moral person (such as a *société*), the effects of winding-up are more far-reaching: article 1844-7 of the Civil Code provides that, as soon as the winding-up order is made, it will cease to exist.

A number of measures are available to deal with insolvent individuals and directors of insolvent moral persons where they have been guilty of misconduct. The court has the power to make directors liable for the debts of an insolvent moral

[133] Art. L 631-7 C.com.
[134] Art. L 631-15 C.com.
[135] On the obscurities of the legislative texts, see M. Jeantin and P. Le Cannu, *Droit commercial: Entreprises en difficulté*, para. 992 ff.
[136] Arts. L 641-2 and 644-1–644-6 C.com.
[137] See art. 2323 ff C.civ. and art. L 641-13 C.com.
[138] Art. L 143-10 C.trav. (in the revised Code, taking effect by 1 March 2008 at the latest, see art. L 3253-2).
[139] Art. L 643-11 C.com.

person.[140] Both directors and insolvent individuals can be declared subject to personal bankruptcy (*faillite personnelle*), which entails certain civic and legal disabilities and means that they cannot be involved in the management of a business (directly or indirectly).[141] Alternatively, they can simply be deprived of their right to manage.[142] They may also be found guilty of criminal offences, including criminal bankruptcy (*banqueroute*).[143]

---

[140] Arts L 651-1 and 651-2 C.com.
[141] Arts. L 653-1–653-7 C.com.
[142] Art. L 653-8 C.com.
[143] Art. L 654-1 ff C.com.

PART II

(D) BEYOND THE PUBLIC LAW/PRIVATE LAW DICHOTOMY

12

Employment Law*

I. Introduction

In the chapter of the first edition of this work dedicated to employment law—essentially *droit du travail*—I pursued a theme and presented an argument about French law rather than conducting a systematic survey of it. My theme was the location of *le droit du travail* in relation to the distinction between public and private law. The argument was that French employment law straddles that distinction more extensively, indeed more fundamentally, than is admitted by its practitioners and even its theorists, who are still rather committed to a strongly institutionalized form of that distinction, and who therefore tend to place it firmly in the domain of private law.

That argument was and continues to be controversial and debatable; it is of course intended to be a provocative one. It obliges the editors of this work to place it, even to isolate it, in a special division of the part of the book which is devoted to substantive law, a division cautiously titled 'Beyond the public law/private law dichotomy?'. It also has the particular effect of conferring upon this chapter the character of an essay, a synoptic overview of its topic; and this in turn makes it especially difficult to tamper with the text of the original chapter without disrupting the development of its essential argument. It was this factor which suggested the approach to be taken to rewriting the chapter for this second edition, the approach being rather partial and limited in its scope, essentially preserving the original essay though with some revision and updating. This stemmed from a view that the most coherent outcome might be obtained by preserving the main argument of the original version more or less intact, and by then adding a conclusion which gives an account of the main developments, both theoretical and practical, which need to be superimposed upon the original argument.

There is a further factor or argument which supports this particular approach; it is a somewhat paradoxical one, but when writing about French law one may

* In revising this chapter for this new edition, I have benefited greatly from discussions with Muriel Fabre-Magnan, Nicola Kountouris, Alain Supiot, and Christophe Vigneau, which have afforded important insights. I must emphasize that the errors, omissions, and infelicities which no doubt remain are entirely my own responsibility. MRF.

allow oneself occasionally to invoke a paradox. The point here is that French employment law has recently entered an acute phase of rapid and probably quite fundamental change; it is felt that nothing less than *un bouleversement* (a complete overturning of the existing order) is in the course of occurring. This will be detailed in the conclusion; but it is worth saying at this point that this sense of *bouleversement* has been heightened, though not by any means solely engendered, by the recent Presidential Election of 2007.

At all events, experience of writing and updating legal texts suggests that the worst moment at which to revolutionize a text is the one at which radical changes in the law are confidently predicted to occur in the immediate future. Sometimes such predicted changes do not occur at all; more often, they occur in a somewhat different form from that which had been confidently expected; more often still, their impact quickly turns out to be quite different from that which had been foretold. So the text which follows is essentially the original one, lightly updated where it is necessary to do so, and followed and concluded by a more tentative *mise à jour* which tries to understand and summarize the work on French employment law which is in progress on the part both of the lawmakers and the commentators.

II. Public or Private Law?

Those embarking upon the study of employment law quickly come to realize, if they had not done so even before opening a single book on the subject, that it is a highly political or politicized legal subject whose boundaries and purposes are more hotly contested than with most legal subjects. In this, French employment law is no different from that of the United Kingdom or other European countries. What is, perhaps, special to the French system is the extent to which one can express those difficulties, or at least focus upon them, by locating the subject in relation to the distinction between public law and private law.

At first sight, it will no doubt seem strange to suggest that there can be a complex or specially significant application of the distinction between public and private law to French employment law. After all, as we have seen earlier in this book, the distinction is so fundamental to the whole structure of French law, to the way in which French law is developed and expounded, that we should expect its application to employment law to have been long since resolved so decisively as to make that issue quite uncontentious and uninteresting.

At one level, there are indeed simple and unequivocal answers to this question. Employment law is seen as a part of private law; the professors who expound the subject, and the texts which they produce, are categorized as such. It follows, or is an associated fact, that employment law, as a private law subject, cannot be applicable to public employees. They are subject to a wholly separate regime, which is part of public law. As both regimes are codified, all this is quite clear and evident. The private law regime, which constitutes the subject of employment law (*droit du travail*), is codified in the *Code du travail*. The separate regime applicable to public employees, which is part of public law and not part of employment law, is codified in the *Code de la fonction publique*. They are separate territories, and employment law is firmly placed in the land of private law.

At another level, however, there are good reasons for regarding the position as much more complicated, and the public/private distinction as much more difficult to apply, so that a legal system such as the French one which insists on treating the public/private distinction as a fundamental one, even as an absolute one, comes under increasing stress in the employment sphere. As the politics and the practicalities of the labour market and the employment situation become increasingly volatile, those tensions are increased. There are great pressures to reformulate the application of the public/private distinction to employment law in response to these changes. By analysing those pressures, we can perhaps appreciate the dynamics of employment law in France at the present day. We need to do this in two different dimensions. First, we should ask, what are the pressures on the confining of French employment law to private sector workers. Secondly, even more significantly, we should ask what are the pressures on regarding French employment law as having an essentially private law subject matter.

If we look, then, at the public/private distinction in French employment law first in terms of the *persons covered*, we find an obvious and progressive breakdown of the earlier certainties. The original or ideal position was that employed workers could be neatly divided into workers under private law contracts of employment (*salariés*) and public employees (*fonctionnaires*), and that those in the former category were within the province of employment law while those in the latter were not, because they were subject to a quite distinct public law regime. This state of affairs, if it ever in practice existed in a pure and simple form, was crucially affected by the enormous growth in the public sector of the French economy, which was progressive through the first three-quarters of the present century but especially strong in the period 1945–75. Even if this tendency was arrested after 1975 and started to go into reverse after 1990, it has still remained a major determinant of the shape of the labour market in France.

This resulted, in particular, in the fact that very large numbers of people came to be employed not only in the service of central or local government, but also in other organizations or enterprises which were either publicly owned or publicly controlled or engaged in carrying out a public service. In relation to those latter groups of workers, there evolved special regimes, for example in respect of the *services publics en régie*, or in respect of the *établissements publics à caractère industriel et commercial*, which were based partly on the *Code de la fonction publique* on the one hand; but partly, on the other hand, on the *Code du travail*. It became conventional to recognize that workers with an intermediate status of this kind were within the scope of employment law,[1] though not everybody recognized the extent to which this kind of convergence threatened the simple classification of employment law as a private law subject.[2]

More recent developments in the labour market and in employment relations have intensified the problems about the classification of employment law in public or private terms, not just with regard to the persons covered by employment law, but also with regard to *the content and character of employment law*. The recent developments in question, not pushed quite as far in France as in the United Kingdom, but nevertheless significant enough, consist in a sort of general re-contractualization of employment relationships, a reassertion of the employers' interest in flexibility, freedom of manoeuvre and managerial control in employment relationships, and of the importance to employers of being free to use the contract of employment to achieve those goals.

One way to analyse the effect on employment law of these changes in employment practice would be to see them as achieving a simple reversal of the trend of employment law in relation to the public/private distinction. That is to say, whereas we might see the earlier growth in importance of the public sector as causing a certain convergence of employment law towards the approaches and attitudes of public law, we might correspondingly wish to see the enlarged size and renewed vigour of the private sector, with all its values and assumptions, as resulting in a simple reassertion of the private law content and character of employment law.

This might, however, amount to a misinterpretation of, or at least to the begging of a set of questions about, the sense in which employment law belongs to and forms part of the realm of private law in France. There are two main different hypotheses to explain this relationship, the liberal hypothesis and the protective hypothesis. Both hypotheses assert that the connecting link between employment law and private law is via the contract of employment; but the linking role of the contract of employment is seen as crucially different in each hypothesis. On the liberal hypothesis, the central function of employment law is to contribute to the general liberal project of private law of validating and implementing an appropriate set of voluntary private agreements, in this case the category of legally recognized contracts of employment.

On the protective hypothesis, however, the contract of employment forms the point of departure for employment law rather than its point of destination. That is to say, the subordination of the employee which forms the central attribute or identifying feature of the contract of employment provides the rationale, not so much for the validation and enforcement of that contract, but rather for its

---

[1] See Despax and Rojot, para. 18.

[2] There are exceptions. Javillier in the introductory part of his manual, *Droit du travail*, on 'La dynamique du droit du travail' devoted chapter 2 to 'Le dualisme du droit du travail', that being a duality between on the one hand *les salariés* and on the other hand *les fonctionnaires et agents publics*.

location in a framework of protection of those interests of the worker which are identified as inderogable or inalienable, such as the interest in certain minimum guarantees of health and safety, and welfare at work.

The choice between these two alternative, indeed ultimately contrasting, hypotheses turns out to tell us important things about the public or private character of French employment law. On the first, liberal, hypothesis, employment law can be viewed not just as part of private law, but also as part of the general civil law applicable, for instance, to all types of contracts mutatis mutandis. On the second, protective hypothesis, however, it becomes more important to maintain the *autonomy* of employment law, precisely so that its protective prescriptions are not submerged beneath the broad voluntarism of the general civil law.

This leads to an important next step; for we find that this claim to the autonomy of employment law is generally associated with the idea of employment law as a species of social law (*droit social*), and as such sustained by an underlying notion of social public order (*ordre public social*). Thus, it could be said 20 years ago (speaking specifically of French labour law) that:

Labour Law more than any other branch of law is an aspect of public order. But here the notion of public order takes on a particular colour: social public order is totally oriented towards the improvement of the conditions of life and work of workers.[3]

Current commentators are less inclined to envisage *ordre public social* as permeating French labour law,[4] perhaps reflecting the decline of the political commitment to mandatory or inderogable legislative labour standards having as their sole purpose the special protection of subordinated workers. Moreover, neither in the past nor in the present has it been admitted by French legal theorists that the presence of the element of *ordre public* in and of itself locates the law in question within the sphere of public law in a strict technical sense. However, we can still conclude that notion of *ordre public social* still significantly associates employment law with public law in the broader sense of that term.

The question whether that is the right or best way to understand the fundamentals of French employment law is no mere academic one. There can be few issues more central to the relationship between law and politics than that of whether the regulation of the employment relationship is developed in the public, constitutional, and social sphere on the one hand, or, in the private, commercial and economic sphere on other. Obviously the reality will turn out to be that both perspectives are to some degree involved; the vital question, which should serve as a prior and general test to be applied to the more detailed descriptions

---

[3] Despax and Rojot, para. 35, attributed by them to Camerlynck and Gérard Lyon-Caen.

[4] Compare, for example, Pélissier, Supiot, and Jeammaud, para. 849: 'French labour law is no longer characterized in the same way by the major role played by the notion of "social public order".'

which follow, is which perspective is the dominant one.[5] It will be useful for British readers, having read this chapter, to ask themselves the question, is French employment law, for all its apparent classification as a private law subject, actually more or less influenced by public law than is the employment law of the United Kingdom?

III. The Sources of French Employment Law and their Hierarchical Relationship

A. Introduction

As we have seen earlier in this book, the exegesis of French law typically involves a systematic analysis of its sources, and a more careful arrangement of those sources in hierarchical order than British readers would generally expect. The *doctrine* of French employment law is no exception. This is not to say that the establishing of the hierarchical order is a straightforward or obvious process as far as employment law is concerned. On the contrary, it not only reveals the tensions about the distribution of normative power which are experienced in most if not all employment law systems, but it actually heightens those tensions to the extent that it requires definitive answers to questions of relative power which can receive more ambiguous answers in legal systems, such as that of the United Kingdom, which do not insist on hierarchical rankings at all or at least so rigorously.

Note, however, that we say, 'to the extent that'; for we should not suppose that the exponents of French employment law, merely because of their perceived duty to think about sources in hierarchical terms, have reached final agreement about the hierarchy of norm-making in employment relations. In particular, as we shall see, large questions remain about the relative normative power of the state and the judges on the one hand, and, on the other hand, the social partners, that is the employers and the workforce especially when operating through the medium of collective bargaining. The following summary eloquently hints at the subtleties, and at the ideological confrontations, which we may expect to encounter in considering how the hierarchy of sources is worked out in practice:

The classical question of the hierarchy of sources nevertheless appears in Labour Law in one very specific respect. It is not so much a question of checking whether the various provisions fit together but of arriving through a combination of sources at a solution able to ensure a social progress in the most efficient way.[6]

---

[5] This is, in effect, the set of questions posed by G. Lyon-Caen, *Le droit du travail—Une technique réversible* (Paris, 1995) a most useful *tour d'horizon* of the state of French employment law at that time.

[6] Despax and Rojot, para. 32.

B. International Law

At various points, we find highly interesting comparisons and contrasts with the treatment of comparable problems in British employment law. We find this right at the top of the hierarchy, where international law is situated (in a sort of complex parallelogram with the French Constitution, in which it is debatable whether the one is hierarchically superior to the other).[7] French employment law is determined in important ways by France's membership of the International Labour Organization (ILO), by adherence to the constitution of the ILO, and by the ILO Conventions which France has ratified.[8] No less significant is the impact of European Community law, the point having been reached where the employment law of any member state of the European Union has to be understood as a combination of EC employment law and domestic employment law. How far does this involve a tension between the dictates of those international systems of employment law and the policies of French employment law? Those concerned with the employment law of the United Kingdom are used to an environment in which the extent of adherence to the ILO is controversial, and in which the primacy of EC employment law seems to have become one of the most divisive issues in the whole legal system.

There seem to be many fewer problems of that kind in French employment law. This may be due to the fact that, as we shall see in proceeding down the hierarchy of sources, the employment relationship is quite highly juridified in France and has been the subject of very extensive state intervention in some respects. The French Constitution and *Code du travail* have generally tended to provide guarantees equivalent to those required by the main ILO conventions, while so far as EC employment law is concerned, the tone has been set by the fact that one of its first and most central provisions, the equal pay requirement of article 119 of the EC Treaty, was actually enacted in order to validate and protect the strong position which French employment law had taken up in this respect. So while French employment law no doubt has many devices for maintaining its own singularity in relation to international and EC employment law, on the whole, with perhaps the exception of some issues concerning immigration and foreign workers, this capacity for singularity seems to be quite easily reconciled with the formal supremacy of international law.

C. The Constitution

That apparent ease of reconciliation is initially a little surprising to a British common lawyer who has expected a hierarchical ordering of sources to be inherently

---

[7] Cf. below, pp. 489–490.

[8] In a significant recent development, the Paris Court of Appeal re-characterized as a contract of indeterminate duration, a purported *contrat nouvelles embauches* on the ground that the termination provisions of the CNE were in violation of ILO Convention No. 158: CA Paris (18th ch.) 6 Jul. 2007, S/06/06992.

difficult. Perhaps the reasons for it start to become clearer as we move through the hierarchy, and realize, in relation to 'the Constitution' that its designation as the primary internal source of French employment law is actually a complex and highly qualified statement, involving the kind of interleaving which takes place, for instance, in relation to common law and equity in English law, and is in reality very far from a simple rank ordering. These complexities are found partly within the Constitution and partly in its relationship with the rest of French employment law: there are issues both of *identification* and of *effectiveness*.[9]

So far as identification is concerned, we can discern two ways of thinking about the relevance of the Constitution to French employment law. One way, perhaps preferred by those for whom employment law is very firmly part of an autonomous body of *droit social*, is to concentrate largely or exclusively on the labour-specific social principles introduced by the preamble to the Constitution of 1946, especially the right to work (*le droit au travail*), the right to freedom of association in trade unions (*le droit syndical*), the right to strike (*le droit de grève*), and the right to supervisory control over enterprise management (*le droit de contrôle*). A rather different view emphasizes that the case law of the Conseil constitutionnel has also given full weight, in relation to employment, not only to those social principles, but also to liberal principles derived from the 1789 Declaration of the Rights of Man and of the Citizen such as freedom of trade and freedom to work (*liberté d'entreprendre, liberté du travail*); this view acknowledges the potential for conflict between social and liberal constitutional values.[10]

So far as effectiveness is concerned, that potential for conflict between constitutional principles means that any one principle has to be of relative rather than absolute application.[11] Moreover, the social rights are generally either expressly stated to be or impliedly held to be intended to be exercised within the scope of relevant legislation (*dans le cadre de la législation*); that represents a kind of *ad hoc* re-ordering of the hierarchy of norms, whereby legislation is integrated with constitutional principle in the particular context. Furthermore, some of the constitutional social principles in particular are treated as so general and aspirational in character as to produce inherent doubt about the extent to which they can be relied upon as concrete norms. The classic example is that of the right to work, though the view is taken that the right to work has been more specifically implemented in constitutional *jurisprudence* than might possibly have been expected or feared.[12]

---

[9] A. Lyon-Caen, 'The Functional and Institutional Organisation of the Regulation of Working Conditions' being the French national report in *The Regulation of Work Conditions in the Member States of the European Community*, Vol 2, *The Legal Systems of the Member States—A Comparative Perspective—National Reports*, Social Europe Supplement 5/93 (Luxembourg, 1994), para. 17.

[10] Javillier, para. 70.

[11] Ibid.

[12] A. Lyon-Caen, (above n. 9), para. 17.

D. Legislation

Our sense of the true complexity of the hierarchy of sources in French employment law is heightened as we go down to the next level, that of legislation. This complexity may come as something of a surprise to a British audience, who may think of the French system as one which is archetypally given to codification, and who might have thought of the *Code du travail* as the perfect illustration of that tendency. It is indeed the case that, since its initial formation in 1910, that Code has been an important symbol of the autonomy, coherence and comprehensiveness of French employment law. There are, however, very real, and probably increasing, difficulties in regarding it as a formulation which is either autonomous, coherent or comprehensive. There are both internal and external complexities which stand in the way of such a view.

So far as *internal complexities* are concerned, these consist mainly in the fact that the Code is made up of a combination of two main kinds or levels of enacted norms, and that the relationship between them is a contentious one. The distinction is between *loi* (parliamentary legislation or statute law) and *règlementation* (executive legislation).[13] To make matters more complicated at the level of terminology, the *Code du travail* is actually set out in three parts, each one with its own initial letter: the first has the prefix L for *loi*, the second is R for *règlement*, and the third is D for *décrets*; but both the latter two parts consist of executive legislation, the first being decrees of the Conseil d'Etat and the second being simple executive decrees as issued, for instance by government departments. A more substantive complication arises from the fact that the boundary between *loi* and *règlement* in employment law is maintained by the Constitution itself; article 34 assigns to the *loi* the role of determining the rules concerning the fundamental principles of labour law, while article 37 assigns regulatory competence to the executive in all other respects.[14] It is difficult to say which arm of government is empowered and which one is restrained by this division of function.

So far as *external complexities* are concerned, there are both vertical and horizontal challenges to the sovereignty of the *Code du travail*. The vertical challenges come not only, as one would logically expect, from above in the shape of international and constitutional norms, but also from below when, as we shall see, the judges exceed their ostensibly interpretative role, or the social partners are accorded high-ranking normative power. The horizontal challenges result from the fact that it is increasingly doubtful whether employment law can be satisfactorily confined to its traditional field of application, namely the private law contractual

---

[13] See above pp. 21–22; and see below, p. 510 as to the re-codification of the *Code du travail*, which at the time of writing is expected imminently to come into effect. References to Articles are to the existing or old version, with the corresponding Articles in the new version shown in square brackets eg [1237-1].

[14] For details of the hostilities which occur across this frontier in the context of employment law, see Javillier, para. 71, text and n. 73.

employment relationship. The *Code du travail* is strongly identified with that field of application, and hence its coverage of employment law is challenged on the one side, as we have seen, by the encroachment of public employment relationships and public law, and on the other side by the growth of semi-independent or fully independent work relationships, bringing into play a wider range of law relating to work and business enterprise, and so breaking down both the autonomy of the *Code du travail* as against the whole body of private or civil law, and the comprehensiveness of its coverage of the field of employment relationships.[15]

E. Judge-Made Law

Next down the hierarchy we come to judge-made law (*la jurisprudence*). The importance of this source is debatable in a way which must be unfamiliar to a British audience accustomed to regarding the superior courts as moving freely and easily from an interpretative role into that of expounding law quite independently of legislative starting points.[16] This is not to say that students of French employment law are free from the necessity of mastering a large amount of case law, for they certainly do have that obligation. But the writers seem to agree that the importance of the *jurisprudence* of French employment law is limited by the extent of its fragmentation or dispersal (*éparpillement*) among a large number of different jurisdictions.[17] At the highest level there is involved not only the Cour de cassation, but also the Conseil d'Etat, and in a different sense the Conseil constitutionnel. At lower levels there are involved not only the specialized industrial tribunals, the Conseils des prud'hommes, but also in various ways the tribunaux d'instance and the tribunaux de grande instance, and, so far as public sector issues are concerned, the tribunaux adminstratifs.[18] As a result, there seems to be less of a possibility than there is in English law of identifying a single body of judge-made law of employment. All that said, it is widely acknowledged that the *jurisprudence* of the Chambre sociale of the Cour de Cassation does play an increasingly important authoritative role in the evolution of French employment law.

F. Norm-Making Powers of Employers and of the Social Partners

In one sense at the bottom of the hierarchy we encounter the norm-making powers of the social partners themselves; but only in one sense at the bottom, for French employment law accords an importance to these powers which is, at least conceptually, unfamiliar to British employment lawyers. Conceptually at least, for when and to the extent that these powers are recognized in the law of the

---

[15] Compare Javillier, para. 16 on the incipient development of *un droit de travail indépendant*, a topic developed at length by G. Lyon-Caen in *Le droit du travail non salarié* (Paris, 1990).

[16] See more generally, above p. 25 ff.

[17] See Javillier, para. 74, referring to A. Jeammaud, 'L'état du contentieux judiciare social' (1993) Dr. Soc. 445; A. Lyon-Caen, (above n. 9), para. 26.

[18] Above, pp. 38 ff.

United Kingdom, it is essentially via the individual contract of employment that these norms take effect, and therefore subject to various sets of conditions for the incorporation of terms into contracts of employment. In France, not only does legislation expressly accord regulatory effect to these norms, but the whole approach to employment law seems more conducive to the acceptance of the normative operation of the social partners as, in and of itself, part of the legal fabric.

That is not to say that such effect is accorded unconditionally and at large. The conditions for the recognition of custom (*usage*) as legally operative norms actually quite closely resemble the conditions for their recognition in English law as validly incorporated into contracts of employment—observance as binding over a long period of time, etc.—though French law, perhaps typically, more carefully requires the meeting of both objective and subjective conditions, but having once recognized a custom, accords it a somewhat more concrete effect. Thus, on the one hand, the custom of an occupation or region is recognized by legislation as one of the determinants of the notice of dismissal to which employees are entitled,[19] while, on the other hand, the circumstances in which a workplace custom may be repudiated by an employer are tightly regulated.[20]

On the other hand, by speaking of norm-making by the social partners, we are not confining ourselves to *joint* norm-making by both sides of industry. Just as French employment law recognizes custom as something distinct from the contract of employment, so it has also for a long time accorded distinct normative force to the employer's power to lay down works rules for the internal management of the enterprise (*règlement intérieur de l'entreprise*). The recognition of this essentially unilateral power harks back to the period before collective bargaining was accorded a central status in French employment law; it nevertheless survives as a primary determinant of the disciplinary and health and safety regime within the workplace. That survival is on the basis of a fairly tight set of statutory controls,[21] which were re-worked as part of the general overhaul of French employment law accomplished by the *lois Auroux* of 1981–82.[22]

G. Collective Bargaining

It is, however, in the sphere of joint regulation of terms and conditions of employment by collective bargaining that French employment law has, traditionally at least, most significantly recognized the normative authority of the social partners. In strong contrast to the British tradition of employment law, in which the

---

[19] Art. L. 122-5 C. trav. [1237-1].

[20] Javillier, para. 76.

[21] Arts. L. 122-33–122-39 C. trav. [1311-1–1321-6].

[22] *Loi* nos. 82-689 of 4 August 1982; 82-915 of 28 October 1982; 82-957 of 13 November 1982; and 82-1097 of 23 December 1982. So called after Jean Auroux, the then Minister of Labour whose report was the basis of the reforms: J.-C. Javillier, *Les réformes du droit de travail depuis le 10 mai 1982*, 2nd edn. with supplement (Paris, 1985).

protagonists of collective bargaining generally sought to strengthen collective bargaining by a voluntarist insistence on its separateness from the legal system, French employment law has concentrated heavily on at once recognizing and endorsing, while tightly controlling, the legal effect of collective agreements. We shall refer later in this chapter to the treatment in French employment law of rights to collective bargaining, and we should briefly draw attention to the importance of the statutory mechanism for the extension of certain kinds of multi-employer collective agreements, by ministerial order, to all employers in a particular sector or sector and locality of industry, or for the enlargement of their area of application.[23] We should also refer to the way in which the major multi-employer, multi-occupational collective agreements (*conventions interprofession-nelles*) quite often assume a meta-status in which they become part of the political and legislative process of the state itself.[24] To the French way of thinking, this makes them a special kind of source of law in themselves.[25]

However, our main concern is with the legislation which determines the basic legal nature and legal effect of collective agreements, mainly contained in articles 132 and 135(2) of the *Code du travail*. What is this legal nature and effect, which makes collective agreements such an important normative source? At the risk of over-simplification, we can say that a collective agreement which comes within this legislation (that is, very briefly, an agreement between one or more represen-tative trade unions and one or more employers which may either cover the whole range of terms and conditions (*convention collective*) or deal with one or more particular aspect of terms and conditions (*accord collectif*)) thereby acquires an *automatic* legal effect which applies *comprehensively to all workers* (*erga omnes*) in the enterprise(s) or establishment(s) and in the occupation(s) which is or are cov-ered by the agreement. The effect is automatic in the sense that terms in individ-ual contracts of employment are overridden by the very fact of the making of the collective agreement. The overriding consists of imposing the norms established by the collective agreement upon the contractual terms which would otherwise apply, except upon individual terms which are more favourable (*sauf dispositions plus favorables*).[26] This overriding effect actually enables collective agreements to vary laws and regulations, normally in favour of the employees concerned,[27]

---

[23] The legislation creating this procedure is basically contained in art. L. 133 C. trav. [2261] See Javillier, paras. 762–774.

[24] Many examples are to be found in the course of Javillier, para. 14, a rich account of post-1980 developments in relations between governments and social partners.

[25] A. Lyon-Caen, (above n. 9), para. 7, referring to 'centralised' and 'institutional' bargaining. But note his misgivings about the risks of a kind of corporatist role for such bargaining, echoed in a rather different way by G. Lyon-Caen, 75: '*Gestion paritaire* (joint management) *de certains services*'. For further reflection on such choices between cooperation and conflict, see Javillier, paras. 30–33 ('*la promotion des relations professionnelles*').

[26] Art. L. 135-2 C. trav. [2254-1].

[27] Normally, but not universally; for the development of exceptions since 1982, see below p. 501 and see Pélissier Supiot and Jeammaud, 132 *et seq.*

provided that they do not undermine the dictates of public policy (*dispositions d'ordre public*) embodied in those laws and regulations.[28]

British readers should not be beguiled by all this into thinking that collective agreements, because they are so obviously approached quite differently in France, are accorded a kind of blockbuster effect, leaving employers or employees power-less in the face of them for ever after the moment of their conclusion. There is a great multiplicity of techniques of argument about the precise effect and duration of collective agreements, which is enabling employers in France to effect, if not a wholesale retreat from collective bargaining, then at least a very significant redef-inition of its nature and scope. However, the conceptual approach to collective agreements remains for the most part intact, and is of such extreme interest from a British point of view, because of the way it expresses a wholly different method-ology in employment law, that it justifies a large place in an extended treatment of the sources of French employment law and the hierarchy in which it is sought to order them. We have placed the great weight of our overall discussion upon that cornerstone; we can afford to be relatively brief in the ensuing survey of some of the main specific areas of French employment law.

IV The Creation and Termination of the Employment Relationship

A. Economic and Non-Economic Dismissals

It will be useful to consider these topics in the reverse order from that of the heading, and to dispose initially of the termination of the employment relation-ship, because the law concerning its creation is rather more interesting from a comparative juridical point of view. Perhaps, however, we should make the point rather differently by saying that the most interesting aspects of the law about the termination of employment are in fact contained in the law about the creation of the relationship and in particular in the law affecting the formation and struc-ture of the contract of employment. Before going on to that subject, we should explain that the *lois* of 1973 and 1975 concerning respectively the control of non-economic and of economic dismissals, as subsequently amended, create a system very broadly similar to that of the United Kingdom, though arrived at by quite a different route.

That quite different route was the following one. French employment law dis-tinguishes sharply between, and has distinct systems for handling, economic dis-missals (i.e. those related to the economic situation of the employing enterprise) on the one hand, and non-economic or personal dismissals (i.e. those relating to the behaviour or performance of the particular worker) on the other. So far as

---

[28] Art. L. 132-4 C. trav. [2251-1].

economic dismissals, or redundancies, were concerned, it was a singular feature of French employment law that, from 1945 onwards, there was (in addition to the legal controls on dismissals in general, controls which were at that time still rather limited) a fairly rigid system requiting administrative authorization from the Ministry of Labour for such dismissals although the employers were in the private sector. This pattern of state control became less and less acceptable to employers, and also less and less attractive to trade unions, who demanded, especially from 1968 onwards, the direct involvement of the workforce in such decisions. It was the main purpose of the *loi* of 3 January 1975 to require information to and consultation with the workforce in relation to economic dismissals[29] (thereby largely anticipating the requirements of the EEC Directive 75/129 on collective dismissals), while still preserving the system of state authorization, which survived until abolished by the *loi* of 3 July 1986.[30] Since the *loi* of 2 August 1989,[31] there has, on the other hand, been a new set of controls on economic dismissals, which is concentrated upon a duty upon employers (with more than 50 employees) to produce a 'social plan' (*plan social,* or *plan de sauvegarde d'emploi*) to rationalize the handling of a redundancy situation and justify proposed dismissals.

This produces a treatment of economic dismissals which is recognizably similar to that of British employment law, though its legislative history is thus very different, and its present state is rather more formally managerialized, via the social plans, than is the case in the United Kingdom. The situation and development with regard to personal dismissals resembles somewhat more closely that in the United Kingdom. The ordinary law of the contract of employment gave rise only to rather scant controls upon personal as well as upon economic dismissals. However, the *loi* of 13 July 1973[32] introduced a whole new set of controls upon dismissals, not unlike those imposed by the British unfair dismissals legislation first introduced in 1971, constructed around the requirement of a real and serious ground for dismissal (*cause réelle et sérieuse de licenciement*). This was supplemented (in a way which goes somewhat beyond British law) by a set of procedural controls upon employers' disciplinary powers contained in the *loi* of 4 August 1982.[33] The adjudication of most of the issues arising under this system by the Conseils des prud'hommes corresponds quite closely to the employment tribunal procedure in British law.

It is worth adding as a major footnote to this discussion of the law about dismissals that French employment law has, since the 1920s, embodied in statute[34] the notion that the contract of employment is made with and attaches to the employing enterprise, so that on the transfer or other re-structuring of the

---

[29]   *Loi* no. 75-5.
[30]   *Loi* no. 86-797.
[31]   *Loi* no. 89-549.
[32]   *Loi* no. 73-680.
[33]   *Loi* no. 82-689.
[34]   Art. L. 122-12 al. 2 C. trav. [1224-1].

ownership of the enterprise, contracts of employment then in force take effect with the new employer. This conception of the transferability of the acquired rights of the employee provided a significant model for the EC Acquired Rights Directive, so that this Directive,[35] which amounted to a bombshell in British employment law, both because of its conceptual unfamiliarity and its unexpected practical impact, causes very little perturbation in French employment law.[36]

B. Creation and Structure of the Contract of Employment

However, despite the interesting character of this recent history of the law of dismissal, it would be fair to say that from the early 1980s onwards, the most important developments in the shape and character of the individual employment relationship have occurred not so much in relation to dismissal, but in relation to the creation and structure of the contract of employment. For it is on this plain that the battle has been waged over the 'flexibilization' of the labour market, that is to say the transformation of patterns of employment from one in which the permanent full-time employment relationship was strongly predominant to one in which the previously atypical temporary and/or part-time employment relationship has become much more central.

It is difficult to judge whether that transformation has progressed further in France or in the United Kingdom, but it is clear that the legal framework within which it has occurred is very different as between the two countries. In the United Kingdom, the law of the contract of employment in particular and the employment law system as a whole impose only very slight constraints upon the freedom to choose between those forms of employment. We can on the whole say that the law of the contract of employment in the United Kingdom does not create sharply defined internal categories of employment, and still less does it enforce such categories upon the contracting parties. In France, on the other hand, the starting point is that of a traditionally very strong insistence on the non-fixed-term contract of employment *(le contrat de travail à durée indéterminée* or 'CDI') as the standard, once almost mandatory, form of the employment relationship.

What form has that insistence, conceptually rather foreign to British readers, taken? It is not that French employment law refused to recognize other categories. On the contrary, it specifies them with full Cartesian elaboration of careful distinctions, differentiating, for example, between the fixed-term contract *(le contrat de travail à durée déterminée* or 'CDD') and the contract for temporary

---

[35] EC Directive 77/187, since repealed and replaced by EC Directive 2001/23.

[36] In French employment law, there was no need for a major internal measure to implement the Directive corresponding to the British Transfer of Undertakings (Protection of Employment) Regulations 1981 (SI 1981/1794) (the now famous 'TUPE Regulations'), and certainly nothing corresponding to the furore over the effect of those Regulations both on corporate re-structuring and on the contracting-out of ancillary services.

work (*le contrat de travail temporaire* or 'CTT'), the difference being that the latter kind of contract is arranged through and with an employment agency. It is not merely that there is a presumption in favour of construing a contract of employment as a CDI. French employment law goes further, both enacting certain specific prohibitions on the use of CDDs or CTTs (for example, they cannot be used for the purpose or with the effect of providing on a permanent basis an employment linked to the normal and permanent activity of the enterprise),[37] and also setting out the situations in which those contracts can be used, impliedly limiting their use to those situations. Moreover, French employment law provides for application to a court for the recharacterization (*requalification*) of contracts, and since 1990 has provided that a purported CDD which is not validly within that category is deemed to have been made (*réputé conclu*) as a CDI.[38]

As is often the case, the legal framework may well be less rigid and constraining in practice than a brief description of it might suggest. Certainly, we know that there has been a continual process of modification and re-modification of this body of law in the last decade, generally tending towards a relaxation of the restrictions on the use of previously atypical precarious forms of employment.[39] Moreover, there has been an important tendency for the state itself to develop and authorize the use of certain special forms of precarious employment and/or training contracts, by way of measures to combat unemployment. Thus for young people there have been created 'orientation contracts' and 'qualification contracts', and for others 'in difficulty with regard to the labour market' there have been successively introduced 'return-to-work contracts', 'employment-initiative contracts', and the part-time 'employment-support contract' (*contrat emploi-solidarité*).[40] These developments, as interesting juridically as they are highly-charged politically, make one realize how much employment law is becoming tied up with the law of job-creation and training (*droit de l'emploi*), and how much that composite body of law is at the very centre of the whole development of law in society in France.[41]

V. Equal Treatment and Discrimination in Employment

The development and present aspect of the law concerning discrimination in employment in France presents an interesting set of contrasts with British law, not so much in terms of detailed outcomes but in terms of a different way of arriving at the normative structure. So it is useful to consider the patterns of development, and the impulses driving that development, of this part of French employment

---

[37] Art. L. 122-1 al. 1 C. trav. [1242-1].
[38] Art. L. 122-3-1 al. 1 C. trav. [1242-12].
[39] For an excellent critical evaluation of these developments, see Javillier, para. 191.
[40] For details and explanations, see Javillier, paras 151, 152.
[41] See further below, Conclusion, at pp 511–512.

law. In particular, it is significant to ask how far that development has been a specific and concrete one, and how far, on the other hand, a development based upon general notions of constitutionally supported fundamental rights.

We look first at specific and concrete developments. As we indicated earlier, the principle of equality of pay between men and women was so strongly embodied in French law[42] that the demand for it to be specifically enshrined in the EC Treaty was distinctly related to the French situation. This undoubtedly broadens out into a wider concern with the relative position of women at work as in society at large, leading to a specific treatment of maternity rights,[43] and latterly of sexual harassment (*harcèlement sexuel*).[44] There is a long tradition of specific provision concerned with discrimination in employment against the disabled (*les travailleurs handicapés*),[45] no doubt in part originally attributable to the results of the two World Wars in France. There are, as we shall see later, many non-discrimination measures associated with the trade union rights of workers, and with their rights to representation in the workplace and with the right to strike.

Underlying those specific developments is the notion, much less familiar to a British reader, that the enacted constitution supports a general principle of non-discrimination, which is ultimately simply a way of expressing the fundamental idea of equality. This notion may be applied in two different, or even opposite, directions. On the one hand, it may be used to demonstrate the need and the justification for legislation about particular kinds of discrimination in employment. On the other hand, it may serve to justify the absence of such legislation, by creating a sense that there is already in place a general treatment of the whole problem. On the whole, the movement seems to be from the deployment of the general principle of non-discrimination in the latter, more negative, way towards its use in the former, more positive, way. This would seem to be the dynamic explaining the enactment in 1992, though not before, of wide-ranging legislation against discrimination in recruitment for employment in the use of sanctions during employment, and in dismissal from employment. The outlawed grounds of discrimination are a person's origin, sex, lifestyle or morals (*moeurs*), family situation, being of a particular ethnicity, nationality or race, political opinions, trade union or cooperative (*mutualiste*) activities, religious convictions, or ill-health or disability.[46] It would be interesting to chart the relative effect in practice of

---

[42] Arts. L. 140-2–140-9 C. trav. [3221-2–3221-9].

[43] Arts. L. 122-25–122-32 C. trav. [1225-1–1225-34].

[44] Arts. L. 122-46–122-48 C. trav., embodying the *loi* no. 92-1179 of 2 November 1992. See especially Javillier, para. 169, n. 79 for a critique of the problems of approaching sexual harassment in terms of the 'abuse of the authority of the employer'; see further on this, M.-A. Moreau, 'A propos de l'abus d'autorité en matière sexuelle' (1993) Dr. Soc. 115. In 1992, sexual harassment in certain circumstances was made a criminal offence: art. 222-33 N.c.pén.

[45] Art. L. 323-1 C. trav. [5212-1–5212-4] and Javillier, para. 187.

[46] Art. L 122-45 C. trav. [1132-1–1134-3], embodying the *loi* no. 92-1446 of 31 December 1992. No general legislation has been introduced concerning age discrimination in employment; in order to comply with the requirements in that regard of EC Directive 2000/78, France has mainly relied on the general legal regime of the *Code du Travail* and the *Code Pénale*, but *loi* no.

this legislation by comparison with the more narrowly focused legislation in the United Kingdom, which is not underpinned in the same way by a general constitutional principle.

VI. Minimum Wages and Working Conditions

As it would be pointless in such a short survey of French employment law to attempt to comment on the whole set of legal controls over wages and working conditions, we shall confine ourselves to describing, still in summary form, two particular sets of arrangements which are of especial comparative interest; they are those relating on the one hand to minimum wages, and on the other hand to the control of working time. They are both areas where there is a high level of legal regulation in France; but as between the two sets of arrangements, there is a crucially different relationship to the collective bargaining process.

Of all the acronyms which abound in French employment law, none has become more demonstrably a household word than the SMIC, the *salaire minimum interprofessionnel de croissance* (i.e. with built-in growth). Introduced by statute in 1970[47] to replace an earlier less dynamic minimum wage system called the SMIG (*salaire minimum interprofessionnel garanti*), the SMIC is essentially a universal hourly minimum wage system which is determined partly by reference to the cost-of-living index but partly also by an annual governmental revision, which is coupled with the possibility that the government may decree an increase outside the annual revision (*une augmentation libre*). The SMIC represents the high water mark of governmental intervention in the labour market in France; it is fixed at a high enough level to be a major determinant of actual wage levels and relativities between wages, and although the rate-fixing decisions have to be taken *après avis de* (meaning, roughly,[48] on the advice of) the tripartite National Commission for Collective Bargaining, the decisions are basically political ones. Indeed, it is positively sought, in an effort to control wage-inflation, to insulate the collective bargaining process from this governmental minimum rate-fixing; there is a statutory prohibition upon the indexation of wages according to the movement of the SMIC without reference to the performance of the enterprise in question.[49]

When we turn, on the other hand, to the legal control of working time (meaning daily working hours, weekly working hours, rules about shift working, night

---

2005-846 of 26 July 2005 was enacted in order to confer special powers to issue *ordonnances* to amend employment law; *Ord.* 2005-901 of 2 August 2005 abolished some of the age limitations upon access to public employment.

[47] *Loi* no. 70-7 of 2 January 1970, see art. L. 141-1 C. trav.

[48] Precise equivalence is disclaimed because that would beg questions about how far the advice of the Commission has to be taken into substantive account.

[49] Art. L. 141-9 C. trav. [3231-3].

work, rest breaks and holidays), we find a very different relationship between legal regulation and collective bargaining. There is a detailed legal regime concerning working time,[50] night work,[51] and rest periods, and holidays,[52] which is constructed upon the basic pillars of the statutory 35-hour week,[53] and the six weeks annual paid holiday,[54] but that summary vastly understates the complexity of the legal regime, and the important point is that the complexities consist largely in an elaborate inter-relating between the legal norms and the collective bargaining process. It has been said that this part of the law is in a permanent state of reform;[55] those frequent reforms usually consist in redefining the circumstances and conditions in which the basic statutory norms can be modified by collective bargaining, whether at enterprise level or at the various multi-employer levels which exist, particularly those at which the agreements *interprofessionels* or *de branche*[56] are reached.

In fact, we could go so far as to say that it is especially in the field of working time that the whole relationship between legal regulation and collective bargaining is being gradually reformed by the creation of new patterns of flexibility around the basic legal norms. Thus, it was in relation to the length of the working week that there occurred in 1982 the first major break with the previously sacrosanct principle that collective bargaining could modify legal norms only in a sense favourable to employees; the *ordonnance* of 16 January 1982[57] introduced, in relation to weekly working hours, the notion of the *accord dérogatoire*, the collective agreement which could derogate from the legal norm in a way which could be unfavourable (*in peius*) and did not have to be favourable (*in melius*) towards the workers affected.[58] The whole notion of the *accord dérogatoire* was further extended, in particular with regard to enterprise-level collective agreements, by an enactment of May 2004,[59] one of the several pieces of legislation often known

---

[50] Art. L. 212 C. trav. [3121].

[51] Art. L. 213 C. trav. [3122].

[52] Arts. L. 221–226 C. trav. [3132–3142].

[53] Arts. L. 212-1 [3121] *et seq.* C. trav. The reduction of the basic working week from 39 hours to the now-famous *35 heures* was initiated by the so-called *loi Aubry I—loi* no. 98-461 of 13 June 1998—and finally carried out by the so-called *loi Aubry II—loi* no. 2000-37 of 19 January 2000 and various Decrees made thereunder. The resulting provisions, as since amended, form an immensely complex regime for the control of working time, in which legislation and collective bargaining (or *règlementation*) are very elaborately intertwined. See Pélissier Supiot and Jeammaud, paras 919 *et seq.*

[54] Art. L. 223-2 C. trav. [3141].

[55] Javillier, para. 342 (this paragraph giving a very useful overview of the recent history).

[56] These terms can be translated as, respectively, 'multi-occupation' and 'single-occupation', but that does scant justice to the particular institutional structures of multi-employer collective bargaining which those terms denote. Cf. Despax and Rojot, ch. V, s. 7, 'Industry-wide Collective Agreements', and Pélissier, Supiot, and Jeammaud at paras 818 *et seq.*

[57] No. 82-41.

[58] Art. L. 212-2 al. 3 C. trav. [3121-53] and see Javillier, para. 95, and for further developments of the *accord dérogatoire* in other fields, para. 749, and also Pélissier, Supiot and Jeammaud, paras 849 *et seq.*

[59] *Loi* no. 2004-391 of 4 May 2004.

as the '*loi Fillon*'.[60] All this explains why the methodology of the EC Directive on Working Time,[61] with its own immensely elaborate set of possibilities for derogation, many of them related to collective bargaining, seems more familiar in a French context than in a British one, and also why, perhaps especially from a French perspective, the Directive reveals the essential 'hesitations and contradictions of EC law in this field'.[62]

VII. Trade Unionism, Collective Bargaining and Workplace Representation

A. Introduction

We could think of this and the next section of the chapter as those in which, having briefly surveyed French employment law as it applies to the individual employment relationship, we conclude by surveying, equally briefly and eclectically, its collective aspects. This is in a sense accurate; but the dichotomy between individual and collective employment law is ultimately a false one, not least in relation to French law. On the one hand, we have seen how a topic ostensibly dealing with the individual employment relationship such as working time has to be understood almost entirely in terms of the law relating to collective bargaining. On the other hand, the part of employment law which we might think of as collective in nature is, in French law, constructed on the basis of a set of positive rights, which are often individual rights in their nature and conception. An obvious example, as we shall see in the next section, is the way in which the right to strike is thought of as an individual right in French law; there are other, more subtle, manifestations of the same thought pattern.

Against that background we can perhaps think of this section as the one which deals with industrial democracy in the widest sense, namely the bases and mechanisms for the identification and representation of the interests and aspirations of people in their work relationships. In French law, we have to approach that subject not only via a complex analysis of what is collective and what is individual, but also by understanding how a set of rights interlock with each other in a very intricate way, of which quite widely differing accounts can be given. The following scheme of analysis will be followed, as perhaps the most accessible one for those using the very different approaches of British jurisprudence. It is a three-part scheme, consisting of:

(1) rights to trade unionism;
(2) rights to collective bargaining; and
(3) rights to workplace representation.

---

[60] After M François Fillon, then Minister of Labour and Social Affairs.
[61] Directive 93/104 of 1993.
[62] Javillier, para. 341.

This corresponds roughly, but not completely, to rights recognized by or under the French Constitution as part of the *ordre public social*. Thus, (1) corresponds directly with the long recognized notion of *droit syndical*, (2) corresponds with the rather less specifically recognized notion of *droit à la négociation collective*, while (3) combines a number of notions emerging more or less concretely such as *le droit de contrôle de gestion*, and *le droit de l'expression des salariés dans l'entreprise*. None of these rights can be regarded as neatly self-contained in relation to the others; the cross-cutting between these sets of rights is elaborate; so we shall continue by trying to show how each of the three headings has its own coherence in relation to the substantive parts of French employment law.

The best way to do that is by considering the choices which confront the makers of employment law between on the one hand protecting liberal and individualistic freedoms in respect of trade unionism, and on the other hand positively securing effective trade unionism as a collective force. The pre-occupations of French employment law have tended historically to be more of the former kind than of the latter kind, not least because of the way that trade unionism has been viewed in pluralist terms, with importance being attached to choice on the part of individuals as to the political and spiritual affiliations which they are expressing through their trade union. We can usefully group together the laws which express those concerns under our first heading of 'rights to trade unionism'.

On the other hand, there has been a powerful impulse in French employment law for much of the last century to maintain a strong system of collective bargaining, and in that particular context there has been a greater willingness to accord to trade unions a protected or monopolistic set of positions. That produces a body of law which has its own coherence of a different kind, which we can identify under our second heading of 'rights to collective bargaining'. We have already described some aspects of this body of law, when we considered collective agreements as one of the normative sources which figure in French employment law, but we need to develop that discussion somewhat further.

That dichotomy between trade unionism and collective bargaining, profoundly important and informative as it is in relation to French employment law,[63] does not, however, serve as a complete basis for our analysis, for there is a third distinct approach to this whole set of issues in French employment law. For at least the past 50 years, there has been a distinct concern with industrial democracy within each individual enterprise. This concern has been developed mainly through the institutional forms of elected workers' representatives (*les délégués du personnel*) and *les comités d'entreprises* ('CEs'—roughly, works councils).[64] Initially, trade unions had a very limited formal place in these structures; latterly they have been accorded a significant role in them. We can usefully discern and bring together,

---

[63] Cf. Javillier, para. 708.

[64] Roughly, because the term has historical overtones of a unitarist or paternalist approach to employment relations, which should be seen as inapplicable, especially since the reforms of 1982.

from initiatives of this kind, a third body of law under the heading of 'rights to workplace representation'.

B. Rights to Trade Unionism

Expanding a little further on each of these three headings, we begin with rights to trade unionism. The foundation of these rights consists in the legislation, originating in 1884, which recognizes freedom of association in trade unions (*la liberté syndicale*) in the form of freedom of trade unions to be established and to exist as bodies with a legal status.[65] Associated with that freedom is an individual freedom to belong to the union of one's choice.[66] This seems to be understood as a freedom of the individual as against the trade union, a duty upon the trade union to allow free access to membership, and French law seems to require unions to recognize as a corollary that individuals have the right not to belong; there is expressly declared to be an individual right to resign from a union.[67]

Rights to trade unionism as against employers are handled rather differently. The exercise of the general right to trade unionism (*droit syndical*) is declared by statute to be recognized in all enterprises 'in respect of the rights and freedom guaranteed by the Constitution, in particular the individual freedom to work (*la liberté individuelle du travail*)';[68] furthermore, it is declared that there is a general freedom of trade union organization in all enterprises (in accordance with specific statutory provisions).[69] The protection of the individual worker or applicant for work from discrimination by reason of trade union membership or activity is covered by its own special statutory provision,[70] as well as being, as we have seen earlier, treated as part of the general law of non-discrimination. Thus far, rights to trade unionism are cast in decidedly individualistic and pluralistic terms.

However, from 1968 onwards there was movement towards also according to the trade unions a more direct right to a collective presence in the enterprise, culminating in the *loi* of 28 October 1982, which not only, as we shall see, gave the trade unions a new role in the institutional representation arrangements (i.e. in the structures for elected representatives and CEs) but also provided for the establishing and functioning of union branches (*sections syndicales*) at enterprise level by representative trade unions.[71] Although these provisions are regarded,

---

[65] See art. L. 411-2 al. 1 C. trav. [2131-2]: '*Les syndicates... professionnels... peuvent se constituer librement*'.

[66] Art. L. 411-5 C. trav. [2141-1]: '*Tout salarié... peut librement adhérer au syndicat professionnel de son choix*'.

[67] Art. L. 411-8 C. trav. [2141-4]: '*Tout membre d'un syndicat professionnel peut s'en retirer à tout instant*'.

[68] Art. L. 412-1, al. 1, C. trav. [2141-3].

[69] Art. L. 412-2, al. 2, C. trav. [2141-6]: '*Les syndicats professionnels peuvent s'organiser librement dans toutes les entreprises*'.

[70] Art. L. 412-2 C. trav. [2141].

[71] *Loi* no. 82-915, arts. L. 412-6–412-10 C. trav. [2142-1–2142-11].

understandably, as part of the general rights to trade unionism (*droit syndical*), the fact that they apply in favour not of all unions but only of trade unions deemed to representative ones aligns these provisions more closely with the rights to collective bargaining, to which we now turn our attention.

C. Rights to Collective Bargaining

As we have indicated earlier, French employment law approaches rights to collective bargaining in a more collectivistic spirit than we generally encountered in relation to rights to trade unionism. That is not to say that it has been prepared to abandon its pluralistic stance to the extent of generally allowing unions to become the sole bargaining agents for particular workgroups on the North American pattern. Indeed, although there has been since 1982 a duty on employers in whose enterprises union branches have been established to engage in annual collective bargaining at enterprise level, that does not involve a full duty to bargain in good faith in order to reach agreement of the kind that exists in American labour law, nor does it require (or even allow) employers to select one union against other unions as a bargaining partner.

However, the rights to collective bargaining in French employment law have been principally located not so much in that relatively recent obligation to engage in annual bargaining at enterprise level, but rather in the much longer standing structures which, as we have seen earlier, accord special normative force and *erga omnes* effect to certain collective agreements and provide for extension and enlargement of certain collective agreements by ministerial order. Although those structures, for their part, have not in principle involved the granting of sole or exclusive bargaining rights to particular unions, they have nevertheless depended upon specific requirements of representativeness (*représentativité*) of the trade union parties to collective agreements which have encroached on the original pluralism of French trade union law.

The law and politics of representativeness are elaborate, thus; the criteria for it not only deal with the obvious question of the independence of the union as against the employer, but also make different requirements according to the level of bargaining, in a way which reflects the particular history and dynamics of French industrial relations.[72] The modern politics include a ministerial order according representative status at national level to a list of the big confederations, and legislation applying an irrebuttable presumption of the representativeness of those unions for statutory purposes at enterprise level.[73] All this suffices to give this body of law about collective bargaining a rather different aspect from that of the basic trade union law.

---

[72] The starting point is arts. L. 133-2–133-3 C. trav.

[73] Art. L. 412-4 C. trav. [2122-9–2122-12] For a full discussion of the current legal position concerning *représentativité syndicale*, see Pélissier, Supiot, and Jeammaud, paras 563 *et seq*.

D. Rights to Workplace Representation

There is yet another aspect or orientation to the third body of law in this area, that concerning rights to workplace representation. We could say that in this area, French employment law has evolved cumulatively, so that it has combined by accretion three originally quite separate and even mutually inconsistent approaches to the representation of workers' interests in the individual enterprise, namely those of consultation with elected representatives of the workforce, representation by trade union nominees, and direct consultation of the members of the workforce.

The first set of strands in this complicated fabric consists in the establishment at the end of the Second World War of a system of elected workers' representatives (there had been earlier patterns in 1917 and 1936), and of CEs in enterprises or establishments employing 50 workers or more. The elected representatives have the role of presenting all individual or collective grievances or claims (*réclamations*) relating to wages, and to the application of employment legislation and of collective agreements.[74] The CE has the object of guaranteeing the employees' collective expression, allowing for a permanent taking into account of their interests in decisions relating to the management and the business development of the enterprise, the organization of work, training and methods of production;[75] the management is subject to specific obligations of information to and consultation with it.[76]

These structures, originally quite disparate from the institutions and approaches of collective bargaining, were crucially transformed by the reforms of 1982, and particularly by the placing, alongside the system of elected workers' representatives, of a system of trade union representatives within the enterprise,[77] and by providing for a first round of elections, both of the workers' representatives, and of the members of the CE, in which the representative trade unions establish the list of candidates,[78] and by also providing for a trade union nominee on the CE.[79]

This account does not, even in summary, do justice to the full extent of structures for consultation at and around enterprise level in French employment law. There are in addition Committees on Health and Safety and Working Conditions,[80] and Group CEs.[81] Broadly speaking, there is reproduced in each of those contexts this particular pattern of industrial democracy which French employment law has

---

[74] Art. L. 422-1 C. trav. [2313].
[75] Art. L. 431-4 C. trav. [2323-1].
[76] Arts. L. 431-5, 432-1 C. trav. [2323-2–2323-5, 2323-6–2323-25].
[77] Arts. L. 412-11–412-21 C. trav. [2143-3–2143-19].
[78] Arts. L. 423-14, L. 433-10 C. trav. [2314-24, 2324-22].
[79] Art. L. 433-1, al. 3, C. trav. [2324-1].
[80] Art. L. 236 C. trav. [4611–4614, 4523].
[81] Art. L. 439 C. trav. [2351–2353].

evolved. There is now an interesting set of issues, as the result of EC Directive 94/95, as to how a further superstructure of European Works Councils is being put in place, and as to how well this new institution can be fitted into the practicalities and the culture of this part of French employment law.[82]

The third distinctive element in French workplace representation arrangements was introduced by statute in 1982–83,[83] and concerns the right of expression in the enterprise. The legislation confers a right on employees to 'direct and collective expression about the content and organization of their work, and about their working conditions'. It is essentially a scheme for direct consultation of the workforce by the management; although the arrangements for this consultation are to be made by agreement with trade union or elected representatives, it is really a right to self-expression by the members of the workforce in person, and includes positive protection of individual freedom of expression in the exercise of this right.[84] Do the various elements in this multi-faceted treatment of workplace representation complement each other? How does their cumulative effect compare with that of a very much less intensively regulated system of workplace representation such as the British one?

VIII. Industrial Disputes and Dispute Settlement

It is quite customary to conclude descriptions of systems of employment by referring to industrial conflict, and to laws and procedures directed to resolving those conflicts. But that can be a misleading framework of analysis, for the legal system may not necessarily be specially oriented towards the resolution of industrial disputes. The legal system, and the employment law system in particular, will, on the other hand, inevitably have an important role in the regulation of industrial conflict, if only in the sense that it will provide an important part of the normative framework within which that conflict takes place; the employment law system will provide many of the rules of the game. So it is with French employment law; mechanisms are provided for recourse to conciliation,[85] mediation,[86] and arbitration[87] on a voluntary basis, but the law is mainly directed to the different end not so much of resolving the conflict but of protecting certain legitimate interests in relation to the conflict. This it does very largely by establishing and then defining the extent of the right to strike (*droit de grève*) and it is to the body of law which does this that the remainder of this section is devoted.

---

[82] See Javillier, para. 463.

[83] *Loi* no. 82-689 of 4 August 1982, art. L. 461 C. trav. [2281], extended to much of the public sector by *loi* no. 83-675 of 26 July 1983, art L. 462 C. trav. [2282].

[84] Art L. 461-1, al. 2, C. trav. [2281-3].

[85] Art. L. 523 C. trav. [2522].

[86] Art. L. 524 C. trav. [2523].

[87] Art. L. 525 C. trav. [2524].

It would be a little bit unkind to say that French employment law proclaims the right to strike for the very purpose of limiting it, but there would be a grain of truth in that statement. For, as we remarked earlier, the very form in which the right to strike is recognized is an assertion of its subjection to detailed legal regulation—'the right to strike is to be exercised within the framework of the laws which govern it'.[88] What form does that process of regulation or limitation take? There are two main operations; one consists of a modification of the law of the contract of employment, while the other consists of a special regime for industrial action in the public sector.

While in British law the establishment of freedom to strike has been seen as largely dependent on adjustment of the law of tort, in French law the right to strike has been centrally expressed in the proposition that the lawful strike is not in breach of the contract of employment. As Gerard Lyon-Caen pointed out,[89] it is the constitutional status of the right to strike which dictates that strike action is not seen as a breach of the contract of employment, (and that it is therefore seen as only suspended): 'striking does not break the contract of employment';[90] the statute which enacts that formula adds the crucial regulatory condition, 'except in the case of gross fault on the part of the employee'.[91] The composite enactment, proposition plus exception, provides a classic example of a cryptic piece of codified law, the so-called 'interpretation' of which by the courts gives them enormous normative authority; there is no single article of the *Code du travail* which has a greater body of exegesis attached to it or of which the *jurisprudence* is more important.

For British lawyers, to whom the treatment of the law of industrial conflict in terms of a positive right to strike is unfamiliar, and to whom its translation into a very specific modification of the law of the contract of employment is also unfamiliar, it comes as a further shock to discover that the assertion of an apparently general and fundamental right to strike is seen as consistent with a very complex and in some ways quite constricting legal regime for industrial action in the public sector, consisting of prohibitions (*interdictions*) on industrial action in some parts of the public sector—police, military services, etc., but also, for instance, administration of justice—and a framework of conditions or restrictions (*l'encadrement*) for industrial action elsewhere in the public sector.[92]

A British audience should not, however, jump to the conclusion that the two domains of industrial conflict law, that of the public sector and the private sector,

---

[88] '*Le droit de grève s'exerce dans le cadre des lois qui le réglementent*': Preamble to the Constitution of the Fourth Republic of 27 October 1946, al. 7.

[89] G. Lyon-Caen, 80.

[90] '*La grève ne rompt pas le contrat de travail.*'

[91] '*[S]auf faute lourde imputable au salarié*': art. L. 521-1 C. trav. [2511-1], originally enacted by the *loi* of 11 February 1950.

[92] See, for some of the most important provisions, arts, L 521-1–512-5 C. trav. [2511-1–2512-4], embodying the *loi* of 31 July 1963 concerning industrial action in the *services publics*; see, for a fuller account, Javillier, paras. 645–652.

are completely conceptually insulated from each other. Javillier, in drawing attention to the constitutional *jurisprudence* which has developed in recent years in the Conseil constitutionnel with regard to the right to strike, comments that there is now a common *problématique* (way of analysing the fundamental problems) as between that Conseil constitutionnel, the Conseil d'Etat and the Cour de cassation which concentrates on reconciling the right to strike with other constitutional rights or principles such as the safeguarding of the general interest, the continuity of public service, the protection of public health and safety, equality, and civil liability.[93]

This extension of the discourse of competing constitutional rights seems to fit in with an even more general development, of which the *Dehaene* case[94] was a major starting point, whereby the right to strike is seen as limited by the notion of the abuse of rights.[95] This leads on to a wide-ranging process of definition whereby the right to strike is identified in terms of the *grève licite*, the lawful strike which is contrasted with *les mouvements illicites* and with abusive exercise of the right to strike.[96] As Javillier indicated at various points, in the end this involves not only a balancing between specific constitutional rights, but an even more fundamental process of reconciliation between those constitutional rights and the whole body of private rights and interests.[97]

IX. Conclusion and *Mise á Jour*

This brings us to the conclusion, not merely of our discussion of the right to strike but of this survey of French employment law as a whole—of which the right to strike is certainly one of the pinnacles. For what we have just seen in the preceding paragraphs is surely an inter-twining, at a fundamental level, of the discourses and philosophies of public and of private law. So we conclude—perhaps very slightly better equipped to answer than at the outset—with the very question with which we began, namely, is French employment law really a matter of public or of private law? In the original edition of this work, that question was left hanging in the air. In this second edition, we can perhaps offer some concluding comments upon that question; they will be ones which reflect both the changes which have occurred between the two editions and the fact, mentioned in the Introduction to this chapter, that French employment currently seems to be in a state of considerable upheaval—an upheaval, we suggest, which is linked to a widespread perception that the mission or direction of French employment law is

---

[93] Javillier, para. 643.

[94] CE 7 Jul. 1950, *Dehaene*, Leb. 426, above p. 170.

[95] Cf. above pp. 373–374, for use of this idea more generally in the context of liability for delictual fault.

[96] Javillier, paras. 653–661; G. Lyon-Caen, 78–80.

[97] Cf. Javillier, para. 653

itself being re-oriented. Although that re-orientation does not consist precisely of a shift of employment law as between public and private law, we shall suggest that it can usefully be analysed in terms of that distinction.

A good starting point for that analysis of the current upheaval offers itself in the shape of the projected re-codification of the *Code du travail*. This project was initiated in 2005, and the resulting re-codification was embodied in an *ordonnance* in March 2007,[98] but not brought into effect, the Government being left with a discretion whether and when to do so until March 2008. This has created a situation of some uncertainty and disorientation, first because of the prospect that if and when the re-codification is implemented, the *Code du travail* will be entirely re-numbered and re-organized, and secondly because of unresolved debates as to whether and how far the re-codification as now enacted would effect substantive changes to French employment law, and finally because of questions about whether further changes might be made in the course of the implementation process.

This uncertainty, and the fact that it ironically accompanies an exercise in re-codification presented as designed to maximize clarity and certainty in the operation of the *Code du travail*, should not occasion too much surprise and is revealing as to the general state of French employment law. For such exercises in re-codification are often, as in this instance, the result of perceptions that the body of law or regulation in question has become over-elaborate and dysfunctional. They often therefore, as in this instance, behind a façade of formal re-organization and rationalization, give some degree of effect to impulses for substantive reform; and they often, as in this instance, become inter-twined with political initiatives for even more radical and extensive changes to the law. This combination of factors produces a state of ferment which we can helpfully analyse in terms of our discussion of the changing location of French employment law between public and private law.

For it is discernible, we suggest, that the location, and even more so the dynamics, of French employment law are rather different today from those of ten years ago, at the time described in the original edition of this work. At that time, it seemed accurate to depict a tendency towards the gradual approximation of the 'public' and the 'private' in French employment law. It still seems correct to identify such a tendency; however, it is a very different kind of approximation, indeed sometimes a diametrically opposed one, which is now taking place. That is to say, ten years ago one could observe what seemed to be a gradual movement of French employment law in a worker-protective direction, broadly speaking consisting of the continuing development of notions of constitutionalism, fundamental rights and *ordre public social* in the workplace, which seemed to intensify the 'public' aspects of French employment law, at least in the broad sense in which English

---

[98] No. 2007-329 of 12 March 2007.

lawyers think about 'public law', though less so perhaps in the narrower sense in which French lawyers understand and define 'public law'.

In more recent years, however, although the gradual erosion of the distinction between the 'public' and the 'private' in French employment law has continued, and might even have accelerated, the whole trajectory of this development has shifted into a market-liberal direction. If previously French employment law was tending to be both aggregated (as between the public and the private spheres) and somewhat 'publicized', now it is still being slowly aggregated as between the public and private spheres, but is also at the same time tending to be generally 'privatized'. The rationale for that tendency has, increasingly, been that of the need for 'flexibility' in employment relations in order to maximize the efficiency of the functioning of the labour market and to minimize unemployment. This is increasingly perceived as such a pressing need as to require the liberalization both of public and private employment law.

That liberalizing tendency has manifested itself in various ways in recent years—for instance, in the gradual attack upon the specially favourable retirement regimes for *fonctionnaires* and public sector workers more generally,[99] and in the cautious retreat from the regulatory excesses of the *35 heures,* hitherto largely concealed behind the freeing-up of enterprise-level collective bargaining *in peius,* which as we have seen culminated in the *loi Fillon* of May 2004.[100] We have also seen the introduction of contracts of employment such as the *contrat nouvelles embauches*[101] which, in the name of job creation, set aside the worker-protective shield of the previously nearly ubiquitous *contrat à durée indéterminée,* in its heyday almost the transposition of the tenured status of public sector workers into the private domain.

This liberalization of employment law is undoubtedly a highly political and politically sensitive activity. In 2006, the then Prime Minister, M Dominique Villepin risked and lost his political capital in an abortive attempt[102] to introduce a further such reduced-protection job-creation contract, the *contrat première embauche,* whose acceptability was undermined by the way in which it was targeted upon young workers. As we have suggested, there are those who discern a similar liberalizing agenda for the *projet Larcher*[103] of re-codification of the *Code du travail*. More prominently, the newly elected President Sarkozy asserts

[99] The crucial reform measure has been the '*loi Fillon (retraites)*', *loi* no. 2003-775 of 231 August 2003, addressing pension provision in both the public and private sectors but significantly re-aligning the special regimes of *fonctionnaires* and public sector workers towards the general regime for the workforce as a whole.

[100] See above, n. 59.

[101] Authorized by *ordonnance* no. 2005-893 of 2 August 2005.

[102] The CPE was to be introduced by art. 8 of *loi* no. 2006-396 of 31 March 2006 on *l'égalitè des chances,* but this was abrogated, without ever properly coming into force, by *loi* no. 2006-457 of 21 April 2006.

[103] So called because the project was launched in February 2005 by M. Gérard Larcher, the Minister tasked with this exercise.

an electoral mandate and firm intentions for a further and quite sweeping liberalization of French employment law—in particular for a further and significant loosening of the *35 heures*, and for the introduction of a *contrat unique* which would comprehensively effect the fusion of the two main existing contract types, the *contrat à durée indéterminée* and the *contrat à durée déterminée,* into a new matrix for standard employment relations which would be somewhat less worker-protective than the *contrat à durée indéterminée* has traditionally been.[104] Finally in this list of actively discussed reform proposals comes one which is analytically complex but which, properly understood, exemplifies and sustains the arguments of this chapter in general and this concluding section in particular. This is the proposal for legislative action to impose a minimum or essential service obligation, *le service minimum,* upon certain groups of public sector workers, especially in the public transport sector, so that the right to strike would be qualified by a duty upon workers, at both collective and individual levels, to ensure the continuous provision of essential public services or utilities.[105]

If this programme of reform is even partially realized, it seems likely further to confirm the tendency towards a market-liberal aggregation of the 'public' and the 'private' in French employment law which has been envisaged in this conclusion. However, if this represents a 'rationalization' of French employment law, it will be one which is profoundly complicated by the legal and political context within which it takes place, and by no means free of its own paradoxes. Thus, for example, if a notion of *service minimum* is introduced, this will, ironically, involve special restrictions upon industrial action for the public sector of the labour economy in order to make that sector behave, in practice, more like the private sector, which is now relatively strike-free; that would be something of a long-term historical reversal of roles between the two sectors. Thus by way of further illustration, if the *35 heures* framework is to be loosened, and if the *contrat unique* is to be created, we can be sure that these reforms, in a further irony, will take the form not of simple de-regulation, but of an ever-more elaborate process of re-regulation, necessary in order to give expression to the refinement of the political and legal compromises which will be involved.

In all this, it must finally be said, the evolution of French employment law is and would be fairly typical of what is happening, in varying ways and to varying degrees, to European national employment law systems more generally. Each system has its own idiosyncrasies, and the 'social model' which is embodied in French employment and social security law is a highly path-dependent one. However, those national systems are already subject to no small amount of supranational coordination from the law and policy of the European Union, and, in an even more fundamental sense, are subject to the strong competitive pressures

---

[104] This idea is detailed in a report of 2004, P. Cahuc et F. Kramarz, *De la précarité à la mobilité : vers une Sécurité sociale professionnelle* (La Documentation française, Paris, 2004).

[105] Legislation moving towards the realisation of that obligation was enacted in August 2007: *loi* no. 2007-1224 of 21 August 2007.

which are imposed by the globalization of national labour and product econ-omies. As to that, we can do no better than to quote in conclusion from Professor Supiot when he says that:

These tendencies destabilize all national employment laws, but each faces them in its own way relying on its own particular spirit, and it would be illusory to think that they are destined to become based on a unique model.[106]

---

[106] A. Supiot, *Le droit du travail,* 3rd edn. (Paris, 2006), 32.

PART III

STUDYING FRENCH LAW

13

Bibliographical Guide and Legal Methods

The present chapter seeks to provide some guidance to students having to deal directly with French legal materials. Various French bibliographical sources will be presented and their potential use explained. Also in order to help the student going to a French university, advice on methods of legal writing and on reading cases will be provided in this chapter.

I. Bibliographical Sources

A. Textbooks

The quest for legal documentation and information should start in all legal systems with a perusal of the relevant textbooks on the subject. They will provide the general background which is necessary to start understanding any subject. Textbooks are written so as to enable their readers to organize their ideas on the subject. It will be easier then to integrate into this framework the analysis of more specific issues. Also references for further reading are listed in this sort of work.

Originally this new category of legal publication was imagined by Dalloz when it created the *Précis* between the two World Wars. Those books were aimed at the student market and this is still reflected in both their content and their price. Various publishers specialize in particular legal topics and most of them have collections of textbooks; these usually cover most if not all the areas of the syllabus. Dalloz, Montchrestien and PUF, are the most famous.

(1) Dalloz: the collection of 'Précis Dalloz' is the oldest and the titles there are often renowned and well written. This collection has existed for years and most textbooks have now been adopted by generations of students. They are often quite thorough but the print is rather small and the presentation concise.

(2) Presses Universitaires de France or PUF: the PUF has now two collections where leading textbooks can be found: the *Collection droit fondamental* which provide good introductions to most courses; it is more recent and aims particularly at first- and second-year students. On the other hand another

collection called *Thémis* covers all topics and provides a more complete account of the law.

(3) Montchrestien: the collection of '*Précis* Domat' have usually very good titles indeed in all topics covered by a university course. The presentation is particularly clear and the references for further readings are often comprehensive.

B. *Traités*

Traités or treatises belong to a much older category of legal writings and they fulfil a totally different function from the standard textbooks. They started to be published during the 19th century and aim at presenting a very complete view of a topic and its relationship to the legal system as a whole. They analyse the law in very considerable detail but also organize all these elements according to a theoretical framework. In fact, the treatises represent an attempt at explaining and reorganizing the whole of an area of law. Authors are very little constrained by space and their theoretical choices and their consequential exposition of the law can be fully explored. These works, therefore, need to be used with care: they are often very voluminous indeed (on average they consist of four volumes) and authors often promote their views and explanations of the law, explanations which might not be shared by the whole academic community. Readers should remember that they are getting a treatment of the legal materials after a number of theoretical choices have been made. Treatises are also published by the main publishing firms mentioned above: to quote but a few of these landmarks: in civil law, the main treatise is *Traité de droit civil*, written or edited by J. Ghestin (published by Montchrestien); in administrative law, the *Traité du droit administatif* by A. De Laubadère (published by L.G.D.J) has been used by generations of students and has been the means by which the author has promoted his ideas on the public service.

C. Casebooks

It is not really possible for any lawyer to avoid coming across a certain number of cases if he or she wishes to acquire an understanding of the subjects studied. There is a close equivalent to the English category of 'cases and materials'; the only difference is that these are only casebooks. Other types of material are not included and so journal articles or legislative provisions will need to be consulted separately.[1] However, there are two main collections of casebooks which present the most important cases in one field and provide a commentary on the decision below. The collection *Les grands arrêts* published by Dalloz presents a number of casebooks reproducing and commenting on the most important cases in an area

---

[1] This might be due to the fact that French universities provide each student with a rather complete set of photocopied materials in the main courses for which he or she is registered. These are called *fiches de travaux dirigés*.

of the law. The cases are presented chronologically and the notes below the cases are extremely thorough. This last point is one of the main differences between this collection and the one entitled *Les grandes décisions de la jurisprudence* which is published by PUF. There, the decisions are organized thematically and the comments are not as elaborate as in the other collection. For a first- or second-year student, it is an ideal presentation of the material. The note below the case not only comments on it but also gives a synthesized presentation of the entire case law; it identifies the various points of interactions between the decision and other case law; it also draws to the attention the general orientations and tendencies of the judges in this area.

D. Law Reports

The knowledge of the cases which can be obtained from the casebooks is only partial and limited and further study of them has to be traced into either law reports or the various journals, as we shall now explain.

It is important to understand that the court system in France is strongly hierarchical and that the cases of the two supreme courts at the top of the private and administrative law courts are highly influential. For this reason, cases decided by the Conseil d'Etat[2] and ones decided by the Cour de cassation[3] are published in separate law reports. The *Recueil des decisions du Conseil d'Etat* also called *Recueil Lebon,* which is published in parts six times a year, contains decisions of the Conseil d'Etat and a very limited number of decisions of the lower administrative courts. The *Bulletin de la Cour de cassation,* which is published in parts ten times a year, contains decisions of the Cour de cassation. However, it is important to underline the fact that these courts decide which of their decisions will be published. The selection is particularly important as far as the Conseil d'Etat is concerned since it is estimated that only a sixth of all its decisions are published, while in the Cour de cassation two-thirds of all its decisions are actually published. However, no lower courts' decisions are published in the *Bulletin de la Cour de cassation.* For the *Recueil Lebon,* the decision whether or not to publish is made by its editorial committee of three *Maîtres des Requêtes* who are all members of the Documentation Centre of the Conseil d'Etat. For the *Bulletin,* the decision is taken by the president of the chamber[4] responsible for the case. The structure of the *Recueil Lebon* is relatively easy to understand: each category of court has its own part in the *Recueil.* The Conseil d'Etat always covers by far the largest proportion of the *Recueil.* The *Bulletin de la Cour de cassation* is divided into two parts: the *Bulletin civil* which includes all the decision of the civil sections, the

---

[2] Above pp. 40–41.
[3] Above pp. 46–47.
[4] Above p. 46.

Chambre mixte, and the Assemblée plénière, which the *Bulletin criminal* includes only the decisions of the criminal sections of the Cour de cassation.

It is also possible to find the decisions of the Cour de cassation and the Conseil d'Etat on the official French portal for the communication of legal information: <http://www.legifrance.gouv.fr/>.

E. Legislation

The second important material that it is necessary to refer to is legislation. There are a number of official and private sources which publish legislative materials.

The first and perhaps most important one is the *Journal official:* the *Journal official* is published everyday and its various series contain most of the official texts. There are five series, but the most important and relevant one is the one containing '*lois et décrets*'[5] in which all the statutes and the important administrative regulations will be included, generally a day or so after they have been adopted.[6] Another two series which are relevant to students are the series reporting the parliamentary debates, *débats parlementaires* and the one containing the *Documents parlementaires;* this comprises the reports and opinions of the committee in charge of examining a bill. This information may be useful if it is necessary to determine the meaning and aim of a particular *loi.*

In order to facilitate access to information for citizens, the *Journal officiel* produces in one single publication all the texts relevant to a specific topic: for instance, the 1958 Constitution is not produced on its own but with the text of the 1946 Preamble, the 1789 Declaration and the most important provisions of the *lois organiques.*[7]

The *Journal officiel* produces also all the codes, regardless of the route by which they have been adopted: through parliamentary legislation[8] or through administrative codification. These publications contain the provisions of the code; no commentary or references are attached to them.

Again, the *Legifrance* website gives access to all primary and most secondary legislations. It is also possible to consult the codes.

In reality, as far as popular codes are concerned, they are also published by private publishing firms; the most famous of these are the 'little red codes' produced by Dalloz. These are brought by students, academics and practitioners alike. To the text of the provision is added a short commentary which makes reference to a long list of cases. Dalloz has also had a tendency to produce compilations of legislation and administrative regulations in one specific area and arbitrarily to

---

[5] Literally, this means 'statutes and statutory instruments'.

[6] The date of publication in the *Journal officiel* is very important indeed: often it determines the date from which a text is valid.

[7] Cf. above p. 21.

[8] Such as the New Criminal Code or the New Code of Civil Procedure.

call these 'codes'.[9] Other publishing companies, such as Litec, have followed this practice and also provide annotated codes.

F. Encyclopaedias

If, having brought together textbook references, cases and legislation on a particular topic, one still needs to understand the subject in more depth, one is well advised to look up the topic in one of the encyclopaedias which all French law libraries possess. These publications are rarely imaginative in their presentation of the law, but they have the advantage of providing a quick and easy access to a great deal of information and long lists of further reading. There are two main collections: the *Répertoire Dalloz*, and the *Juris-Classeurs (Éditions Techniques)*.

The *Répertoire Dalloz* has the advantage of being integrated with the *Codes Dalloz* and the *Recueil Dalloz Sirey*; this means that there are references in both the *Codes* and the *Recueil* to the items contained in the relevant *Répertoire*. The items are organized alphabetically. There are a number of *Répertoires* for each of the main subjects: *Répertoire civil* (8 volumes), *Répertoire du droit commercial* (5 volumes), *Répertoire du droit du travail* (3 volumes), etc.

In the *Juris-Classeur*, the organization changes according to the subject matter: if the area of law is codified (as in the case of the civil law, for instance), the structure of the *Juris-Classeur* follows the sequence of the clauses of the code in question; in other areas, the *Juris-Classeur* is organized around a thematic plan as in the *Juris-Classeur Droit Administratif*, lastly, the *Juris-Classeur* is sometimes organized alphabetically. The high reputation of *Juris-Classeur* is well-deserved and at the beginning of each of their articles an extremely complete bibliography is provided and many cases are referred to in the body of the text.

G. General Journals

Journals in France can be divided into two main categories: the general journal covering all fields of law and the specialist reviews concentrating on one area of the law.

There are three main general journals: *le Recueil Dalloz Sirey* (D), *La Semaine Juridique* also called *le Juris-Classeur Périodique* (JCP), and *la Gazette du Palais* (GP). In these three journals, can be found articles, cases and commentaries,[10] and legislation. In order to be able to use these, it is quite important to know how this mass of information is organized. They follow approximately the same pattern: articles in the first part, case law in the second, and various further items of information in the third part (legislation, summaries of other cases, etc). This

---

[9] See the *'Code administratif'* which in effect does not exist.
[10] Since cases in France are not very long it is quite easy to reproduce them in full in the various journals and reviews.

is important to realize as each part has its own pagination system. The reference will therefore give the part in which the article or the case is to be found and the page: for instance 'ROBERT Jacques "De la cohabitation" D 1986 I (or Chron) 179' means that the article written by Jacques Robert is published in the *Recueil Dalloz Sirey* in the volume for 1986 in the first part at page 179.[11]

There are some slight differences between these three general journals and these should be recounted briefly. *La Gazette du Palais* is published in two semesters and the Roman number in the reference indicates which volume is referred to. The *Gazette du Palais* is particularly intended for those practising lawyers who are involved with the courts and the bar. The articles are concise and often deal with questions, cases or legislation under discussion at the time. It reproduces a great number of cases of the lower courts (which do not get officially reported).

The *Recueil Dalloz Sirey* on the other hand contains longer articles and some excellent commentaries on recent cases. It also gives closer attention to legislation, reproduces and comments on it.

The *Semaine Juridique* is divided into four parts: articles, cases, legislation and summaries of cases. To avoid confusion, it is important to know that there are different editions of the *Semaine Juridique*: a general edition, an edition entitled 'commerce and industry', one aimed at notaries (*édition notariale*), one aimed at companies (*Entreprise*) and one covering issues of administrative law (*administrations et collectivités territoriales*).

H. Specialized Reviews

Along with these general journals, there is a great variety of more specialized reviews in each of the subject areas of the law. These publications are aimed largely at students and academics in general. Although it would be impossible to provide here an exhaustive list, they include:

(1) Civil law: *Revue Trimestrielle du Droit Civil* (RTDCiv);
(2) Commercial law: *Droit des Sociétés; Revue Trimestrielle du Droit Commercial* (RTDCom);
(3) Public law: *Revue du Droit Public* (RDP);
(4) Administrative law: *Actualité Juridique-Droit Administratif* (AJDA); *Revue Française de Droit Administratif* (RFDA).

Within the broad category of specialized reviews should be distinguished a number of publications which deal with more theoretical issues or are interested in a more inter-disciplinary approach. These include: *Revue Française de Théorie Juridique (Droits); La Revue de la Recherche Juridique (Droits Prospectifs)* (RRJ); *La Revue Internationale de Droit Comparé* (RIDC).

---

[11] It should be noted that sometimes instead of putting 'I' to indicate the part, it says Chron. or Chr. which means *chroniques* that is to say articles.

I. *Les Mélanges*

It is customary that when a professor retires, a collection of essays (*mélanges*) is produced by his or her colleagues, former students and intellectual followers. The essays which are written are often interesting because they tend to present a particular person's view of one aspect of the law or on the whole of an area. Moreover, since they are meant to be a personal view, they tend to be more controversial in their approach to questions and therefore represent a different type of writing from articles found in journals and reviews. They are often recommended reading for students and their style and presentation makes them easy to be understood.

J. Specialized Books and Research

For a person who intends to get to know a particular subject in depth, it is useful to find out about the various doctoral theses which have been written on the topic. Libraries usually have a separate card and computer index for doctoral theses, which can be available on paper but more and more they may be consulted on micro-fiches. Doctoral theses are a very interesting source of information and should not be neglected. The best ones are often published in a separate series: the publishing houses LGDJ, Economica Pedone, and Dalloz have all acquired a sound reputation for works of this type.

Conference proceedings should not be ignored and important conferences which take place on a regular basis are published and represent landmarks: for example, the proceedings of the annual conference of the *Association des Constitutionalistes Français* are very informative. Some conference proceedings have a systematic outlet such as the *Archives de Philosophie du Droit*.

K. Legal Databases and CD-Rom

There are a number of legal databases which are available as a tool for further research and a great number of French university libraries provide their users with access to these, but for some it is possible to gain access to them from home via the Internet. Websites containing information on French law are now being developed. A particularly helpful site is that set up by the Ministry of Justice which contains information on courts, judicial statistics, and legal personnel.[12]

As far as French documentation is concerned, the Government since 1983 has adopted a policy of cooperation in order to organize the market and make it more accessible to consumers. The Journaux Officiels is now in charge of collating all official texts (national and European) and decisions produced by national courts. These are made available on the official French portal for the communication of legal information: <http://www.legifrance.gouv.fr/>. The consumer

---

[12] <http://www.justice.gouv.fr/>.

has the advantage of one single point of access to a considerable amount of legal materials.

In the private sector, the main database is LEXIS which is also well-known throughout Europe. It contains at present the largest amount of legal information in the world on both cases and legislation.

II. Legal Methods

Having perused a certain amount of French academic writings, a reader will be aware that most articles or commentaries follow a rather strict model of presentation and method. Methods of legal writing are given a large place in French legal education: essays, articles and doctoral theses must be drafted according to the famous two-part *plan* (or essay structure). Cases that students will be required to comment on must also be tackled in a specific manner. At first, these methods are difficult for a foreign student to master, but it is important to emphasize that an essay which is not organized around a two-part *plan* is unlikely to meet with the approval of its marker.

Students might find it useful to consult some of the books on legal method that Dalloz and Montchrestien have started to publish: Dalloz has a series on legal method but it does not really address the needs of undergraduates, but the series entitled *Travaux dirigés* could be useful: each book covers a French university course and is divided into the subjects normally covered in *Travaux dirigés*. Sample essay questions and commentaries are provided with corrections. Similarly, Montchrestien publishes a series of works on legal methods which is well worth investigation.

A. The Two-Part Plan

To decide on the organization of an essay is to make a deliberate choice, a choice that is based on the analysis of the materials which have been collated. There is no point in adopting the various headings which may have been encountered in textbooks or articles, as the subject of the essay is not likely to exactly fit any of these. For the *plan* must not bear a loose relationship only with the title of the essay which is set, but must directly address it. We shall explain this by reference to the analysis of a sample essay title.

Essay title: 'The Role of the Conseil Constitutionnel in the 1958 Constitution'

1. Analysing the title of the essay

The first step is to imagine why the subject was set, to determine what is the value of the question (behind what may appear at first sight a rather benign title may lurk after reflection some very considerable problems). Although this is not always easy to establish, once an answer to this question is found it is likely to determine the direction which the work will take. Then a list of the issues that you think are relevant to the title, should be drawn up and this list should be comprehensive. The exact wording of the title of the essay must be studied minutely to make sure that you know what each particular term means, so as to avoid misunderstanding what is required of you.

In the present title, there is no word which could really create confusion. However, what is required to be analysed here is the *role* that the Conseil constitutionnel has created for itself. There is therefore little point in discussing, for example, the membership or appointment procedure of the Conseil (unless you can show a clear correlation between these and its role).

2. Selecting and interpreting the data

Once you have established what you think is required of you, you need to select from the reading already done, the specific and necessary information to enable you to address the essay title. At the same time, it is impossible to begin to select what you need unless you have an idea of what you want to demonstrate, the propositions that you wish to establish. The French *plan* is NOT an arbitrary structure (although it seems so to all beginners). It is perfectly adapted to French legal ways of thinking and provides a structure to order your thoughts and material. Indeed, you will be surprised to see how much in French law—theories, concepts, approaches—are divisible into two.

It is quite clear from the discussion in Chapter 5 that the role of the Conseil constitutionnel has changed radically from what was originally envisaged by the drafters of the Constitution of the Fifth Republic. This point could form your central idea, your thesis; it will then be up to you to return to the material which you have already read in order to find specific support for it.

3. Choosing a two-part plan

The student must appreciate the fact that there is no one single right *plan* for any given essay. On the same essay title there could a number of possible *plans* and they could all be valid: each would represent a slightly different picture or present a different angle of the subject. Clearly then constructing a *plan* always requires a choice as you are providing your reader with your view on the subject (though this view will naturally be divided into two parts because your argument will demand this).

For example, in the sample essay title noted above, the following *plans* could be adopted:

I. The Conseil constitutionnel which was created in order to protect the executive

II. Has in fact turned against it;

   or

I. The Conseil constitutionnel which was created to regulate the behaviour of political institutions
II. Has in fact become a defender of civil liberties.

Many more combinations are possible and appreciating this is extremely important. For since an essay defends a *view*, not only is it impossible to cover all aspects of the question, but such a coverage (or attempted coverage) is not really desirable: this is not the aim of the exercise. In fact, if you look again at the above suggested *plans*, you may not agree with some of the propositions which they include. Nevertheless, these *plans* reflect a tenable opinion and the main part of the essay should provide arguments to justify this position.

4. Drafting the essay

The introduction to your essay must be written with great care and it should unfold the line of reasoning which has led you to adopt your chosen *plan*; you need to convince your reader/examiner of the appropriateness of your choice. It is recommended that you start by defining and analysing briefly the main terms of the title of the essay and then you should identify the question or questions which you think it raises and present the *plan* which you intend to use in analysing them. For example, as regards either of the *plans* suggested above, you may feel the need to explain your starting point: the contrast between the role which the Conseil constitutionnel now assumes and the one which the drafters of the Constitution had originally intended for the Conseil.[13] Your introduction should contain a clear argument that is articulated through the *plan*. You cannot use the English style of general introduction and leave the statement of your argument to the conclusion.

The body of your essay should be divided into two clear parts which will be themselves divided into two, etc. (the divisions of the subparagraphs should be made on the same basis as the division of the whole essay). It is recommended to write out the headings themselves, especially if you are inexperienced in this style of presentation as this will show the reader immediately the line of your argument. Having the title actually in front of you will allow you to check that what you are writing is consistent with the idea 'advertised' in the heading. In writing the body of the essay itself always ensure that each argument which you put forward is supported by facts, evidence or authority (cases, legislation, empirical studies, statistics, etc).

5. The conclusion

The conclusion of your essay is *not* meant to provide a summary of all its arguments but instead must lead naturally to a further question, to a larger debate

---

[13] For instance, it might be argued that the Conseil constitutionnel was not created simply to defend the executive. But in the introduction you would have to counter this argument by contending that the protection of the executive was the main reason for its creation even though it was also given other duties.

(though still one related to the central argument which you have defended in your essay). Thus, in the sample essays given above, the question of judicial activism or the legitimacy of constitutional control undertaken by the Conseil constitutionnel are appropriate issues to be raised at this stage.

B. Reading and Commenting on Cases

French law students are often required to comment on cases for their *travaux dirigés*[14] or for their examinations. To enable a foreign student to perform this task easily, it is important to provide him or her with some guidelines as to how a case should be read. The decision of the Conseil d'Etat of 20 October 1989 *Nicolo*,[15] which is reproduced at the end of this chapter, will be used to serve as an illustration of the suggested manner of writing a commentary.

1. *The structure of French cases*

French judgments are made up of various elements which fulfil different functions. There are some differences between the various courts but the general organization is the same:

(a) Les visas

This section of the judgment starts with '*vu...*' (having seen) and then cites the legal provisions which are often at the centre of the dispute (parliamentary or administrative legislation, articles of the Constitution, etc). Seven *visas* were included in the decision of the Conseil d'Etat taken as our example. The *visa* quoting the Constitution and its article 55 is the most significant one. In fact, it signals a departure from the previous case law.

(b) Les attendus *or* les considérants

These constitute the main body of the judgment and contain the reasoning of the court. They present the facts of the case, the arguments of the parties and then develop the legal propositions on which it will rely. All this is done in very few words. The reason for the name of this part of the judgment lies in the fact that each different step in the line of reasoning starts with '*attendu que...*' or '*considérant que...*'.[16]

The judgment printed below contains three *considérants*: the first one explains the French legislative provisions concerning the election of French representatives to the European Parliament; the second quotes the relevant treaty provision and proclaims their compatibility with the French legislation; the third rejects the arguments put forward by Nicolo.

---

[14] *Travaux dirigés* are the equivalent of supervisions or tutorials.
[15] CE Ass. 20 Oct. 1989 *Nicolo*, Leb. 190, concl. Frydman.
[16] This is often translated loosely by 'whereas...'.

(e) Le dispositif

This is the actual 'solution' of the matter before the court, the equivalent of the order which an English judgment would often make. It starts with the phrase *'Par ces motifs'* or the verb *'Decide'*. In the Conseil d'Etat's sample judgment the *dispositif* rejects the request of *Nicolo* to annul the election of the European Parliament.

2. *The art of writing a commentary on a case* (commentaire d'arrêt)

Like essays, a commentary on a case will need to be organized around a number of ideas. However, there are some differences between them which require a little more explanation.

(a) The introduction

The introduction of a commentary has rather strict rules and a number of elements must be absolutely present. The decision to include these elements was not a random one as they aim at ensuring that you have understood the decision properly. The French judicial style of prose is very concise and it is quite possible to miss a point totally or even to understand the opposite of what was meant. It is therefore considered important to force the student to reproduce a certain number of the essential elements of a decision and so make sure that the fundamental points of the decisions have received proper attention.

The introduction must contain:

(1) the court:[17] in our sample case this is particularly important since the case came before the Assemblée, a choice which signifies that an important point had to be settled;

(2) the date: in our case, 20 October 1989;

(3) the point or points of law: here, only two or three lines are required as you are only indicating the issue. In our case, the question was whether the French organization of elections to the European Parliament breached the requirements of the treaty of the European Economic Community;

(4) the facts: again, only a few words by way of summary. Thus, in our case, Nicolo, a French citizen, requests the annulment of the European Parliament election of 18 June 1989; he argues that the inclusion on the electoral roll of all the electors from the French overseas territories contravenes the Treaty of the European Economic Community;

(5) the procedure: this should describe whatever decisions have been taken already, at what date, and what were the arguments of the parties on these occasions. All this needs to be presented very briefly. On the other hand, on occasion a lot may have to be said under this heading. In our case, however, this is the first instance and there is little to say.

---

[17] For instance, its level in the hierarchy will be relevant when determining the importance of the decision.

(b) The commentary

The functions of any commentary are threefold:

(1) to explain the meaning of the decision. The commentary should therefore include an explanation of the court's reasoning by reconstructing its arguments and also clarify the methods of interpretation which it adopts. For example, in our own case, it is important to state that this decision is a departure from an established case law. For the first time, the Conseil d'Etat accepts to check the compatibility of a French legislation with a Treaty provision. The case is a real landmark;

(2) to analyse its value. The student is required in the commentary to evaluate the court's decision by determining whether the solution which it adopts fits in logically with the rest of the case law, whether it respects the ideals of morality and justice and whether it takes into account any economic or social realities which may apply. In doing so, a student may certainly make use of criticisms already voiced by commentators. For example, in our case, it is important to explain the growing importance of European Community legislation. The previous position of the Conseil d'Etat was becoming increasingly difficult to sustain; it needed to accept the changes that were taking place in the European Community arena. In fact, one might argue that it was high time that such a change occurred;

(3) to judge its implications. The commentary should therefore include discussion of the impact which the decision has had in relation to subsequent cases (if it is an old decision) or which the decision is likely to have (if the decision is a recent one). In our own case, it would be necessary to compare the solution in *Nicolo* with the relevant case law of both the Conseil constitutionnel and the Cour de cassation. It would also help to discuss the case law of the European Court of Justice in relation to this issue. This will enable you to predict the probable evolution of this new line of cases.

While the commentary should cover these three points, the organization of its structure should be determined according to the content of the decision. For example, if the decision changes an otherwise established case law, the implication of this new direction must be studied in depth. In the light of this, part II of the essay should be dedicated to it, while the meaning and value of the decision should be re-grouped and tackled in part I. (Our own case should be included in this category.) On the other hand, if the decision is merely the faithful follower of a long line of cases, the part on its implication will be much smaller, but the analysis of its meaning and value will have to place it in relation to the others, and to outline the general reasons and ideas behind the established case law.

Until now, our discussion has assumed that the decision to be commented on addresses only one point of law. This is rarely the case and often students will be confronted with cases which tackle two or sometimes three issues. The student must cover all the points in his or her commentary, but may want to give each point different amounts of space in the essay in accordance with their relative importance. However, students should be warned that this sort of evaluation can be dangerous, as their perception of the significant points could well differ from what the examiner will require. Certainly any such choice on the part of a student will have to be explained and justified in the body of the commentary.

Finally, the conclusion of the commentary should be constructed on similar principles as for an essay.

3. *Sample case*

Conseil d'Etat, Assemblée

20 October 1989

Vu la requête, enregistrée le 27 juin 1989 au secrétariat du Contentieux du Conseil d'Etat, présentée par M. Raoul Georges Nicolo, demeurant 26, avenue de Joinville à Nogent-sur-Marne (94130), et tendant à l'annulation des opérations électorales qui se sont déroulées le 18 juin 1989 en vue de l'élection des représentants au Parlement européen,

Vu les autres pièces du dossier;

Vu la Constitution, notamment son article 55;

Vu le Traité en date du 25 mars 1957, instituant la communauté économique européenne;

Vu la loi n° 77-729 du 7 juillet 1977 ;

Vu le code électoral;

Vu l'ordonnance n° 45-1708 du 31 juillet 1945, le décret n° 53-934 du 30 septembre 1953 et la loi n° 87-1127 du 31 décembre 1987;

Après avoir entendu:

– le rapport de M. de Montgolfier, Auditeur,

– les observations de la S.C.P. de Chaisemartin, avocat de M. Hervé de Charette,

– les conclusions de M. Frydman, Commissaire du gouvernement ;

Sur les conclusions de la requête de M. Nicolo:
Considérant qu'aux termes de l'article 4 de la loi n° 77-729 du 7 juillet 1977 relative à l'élection des représentants à l'Assemblée des communautés européennes "le territoire de la République forme une circonscription unique" pour l'élection des représentants français au Parlement européen ; qu'en vertu de cette disposition

législative, combinée avec celles des articles 2 et 72 de la Constitution du 4 octobre 1958, desquelles il résulte que les départements et territoires d'outre-mer font partie intégrante de la République française, lesdits départements et territoires sont nécessairement inclus dans la circonscription unique à l'intérieur de laquelle il est procédé à l'élection des représentants au Parlement européen;

Considérant qu'aux termes de l'article 227-1 du traité en date du 25 mars 1957 instituant la Communauté Economique Européenne : "Le présent traité s'applique ... à la République française"; que les règles ci-dessus rappelées, définies par la loi du 7 juillet 1977, ne sont pas incompatibles avec les stipulations claires de l'article 227-1 précité du traité de Rome;

Considérant qu'il résulte de ce qui précède que les personnes ayant, en vertu des dispositions du chapitre 1er du titre 1er du livre 1er du code électoral, la qualité d'électeur dans les départements et territoires d'outre-mer ont aussi cette qualité pour l'élection des représentants au Parlement européen ; qu'elles sont également éligibles, en vertu des dispositions de l'article L.O. 127 du code électoral, rendu applicable à l'élection au Parlement européen par l'article 5 de la loi susvisée du 7 juillet 1977; que, par suite, M. Nicolo n'est fondé à soutenir ni que la participation des citoyens français des départements et territoires d'outre-mer à l'élection des représentants au Parlement européen, ni que la présence de certains d'entre-eux sur des listes de candidats auraient vicié ladite élection ; que, dès lors, sa requête doit être rejetée;

Sur les conclusions du ministre des départements et territoires d'outre-mer tendant à ce que le Conseil d'Etat inflige une amende pour recours abusif à M. Nicolo:

Considérant que des conclusions ayant un tel objet ne sont pas recevables;

DECIDE:

Article 1er: La requête de M. Nicolo et les conclusions du ministre des départements et des territoires d'outre-mer tendant à ce qu'une amende pour recours abusif lui soit infligée sont rejetées.

Article 2: La présente décision sera notifiée à M. Nicolo, à M. de Charette, mandataire de la liste l'Union U.D.F.–R.P.R., aux mandataires de la liste de rassemblement présentée par le Parti Communiste Français, de la liste du Centre pour l'Europe, de la liste Majorité de Progrès pour l'Europe, de la liste Les Verts Europe-Ecologie et de la liste Europe et Patrie et au ministre de l'intérieur.

Index